THE HOME FRONT

THE HOME FRONT

New Zealand society and the war effort, 1914–1919

STEVEN LOVERIDGE AND JAMES WATSON

MASSEY UNIVERSITY PRESS

CONTENTS

NORWICH, UNION FIRE INSURANCE SOCIETY.
COMMERCIAL HOTEL
T. C. MUTUAL LIFE
CONFECTIONERS

INTRODUCTION
TOWARDS 1914

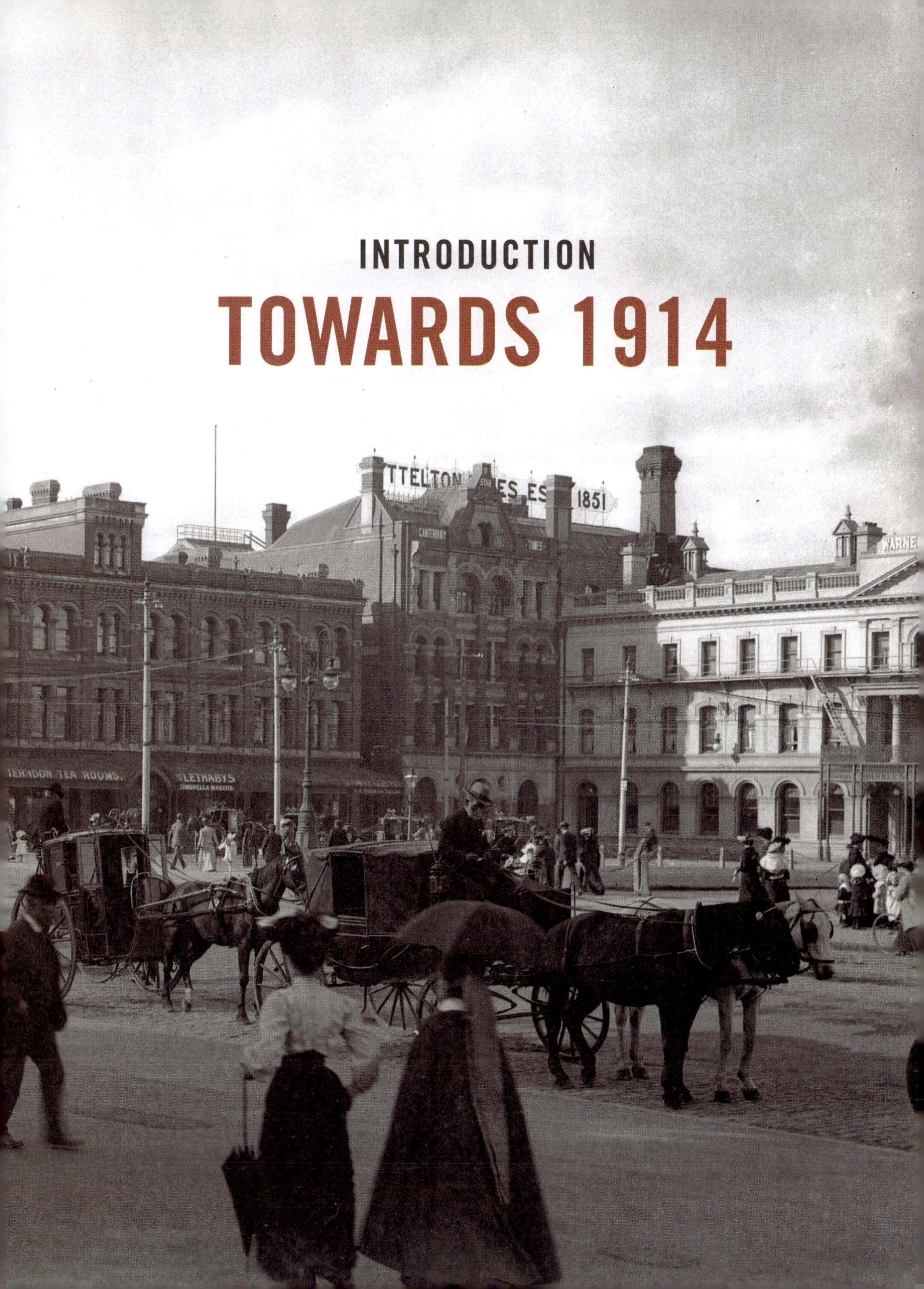

previous pages
An Edwardian city: Cathedral Square, Christchurch, in the early twentieth century.
CANTERBURY MUSEUM, 2005.36.154

Fiction, film and myth have conspired to portray the years leading up to the outbreak of the First World War as a tranquil, golden, innocent era. In fact, when the war was declared New Zealand was a small, remote but also interconnected part of a volatile world, and its own society was far from settled.

In the nineteenth century its demography had rapidly transformed. In 1840, the non-Māori population stood at under 1000. By 1881 this had ballooned to 500,910. High immigration and birth rates then caused the settler population to effectively double, to nearly 1.1 million by 1914.[1] The vast majority of arrivals came from the British Isles, though there were some notable streams from western, central and southern Europe and parts of Asia.

This expansion had an enormous impact on Māori, who were already undergoing a cultural transformation brought about by European technologies, goods and ideas. Some of these developments proved devastating, particularly the acquisition of firearms, which resulted in, potentially, 20,000–30,000 Māori deaths during the intertribal Musket Wars between 1807 and 1845.[2] Together with the impacts of introduced diseases and displacement, the Māori population likely fell from some 100,000 to 120,000 in 1800 to around 41,000 by the start of the 1890s.[3] Settlers' efforts to acquire and develop property also led to a rapid alienation of Māori land, both through voluntary sales and, in many cases, under pressure.

These dynamics, and questions of sovereignty, fuelled a series of localised conflicts in the 1840s that escalated during the 1860s, with major clashes in the Waikato, Taranaki and the Bay of Plenty. Known collectively as the New Zealand Wars, these battles are estimated to have killed 2154 anti-government Māori and 745 British imperial and colonial troops and kūpapa (Māori fighting for the Crown). In the aftermath, Māori lost even more land to confiscation.[4] In 1914, these actions, still in living memory, remained a source of enduring bitterness.

By 1911 New Zealand's urban population had overtaken the rural and just under a third of the population lived in the four urban centres of Auckland, Wellington, Christchurch and Dunedin.[5] Forty-nine per cent, however, lived in the counties, most with populations of only a few thousand, and in towns with populations in the hundreds.[6] Despite some vestiges of a rougher frontier existence, cities and towns had rapidly acquired modern amenities and more genteel features: parks, halls, theatres, galleries, museums and libraries.[7] There had been mammoth efforts, too, to develop facilities and infrastructure, notably in the 1870s under Julius Vogel's public works scheme.[8] Over 400 miles of railroad were under construction each year between 1873 and 1876 and the 700 miles of telegraphic line of 1866 had expanded to almost 3000 in 1875. In 1877 this network was integrated into the wider imperial system, allowing rapid communication across the world and for distant events to become local news.[9] This occurred alongside a flourishing local press. As the French geographer and economist André Siegfried, who visited at the turn of the twentieth century, observed, the newspaper held 'a very high place in New Zealand. Everyone reads it, and there are few people ignorant or old-fashioned enough not to be interested in the news.'[10]

From the early decades of the colony, economic activity was heavily centred on land clearance, farming, small-scale manufacturing, construction and extractive industries — notably mining (gold, coal and gum) and timber milling.[11] By 1914, nearly half the male workforce still worked on the land, notably in agricultural activity. The local advent of refrigerated shipping in the early 1880s underpinned an economy heavily invested in long-distance international trade with the British market. New Zealand's exports to Britain, largely meat, dairy products and wool, had grown from 37 per cent in 1861 to 79 per cent in 1913.[12]

This economy also employed large numbers of men in the processing and transportation industries, including freezing works and waterfront work, as well as in mining the coal used for shipping and to heat homes and businesses. However, the white-collar sector was also growing as work became more specialised and secondary education expanded. Many men had jobs as clerks, shop assistants, factory workers, on the railway, as public servants and within the professions. The number of women drawing an income also rose steadily between 1881 and 1911 as paid work between leaving school and marriage became common.[13] Labour was also becoming increasingly unionised. In 1900 there were 175 registered unions with a total membership of 17,989; in 1914 there were 403, with 73,991 members.[14] By 1919 New Zealand was among the most unionised nations in the world.[15]

Constitutionally, the country remained subordinate to British authority in various ways. London's Colonial Office remained the major point of contact in managing foreign affairs, and a local representative of the Crown was present in the figure of the governor. In 1914 this post was held by Arthur William de Brito Savile Foljambe, the second earl of Liverpool, who had arrived in December 1912.[16] London had long recognised, however, the difficulty of direct rule over settler populations. In what may seem like a paradox, imperial rule came with effective self-governance and a democratic franchise far more advanced than in Britain.[17] In 1852 New Zealand was granted responsible government, with an elected House of Representatives and an upper Legislative Council, though there was a significant degree of governance and development at provincial level. In 1876 the provinces were abolished and a central government was established in Wellington, which had been the capital since 1865. This government was elected under an increasingly widening franchise that was extended to Māori males in 1867, to all men in 1879 and, in a global first, to all women in 1893.[18]

Towards 1914 many approached this history against a general optimism that the modern age was one of unprecedented material and moral progress. An official booklet for the New Zealand International Exhibition held in Christchurch over the summer of 1906–07, for example, proclaimed that the event showcased 'a wild country made fit for civilised men' and marvelled that this had occurred within a lifetime: 'Men still living saw New Zealand when not a European town or village stood upon its shores, except one or two rowdy bay-townships, where whaling ships came for three main "supplies" of the rough old whaling days — wood, water and temporary Maori wives.'[19]

A sense of New Zealand identity had also been growing alongside nineteenth-century developments. As Siegfried noted, 'in many respects New Zealand is still, in the proper sense of the word, a colony, in other ways she is already a nation, whose national beauties and whose history, with its crises of tragedy and romance, have already stirred in her citizens a real love of her'.[20] Various touchstones are apparent within this identity. From the 1870s, for example, the country had often been described as 'Maoriland', a term evoking 'a world of saccharine fantasy' and Victorian literary forms including stout-hearted pioneers, fierce Māori warriors and dusky Māori maidens.[21]

Into the twentieth century, a laundered commemoration of pioneering audacity and self-reliance was widely held as an exemplary model for national and masculine character.[22] Competing with the celebration of frontier heritage, however, was New Zealand's growing distinction as a land of advanced social reforms: women's suffrage in 1893, the establishment of industrial arbitration in 1894, which was said to make New Zealand a 'land without strikes', and the 1898 introduction of old age pensions. This reputation was greatly boosted by a series of visiting international observers who described the country as the 'birthplace of the twentieth century', the 'political brain of the modern world' or the 'social laboratory from which the world should learn much'.[23]

This developing identity also spurred some sense of a distinct destiny, including the 1901 decision not to become the seventh state in the newly constituted Commonwealth of Australia.[24] It also informed ideas of acquiring an empire in the Pacific; an ambition which gained some ground in 1901 when the Colonial Office assented to New Zealand administrating the Cook Islands, previously a British protectorate.[25] However, this sense of national distinction occurred alongside an increasing orientation towards the British Empire. In Siegfried's words, a 'thousand signs' made it apparent that 'it is London which is the capital for New Zealanders and that they derive thence their ideas, their fashions, and their watchwords'.[26]

This closeness was underwritten by a transnational infrastructure that carried New Zealand produce to the British market, and Siegfried's ideas, fashions and watchwords back to New Zealand media and consumers (in 1913, 60 per cent of imports came from Britain).[27] In 1907 the country was proclaimed a British dominion, rather than a colony, and although this new status brought no constitutional change it complemented a sense of progress and an ongoing relationship with the empire.

New Zealand's reliance on Britain to meet its defence and economic interests, and sometimes brazenly stated expectations that the empire should work for its benefit, could, cynically, be seen as sufficient explanation for such attachment to 'Home', as Britain was conventionally known. Certainly, trade with Britain underwrote a standard of living claimed, by the turn of the twentieth century, as among the highest in the world, and New Zealand's regional defence was guaranteed through the Royal Navy, overwhelmingly funded by British taxpayers.[28] However, cynicism alone is insufficient in explaining the strength of the moral relationship, and the hardships New Zealand endured to sustain and honour it. The overwhelming sentiments of mass culture and mass politics saw New Zealanders presenting themselves as distinct, perhaps superior, Britons who, as part of a global empire, were entitled to British cultural achievements, prestige and preference.[29]

Another strand within the country's identity derived from ideas of racial harmony. Even the New Zealand Wars were interpreted to fit this narrative. In April 1914 some 5000 people, including a small number of Māori and Pākehā veterans, gathered to recognise the fiftieth anniversary of the Battle of Ōrākau. The *New Zealand Herald* proclaimed that this most famous encounter of the Waikato war marked 'the final acceptance of the British mana by a heroic and warlike native people' and as laying the ground for 'a just and generous reciprocity which is everywhere regarded as an example to the civilised world'.[30] Proponents of the mythology of racial harmony and progress could point to decades of considerable intermarriage and of economic and cultural engagement. By 1912 more Māori were attending public schools than native schools; a professional class of Māori schoolteachers, clergymen, nurses, solicitors and doctors had emerged; and Māori leaders such as Āpirana Ngata, Māui Pōmare, Sir James Carroll, Peter Buck (Te Rangi Hīroa) and Paraire Tomoana — typically grouped together as the Young Māori Party — worked as members of Parliament to improve Māori health, living and social standards.[31] Carroll had been the first Māori to win a general rather than a Māori seat, the first to enter Cabinet and the first to serve as acting prime minister, in 1909 and 1911.

Claims of racial harmony, however, were not so clear-cut. Some iwi, bitter about land confiscation and resentful of European authority, found autonomy in physical isolation, economic self-sufficiency and the enduring authority of tribal institutions. The Kīngitanga movement, based in Waikato, had arisen in the nineteenth century with the ambition of bringing Māori under a unified sovereignty.[32] Although pan-tribal legitimacy and independence had proved unobtainable, the movement held significant authority across the central North Island and within the tribes of Waikato, Maniapoto and Ngāti Hauā. At the time of the Ōrākau commemoration, Te Rata, the fourth Māori king, was drawing up plans to travel to Britain and lay grievances before the British monarch as a partner under the Treaty of Waitangi.[33]

Significant parts of Tūhoe, and some of Ngāti Awa and Whakatōhea, also sought autonomy by following the leadership of the Tūhoe prophet Rua Kēnana.[34] By 1914 Rua had built a reputation with claims that a vision declared him to be the prophet foreseen by the New Zealand Wars guerrilla leader Te Kooti, that he was the second son of God and the brother of Jesus Christ.[35] In 1907 Rua and his Iharaira (Israelites) relocated to the settlement of Maungapōhatu, cleared from some 800 hectares of dense bush deep in the Ureweras. Various regulations were set with playing cards and, for a time, alcohol forbidden, hair grown out, worldly goods surrendered, an ethos of cleanliness and communitarianism cultivated.

above Rua Kēnana's meeting house at Maungapōhatu. The people on the external staircase include Rua (third from left) and several of his wives and daughters. AUCKLAND LIBRARIES HERITAGE COLLECTIONS, 7-A3323

left The Māori King Te Rata and his delegation before their departure to Britain. From left: Te Rata Mahuta Pōtatau Te Wherowhero, Tupu Taingākawa (seated), Mita Karaka and Hōri Tiro Pāora. AUCKLAND WAR MEMORIAL MUSEUM TĀMAKI PAENGA HIRA, PH-PR-175

Furthermore, citing biblical sanction for polygamy, Rua would ultimately take 12 wives.[36]

There was great curiosity about the Māori messiah and his 'new Jerusalem'. Critics denounced him as a fraud; the Ringatū Church, in which he had begun his religious life, dubbed him a heretic; and the Anglican Church regarded him as an obstacle to proselytisation. Official eyes noted his threatened defiance of the dog tax, the 1907 Tohunga Suppression Act and his involvement in sly-grogging.[37] Others admired him as a reforming figure and praised the cleanliness and industriousness of his followers.[38] Rua's charisma and compelling physical presence were also commonly remarked upon.[39]

A sense of moral progress formed another recurring theme in the way in which New Zealanders presented themselves. The retreat of frontier conditions was accompanied, between 1880 and 1910, by dramatic declines in rates of violence, crime and public drunkenness.[40] This partly reflected new efforts at social regulation in what has been termed a moral crusade to raise the population's physical, mental and moral condition.[41] Such campaigns were spearheaded by secular progressives and the Protestant middle class. Although New Zealand had no state church, churches held influential voices and Christianity and civilisation were often linked together. In early 1914, for example, planning for the December centenary of missionary Samuel Marsden's first New Zealand sermon called for a recognition of 'his magnificent services in the cause of Christianity, civilisation, and colonisation'.[42] The progressive drive was manifested in various causes including campaigns for the female franchise, the temperance movement, efforts to curb sexual impropriety and censor 'offensive' material, attempts to improve public hygiene, the offering of health services for mothers and babies (especially via the Plunket Society), the promotion of eugenics, and the restriction of non-white immigration. In 1914 the two great campaigns were efforts to introduce biblical instruction into the school syllabus and lobbying to restrict or prohibit alcohol. Temperance reformers achieved some successes. Thanks to 1893 legislation, licensed premises in a constituency could be closed by a 60 per cent vote and various areas consequently went 'dry'. In 1911 a referendum showed that 56 per cent of voters favoured national prohibition, just short of the three-fifths required.[43]

Opposition to these campaigns often reflected social faultlines. One of which was class. The editor of *NZ Truth*, a leading populist newspaper directed at workers, denounced reformers, notably prohibitionists, as puritanical 'wowsers' and 'gospel-grinding gasbags'.[44] Moral campaigns could also divide the Protestant majority from the Catholic minority (some 13 per cent of the population), since most Catholics came from working-class backgrounds and had different attitudes to alcohol and gambling. The fact that the overwhelming majority of New Zealand Catholics were of Irish heritage sometimes constituted another faultline: Protestant–Catholic antagonism had some history in New Zealand. There had been a 'comic opera "Fenian Riot"' on the West Coast in 1868 and Timaru and Christchurch witnessed clashes between Orangemen and Catholics in 1879.[45]

As the new century approached, the most significant Catholic–Protestant antagonisms centred on the education system.[46] Fearing that non-sectarian religious instruction could become Protestant proselytisation, the New Zealand Catholic Federation laboured to establish their own schooling system and campaigned for state funding. That they did this while insisting that state schools remain strictly secular, to accommodate the number of Catholic children who could not be placed in Catholic schools, raised ire and accusations of hypocrisy, especially from Protestant groups campaigning for biblical instruction in state classrooms.[47] A series of political–cultural issues further stoked antagonisms. Catholics were rumoured to be over-represented or specially favoured in the public service, though official investigation suggested that this understanding was 'unsupported by facts'.[48] Moreover, the Vatican's 1908 Ne Temere decree, which ruled that interfaith marriages were invalid unless a Catholic priest was present, was seen both as papal intrusion into civil law and as an accusation of illegitimacy and bastardry. The great question of Home Rule for Ireland had some resonance, too. Orange groups had organised anti-Home Rule meetings in several centres in 1906, and in May 1914 one newspaper was captioning pictures of British troops arriving in Ulster as 'Under The Shadow of Civil War'.[49]

Interdenominational relations were, however, largely defined by well-tempered discontent, with polite society asserting that old-world quarrels should not be replicated in the new and that attacking an individual's religion was unseemly, if not bigoted.[50] Into the twentieth century, Catholic leadership increasingly favoured gentle persuasion and appealing to the fair-mindedness of the non-Catholic majority in pursuing its interests. For example, Auckland's Catholic bishop, Henry Cleary, diligently sought to cultivate interdenominational goodwill and has been described as 'the most eminent supporter of an integrationist line'.[51] By 1914 the fruits of this work included free rail travel for teachers in Catholic religious orders, as well as permission for Catholic pupils to compete for state secondary scholarships and, if successful, accept them at Catholic schools.[52] Moreover, many Catholics, too, were influenced by the wider mood of imperial loyalty, often presenting the empire as an Anglo-Celtic project in which Ireland had contributed to British achievements and heritage.

Rapid social and economic change was accompanied by a sometimes volatile transformation of politics. Between 1893 and 1906 the political scene had been dominated by the figure of Richard Seddon, whose nickname, 'King Dick', hinted at his centrality in New Zealand politics as the Liberal Party he headed blazed a trail of reforming legislation. An English migrant, Seddon had come from a varied background, including mining on the Australian and New Zealand goldfields, running stores and hotels, working as a lay litigant representing miners and serving as mayor of Kumara.[53] Though opponents derided his common background, Seddon was in tune with an age of mass politics and turned a homespun manner to his advantage. He possessed immense skill in handling crowds, creating an impression of boisterous friendliness and pragmatism. Tall and barrel chested, and weighing some 280 pounds, he physically embodied his larger-than-life persona. Despite a robust constitution, by the turn of the twentieth century his health was deteriorating and he developed a heart condition. He died on 10 June 1906 while returning from a visit to Australia. His legend remained a potent force for some time as later politicians presented themselves as heirs to his humanitarian programmes and populist style of leadership.

above Rua Kēnana, around 1908. At this time a correspondent meeting with Rua described him as 'Apparently 40 years of age, slim built and tall, his long wavy hair worn as in the pictures of Christ'. He also noted Rua was a 'very charming personage, and the reverse of the overbearing despot one expected to meet'. ALEXANDER TURNBULL LIBRARY, 1/2-C-008873-F

right A genial and genteel 'financial wizard', in 1906 Sir Joseph Ward became prime minister and sought to preserve the Liberals' standing within New Zealand politics. ARCHIVES NEW ZEALAND, R18339408

Sir Joseph Ward, presented as the Liberals' great hope, stepped into the vacuum Seddon left. Born 1856 in Melbourne to an Irish Catholic family, Ward had immigrated to New Zealand early in his life. An urbane technocrat, he had readily accepted a knighthood in 1901 and personified a debonair style that was apparent in his affinity for cigars and gadgetry, his practice of waxing the ends of his moustache — which he was wont to worship 'with the rapt devotion of a Hindoo contemplating the problems of Nirvana' — and habitual smart dress; cartoonist David Low considered that Ward 'always dressed as though he had a lunch engagement at Downing Street'.[54] In 1883 he had married Theresa De Smidt, a noted beauty with a keen business acumen who was an important source of psychological support; the couple had five children.[55]

By the turn of the century, despite sectarian sneers over his Catholicism and personal humiliation over his involvement in the Colonial Bank's bankruptcy during the 1890s, he had built a notable career straddling business and politics, with a reputation as a 'financial wizard'.[56] Ward skilfully aligned his expertise with a formidable capacity for work and, in the words of his biographer, 'It is probably not too much to say that no other politician in our history has had a greater impact on so many aspects of the country's development.'[57] His belief in progress was complemented by 'one of the brightest and sunniest natures that man was ever blest with. Hope, hope, bright beautiful hope is through him warp and woof.'[58]

This positivity would be tested as the political landscape shifted. Under Seddon, the Liberals had governed on a broad base of urban and rural support. In the early years of the new century, however, and notably after Seddon's death, this consensus and dynamism appeared unsteady, and in the 1908 general election the Liberal Party effectively offered no policy, largely from fear of the centrifugal forces on its left and right flanks. On the left, the future of the Liberals' traditional cooperation with the labour movement, the so called 'Lib-Lab alliance', came into question as parts of the labour movement drew influence or inspiration from the global rise in radical labour politics including socialist, communist, anarchist and syndicalist traditions. This development, however, also intensely divided the labour movement over objectives and tactics. Many, and especially the older generation, the craft unions and the skilled workers, embodied an ethos that was 'sentimental rather than intellectual, Christian rather than Marxist, anti-poverty rather than anti-capitalist'.[59] Such moderates tended to be more concerned with local conditions, and to favour piecemeal reforms and some continuation of the alliance with the Liberals.

Conversely, more militant elements, particularly within the maritime and mining industries, favoured radical action to confront what they saw as an unjust status quo. They sought the creation of large unions able to force direct action and reject state arbitration — 'labour's leg-iron' — and to raise worker solidarity across industries. To such ends, the Federation of Labour, later the United Federation of Labour, was founded in 1909. Its members were popularly nicknamed the 'Red Feds'.

Among the Red Feds were a number of activists who soon became prominent national labour leaders. All originated from humble backgrounds, had cut their political teeth in more radical scenes, mostly within the Australian labour movement, and had arrived in New Zealand in the

above left After his arrival in New Zealand in 1912, Henry (Harry) Holland emerged as a major figure within the labour movement, progressive causes and national politics. ALEXANDER TURNBULL LIBRARY, 1/1-018348-F

below left Robert (Bob) Semple's pugnacious nature and boxing experience gave him the nickname 'fighting Bob'. His rhetorical jabs were dubbed 'Sempleisms'. ALEXANDER TURNBULL LIBRARY, 1/2-044054-F

above right Patrick (Paddy) Webb arrived in New Zealand in 1905, and by 1913 had risen from general labourer to labour organiser and Member of Parliament for Grey. ALEXANDER TURNBULL LIBRARY, 1/2-044394-F

below right Peter Fraser emigrated from Scotland in late 1910 and became a major figure within militant labour politics as a result of his forceful personality, organising abilities and sharp oratory. ALEXANDER TURNBULL LIBRARY, 1/1-018354-F decade before 1914. Henry (Harry) Holland, for example, had come to New Zealand from New South Wales in 1912, aged 44, to work as an organiser for the Federation of Labour and as an editor for its newspaper, the *Maoriland Worker*. Slightly built and radiating an air of sincere intensity which a contemporary described as 'Napoleonesque', Holland was given to bellicose rhetoric accented with Marxist doctrine.[60]

Robert (Bob) Semple, who had arrived from Victoria in 1904 to work on the coal fields, was equally bellicose; he soon became involved in union organisation and, later, was a full-time organiser for the Federation of Labour. The 'outstanding personality in the militant union movement', he has been described as a 'spell-binding, apocalyptical evangelist of theatrical extravagance, emotional rather than logical, completely egotistical, vicious in his criticism of others but very sensitive to comments about himself, a coiner of unforgettable abuse not a deep political thinker'.[61]

Patrick (Paddy) Webb was another Victorian immigrant turned New Zealand labour leader. Genial and prematurely bald, and affectionately described as 'a likable little urchin',[62] Webb had arrived in the country in 1905 and found work in the mines while making his mark in union affairs. Though he opposed a more aggressive industrial policy, he was prominent in attacks on the arbitration system, notably in the 1908 'tucker-time strike' in which he and six other miners were sacked for taking 30 rather than the prescribed 15 minutes for lunch. The resulting strike by the Blackball Coal-miners' Union knowingly breached arbitration agreements and the union refused to pay the resulting fine, signalling its willingness to challenge the system.[63] Webb's prominence was further established when he became the inaugural president of the Federation of Labour.

Peter Fraser was another rising talent. He arrived in New Zealand from Scotland in 1911, aged 26, to work on the Auckland waterfront. Lanky, with thinning hair and thick spectacles, Fraser possessed a studious air and an austere manner. Like his fellow Red Feds, he was soon involved, and increasingly influential, in the labour movement, becoming an executive member of the Federation of Labour. His incisive and tireless work, and quick and cutting wit, made him an effective soap-box lecturer with a mantra of 'educate, agitate, organise'.[64] He identified himself as a 'revolutionary socialist', noting that 'any working class movement that is not revolutionary is reactionary. It must be either for the perpetuation or the abolition of the present Capitalist system.' He was also explicit that the revolution had to be won by democracy, 'the slowest, the least picturesque, the most ponderous, but still the only sure method of social transformation'.[65]

The labour movement had also developed a parliamentary presence, inspired by similar organisations in Britain and Australia. A series of minor and often fractious parties formed on the left of the Liberals, and in 1911 four MPs were endorsed by various labour groupings; in 1913 by-elections two more, including Webb, joined them. This grouping ranged from Wellington South MP Alfred Hindmarsh, remembered as pleasant, cultured and suspicious of socialist militants, to the inflammatory, if not demagogic, Grey Lynn MP John Payne. In January and July 1913, two conferences attempted to unify factions and led to the founding of the Social Democratic Party.

The Red Feds had a notable presence within the second conference, at which Holland called for the 'abolishment of the wage system' and submitted a revolutionary preamble to be added to the new party's constitution: 'The working-class and the employing-class have nothing in common. There can be no peace between them so long as hunger and want are found among millions of working people, and the few, who make up the employing class, have all the good things in life . . . It is the historic mission of the working class to do away with capitalism.'[66]

Developments on the Liberals' left were accompanied by reactions on the right as the Reform Party coalesced in 1909. It identified itself with a vision of New Zealand as a property-owning, meritocratic democracy and opposed socialism by advocating property rights, self-reliance and economic independence. Its promise of honest, efficient and fair government for all classes came with charges that cronyism left the Liberals subservient to union demands and that Catholics were favoured in political appointments.[67] Although Reform possessed more urban support than is sometimes appreciated, its major support base lay in rural New Zealand.[68] This rural backing hardened as trust in the Liberals was eroded over perceived concessions to the Red Feds and over debates about land holding. Most farmers strongly favoured freehold tenure over leasehold schemes in which the state would maintain ownership of Crown land and lease it to tenants. Championing freeholding, Reform framed the debate as a question of 'serfs of the Crown or every man his own landlord'.[69]

Having won the 1894 Waitematā by-election, and become increasingly prominent within the developing Reform movement, William Massey was formally announced as leader of the Reform Party in 1909.[70] Born in 1856 in the small Irish town of Limavady in Ulster, Massey had travelled to New Zealand, aged 14, to work on his father's farm in West Tāmaki. In 1882 he married his neighbour's daughter, Christina Paul, with whom he had seven children, two of whom died in infancy. Christina Massey would later replicate her keen involvement in Auckland women's, charitable and community groups at a national level.[71]

Massey fell short in many of his age's heights of gentlemanly refinement. His penmanship destroyed nibs, his choice of attire was described as failing 'to appeal to the tailors of Wellington' and his efforts at shaving could leave on his chin 'a gruesome patchwork of sticking plaster'.[72] He was, though, no uncultivated rustic. His parliamentary speeches made familiar use of biblical and Shakespearean verse, and books, notably Victorian poets and novelists, were cherished in his household.[73] In this sense he was neither the first nor the last New Zealand politician to successfully champion a common air over sophisticated graces and, like Seddon before him, he turned down a knighthood to preserve a common touch.

Indeed 'Farmer Bill' often presented himself as representing New Zealand's bold-hearted, plain-spoken rural aspect. He habitually peppered his stump speeches with references to 'fellow sons of the soil' and burnished a political legend that he was on a haystack when an invitation to stand for a seat was hoisted to him on a pitchfork.[74] His bluff, tenacious and often combative political style was matched by a staunch readiness to confront those he considered to be transgressing legal and social boundaries with a sense that offenders should suffer the consequences. He could embody this conviction at a remarkably personal level: when he received death threats during labour unrest he refused to deviate from his habit of early

Immigrant, farmer, politician, party leader and prime minister: into the twentieth century, William Ferguson Massey emerged as a formidable and enduring force in New Zealand politics.
ALEXANDER TURNBULL LIBRARY, 1/1-001538-F

morning and late night walks to and from Parliament, though he elected to carry a revolver whilst doing so.[75]

Political tensions became increasingly obvious after Seddon's death and as frictions between labour and capital increased. Worsening industrial relations challenged New Zealand's reputation as a 'land without strikes'. Between 1894 and 1905 there had been no strikes by registered unions; in 1906 there was one; by the end of 1911 there had been another 41.[76] Events came dramatically to a head after the inconclusive results of the 1911 general election when Liberal defections allowed Reform, in 1912, to form a government and end the Liberals' long reign. In toasting the new prime minister, Ward ambiguously wished Massey as long a time in office as he deserved. Massey retorted by wishing the same for the Liberals in opposition, adding that he thought it would be a considerable measure.[77]

The exchange was not untypical of Massey and Ward's interactions, which reflected the cut and thrust of political theatre, parliamentary decorum and measures of authentic, and not always well-concealed, enmity nursed over long careers.[78] Ward's biographer notes that he considered Massey a 'political parvenu' and 'little more than an uncultivated bigot' while Massey made some sport of pricking Ward's ego in parliamentary debate.[79] There was also a religious divide. Massey was a former Orange Lodge grand master, and Reform's campaigning had alleged that Ward was using his office to favour his fellow Catholics.[80] Conversely, devotion to the British Empire formed a point of unity — their commitments to imperial loyalty 'were perhaps measurable only in micromillimetres'.[81] Massey, influenced by British Israelism, saw the empire as possessing a divine purpose, while Ward has been described as 'the perfect lay spokesman' for the Catholic social elite's conceptions of the 'Anglo-Celtic Empire' and as turning 'the identification of Catholics with Imperialism into almost an art form'.[82]

Once in power, Reform attempted to restore harmony by confronting Red Fed industrial action and driving unions back into the arbitration system. In November 1912 the Coromandel gold-mining town of Waihī became a flashpoint as the government strengthened the local police presence to deal with a major strike that had started in May. The situation escalated into open violence with the police and non-union workers squaring off against unionists; the unionist Fredrick Evans was killed during the skirmishes. Though the strike was soon broken, Holland soon proclaimed Waihī 'but a skirmish of the advance guard in the great class war'.[83]

Greater unrest was certainly unleashed in the Great Strike of the following year as a series of industrial actions erupted between mid-October 1913 and mid-January 1914.[84] The origins lay in disputes at a Huntly coal mine and on the Wellington waterfront, but escalated to a general strike that ultimately involved some 14,000 strikers in a number of centres, though concentrated in mining and waterside areas.[85] Facing port closures that would leave their produce unshipped and valueless, the Farmers' Union helped to organise rural volunteers as police specials, dubbed 'Massey's Cossacks' by labour activists. The government was also prepared to deploy the military if necessary, and Wellington was described as 'an armed camp' in which the 'sinister sound of massed hoofbeats' signalled the movement of hundreds of specials into the city.[86] Militant rhetoric of class war was met by press commentary denouncing anarchists and 'IWW methods' — referring to the syndicalist Industrial Workers of the World.

above Mounted special constables, armed with long batons, ride down Wellington's Tasman Street during the Great Strike of 1913. ALEXANDER TURNBULL LIBRARY, 1/2-049059-G

below Soldiers with fixed bayonets on Wellington's Buckle Street during the Great Strike. ALEXANDER TURNBULL LIBRARY, 1/2-049061-G

The pitched street battles and serious riots that followed constituted the most disruptive episode of civil unrest in modern New Zealand history.

By the end of 1913 the strike had largely broken, with most unions agreeing to return to work under the arbitration system, though enmity between Reform and militant labour had been entrenched. Webb proclaimed that 'Massey has got to go', and even unionists who had opposed the strike were disquieted by the way in which it had been routed.[87] Labour was left in some disarray as various militants lost their positions. Holland, Semple and Fraser were among those charged with inciting violence. Holland was sentenced to 12 months' imprisonment but Semple and Fraser were released, seemingly in an effort to reduce tensions.[88] Perhaps most significantly, the strike left many socialist and labour leaders reassessing the merits of direct action over the need to build institutional power.

Modernisation, the orientation towards Britain and the significance of mass politics were all evident in the unprecedented military reforms undertaken before 1914. Into the twentieth century the British Empire's strategic position shifted as an era of 'splendid isolation' became less certain. The rise of rival powers raised prospects of relative decline, and the prolonged struggle of the South African War (1899–1902) raised anxieties that British power might be in absolute decline. To consolidate regional interests and improve security, London brokered a series of strategic alliances and agreements, including the 1902 Anglo-Japanese alliance and the 1907 Triple Entente with France and Russia. In this same period antagonisms within Anglo-German relations developed, notably around Germany's effort to build a fleet intended to challenge British sea power.[89] The result was a naval arms race and the withdrawal of Royal Navy assets from the Far East for concentration in the North Sea.

New Zealand shared this sense of heightened anxiety. During the nineteenth century both France and Russia had become established bogies in the public mind, and the Anglo-Japanese alliance did little to ease concerns about Japanese power, which flared after that country's shock victory over Russia in 1905 and was sometimes taken as evidence of an awakening Asia, crudely presented as the 'yellow peril'.[90] Furthermore, in 1912 the minister of defence was receiving reviews of the strategic situation which noted Germany as 'our probable opponent in the next great war'.[91] British sea power was considered as essential to regional and national security. As the *Evening Post* sombrely noted in 1908, 'Great Britain can defend the Atlantic; she can defend the Pacific just as certainly; whether she could, if pressed in both oceans, defend her possessions in each equally is a grave question.'[92]

Anglo-German antagonism had another aspect highly relevant to New Zealand. In the last decades of the nineteenth century, German imperial rule had been formalised in several South Pacific territories. Two major possessions, German New Guinea and German Sāmoa, were annexed in 1884 and 1899 respectively and several small islands, like the Marshalls, the Marianas and Carolines, were acquired between those dates. Various political and commercial interests in New Zealand regarded this expansion as thwarting their own Pacific ambitions; Australia expressed similar sentiments, particularly towards New Guinea. In 1900, New

Zealand Chief Justice Sir Robert Stout boldly claimed that the establishment of German rule in Sāmoa had 'created a second Alsace', comparing New Zealand ambitions for Sāmoa to the region France had lost to Germany in 1871.[93] The German East Asia Squadron, stationed at Tsingtao in China, with its core of two modern armoured cruisers, SMS *Scharnhorst* and SMS *Gneisenau*, was also taken as a significant concern.

Germany also carried out 'surveillance and other intelligence tasks' in New Zealand through visits by German naval vessels as well as by 'reporters', 'confidants' and 'informants' based in the country.[94] Police were employed in countering potential espionage and undercover officers were ordered to ascertain the 'identity, destination, and object in view' of 'all Foreigners frequenting Forts or Defences' and then all overseas travellers. For one Wellington detective, this work was ordered to take precedence over 'all other duty he may have in hand'.[95] Other authorities concluded that seizing Sāmoa would be a likely New Zealand objective in the event of hostilities with Germany, and in late 1912 and early 1913 plans for this contingency were drawn up and approved by London.[96]

New Zealand's major response to this mood of anxiety was a strategy of defence reform and greater cooperation with Britain.[97] For example, as efforts to boost British sea power grew, New Zealand's annual subsidy for the Royal Navy was increased from £40,000 in 1903 to £100,000 in 1908.[98] In 1909 Ward announced that New Zealand would gift a dreadnought to the Royal Navy: the battle cruiser HMS *New Zealand* was subsequently launched in 1911. In 1913 an agreement was secured with Britain for the loan of HMS *Philomel* for use as a training ship to build local naval power in cooperation with Australia, which was creating a regional naval capacity.[99]

Defence cooperation was also evident in New Zealand's involvement in the South African War, in which some 6500 New Zealand soldiers, along with doctors, nurses, vets and some 20 schoolteachers, served.[100] By 1913 there was a clear objective of efficiently preparing and dispatching an expeditionary force that could operate alongside imperial forces. 'We want,' the minister of defence publicly stated, 'to be in a position to say to the Mother Country that we have always at her disposal a permanent organisation by which we can send about eight thousand men to any part of our Empire where their services may be needed.'[101]

This strategy led to a significant overhaul of New Zealand's amateur military tradition. In 1898–99 defence expenditure totalled £124,947 (2.6 per cent of total government expenditure); by 1912–13 this had leapt to £1,257,498 (11.3 per cent).[102] The flagship policy of the reforms was introduced by the Liberals, with support from Reform, in the 1909 Defence Act. This established a Territorial Force to replace the Volunteer Force and introduced a system of compulsory military training. In the original text of the legislation, boys enlisted in the Junior Cadets at 12, graduated to the Senior Cadets at 14 and were transferred to the General Training Section at 18. Between 21 and 30 they were included in the Reserve. A British Army officer, Major-General Alexander Godley, was appointed as commandant to oversee the implementation of this scheme and arrived in New Zealand in December 1910.

These reforms also occurred in the context of a distinct public mood that emphasised valour, adventure, physical assertiveness, involvement in patriotic activities, a glorification of history and the notion that military training could instil physical fitness and civic-mindedness in the young.[103] A National Defence League and a Navy League, founded to advocate for defence reforms, claimed thousands of members, branches across the country and patronage from leading public figures.[104] Volunteer movements and rifle clubs were part of the social fabric and community life, especially in small towns.[105] Huge celebration surrounded the 1910 visit of Lord Kitchener, 'the great military organiser of the Empire', and when HMS *New Zealand* toured the country in 1913 it is estimated that almost half the population visited the ship.[106]

The preparation for war, however, occurred alongside a growth in the pacifist and anti-militarist movements. These were inspired partly by the progressive internationalism spreading at the turn of the century, which believed that growing material and moral progress made war, or at least a war between the great powers, untenable. The elements identified with this progress included democracy, capitalism, socialism, growing female influence in public life and evidence of international cooperation such as the disarmament discussions raised at The Hague Convention of 1899. Although peace movements were active before 1900, the introduction of compulsory military training stimulated opposition from an array of pacifists, labour groups, non-conformist religious adherents, civil libertarians and women's groups.[107] Common objections to the scheme included the denial of individual liberties, the militarisation of youth, allegations that camp life promoted immorality, and the sense that all expressions of militarism must be fought in order to secure peace.

Christchurch, in particular, emerged as a heartland of this new anti-militarism. The Anti-Militarist League was founded there in June 1910, with branches later opening in Rūnanga, Blackball, Huntly and Waihī. In May 1911, Christchurch Baptist lay preacher Charles Mackie founded the National Peace Council as an umbrella organisation for church, community and political groups concerned with peace issues; by December 1912, the council claimed 16 branches and 30,000 affiliated members.[108] The organisation also maintained international connections and was instrumental in importing and distributing overseas peace literature, including an abridged copy of English economist Norman Angell's 1910 *The Great Illusion*, which argued for the link between economic interdependence and peace.[109] In February 1912 the Passive Resisters' Union was founded, also in Christchurch, with branches in Wellington, Auckland, Millerton and Rūnanga.[110] In Auckland, Quaker Egerton Gill founded the New Zealand Freedom League as an umbrella organisation uniting small local groups. After its first meeting, the League was most concerned with having the compulsory clauses of the Defence Act repealed.[111]

The labour and women's movements also became forums for some anti-militarism, and the 1913 Unity Conference included discussion on the Social Democratic Party's position. Though some delegates spoke in favour of compulsory military training, the conference eventually decided, by 1987 votes to 44, on a resolution to the 'repeal of the present inadequate Defence Act, and the creation of a citizen army on a volunteer basis, democratically organised with a standard wages while on duty, which shall not be used under any circumstances in time of industrial disputes, together with practical measures for the promotion of peace'.[112] Likewise, a Housewives' Union, founded in Christchurch in 1912 under the dynamic leadership of Ada

above left Charles Mackie committed himself to pacifism, founding the National Peace Council as an umbrella organisation for the peace movement. CANTERBURY MUSEUM, 1980.175.51548

below left Egerton Gill founded the New Zealand Freedom League as a unifying organisation for Auckland-based peace groups. ALEXANDER TURNBULL LIBRARY, PA1-F-129

above right By 1914 Ada Wells was a veteran social campaigner — notably in the suffrage movement — and one of the first women to win public office. ALEXANDER TURNBULL LIBRARY, 1/2-C-016534-F

below right When he became the minister of defence in 1912, James Allen stepped into a role that would give him enormous powers and responsibilities. ALEXANDER TURNBULL LIBRARY, 1/1-013396-G

Wells and Sarah Saunders Page, protested that schools were being turned into 'recruiting grounds for savage warfare', called for women to resist the Defence Act and to campaign for peace.[113]

The implementation of compulsory military training led to confrontation with the anti-militarist movement, most violently in Christchurch. Officials hounded anti-militarists, editorials criticised them, the public abused them and their meetings were broken up. Counter-blows included dispensing pamphlets, disrupting drilling sessions and vandalism. In Christchurch, 'To hell with Godley' and 'We have nothing to defend' were painted around the city and a trophy gun, captured in South Africa, was removed from Victoria Square, painted red and rolled into the Avon River.[114] Some boys who refused to register or take an oath were imprisoned when they refused to pay the resulting fines. Between 11 July 1911 and 30 April 1914, 6876 boys were convicted; from 1 May 1913 to 30 April 1914, 234 were incarcerated for refusal to pay fines.[115] Resistance was remarkably concentrated in the Canterbury military district, where counts of absence from, or obstructions of, parades were twice that of Otago, counts of non-registration were more than four times higher than Wellington, and counts of refusing the oath in the territorials were nearly 17 times higher than Auckland.[116]

With the formation of the Reform government came a new defence minister determined to bring the system into line. James Allen was born in 1855 in Adelaide, Australia. He moved to Dunedin and then England and was orphaned before he was 10. Aged 22 he graduated from Cambridge with a law degree and returned to Dunedin with his cousin and wife, Mary Jane Hill Richards, with whom he would raise six children. Here he gained some of his experience in the administration of education, serving as chancellor and vice-chancellor of the University of Otago, and as a board member of Otago Boys' and Girls' High Schools. He also established business activities and had successful coal-mining investments.[117]

Allen made his move into national politics in 1887 with a surprise victory over Premier Sir Robert Stout for the Dunedin East electorate. Although touted as a potential leader of what became the Reform Party, he ultimately became a lieutenant within Massey's hierarchy. This reflected not only Massey's willingness to promote men smarter than himself but also Allen's strengths and weaknesses, which made him 'more of an administrator than a politician'.[118] Intelligent, practical and diligent, he had, as the following years would prove, a capacity for work described as 'simply prodigious'.[119] However, his stoic and almost patrician demeanour gave him an air of dourness and parsimony, characteristically unsoftened by levity. In politics he often matched Massey in resolute conviction, though he was more receptive to new ideas and consistently pushed for reforms, efficiency and economy; in the process he became an outspoken critic of Ward's financial policies. A committed Anglican, Allen was a notable supporter of the Bible in Schools movement. He also established himself as a leading opposition spokesman on military matters; he was an active member of the Volunteer Force from April 1891 and president of the Otago branch of the Navy League from 1912. In that year, he took up the defence portfolio, adding it to his other responsibilities as minister of finance and of education.

In overseeing the defence scheme, Allen sought to stand fast while making reforms. The

Junior Cadets were abolished, though the maximum age of the general training section was extended to 25. Allen also worked to make the system less contentious: disputes over unpaid fines were to be avoided by taking them out of wages, scandals over imprisoning objectors alongside common criminals were to be circumvented by holding objectors in military detention centres, and new legislation would offer an alternative means of service for those with religious convictions.[120]

However, unions seethed over tampering with wages and 13 objectors placed in detention on Rīpapa Island in Lyttelton Harbour became something of a cause célèbre in 1913 when news got out that they were staging a hunger strike in response to their treatment. Labour's Unity Conference, then in session, facilitated a 400-strong march on Parliament, demanding their release. When the prisoners were released they were met by a crowd of 2500 sympathisers and subsequently toured the country to promote a repeal of the Defence Act.[121]

However, the vast majority of boys complied with the provisions of the Defence Act — 83.31 per cent in 1913–14, against 10.44 per cent listed as absent without leave and 6.25 per cent listed as absent with leave — and supporters of the scheme were growing frustrated with those they considered to be flouting the law and communal obligations.[122] Editorials called for tougher treatment: 'We have precious little sympathy with the silly, notoriety-craving youths, who, in Christchurch, persist in defying the law with regard to military training, and so far as actual deliberate breaches of the Defence Act are concerned we hold that those who commit them deserve no leniency, but should be made to obey the law, even if the form of punishment were ten times more severe than it is at present.'[123]

Such attitudes towards 'shirkers' had repercussions for those citing religious objections to taking oaths and other aspects of military training. Military authorities could exempt boys on religious grounds, but a 1912 amendment proposing a broader recognition of conscientious objection was decisively defeated in Parliament, and when the government asked local bodies to provide work for the few religious objectors, most refused.[124] In June 1914 Massey, with characteristic conviction, announced that his administration would 'stand or fall by the principles of the Defence Act'.[125]

That month was the height of a European summer that would later be mythologised as the final days of a more innocent age. In New Zealand it was winter, but the rhythms of everyday life continued alongside the great issues of the age. Social events were held, including gatherings to mark the ninety-ninth anniversary of the Battle of Waterloo; farmers stated their assessments of the last season and made predictions for the season to come; the latest films and fashions were advertised; births, deaths and marriages were announced. At the end of the month, news arrived that the presumptive heir to the Austrian throne and his wife had been assassinated.

CHAPTER ONE

CRISIS

previous pages
The battle cruiser HMS *New Zealand* arriving in Lyttelton on 13 May 1913. A gift to the Royal Navy, the ship was viewed by an estimated 500,000 New Zealanders during its 10-week sail around the country. NATIONAL MUSEUM OF THE ROYAL NEW ZEALAND NAVY COLLECTION, ABT 0060, PHOTOGRAPHER UNKNOWN

On 28 June 1914, the Austrian Archduke Franz Ferdinand and his wife, Sophie, the Duchess of Hohenberg, were assassinated while visiting the Bosnian city of Sarajevo. The assassin, Gavrilo Princip, was a young radical and a member of a revolutionary group with links to Serbian officials. The resulting confrontation between the Austro-Hungarian Empire and Serbia soon escalated into the 'July Crisis' and climaxed with the outbreak of a general European war by early August. Such a development was both long anticipated and shockingly sudden. Although tensions and sabre-rattling were certainly apparent, prior international crises carrying threats of war had been settled through diplomatic solutions, and in 1914 Anglo-German relations appeared less menacing than was the case five years earlier.

Most New Zealanders learnt of the assassinations through newspaper editorials that conveyed the opinions of a number of relatively well-informed commentators. Many papers reported the assassinations alongside the losses the Austrian royal family had suffered in recent years.[1] The government's initial reaction was restrained and diplomatic: a condolence telegram, denouncing 'the terrible crime which has been perpetrated', was promptly sent to Vienna via the colonial secretary.[2] General sympathy was, however, tempered with some reproach; the *Auckland Star*, for instance, criticised the Austro-Hungarian 'forward policy' to confront Balkan nationalism.[3] Conversely, the *New Zealand Herald* sympathised with Austria's 'dominant Teutonic element', and hoped that antagonisms within Anglo-German relations would soon be transcended:

> Even in the heat of international rivalries and jealousies, we need not forget that Germans and British are antagonistic only because they desire the same thing and because our German cousins seek to oust us from the position in the world we inherit from our fathers . . . We have much more in common with the Germans and with the German-Austrians than we have with the Russians, and have had enough experience of the burden of Empire to understand and sympathise with the position of Austria in Central and Southern Europe.

Indeed the paper declared the Balkans a 'zone of anarchy, the breeding-ground of the syndicalist movement', and drew a connection between the lawlessness of the assassinations and the previous year's general strike.[4]

Another major theme in the initial commentary was some recognition of the potential implications of the assassinations for regional and European stability. The Christchurch *Star* presciently, if rather vaguely, anticipated that '[a]ll Europe will be thrown into a state of turmoil . . . [it] would be a bold prophet who would venture to predict the end of the complications that will ensue'.[5] Its rival, the *Sun*, believed that 'the possibilities of local and Near East conflagrations are very pronounced'.[6] Wellington's *Dominion*, too, warned that 'the nations of Europe are armed to the teeth' and that the consequences of assassination might be 'far-reaching'.[7] However, the incident rapidly died down in the New Zealand press and was rarely referred to over the first three weeks of July. Those who did mention it noted that a potential war between Austria and Serbia could destabilise the European order and that a general war was possible. The *Dominion*, for example, remarked that 'Russia is not likely to stand idly by and see Austria increasing her power and prestige in Eastern Europe, and if Russia should take a hand in the fray it is impossible to say where the trouble would end'.[8]

The crisis escalated on 23 July when Austria–Hungary delivered a severe ultimatum to Serbia. Within days several newspapers prematurely announced, often in banner headlines, that Austria–Hungary had declared war on Serbia and editors again warned that the whole Triple Entente — Russia, France and Britain – might soon become involved.[9] The threat was commonly described as 'Armageddon' and many papers demonstrated a sense that history was being made. 'Historians of the future,' noted the *Nelson Evening Mail*, 'will turn to the year 1914 as marking great changes in world affairs. What those changes will be it is impossible to say now. We stand on the threshold of great upheaval, and the fate of Empires hangs in the balance.'[10] Many of those following the news felt the same. As Auckland clerk Harrold Ennor noted in his diary, 'Things look black in Europe just now. Serbia refused to punish the assassinator of Austria's Crown Prince and war has been declared. It is quite possible that Russia, France, Italy and England may be drawn into the quarrel.'[11]

The Auckland dailies continued to duel over whether Serbia or Austria–Hungary was more culpable. The *Auckland Star* declared that 'Austria has simply seized upon this tragic incident as an opportunity for putting into operation the plan that she has long since carefully matured'.[12] The following morning the *New Zealand Herald* reiterated its view that 'there can be no sympathy for Servia [sic]' and that the other powers should strive to persuade Russia not to intervene.[13] It described the latter as 'little more than an Asiatic autocracy, which by force of circumstances and natural energy has become fastened upon the eastern flank of civilisation'. The *Southland Times* went further and argued that no one wanted war except for Russia.[14]

On 28 July, a month after the assassination, came the first parliamentary mention of the crisis, when Massey read the latest telegram from the Colonial Office to the House: '"His Majesty's Government has not received any intimation of the outbreak of war." It was to be hoped, even now, that war would be averted.'[15] Massey had also alluded to the crisis earlier that day, when opening the Agricultural and Pastoral Conference in Wellington. Speaking of 'the bright prospects ahead of New Zealand', he also noted that 'there was only one trouble, and it might prove to be a serious one . . . the war cloud that threatened in the Northern Hemisphere. When a war started there was no telling where it would stop.'[16] He concluded with a statement that embodied his attitude throughout the conflict and drew applause: 'If the Great Empire to which we belonged happened to become involved he was quite sure the different parts of the Empire would stand together as they had done in past years.'

At 11 a.m. on 28 July, Austria–Hungary declared war on Serbia. Time difference meant the news was announced in New Zealand on 30 July by the governor, who also noted that Russia had ordered a general mobilisation of its military forces, increasing its readiness for war. These events clearly increased the possibility of a general European conflict, and potentially British involvement. An Admiralty message received on 30 July noted 'that war appeared imminent', an obvious escalation from the 27 July position that war was 'by no means impossible'.[17]

A quickly assembled 'war council', consisting of Massey, Godley and Captain Herbert Marshall (New Zealand's senior naval officer), sanctioned various mobilisation and defence measures, including instructions for military district headquarters to post guards at sensitive sites, 'as unostentatiously as possible', and to man coastal defences.[18] This decision was born of the long-standing fear of a naval raid and with the German East Asia Squadron in mind, which was reported as possibly as close as Sāmoa.[19] In case of potential sabotage, guards were posted at radio stations and cable-landing points and on every railway bridge and tunnel. They remained on a round-the-clock watch through August.[20]

These precautions ultimately proved more hazardous than enemy action. Besides the extinguishing of lighthouses, until 15 August, from 4 August regulations required vessels entering the main ports to be cleared by a naval officer. The captain of the small steamer *Wakatu* was not aware of this when entering Lyttelton Harbour early on 5 August and a warning shot was fired from Fort Jervois on Rīpapa Island. Two days later some confusion as to whether the coaster *Breeze* had been cleared led to another Fort Jervois warning shot, which exploded astern of the ship — and raised questions about the accuracy of the gun or the gunners. A fortnight later, when the Takapuna battery in Auckland fired a warning shot to halt the scow *Three Cheers*, the shell exploded midway between the offending vessel and a passenger ferry headed for Rangitoto.[21] These precautions would also lead to New Zealand's first service-related death of the war: territorial Robert Hislop died on 19 August after falling from a rail bridge.[22]

On the outbreak of the Austro-Serbian war, the Austrian consul announced that local reservists must now return home to report for duty: he expected about 100 men to sail on 10 August.[23] This summons, however, provoked a strong reaction from local Croatians, largely from Dalmatia, who constituted by far the largest section of Austria–Hungary's imperial subjects in New Zealand.[24] On 30 July a meeting of Croatians in New Plymouth claimed that they were 'not Austrian subjects by free will, but by the point of the bayonet'. They were, they declared, 'now subject to the Union Jack, where they get justice and freedom'.[25] A Croatian Independence League formed in Auckland and raised the substantial sum of £250 in two days to pay the passages of Slavs who wished to volunteer for the Serbian Army.[26] Nearly a dozen protesters demonstrated outside the Austrian consulate in Auckland's Customs Street East, shouting 'Down with Austria', though ambitions to burn an Austrian flag were thwarted by difficulties in obtaining one.[27]

Despite the threat of a wider war, some nursed hopes that a major conflict could be averted and many looked to the British foreign secretary, Sir Edward Grey, and British diplomatic proposals for a conference to peacefully resolve the crisis or limit the war.[28] On 1 August Lord Liverpool was applauded when he remarked that '[t]he position as regarded the war was very uncertain at the present moment, and he was sure all those present would join him in the hope that the prospects would brighten very soon'.[29] There was also, however, anxiety and uncertainty, as the *Dominion* noted: 'the situation has darkened . . . The dangerous rapidity of events is outstripping the efforts of diplomacy.'[30]

On the evening of 31 July, Massey announced in Parliament: 'As far as it is possible to judge from information received there is no occasion for serious alarm but under existing circumstances we have to prepare for possibilities.' He requested the House to approve the creation of an expeditionary force of volunteers 'if the occasion arises'. This offer, influenced by news that Canada had offered a substantial force, signalled to the authorities in London and to the patriotic New Zealand public that his government would fully support the empire in the crisis. Any reluctance to follow the Canadian example would have been regarded by a very large section of the population as strangely unpatriotic and would have allowed Ward to characterise Massey as neglectful of imperial responsibilities. In contrast to the parliamentary response to the outbreak of the South African War, when some radical Liberals opposed sending New Zealand troops, MPs were unanimous in supporting the offer. Both sides of the House applauded, and all MPs stood to sing a verse of 'God Save the King'.[31] Ward announced that his MPs would 'gladly co-operate with the Government in assisting it to defend this portion of the Empire and the Empire as a whole'. A thoroughgoing imperialist, Ward also knew that an election had to be held by the end of the year and he had high hopes of returning to power. Anything suggesting that the Liberal Party was not responding patriotically to the crisis threatened that prospect.

On 1 August the possibility that a regional war between Austria–Hungary and Serbia might develop into a continental war was confirmed as Germany declared war on Russia and began an invasion of Luxembourg. When this news arrived in New Zealand, at 5 p.m. on Sunday, 2 August, many editors sent messages or copies of the special editions to local churches so that those officiating could tell their congregations. Most clergymen mentioned the development in their sermons and offered prayers for peace, though the frequent singing of 'God Save the King' seemed to indicate an acceptance that the British Empire might become involved.[32] Dr Alfred Averill, the Anglican Bishop of Auckland, probably spoke for many when he said, 'It is monstrous even to think of our Empire being dragged into the conflict . . . it is monstrous that there should be a resort to war on our part as the price of the Triple Entente. Of course, if it is our duty, however sad as it may be, we shall not be found to fail.'[33]

The Executive Council — members of the Cabinet plus the governor — immediately met at Parliament, while 'interested members impatiently paced the lobbies and discussed the possibilities of the situation'. Alongside 'deep regret at the outbreak of such a disastrous conflict . . . members one and all declared a confident belief in the ability of the British race to weather whatever storms might descend'.[34] The council met again the next morning and

BLACK OUTLOOK.

WAR DECLARED.

BETWEEN AUSTRIA AND SERVIA.

OFFICIAL ANNOUNCEMENT.

WAR FEELING IN AUSTRIA-HUNGARY.

PATRIOTIC DEMONSTRATIONS IN RUSSIA.

ACTIVITY IN BRITISH NAVAL CIRCLES.

A cable message from London received at 8 o'clock this morning conveyed the bare information that war between Austria-Hungary and Servia had been declared. About an hour later this was confirmed by receipt of the following message:—

(By Telegraph.—Press Association.—Copyright.)

VIENNA, 28th July.

It is officially announced that Austria-Hungary has declared war on Servia.

The proposal made by Sir Edward Grey (British Secretary of State for Foreign Affairs) that the Ambassadors for France, Germany, and Italy should confer with him in London did not receive Germany's approval, although Italy urged her ally to fall in with it.

In Austria-Hungary there is a very strong war feeling, and in the Russian capital there have been significant patriotic demonstrations. In England there is much activity at naval depots.

above Members of the Post and Telegraph Guard posted to Cable Bay, Nelson, as part of the national security measures enacted during the crisis. ALEXANDER TURNBULL LIBRARY, 1/1-011487-G

left A cable news report noting the outbreak of an Austro-Serbian war and the threat of a wider European war. EVENING POST, 29 JULY 1914, P. 7

afternoon, but Massey made only a few remarks to waiting journalists following the earlier meeting, denying any official reply to his 'offer' of 31 July and maintaining that it was not an offer, anyway, 'until Parliament agrees'.[35]

Again there were reactions from foreign consulates in New Zealand. The French consul, doubtless expecting that Germany's declaration on France's Russian ally would result in a Franco-German war, announced on 3 August that 'all French subjects, including reservists' would be required to report to local agents of France as part of the general mobilisation.[36] The following day the German consuls in Auckland and Wellington advised German soldiers and citizens liable for service to travel home or report to the consulate.[37] That same day Lyttelton mayor J. R. Webb noted that New Zealand 'could not help feeling sympathy with those who had been plunged into conflict' and added his fear that Britain 'would be brought into the broil, in which all nations would suffer'.[38]

With the Triple Entente and the Central Powers — Germany and Austria–Hungary — now mobilising for war, British involvement became a distinct possibility, though a great deal of uncertainty remained. New Zealand's newspapers disagreed over Britain's moral obligation to support Russia and France, given that it had no formal treaty, though some argued the Triple Entente entailed a moral, if not a legal, duty. Christchurch's *Press*, for instance, considered that the empire was obliged to help its 'friends' and was somewhat critical of London for not pledging its assistance to France and Russia unequivocally at an early stage.[39] The *Ashburton Times* made a similar point: 'if the Triple Entente and the Entente Cordiale stand for anything — if they are anything but meaningless phrases — it is quite conceivable that Great Britain, also, will be drawn into the international maelstrom which those fateful bullets have created'.[40] Similarly, the *Oamaru Mail* declared that Britain 'will assuredly honor the obligations placed upon her by the unwritten entente'.[41] Late in the crisis, the *Poverty Bay Herald* claimed that British neutrality would 'forfeit the honourable esteem of countries which have been led to rely upon us for help'.[42]

Other newspapers questioned any moral commitment to the Entente. Dunedin's *Evening Star* reacted negatively to the news that a prominent St Petersburg newspaper 'seems to count on the active and practical sympathy of England in the event of Russia and France being drawn into the maelstrom'. It declared that '[t]he sincere prayer of Britons throughout the Empire will be "We trust not"'.[43] Wellington's *Evening Post* felt the same and took heart from Italy's announcement that it would be neutral despite its defensive alliance with Austria–Hungary and Germany: 'Fortunate are the countries that hold aloof from the threatened carnage. Italy may be one, and Britain, it may be hoped, will be another.'[44]

After Germany's declaration of war on Russia, though, the New Zealand press was almost unanimously of the view that the security of Britain, and of its empire, including New Zealand, was at stake. As the *Timaru Herald* pointed out, both self-interest and loyalty would ensure that the dominions joined the war, 'since the safety of Great Britain is the safety of the Empire'.[45] The *Grey River Argus* was more explicit:

'STAR' EXTRA

FRANCE INVADED

BY GERMAN ARMY.

No Declaration of War.

(Received 10.20 a.m.)

LONDON, August 2.

Though France was not notified of a declaration of war, Germany to-day invaded France at Circy.

Printed and Published for the Proprietors, "The Brett Printing and Publishing Company, Limited," by Henry Brett, of Lake Takapuna, Journalist, at the Office of the Company, Shortland Street, Auckland.

MONDAY, AUGUST, 3, 1914.

A newspaper extra, printed on 3 August 1914, announcing a German invasion of France. However, Germany had not yet invaded and Berlin would issue a declaration of war on 3 August. ALEXANDER TURNBULL LIBRARY, QMS-0680

> If France and Russia are defeated in the present struggle and Britain stands aloof and allows this to take place, Germany will become the overlord of Europe and will then be in a position to compel the European nations to combine for the conquest of England which will then stand apart in dreary isolation, surrounded by enemies on all sides. This would be the beginning of the end of the British Empire . . . Japan would undoubtedly seize the opportunity of becoming possessed of India and any of our Pacific possessions that took her fancy. Australia and New Zealand . . . could offer at best a poor opposition to the well trained soldiers of Japan . . . The motto of Britain at present must be: 'Now or Never'.[46]

With an eye to the recent naval arms race, other editorials also concluded that victory over France and Russia would make Germany too powerful economically and militarily for Britain's safety and would put its forces in vital strategic positions just across the Channel and North Sea.[47] The *Evening Star*, which had denied Britain's moral obligation to assist fellow members of the Entente, had already accepted that, for its own security, Britain could not stand aside and see France defeated.[48] The *Evening Post* also came to regard as too dangerous the prospect of Germany defeating France and receiving a massive indemnity that could be spent on dreadnoughts 'to crush Britain'.[49] It also emphasised the threat represented by German control of the Low Countries and the Channel ports, which could be used to threaten an invasion.[50] Curiously, the idea that the British Empire was bound by treaty to confront any violation of Belgium's neutrality featured very little in editorial discussions.

Although many accepted the logic of standing by Britain, several commentators, publicly and privately, continued to note their dismay at developments. On 2 August, William Skinner, a prominent New Plymouth land surveyor, wrote in his diary: 'Now we are in for a most awfull [sic] war, as France must go to Russia's assistance, & England can scarcely hope to keep out of it this will be one of the most dreadful wars of all time.'[51] Some marked a particular sadness at the possibility of an Anglo-German conflict. On 1 August the *New Zealand Herald* stressed that German immigrants were welcome in New Zealand, that German cultural and intellectual achievements were admired, and that kinship should trump foreign policy: 'in religion, in national aspirations, in social tendencies and in ethical conceptions, British and German are one and the same'.[52]

On 4 August Dunedin's evening newspaper declared 'that the German people are perhaps the most intelligent in Europe, and they are as much concerned in peaceful industry and commerce as we ourselves'.[53] The same day the editor of Hokitika's newspaper pleaded that a war should not affect personal friendships, 'some of them long-standing and greatly cherished. For our own part, we know many Germans for whom we entertain the highest regard and admiration. We admire the German nation for their many fine qualities of thrift, of thoroughness, of dogged pertinacity.'[54]

Unsurprisingly, the *Maoriland Worker* had a very different interpretation of the causes of the crisis. Its only pre-war editorial placed the blame on the capitalist system:

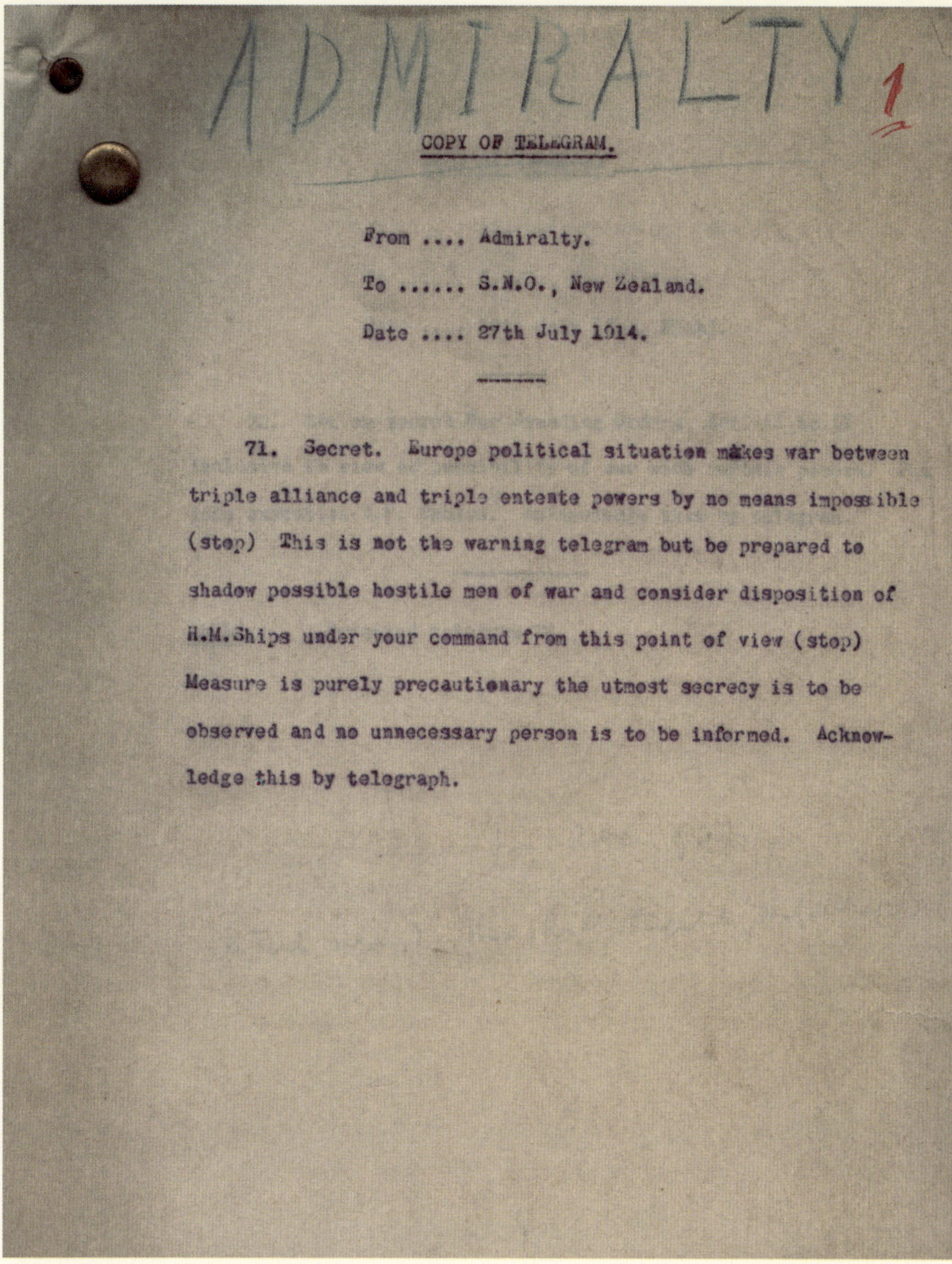
ADMIRALTY 1

COPY OF TELEGRAM.

From .... Admiralty.

To ...... S.N.O., New Zealand.

Date .... 27th July 1914.

---

71. Secret. Europe political situation makes war between triple alliance and triple entente powers by no means impossible (stop) This is not the warning telegram but be prepared to shadow possible hostile men of war and consider disposition of H.M.Ships under your command from this point of view (stop) Measure is purely precautionary the utmost secrecy is to be observed and no unnecessary person is to be informed. Acknowledge this by telegraph.

A British Admiralty telegram to New Zealand authorities advising on the critical situation in Europe, the possibility of war and the prospect of precautionary measures being ordered. ARCHIVES NEW ZEALAND, R13344128

> For despite all the tall talk of 'patriotism', 'loyalty[']', 'fatherland', and the like, the propelling force back of the whole bloody and damnable conspiracy is DIVIDENDS, DIVIDENDS, DIVIDENDS! Soon Britain may, because of her alliance with France and because of certain financial interests involved, or anxious to be involved, be dragged into the human maelstrom . . . Then will be utilised all the force and ingenuity of the capitalist class to arouse us into a state of frenzy, dubbed by them patriotism.[55]

The editor urged New Zealand workers '[t]o keep cool heads and not be blinded into silly volunteering as part of expeditionary forces to bolster the vested interests of plutocracy'. He also referred to a hope, nurtured by many socialists, that industrial action would halt war. 'Would that the workers were organised sufficiently to stop this mad murder-mongering now! Would that they could declare a general strike and paralyse the military demons . . . Whether our comrades will undertake the task or not it is difficult to say, but if ever such a step ought to be taken now above all others is the time.'

However, unlike its British counterpart, the *Daily Herald*, the *Maoriland Worker* did not call for such a strike in New Zealand, possibly chastened by the outcome of the previous year. However, 'John Ball', a columnist in the newspaper, urged readers to take heart from reports that socialists in a number of European countries were opposing involvement in war.[56] In its only editorial related to the crisis, *Truth* confined itself to contradicting any assertions that socialist or anarchist movements were responsible for the rash of assassinations in recent years, including those in Sarajevo. A cartoon in the same edition portrayed a stalwart John Bull endeavouring to keep 'the dogs of war' from savaging 'Europa', wielding a whip labelled 'diplomacy'.[57]

Officials were also now openly speaking of British involvement in the conflict. In a speech at Takapau in Hawke's Bay on the evening of 2 August, William Fraser, minister of public works, dismissed the idea that the expeditionary force was destined for European battlefields: 'They could not send men to the front from here. That was nonsense; the great thing was to show the Old Land that we were heartily with her, and intended to back her up on every occasion, to the fullest extent of our power.'[58] Two days later, he clarified his remarks by saying that 'it would be nonsense to send men from here to Europe, because it would be impracticable. Canada had offered troops, but Canada was in a very different position, being only six days from Europe, while we were about 50 days. It was quite possible, however, that an expeditionary force from New Zealand might be used somewhere in the Pacific or in this hemisphere for Imperial purposes.'[59] Given that, on 2 August, London had suggested that New Zealand might send an expeditionary force to Sāmoa, and that any mention of this was forbidden, Fraser's reference to 'the Pacific' seems rather unwise, though there were other German possessions in the region.

Massey maintained the even demeanour he had so far displayed, stating that his government was taking the situation seriously, calling for solidarity but avoiding any specific prescription. On the afternoon of 4 August, he publicly summarised the measures that had been put in place, including the mobilisation of the naval volunteers, the handover of control of the New Zealand Navy to the Admiralty (as envisaged in the legislation establishing the local force), the introduction of censorship on telegrams, the manning of port defences and the requirement that ships entering ports submit to examination. He appreciated that 'in all parts of the Empire Imperial questions were being considered above party. There was no necessity for anything in the way of panic or for the indulgence in Jingoism. He was sure that Parliament, people, and Government of New Zealand would do their duty, although it might mean that sacrifices would have to be made. But they would do their duty, and do it under any circumstances that might arise.'[60] Calling for an adjournment, which was agreed to, Massey noted, 'I do not propose to take any contentious measures to-day, as I am afraid the thoughts of honourable members are, like my own, on events occurring in Europe, and not on the business of the House.'[61]

During the first days of August reaction to the crisis moved beyond commentary and official preparation. Some rushes to stockpile goods suggest that sections of the public were seriously considering the likelihood of a war that would probably lift prices and disrupt supplies.[62] On 1 August Wellington and Canterbury flour prices increased by £1 per ton and two days later prices in the capital went up by another £1.[63] A day later Ashburton bakers advertised that they were raising the cost for a 4-pound loaf from 7d to 8d, roughly 14 per cent, in response to what was now a £2 per ton increase in the flour price.[64]

According to one grocer, 'Sugar is also much sought after and perhaps next to that is kerosene. People are buying a lot of stuff in large quantities, no matter whether there is a prospect of a rise or not. We have also had a big run on dried fruits, such as currants, raisins, etc.' 'One rise scares them,' said another. 'Nothing touches a housewife more deeply than a drain on her purse. Flour is up, for a time at least. We are selling 200 lb. bags where we used to sell 25 lb. lots. There is a great demand on oatmeal and sugar too, and we are also getting rid of a lot of petrol.'[65] Such large-scale purchasing only hastened price increases, and because buying in bulk required either cash or credit, poorer people lost out while anyone in the supply chain — growers, millers or bakers — still holding stocks of wheat or flour when the price went up stood to make a windfall.

In the last days of peace crowds gathered in civic centres and outside newspaper offices. Later accounts saw these gatherings either as embodiments of admirable public unity and idealism or as manifestations of a haunting naivety about the coming catastrophe. Major Fred Waite's 1919 history of the Gallipoli campaign was a classic example of the former:

> . . . recognizing to the full the gravity of the step, New Zealand placed all her resources at the disposal of the Mother Land . . . It was instinctively recognised that Britain must stand by France and Belgium, and when the news of that momentous decision did come the great wave of enthusiasm swept anew over the countryside.[66]

More recent scholarship, however, reveals 'an altogether more complex picture' of the manner in which people reacted to the prospect of war; one historian, summarising transnational research, writes that 'the myth that European men leapt at the opportunity to defeat a hated enemy has been comprehensively dispelled'.[67] Within New Zealand, crowds expressed enthusiasm for the war, horror at such a possibility and resolutions to dutifully pull together.

In a society given to such events, public gatherings and communal singing also helped to relieve collective anxieties. Large numbers took to the streets throughout the country. On 4 August in Auckland a dense crowd on Queen Street was

> anxiously awaiting the posting of any fresh war news at the *Herald* office. Snatches of patriotic songs and the National Anthem helped to relieve their feelings, while at intervals rousing cheers were given for territorials in uniform, who happened to pass along the street. When the Garrison Artillery Division paraded on the wharf at midnight, a crowd of between 200 and 300 civilians cheered them to the echo as they embarked for the forts.[68]

When the Garrison Artillery's mobilisation was announced at the beginning of the Northern Boxing Association's carnival, the audience of nearly 3000 rose to sing the National Anthem and 'Rule Britannia', 'afterwards cheering wildly'.[69] In Whanganui a large crowd, gathered outside a newspaper office in the evening to get the latest news, sang patriotic British songs and the 'Marseillaise' to the accompaniment of a Salvation Army band.[70] There were comparable expressions of solidarity from some Māori. In the Bay of Plenty, Te Arawa sent a telegraph to the government on 3 August, signed by several chiefs: 'We of the Arawas, as our forefathers before us offer our services to our King and country in whatever clime and whenever you see fit to call us.'[71]

Some of these demonstrations were certainly boisterous, even bellicose, especially when young middle-class men were involved. On the evening of 4 August between 200 and 400 university students, mostly male and some in cadet uniforms, marched to Parliament to cheer, sing patriotic songs and call for the prime minister.[72] There was some disappointment when Massey informed them that war had not been declared in London, despite an American report to that effect. However, cheers followed when he added that he thought such a declaration was imminent and suggested that New Zealanders might be sent to the front. The crowd then proceeded to the Royal Oak Hotel on Cuba Street, where Ward was staying. He, too, was cheered when he said that New Zealand involvement was inevitable. In stating his expectation of a difficult struggle he expressed a sentiment that would be widely used, both approvingly and cynically, during the war: 'if the necessity arose our men and our money would be used to the last man and the last shilling to keep flying the old flag under which we had lived for centuries'.[73]

That same evening, in Christchurch, some 30 to 50 students marched from Cathedral Square to Victoria Square during rush hour.

> The numbers grew as they marched along, cheering and singing, for the inevitable small boy trailed behind and the curious male, wanting to know what it was all about, also drifted alongside in numbers. There must have been almost two hundred persons gathered about the Queen's Statue at a quarter to six, and they there learned from one of the young men elected to speak . . . that although there was no further war news to be imparted the demonstrators

> were prepared to be excessively patriotic under all circumstances . . . [T]he cheerful patriots marched back to the Cathedral and made another little stop outside the tram shelter, where more singing and more cheers were given, for the benefit of the six o'clock homefarers this time. They were mildly interested.[74]

Some at public gatherings were vehemently opposed to any involvement in the coming conflict. On 1 August, in Christchurch, the Passive Resisters' Union had called an anti-war meeting in Victoria Square. It attracted some 20 to 30 spectators when it started at 8 p.m. — most people were at a charity concert in Cathedral Square — but the crowd eventually swelled to around 250 as alternative Saturday-night attractions dwindled and news spread that there had been some minor confrontations with hecklers. In the words of one speaker, the 'armament trusts' and 'money bugs' of Europe had been engineering the developing conflict. The meeting passed a resolution condemning 'any efforts on the part of the New Zealand Government or legislators to incite our young men in any way to leave the Dominion to take part in a European war'.[75] On 3 August a public meeting of the Wellington Branch of the Social Democratic Party had passed a resolution noting 'our abhorrence of the pseudo-patriotism, that is the outcome of Jingo sentiments, fermented by and in the interests of financial groups, that thrive by inculcating the spirit of hatred and international jealousies, in order to plunder the public'.[76]

Ultimately, the last days of July and the first days of August were a time of uncertainty and prolonged tension for much of New Zealand society. Questions of whether Austria–Hungary and Serbia would go to war, whether that confrontation would bring a more general war and whether the British Empire, and New Zealand, would be a spectator or a participant weighed heavily on many minds. As one witness later recalled, 'there were hopes, fears, doubtings, but an ever-increasing undercurrent of certainty that war would come'.[77] For New Zealand, that certainty arrived on 5 August.

CHAPTER TWO

WAR IS DECLARED

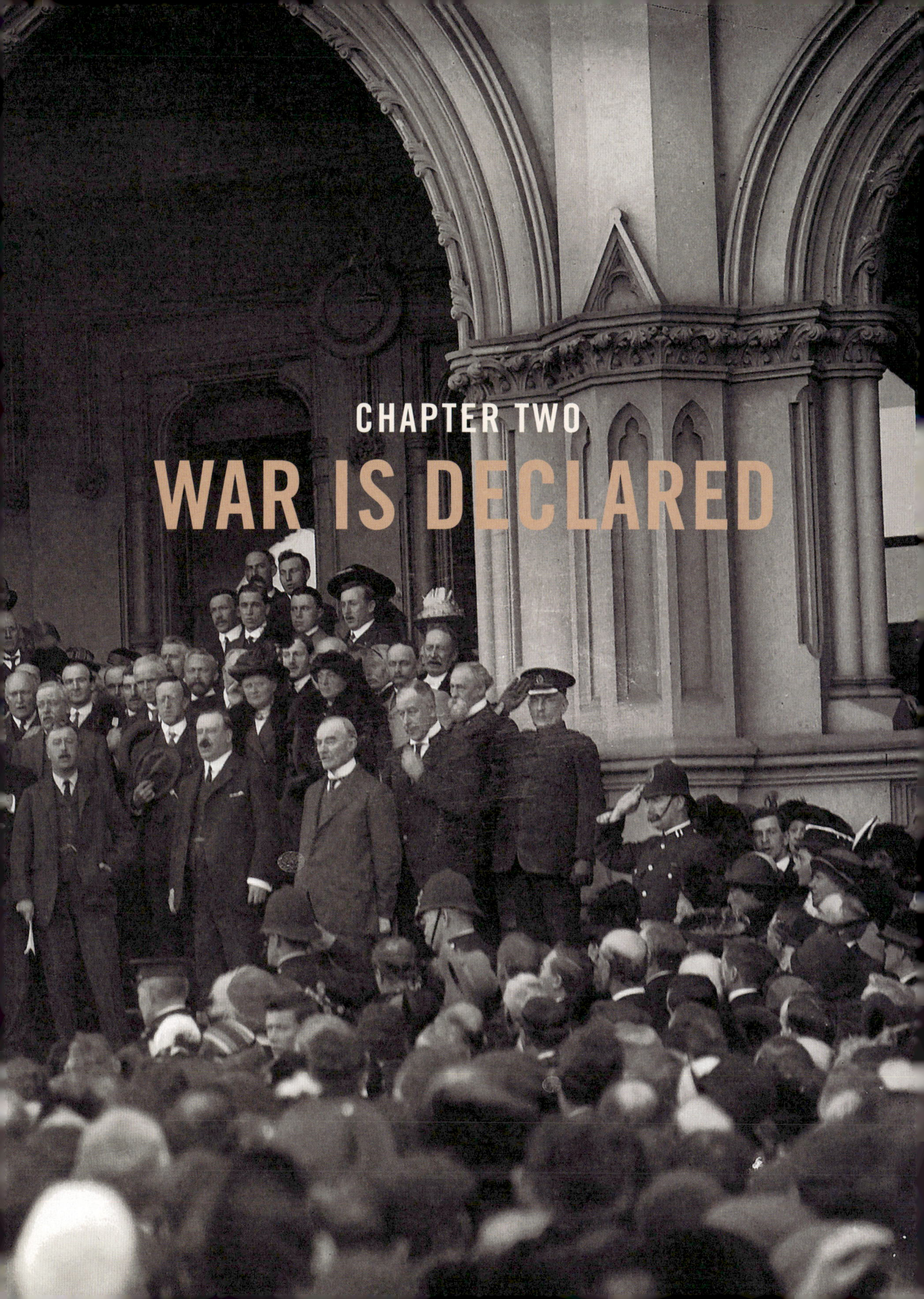

previous pages
The governor, the second earl of Liverpool (centre and holding a telegraph), announces Britain and New Zealand's state of war with Germany to a large crowd outside Parliament on 5 August 1914. ALEXANDER TURNBULL LIBRARY, 1/2-048457-G

On the morning of 4 August 1914, Germany invaded Belgium as part of its war plan against France. The invasion transformed British parliamentary opinion, which had hitherto included significant support for a conference to resolve the crisis and calls to remain neutral in a continental conflict. On 27 July, three-quarters of the Cabinet had been against British intervention and Prime Minister Herbert Asquith had described the looming confrontation as 'still not a British war'.[1] Following the invasion, politicians broadly unified behind British involvement. Conservatives argued the need to prevent a victorious Germany from holding the Low Countries and to preserve Britain's honour (the modem synonym would be 'credibility'). Liberals emphasised the need to uphold the rule of law, maintain the rights of small nations and resist what they saw as Germany's aggressive militarism. An ultimatum to Germany, stating that Belgium's neutrality must be respected, was dispatched and set to expire at midnight.

In bright winter sunshine on the morning of 5 August, a Wednesday, notices were posted around Wellington stating that the governor would make an important announcement outside Parliament Buildings at 3 p.m. It was understood, however, 'that the announcement did not involve a declaration of war'.[2] At the appointed time an official party assembled on the steps before a crowd thought to number between 12,000 and 15,000. Lord Liverpool, demonstrating a sense of drama, slowly read a telegram of appreciation from King George V for the support of the dominions during the crisis, followed by his reply, which affirmed New Zealand loyalty. He then announced, 'Fellow subjects: Since I sent out that notice this morning, I have got another telegram. It is very short. I will read it to you: "War has broken out with Germany."'[3]

In a legal sense, Britain's declaration of war meant New Zealand and the other dominions were automatically at war too. However, that legal reality did not compel any particular response, and as one historian notes, 'In principle the dominion governments were free to cheer from the sidelines, or to make only token gestures of support.'[4] In practice, however, there was a general commitment to stand with Britain. Such sentiments dominated the official speeches made immediately after the declaration. In stressing the gravity of the situation, Massey called for solidarity and calm:

> I trust that we are all of one way of thinking: that the British people and the Empire are to-day face to face with the most serious crisis ever experienced in the history of the Empire, and we are confident that we shall come through successfully. We must take notice of the very earnest advice contained in the last announcement of the message from His Majesty the King: we must 'stand together, calm, united, resolute, trusting in God,' and I am glad to say that not only in New Zealand does this feeling of confidence exist but it obtains throughout every part of the Empire. The whole British people are to-day able to present a united front to our enemies . . . My advice at the most trying moment is to keep cool, stand fast, do your duty to New Zealand, and to the Empire.[5]

Ward, too, considered that the British Empire was 'entering upon the greatest crisis in her history'. Although imperial rulers had 'done nothing to provoke or precipitate war; on the contrary, they have done all that is humanly possible to avert it', Britain could not 'stand aside and let powerful friendly nations go on without taking their part'. He trusted that people throughout the empire would 'stand united, with undoubted courage and inflexible determination, and they will leave nothing undone to defeat the enemy, which I earnestly pray, under the guidance of Divine Providence, may soon be brought about'.[6]

News that the country was at war spread rapidly by word of mouth and telegraph to New Zealand's major cities and towns. As during the July Crisis, the most obvious reactions to the news were on the streets. At the initial reading of the declaration outside Parliament Buildings, for example, the crowd responded with 'a wild burst of cheering . . . A verse of the National Anthem was sung and cheers followed cheers for several minutes.'[7] On the evening of 5 August, an estimated 15,000 to 20,000 people, a large proportion of the city's population, gathered in Wellington's main streets. Lambton Quay and Willis, Manners and Cuba streets became 'so densely crowded in places that it was difficult for the ordinary traffic to get through' and a marching parade, accompanied by a band, patriotic songs and cheering, was held.[8]

There were comparable scenes in central Auckland: 'As the evening wore on feeling became more intensified, and groups of young men, waving Union Jacks, marched up and down Queen Street, cheering and singing national airs. Sometimes the crowd forming these processions swelled to a couple of thousand, and traffic in the main thoroughfares was frequently blocked.'[9] When the government's call for volunteers was announced, the next day, the crowd in Queen Street, outside the *Auckland Star* office, 'immediately . . . stampeded up Shortland Street, and the scene was one of wild enthusiasm when those in a position to see called out the news to the surging hundreds who blocked the full width of the street. Flags were wildly waved, and the cheering was tremendous.'[10] There was another, smaller, parade in Queen Street the following evening.[11]

Dunedin's first outdoor patriotic demonstration, also on the evening of 5 August, began when the Salvation Army Band struck up some 'national airs', including 'God Defend New Zealand', at the Dowling Street steps. By the time the crowd reached the town hall to hear speeches from various hastily contacted notables, it was estimated at 2000 and noted as being in fine voice. Meetings organised for the following evening packed the Garrison Hall, with thousands more waiting outside, and the Early Settlers' Hall.[12] In Christchurch the initial reaction appears to have been quiet: 'Everywhere people discussed the expected and judged future possibilites [sic], but no excitement was shown. Patriotic feeling was expressed in quiet confidence in Britain's attitude and her ability to bring the war to a satisfactory conclusion.'

The 'more youthful part of the community' showed its 'fervour' at the evening picture shows, standing to cheer when portraits of the king and queen were shown and singing the National Anthem. And after its parade at the King Edward Barracks that evening, the Cadet Bugle Band sparked singing and cheering from large, flag-waving crowds as it marched through the city streets playing several 'songs popular at the time of the South African War'. On 8 August, a Saturday, the *Sun* estimated that 10,000–12,000 turned out for a meeting in Victoria Square that was preceded by a long procession which wound its way through much of the central city, cheered by watching crowds.[13]

There were some very big patriotic gatherings in the larger provincial towns, too. On the Saturday night 'not less than 6000' assembled in Invercargill's Post Office Square; the same evening, a modest 2000 turned out in Whanganui. At Palmerston North crowds gathered outside newspaper offices and the *Manawatu Times* maintained that the multitude outside its office on 7 August greatly outnumbered an election night crowd.[14] In Gisborne, on the night of 13 August, a 'korero' given by the local Savage Club, a male social association for those interested in literature, music and art, filled 'every nook and corner' of the Opera House.[15] In Timaru on the Wednesday evening 'large numbers of people walked the streets' in scenes described as 'reminiscent of the Boer war times, people singing snatches of patriotic songs in the streets, at intervals'. The next day a public meeting called by the mayor packed out the Olympia Theatre.

Between 3000 and 4000 people assembled on Napier's Marine Parade after war was announced, with local bands playing 'the English, French and Russian Anthems'.[16] The same kinds of celebrations were seen, too, in slightly smaller towns — New Plymouth, Stratford and, memorably, Hastings. After some 1000 gathered in Heretaunga Street on the evening of 6 August to hear and cheer the playing of patriotic airs, 'the more sober-minded enthusiasts' listened to speeches delivered by the mayor and councillors from the fire escape balcony of the Pacific Hotel, but 'the youths of the town gave free rein to their patriotic ardour by numerous demonstrations accompanied by some uncalled for rowdyism'. 'A Union Jack was obtained from one of the hotels, and with this attached to a stalwart pole, the crowd paraded up and down the street singing patriotic songs and giving vent to their overflowing loyalty in every possible manner. To add to the din, some of the party hied away to a motor garage, and returning armed with a kerosene tin apiece, assisted to swell the noise, which was becoming hideous.'[17]

There were also remarkable turnouts in relatively small towns. 'Upwards of 2000 persons' were said to have gathered at Motueka's cricket ground on the Sunday following the declaration of war, with proceedings described as 'remarkably enthusiastic throughout'.[18] In Temuka the following evening 'a huge procession formed up, headed by the Temuka Municipal Band, the

Pipe Band, Boy Scouts, and Fire Brigade', who 'marched from Henry's corner to the [Dominion] Theater, which was packed in every part, many people being unable to gain admission'.[19] People from Fairlie and the surrounding district overflowed its local hall the next evening.[20] Wairarapa people packed the drill hall in Masterton on the Saturday afternoon, while in Feilding around 1000 gathered at the Soldiers' Monument in the Square that night.[21] A meeting called by the mayor of Greymouth on the Monday evening 'crowded' the town hall 'whilst the dress circle was fully occupied by members of the fair sex'.[22] It resolved to 'unswervingly support the action of the Government in equipping and dispatching an expeditionary force to give assistance to the Imperial Government wherever required'. A committee that included local MP Paddy Webb was elected to raise funds to help equip the force.

Within and beneath all this congregating, cheering, singing and marching, however, were more complex intellectual and emotional reactions. Generally, the significant contrast was between those who saw the war as a great adventure and those who saw it as a terrible duty.

The *New Zealand Herald* asserted that the war would ennoble society: 'All that is noblest and best in us rises to the challenge of circumstance. We know that we are the custodians of a sacred trust, the guardians of the national life of the British . . . War! There is no conception more inspiring, no condition nobler, no call that rings more grandly in the ears.'[23] There was similar enthusiasm, continuing from public rallies during the July Crisis, among many young men: 'most of the noise and impetus came from "boys and youths"'.[24] This eagerness could result in some frenzied incidents. When his mother refused to give him permission to enlist, for example, 19-year-old Edward Charles Stewart threatened to shoot family members before running amok and bayoneting a large photo, the bathroom door and the family piano.[25]

But there were more sober commentary and reactions. After the declaration Massey told Parliament, 'We are all anxious for peace. We all detest war; but we do not want peace unconditionally. We do not want peace at any price; we want peace with honour.'[26] As during the July Crisis, many gathered in the streets less out of eagerness for war and more for reassurance in a deeply troubling situation. According to one reporter, 'behind the outward expressions of patriotism there was an evident feeling of anxiety'.[27] Such tension was seen at Liverpool's announcement of war: '[h]ats and hands were raised in the air, but the face was one of strained emotion. Old men on the outskirts of the crowd were seen with tears tracing their cheeks and women with handkerchiefs to their eyes.'[28]

Another correspondent remarked that there 'were rather feeble cheers at first, as the people appeared somewhat staggered, but after a slight pause they were followed by hearty cheers'. Many, however, 'were visibly affected by the gravity of the announcement'.[29] In the words of the *Free Lance*, 'nobody was particularly surprised, some were relieved, many were enthusiastic. For days the people had been under strain of suspense, and the strain was becoming intolerable.' They were 'impatient to know what was actually taking place on the other side of the world. There had grown up feeling that war with Germany was inevitable [and] that only by the stern correction of German and Austrian aggression and arrogance could the peace of the world be made secure.'[30]

Lewis Coster, a farmer from Onaero near Waitara in north Taranaki, wrote a sad letter to

Lillian Beauchamp: 'This war is going to be very serious dear & we may all be needed yet. I do hope Germany gets quietened down soon as after a war there is always such depression & misery & so many fine chaps loose [sic] their lives & it means so many widows & orphans does it not[?]'[31] Even the *Maoriland Worker* acknowledged that 'the spirit of jingoism is not nearly so pronounced as was the case during the Boer War' and that 'everyone can realise that this scrap is not a mere holiday with certain victory facing us'.[32] Such views were common even during the initial gatherings. A meeting held in the Ōamaru Municipal Opera House after church on Sunday, 9 August was so full that hundreds of people could not get in. The speeches expressed regret and foreboding over what was said to be a just war. 'The whole meeting,' said the *North Otago Times* reporter, 'was pervaded with a deep sense of reverence, and the quiet patriotism of the gathering made itself felt to one.'[33]

New Zealanders approached the war with a multitude of reactions — confusion, anxiety, excitement, fear, enthusiasm and stoic resignation. Many may have felt a little of each, simultaneously or intermittently. As one woman wrote two days after the declaration: 'Isn't the War dreadful? One seems to think & talk of little else just now . . . How splendidly all colonies are offering help. I do hope that they won't need our men. That it may soon be over.'[34]

Great adventure, terrible duty and uncertainty all coalesced in a remarkable burst of solidarity that proved capable of rallying diverse, sometimes divided, social elements. There was an entrenched sense that the situation went beyond party politics, and Ward called for 'union in spirit and deed' with the government.[35] The response from the labour movement was still more revealing of the outbreak of goodwill, and the Arbitration Court suspended operations as unions promised not to strike. As labour historian Erik Olssen notes, 'The overwhelming majority of union members, like the overwhelming majority of workers (most of whom were not unionised), supported the war. Indeed the issues central to the war — playing by the rules, treating small and weak players fairly — resonated powerfully with most workers and union members.'[36]

In this spirit John Paul, a member of the Legislative Council and a leader in the Dunedin labour movement, declared, 'In perfect unanimity with all classes [organised labour] has declared that peace would be a hollow unreality until the wings of the German eagle are clipped, and the Kaiser's bombastic war policy is reversed.'[37] Likewise, *Truth* denounced Germany's 'war-mad monarch' and called for an assertion of British justice to punish German militarism:

> All we know is that Britain has been drawn into the maelstrom unwittingly, and he would be a spunkless sort of a Saxon or Celt, Colonial or British-born, who would refuse to respond to the Empire's call, now that she has espoused the cause of weaker nations, who, for the time being, are the victims of the military madness of the bellicose braggart War-Lord of Germany. Truly, it is now 'My country, right' — there is no question of it being wrong — the really magnificent and spontaneous outbursts of loyalty from all parts of the British Empire show how unanimous and united the Empire can be when given a just cause.[38]

Remarkably, this detente also extended to militant labour. On 8 August, Wellington waterside workers who belonged to the union defeated in the 1913 strike gathered in Post Office Square, where unionist James Bruce proclaimed: 'The last time we assembled here . . . we were fighting an industrial battle. Today we are fighting for our very existence.'[39] The Waterside Workers' Band, 'famous' during the strike, played 'God Save the King' and the 'Marseillaise'.[40] In Christchurch, Hiram Hunter, the national president of the Social Democratic Party, declared, to loud applause: 'Some little time ago there was trouble in this country between two parties — the workers and the employers. At that time my feeling was: "My class, right or wrong". This time it is on a broader basis, and I can say it is "My country right or wrong!"'[41] Peter Fraser wrote to a Wellington newspaper to proudly declare that 'the majority of Socialists almost everywhere are agreed that the most desirable outcome of the present situation is the defeat of Prussian militarism . . .'.[42] In response, Massey praised the Red Feds for adding 'a bit of white and blue' to their colour and released six of the 10 imprisoned for offences during the 1913 strike, including Harry Holland.[43]

Both Catholic and Protestant commentators in New Zealand upheld Irish rapprochement as exemplary, as factions in Ireland spoke of the need for unity and as the controversial Home Rule bill was shelved for the duration. Massey told a cheering patriotic meeting on 12 August 1914 that 'the two great sections of the Irish people were looking at each other along the barrels of their rifles, but today they are standing side by side and shoulder to shoulder ready to fight for their country and their Empire'.[44] As 'A Bunch of Shamrocks' wrote to the editor of the *Poverty Bay Herald*, 'We may be Ulstermen or Nationalists, but we are, above all, Irishmen . . . We are all children of the "little green flag with its harp of gold," and the manner in which both parties have agreed to sink their differences and stand shoulder to shoulder at the call of Empire is a splendid tribute to the patriotism of the Irish nation.'[45] Although the Papacy's position of neutrality created some awkwardness for Catholic commentators, the plight of Catholic Belgium was readily emphasised as signalling that Catholics were at the centre of the war.

Many iwi, particularly those who had fought alongside government forces in the past, were keen to be involved. On 5 August, Ngāti Apa of Rangitīkei sent Massey a telegram, signed by chief Rangi Marumaru: 'On behalf of and at the request of some of the leading members of the . . . tribe, we wish, and feel it a duty, to offer ourselves for service to the Government for the defence of the Empire and its mana in the present European crisis.'[46] Shortly after the declaration, Nau Paraone Kawiti was 'empowered' to cable Massey that, as 'British subjects under the Treaty of Waitangi, we, the Ngapuhi people, wish to convey through you to His Most Gracious Majesty, King George the Fifth, in this most trying epoch of his Empire, an assurance of our loyalty and devotion, and that we are ever ready and willing to in any way assist in the defence of this Dominion against his enemies'.

In the Hawke's Bay settlement of Wairoa, '[n]atives assembled at the Land Court called on Judge [Robert] Jones to explain the European crisis. They thereupon passed a resolution offering their services to the Government for the defence of the Empire. A great haka demonstration followed.' A large patriotic gathering in Kaiapoi, north of Christchurch, 'expressed the hope that those Maoris who were offering to serve their country would not be rejected'.[47] At a

Te Puke meeting later in August, W. K. Wihapi, who was a Land Court interpreter, said Māori 'realised that they were under one flag and one King'. He also introduced Winiata Matea, who was 'taking a great interest in the war, and who had been instrumental in collecting a substantial sum' for the local Patriotic Fund. He 'hoped the King would be successful in the war. The Maoris could not do much, but they would do what they could to assist. He concluded by handing the Chairman £2 as a personal contribution, and was loudly applauded as he resumed his seat.' [48] A week after war was declared, Massey could say that 'scores of offers of active service had been received from the Maoris'.[49]

By the beginning of September, organisational efforts were under way. A large patriotic festival in the Hawke's Bay village of Waipatu attracted Māori from all over the region and featured speeches by Māui Pōmare and Āpirana Ngata, MPs for Western and Eastern Māori. Pōmare claimed enthusiastically that 'the Maoris of the Dominion have expressed as with one voice unswerving loyalty to the British throne. They recognise that the British cause is their cause; that the British King is their King; that the God of the British is the God of the Maoris too.'[50] Shortly afterwards an Auckland conference of representatives from Ngāti Whātua, Te Uri o Hau, Te Arawa, Te Aupōuri and Ngāpuhi decided to canvass members of their tribes for contributions.[51]

Members of several long-established communities with Germanic heritage also signalled their devotion to the British cause. In Stratford, Gerald van Heck, who conducted the orchestra at Bernard's Pictures and was an eminent violinist, placed a notice in the local newspaper informing readers that while he was 'of German extraction', he was an 'Englishman born in London', and that he 'fought with the British in the Boer War and was seriously wounded'. Furthermore, 'if the authorities would pass him [he] would again offer his services for the front against Germany'.[52] In Halcombe, in Manawatū, H. H. C. Dierks, the pastor of the German Lutheran Church, took a collection for the War Fund and emphasised that 'our people are true to the British nation'. He cited a meeting held the previous night in the 'German school room . . . to consider the advisability of helping the British Empire in its time of trouble'.[53]

Outside Nelson, the small town of Sarau, renamed Upper Moutere during the war, organised a meeting that arranged for a loyalty declaration to be published in newspapers, and raised money to purchase a horse for one of the two local recruits who had been accepted for the expeditionary force.[54] As the *Colonist* noted, 'with a declaration of such frankness, such reasonableness and such sweetness as that which our Moutere friends placed before the public eye, what risk now of their misunderstanding us, or any of us misunderstanding them?'[55] On 17 August those at a meeting in the little settlement of Pūhoi, north of Auckland, whose population was overwhelmingly of German extraction, albeit from within the Austro-Hungarian Empire, 'affirmed the loyalty of the settlement to the British Empire, and offered to render any assistance possible'. They also donated £75 to the Patriotic Fund.[56]

Several contentious political issues were also shelved, theoretically, for the duration. A bill to hold a national referendum on the prohibition of alcohol, before a select committee when war was declared, was suspended. Likewise, the Bible in Schools League agreed to the withdrawal of the Religious Instruction-in-Schools Referendum Bill 'in view of the crisis' and so that 'nothing should hinder the closest union between every section of the community'; it also announced it was suspending campaigning, and donated £1000 to the War Fund.[57] Such behaviour, said Ward, 'shows clearly to my mind, what I and every one of us have believed hitherto of New Zealanders — that in times of stress and trouble every class in this country will do what it can to help'.[58]

This solidarity, however, was not unconditional. James Bruce called for New Zealanders to 'sink all differences' but also acknowledged that '[w]hen the conflict is over we shall probably resume our fight'.[59] Officials within the labour movement differed over the degree of support they should give to the war. Two days after 'the prominent Labour leaders of Auckland' had offered 'a Labour Regiment for service at home or abroad', the Auckland Trades Union Secretaries' Association repudiated this, supporting instead 'a National Reserve, for defence purposes only'.[60]

Some solidarity from communities with German connections was borne in hope of soothing suspicions. A number of people beyond the district had questioned 'the attitude of the Moutere German residents, and . . . some doubts and misgivings seemed to be entertained as to their loyalty'.[61] The statement by the Sarau residents also asked 'fair-minded people' to show 'their indulgence and a certain amount of latitude for the sympathy and sentiment for the land of their birth of those who had been born and lived their youth in Germany, and whose relatives lived there', adding that 'such sympathy is not disloyalty'. As the meeting had 'expressed again and again . . . the residents of German extraction, who for so many years have made their homes here without molestation on terms equally with the rest of the community, and enjoyed the protection and assistance of the Government of this colony, will stand shoulder to shoulder, man for man, with any other inhabitants of the colony to defend its shores and institutions, their homes and families against any foe whatsoever. We unhesitatingly state that her foe is our foe.'[62]

Although a number of Māori were 'quite elated' and 'willing and anxious' to undertake overseas military service, some offers were apparently conditional on serving in the defence of New Zealand itself.[63] For example, 'a large and influential gathering of Natives from the Wanganui and Taumarunui districts met . . . and discussed the question of forming a corps of Territorials drawn from all the Natives of the Wanganui River district', but for 'exclusively defence purposes'.[64] Another large gathering at Pariroa, near Pātea in Taranaki, decided that though 'all the young men [must] volunteer and be drilled for service in the protection of the Dominion', since 'no outside foe has ever invaded New Zealand it would not be right for Maoris to go abroad in defence of the Empire'.[65] Some Pākehā made similar points. While accepting the war's necessity, the *Inglewood Record and Waitara Age* asserted that New Zealand's interests and welfare should be prioritised:

> We cannot see the startling necessity for sending men to die on foreign soil in somebody else's quarrel. Is it a fair deal merely on the grounds of sentimentality to take away the very flower of our population to die at the hands of an enemy devoid of honour and whose cause has not a particle of justice in it[?] What is to happen in the future to New Zealand and the Commonwealth devoid of population and with nothing but the medical inspectors' rejects

"HOLD THE FORT FOR I AM COMING."

An *Observer* cartoon by William Blomfield captures the eagerness of some for active participation during the first period of the war.
NEW ZEALAND OBSERVER, 5 SEPTEMBER 1914, P. 1

> to repopulate our country, occupy and cultivate our idle lands and at the same time defend our dominion from the many nations who look with jealous eyes on our unoccupied country and gloriously fertile lands?[66]

As well as not being unconsidered and unconditional, support for the war was not universal. The clearest public opposition came from the West Coast mining township of Rūnanga (population around 1750), a stronghold of the Social Democratic Party and the Federation of Labour. Three members of the borough council, James O'Brien (later a long-serving Labour MP for Westland), John Arbuckle (an official in the Miners' Union) and the Reverend Moses Ayrton (Methodist clergyman and Social Democratic Party activist), opposed the mayor's proposal that the town clerk should canvass local businesses for contributions to the War Fund.[67] O'Brien was 'not in favour of the war, and the Council should not do anything to assist it'. The trio's attitude was widely reported and roundly condemned, not least by the local *Grey River Argus*, which became embroiled in a heated exchange with Ayrton, who had not read the paper but understood it 'vomited filth'.[68]

Although the re-election of these councillors, and three more from the Social Democratic Party, the following year, suggests that most Rūnanga electors did not share the *Argus*'s hostility, there was clearly also plenty of local patriotism and support for the war. A meeting of 'residents of Runanga and State Collieries' on 8 September drew 'over 250' people and formed a branch of the Patriotic League to canvass for funds and hold a series of concerts.[69] The Miners' Union made its hall available free of charge for both the meeting and the concerts, and the district's miners agreed to a levy of between 2s and half a crown per member 'to be devoted to one of the war funds'.[70]

Henry Reynold, the secretary of the Christchurch Anti-Militarist League, condemned the war as a consequence of militarism:

> In the light of present international events in Europe, anti-militarists feel that they can well afford to maintain silence, the general outbreak of war, with all its horrors, being in their opinion sufficient proof of the rectitude of their purpose and endeavours, and ample evidence also of the fallacy of the faith built upon the old pagan motto: 'If you want peace prepare for war.' Coupled with these facts, the League also wishes to point out with emphasis that it is mainly due to the inordinate elevation and glorification of the military ideal that the unparalleled situation has arisen in Europe to-day, and particularly so with regard to the attitude of Germany, the home of conscription.[71]

The *Maoriland Worker*'s initial response also built on its pre-war anti-militarism, but it generally criticised the conflict in the abstract, as being caused by capitalism and the 'interests' that it fostered. In a rare excursion into specifics, it announced that since Britain's involvement, 'we confess we are anxious for our race, together with the French and Belgians (upon whom the fight was arrogantly forced) to emerge triumphant'.[72] The paper nevertheless denounced any display of patriotism.

Lastly, as historian Monty Soutar has suggested, Māori support for the war came from 'iwi whose experiences with the Crown made them more amenable to notions of civic responsibility and service . . . they were motivated by ideals of patriotic service and the obligations of citizenship inherent in the Treaty of Waitangi'.[73] This ethos was far less visible among tribes in Waikato, Taranaki and the Bay of Plenty who had opposed the government in the wars of the 1860s and 1870s and had suffered devastation and land confiscations. King Te Rata and his party were returning from their mission to present Māori grievances to King George V in London when war broke out and the steamer on which they were travelling was delayed at Gibraltar; they reached Auckland in late September.[74] As the *King Country Chronicle* noted, previous discussions about possible participation in the war had been postponed until the king's return, though the reporter was optimistic: 'the arrival of Rata will probably see the movement placed on a definite footing, and active steps taken to organise the local contingent'.[75]

If the declaration removed the suspense of the July Crisis, in the first hours and days of the war there were enduring uncertainties about what the conflict would mean for New Zealand. Rumour-mongering and speculation were inevitable. As early as 11 August the *Southland Times* was complaining of a great many inquiries by those wanting to verify hearsay: 'We are asked whether it is true that the German North Sea fleet has been annihilated; whether it is true that the battle cruiser New Zealand has been sunk; whether it is true that there is a Japanese cruiser off the Bluff; whether it is true that the Germans have entered Paris.'[76] In Christchurch the *Star* was facing similar problems: 'That story about the loss of nineteen British Dreadnoughts is still circulating actively around the suburbs, and we should not like to say how many people have paid twopence to ring us up about it.'[77]

However, the press was also vulnerable to false information. Many news stories published in the early days of the war, mostly on the basis of cables from overseas, were seriously misleading or untrue, leading some editors to express exasperation with the cable news they were receiving.[78] There were, for example, various fictitious reports of naval clashes in the North Sea, but perhaps the most egregious was the 'news' that the Netherlands had declared war on Germany, which was repeated as fact by Massey in the House.[79]

The situation was not helped by businesses that exploited the hunger for news by publicising rumours in their shop windows. On 25 August, Gilbert Henry Price, a tobacconist in Wellington's Mercer Street, was convicted of 'knowingly propagat[ing] false war news to the alarm of His Majesty's subjects'. He had posted a notice carrying a report of a naval engagement in the North Sea in which ten German warships and five British had been sunk, 'including H.M.S. Collingwood, on which the King's second son is reported amongst the casualties'. Even the display of a reprinted article lampooning the reporting of the war by daily newspapers 'made the sidewalk opposite impassable, and men fought their way close enough to read [it]'. The police warned shopkeepers to remove such 'skits' or face prosecution.[80]

There was particular worry about the whereabouts of the German East Asia Squadron, which had steamed out of Tsingtao and was now at large in the Pacific. Fears were only heightened by reports that some vessels had visited Sāmoa on 14 September and had shelled the Tahitian town of Papeete on 22 September. James Allen described New Zealand's coastal defences as 'ample' and boasted that the gunners would enjoy 'an evening's sport' if the battleships attempted to enter Auckland or Wellington harbours, but public doubts appear to have remained.[81] On 28 September, George Bollinger noted a rumour that the German squadron had recently sailed through Cook Strait.[82] A month later, Annis Hamerton in Inglewood wrote to her daughter-in-law, 'I shudder when I think of what one could do in an hour in poor little N[ew] P[lymouth] it is a strange anxious time.'[83] Such concerns did not vanish until early December, when the bulk of the squadron was destroyed by the Royal Navy at the Battle of the Falkland Islands.

Pre-war defence planning for an expeditionary force provided some sense of the role New Zealand would play, but questions soon appeared about its deployment and role. Shortly after war was declared, Allen noted that some 7000 volunteers would be raised but that 'it was impossible' to say where they might serve 'because at the moment there was no call to send anyone out of the country'.[84] Massey was willing to be more speculative, noting that New Zealand volunteers might serve 'perhaps in India, perhaps in Egypt, perhaps on the Continent of Europe', with 'garrison duty' likely but service at the front possible.[85]

Curiously overlooking Sāmoa, one 'close student of war' hypothesised that New Zealand troops might attack German colonies in New Guinea or South-West Africa, deeming it 'unlikely that the New Zealanders would be sent to the front, or Australians either. After all, it was a matter for very highly trained troops in the European battlefield.'[86] Massey also noted the enthusiasm of many Māori to be involved, but cautioned, 'I am aware that the Imperial regulations may prevent any members of the Maori race from taking service abroad.'[87]

Many assumptions also reflected a widespread sense that the conflict would not last long. Although Britain's newly appointed Secretary of State for War, Lord Kitchener, commanded enormous respect, few New Zealanders appear to have accepted his much-reported suggestion that the war would last for three years.[88] The editor of the *Sun* in Christchurch was taken aback by the same prediction from the *Sydney Daily Telegraph*, which also thought that the war would cost New Zealand £10 million. 'We may be in for a long war,' he responded, 'but it will be an extraordinary thing if Germany can resist the combined pressure of three first-class Powers for anything like the period mentioned.'[89] Massey seems to have spoken for many when he returned to the House on 5 August after the reading of the declaration: 'I hope and believe that the war which has just broken out will not last long, and I hope and believe that within a comparatively few months — to say weeks would be too much to expect — within a few months the Imperial authorities will be able to announce to us that peace with honour has come for the British Empire.'[90]

Mirroring the common idea of a decisive, knockout blow, Ward envisioned the war ending around the end of 1914 or a few months later. He argued that the Central Powers would be unable to stand the financial strain, Germany would be unable to feed its population now food imports had been cut off, and 'the naval engagement which must inevitably take place' would result 'in a victory for the British fleet'. The *Dominion* agreed: 'Everything indeed points to a short war, for the financial strain is too great to be long sustained.'[91] At the end of August one minister suggested that 'it may last for a year, or perhaps more' and Massey soon declared, 'I think it will last twelve months. I do not see how the food-supplies can be kept up for longer than that.' By mid-September he was hoping that 'by the 1st December we will be able to say that the war will have very nearly reached its termination'.[92]

Such expectations were also evident in economic forecasts. As one Dunedin businessman connected with the frozen-meat trade commented, 'Fortunately the season is practically over for the year, and all the freezing works will close within the next few days. If the present situation had arisen in the middle of the freezing season, there would have been only the local demand to deal with . . . No war on the scale of this gigantic European outbreak is likely to last till December, and until that month the export of frozen meat does not count.'[93]

With the expectation of a relatively short war, some argued that New Zealand's involvement could only be limited. The *Maoriland Worker* ridiculed the whole notion of an expeditionary force: 'We fail to see how the action of the N.Z. Government in dispatching a mere handful of troops to a point not yet disclosed, but somewhere in Europe, which cannot be reached under seven weeks, will in any measure affect the ultimate verdict.'[94]

CHAPTER THREE
TO ARMS

previous pages
A final farewell between soldiers on a troopship and a crowd on a wharf. The streamers connecting those aboard and those on the wharf were torn as the ship departed, symbolising a parting of ways. ALEXANDER TURNBULL LIBRARY, 1/2-152620-G

For New Zealand, the period between the declaration of war and the end of April 1915 has been dubbed a 'phoney war'.[1] In one sense the country's new belligerent status was highlighted by news of the situation overseas, the relative novelty of columns of soldiers mustering for training and the martial spectacles that accompanied the departure of troops — first the Advance Party of the New Zealand Expeditionary Force (NZEF) to German Sāmoa in August, to capture the wireless station and secure a territory imperialists had coveted for decades, and then the Main Body in October.

However, as New Zealanders learnt of critical battles in Europe there developed a frustrated sense that the country was not properly committed to the war. The action in Sāmoa was quick and bloodless, with an occupation formally declared on 30 August, sometimes incorrectly claimed as the first German territory captured in the war.[2] The Main Body, too, was denied any immediate action; originally destined for the Western Front, it was redirected to Egypt following the Ottoman Empire's entry to the war on the side of the Central Powers on 1 November. Some frustrated patriots made remarkable efforts to translate sentiments into action and displayed antagonism towards anything considered to be a 'business as usual' mentality.

Early in the war, the often confused reactions to the July Crisis and the instinctive rallying after 5 August gave way to more confidently asserted convictions about the nature of the conflict. Germany's conduct in invading and occupying Belgium would prove crucial in this process. The invasion itself was a breach of Germany's legal obligations to guarantee Belgian independence and neutrality, and the impression that Berlin was displaying contempt for international law was greatly strengthened by a widespread reprinting of the German chancellor's remarks that the Treaty of London was merely a 'scrap of paper'.[3]

In the first six weeks of the invasion, the German military killed thousands of civilians. Modern estimates place the total deaths at 6500; the subsequent predatory occupation created conditions responsible for the deaths of 250,000 more.[4] These killings were the result of both spontaneous actions, in which inexperienced troops fired on civilians they believed were acting as guerrillas, and sanctioned mass executions influenced by Schrecklichkeit doctrines intended to dominate occupied areas by cowing the local population. Translated into English as 'frightfulness', the term, and its connotations, became staple ingredients in anti-German propaganda.[5] The invasion also destroyed prized cultural heritage. The burning of Louvain's Catholic University Library, with its irreplaceable collections of medieval, Gothic and Renaissance manuscripts, would prove a particular touchstone of brutality.[6]

These actions would soon be cited in sensationalised propaganda about the 'rape of Belgium', featuring brutish German soldiers bayoneting babies, chopping the hands off children, raping women and immolating cultural treasures. Reports on the invasion, massacres and destruction were given prominent space in New Zealand papers. Alongside articles from war correspondents and Belgian refugees, an Auckland man, R. White, added an eyewitness account in December. He had been a special constable at Folkestone, where many thousands of Belgian refugees landed in Britain, and claimed to have seen signs of atrocities. 'There was a soldier who had one ear torn off by a German bayonet, and a particularly pathetic case was that of a male child, only a few months old, which had both its hands cut off.'[7]

The recurring stories of children with purposely severed hands are now regarded as an urban legend, exaggerations of all too real cases of collateral injuries, but they appear to have been widely accepted at the time.[8] Photographs and commentary on devastated Louvain were conspicuous, too. At the end of August, the *New Zealand Herald* wrote: 'A week ago Louvain was a city of about the population of Dunedin . . . Today Louvain is a heap of ruins, its 45,000 citizens are homeless dependents . . . its wonderful churches, its great public buildings, its pictures, its statuary, its every relic of centuries bygone have been destroyed.'[9] In response, the University of New Zealand passed a resolution to write a letter to its Louvain counterpart, expressing its 'indignation and deep regret . . . That such destruction should have been caused by a nation calling itself cultured and civilised is amazing to us in New Zealand. We desire to send you our deepest sympathy with you and the people of Belgium generally in the great loss that has befallen your nation.'[10]

Reporting on Germany's record in Belgium was central in defining the sense of the war and crucial in mobilising the psychological and emotional resources that drove commitment to the conflict, in justifying the enormous hardships, and in providing some of the war's most profound meanings, highest ideals and impassioned animosities. This process was relatively decentralised, as journalists, priests, musicians, cartoonists and businesses all expressed their understandings of the war. The New Zealand government was also involved, commissioning school textbook content, posters and paintings from appointed war artists at the front.[11]

In a society that sanctified notions of legality, heritage, property, knowledge and chivalry, many saw the 'rape of Belgium' as an indication that the war against Germany was a struggle between a civilisation based on the rule of law and a barbarous military autocracy. At the end of August the First Lord of the Admiralty, Winston Churchill, touched on this motif of a 'war for civilisation' in an interview: 'The war began as a war of honour, and it was now one of self-preservation. The British democracy with a limited monarchy, ancient Parliament, and ardent social and philanthropic dreams, was now in deadly grapple with the formidable might of Prussian autocracy rule.' When the interview was interrupted by news of the destruction of Louvain, Churchill asked, '[W]hat further proof was needed of the issue?'[12]

New Zealand commentators reinforced the theme. In the first weeks of the war, the

Pictures of the destruction of heritage in Ypres, Belgium, reproduced in an Auckland newspaper. Such images were highly influential in shaping the sense of the conflict as a war to save civilisation from barbarism. AUCKLAND WEEKLY NEWS, 14 JANUARY 1915, P. 35

New Zealand Tablet, the country's major Catholic publication, lamented the war but proclaimed it as 'a matter of self-preservation'.[13] In an address to the Southland Teachers' Institute entitled 'A Study of the German Mind', the Reverend J. W. Shaw asserted that Germany's invasion and actions demonstrated the march of autocracy and argued the need to defend the liberal values he argued that Britain had nurtured and spread. As he concluded, 'We owe it to our fathers who fought and died for liberty and into whose labours we have entered, we owe it to the generations yet unborn, to civilisation, to humanity, that we in this the supreme day of testing should summon every resource of our vast Empire, should willingly accept any sacrifice demanded, to trample into the dust the foul monster that would corrupt and enslave the world.'[14]

Alongside appeals to higher duties were those to self-interest; Belgium was presented as a foretaste of what could be expected from a victorious Germany. Many speculated that a defeat of British power would leave New Zealand vulnerable and a possible spoil of war. Massey, for example, argued that fighting for the British Empire and for New Zealand were one and the same. 'If Britain did not win — but they were certain she would — the German flag, instead of the British flag, would fly over New Zealand.'[15]

The *Auckland Star* felt the same: 'if England's naval strength were once effectually broken, there would be nothing to prevent Germany from transporting troops and munitions of war to this side of the world, seizing our chief towns and establishing in these countries that reign of terror which she has employed so effectively in Belgium'.[16] 'If Germany were successful in her piracy,' the *New Zealand Herald* warned, 'German officers would swagger on the streets of Auckland, New Zealand women would be treated as Belgian women have been treated, and every New Zealander who wanted to say what he thought about the Kaiser would have to go into exile if he did not care to be shot.'[17] Other editorials asked readers to imagine 'Queen Street, Ponsonby Road, Khyber Pass and every street that guns can reach carpeted by slaughtered innocents! Hamilton as Louvain; Takapuna as Liege; Whangarei and the furtherest farms given up to "frightfulness!"'[18]

Rumours of German designs on New Zealand, said to be 'an open secret in well informed circles', lingered throughout the war.[19] In early 1916 various New Zealand papers reprinted an excerpt from a German newspaper, the *Lüneburgerheide Nachrichten*: 'As soon as Germany has command of the seas we would advise our Government to turn its attention towards an island called New Zealand. It would not take much to get possession of it because they have only boys as soldiers, and are too far away from Britain to get any help from there . . . The first nation of the world — Germany — ought to be in possession of it.'[20]

In June that year, Liberal MP Willie Field cited, in Parliament, a rumour that a map had been discovered during the campaign in German South Africa that showed New Zealand as part of the German Empire: 'It would be one of the first places taken if the Germans won.'[21] These seemingly far-fetched fears could validly point to a history of territory and colonies changing hands in post-war settlements; a pattern the Sykes-Picot, Brest-Litovsk and Versailles treaties continued. Furthermore, although the containment of the German High Seas Fleet and the neutralisation of the East Asia Squadron restricted German naval power, plans for naval raids on Australian and New Zealand coastal facilities and towns did exist, at least on paper. This 'ruthless warfare', as it was known, aimed to disrupt shipping, demoralise populations and build pressure to keep troops at home.[22]

A second and enormously influential conception of the war was as an idealistic crusade. This crusading narrative, rather than just calling on New Zealanders to defend a way of life, also pledged that victory would create a better world. Famously, in August 1914 the English author and commentator H. G. Wells published the pamphlet *The War That Will End War* proclaiming, 'This is now a war for peace . . . This, the greatest of all wars, is not just another war — it is the last war!'[23] Reporting on this, one New Zealand paper observed, 'Into this war we have gone with clean hands — to end the reign of brutal and artful internationalism for ever.'[24]

Crusaders also conceived of the war not as a conflict driven by self-interest but rather as a struggle to defend great intangible values. As the Anglican newspaper *Church Envoy* put it in September, 'not for lust of territory, not for commercial or any material gain are we at war. No new territory do we require or desire . . . There is one answer and one answer only to the question "Why are we at war?" That which is at stake is our honour and self respect.'[25] Since it was argued that Britain and New Zealand could have remained neutral, some who saw the war as a crusade also regarded the British position as uniquely selfless. A poem, written for a Wellington patriotic event, imagined the dead setting out their motivations for fighting:

> 'I fought as I was ordered,' a German sighed,
> For his wounds, he could not stand,
> 'They said that we wanted Belgium,
> So, I died for the Fatherland . . .'
>
> What had once been a Belgian spoke:
> 'My wife and child were slain –
> I can see their tortured bodies still
> Amid the burning grain.'
>
> 'I fought for the truth,' said a Briton
> 'No one made me come,
> But my friend had gone and my country called,
> So I followed the beat of the drum.'[26]

Those outside the patriotic consensus also sought to make sense of the developing war. On 5 August a *Maoriland Worker* columnist expressed a view held by some socialists internationally that the war would transform the political order: 'This war, my beloved, WILL END CAPITALISM! Do you get that? After capitalism, what? SOCIALISM!' In December the paper restated the point and thanked the Kaiser for 'exploding for us, among other bombs, the bromidial fallacy that vast armaments insure peace. When things get bad enough they tend to cure themselves . . . At the close of this war, which famine will dictate shall be brief, there will be for sale a fine job-lot of second-hand crowns.'[27]

Despite some hopes that Te Rata's return to New Zealand might spur Waikato commitment to the war, the Kīngitanga emerged as a hub of non-commitment. Though the official position was that Māori should enlist, or not, as they saw fit, numerous accounts attest to less than neutral dispositions.[28] *Te Paki o Matariki*, the official newspaper of the Kīngitanga, argued that many belligerents had good reasons to be at war. King George V and Kaiser Wilhelm II were fighting over sovereignty and Germany was at war with France, Belgium and Russia over land; it was 'right for those nations whose land is close to Germany to fight as they are fighting over their own land interests'. Conversely, the United States and China and, incorrectly, Japan were not involved because they lacked territorial interests. Given this, the paper concluded, Māori had no basis for involvement. Further, under the Treaty of Waitangi Queen Victoria had promised to protect Māori, and enlistment threatened this protection. Lastly, the 1881 declaration of the second Māori king, Tāwhiao, that warfare should be banished was cited and Te Rata proclaimed that Māori should not search for war but rather should abstain from fighting until conflict came to New Zealand.[29]

The new circumstances of war also brought new views of fellow belligerents, enemies and allies. Belgium and to a lesser extent Serbia were presented as martyrs for the Allied cause, and Belgium was often depicted as an abused woman suffering at the unchivalrous hand of the enemy. Under this interpretation, Britain was right to avenge Belgium and had a duty to alleviate Belgium's suffering. As one editorial put it,

> In her hour of trial Belgium has turned for aid to the great nation that has ever fought for the liberties of struggling nationalities, and how the Belgian people trust our answer to their appeal . . . Betrayed by their German guarantor they oppose him on their violated frontier, firmly believing that Britain will succour them before their freedom is lost. Surely this is enough in itself to justify the mustering of troops in all the free states of the British, and the swelling from our abundance of the Patriotic Funds that are to relieve and minimise the hardships of war.[30]

In October 1914, Māori in the Northland settlement of Waipū hoisted a Belgian flag under the New Zealand ensign in a service that equated British actions in Europe with the 'paternal care' shown to Māori.[31]

More curious were the shifting perceptions about France, Russia and Japan, Allied powers that had recently been considered rivals, antagonists and potential security concerns. The Anglo-French rivalry had generally diminished in the decade before 1914 and there was some rapprochement, if mixed with customary cultural sniping at 'Gallic decadence' and 'Anglo uncouthness'.[32] The outbreak of war furthered this accord, with the French, like the Belgians, presented as victims of Germany's invasion of Western Europe, and as mounting a heroic defence of their homeland and democratic values. Images of the French Tricolour beside the Union Jack, John Bull standing in solidarity with Marianne or comradeship between British Tommies and French Poilus were common. As a 1916 pamphlet noted, 'Since the beginning of the war, we have discovered that the kind of hero-worship we had bestowed upon those we now call *Huns* and *Vandals* (the latter word is really more appropriate) was entirely misplaced; we had wrongly judged the French nation when we judged it frivolous, degenerate, and senseless.' Instead, the war had revealed an indomitable French spirit willing to endure despite horrific losses.[33]

Unity with Russia was perhaps more difficult, and early efforts at sketching the qualities of Britain's Russian ally were not overly flattering. The *Oamaru Mail*, for example, noted in September 1914:

> The main asset of the Russian army is Ivan Ivanoff, the Russian soldier, unimaginative, uneducated, docile by the circumstances of his lot, he is the best material for the manufacture of the soldier that has to die in heaps in the world. Unimaginative, he is tenacious and fearless; uneducated, he is devoid of class ambitions and sensitiveness; docile, he may be herded to death or led to victory with equal lack of interest in the event in which he is but an animate pawn.[34]

Within months, however, character sketches of 'Tommy's Russian brother' had adopted a more positive focus on qualities of doggedness, stoicism and lack of pretension. In January 1915 the *Evening Post* considered the Russian soldier 'on the whole . . . very fine indeed':

> They set little value on, their own lives or on anybody else's when it is a question of duty or of fighting. 'Sbezn copjeka' (Life is a farthing) is one of their favourite proverbs. Their religious character is seen in conflict, for they look on a battle, not as a sanguinary fight, but as the defence of their faith, Tsar, and country. The average Russian, even of the lower classes, is extremely fond of his native country (matooshka Roosija), our little Mother Russia, as he calls her, although she is frequently a very severe parent to him.[35]

Attitudes towards Japan would make a similar transition as the Japanese military acted to capture the German base at Tsingtao, claimed German territory in the Pacific and gave New Zealand naval assistance. One editorial, marking the visit of the Japanese cruiser *Ibuki* to the capital, praised the conduct of the Japanese sailors and believed that 'the citizens of Wellington were enabled to secure a broader and, let it be hoped, a permanent understanding of the true Japanese spirit'.[36] However, underlying suspicions of Japanese expansion remained. Days into the war, the Christchurch *Star*, while describing Japan's loyalty to the alliance as 'admirable', worried about a Japanese seizure of Germany's Pacific possessions.[37] In December the *New Zealand Herald* admitted that 'Japan has discharged her treaty-obligations loyally and honourably', but 'refuse[d] to think that this is satisfactory to New Zealanders, or that either in war or peace they will be content to bask for ever under the Rising Sun of the Mikado'.[38]

New Zealand government officials were thinking along similar lines: during May 1915 discussions on the post-war Pacific, they bluntly informed London that they would never be convinced 'that in the future our peril is not from Japan'.[39]

As the war continued, both sides attempted to court neutral powers. When several joined the conflict on the Allied side — notably Italy (April 1915), Romania (August 1916), the United States (April 1917) and Greece (officially in June 1917) — it was used as evidence of burgeoning military power and the solidarity of global opinion against Germany.

Austria–Hungary was relatively ignored as an enemy power, as was Bulgaria, which entered the war in October 1915. Both were generally portrayed as opportunists, pale versions of Prussian autocracy or lackeys being unwittingly or unwillingly exploited by Germany.[40] The Ottoman Empire was also presented as a German cat's paw, though such sentiments were often mixed with Edwardian conceptions of 'the unspeakable Turk':

> Never have the principles of Machiavelli been applied with all their cunning and cruelty as they have been by Germany. She is quite prepared to stir up the religious fanaticism and bloodthirstiness of the Turk and the awful passions of the Turcomans in Asia Minor. Here is a nation crying out to Europe, and the Poles in particular about the Asiatic barbarism of the Russians and proclaiming her leadership in culture. And, on the other hand, seeking to enlist the help of the most bloodthirsty races in the world — the Turks and the Turcomans of evil fame in Armenia.[41]

Oddly, though, such sentiments would later stand alongside admiring, if often patronising, descriptions of the character and conduct of Turkish soldiers — 'Abdul is a white man', 'The Turk is a sport'[42] — as notions of Turkish backwardness and unrestrained barbarism became less tenable once the Gallipoli campaign became deadlocked. Ideas of a worthy adversary were also facilitated by the understanding that the Turks were enemies due to German manipulation, rather than innate villainy.[43]

The most discussed and examined enemy was, of course, Germany. Early on there was a strong tendency to blame the conflict on the German government, and particularly the Kaiser, rather than the German nation: 'Our quarrel is not with the German people but with the German machine, the military machine, which, machine-like, is without a conscience, without a soul, without tenderness or feeling of any sort.'[44] Some more liberal commentary was openly Germanophilic and at the large patriotic meeting called in Ōamaru after church on 10 August, the Reverend J. A. Lochore felt compelled to 'put in a word for the German people'. They possessed 'many of our own characteristics, and were only driven into this war by the mad militarists who were ruling the country'. He hoped New Zealanders 'would not condemn any Germans with whom they might mix, as had been done in many instances. They should remember that these people had as little part in the causing of the war as they themselves.'[45]

The *Maoriland Worker* also stressed a difference between militarists and the masses: 'if anyone asks, Who lifted the lid off Hell? Let the truthful answer be: William Hohenzollern.' After an extended denouncement of the Kaiser, a 'mastoid degenerate' with a 'shrunken soul'

"BELGIUM WEEK" IN AUCKLAND: SCENES IN CONNECTION WITH THE STREET COLLECTION, PROCESSION, AND SPORTS HELD IN AID OF THE RELIEF FUND.

Various photographs from Auckland's 'Belgium week'. The total takings, £2338, were reportedly the largest sum raised in a single day in Auckland. AUCKLAND WEEKLY NEWS, 19 NOVEMBER 1914, P. 39

whose torching of Louvain outshone Nero's 'carelessness in the use of fire', the paper noted that '[t]he emperor does not represent the true Germany': 'Our hearts are with Germany — the Germany of invention, science, music, education, skill — but not with the War Lord.'[46]

The demarcation between the German military and wider Germany was soon challenged. As one study notes, 'The arrival of the atrocity stories demanded answers. Answers to questions of what had failed so badly in German culture to produce a nation capable of such horrors?'[47] A major early talking point was the October 1914 'Manifesto of the Ninety-Three', in which that number of prominent German intellectuals declared their unequivocal support for their nation's conduct in Belgium. 'It is no exaggeration to say,' wrote the *Auckland Star*, 'that the Germans have been sedulously taught by all their leading thinkers and writers to regard themselves as superior to all other nations in everything that makes for the highest and best civilisation, till they have actually come to believe in their own inherent right to lead the world, and if necessary to assert their claim to leadership by war.'[48]

Various critics rejected the argument that the 'true Germany' was represented by its scientific, industrial and cultural achievements and sought links to contemporary actions in German history, philosophy and the words and deeds of figures such as Frederick the Great or Friedrich Nietzsche, Friedrich von Bernhardi and Heinrich von Treitschke. Prussian militarism, materialism, relativism and a lack of Christianity were also cited as malign influences that had led a once great civilisation astray. In the words of the *Grey River Argus*, for example, 'the Germans are a great and strong people; they are, indeed, of the same stock as ourselves . . . The evil idea of conquest has been deeply rooted in their minds by three generations of culture, their military machine is the most terrible that has ever been constructed.'[49]

Other explanations asserted that 'Hunnish behaviour' was an innate expression of 'racial character'.[50] By October 1914, the *New Zealand Herald*, two months after stressing the blood-bound nature of Anglo-German kinship, was arguing that '[i]t was long believed in Europe that the Prussian was a half breed, the bi-product [sic] of that vast wave of Mongolian invasion which rolled westward from Asia centuries ago'.[51] 'Rumour has it,' said the *Otago Daily Times*, 'there is a strain of Tartar blood in the Prussians . . . Certainly, the photographs of his Imperial Majesty do betray a Tartare [sic] likeness . . .'[52]

The way the enemy was conceptualised had major implications for anyone in New Zealand who might be associated with those powers. In August 1914, Nelson's *Colonist* spoke of Germans who 'have so closely identified themselves with the Dominion's life and nationality that there can be no question of their fidelity to the country that has given them a far greater degree of prosperity than that which the Old World offered'.[53] Ideas that blood and loyalty ran together, however, undermined this separation. In December the *Evening Post* printed a letter advocating that, 'While Germany and Britain are at war the place for all Germans is Germany, failing that . . . a concentration camp. The only safe way is to arrest all Germans, beginning with the richest, the most influential, and the seemingly most loyal . . . We cannot afford to trust any person with German blood in his veins.'[54]

Accordingly, those who might be associated with enemy nations were sometimes the focus of public attention and angst, notably the 4015 individuals listed in the 1911 census as born in Germany. Those who might have ancestral links with Germany and subjects of enemy empires could come under suspicion, too.[55] Although the sympathies of the Croatian community were firmly with the Allies, or against Austria–Hungary, many were unnaturalised and thus officially Austrian subjects. There were also Syrians (overwhelmingly Christians from Lebanon), German-born Poles, and individuals, frequently Jewish, from within the Russian Empire who had inherited German names.

One Pole lamented, 'At home we were persecuted by the Germans and now, here in New Zealand, we are regarded as Germans.'[56] There was some sympathy for this difficult position. When Dunedin city councillor John Carroll protested that local Syrians should be interned, *Truth*, among others, reprimanded him, noting that they were decent Christians and that those under Ottoman rule were there by compulsion.[57] Lastly, associations with the enemy could expand to include accents and names. In May 1915 Johan Wielaert, a Dutchman with Belgian heritage, was assaulted in a Hamilton hotel by a patron who objected to sitting next to a 'German'.[58]

Feeling vulnerable, many sought to signal their solidarity with Britain and/or shared animosity to enemy belligerents. In December 1914, Schneideman Bros, 'The Empire Tailors', took out a full-page newspaper advertisement announcing that they were 'true British Subjects (formally of Riga, Russia)'.[59] In April 1915, H. B. Sorenson, a candidate in the Christchurch municipal election, proclaimed that he was Danish, had been in New Zealand for 53 years and, if he were younger, would be fighting against his country's enemies as '[t]he Danes had the greatest reason to hate the Germans'.[60]

In Auckland, members of the Syrian community donated a substantial sum to the Patriotic Fund and stated a willingness to enlist: 'we hope to show to the British nation that our patriotism to the King and country does not end in mere words'.[61] Palmerston North Syrians subscribed the sum of £13 'in gratitude for privileges enjoyed under the British flag, and especially for the protection afforded to their country in the Lebanon incident in 1860'.[62] A New Zealand-born son of Polish settlers who volunteered in 1915 recalled, 'I wanted to go to the war, to take a little revenge for the sake of my parents who had suffered so much at their [German] hands.'[63]

Suspicion was most widely manifested in concerns about potential spying and/or sabotage.[64] As the *Auckland Star* later recalled, 'the fun commenced' during the early weeks of the war: 'There were stories of trading with the enemy. Powerful wireless installations were said to be operating in all sorts of places that many an Aucklander had never heard of. There were furtive masonic signs passing between Germans in the street, there were winkling signals from lonely beaches, and on every hand the Germans were a planning and a caballing.'[65] Such anxieties were greatly fostered by international spy stories, and in October 1914 a Reform MP suggested in Parliament that all 'foreigners' should be required to report to the authorities 'as there is a general feeling of insecurity throughout the country'.[66] Many fears focused on possible communications with the German warships at large in the Pacific and on the new, still mysterious, medium of radio. As the *Free Lance* noted in early September,

> It is rumoured that undecipherable code messages picked up at New Zealand wireless stations are discovered now to have been sent by a naturalised German holding an office of responsibility in a New Zealand Government department, and that a brother of this man's (also a civil servant) left the Dominion suddenly just before the outbreak of war. This rumour is exceedingly serious. If there is truth in it, we are menaced by a very great danger. There is evidence enough of the ubiquity of German spies in Europe.[67]

The subsequent discovery of a naturalised German who had illegally acquired wireless equipment only heightened popular fears: one newspaper headlined its story 'Suspected German Spy'.[68] Police announced that anyone with unlicensed wireless equipment would be interned as a prisoner of war; this man was charged, convicted and, unable to pay the fine, incarcerated.[69]

Despite the fanciful nature of most allegations of enemy spying, at least one German agent was active in New Zealand. The former German consul in Auckland, Karl/Carl Seegner (aka 'informant/confidant 6301') was part of a network collecting and forwarding pertinent local information to a secret war intelligence section in Sydney.[70] In early 1916, Seegner and his former private secretary were arrested and interned under the Defence of the Realm Act. According to the *Dominion*, 'the action of the authorities in the matter was due to the suspicions aroused by the persons named in connection with their recent movements'. Although both the military authorities and the police were observing 'strict reticence', the paper described mysterious meetings in the Auckland Domain and threats against the men.[71] Whether New Zealand authorities were aware of Seegner's intelligence role is unknown.

Wartime animosity towards 'enemy aliens' also reflected economic and class issues. These were apparent in the case of George von Zedlitz, an unnaturalised German professor of modern languages at Victoria College who had married into a prominent Wellington family. In the days after Germany's declaration of war on Russia, but before the British declaration, von Zedlitz had visited the German consul and offered his services in a non-combatant role.[72] The claim that he had sought to aid Germany was soon joined by broader suggestions that an enemy alien should not hold public employment and allegations that he was disloyal.

By the end of February 1915 the *Dominion* was noting that 'various correspondents' had asked 'how it is that in Wellington we have a Chair of Modern Languages at Victoria College held by a German subject. Frankly, it is a little puzzling that the College Council does not appear to have concerned itself in the matter. It may have good reason; but surely the staff of, say, the University of Louvain could, if desired, provide us with a scholar to whom such a post would be welcome.'[73]

The *Maoriland Worker* presented the professor's retention of his job, even as ordinary workers in government employment were dismissed, as a 'glaring instance of class distinction and social influence':

> if there are dangerous Germans, they must be looked for in the upper classes, to which the aristocratic Professor belongs, and who makes no secret of the fact that his interests

> lie in Germany, where he hopes to inherit large and noble estates . . . Yet he is allowed to continue to draw during this war out of the State's coffers an annual salary of £800, while his countrymen in the public service, who probably only received the fifth part of this sum, have been dismissed.[74]

The *Marlborough Express* was of like mind: 'The special tolerance which is being extended to the Professor may be interpreted by not a few people as being due to the fact that the gentleman in question is a member of the Wellington Club, and has influential friends in the so-called "society" circles of Wellington.'[75] For the meantime, however, the Victoria College Board declined von Zedlitz's offer to resign and stood firm against criticism.

Economic contraction in Northland's gum industry and heightened competition for fewer local body public works also contributed to deteriorating attitudes towards local Yugoslavs.[76] Some commentators proved decidedly unsympathetic. *Truth*, for example, said: 'The most mischief-making of all the nationalities which have been permitted to land in New Zealand are the Croatians, who, up till now, have been quite content to style themselves Austrians, or have permitted others to style them Austrians.'[77] At the end of November 1914 a Croatian who had won a tender for a roadwork contract with the Hobson County Council gave it up because 'he was in fear of serious molestation . . . owing to the bitterness of British labourers being vented upon him and his party'. Frank Pavlovich, a young 'native of Herzegovina', committed suicide after complaining to the local constable that he and a Yugoslav contractor had been subjected to abuse after securing a large road contract. Fearing for his life, the other man did not carry out the work.[78]

Threats and acts of violence towards those associated with the enemy began shortly into the war. On 6 August, a German resident of Whanganui received telephoned threats telling him that he had 'an hour to clear out of the town'. The following evening, in Wellington, four windows in the office of the German consul, Eberhard Focke, were smashed. In Bluff, in October, a party of armed men called on a Mr Nichol, demanding to know the whereabouts of his German gardener. When they were told to leave, they fired several shots at the gardener's cottage; there were no injuries and the police soon arrived and made arrests.[79] Such acts, along with reports of violence against Germans in other parts of the empire, were publicly condemned.[80] The *Wanganui Herald* called the phone threats 'a cruel and senseless jest' by people who had 'lost their sense of British fair play', and the Wellington vandalism was denounced as the work of 'a few irresponsible excited boys'.[81] Repairs were paid for through public donations and a local newspaper reminded the public that Focke, who was a naturalised subject, had been an esteemed resident of the capital for 35 years and that his son had served in D Battery.[82]

Violence often flared in reaction to wartime events. For example, shortly before Christmas 1914, German warships shelled British seaside towns, causing the deaths of numerous women and children. Then, in late December, came the 'Ruahine tragedy', in which a drunken 21-year-old dairy farm worker, Arthur Rottmann, murdered his employer, his employer's wife and their baby.[83] For some, the case was seen as an example of inherent German brutality and of the danger local Germans posed. In Gisborne on New Year's Eve 1914, around 2000 locals gathered outside a butchery owned by 35-year-old Friedrich Wohnsiedler. Born in Eberbach, Germany, he had lived in New Zealand since 1902 and his naturalisation papers had been signed on 4 August 1914.[84] The crowd threw stones to smash the windows of the building while the terrified Wohnsiedler family hid upstairs before escaping out a back door. The small and hard-pressed band of police present was unable to prevent the attack.

Although press condemnation was universal, some commentary betrayed sympathy for the motives, if not the methods, of the rioters. In particular, some criticised the government's 'characteristic flabbiness' in not interning enemy subjects, giving 'hoodlums' an excuse to run amok.[85] The editor of the *Poverty Bay Herald* attacked the 'namby-pamby treatment of enemy subjects', and declared that internment was necessary, 'not alone for their own security, but in order to guard against the public mind becoming inflamed against people who thoughtlessly do business with these aliens, and against the peace being thereby disturbed'.[86]

Those of a conspiratorial bent asserted that the government was riddled with 'pro-Germans', a term that could embrace anything from attachment to German culture to more sinister notions of treasonous intrigue.[87] Such resentments were further stoked by the not insignificant numbers of German farmers or merchants who were flourishing, or allegedly flourishing, thanks to the war. They, it was said, might emerge from the conflict better off, while British people suffered death, wounds and financial hardship. The wealth and education of well-known members of Dunedin's German Jewish community was certainly a salient factor when the local Municipal Association asked Mayor John Shacklock to arrange greater 'supervision' of 'German residents', including those who were naturalised.[88]

By 1915 calls for more extensive internment procedures were gaining traction. In January, a large meeting of Auckland justices of the peace advocated the internment of 'all male alien enemies in New Zealand, whether naturalised British subjects or unnaturalised, during the war, and urg[ed] that they should be treated kindly and in a humanitarian spirit, but should be prevented from causing any mischief to the community'.[89] The following month 'loyal British subjects of the Masterton district' petitioned that all the local 'enemy subjects' should be interned 'as several of them have been expressing their opinions freely against the Allies'. The petitioners feared 'that when the enemy meet with a crushing blow, which will assuredly happen before long, some of the above enemy subjects will be acting dangerously towards us'.[90] The move may have been given impetus by an incident the previous month when local barber Otto Thiel had been arrested on suspicion of being a spy, revealed as a German reservist and interned, though not charged with spying.[91]

Both these proposals were condemned, especially the suggestion that naturalised citizens should be detained. Some aligned this position with patriotic pride. As one letter to the *Colonist* said, 'We Britishers usually pride ourselves on . . . a love of fair play and justice . . . the ability to keep our heads and not get "panicky" in critical times. The letters of some of your correspondents on the subject of alien enemies seem to indicate a lack of these British characteristics.'[92] The *Star*, a Liberal paper, was particularly scathing about the JPs: 'If these sapient individuals had made investigations anywhere beyond the radius of the village pump, they would have discovered

above German prisoners being escorted through Wellington on 11 August 1914, bound for the Alexandra Barracks in Mount Victoria. The following day they were moved to Matiu Somes Island. AUCKLAND WEEKLY NEWS, 20 AUGUST 1914, P. 49

left Friedrich Wohnsiedler's butchery in Gisborne after it was vandalised on New Year's Eve 1914. GLENN REDDIEX COLLECTION that some of the earliest and worthiest of our pioneers were representatives of the German race, and that numbers of their descendants are loyal and patriotic New Zealanders serving at the front.'[93] A Masterton newspaper labelled the local petition 'silly' and was embarrassed when it drew condemnation from as far afield as Ashburton.[94]

Once war was declared, many New Zealanders were eager to be involved. The military commitment formed a clear focus and by 10 August ideas of garrison duties somewhere in the empire had disappeared as Massey announced that New Zealand men could expect to play an active role in the fighting: 'within a few weeks after leaving . . . they will find themselves at the front, and probably in the firing-line'.[95]

There was enduring haziness, though, about some aspects of service. For example, Māori eager to enlist faced uncertainty as officials pondered imperial regulations regarding the use of 'native troops' in wars between Europeans.[96] Massey thought there should be no problem with Māori serving in India or Egypt and Allen could not see any difficulties with 'half-castes' enlisting.[97] In early September, London accepted the offer of a Māori contingent of 500 volunteers, originally intended for garrison duty. Women desperate to serve overseas as nurses waited still longer for official confirmation. Allen took considerable time to bow to pressure, particularly from the determined Hester Maclean, head of the nascent New Zealand Army Nursing Service (NZANS). As she wrote in the nursing journal, *Kai Tiaki*, in October 1914, 'Britain's sons are eager to save her. Her daughters too, are all for helping.'[98]

Not until 7 January 1915 did a cable go to the War Office in London offering 50 trained New Zealand nurses. Acceptance came on 25 January. Ultimately some 550 served with the NZANS; others nursed with other organisations such as Queen Alexandra's Imperial Nursing Service.[99] There was a surge in interest in the profession and the number of nurses rose even as many of the country's experienced sisters left for overseas. In August 1915 the superintendent of Waikato Hospital was struggling to cope with the number of applicants for nursing training: there was a waiting list of over 100 and four or five further applications coming in each day.[100] Other women left New Zealand on their own initiative — some, too, were already in Britain when the war broke out — and took up an array of war-related roles, as doctors, ambulance drivers, munitions workers, members of the YMCA and the Red Cross, and serving with the Voluntary Aid Detachment.[101]

There was a rush of volunteers for the NZEF and, as one study notes, 'without any sort of recruiting stimulation New Zealand raised and equipped almost 10,000 soldiers by the third week in August'.[102] Many more volunteered but were turned down — in 1914 more than 25 per cent of applicants were rejected as medically unfit.[103] However, comparing enlistment rates across the four military districts somewhat complicates the picture. Wellington, for example, received a rush of 5541 applications for the 2000 spaces each district was assigned. The Auckland response was comparable and Canterbury had 'practically no difficulty'.[104] Otago, however, was unable to fill its quota in time, largely because it had a significantly smaller pool of eligible men: 18.5 per cent of the nation's male population against Wellington's

31.7 per cent, Auckland's 24.7 per cent and Canterbury's 24.9 per cent.[105]

The backgrounds and motivations of those volunteering have been an enduring point of interest. A survey of the NZEF in mid-November 1914 gives some sense of who these men were. They were young: 5300 (63 per cent) were under 25, 1614 (19 per cent) under 21; only 89 men were over 40 and the mean age was 25.9. They were overwhelmingly — 7992 (94 per cent) — unmarried and childless. Religious affiliation was broadly representative of the general public: 87 per cent identified themselves as Protestant and 12 per cent as Catholic. Most, 82 per cent, had some experience of military training before they enlisted, almost half by choice. A disproportionate number came from rural backgrounds, which gave the NZEF a 'strong rural flavour' that persisted even when its composition later became much more urban.[106]

These, then, were largely men with few responsibilities to hold them back and with social, ideological, temperamental, and potentially economic, enticements to go. From the beginning, men in manual work, often casual, remained the backbone of enlistments.[107] Days after war was declared, Taranaki station owner Duncan Stevens noted in his diary that '[a]ll the bushmen called in the morning & R. Fulton, Yarrell & Baldwin left for Waitara to volunteer for the front'.[108] On the other side of the North Island, bushman Charlie Clark and his mates did the same: 'I went into Gisborne and all the bushmen from the district were in and there were bushmen out on the town . . . So we had a few drinks and we all marched over and put our names down to go into the War.'[109] The same happened in the towns and cities. By November 1914 the *New Zealand Herald* was reporting that boarding houses were emptying, 'the men mobilised for service being largely of the boarding and unattached class'.[110]

Being young also meant greater impulsiveness. 'There was a parade called for the Territorials,' George Skerrett recalled, 'and I volunteered. I don't know why, I think it was because I wanted to be with my mates.'[111] Many attempting to enlist were under the minimum age of 20. After Reform MP David Buick pointed out that this was 'causing much concern amongst parents', Allen assured him that the 'next portion' who enlisted would have to produce birth certificates. He later expressed his preference for a minimum age of 22 rather than 20.[112]

Economic opportunity seems an unlikely spur to enlistment but may have had some influence. Relative to a British Tommy's pay of 1s a day, a New Zealand private was paid 'a princely sum' of 5s a day — an annual total of £89 9s.[113] Relative to New Zealand incomes, though, this figure was meagre; a general labourer could earn 8–10s a day and a clerk, depending on experience, might earn between £120 and £250 a year.[114] Moreover, the New Zealand economy appears to have been expanding at the time, offering more employment opportunities. Nevertheless, those in less stable employment may have found enlistment, for what they thought would be a relatively brief overseas adventure in the off-season, with food, clothing and accommodation (of a sort) provided, an attractive prospect.[115] Charles Kerse certainly thought so. 'Some of these chaps,' he told his mother, 'will have more money than they ever had before.'[116] Significant, too, was the fact that the war began during the seasonal dip in agricultural jobs, when relief work was prioritised for men with dependants.[117]

Some cited a sense of responsibility as their motivation for joining up. Cecil, soon to be Private, Malthus thought 'it was the urgent duty of every able-bodied man to consider the question of enlisting'.[118] A desire for adventure or an escape from routine certainly played a part, and no doubt the prospect of a 'free' visit to relatives in Britain and the chance to see famous locations also appealed. Confirmation that New Zealanders would be assigned a combat, rather than garrison, role seems to have accelerated volunteering, indicating that many were keen to partake in a meaningful action.[119] As an officer at Awapuni Military Camp remarked, initial enlistments had been 'rather slow' until it was announced that European service was intended: 'from then onwards enrolment had proceeded vigorously. I would not have enrolled myself for garrison duty in India or Egypt . . . That would only have meant constant drill and we should have been left out of the fighting. You see we want to be in it.'[120]

Escape from domestic responsibilities could also be a motivation. In December 1914, Trooper Albert Landsdown was ordered off a transport when his wife appeared, claiming that they had eight children for whom he had not made adequate provision.[121] In an age when husbands were the sole or major breadwinners, the whole question of married men volunteering was controversial. A Christchurch newspaper declared that 'so long as the services of single men are available, married men should not be allowed to take their places in the ranks' and even the appointment of married officers and non-commissioned officers 'should be made only with the greatest circumspection'. It concluded that '[t]he man who goes to war without having made adequate provision for those at home is not a patriot. He is a scoundrel.'[122]

Most young, single men, especially in New Zealand's many tight-knit communities, were also sensitive to the widespread expectation that they ought to volunteer. In November 1914 George Knight told his mother:

> I feel that the next time an appeal for recruits is made in Dannevirke, I must enlist. It is not a resolution made on the spur of the moment but has been well thought out . . . When I was home & saw the soldiers going off I felt sort of mean & wanted to hide because I was not there & have dreaded anyone asking me if I am going or want to go . . . Of course I don't like to leave Home & I know that Home doesn't want to loose [sic] me but I feel I must. There is a piece of poetry, it was in the paper. 'What would you do Sonny[?] I wasn't amongst the first to go but thank God I went.'[123]

One soon-to-be recruit felt the pressure during a male-only Sunday sermon that outlined 'the horrible brutality of the Hun and the poor little Belgian children'. The preacher 'made the most of it. Monday morning came and everybody rushed to the recruiting office including me and my brother.'[124] In other cases, communities reinforced the sense of expectation by lauding the involvement of their members. The *Tablet*, for example, praised Catholic representation within volunteers: 'Lip loyalty is cheap and easy, but the real thing is a matter of deeds rather than words.'[125] Labour leaders voiced similar sentiments. Early in September 1914 John Paul noted that:

> Organised Labour will be well represented in the Expeditionary Force. Several prominent unionists of my personal acquaintance have volunteered, and some of the unions have

above The Greymouth contingent of the Main Expeditionary Force marches past the town's post office in 1914. CANTERBURY MUSEUM, 1976-96.2

below Nelson members of the New Zealand Expeditionary Force at an official farewell before their departure. ALEXANDER TURNBULL LIBRARY, 1/2-025645-G at least temporarily lost valuable and loyal members. So far, I think, the Auckland Hotel and Restaurant Employees' Union holds the record for the number of members who have volunteered and been accepted. The number of members of this union who are going on active service is stated to be 168 — a very commendable record.[126]

On 24 August the *Dominion* reported that over 40 members of the Wharf Labourers' Union had joined up and that they would be exempt from fees but keep their memberships while they were away.[127] Much also rested on understandings of ideal gender roles. As Mary Downie Stuart pointed out, in her capacity as president of the Otago and Southland Women's Patriotic Association,

> Since the most primitive times — it has always been the same, we women the home keepers must find our duty there, you men, the home guardians, must go out & meet the enemy. The defence of home & country has always been the traditional duty of the man . . . No one pretends it is not hard to let you go, but you would not be the men we love & are proud of if you had any other instinct — than to go. I know that most men want to go — but for various reasons cannot. So we congratulate you who are able to go, because you have found the way open to fulfil your natural inclinations.[128]

Māori volunteering for what became known as Te Hokowhitu-a-Tū (the 70 twice-told warriors of the war god Tū) exhibited many of the same dynamics as Pākehā communities. Established networks facilitated recruitment and most volunteers had been well educated, many at Anglican schools like Te Aute, St Stephen's and Te Rau Māori Theological College.[129] Soon after war was declared, Alec Takarangi, a Te Aute graduate and renowned rugby player, was 'acting as "recruiting agent", and his office was . . . quite a base for the handing in of the names of those ready and willing to serve their country'.[130] Recruitment relied heavily, though, on the emergent Native Contingent Committee, chaired by Māui Pōmare and with Carroll, Ngata, Buck and Taare (Charles) Parata as prominent members.

The committee agreed on recruitment quotas for each district; men were often attracted to enlist, trained and sent on a tribal basis. Under this system, Northern Māori were to recruit 100, Western Māori 180, Eastern Māori 180 and Southern Māori 40. If one district could not fill its quota, others would make it up, a process that left recruits 'with the impression that they had been chosen as envoys of their tribes'.[131] At the beginning of September, Ngata announced that '[t]hree hundred men of the Arawas and 300 of the Wairoa natives — two good fighting stocks — had already offered their services'.[132] There was personal conviction behind the committee's work: by 1916 both Carroll and Ngata had sons at the front and one of the latter's closest friends had been killed. Peter Buck (Te Rangi Hīroa) had volunteered and was serving as a medical officer.

The shame directed at non-participants proved another source of motivation to volunteer. This dynamic drew on established gender relations in which women were deemed responsible for setting the moral pace and ensuring masculine dutifulness.[133] In the first months of the

above Collected clothes being sorted for dispatch to troops. The woman second from the left is J. A. Nash, the wife of the mayor of Palmerston North. MANAWATŪ HERITAGE, 2007_A14_WAR_0001

below Organisers working in a supply depot established under the Lady Liverpool Fund. ALEXANDER TURNBULL LIBRARY, 1/1-008352-G

above Members of Wellington's 'Spinsters Club' knitting socks for soldiers. ALEXANDER TURNBULL LIBRARY, 1/2-030986-F

below Pupils from Iona College, in Hawke's Bay, fundraising for Belgium in 1915. The presence of United States flags, alongside British and Australian ones, likely reflects an affiliation with the Commission for Relief in Belgium, a predominantly American organisation. ALEXANDER TURNBULL LIBRARY, PACOLL-5600 war, some women, individually or in groups, began accosting men, particularly those who were young and able-bodied, and attempted to pressure them into enlisting. Particularly vindictive was the practice, started in Britain and imitated in New Zealand, of giving or sending white feathers, denoting cowardice.[134] In November 1914 the *Sun* in Christchurch implicitly commended the practice, not specifically to encourage volunteering, but rather to shame territorials who were not attending parades. Newspaper correspondence in Dunedin the following month indicated that white feathers were being handed out in considerable numbers.[135] In some cases it proved effective: 'I didn't want to go but I was single, 27 and I was getting white feathers handed to me . . . and I said "to hell with it, I'm going." No I'm no hero I didn't want to fight but I couldn't stand that.'[136]

There was soon a backlash, however, especially when cases of indiscriminate shaming were publicised. A notable example was a young man in Britain who was unfit for military service and apparently committed suicide after being sent a feather.[137] Letters to the editor brought calls for British fair play and explanations that many men wanted to enlist but were unable to do so for legitimate economic or medical reasons. One correspondent reasoned that 'mean and underhand reflections on our manhood should not be made until the number of men required for our New Zealand forces exceeds the number responding'.[138] Local newspapers, including the *Sun*, also began to condemn feather giving.[139] In February 1915, the *Star* cited two Christchurch cases:

> Two brothers were working in an office: one engaged to be married. It fell to the portion of the one unattached to enlist, and he lingered for two months in the city to complete an examination. In that time he received five white feathers from girls of his acquaintance. Another case is one in which a man who had applied for enlistment was upbraided. Each of these feathers sent is a symbol of disgrace to Christchurch girls.[140]

The desire for involvement also underwrote enormous charity efforts. Women were essential in this endeavour, providing countless hours of unpaid labour. In the words of historian Margaret Tennant, 'Women had always provided the workforce behind charities, even when men provided leadership or controlled the finances.'[141] Existing social networks and organisations such as the Women's Christian Temperance Union (WCTU), the Red Cross and the Victoria League were mobilised, and more than 1000 new bodies were formed during the war.[142]

Many socially active women explicitly defined charity as the appropriate means for women to contribute to the war effort. A day after the declaration, for example, the Countess of Liverpool made an appeal from Government House: 'At this moment of our Empire's need I desire to appeal to the women of New Zealand to assist me in trying to provide any necessaries which may be required for those portions of the citizen army which are now mobilising for any service which may be required of them.' She called for women to organise committees across the country able to take contributions in funds but also appealed that women 'could not do better' than to help provision knitted and woven goods for the NZEF.[143]

As a book of knitting patterns later produced under her name put it, 'For the Empire and for freedom, We all must do our bit; The men go forth to battle, The women wait and knit.'[144] Many other members of the social elite took up prominent roles. Christina Massey, for example, was the vice-president of both the Countess of Liverpool Fund and the Red Cross Society; she was later active in the Women's National Reserve. In 1915, Miria Pōmare, the wife of the MP for Western Māori, and Lady Liverpool formed the Māori Soldiers' Fund, drawing upon the resources of Māori women's committees around the country to provide comforts to Māori soldiers.

Most of the initial emphasis was on supplying and provisioning the NZEF and ensuring that the troops were well equipped with 'comforts'.[145] By 7 November 1914, less than three months after its formation, the Otago and Southland Women's Patriotic Association had issued the region's soldiers with 1600 full kits containing 33,600 articles of clothing.[146] Other charity work focused on civilians, both New Zealanders affected by war-related economic disruptions and those much further away. In the second week of the war a number of wealthy Christchurch individuals established a Poor of Great Britain and Ireland Relief Fund to send meat, dairy products and other produce 'for the relief of those at Home'.[147]

The plight of Belgium, though, quickly became a key focus. On 22 August the *Hawke's Bay Tribune* announced that it was opening a fund 'for the relief of the numberless Belgian families that have been rendered homeless and driven to distress by the ruthless invasion of their country'. Similar funds were then established elsewhere; in Christchurch the British fund was relaunched as the Poor of Great Britain, Ireland and Belgium Fund.[148] On 13 November an Auckland street collection for the Belgian Relief Fund set a new record for the city, eclipsing a similar drive for the Patriotic Fund a few weeks earlier.[149]

In the month to 18 January 1915, over three-quarters of the £6279 received by the Otago Patriotic and General Welfare Association was specified to be for the Belgians.[150] Ninety-seven per cent of the £4617 donated in March and April was for Belgian relief.[151] Up to September 1915 the executive of the Canterbury Patriotic Fund considered that the Belgian Relief Fund had 'a prior claim' on the public's generosity and awaited the return of wounded soldiers to New Zealand before it launched its own major effort. Consequently, a much higher proportion of donations from Canterbury went to the Belgians during the war — almost all of it before the end of 1915 — than was the case in either Auckland or Wellington.[152]

Fundraising extended even to Māori in areas that had suffered land confiscations: a number donated stock or cash at Ōkato in Taranaki, and in the King Country H. Hetet collected the large sum of £110 from 'the natives of Te Kuiti'. In Whakatāne, in September 1914, the 'Tuhoe natives, who have held several meetings at Ruatoki for the purpose of arranging means of raising money in aid of the Empire Defence Fund, decided . . . to offer the Government a block of 1600 acres, to be sold by the Government at the highest market price, and that the whole of the money raised thereby be given to the Defence Fund'.[153]

Appeals for war causes could, however, create headaches for other operations funded by public donations. At the beginning of October 1914, Archdeacon Neild in Auckland complained

above Attendees of the Lady Liverpool Fund Conference, primarily established to support soldiers and their dependants. Front row, fourth from right, is Christina Massey, the wife of the prime minister. MANAWATŪ HERITAGE, 2011P_PG125_006118

left The front cover of *Her Excellency's Knitting Book*. Published in August 1915, the 193-page book contained knitting patterns for socks, balaclavas and gloves. TE PAPA, GH003690

above Māori soldiers awaiting departure. ALEXANDER TURNBULL LIBRARY, 1/2-011079-F

below East Coast volunteers for the Native Contingent gather for a photograph in Napier in October 1914. Vigor Brown, Napier's mayor and Member of Parliament, is seated in the centre between Āpirana Ngata and Arihia Ngata. TAIRAWHITI MUSEUM that 'many people who had promised donations to the Melanesian Mission had withdrawn their promises, as they desired to give to the patriotic and war funds instead. "I don't call that patriotism," he said, "I call that robbing God. Unless things change, I can see the withdrawal of the missionaries and the Southern Cross, and the stoppage of Christian work in Melanesia."' He was not asking the public 'to support the mission with money that might go to the war funds, but . . . promises should be kept, even if to do so meant a little sacrifice in forgoing a luxury or two'.[154]

Priorities could also be a problem with war-related causes. In February 1915, for example, the Commission for Relief in Belgium, an international though predominantly American organisation, appealed to Australians and New Zealanders for £75,000 a month in money or food.[155] This prospect crystallised concerns that the dependence on voluntary contributions meant the burden was not being equitably borne and the mayors of Christchurch and Dunedin called for a tax to meet the commission's request. After gaining assurances that the food provided by the commission would not fall into enemy hands, the government agreed to contribute £5000 each month and a pound for pound subsidy on voluntary donations up to that amount.[156]

Measuring the scale of such wartime donating work proved a monumental task for the Department of Internal Affairs, but it eventually calculated that around £2 million had been collected in the 17 months to the end of 1915, an amount roughly comparable on an annual basis to the £1.3 million in land and income tax for the 1913/14 tax year.[157] The department's total was almost certainly an underestimate. The record-keeping of many of the organisations involved was decidedly ad hoc; also, donations made directly to funds overseas or the Red Cross were not included and nor were gifts from individuals to soldiers.

The farewells to departing troops that marked the early months of the war would become a regular occurrence over the following years. Just days after the declaration people gathered at railway stations to send off men accepted for the 1413-strong 'Advance Guard' bound for German Sāmoa, though that destination was not publicly known. The Samoan Expeditionary Force, as it was subsequently called, was ready to depart by 11 August but was delayed owing to a potential threat posed by the East Asia Squadron. While the Admiralty believed that German ships could be as close as New Guinea, they argued that the Australian Squadron represented an effective deterrent. Captain Marshall, however, pleaded for a stronger escort, and HMAS *Australia* and the French cruiser *Montcalm* were assigned to this task.

On the morning of 14 August crowds watched the soldiers march through Wellington to assemble in the Basin Reserve for an inspection and an official farewell. An estimated 5000 listened to the official speeches which stressed pride in the troops and the gravity of the situation. 'You are going forth,' Massey told the men, 'to uphold the honour of New Zealand and to fight for your King and country in the greatest crisis that the Empire has ever seen. That you will do your duty and do it well goes without saying.'[158] The next day the *Moeraki* and the *Monowai* steamed out of Wellington Harbour, carrying the first of the tens of thousands of

New Zealanders who would serve overseas.

Through the rest of August, masses of men marching through familiar landscapes, en route to training camps where the Main Body of the NZEF was being formed and equipped, became a common sight. They were an early part of an exercise described as 'one of the largest organisational feats' in New Zealand history.[159] The prevalent martial mythology that New Zealand men were 'natural' soldiers was burnished in press coverage. The *New Zealand Herald*, for example, considered the average young New Zealander, especially if living in the country, as 'half a soldier before he is enrolled. He is physically strong, intellectually keen, anxious to be led though being what he is will not brook being driven a single inch. Quick to learn his drill, easily adapting to the conditions of life in camp since camping usually is his pastime and very loyal to his leaders when those leaders know their job.'[160]

More sober voices mixed pride with an awareness that effective soldiers required effective training. 'Training, discipline, and organisation,' said the *Evening Post*, 'are needed before a collection even of the most soldierly units can be converted from a mob into an army, and with all these things New Zealand's Expeditionary Force has yet to be supplied.' The *Observer* picked up on Kitchener's statement that he was not going to use 'half-baked' troops and noted '[i]n the military sense the whole of the New Zealand territorial force is not even half-baked — it is unequivocally "slack-baked"'.[161]

With no permanent training facilities, mobilisation camps were established in each of the four military districts. Facilities were ad hoc: most troops slept under canvas in available open spaces. Auckland's recruits camped at Alexandra Park racecourse; Canterbury's at Christchurch's Addington Racecourse (soon relocated to Sockburn Park after an outbreak of scarlatina);

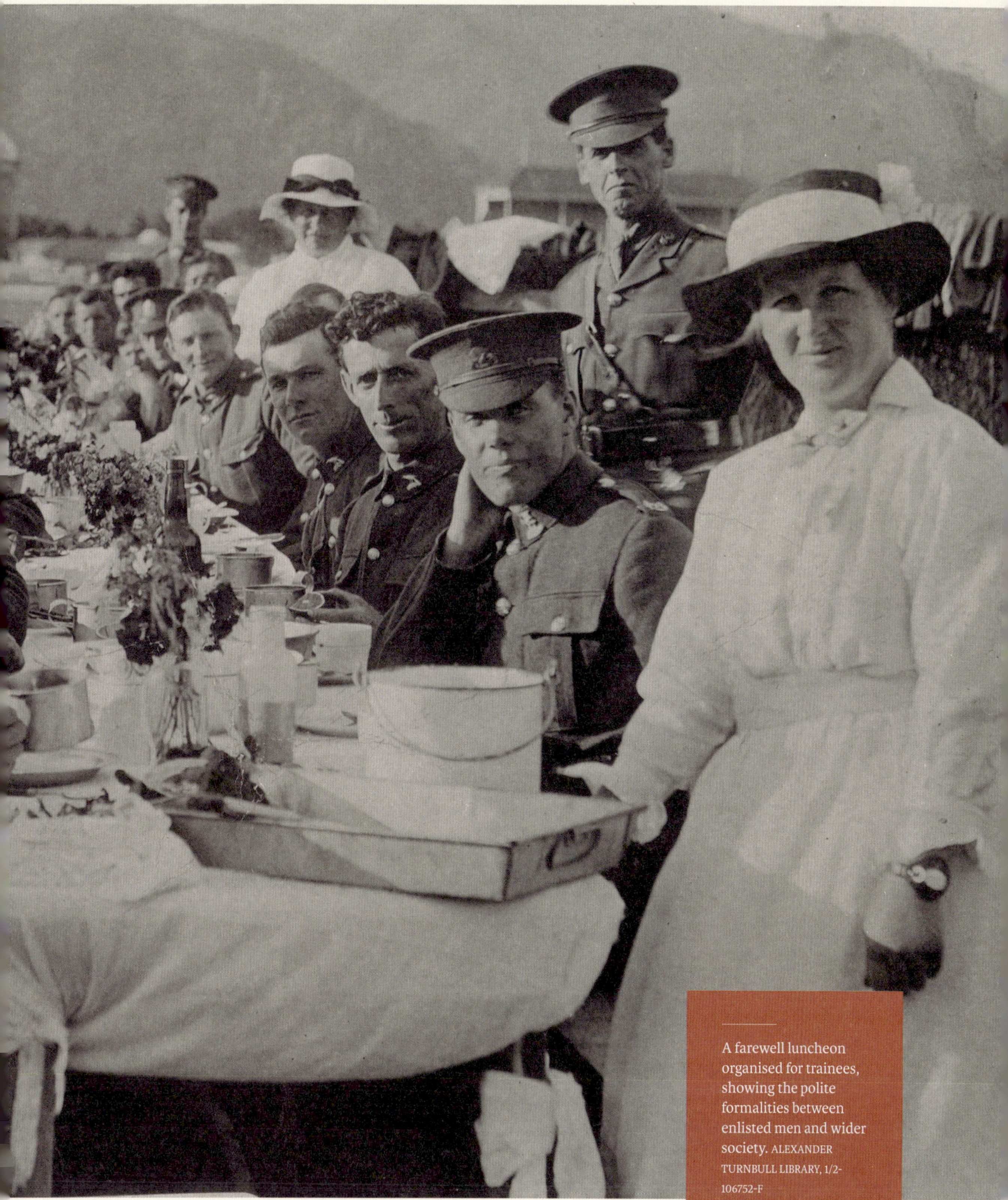

A farewell luncheon organised for trainees, showing the polite formalities between enlisted men and wider society. ALEXANDER TURNBULL LIBRARY, 1/2-106752-F

Otago's at Tahuna Park; and Wellington's at the Awapuni Racecourse in Palmerston North. Each camp accommodated the district's infantry and mounted rifle contingents; the much larger Awapuni camp also accommodated the country's artillery, signallers, engineers, Army Service Corps and the Mounted Field Ambulance units. Soldiers for the Māori contingent were trained at Avondale, alongside the Engineers' Tunnelling Company, between October 1914 and February 1915.[162] Both were subsequently relocated to Narrow Neck, on the North Shore.

In the early months of the war, the camps were more than just places where civilians became soldiers. Because they were in or near urban areas, they were also the subject of great public interest — there were open days, for instance — and recruits could head into town on their days off. In a forerunner of its later role as the most militarised New Zealand city, with Linton and Waiōuru camps and Ōhakea Air Force Base established there, Palmerston North was especially energised by the nearby Awapuni camp:

> Everywhere in the evenings and on Saturday and Sunday afternoons, when the troops get leave there is to be seen the soldier in his khaki uniform — parading the streets, patronising the shops and various places of refreshment and amusement, going in and out of houses where he is invariably welcomed, and driving about in taxi-cabs, motor-buses, and vehicles of all descriptions . . . The change in the town is equally apparent. In almost every shop window appear the colours of the national flag, many of the citizens are wearing red, white and blue, and everywhere the war is the sole topic of conversation . . . Palmerston at the same time is crowded with visitors, the mothers and sisters and fathers and brothers of the troops, who are seeing as much of them as possible before they leave for Europe.

When an estimated 7000 people visited the camp one Sunday, '[o]utside the gates stretched a succession of closely-packed vehicles . . . fully half a mile long — a spectacle which those who saw it will not readily forget'.[163]

There were undoubtedly some drawbacks. Locals had to get accustomed to the sounds of machine guns and rifles, and long columns of marching troops could hold up traffic. There were problems with bad behaviour on leave days, such as brawling and indecent bathing, but drunkenness was the most common issue. The city's businesses, especially the hotels, were happy, but some moral guardians were less so as they confronted 'the discrepancy between their noble idea of a crusade and the army of non-teetotallers'.[164] In February 1915 a Wellington magistrate declared it 'a deplorable fact . . . that when one takes up the papers each morning there is something to read about a disturbance in which troopers have taken part'. He was speaking at the trial of a trainee private and another man who had been discharged from the army for numerous offences. They had brawled outside the Duke of Edinburgh Hotel in Manners Street, pitting much of a large crowd against the police officers who were attempting to arrest the private for drunkenness. The prosecuting police inspector considered that lives had been endangered, while one defence counsel argued that if all those involved had been arrested 'there would have been a parade of quite a dozen soldiers before the Court'. The same day another soldier was convicted of violently resisting arrest when drunk in Featherston Street.[165]

Pickets of military police, known as 'Red Caps', became another sight in parts of wartime New Zealand. Corporal William McKeon recalled an incident when he was on guard duty:

> Just prior to midnight, the camp police brought in a prize exhibit, a soldier who had been very definitely on the loose. He was out cold, and was dumped on a bench in one of the cells . . . He was in a shocking state, filthy and smelling to high heaven of stale liquor . . . It was subsequently found that he was one of the camp cooks who had been A.W.L. [absent without leave] for over a week and was picked up in Featherston township after a stupendous pub-crawl in Masterton, Carterton and Greytown.[166]

Absence without leave was a sizeable problem. In January 1915, Herbert Knight of the Third Reinforcements noted, 'We got paid the day before the races. We were supposed to be in camp directly after the races and about 300 were in town for a couple of days without leave. They sent in two or three lots of pickets to get them but I don't think they got them all.'[167] The most significant episode of indiscipline appears to have occurred in Dunedin one Saturday night in September 1914, when almost 1000 men broke out at Tahuna Camp because general leave was halted.[168]

By this time, the final preparations to deploy the Main Body of the NZEF were nearly complete. On 22 and 23 September respectively the Otago and Canterbury troops left camp and boarded transports at Lyttelton and Port Chalmers to sail to Wellington, from where, with local troopships, they would depart on 25 September, and rendezvous with the Auckland vessels in the Tasman Sea. As the *Southland Times* reported, the mounted men of the Otago section of the NZEF left Dunedin's Tahuna Park shortly before daybreak on 22 September. There was 'no fuss, and the only sound distinguishable for any distance was the call of the bugle, which rang out clearly in the morning air. There were few people to witness the departure of the men, but there were one or two, including ladies, and these, together with a few of the comrades in arms of the departing Expeditioners, gave hearty cheers which floated out on the breeze like the sound of a Clarion.' The infantry went to Port Chalmers by train. Although there was no formal farewell ceremony, 'the town was given an opportunity to say au revoir to the departing troopers' and the mayor boarded the troopships to wish the men bon voyage and make a speech.[169]

The Canterbury troopships, *Tahiti* and *Athenic*, 'officially known as His Majesty's Transports Numbers 4 and 11 respectively', steamed out of Lyttelton Harbour on the evening of Wednesday, 23 September 'with as fine a lot of soldiers as ever went off to war. They had a good send-off in spite of the official bungling that deprived them of anything in the nature of a public farewell.' Throughout the day, the news had 'circulated freely through the city that the troops were moving', and hundreds took the train through the tunnel to the port to say goodbye 'and give our boys a final cheer'. But the public were not allowed onto the wharf until all the troops were aboard, about five o'clock. 'The transports,' said the *Sun* reporter, 'then presented a wonderful sight. Khaki figures swarmed as they could stand on the decks, perched on the life-boats, and crowded on all over the vessels. Packed as close every inch of space, they looked as thick as bees. The boys were in high spirits and exchanged boisterous greetings and good-byes with their friends and relatives on the wharf.' Darkness was beginning to fall as the transports 'steamed towards the heads'.[170]

That same day, in Auckland, the soldiers marched through the city for a brief review at the Domain Cricket Ground, attended by between 15,000 and 20,000 people, undeterred by a bitter north-easterly wind and occasional driving rain. Then, accompanied by two bands, the troops paraded to the foot of Queen Street, 'cheered every yard of the way by crowds who thronged the footpaths — behind lines of cadets and boy scouts — who had invaded windows, roofs and verandah-tops, and, indeed, every point of vantage'.[171]

In Wellington a half-holiday was declared for the 24th and a record crowd of 25,000 to 30,000 people packed a farewell event held at Newtown Park. This, in the view of the *Evening Post*, 'was a quiet, dignified, solemn, and impressive ceremony, without the slightest touch of jingoism in it, and will pass down to posterity as a striking example of the attitude adopted by the citizens of the Empire City in the great tragedy that has befallen mankind, and of how they despatched their soldier sons, the flower of the New Zealand Army, to fight upon the battlefields of Europe.' There was sorrow, too, for those looking down from the park banks at the men drawn up on the grass: 'Tears there were, surreptitious tears, sometimes, but then those for whom they were shed were down below and could not be troubled by them, and there comes a limit to self-control.'[172]

After the pomp and the speeches, a hymn and a psalm, the troops marched through the city. 'The only note of colour in the long stream of men was imparted by the uniformed bands. For the rest, it was a long, swinging, mud-coloured ribbon of men — and khaki means mud. The men were not got up for a show at the Horse Guards. They are going into action, therefore their extremely serviceable clothing, made of good and pure New Zealand wool, will be just the thing for the northern winter into which they are going.' In light rain the crowds packed under the verandahs and cheered as the men went by.[173]

The sense of a final goodbye, however, was marred by a potential crisis. Just before 7 p.m. on the night of 24 September, the governor received a telegram from his counterpart in Australia, Sir Ronald Munro Ferguson, stating that the transports could be at risk from German warships. An hour later Liverpool dispatched a telegram recalling Auckland's transports and the Canterbury and Otago contingents were disembarked in Wellington.[174] Massey was notably shaken by the news, as one of his ministers later recalled: 'I found him sitting at the head of the Cabinet table, his head on his hands, and great beads of perspiration standing out on his large head. Without a word he pointed to a telegram on the table.'[175]

A three-week impasse followed with the British Admiralty over the safety of dispatching the troopships without a stronger escort.[176] On 3 October the Admiralty made a further attempt to persuade the New Zealand government to allow a departure,[177] but Massey adamantly refused: 'I took the signal ordering the ships to sail to the Governor-General (Lord Liverpool) asking him to amend the time of sailing by five minutes . . . [He] seemed somewhat puzzled, and asked me, "But why five minutes?" . . . "Because, sir", I replied, "it will take me exactly that time to write out my resignation!"'[178] Liverpool's report to London noted that the government considered changes to the provision of escorts as a breach of faith, that Massey would resign if overridden and that the reason would probably become public knowledge.[179] With no wish to trigger a political crisis, arrangements were made to have HMS *Minotaur* and the cruiser *Ibuki* added to the escort.

During this period the Auckland contingent had been shipped to Wellington, where the troops were kept busy with further training and were entertained by the locals. By mid-October, the escorts had arrived and the Main Body prepared to leave on the morning of the 16th. The 8499 men who embarked remain the largest group to leave New Zealand at one time. The morning was 'clear, but very grey' and although news of the departure had been restricted, word of mouth brought crowds to the waterfront and around the harbour, with some on boats. There was 'much waving of handkerchiefs on shore, and occasionally the voices of the men on the ships came across the water cheering'. The ships' bands played the National Anthem and popular tunes, and one witness described the mood as calm and confident: 'There was a little weeping, but at the back of it all a solid satisfaction, a high sense of a great thing doing.'

Another noted that 'many a mother, sister, or sweetheart smiled bravely to hide tears as she looked across the water to big quiet hulls that carried the loved ones, some of whom perhaps would not return'. As the vessels steamed away, the sun broke through the clouds, which one observer took as a sign that 'after the dark hour of parting shall come the happiness of reunion when the black fog of war has rolled away'.[180]

With the departure of the Main Body, New Zealand's enlistment system turned to training regular reinforcements to maintain the strength of the NZEF. Under pre-war calculations, based on study of the Russo-Japanese War, the reinforcement rate was set at 5 per cent. Three months into the war, however, and in light of heavy casualties in Europe, these rates were revised to 15 per cent for infantry and 10 per cent for mounted rifles. This committed the country to dispatching almost 3000 troops every two months.[181]

Further changes came from the decision that the two-month training period would be extended to four, beginning with the Fourth Reinforcements, and because so many trained instructors had departed with the Main Body and the remaining expertise needed to be more efficiently used, training was centralised at a national camp. This was established at Trentham Racecourse, just outside Wellington. The capital therefore became the main supply and recreational centre for enlisted men as well as their port of departure, the place where the troop transports were serviced and the place where relatives and friends gathered to farewell soldiers.[182]

By May 1915, nearly 17,000 New Zealanders had departed. Among them were the first men of the Native Contingent and the first women of the NZANS. On 14 February 1915, 518 Māori left Wellington on the SS *Warrimoo*, bound for Egypt. As with other farewells, commentators, both Māori and non-Māori, described them as the flower of their generation and tasked them with living up to past glories.[183] These themes were linked with statements of the Māori duty to the empire. Tureiti Te Heuheu Tukino, paramount chief of Ngāti Tūwharetoa, and Kingi

above A Wellington crowd gathered to farewell departing soldiers moving past lower Cuba Street. ALEXANDER TURNBULL LIBRARY, 1/2-008482-G

below Members of the New Zealand Army Nursing Service outside Parliament before their departure on 10 July 1915. ALEXANDER TURNBULL LIBRARY, 1/1-008879-G

Topia representing the Whanganui tribes, urged the men 'to be strong and of good courage, to face the foe without flinching, and to uphold the mana of the Great White King whom they had sworn to serve'.[184] 'Be truthful; be honourable,' said Hari Wahanui, a rangatira from Otorohanga. 'You carry the honour of the Maori race in your hands. Be brave, and remember the flag you have flying over your tents. With reference to your religious beliefs, don't forget that you aim for one heaven. Fear God, read and study your Bibles, and may the British reign over us for ever.'[185]

Such sentiments were mirrored by those Pākehā commentators who cherished notions of racial harmony and saw Māori as uplifted by British governance. The *Evening Post* claimed that 'time has enabled the Maori to give wonderful testimony to the British genius for colonisation and Government'.[186] Auckland's Anglican bishop described Māori volunteers as 'assembled and anxious to stand shoulder to shoulder with their European friends and fight the foes of England . . . We have every reason to marvel at such progress.'[187]

Two months later, on 8 April, another large crowd gathered on Wellington's Glasgow Wharf to farewell the first 50 nurses of the NZANS, though other nurses were already working overseas. Nearby buildings were decorated with bunting, officials presented the nurses with parting gifts and a band played popular tunes including 'The Girl I Left Behind Me', the 'whimsical incongruity' of which was reported to bring the crowd to good cheer. Shortly after noon, as the steamer *Rotorua* pulled away, the streamers thrown from the upper decks, and held by those on the wharf, snapped. 'It was an inspiring spectacle — representatives of New Zealand's womanhood going to take their share in the noblest form of service in the field to which so many of our men have already gone.'[188]

CHAPTER FOUR

THE EMERGING WAR ECONOMY

previous pages
A traction engine hauling grain in Feilding. MANAWATŪ HERITAGE, 2007N_GS25_RTL_0801

Before 1914, influential intellectuals had argued that a war between the major powers would be economically irrational, if not impossible, and ultimately ruinous. Such assessments loomed as global trade and finances were rocked by disruptions in the early months of the war. With reference to leading figures in this school of thought, a *Grey River Argus* editorial remarked that war had come 'in spite of M. de Bloch and Norman Angell'. It noted, however, that a rapid collapse of efforts to maintain the war might provide 'a practical demonstration of the correctness of their theories'.[1] Particular nervousness focused on disruptions to trade with Britain. There had been warnings, too, that war would destabilise international money markets and send interest rates soaring, potentially serious given New Zealand's reliance on borrowing.

In this climate, the outbreak of war prompted a major economic downturn. As the *Evening Post* noted, 'Some merchants cabled at once cancelling orders given to firms in the United Kingdom, on the Continent, in the United States and Canada, and in Australia. Building and other large contracts on the point of signature were cancelled; orders to local tradesmen and manufacturers (except for foodstuffs, coal, and other prime necessities) were countermanded; salaries and wages — not fixed by awards — were reduced and staff were put off.'[2] There had already been some disruption following a sharp fall in the value of gold-mining shares after news of Austria's declaration of war on Serbia arrived on 28 July.[3] Trading in other stocks on New Zealand exchanges appears to have come to a virtual standstill as investors held back.

There was a similar dynamic in the land market. As one Manawatū newspaper commented, 'A foolish effect of the war scare is already being felt in the Wairarapa. Negotiations for the purchase of one or two large estates in the district which had been practically completed having been abruptly abandoned.'[4] A farmer in back-country Manawatū, hoping to sell and move to a property in Hawke's Bay, told a real estate agent, 'we had an offer from a buyer, and everything was just about settled when this war was declared, now unless we can purchase ourselves we will, I think, be in a very awkward position'.[5] The prohibition on the use of code in telegrams caused other difficulties. An Upper Hutt sawmilling firm, May Morn, had to lay off 100 workers because banks would not accept uncoded instructions from the British owner to pay wages.[6]

Others took a positive approach. On 1 August a *Press* editorial informed readers that, thanks to the 'prudent finance' of finance minister James Allen, the government would not need 'to go to the London market for some months, by which time, it is to be hoped, the present trouble will be over-past'.[7] Three days later, the chairman of the Bank of New Zealand, Harold Beauchamp, moved to calm business sector anxiety about the flow of credit, particularly in light of the news that the bank rate in Britain had been raised to 10 per cent, the highest since 1866. There was, Beauchamp declared, 'no fear of the banks calling up their overdrafts or any such foolish proceedings. Such an act would be sheer madness and would precipitate a financial crisis.'

Allen was similarly soothing: 'If war continues for any length of time, more especially if Great Britain becomes involved, the price of money will inevitably rise; but the conditions on the Continent are such that a long campaign is improbable. It is expected that the Continental nations will be forced owing to the lack of food supplies and money to speedily come to terms.'[8] There were, however, calls for caution in spending and Massey advised people to 'husband their resources'.[9] The mayor of Wellington announced that the unsettled state of the money markets would mean holding back 'any important financial negotiations for the present on a very big loan for public works in the city'. Like others, he did not seem to envisage a long delay.[10]

The British entry into the war had other effects on business and financial arrangements. Initially there were fears that anxious savers would withdraw their money en masse and that the resulting bank closures would severely disturb business. During the first week of the war, the postmaster-general, responsible for the Post Office Savings Bank, referred to 'a mild run on savings-banks in some centres', which had led to a temporary limit on withdrawals without seven days' notice to £2 per week.[11] The newly minted Banking Act appears to have headed off any serious run on the gold reserves of the commercial banks by providing a state guarantee for their bank notes. Nevertheless, the banks protected their gold reserves by paying out only in notes.[12]

Some people certainly chose to hold on to their gold sovereigns and to spend their paper pounds, which were officially of the same value. A week after the British declaration of war, Harrold Ennor noted in his diary, 'My gold takings to-day dropped to £7 while my notes went up to over £300.'[13] The virtual disappearance of gold coins from everyday New Zealand commerce was a lasting legacy of the war: in 1920 a Christchurch newspaper correspondent declared, 'Today, not one person in 100 has a gold sovereign in his pocket.'[14] A more short-term effect, noted in 1915, was that bank notes became significantly grubbier, mainly because local banks could not get new notes printed in London.[15]

The banks appear to have tried to maintain commercial activity by not calling in loans, despite some falling off in deposits. But advances still had to be secured against something tangible in a season when 'New Zealand had nothing ready to send away that the rest of the world wanted. That being so, the producers or shippers, as the case might be, had nothing upon which they could go to the banks and ask advances upon.'[16] Nevertheless, between the end of June and the end of September 1914 advances had increased by £500,000 despite a similar fall in deposits, meaning that the banks had expanded the money supply by roughly £1 million.[17]

The government took early legislative action to prevent a widespread foreclosure of mortgages that might harm farmers in particular. This required the Supreme Court to approve forclosures, and permission would not be granted if the mortgagor was still paying interest. When introducing a later amendment that allowed parties to opt out of the legislation, the government admitted that 'the effect of the measure [had been] to tie up money to a certain extent'.[18]

Declining business confidence also resulted in considerable unemployment. A fortnight after Britain entered the war, over 400 men had registered as unemployed with trade unions in Auckland. A little later it was reported that, in Port Chalmers, '[t]he depression is more marked than during the recent maritime strike and the ironworkers are now affected': the remarkable claim was made that '75 per cent of the people are out of employment' there. In mid-September trade union official and politician Ted Howard said that there were 1000 out of work in Christchurch.[19] As late as November the Labour Department was reporting that in Auckland '[t]here is still a large number of unemployed — an average of two hundred men calling at the office each week'. In Christchurch many 'pick-and-shovel men' remained out of work, while lack of investment in Invercargill meant that 'a considerable number of men [were] out of work, mostly labourers'.[20]

Several export industries were also affected. Kauri-gum digging, which employed over 3000 individuals and supported much of the economy north of Auckland, was especially hard hit. On 7 August Vernon Reed, Reform MP for the Bay of Islands, declared that '[t]he market for gum is in Europe, and is gone, and there is no question of export'. He called for the government to temporarily take in gum, advancing the owners half its value, until the crisis passed, and such a system was adopted two months later.[21]

At the other end of the country, the export of frozen rabbit carcasses to Britain was held up, with 100,000 crates detained in stores in Otago and Southland.[22] Timber milling, an important industry in several parts of the country, suffered from the loss of all export orders. This, combined with a halt to much local building, led some King Country sawmills along the Main Trunk Railway to close within a few days of the outbreak of war.[23] One miller thought everyone would suspend operations if the war lasted more than a month. Early in November some mills claimed that they had to cut weekly working hours from 47 to 32, because of slack demand.[24]

Flax milling, particularly important in the Horowhenua and Manawatū districts — the flax was used to make rope — was also hit hard by lack of demand in London and increased freight charges.[25] In late August 1914, the Social Democratic MP for Ōtaki, John Robertson, led a deputation to Massey on behalf of the flax workers and claimed that the 600 men normally employed at this time of the year were not in work and that another 600 would soon be in the same predicament.[26] In early November J. Liggins, 'a well-known flaxmill owner', reported that Tokomaru, usually 'a thriving little township, is now like a deserted village since the flaxmills were closed'. The following month Alfred and Louis Seifert's mill at Miranui, near Makerua, which employed 170–180 men, had temporarily ceased operations.[27] It was well into 1915 before overseas demand picked up and flax mills went back to full production.[28]

New Zealand's great pastoral exports, wool, meat and dairy produce, did not suffer any great disruption and provided some much-desired stability. Most of the production from the 1913–14 season had been sold and dispatched to overseas markets. The new season would not normally start until the middle of September, when the first butter would be shipped, followed by wool and meat exports, which usually began in November and peaked in summer. Strangely, apprehension in the sector was not about enemy action as some had feared — that worry faded as the Royal Navy began sweeping German naval units from the world's oceans — but rather about the military demand for ships.[29] Eight of the refrigerated vessels that normally operated in the 'home' trade from New Zealand were converted into troop transports to carry the NZEF, and three others were among the 20 ships conveying the Australian Imperial Force.[30]

Possibly lulled by the assumption that the war would be over quickly, Massey dismissed concerns that removing these ships would create serious problems in the coming season. In late September he was confident that there would be sufficient vessels, though he mentioned having to pay the owners of the troopships to bring them back wholly or partly without cargo. Ward pointed out that it appeared meat exports would be larger than in previous seasons and that the completion of eight new ships had been delayed by the war. He recommended that non-refrigerated vessels should be fitted out as transports so that some of the refrigerated ships could return to their usual role, a suggestion Massey dismissed.[31]

The prime minister again claimed that there was no problem when he opened his election campaign in November, despite the fact that the postponed departure of the Main Body had delayed the return of the transports by three weeks.[32] Massey's assurances looked increasingly questionable as the season opened. A torrent of telegrams flowed between Wellington and London as Massey desperately sought to avert a crisis that would damage both the New Zealand economy and his own credibility, particularly with farmers. The war was clearly expanding expectations of government; in peacetime it had generally been accepted that shipping arrangements were settled by the industries involved.

By the new year these problems were beginning to take hold. In February some of the Christchurch freezing works were either closed or working short time because of lack of shipping, while the secretary of the Timaru Grain and Wool Store Workers' Union had a narrow escape: 'The storage capacity at the freezing-works was about exhausted when some "meat" steamers arrived in port and relieved the congestion, thus enabling the works to continue their activity.'[33] The following month lack of shipping meant curtailed work in Auckland freezing works; those around Palmerston North were forced to close, one with over 50,000 carcasses in its chambers; in Masterton only 250 men were employed, rather than 300; and in Nelson the works closed for two weeks. In May the industry in Napier was only working three-quarter time for the same reason.[34]

The cost of living also rose rapidly during these early months of the war. The run on groceries in the last days of peace quickly subsided: on 7 August a Christchurch grocer, noting the fall in business, believed 'everyone must have got pretty well stocked up with necessaries now, and judging by the orders some people have given they must be victualling themselves for about six months!'[35] If he was correct, those with stockpiles would be in a good position as prices ballooned over the following months. By the end of 1914 the average cost of foodstuffs purchased by a typical household in the four main centres had increased 9.41 per cent. By the end of April 1915 this had risen to 13.33 per cent and 16.5 per cent by August 1915, only a little less than the rise over the previous 20 years.[36]

These price rises included goods central to many diets. In the four main centres the average price of a 2-pound loaf started to increase a few weeks after the outbreak of war and accelerated over the summer, plateauing from March 1915 at about a quarter higher than the August 1914 level. The retail price of flour rose earlier, and by much more, levelling off at around two-thirds higher. The prices of other staples also increased. The price of eggs, generally produced by wheat-fed hens, rose at a similar rate to flour, as did oatmeal, grown entirely in New Zealand, frequently exported, mainly to Australia, and widely consumed as porridge. Oat prices firmed early in the war and rose by a third by the end of April 1915. Besides a decrease in supply owing to dry weather, this also reflected some 'anticipation of the demand caused by the troopships requiring good quantities' for the horses they carried to war.[37]

Potatoes, also locally grown, were up by just over a quarter by April 1915.[38] The price of sugar, another substantial item in New Zealanders' diet, rose by about a quarter by the end of 1914. Apart from a limited amount imported mainly from the Dutch East Indies, sugar was supplied entirely by the Auckland refinery of the Australian-based Colonial Sugar Refining Company, which lifted the bulk price of refined sugar three times in the first few months of the war, citing the increased cost of its raw material. This no doubt piqued pre-war suspicions that the company was exploiting its near-monopoly position, as did the announcement of a strong profit for the previous year and the discovery that it was illegally paying commission to wholesalers.

Dairy prices stayed relatively stable as spring brought the usual flush of production but then rose sharply and were 16.14 per cent up by April.[39] Strong British demand for butter maintained the price during the spring, but then drought across the Tasman pushed prices up dramatically in early 1915 as Australian merchants bought New Zealand stocks normally held to supply the local market during the following winter.[40] At the end of April the price of butter was around 17 per cent higher than at the start of the war. As the manager of an Auckland grocery asked, 'How can poor people be expected to pay 1/6 per lb for butter? . . . Families who were getting four and five pounds per week are now ordering three and four pounds. They say they must do so in order to live within their incomes.'[41] It was said that 'many of the poorer people are buying roast beef dripping from the restaurants at sixpence per pound. It is only at a time like this, when prices are so high, that people in such a prosperous country as New Zealand turn to dripping.'[42]

If some New Zealanders refused to accept that the price of an imported commodity like sugar must rise, many more rejected the idea that the price of a locally produced commodity should lift with overseas prices. As the *Sun* observed, '[i]t is strange that the country which produces the article should have to pay as much for it as the country which imports it, solely because the butter factories realise an opportunity for enhancing profits'.[43] More sharply, the *Maoriland Worker*

above Horse-drawn carts, likely in Northland, transporting milk cans. ALEXANDER TURNBULL LIBRARY, 1/1-006307-G

below The interior of the main office of the Department of Imperial Government Supplies in Lambton Chambers, Wellington. WILL LAWSON, FOOD-SHIPS FOR BRITAIN, P.26. ALEXANDER TURNBULL LIBRARY, PAM 1918 LAW 4034 declared, 'Because the people of England are being plundered by the treacherous exploiters there, the exploiters here must be allowed to also plunder the people of New Zealand.'[44]

After a brief dip in livestock prices, likely caused by sellers demanding cash in the uncertain early period of the war, the operations of export meat traders and an awareness of high prices being paid in Britain began to drive up local meat prices.[45] In late September it was reported that '[t]here is a scarcity of fat cattle in the Hastings district and butchers are at their wits' end to know where to procure supplies. Prices are exceptionally high, and the majority of the stock finds its way to the freezing works [i.e. to the export market].'[46] Meanwhile Dunedin's Burnside market witnessed its highest beef prices ever.[47] At the end of October it was reported from Balclutha that a milch cow (one kept for milk) worth £6 or £7 had sold at more than £13 as a 'fat' (for its meat).[48] This was seen as 'proof positive of the boom in cattle caused by the war and the prospects of an unlimited demand for the "Tommies" both British and French'.

Retail butchers, who had to deal directly with angry customers, appear to have endeavoured to hold prices down and, like bakers, approached government ministers for help. At the end of November 1914 the average cost of meat in the four main centres was 7.56 per cent higher, though this increase had halved by the end of April 1915.[49]

Prices of other household goods that were entirely or largely imported continued to rise, as they had just before the war. In some cases, potential disruption and loss of shipping threatened shortages. For example, the supply of Mediterranean sultanas and raisins was suddenly restricted, while imports of cream of tartar, produced largely in France or Germany and generally carried in German ships, was for a time no longer available.[50] Many wholesalers, however, almost immediately raised prices on existing supplies. Three weeks after the declaration of war a retail chemist in Whanganui protested that wholesalers in Wellington had doubled the price of codeine and morphine preparations, put quinine up 50–75 per cent and the disinfectant Lysol 25 per cent, and raised the price of all other imports by at least 10 per cent.[51]

The British government's embargo on exports of medical supplies was given as the reason, but the increases were clearly on current stock. In April 1915, responding to accusations of exploitation, well-known Auckland merchant A. J. Entrican stated that he and his colleagues had met daily for a week after the declaration of war and had never suggested raising prices more than 5 per cent. He argued that '[m]erchants had to replenish their stocks, and the value of goods already held was not what they had cost, but the amount for which they could be replaced'.[52] This point was not likely to be readily accepted by consumers.

The spike in the cost of living in the first year of the war had a major impact on many working people. Although some relief came from the relative stability of housing rentals, Labour Department officials repeatedly noted a decrease in spending on 'luxuries' during 1915.[53] Many Dunedinites were 'going in for repairs in lieu of buying boots' and a report from Gisborne observed that 'the smaller retailer, who is depending more particularly on the wage-earner for support, complains of slackness of trade'.[54] And as male customers enlisted, shopping patterns changed. 'With the departure of the Expeditionary Force,' said one Dunedin manager in December 1914, 'there vanished many of our most constant visitors and our freest spenders':

> Our best customers . . . are the young men from 20 to 35 years of age. From 20 to 30 the average man is very particular about his attire. He must have the most modish of shirts and socks, of natty ties, of felt hats, and of 'bubbly-toed' boots and shoes. After 30 he gets married, as a rule . . . They don't come to us so often after they take the plunge, and we notice that they tend to become less particular about 'modishness' and pay more attention to quality and price.[55]

Besides rising living costs, award wages were effectively frozen early in the war because the Arbitration Court, clearly anticipating a short war, had decided to hear no new disputes during the conflict, on the grounds that it might cause severe disruption.[56] The court did, though, continue to hear cases about the enforcement and interpretation of awards, and applications by workers to come under them, plus compensation for workplace injuries. Conciliation councils continued to forward agreements to the Arbitration Court to be registered as awards, but only if both employers and employees agreed.

It soon became evident that employers were not inclined to accept proposals that involved any increase of wages or improvement of conditions, despite clear evidence of a large increase in the cost of living and, by the new year, of considerable prosperity in some quarters, especially in farming. Consequently, a growing number of disputes were referred for the eventual consideration of the Arbitration Court. The resulting discontent increased with the news, in January 1915, that the New South Wales Arbitration Court was to resume hearing claims for wage increases. By the beginning of March there was also news of strikes in the engineering industry on Scotland's Clydeside.[57]

John McCullough, the union representative on the Arbitration Court, urged the reopening of the arbitration system. He noted the New South Wales situation and pointed out that '[f]irms and companies were manifestly benefiting from the war and yet the cost of living to the worker considerably increased'.[58] After hearing representations from both employers and workers, it was announced on 26 March that the court would again consider applications for new awards. Even conservative newspapers agreed that no less could be done. The court resumed operations in April 1915.

Paradoxically, war conditions also stimulated economic activity. The government's commitment to raising and equipping the expeditionary force was a major economic accelerant. In 1915 a New Zealand soldier's equipment consisted of two sets of tunics and trousers; a pair of puttees; a greatcoat; a hat and a puggaree (a scarf to protect the wearer's neck from the sun); a cap; a pair of braces; two pairs of boots; a pair of shoes; two pairs of underwear; two shirts; two undershirts; a denim suit; three pairs of socks; a kit-bag; a holdall; three blankets; two towels; a cholera belt (a band, often made of flannel, worn under the uniform supposedly to ward off the disease); a sea-kit; a jersey; a 'housewife' (a small sewing kit); a knife; a fork; a spoon; a plate; a mug; a mess tin; a water bottle; a waterproof sheet; a rifle; a bayonet; webbing; an entrenching tool (for digging); a pull-through (a cloth for cleaning gun

BUSINESS AS USUAL—THE ARBITRATION COURT RE-OPENS.

The Arbitration Court, which was suspended on account of the war, has been opened again A long list o disputes has been filed. —*News item.*

The Employer: What with these demands and the War Tax I can see I am in for lively times.

The resumption of Arbitration Court hearings in April 1915 was a tacit acknowledgement that the initial perceptions of both wartime solidarity and a short war were shifting. NEW ZEALAND FREE LANCE, 31 MARCH 1915, P. 3

barrels); an oil-bottle; a protector; and an identity disc. Together this kit cost £17 15s 7d per soldier and tens of thousands of orders were being placed.[59] The result was a huge demand for suppliers and some manufacturers saw an opportunity to broadcast the quality of local goods. 'It may be,' said the president of the Wellington Provincial Industrial Association, 'that the war will teach a lesson even better than that taught by the holding of an exhibition.'[60]

As early as 4 August 1914 the Christchurch firm of O'Brien & Co., already a contractor to the government, received an order for 5000 pairs of their 'regimental boots' and were asked to arrange to supply the same number again.[61] At the end of August clothing factories in Wellington were said to be working 13-hour days making uniforms.[62] In early 1915 a uniform shortage meant that territorials had to attend training camps in civilian clothes, despite seven firms having contracts to supply uniforms.[63] One man involved in the industry maintained that '[a]lmost every manufacturer in the Dominion was busily engaged in making uniforms' and the main limitation on output was a shortage of skilled labour.[64] Supplying army boots was another major endeavour. By the end of August 1914 10,000 pairs had been ordered from five large firms: the Northern Boot and Shoe Company (Auckland), R. Hannah & Co. (Wellington), M. O'Brien & Co. and Skelton & Frostick (Christchurch) and Sargood, Son & Ewen (Dunedin).[65] All were working under high pressure. Some patriotic funds also appear to have purchased boots for their local contingents.

The training camps also had an impact. Nearby shopkeepers, publicans and landlords experienced good times, although their customers were doubtless less happy about the accompanying price increases and their counterparts in other parts of the country probably experienced downturns. In the spring of 1915, the capital was the only main centre in which rents rose, perhaps because of 'the military activity of the Dominion being centred in the vicinity of Wellington; while Palmerston North, the only other large town to rise, has also benefited from this cause'.[66]

Selling goods directly to the soldiers in camp could certainly be profitable. In February 1915, Trooper Arthur Lush at Trentham noted that the *Auckland Weekly News* was 'one of the papers regularly sold in camp by an enterprising old man who must be making 25/- per day profit on dailies alone'.[67] Gifts for departing troops formed another market, with wristwatches, cameras, shaving sets and diaries proving particularly popular items. Within days of the declaration, merchants nationwide were promoting such items. By 11 August, for example, Wairarapa-based H. Beale & Co. was suggesting that '[a]n appropriate gift for our boys who are leaving these shores to uphold the honour of the Empire would be an auto-strop safety razor'.[68]

Others soon benefited from the exclusion of imported goods made in Germany or by firms identified as German-owned. Early in November 1914, the *Wanganui Herald* reported on what it termed the 'so-called "British" Mannesmann Tube Company', which was almost entirely owned in Germany. This firm had been 'the stumbling block to the progress of the locally-owned Spiral Steel Pipe Company . . . [its] strongest competition . . . for several years past'. Just before the war, in fact, 'the directors of the local concern had . . . practically decided to "throw up the sponge," as it was impossible to compete under existing circumstances with the foreign firm'.

Now, though, Spiral Steel would surely have 'a new lease of life, and . . . the public bodies of New Zealand will recognise that it is to their interests to support local industry, especially when the product of that industry is of equal quality to the foreign article and is as cheap as the imported manufacture'. By September 1918 the paper could report that, despite a 'slack period' in the first year of the war, the company had supplied 'ten Government Departments and military camps, 15 freezing companies, and 55 local bodies with pipes'.[69]

Soaring export prices flowed through into the rural sector. Meat producers and processors were the first to experience a massive boost, and from the outset it was clear that beef would be particularly in demand as the meat favoured by British and French armies. Companies that already had meat in transit to British, Allied or neutral markets at the beginning of August 1914 benefited from the jump in prices that came when war was declared. At the end of that month, a freezing company on the North Island west coast was anticipating 'a profit on one shipment only of £10,000 in excess of the original profit that was anticipated before the war broke out'.[70] As Massey, who had extensive contacts in the primary industries, explained, 'a number of the large meat firms received orders through their agents in London for large quantities of beef at almost any price. Stock had been purchased accordingly, in some cases at extreme rates.'[71]

In January 1915 the Auckland representative of Vestey Brothers, a major British meat company, revealed that a local subsidiary had offered to buy beef at 10 per cent over the prevailing price in order to fill a contract for 600 tons a month to be shipped directly to French ports for Allied forces.[72] The following month, in Whangārei, it was reported that 'old bulls, that under ordinary circumstances are worth the value of their hide, have increased in value, up to as much as £10, and the country has been scoured for them'.[73] By April 1915 London prices for New Zealand beef were 51 per cent higher than a year earlier. Sheepmeat prices had also risen strongly: both lamb and mutton were over 31 per cent higher than in April 1914.[74]

As the new wool-selling season opened in November 1914, it rapidly became evident that prices would be dramatically higher and that the needs of the military would shape demand. One wool buyer warned of an impending fall, especially in crossbred wool, though he wisely added that he and his ilk were 'the worst prophets in the world concerning the wool market, and I may be wrong'.[75] He was seriously wrong. Subsequent wool sales generally confirmed the upward trend; crossbred wools, the stronger and coarser fibres that made up most of New Zealand's clip, were greatly in demand in Britain for making uniforms.[76] At the November Wellington sales, crossbred wool was up around 14 per cent on the comparable sale in 1913 and in February it was up about a quarter more.[77] By then even crossbred wool classed as 'inferior' was drawing prices as high as, or higher than, merino. The following winter an 'expert' declared that '[t]he prices received during the past season for crossbred were easily a record, and the pastoralists simply coined money'.[78]

The pattern was the same for dairy products. Between the beginning of 1914 and the beginning of 1915, prices for New Zealand butter in London increased by around 20 per cent. In April 1915, with a shortage across the Tasman, 10,000 boxes of butter were sold to the Australian government at prices higher than bulk sales in New Zealand. The rise in the price of cheese, like beef in demand by Allied armies, was more considerable, at 32 per cent to January and 49 per cent to April.[79]

The introduction of a commandeer system added much-needed stability. As British demands for various goods and materials surged, formal arrangements were made with several countries to purchase the entire national output of particular commodities, at fixed prices, beyond the requirements of their domestic markets.[80] New Zealand was relatively late in coming to such an arrangement; the Queensland government began exercising powers over meat exporting on 3 February and New South Wales passed comparable legislation on the night of 11 February, apparently immediately after the request was received from London.[81]

It was not until six days later that Massey confirmed that his government had received a request to commandeer New Zealand meat and he stated that 'the matter requires the most careful consideration, and a decision will not be arrived at for some little time'.[82] A conference was arranged with representatives from the shipping and freezing industries and the Board of Agriculture to determine how the system might operate, and the government sought assurances that the country's lamb trade would be included.[83] On 3 March it was announced that all frozen meat for export was to be purchased by the New Zealand government at a fixed, above market, price, which would be reimbursed by London. Other major goods came under the commandeer as the war progressed: cheese from November 1915, wool from November 1916 and butter from November 1917. Considerable quantities of scheelite (tungsten ore), Glaxo (a milk powder product), canned rabbits, hides and skins were also bought.[84]

This requisitioning has been mistakenly characterised as the cause of higher wartime prices for exporters.[85] It was the war itself that brought high prices; the commandeer was partly a means by which those prices were kept down while ensuring that producers would have a secure market. As the chairman of the Wellington Meat Export Company remarked, the arrangement was 'for war supply purposes, and with the object of preventing undue inflation of Home market values. The prices arranged here were on times market parity, and assured to growers a continuance of the then good prices'. Similarly, a Southland newspaper recognised that '[p]rices will not rise as high as they might do if free competition were allowed, but that must be borne in the interests of the Empire by those who have stock for sale'.[86] The commandeer also placed a ceiling on the local price of beef and sheepmeat, though it is unclear whether this influenced the government's agreement to introduce it. To some extent the commandeer provided the dominions with the system of 'imperial preference' they had been seeking for years.[87]

On the same day frozen meat was requisitioned, the Imperial Government Meat Supply Branch, later renamed the Department of Imperial Government Supplies, began managing the commandeer. Operations began on a small scale under Assistant Public Service Commissioner Robert Triggs, with just five staff squeezed into a small room in Wellington's General Post Office Building. However, by 1918 the department had 59 staff located in Lambton Chambers on Lambton Quay and was coordinating with 85 wool and skin brokers, 40 freezing works, 33 wool-scouring works, 23 fellmongeries and a number of other industries.[88]

Recovery from the disruption caused by the outbreak of war occurred as production generated substantial economic activity and as enlistment began to contract labour supply; by mid-1915 demand for workers exceeded supply in most sectors.[89] The onset of this recovery, however, varied across the country. It seems to have occurred relatively early and strongly in Wellington, and in November 1914 the Labour Department reported '[g]eneral satisfaction . . . with the condition of trade and labour prevailing. The worker, especially the skilled tradesman, feels more secure in the tenure of his employment than he has since the outbreak of the war.' Conditions in Palmerston North a month later were less positive: 'Business generally has been quieter than usual for the season of the year, on account of the feeling of uncertainty as to how long the European War is going to last, and many skilled artisans are working only half-time, and consequently are husbanding their resources.'

In January 1915 there were more swagmen about in Pātea than 'for a long time past', and in Greymouth several sawmills were 'having extended holidays, due to the marked decrease in the demand for timber'. Even in April a number of contracts for private dwellings in Christchurch had 'been countermanded, and there is an inclination to hang on to money rather than invest in house property'.[90] It was not until then that numbers of men assisted by the department to find work were lower than in the same month in 1914.

Unemployment was mainly combatted by the long-established practice of central and local government public works. These, Massey declared, would be continued and probably increased as '[t]he Government realized that it was their duty to prevent hardship in every way'.[91] This solution absorbed and effectively obscured the continuing level of unemployment; such men were not regarded as out of work. In November 1914 the Labour Department sent 629 men to public works, and 335 to private work.[92] As late as March 1915 Allen made it clear that 'even if they had to go to the London market and pay high rates, it was essential from the Government point of view to keep the works going, in order not only to develop the country, but [also] to prevent any possibility of unemployment'.[93]

Most public works were far from the towns, where most of the unemployed lived, and so there was also agitation for local bodies to provide work. In August, local bodies in the Northern Wairoa district were 'pushing forward arrangements to proceed with loan expenditure in order that there may be as little unemployment as possible': street improvements, a water supply scheme; and road, bridge and drainage work. In September the Christchurch City Council had 17 men on what were effectively unemployment relief works. The New Plymouth Borough Council 'put an amount of work in hand so as to keep as many men as possible employed during the time trade was dislocated'.[94]

Tensions emerged as some sectors started to boom while others stagnated. As early as three months after the declaration of war, deposits at the Post Office Savings Bank had started to exceed withdrawals by a wide margin. Investigating where this money was coming from, Allen noted that 'to a very large extent it was coming from the small farmer'.[95] Many resented this bounty, and a perception grew that farmers were exploiting the public. It was widely assumed that because some were profiting from shortages, they were also causing them and therefore punishment was required. Opposition politicians and trade unionists called for the government to seize wheat from those holding it, arguing that inaction was effectively collusion with exploiters.[96] In a March 1915 letter accompanying his extremely large donation of £1000 ($150,000 in contemporary values) to the Belgian Relief Appeal, wealthy Manawatū farmer P. A. McHardy wrote:

> Since the outbreak of hostilities produce of nearly all descriptions has greatly risen in value: such a rise is to a great extent due to the war, the vast armies needing same for consumption and clothing . . . As a producer and one who is deriving increased revenue from the efforts of those who are dying fighting, enduring hardships, and torture, having their country laid waste and their homes destroyed, it is my duty to return something to those who are so nobly defending our existence . . . The increased price of produce, is in my opinion, conscience money or ill-gotten gains, gains derived from the British and their allies on land and their fleets at sea.[97]

Some of the developing tensions were evident in April 1915 when a Foodstuffs Commission, appointed to inquire into the prices for food and drink and to advise on whether maximum prices should be set, told Massey that it had uncovered no evidence of exploitation and that the increased prices of both imported goods and exported commodities were due to higher prices overseas.[98] Nothing could be done about the price of imports, while export prices could be reduced locally only if quantities were reserved for the local market at a lower price than could be obtained overseas, which the commission considered impracticable. Such conclusions were never going to be accepted by many New Zealanders, who regarded price rises as the result of 'rigging'. Even those who might have accepted the broad thrust of the findings were disappointed by the commission's work. They had envisaged it acting rather like the Arbitration Court, using judicial authority and Labour Department staff to investigate individual cases and making examples of perceived exploiters through prosecutions under the Regulation of Trade and Commerce Act. As one editorial put it,

> The man in the street who pays higher prices than seem reasonable for foodstuffs and other necessaries can only conjecture as to the cause . . . He may suspect that the baker, who is selling bread based on a flour cost of £17 per ton, has really obtained supplies at £15, and he may wonder why some anticipated shortage of butter a few months hence should send the price soaring immediately. The average consumer is utterly unable to prove exploitation, but a Royal Commission, with full power to call for person and papers, is in a superior position.[99]

Andrew Fairbairn, a Christchurch merchant who had served on the 1912 Cost of Living Commission, declared that he had provided detailed evidence that his competitors had exploited the public by raising their prices on goods imported before the war by 10–90 per cent. That the commission could not produce the transcript of his evidence was taken as further evidence of its incompetence. The *Star*, accusing the commission of working in 'devious subterranean ways', decided that '[t]he whole question of the forcing up of food prices

An Illustrated Journal of Information and Racy Comment upon the Topics of the Hour.

Vol. XVII. –No. 908. FRIDAY, DECEMBER 7, 1917. Threepence.

The new order of the Defence Department requiring all privates to wear the regulation uniform two sizes too large is causing widespread dissatisfaction. –*Newspaper item.*

"WHEN I FIRST PUT THE UNIFORM ON."

The Girl in Blighty—Who is your tailor, Tommy, in New Zealand! Does he expect you to grow into your uniform!

above Boot manufacturing at Staples & Coy in Wellington. ALEXANDER TURNBULL LIBRARY, PA1-O-367-030

left Issues around the quality of military supplies is the focus of this cartoon as 'the girl in Blighty' asks a New Zealand soldier whether he is expected to grow into his uniform. The presence of a smartly outfitted Australian, enjoying female attention, adds to his humiliation. NEW ZEALAND FREE LANCE, 7 DECEMBER 1917, P. 3

PHANTOM WHEAT.

Prime Bill: There is absolutely no wheat in the country. My friend over there and my Food Commission say so.

The suspicion that price increases and shortages of goods were caused by exploiters persisted throughout the war. This *Observer* cartoon depicts the capitalist caricature 'Mr Fat' concealing wheat from the public and a seemingly credulous Massey.
NEW ZEALAND OBSERVER, 30 JANUARY 1915, P. 1

demands ventilation even if it does involve the fall of a Ministry in war time. The country at the present time is over-stocked with pseudo-patriots who try to stifle honest criticism by yelling "Rule Britannia", but the public are slowly learning to distinguish the real gold from the spurious article.'[100]

Fairbairn's points, given additional weight by the fact that he was himself a merchant, were widely publicised and accepted. His credibility was enhanced when, in May 1915, he won an out-of-court settlement of £2000 from Wellington's Levin & Co. after claiming that they had set unlawful conditions when he sought to purchase from them shortly before the war.[101] His decision to distribute the balance of the money after legal fees to his affected customers lifted his standing even higher. From the point of view of his fellow merchants, the commission and the government, it was perhaps something of a relief that the developing controversy was overshadowed by the dramatic news from Gallipoli.[102]

The notion that war profiteers were enriching themselves by charging outrageous prices for shoddy military supplies then became another focus of public debate.[103] An excerpt from a New Zealand soldier's letter, printed in New Zealand newspapers in April, tended to confirm the poor quality of early uniforms. 'The uniforms [for mounted men] are made in England, and there is as much difference between our new uniforms and the New Zealand article, as between chalk and cheese. These English uniforms are made to last, and are not like the New Zealand stuff.'[104]

Godley's criticism of some boots further fuelled concerns, as did an outburst by the commander of the Auckland Mounted Rifles, Colonel Charles Mackesey. 'I saw the soles come off the men's boots on the first march. There may have been others — there undoubtedly were, that I did not see. This does not say much for New Zealand bootmakers. FELLOWS WANT FLOGGING.'[105] The *Observer*, which thought that 'the officers of the stores department should be court-martialled', also led the charge when it came to accusations that poor-quality saddles were being supplied. Clearly drawing on skilled advice, it published a catalogue of serious defects found in a number of the saddles and, although it denied that it had produced them, L. Marks & Co. agreed that such saddles were used by the army.[106] An Otago soldier in Egypt felt that 'the equipment of the New Zealand men compared very unfavourably with that of both the Australians and the English Territorials'. The Patriotic Committee member reporting this said he understood that saddles had been sent back to New Zealand as 'unsuitable for military purposes'.[107]

In fact, the Defence Department itself seems to have been largely responsible for the poor quality. The military may have been well prepared for war in some ways in 1914, but not when it came to supply arrangements. Early volunteers were expected to supply their own equipment, which was not then inspected by anyone competent to assess it. Moreover, the standards specified appear to have been extremely low, thanks to departmental ignorance about what was really required, a reluctance to call in independent civilian experts and an ethos of economising. Auckland boot manufacturers urged the government to set a higher standard, claiming existing boots could wear out in as little as a month of active service.[108]

When tenders for boots for the Māori contingent were called, some bootmakers either declined to participate, complaining that the selected pattern was so unsuitable that it would bring their trade into disrepute, or provided samples they considered more durable. By November a better pattern had been adopted.[109] A letter received in March from a New Zealand soldier in Egypt declared that the 'marvellous' new boots were 'more like Sunday boots. They are said to be the best boots ever made for the Army, and are supposed to have cost the Government 18s per pair.'[110]

The Defence Department effectively had to learn on the job as it built up knowledge of the country's production capacities and a robust tendering system. Rather than purchasing through the Public Service Tenders Board, a separate system was put in place, modelled on that in the British Army. Tenders had to be considered by a committee of three officers — so no one officer might be made the target of corrupt suppliers — and make recommendations to purchase, which were then generally accepted by the higher authorities. The committee, however, became effectively the Director of Stores, Major James O'Sullivan, and two of his subordinates. In addition, many orders were placed by getting a limited number of quotations or simply by direct purchasing, practices that were strictly forbidden but which allowed supplies to be secured quickly.

Understandably, quotations and direct purchasing were used more frequently to rapidly equip the Samoan expedition and the Main Body, but this approach remained very common; anticipating the needs of the steady flow of reinforcements and their troopships and calling for tenders in advance was rare. At the very least, this greatly reduced the chances of getting the lowest possible prices and meant orders were disproportionately placed in Wellington. At worst, it opened up considerable opportunities for favouritism and corruption. In at least one major area — the provision of uniforms — the relationship between those ordering and those supplying does appear to have been excessively close.

Wellington tailor and clothing manufacturer Abraham Levy had a good deal of contact with the military in the capital before the war because his firm made a lot of territorial officers' uniforms. In 1913 he was awarded the contract to make the uniforms for the other ranks, despite Kaiapoi Woollen Mills, which then held the contract, tendering at the same price. The usual practice would have been to award the contract to Kaiapoi, a much larger Christchurch firm that had proved entirely satisfactory.

Following the outbreak of war, Levy's firm appears to have successfully tendered to supply what was now a vast number of uniforms by offering the lowest price. Lacking the capacity to produce the necessary quantities, Levy's seems to have then subcontracted much of the work to other Wellington firms. Nevertheless, Defence Stores had to sign with further firms, including Sargood, Son & Ewen of Dunedin, to meet its requirements. Yet in February 1915 Levy's was awarded a contract to supply all uniforms for a year from 31 March, without further tenders being called.[111]

Such behaviour sparked anger from those businessmen, particularly in other centres, who felt they might have secured at least some of this work had they been allowed to tender. There were also rumblings from the public service, which was obliged to monitor the comparatively recent purchasing regulations. In late February 1915 the public service commissioner asked

Allen why the Defence Department did not appear to be following public service regulations, despite Godley having confirmed that it would.[112] Allen, who seems to have had little operational knowledge of Defence's purchasing, asked Godley's successor, Colonel Alfred Robin, why the regulations were not being adhered to. Robin maintained that Godley had wanted the Defence Department to be 'self contained' and had intended that the regulations should be followed 'as closely as the Defence requirements from time to time would admit'.[113]

After extensive inquiries, R. B. Morris of the Public Service Commission presented a damning report, which Allen forwarded to Robin, asking for immediate action 'to stop any exploitation of soldiers by Levy & Co. or anyone else if you are satisfied that the report is correct'. The colonel suggested a military court of inquiry but Attorney-General Alexander Herdman quashed the suggestion in favour of a largely civilian one.[114]

NEW ZEALAND HERALD - ONE PENNY

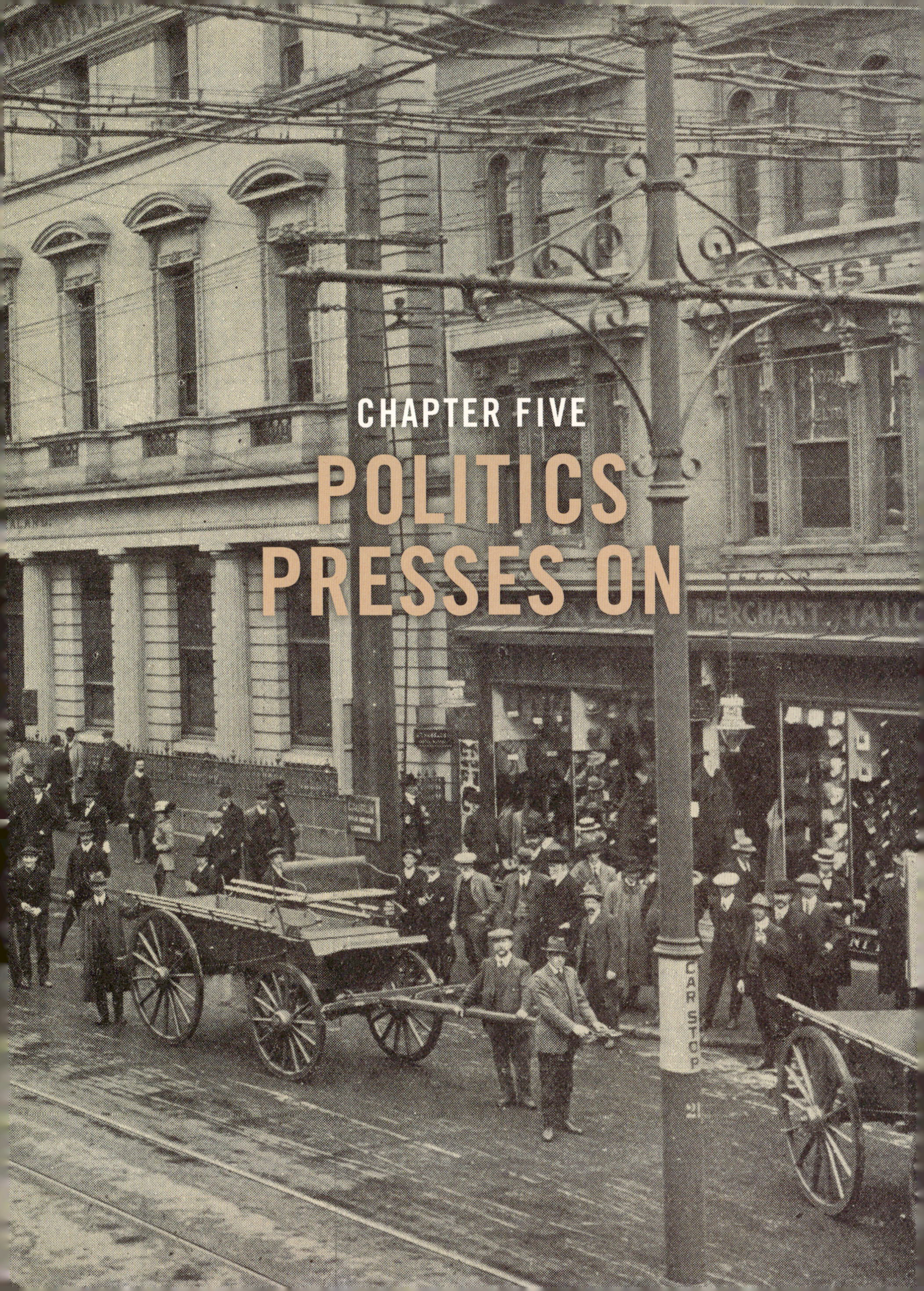

CHAPTER FIVE

POLITICS PRESSES ON

previous pages
Military wagons built by Auckland Coachbuilders for the Defence Department are paraded through Queen Street in 1914. AUCKLAND WEEKLY NEWS, 3 SEPTEMBER 1914, P. 38

From the outbreak of the war, the government was presented with an array of enormous challenges, and in response it began to acquire and exercise unprecedented powers. As with other aspects of the early war, this process was often ad hoc as authorities dealt with new and evolving realities. The legislative muscle for such activity was provided by the War Regulations Act, passed on 23 October 1914 without debate, which empowered the governor in council to make such regulations 'as he thinks necessary for the prohibition of any acts which in his opinion are injurious to the public safety, the defence of New Zealand, or the effective conduct of the military or naval operations of His Majesty during the present war'.[1] Regulations could be made without reference to Parliament, superseded conflicting legislation and were continuously added to throughout the war.

This unconstrained design has been seen as a reflection of Solicitor-General John Salmond's philosophy of 'the law as a tool of the state', which could justifiably be used in emergencies.[2] In his words, 'extrajudicial force may lawfully supersede the ordinary process and course of law, whenever it is needed for the protection of the state and the public order against illegal violence'.[3] Actions under the legislation were to be restrained by political expediency and a sunset clause, which noted, initially, that the act would operate until 1 August 1915, 'and no longer'.[4]

Despite the extraordinary circumstances, the unprecedented powers and the pledges of solidarity, the eternal nature of politics was soon confirmed. The opposition demonstrated greater enthusiasm for a truce between parties, proposing that the imminent presentation of the Budget should be postponed, to avoid plunging into the 'cauldron of hot party politics'.[5] In perhaps the most striking example of a belief that the war would be short, 'Ward's first lieutenant', George Russell, asked for a postponement of perhaps a week until the parties 'may be able to resume their normal condition. Then we will be prepared to meet the Government in party conflict.'[6] The six members of the labour group, allied with the Liberals, also emphasised their support for a patriotic party truce, despite their deep-seated animosity towards Reform. Even militant Paddy Webb declared, on 11 August, that '[s]ince the war started, we on this side of the House have fully recognized that this is no time for party contention and party wrangling'.[7]

Massey immediately rejected the idea of postponing the Budget reading and did not address the question of bringing Ward into the administration. Indeed, the government generally showed remarkably little inclination to cooperate with its opponents. The opposition elected to leave the House en masse when Allen rose to read the Budget, which contained criticisms of his predecessors' policies. Accusations that opponents had resorted to 'party' soon became a bone of contention.[8]

The most heated exchange came on 18 September, when the question, 'Is this a party speech?', directed at Francis Fisher, the minister of customs, led the latter to declare, 'Yes; I am sick of this rubbishy talk about party.'[9] 'The honourable gentleman,' responded Russell, 'is a true German so far as his tactics in warfare are concerned.' Eventually Massey lost his short temper. A Liberal member described the scene: 'Fancy the Premier, leaning over from his seat, shaking his fist, and shouting "I'm a better man than ever you were".'[10] The attorney-general also returned fire, claiming that Russell 'would rather see the Germans overrun Europe than that we should occupy the Treasury benches'.[11]

The general election, due in December 1914, was doubtless looming in many minds. Ward, afraid that a wartime election would favour the government, suggested a postponement until March, or possibly June, 1915, but was rejected.[12] As the election approached, the opposition felt increasingly obliged to criticise the government. The cost of living was a leading issue, but military matters were also raised and Liberal and Labour MPs cast themselves as the champions of the ordinary soldiers and their families. Regarding the departure of troops from Lyttelton to Wellington, a Christchurch Liberal MP asked, 'Why were the officers' friends allowed on the wharf and the wives and sweethearts of the rank and file not allowed there?' A Social Democratic MP accused officers of eating all the chocolates donated to the Awapuni Camp, while the Liberal Party's Harry Atmore alleged political influence in officer appointments: '[I]t appears to me that fitness was not considered, but in some cases family connection and in other cases the amount of wealth their parents had.'[13]

As the war proceeded, public demand to resolve the 'enemy alien problem' began to place the government in an unenviable position. Generally, officials urged restraint and resisted calls for extreme measures or arbitrary reactions. Allen consistently opposed interning all enemy aliens, even those who had been military reservists in their younger days: 'Some of them have been in the country for twenty, and thirty, and forty years, and it becomes a very ticklish matter to have to deal with them as you deal with a prisoner of war, until you know definitely that they are hostile.'[14] Massey backed him, declaring that a man should be 'known by his work' and that indiscriminate measures were unwarranted. Although noting that 'a number of Germans' would doubtless sympathise 'with their people and against us', he also observed that 'there are Germans in New Zealand who are old settlers, who are naturalised British subjects, and I have reason to believe that even in the present crisis their sympathies are with Britain'.[15]

This generally liberal attitude had some wider influence. Initially, Germans who were naturalised British citizens were not subject to any official action; though those who had been naturalised as British citizens outside New Zealand, generally in Britain or Australia, were made subject to the same restrictions as enemy subjects.[16] Similarly, there were, at first, no restrictions on military service for those born in New Zealand, regardless of German parentage. There could be less formal restrictions, however: in October 1914 Parliament was told of a man who had been defending Auckland's forts but had been transferred to another position.[17]

There had been some official actions before the declaration of war. On 3 and 4 August, Auckland police visited German residents to collect their names and to instruct them to report to their local police stations. All enemy subjects were subsequently required to register at the nearest police station and to obtain a police permit to travel 20 miles from their homes.[18] Karl Joosten, the German consul in Christchurch, who had been naturalised eight years earlier, collected the names of local German and Austrian reservists on his own initiative and supplied them to the police 'to prevent any friction that may arise between German subjects and the local authorities'. He stated firmly that 'New Zealand is my home and neither Germany nor any other State would influence me to do anything contrary to my country's interest'.[19]

After 5 August, police prevented any known or suspected German and Austrian military reservists from leaving the country and various arrests, including the members of a touring German band, were reported across New Zealand. Others were required to pay a £100 bond, supply character witnesses and report daily to the police.[20] Likewise, the four German consuls, all naturalised, had their records seized and Joosten was briefly detained by the police when his attempt to purchase waterproofed overcoats fuelled an allegation that he had tried to 'secure contracts for clothing for the German Army'.[21]

On 12 August 1914 around 90 Germans were marched from Alexandra Barracks on Buckle Street, Wellington, where they had been detained, to the wharves to be interned on Matiu Somes Island in Wellington Harbour, a former quarantine station turned internment camp.[22] Additional internment sites at Motuihe Island in the Hauraki Gulf, Rīpapa (often called Ripa) Island in Lyttelton Harbour, Auckland's Devonport Barracks and Featherston Camp in Wairarapa would later be used for the same purpose.[23] By October those interned included some German officials taken prisoner after the capture of Sāmoa.

Early reports of internment conditions were positive. A German who had been temporarily detained on Somes told a reporter that the 80 or so men 'were being well looked after':

> The food was good and there was nothing to complain about as regards the accommodation. The members of the party were all housed at the quarantine station, being divided into groups of ten, each group having a large room to itself. They were allowed the free run of the island, and some of them indulged in fishing, at least one good haul having been reported. Practically the only restriction placed upon them was that they were not allowed on the wharf when the tug-boat was there. Reading matter was available, including a supply of the daily papers.[24]

Yet the guards took security very seriously: a sentry fired twice when a fishing party approached the island too closely and a second shot passed 'through the coat and waistcoat of one of the occupants', grazing 'the skin of his abdomen'.[25] Internment also, of course, ruptured relationships. After her German reservist husband was interned, one woman, 'a colonial of English parentage', noted that she had been left destitute.[26] At the behest of the former German consul, the mayor of Wellington gave assurances that the dependants of detained Germans in the city would be eligible for assistance from his distress fund on the same basis as anyone else.[27]

In mid-August the authorities released those internees who could get a British citizen to vouch for them and who were prepared to affirm that they would abstain from words or deeds hostile to the British Empire, would not leave their home localities or attend gatherings without permission, and would report to the police as directed.[28] On the 19th, a proclamation from the governor confirmed the civil rights of 'peaceable' enemy aliens, who were considered 'within the peace and protection of His Majesty, and . . . they may sue and plead accordingly in all Courts of Justice in the Dominion in respect of all contracts, rights, injuries and other causes or matters, saving always the prerogative right of His Majesty in time of war to do with such persons, and all other of His Majesty's enemies, in all respects according to his good pleasure'.[29]

Further-reaching measures loomed, however, and were given a legal footing in November, when war regulations defined enemy aliens as including 'any person who has been naturalised in New Zealand and who would have been an enemy alien had he not been so naturalised'.[30] In December, Herdman announced that all enemy subjects, with the exception of Serbs and Croatians, were to be suspended from the public service until 'careful inquiry' satisfied the public service commissioner that they were 'absolutely loyal'.[31] The government appears to have considered this as also applying to the university colleges, which were largely state funded. This resulted in a stand-off when the board of Victoria University College declined to dismiss von Zedlitz, embarrassing Herdman, who was a member of that body. The chairman of the University College Council, Henry Ostler, replied that the government had told it soon after the outbreak of war that von Zedlitz was 'living peaceably' and therefore came within its assurance that such enemy subjects could sue for breach of contract.[32]

Before the war, Britain's Committee of Imperial Defence had undertaken detailed planning regarding censorship of information that could be exploited by enemy powers; measures were rapidly introduced in August 1914. New Zealand's Defence Department was instructed to introduce equivalent measures. Colonel Charles Gibbon, a British officer with experience as a staff captain in the Intelligence Branch in India, arrived in New Zealand in April 1914 and was appointed both chief censor and chief of the general staff.

News media were the major focus of censorship. Britain quickly set up an official Press Bureau in which military and civilian censors vetted all cables and telegrams. Cables to the United Press Agency were censored there, and because it was a way-station in a cable's journey, again in Australia before reaching New Zealand censors. Newspaper editors, concerned that local officers would become 'supercensors, or censors of censors',[33] were assured that cables passed by the British censor would not normally be subject to further censorship. However, New Zealand censors clearly used some discretion in approving cables, indicating that, from the start, they played a role beyond purely preventing the spread of information that could advantage the enemy. In late August, the censor in Auckland effectively acknowledged this: 'If, for instance, a message came through indicating a great naval or military reverse, and we doubted its authenticity, we would probably hold it pending official confirmation rather than let it go forth to create a possible financial panic.'[34]

Even *Truth*, hardly the natural ally of the military authorities or censorship, reluctantly approved of such prudence: 'The censor is a very nasty person to have about the premises, but it sometimes happens, as in the present instance, when there is a danger of panic, that the individual with the blue pencil can exercise a very sobering influence.'[35] A small Central Otago newspaper noted another concern: 'If certain events came to pass, the divulgement of which might encourage foes and dishearten friends, we could not expect the patriotic censors to pass them on to the aforesaid friends.'[36] Given Gibbon's heavy workload, a senior Post Office official, H. W. Harrington, was appointed deputy chief censor and, together with eight assistant censors, relieved Gibbon of most cable censorship work. Harrington, based in Wellington, had staff there and at the cable landing stations.

Media content was also managed by what has been called 'loyal co-operation'.[37] On 7 August 1914 the Defence Department sent a circular to the country's newspapers and periodicals emphasising the importance of not printing information concerning 'British naval movements in the Pacific, any movements of ocean steamers, any special coaling arrangements or hire of colliers, any reference to mercantile traffic routes, and also the destination of a possible expeditionary force or the time of its departure'.[38] Although editors were happy to comply, self-censorship was not universally implemented, at least not to the standard officials sought, especially when their interests differed from those of editors. As one study has pointed out,

> While the government desired enthusiastic press support, it was, with its strict censorship regime, very conscious of the risks involved when papers published stories, or printed soldiers' letters, that differed from the 'official' line. Newspapers, on the other hand, saw their primary role, in peace and in war, as providing their readers with news of importance and interest as soon as possible. This approach was inextricably coupled with the fact that newspapers were commercial businesses and the most marketable news was up-to-the-moment, unvarnished information about campaigns, battles and casualties.[39]

Dunedin newspapers seem to have been particularly inclined to sail close to the wind. On 6 August the *Otago Daily Times* printed an observer's suggestion that the NZEF 'might be sent to attack the German colonies, such as German New Guinea and German South Africa'. A few days later the *Otago Witness* declared that the force might be 'going to Europe, which the boys hope, or it may be to Samoa, which the fathers and mothers fervently hope. Or it may be to South Africa, where the boys are willing to go; and the fathers and mothers are indifferent as to their destination.'[40] The ingenious parliamentary reporter for the *Evening Star* found a way of telling its better-read readers that the preparations taking place in Wellington were for an expedition to Sāmoa, home of Robert Louis Stevenson.

> Of course, the departure of fighting men and machines always kindles the imagination, and one could hardly keep from remembering that direct opening to one of Robert Louis Stevenson's most entertaining essays: 'So I saw the island first when it was neither night nor morning. The day star sparkled like a diamond, and the wind came up from the sea with the smell of wild lime and vanilla.' It is odd how the fancy of men who go down to the sea turns on (to quote Stevenson again) brown faces and a kindly sun.[41]

A Christchurch evening newspaper was more direct. On 11 August the *Star* denounced the publication, by its rival the *Sun*, of a rumour that 600 men would leave for Sāmoa the next day.[42] The *Sun* responded sharply, complaining that self-censorship of such reports was unnecessary because they could not be sent overseas by cable without being censored officially. 'The military mind is invariably narrow, impractical, and frequently unintelligent in regard to these matters. The spectacle of uniformed gentlemen with a plenitude of brass buttons on their coats, and an absence of common sense in their heads poring over obviously commercial telegrams, trying to discover in a quotation for cheese some sinister piece of espionage, would be humorous were it not fraught with so much inconvenience to the public.'[43]

In September, the *Star*, which had been scrupulously following official requests to print nothing about the imminent departure of the Main Body, became so exasperated by ministerial announcements revealing the date that it declared 'we have instructed our staff to obtain . . . any news that may be available in regard to the doings of our local expeditionaries, and this will be duly published'.[44] This contest between press hunger for news and the authorities' wish for discretion would continue throughout the war.[45]

Censorship was also applied to the postal service. Although postal censorship had been discussed by the Committee of Imperial Defence before the war, operations began with some confusion and a request to London for specific instructions was met with the reply that there were none.[46] Attempting to meaningfully review information sent through the post was a daunting prospect. Beyond notions of the 'customary sacred privacy of mail in transit' was the sheer scale of information, with an estimated six million items posted each week.[47] However, operations and procedures, if often ad hoc, were developed and by late August authorities were organising means to intercept and analyse postal correspondence.[48]

Although this work was ultimately overseen by Gibbon, the day-to-day management fell largely to deputy chief postal censor Walter Tanner, a postal worker and son of a Liberal MP, and a team made up mostly of Post Office men, who consulted experts in handwriting and foreign languages as needed. A main postal censorship office was established in Wellington's General Post Office, but mail was also examined in Auckland, Wellington, Christchurch, Dunedin, Devonport, Motuihe Island, Matiu Somes Island, Nelson, Bluff and, after its occupation, Sāmoa.[49] The specialist equipment used to open, copy and reseal mail included electric irons, duplicating carbon paper, gummed strips and censor stamps.[50]

Although all mail was liable to censorship, the limits of what the nine postal censors could review imposed some tough constraints. Accordingly, mail addressed to hostile and neutral countries was examined on a routine basis; incoming and internal mail was checked more selectively.[51] Trans-Tasman cooperation provided some further reach, as Australian postal censors forwarded relevant excerpts from mail sent from New Zealand to Australians who were under surveillance. Selected letters were opened and searched for information of military value to the enemy, enemy propaganda and seditious literature.

In some cases, excerpts were sent on to relevant authorities and used to inform such operations as locating defaulters or suppressing banned literature. Although an official stamp notified recipients that their mail had been 'passed by the military censor NZ', some letters known to have been posted never arrived; examples survive in Archives New Zealand.[52] Ultimately, this operation opened and examined over 1.2 million letters, postcards and packages over the course of the war in what has been called 'the largest state intrusion into . . . private life in New Zealand history'.[53]

After the departure of the Main Body, New Zealand's primary wartime task was to secure, train and send away regular reinforcements to maintain, and subsequently expand, the strength of the NZEF. From the beginning, Allen emphasised the need for a sustained and sustainable effort. As a June 1915 Defence Department report noted, 'We have to prepare for war which may last for three years. It would be an everlasting disgrace to New Zealand if before the war came to an end she had to confess that she could not maintain her Expeditionary Force in the field.'[54]

This ideal of husbanding the country's strength and generating an ordered stream of reinforcements was, however, entirely at odds with the patriotic spirit of the early months of the war. Many seemed to envision a 'knock-out blow' that would end the conflict, and expressed confusion and irritation that men willing and wanting to serve were waiting in New Zealand rather than turning the tide of battle overseas.[55] Significantly, the *New Zealand Herald*, which supported Reform, was overtly disparaging of the Defence Department's approach:

> On the one hand there is the State and its recruiting system, on the other there is the great number of men able and willing to take up arms in its defence; there is evidently need of a little more co-operation between the two. The men, for their part, have shown their willingness to do their share; it is the State, with its cut-and-dried system, its absurd officialisms, and its lack of comprehension, which is chiefly at fault.[56]

Some called for an expanded commitment and there was talk of raising a second expeditionary force. Those who, incorrectly, thought New Zealand's contribution was smaller than that of other dominions, also considered that the Defence Department, and often Allen himself, was thwarting the country's desire to do its part.[57]

There was public frustration, too, about 'being in the dark' regarding enlistment.[58] Through the early months of the war the Defence Department, facing an unprecedented situation with a diminished staff, thanks to the many enlistments, struggled to communicate its recruitment needs and processes to the public. There were no official appeals for volunteers,

10 THE EVENING POST, MONDAY, FEBRUARY 15, 1915.

NEW ZEALAND EXPEDITIONARY FORCE

REINFORCEMENTS

To the Manhood of New Zealand between the ages of 20 and 40 years.

HALT!

YOUR EMPIRE CALLS YOU, AND—ENGLAND EXPECTS!—

IN order to maintain a regular supply of REINFORCEMENTS for the NEW ZEALAND EXPEDITIONARY FORCE, every man of the required age who is a British subject and is medically fit owes a duty to his EMPIRE.

REGISTER YOUR NAME AS A RECRUIT TO SERVE YOUR KING AND COUNTRY.

Due to the patriotism of your forefathers, ENGLAND is to-day able to assert the principle of JUSTICE and RIGHT. Are you by your neglect going to deprive our Empire of this privilege and power?

PROVISION IS MADE FOR YOU WHEN SERVING YOUR COUNTRY to receive PAY at the following rate: As a Private, from the day of leaving for Camp you will receive 4s. per diem for seven days in the week. This will be paid to you in full at intervals of ten to fifteen days for the first calendar month. After that date the daily rate will be 5s. You will be fed and clothed until discharged. Arrangements can be made to enable you to allot any portion of your pay to relatives or friends, or to a bank until your return, but only 2s. a day can be drawn after embarkation. The balance, if not allotted, will be held as deferred pay, and paid to you on discharge or on return to New Zealand.

REGISTER NOW

Registration-cards can be obtained from any post-office or Defence Office. When filled in, send to the nearest Defence Office, or to the Officer commanding your Unit.

DON'T GIVE UP WORK UNTIL ORDERED TO DO SO.

Don't feel for the rest of your life you shirked your duty when your Empire's existence depended on your help.

GOD SAVE THE KING!

CONDITIONS.—INFORMATION FOR INTENDING RECRUITS.

1. HOW TO ENLIST:—
Apply to the nearest Defence Office or Post-office for information and registration-card. Fill in the card and send it to the nearest Defence Office (no stamp required). When you are called on for medical examination do not give up your civil employment. Medical examination is only a stage in the proceedings, after which you return to work and wait until you are ordered to parade. Due notice will be given so that arrangements may be made to settle private affairs.
Serving Territorials must register through their Unit Commanders.

2. ACKNOWLEDGMENT or REGISTRATION:—
Registration-cards received by the Defence Authorities will be acknowleged. The acknowledgment will be given a registration (serial) number, which should be referred to in all subsequent correspondence.

3. CHANGE OF ADDRESS:—
Intending recruits who change their place of residence must notify the Defence Office with whom they registered. Should they go to another district they must re-register in the new district.

4. TERMS OF ENLISTMENT:—
Enlistment is for the period of the war and until such time thereafter as may be necessary for return and discharge in New Zealand.

5. OATH OF ALLEGIANCE:—
Every soldier is required to take the Oath of Allegiance to His Majesty the King in a prescribed form.

6. REQUIREMENTS:—
Age must be between twenty and forty years.
Height must be over 5ft. 4in.
Weight must be under twelve stone.
Fit for service.

7. MEDICAL TEST:—
The medical examination requires, amongst other matters, that a recruit should have good eyesight, good hearing, no ruptures, no defects, not subject to fits, and be possessed of sufficient teeth for efficient mastication.

8. VACCINATION AND INOCULATION:—
In the interests of himself and of his comrades, every soldier is required to have been vaccinated and inoculated for enteric. No recruit will be accepted unless he agrees to vaccination and inoculation.

9. EQUIPMENT:—
All equipment, clothing, blankets, etc., will be provided free by the New Zealand Government.

10. TRAINING:—
Before leaving New Zealand men are liable to be trained for four (4) months at Trentham or for any shorter period ordered.

11. PAY:—
Men who enlist for service with the Expeditionary Force receive pay at Territorial Force rates for the first month in camp—that is, 4s. per day in the case of privates. The whole of this money is paid direct to the men at intervals of ten to fifteen days.

At the end of the first month pay is increased to Expeditionary Force rates—that is, 5s. per day in the case of privates. From this pay is deducted any allotments that the men desire to make.

Only 2s. a day can be drawn after embarkation, the balance, if not allotted, being held as deferred pay, and paid to the soldier on discharge or on return to New Zealand; in case of death, paid to next-of-kin or legal representative.

By early 1915 the Defence Department was seeking to better inform the public about the enlistment process and potential recruits about the requirements and conditions of service. These posters were distributed in public spaces and reproduced in newspapers. EVENING POST, 15 FEBRUARY 1915, P. 10

clear information on how men should enlist was lacking, and the Defence Department almost seemed to spurn the patriotic societies offering to help organise local recruitment. 'It was far better,' Allen claimed in November, 'that recruiting should be in the hands of the Defence Department and that applications should go in the first place to the local defence office . . . it was obvious that the local defence officer was likely to know more about the volunteer than anyone else.'[59] Complaints from would-be volunteers about lethargy bound in red tape were common. Some added despondently that they had made what turned out to be premature financial arrangements, or pre-enlistment drinking binges that swallowed their available funds.[60]

Many appeared to think that the country could do more, and announcements, made in April, that New Zealand would raise two additional 1000-man infantry battalions and a 500-strong artillery unit seemed proof of this.[61] Allen, however, tried to impress on the public the hard fact that a lack of officers, equipment, infrastructure and logistics prevented any rapid escalation of commitment: the nation, he said, 'had to look 12 months, or possibly two years, ahead for a continual supply every two months'. He pointed out, too, that New Zealand had fulfilled its promises and had done more in per capita terms than the other dominions.[62]

Efforts to better organise and standardise the recruiting process were under way by the end of 1914 and came into force in the first months of 1915.[63] Posters and circulars outlined how men could register so they could be called up when space was available. Until then they should remain in their jobs. Thousands of copies were distributed to the country's post offices, police stations and drill halls and reproduced in newspapers.[64] Recruits could also register at a post office and receive an acknowledgement and an appointment for a medical examination. Local recruitment committees also became more significant, manning recruiting stands and organising patriotic events. By December 1914 Allen was noting 'the great value' of local efforts and by mid-April 1915 he was offering high praise: 'I am grateful to the various recruitment committees which have kept the thing going so splendidly . . . I would much rather the work be left in their hands . . . no one could do it better.'[65]

Defence's initial passivity about recruitment can partly be explained by the ready supply of volunteers. As Robin noted towards the end of 1914, 'So far all the men required have been obtained without difficulty, and in a sense more than required.'[66] By 31 May 1915, 8690 men had registered for service in the Wellington district, 6147 in Auckland, 4957 in Canterbury and 4585 in Otago. Although a number did not turn up to their medical tests, and others failed them, the total significantly exceeded requirements.[67]

The situation across districts was more complex, though, as Canterbury fell over 100 below its quota for the third draft and Otago fell short for the second, third, fourth and fifth drafts. Surpluses from Auckland and Wellington, which amply exceeded their quota for every draft, were again used to make up the shortages.[68] Local recruitment campaigns and editorials urged Otago to 'wake up' and asked if men had to wait until 'a German cruiser drops shells on the Octagon' before they would enlist.[69] But the numbers enlisting reflected Otago's smaller pool of eligible men and, when measured in per capita terms, the district's enlistment rates were, in Allen's words, 'very satisfactory indeed'.[70]

To secure additional funding for the war, the government passed the Public Revenues Amendment Act in August 1914, empowering it to borrow £2 million in Treasury bills for the rest of that year.[71] Allen, as finance minister, anticipated that about half of the money would be spent on public works and the rest on war costs.[72] The intention appeared to be to pay both interest and principal after the conflict out of existing sources of revenue, which had been proving increasingly lucrative before 1914. The hope was that the war would be over before other measures, such as a war tax or a conventional loan, would have to be considered. A loan was decidedly unattractive given the prevailing London interest rates. In a statement not devoid of political point-scoring, Allen noted that even the short-term loan floated by Ward, due in December 1914, could not be refinanced, probably because the government was unwilling to pay the prevailing interest rates.[73]

Throughout 1914 the government resisted any suggestions of war taxation. 'As far as I can see,' said Massey in August, 'there will be no war tax for some time to come. I hope we may be able to avoid it altogether.'[74] In November, he judged that it would be 'most foolish to impose a war tax' as '[t]he industries of the Dominion would stagnate and thousands would be thrown out of employment, because wages payments would be interfered with'. Existing taxation would be sufficient to service the '£2,000,000 — probably more' that the war effort was estimated to cost.[75]

Allen also tapped into public readiness to demonstrate 'practical patriotism'. On 9 August he announced the establishment of an Empire Defence Fund, which also came to be termed the War Expenses Fund or just the War Fund.[76] Donations from local authorities, companies and individuals could be paid into it. All sorts of gifts in kind, including horses, were also sought, and if suitable, would be transported free to military district headquarters.

The government may have missed an opportunity to impose a war tax while patriotic feeling was so high. Less than a week after the declaration of war a meeting of leading Auckland businessmen agreed that expenses could only be adequately and equitably met through taxation rather than donations. J. H. Upton, who 'had put his name on the Mayor's list for £100',

> did not imagine for one moment that he was going to get off with £100, or several hundreds: possibly they would be lucky to get off retaining half the property any one of them possessed. If they all got off by paying double the income tax they would be able to thank God for it. This was no Boer war but the greatest military upheaval the world had ever known. A motion such as that suggested would encourage Parliament in its action. It was quite conceivable, of course, that Parliament would decide to treble the income tax. He wanted to see the Government do a wise thing in putting the saddle on the whole beast, instead of leaving it to a few of those citizens who were most open-handed.[77]

Upton was not alone. In late August, representatives of many Taranaki co-operative dairy companies met in Hāwera to hear the chairman of the National Dairy Association propose that each company contribute 0.5 per cent of its profits to the patriotic funds. This effectively meant that shareholders in those companies would be taxing themselves. The move was justified on the basis that 'if they went round with subscription lists it frequently happened that the man worth £30,000 or £40,000 put his name down for half a crown, whilst a man with only a thousand or two would pay £20 or £30'. In case patriotism was not enough, the representatives were reminded that the Royal Navy was vital to protecting their trade and that by taking on the war risks insurance on cargoes bound for Britain, the government had saved exporters perhaps as much as 6 per cent of their returns.

They agreed to make the recommendation, though one of its strongest supporters admitted that possibly a war tax 'on incomes firstly and on property secondly, would be the fairer basis and may eventually be put into operation'.[78] In March 1915 the Gisborne Patriotic Committee told James Allen that 'there were certain sections who were well able to subscribe but who had not up to the present given a penny, and it was to get at these that the committee would welcome a war tax'.[79] Such ideas mark early examples of concerns about 'equality of sacrifice', in which all were expected to contribute to the war as they were able. These would intensify as the war continued.

There was some early discussion about how a reasonably equitable war tax might be structured. In March 1915, the Bank of New Zealand's Harold Beauchamp proposed a levy of 1 per cent on the value of all exports and imports, estimating that this would bring in £500,000 each year and could meet the full costs of the war, assuming it ended around the end of 1915, in about 14 years. While conceding that exporters, notably farmers, would end up paying both on their exported produce and the imports they used, he reasoned that 'as a class the producer has greatly benefited, is benefiting, and is likely to benefit still further from the war' but this was not the case for the 'non-producing class [who] are not so directly benefiting; on the contrary they have to pay more for New Zealand produce consumed in the country in consequence of its enhanced value outside'.[80]

This argument was unlikely to go down well with most farmers, a group strongly represented among the government's supporters. Speaking during a visit to Gisborne, Allen did not address Beauchamp's suggestion, but said the government could borrow substantial funds from the flush Post Office Savings Bank, rather than seek funds on the London money market.[81] Again, the government was looking to borrow from those who were benefiting most from the war rather than tax them.

The financial situation shifted in early 1915 when the British government took out a massive war loan of £350 million at an effective interest rate of 4 per cent and agreed to advance portions to the dominions at the same rate.[82] This meant the New Zealand government was able to use Britain's extremely high 'credit-rating' and the patriotism of its investors to obtain what was regarded as cheap money to repay both the Treasury bills it had issued and Ward's loan, a total of £5.25 million.[83] In March 1915 Allen announced that the same facility would be available for any future war finance and that he estimated a direct cost of £5 million to New Zealand by the end of the year, 'if the war continued [to] that time'. He also acknowledged that some increase in taxation would be necessary to finance the loan. A month later Massey likewise, albeit reluctantly, signalled his acceptance: 'I cannot help thinking . . . that there are a good many people asking for a war tax now who will be sorry when it arrives. But come it must, when Parliament meets.'[84]

Rising living costs, and particularly wheat prices, presented the Reform government with another complex challenge. Massey was undoubtedly correct in his repeated claims that there would have been a wheat shortage even without the war. The long-term decline in local production had been exacerbated by unprofitable recent seasons and a relatively poor harvest, thanks to dry conditions in major wheat-growing areas. Also, cheap and abundant Australian wheat, which had led many local producers to abandon wheat-growing, suffered a massive check owing to drought in 1913–14. Prices soared and neither wheat nor flour could be cheaply imported from across the Tasman. The war did somewhat compound the problem by making it more expensive and difficult to import wheat from further afield as prices rose in Europe and shipping became scarcer and more costly.

Although he argued that markets should generally be unfettered, Massey was inclined to seek solutions, especially in view of the approaching election. State efforts to control prices were announced as to protect New Zealanders from price manipulation by 'rings' and 'trusts'; the belief that such bodies existed was widespread and was shared by many Reform supporters and sometimes by Massey himself. The same afternoon that war was declared, the prime minister pledged that 'if there is any evidence to show an intention to exploit the community by unduly increasing prices of foodstuffs on account of what has taken place in Europe the Government will ask Parliament to take drastic action'.[85]

On 7 August grain exports were banned and efforts were made to bulk-purchase wheat and flour from overseas markets. New Zealand does not appear to have used state purchasing in this way before, even when prices had risen to similar levels in 1907. Only 45,000 bushels were obtained in Australia before word leaked and the prices asked of those buying for New Zealand made the operation unfeasible.[86] Some 400,000 bushels were ordered from Canada and Massey appealed to farmers to plant cereals, citing predictions that the war would create a world shortage by early 1915.[87]

Mixing patriotism with economic incentives, he pointed out 'that the food supply may be a determining factor in the great struggle, and farmers who endeavour to help their country by providing this class of produce may find that in serving the Empire's interests they have served their own'.[88] He did not say that it would also keep prices in New Zealand lower than they might otherwise be. Although it was late in the season to begin working the ground, additional acreage does appear to have been sown.[89]

On 10 August the government passed the Regulation of Trade and Commerce Act, establishing 'standard prices' and giving itself sweeping powers to launch investigations into pricing and to fix maximum prices. Massey later admitted that he hoped that the act alone would 'prevent exploitation of the public'.[90] There was also the Foodstuffs Commission, appointed in late August. Massey again hoped that a show of will would produce results and later maintained that as soon as the commission was asked to deal with meat prices, 'the stock yards were filled, and the difficulty which had prevailed in one part of the country disappeared immediately'.[91]

Wheat and flour prices became the commission's major focus and after hearing submissions around the country, it recommended a wheat price of 4s 9d per bushel and a flour price of £11

15s per ton as legal maximums at the South Island ports that shipped most production. Both these rates, made official on 29 September, were significantly below those that had been ruling in the market. The commission had in fact earlier settled on 5s 3d and £13, before changing its decision.[92]

The commission enjoyed some success when it came to the sugar industry, where the show of will seemed to achieve the desired results. Apparently fearing that its New Zealand business might be taken over and run by the government, the Colonial Sugar Refining Company proposed that, in return for a guarantee that this would not happen, it would supply sugar to the local market at no more than £20 a ton, a little higher than it had set previously though notably lower than the current British price of £33.[93] No restrictions were to be placed on imports, so sugar could be brought in at less than £20 a ton if merchants could obtain it. In early 1915 the government agreed to the deal and Massey was able to boast that the country enjoyed the cheapest sugar in the British Empire. This did not, of course, satisfy critics, who continued to imply that it should be cheaper still.[94]

The new fixed price for flour was another matter: it caused a storm of protest from most of the country's millers, as those who had recently bought wheat were now faced with making flour at a loss. Some threatened to stop production. Massey claimed that those primarily affected were the smaller millers, who bought only enough wheat for immediate needs, whereas the bigger mills had purchased large quantities early in the season at pre-war prices.[95] Suspicions arose that the large millers had attempted to squeeze out the smaller ones by persuading the commission to set such a low flour price.

The government sought some goodwill by announcing that imported wheat would go to the small mills, but it also hinted that it might take over running of 'one or two' mills 'for the purpose of ascertaining the cost of production and the buying prices of wheat and the selling prices of flour'.[96] But wheat-growers and holders also refused to sell at the price set. On 2 October it was reported from Christchurch that business in wheat was at a complete standstill.[97] At a meeting of the Timaru branch of the Farmers' Union a few days later, C. N. Orbell wanted to know 'how the Government could make a farmer sell at the price stated. If the Government intended to seize the grain they would find they had some difficult men to deal with.'[98]

With the market deadlocked, the prospect of bread scarcity loomed. A survey indicated that the country held around 1.1 million bushels of wheat, enough for nearly two months at a normal rate of consumption.[99] Three-quarters of that amount was held by millers so they could continue to make flour until the new season. The government asked the Foodstuffs Commission to take further evidence and on 20 October it set out new fixed prices for wheat and flour at the level it had originally favoured. The import duty on wheat and flour was also suspended until the end of February 1915, when the new season's local wheat would start to become available.[100] The government was clearly looking to imports to dissuade those holding wheat from demanding still higher prices.

However, despite the increase in the official wheat price, in late November the Flourmillers' Association told Dunedin bakers it had no flour available 'as farmers resolutely declined to

Soldiers of the Canterbury Mounted Rifles and the Canterbury Infantry Regiment embarking on HMNZ *Tahiti* and HMNZ *Athenic* at Lyttelton on 23 September 1914.
ARCHIVES NEW ZEALAND, PC4/1569

sell at the price fixed by the Government'. A few days later five out of six mills in the city were 'practically closed down' and orders from bakers to mills in Ōamaru, Timaru and Christchurch had proven fruitless. It was claimed that some South Canterbury wheat sales were going through at up to 6s 3d per bushel and that this was achieved by charging 5s 3d for the wheat and making up the difference in the price of the sacks or other 'charges'.[101] An announcement from the Wellington Master Bakers' Association a fortnight later, that bread prices in the city would shortly go up 12.5 per cent, led to revelations that millers were also finding loopholes in price controls. At least one miller was saying that the flour he sold was coming out of his stores and therefore not subject to the proclamation.[102]

In response to such practices Massey was firm that 'the Government will not allow any storing of wheat supplies for the purposes of exploiting the public' and issued instructions 'that persons holding more than 10,000 bushels of wheat should be notified that unless they do not [sic] dispose of the surplus within 14 days for the purpose of it being ground into flour the Government will take it at a fair price'.[103] This was directed at grain merchants, who, on 18 November 1914, had been holding 132,868 bushels, with over 90,000 in Timaru alone. By 19 January 1915 Timaru merchants were holding only 7400 bushels, which suggested that the warning may have worked, although the imminent arrival of state imports and the approach of the new season would also have had an effect.[104]

The Reform government was never likely to confiscate wheat from farmers, and such a policy would almost certainly have exacerbated and prolonged the crisis. Although some took advantage of the situation to sell wheat at increased prices, the quantities they held were comparatively small and their confiscation would not have yielded enough flour to see the country through. Seizing wheat would also have discouraged farmers from carrying sown crops through to harvest and from further wheat-growing. Angry trade unionists might demand that the government force farmers to produce wheat, but it was unclear how that could be done without an army of inspectors, forced investments of labour and endless legal wrangling. As one study of transnational economies during the war has pointed out, 'in richer countries the government paid more to the food producers, and this worked, but in poorer countries . . . the government wanted to pay less and this had entirely predictable results. The willingness of farmers to participate in the market was still further undermined.'[105]

Massey's tough talk doubtless did no harm to his image as a strong leader before the December election but almost immediately afterwards he appeared to backtrack. 'It is being said that wheat is being privately held here for high prices. That is not so. Very little wheat is being held, so little that it can make no difference to the supply price . . . Nothing can keep prices down when the wheat required is not in the country.' He pointed to the failure of New South Wales' Labor government to maintain set levels of wheat and flour prices, an attempt that had featured some seizures at fixed prices.[106]

After delays caused by wartime conditions, the wheat import arrived late January 1915.[107] The government became a flour and grain merchant, allocating 75 tons of flour and more than 2000 sacks of wheat to hard-hit Dunedin. The wheat was sold to millers at 5s 9d a bushel, which meant a loss to the government of between 3d and 6d a bushel.[108] Anticipating a strong demand for a product that was both subsidised and yielded more loaves per ton than local wheat, it also established a system of rationing between the country's flour mills. Applications for allocations were made through chief postmasters and a national Wheat Distribution Board determined who would buy the wheat, which was provided on the condition that the resulting flour should be sold at £15 a ton, with 10s added if necessary for delivery costs.[109]

The use of merchants' stocks and imported supplies bought time, but the country only narrowly avoided exhausting its wheat supplies before the new harvest.[110] Although potatoes and oatmeal were available, a lack of wheat or flour would have shaken most households and some major industries. The problem was also likely to continue. The 1914–15 growing season was dry and the harvest again promised to be poor. With November 1915 stocks predicted to be even lower than those at the same time in 1914, Massey arranged an option to buy over a million bushels of Canadian wheat for a July delivery.[111] Wheat-growers, however, demanded still higher prices for the new season's crop: over 7s a bushel in some cases.

Accurate statistics on production and stocks were considered essential and Massey insisted on monthly returns from threshing mills, and fortnightly returns from every flour miller and grain merchant, including quantities in store and the prices at which they were being sold. By early March he was more optimistic about the harvest, which, 'along with the probability of the Russians being able to get wheat through the Dardanelles in the not far distant future', was likely to reduce prices.[112] The precedent for increased state intervention in the economy had also been established and further possibilities were soon raised. As the price of bread in Auckland increased to 10d for a 4-pound loaf in March 1915, and seemed set to rise higher,

above Massey and Ward share the stage at a fundraising event held days before the 1914 general election. AUCKLAND WEEKLY NEWS, 10 DECEMBER 1914, P. 50

left Annie Thomson farewells her son, Sergeant George William Ladd Thomson, from Timaru, in October 1914. AUCKLAND WAR MEMORIAL MUSEUM TĀMAKI PAENGA HIRA, PH-2003-1-36

Massey startled some of Reform's strongest supporters by saying that 'if there are any further increases in the price of bread, the Government will establish bakeries in the four principal centres of the Dominion, with the object of regulating prices'. This seemed to work: the Auckland Master Bakers' Association decided 'almost unanimously' against a further increase in the price of bread.[113] A government that boasted of its devotion to private enterprise had again proclaimed that it was prepared to greatly extend state activity in a crisis.

A few days out from the 10 December 1914 general election, one editorial concluded, rather sweepingly, that, 'Contrary to the expectations of some of the leading politicians, the great world war has not affected the course of the elections in the slightest degree.'[114] While somewhat overstated, the election was a firm demonstration of the continuation of domestic politics. There was certainly little to distinguish between the candidates concerning the war. Ward had said nothing that might deter patriotic Liberals, who were constantly reminded that Reform had been very critical of his offer of a dreadnought and that it was his administration, not Massey's, that had introduced compulsory military training. On 2 December George Russell, the leader of the party's more radical wing, told a large audience at Port Chalmers that

> the Liberal party was led by the greatest Imperialist in the Dominion, and whatever was necessary to give full effect to the wishes of the Imperial authorities and the patriotism of the people of New Zealand would be provided by the Liberal party in the matter of men, food, and equipment. There would be no halting in the work of assisting the Empire, and a change of Government would possibly mean greater energy and assistance to the Mother Country than was being shown at the present time.[115]

Those in the labour movement seeking political office also emphasised their support of the war. Representing the Social Democratic Party, Webb told a Reefton audience, 'once war had broken out, it was the duty of all — no matter what their views previously had been — to stand together. In such a case there should be no party. It was no time to argue about the war.'[116] Dan Sullivan, standing for the Avon seat in Christchurch, denied that the party would, during wartime, seek to abolish compulsory military training: 'The Social-Democrats were as loyal as anyone else, and cohesion was needed to bring the struggle to a satisfactory conclusion.'[117] Peter Fraser insisted that 'the majority of Socialists almost everywhere' — and he included those in Germany — 'are agreed that the most desirable outcome of the present situation is the defeat of Prussian militarism'.[118] Palmerston North candidate James Thorn declared that 'while there was need for navies — and there would be for some years to come — the best thing we could do was to aid the Imperial authorities in making their Navy supreme'.[119] Harry Holland, standing in Wellington North, appears to have said nothing against participation in the war and declared himself strongly in favour of a war tax.[120]

Candidates selected by Labour Representation Committees took a firmer stance. David McLaren in Wellington East was confident 'in the ultimate success of the British Empire. But all in New Zealand should contribute towards this — the wealthy, that could afford it, in money, and all classes in men.'[121] Francis Moore, standing for Wellington Suburbs, maintained that 'New Zealand had to do its utmost to overthrow German militarism, which had to be destroyed no matter what the cost'.[122] Sitting labour MPs William Veitch in Whanganui and the firebrand John Payne in Grey Lynn were of the same mind.

Reform was more willing to make the war an election issue. Its campaign book cynically pointed out that the United Federation of Labour and the Social Democratic Party were affiliated to the International Socialist Bureau, headquartered in Berlin.[123] Fraser repudiated this in a public letter claiming that, until the war, the bureau's offices had been in Brussels. This effort was undermined, though, by its appearance beside an editorial comment noting that the constitution of the 'Red Federation of Labour' had a clause stating that '[i]t shall become affiliated with the International Secretariat of Berlin, the headquarters of the International Trades Union Movement'.[124] The perception that the Social Democrats were associated with their German counterparts was no doubt damaging anyway, particularly among those aware that the latter had voted for the war credits necessary for Germany's military effort.[125]

Reform candidates further played the war card by arguing that Liberal cooperation with the Social Democrats, to avoid splitting the 'progressive' vote, could result in Ward heading a government short on resolve to pursue the war. In what the *Sun* described as a 'manifesto', Massey made it clear that although he and his colleagues 'have never questioned the willingness of the Opposition to co-operate with the Government for the good of the Empire . . . a party which involves itself with the Social-Democrat Party and the Red Federation in order to capture the Treasury benches cannot hope to do as good service as the Reform Party can do for New Zealand and the Empire'.[126]

The major pre-election bouts, though, had nothing or little to do with the war. Memories of 1913 hung over campaigning and, in its aftermath, Fraser maintained that '[t]he Reform Party made the strike of last year the predominating issue of the contest'.[127] It was certainly in their interest to do so. Many Liberals had considerable sympathy for the government's handling of the strike, as a New Plymouth newspaper made clear, even while calling on electors to vote for the local Liberal candidate. 'The Government, in our opinion, rose magnificently to the occasion when it was faced with the "Red Fed." crisis last year, and discharged its duty splendidly. For what it did it deserves the gratitude of the country.'[128] Reform's warnings about undue Social Democrat influence over the Liberals were pitched far more at domestic politics. As Holland told a receptive audience in Wellington on 8 December, 'the only answer the Government could give was "Red Fed, Red Fed, Red Fed". It had even called Sir Joseph Ward a "Red Fed". He did not think that was fair to the "Red Feds."'[129]

If voters needed any reminder of the disorder that had accompanied the strikes, it was provided by the repeated disruption of Reform meetings in Wellington and Auckland by those who had supported the industrial action. When, on 9 December, Massey described 1914 as 'the dirtiest election I have ever experienced', he was referring largely to 'the hoodlumism that has disgraced the fair city of Auckland during the last few weeks'.[130] The night before, when he had arrived at a meeting in Ponsonby for MP James Bradney, a tyre on his car had been slashed and other damage done. Apparent sabotage of the engine powering the electric lights in the hall created a lot of smoke and forced the meeting to close. 'Outside the hall there was a scene of wild excitement. Many hundreds of people, largely of the Federationist element, crowded around the building, and the police — there were 22 of them under Sergeant Rutledge — had all their work set in keeping them in order.'[131] A stone was thrown at Bradney and his daughter was trampled when she fainted.

The Liberal *Auckland Star* strove to dissociate the political opposition from these events and put the blame elsewhere: 'We have never hesitated to denounce and condemn the dangerous anarchism of the "Red Fed." type, which was the source of the trouble at Waihi two years ago, and which was chiefly the cause of the great strike last year; and we have no doubt that the disturbance last night was due to the malign influence and activity of the same lawless and desperate minority who regard all representatives of authority as their natural enemies.'[132]

This was clearly an awkward position, given that individuals who were emphatically Red Feds were calling on their supporters to vote Liberal, when the Liberal party's leadership had discouraged candidates from standing against some outspoken Red Fed supporters, and when Ward had directed Liberal votes cast by the NZEF in select districts to go to Social Democratic Party candidates. One Liberal candidate protested that this meant that votes cast for him by family members would now be cast against him. Similarly, Liberal campaign pledges to act against 'bogus unions' that had been organised to break the strike drew a clear line on the issue and appeared to align them with the strikers.[133]

The other big issue during the election campaign was the rapid rise in the cost of living. This gave the opposition considerable ammunition, which it used unstintingly. For the December quarter of 1914, the government statistician calculated an average increase of 6.5 per cent in the cost of living since the start of the war.[134] With most wages effectively frozen and economic activity disrupted in most towns, many working people were suffering particularly severely. A fortnight before the election an estimated 2500 people gathered in Christchurch's Cathedral Square to pass resolutions condemning the government for not seizing wheat and flour from those who were allegedly cornering the market and calling for the application of heavy penalties under the Regulation of Trade and Commerce Act.[135]

The deaths of 43 men in an explosion in a Huntly coal mine on 12 September probably also told against the government. At the beginning of November, John Payne was removed from the House for the day after describing the deaths as 'murder' and directing some responsibility towards Massey as minister of labour.[136] During the election campaign opposition candidates made similar claims. Peter Buck (Te Rangi Hīroa), standing for the Liberals in the Bay of Islands and speaking at the mining settlement of Hikurangi, declared that 'the Reform party had failed to introduce mining legislation to prevent the accident . . . The Government must accept the responsibility of being guilty of manslaughter.'[137]

Massey was also accused of corruption. It was alleged that he owned a considerable share of a large estate known as 'the ostrich farm', through which the Waiuku railway line was to run. Construction of the line had been approved shortly before the passage of legislation that made owners of land through which new railways ran liable for some of the cost of their construction.[138] Another Reform MP was said to own a majority interest in the block, and the fact that the manager of the Huntly mine was also a partner provided a tenuous link to the disaster and the inadequate supervision of safety measures leading up to it. Massey doubtless had such accusations in mind when he spoke of 'slander, calumny and misrepresentation', along with disorder, making the campaign 'dirty'.[139]

The election, held on 10 December 1914, with the Māori vote on the 11th, had an even higher voter turnout than in 1911, which had itself been a record.[140] There was a massive swing in the share of the popular vote going to the Reform Party — from 35.45 to 47.1 per cent, the highest level it ever received in an election — and much smaller increases in the Liberal proportion (41.1 to 43.1 per cent) and that of labour and Social Democratic Party candidates (8.8 to 9.6 per cent).[141] Reform's increased share of the popular vote was partly the result of the virtual disappearance of the vote share that went to independents in 1911, as several previously independent candidates now formally joined Reform and the Liberals. The industrial unrest of 1912–13 also appears to have solidified most of the existing rural and small-town discontent with the Liberals to Reform's advantage.

Yet Reform's triumph in the popular vote was not reflected in its parliamentary majority: it suffered a net loss of seats and seemed, for a while, on the brink of defeat. The electoral arrangements of the Lib-Lab alliance yielded dividends, albeit largely to the Liberals. In electorates where sympathy for the strikers was strong, Reform lost heavily — to Liberals in Auckland West and Wellington Central, and to a labour candidate in Dunedin North. The same would have happened in Dunedin Central to a labour candidate if a polling clerk had not made a mistake.

Small swings to the Liberals, particularly in the larger settlements in the electorates, gave Taumarunui, Hawke's Bay and Wairarapa to Ward's men and almost saw the opposition into government. Conversely, the erstwhile Liberal Willie Field, now standing for Reform, took Ōtaki from the Social Democratic Party, while Reform candidates captured Nelson and Motueka. In all three seats there was a particularly large swing to Reform in farming areas, again suggesting that the disruption associated with the strike had exerted a strong influence.

The uncertainty that followed the initial declaration of results was prolonged for more than six months as the Reform MP for Dunedin Central sportingly resigned to enable a new contest to be held and successful court actions forced by-elections. Within a few days of the election it seemed likely that the formation of a government, by either side, would depend on the vote of Tau Henare, the newly elected independent MP for Northern Māori. Asked which way he would vote, Henare's response, 'I give you two guesses', became proverbial. On 16 June 1915, though, shortly before Parliament met, Massey could 'say emphatically that there is no reason for the slightest doubt as to the attitude of Mr Henare . . . He has promised to support the Reform party, and will do so.'[142]

HE
OUR WO
SHIPPING BERTHED.

CHAPTER SIX

COMMITMENTS ESCALATE

previous pages
An illuminated display on Queen's Wharf, Auckland, during a 1915 Queen Carnival event.
ALEXANDER TURNBULL LIBRARY, 1/2-001651-G

From late April 1915 the nature of New Zealand's war took a brutal turn. Knowledge that New Zealand soldiers had engaged at Gallipoli strengthened a sense that the country was finally making a real contribution, but as the campaign stretched out over the rest of the year, long casualty lists, returned wounded and letters from the front gave some sense of the costs of that contribution. The redeployment of New Zealand's forces to the Western Front and the Sinai Campaign in 1916 further emphasised the scale and costs of the war. Over this same period, the country's war effort expanded enormously, requiring more from people more of the time. Highly significant, too, were the introduction of conscription, in mid-1916, and the development of a culture that sanctioned loss as sacrifice for a greater cause.

In Europe, the bloody clashes of the war's opening months resulted in hundreds of thousands of casualties. Some New Zealand families had links to this carnage and anxiously awaited news of relatives serving in British forces. At the beginning of September 1914 Captain Harold Williams from Napier was the first New Zealander to be reported wounded at the front.[1] In October Captain Henry Walker from Auckland, serving with the Royal Warwickshire Regiment, appears to have been the first New Zealander reported as missing, although a fortnight later his parents received a telegram from their son, 'reporting himself safe and well'. He was later killed.[2]

Captain Walter Russell of the Northamptonshire Regiment was possibly the first New Zealander to be killed in action, on 28 October 1914.[3] A few members of the New Zealand Expeditionary Force also died in training or on the voyage to Egypt, and Private William Ham of Ngatimoti in the Motueka Valley was killed in February 1915 during the Ottoman Empire's unsuccessful invasion of Egypt.[4]

Nevertheless, by April 1915 New Zealand had effectively been spared mass casualties and nine months into the war almost all the New Zealanders who would ultimately be killed during the conflict were still alive. Towards the end of March, James Allen was largely justified in telling a Gisborne audience that they were 'very fortunate' to be living in New Zealand, 'for no country had suffered less than they had. They must be willing to bear their share of the burden of the Empire and he was sure they would do it very willingly.'[5] The *Evening Star* made a similar point in a harsher fashion: 'We are too favored; the hand of the aggressor has not smitten us; we still think, feel, and act as we did nine months ago. War! What is war to us? We shall be all right; the Germans will not touch us; why should we worry? These terms are the commonplaces heard daily on our streets.'[6] This 'fortunate' and 'favoured' status was soon brutally challenged by news from Gallipoli.

Throughout February and March 1915, New Zealand newspapers closely followed the abortive efforts by the British and French navies to force their way through the Dardanelles and attack Constantinople (now Istanbul), the capital of the Ottoman Empire. By the end of March there was an awareness that troops would be landed, possibly to conduct 'regular siege operations', and that the NZEF was likely to be involved.[7] Their location in Egypt made this a strong possibility, and letters from New Zealand soldiers, though posted several weeks earlier, mentioned preparations for movement and the Dardanelles as the probable destination. As a 'Napier boy' said in a letter to friends written at the end of February, 'it is surmised we are to attack the Dardanelles. There are a number of transports at Alexandria, and the Australians are embarking already. No doubt the Turks will offer a violent resistance to us approaching the heart of their empire.'[8]

On 9 April, Massey told an audience at Waiuku that French troops had arrived in Alexandria and that a British force would probably join them to attack the Dardanelles. Three days later press reports originating in Paris and London specifically mentioned New Zealand participation.[9] Speculation was abroad too. When the *Poverty Bay Herald* reported the death of Trooper Tom Mossman on 14 April, it claimed that 'the unfortunate young man had been shot at the front [and] it is considered possible that it was at the Dardanelles, because recently the parents of another local young man who is serving in the same company as the deceased received a cable from that locality'. Mossman had actually died of disease in Egypt and was buried in Cairo.[10]

However, subsequent news of a build-up of Allied troops on the island of Lemnos, not far from the Gallipoli Peninsula, made no mention of the NZEF. Nor did the early reports of the landings, the first of which was received on 26 April. It was not until 29 April that New Zealand involvement in the Gallipoli landings of the 25th were reported to the public. Banner headlines proclaiming 'New Zealanders Take Part in Dardanelles Attack', 'SPLENDID GALLANTRY' and 'NEW ZEALANDERS PRAISED' were based on the governor's release of a telegram from the British government offering 'their warmest congratulations on the splendid gallantry and magnificent achievement of your contingent in the successful progress of operations in the Dardanelles'.[11] Press commentary proudly celebrated that New Zealand was now directly involved in the fighting. The *Press* noted that New Zealanders now had the 'joy and satisfaction of knowing that when the test of battle came they were not found wanting', and the *New Zealand Herald* noted that the duty entrusted 'to our Force was difficult and that its successful achievement was no small feat of arms'.

In the words of the *Auckland Star*, 'our boys' had acquitted themselves in a manner that was a 'tribute to God's Own Country, and the sort of patriotism it inspires'.[12] Private correspondence voiced similar sentiments. On 2 May Christchurch woman Kate Commons wrote to her 19-year-old son Kenneth at Gallipoli, 'we realise everything much more seriously now that our boys are actually in the fighting line. We are all so proud & thankful for the commendation you have won.'[13] Later in the war, departmental officers, responding to an official questionnaire on the mood among new recruits, noted that a desire to emulate 'the deeds of heroism on Gallipoli' remained an inspiration.[14]

In Wellington on 29 April, government departments were given the afternoon off 'in celebration of the success of the Dardanelles operations', schools were closed, church bells were rung and 4000 to 5000 people gathered outside Parliament.[15] Both Massey and Ward addressed the cheering crowd and the prime minister declared, 'Our New Zealand soldiers, our boys, have done well, and the country has done well.' No longer, however, did he think the war would soon be over, and he noted that more manpower would be needed.

> We have sent on active service 17,000 men, the best and brightest in this community. I include the Native contingent and the men at Samoa. In a few months, if the war lasts, and I believe it will last, because the end does not appear to be in sight, New Zealand will have 25,000 men on the other side of the world fighting for their King, for the Empire, and for their country . . . I feel absolutely certain of this, that if another 25,000 men are required from New Zealand (and they may be required) they will be forthcoming from the manhood of this country . . . No sacrifice on our part is too great to keep the Old Flag flying, with all that it means to us in the way of liberty and freedom.

It was left to the mayor of Wellington, John Luke, to sound a more sombre note in addressing the parents of 'our boys': 'You will need to brace yourselves up for some news that will take out of you some of the enthusiasm of today, but you will have the support of every man and woman in New Zealand in your hour of trial and sorrow.'[16]

News of involvement at Gallipoli was quickly shadowed by speculation, rumour and scraps of information about casualties. However, both distance and the chaotic circumstances of the campaign hampered official communications and letters sent from the Dardanelles took at least six weeks to arrive. It was not until mid-May that official casualty figures were printed; detailed reports did not appear until the following month. The Defence Department used the telegraph to meet the challenge of reporting information about casualties half a world away to anxious next of kin. Regularly updated casualty lists became a feature of wartime society and the newspapers printed 'rolls of honour', often accompanied by photographs, listing the latest details of soldiers who had been reported missing, injured or killed. By the start of June 1915 total casualties stood at 1750; by September, after heavy fighting in August, the total had risen to 6138.[17] By the time the Allied evacuations from Gallipoli came to an end in December 1915, some 7300 New Zealand casualties were reported, of whom 2779 were dead.[18]

The wait for news, during the Gallipoli campaign and throughout the rest of the war, placed families and loved ones in an agonising limbo, described by one commentator as a 'sickening apprehension'.[19] As one mother of a recently enlisted son wrote, 'I find I cannot reason anything out, & get fearful when I try to reconcile all that it means with all we have been taught of the Christian life. I suppose we are not meant to think — just suffer!'[20] The arrival of news also strained nerves, and the delivery of more than 16,000 telegrams announcing deaths between 1915 and 1918 associated telegram boys, and later some girls, with dire news.[21]

Noting that 'I have often heard my people say "I dread the very sight of a Telegraph boy",' one Dunedin clergyman recommended to Allen that official condolences — sent on behalf of the king and queen, the governor and Massey and Ward — be limited to spare additional stress: 'I was in the home of one of my people shortly after the receipt of your wire informing them of the death of their son. Then came the two sympathetic wires. The family was so staggered that no one had courage to open these telegrams & I had to come to their assistance. The first thought in the minds of the girls was "the announcement of the death of another of the brothers".'[22] Allen persuaded Liverpool to post letters instead and Massey and Ward agreed to stop sending telegrams.[23]

The mounting casualty lists clearly had an effect on the public mood. As politician George Fowlds observed, 'with a daily list of New Zealanders killed and wounded the horrible character of the war has been brought home to us'.[24] By 30 May, the tone of Kate Commons' letters to her son had altered markedly: 'These are anxious times and we are so thankful as day after day passes and your name does not appear in the casualties.' On 13 June she wrote, 'you will imagine how thankful we are as each day passes & we hope that you are still unscathed. I pray unceasingly that you may be spared.'[25] Writer Eric McCormick would later recall that 'the mere sight of casualty lists in the paper brought tears to my mother's eyes'.[26]

The ideal of a 'good death', a proper funeral and a conventional mourning process was shockingly replaced by an abrupt awareness of the usually violent death of a loved one far away.[27] Overwhelmingly, those who died were young, leaving parents to endure the worst of all grief, the loss of a child.[28] Hundreds of families lost more than one child; some lost three and even four sons. Grief took many forms. Often numbness and shock came first, followed, perhaps, by feelings of disempowerment, frustration, anger, guilt and despair. Uncontrollable crying and problems with sleeping and eating were typical, and extreme cases could include hallucinations.

Before he enlisted, Private George Belcher, who was killed at the Somme in March 1918, had been a brickmaker and superintendent of the Bible class at St Jude's Anglican church in Auckland's Avondale. When two members of the congregation paid a visit to his brother, John, they 'found him at home looking very dirty & fat he sat in the room without coat or waistcoat in his stocking feet & his hands very dirty he repeated I knew it all along I knew he w[oul]d never come back, none of them will come back!! . . . It made one feel sad, it was altogether dreadful.'[29]

After 61-year-old Gustav Diehl died suddenly at his Wellington home on the evening of 29 November 1915, medical evidence pinpointed the cause as pneumonia and bronchitis, but also spoke of a heart that 'was not in a healthy condition'. Since his 25-year-old son Ralph had been killed at Gallipoli on 23 October, he had 'complained of feeling unwell'.[30]

Outward resignation could conceal terrible pain, and Massey recalled that Henry Okey, the

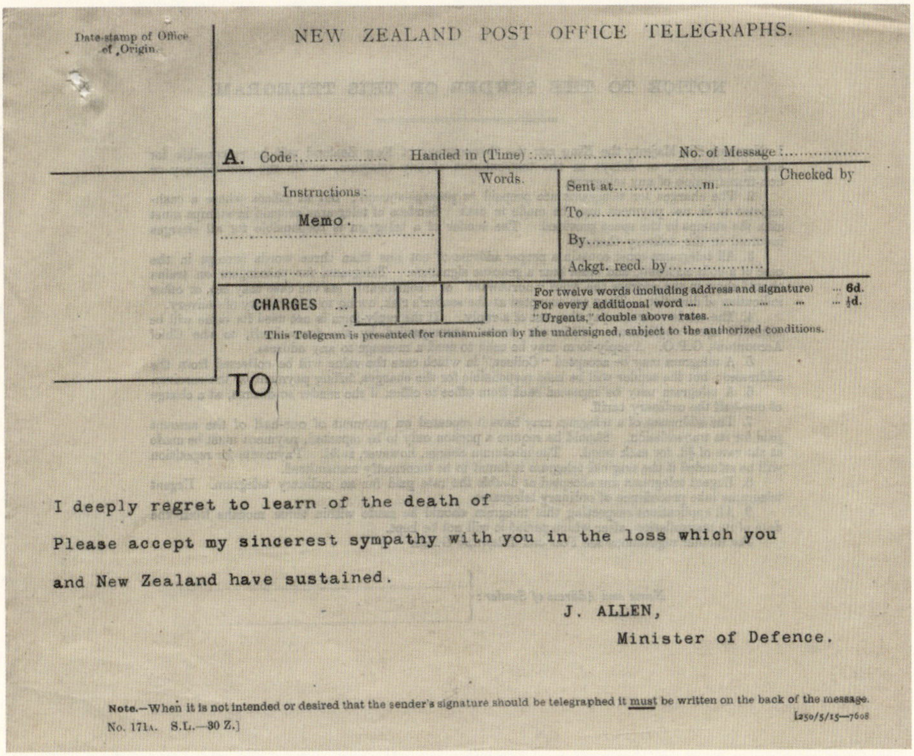

NEW ZEALAND POST OFFICE TELEGRAPHS.

Date-stamp of Office of Origin.

A. Code:.................. Handed in (Time):.................. No. of Message:..................

Instructions: Memo.	Words.	Sent at..................m. To.................. By.................. Ackgt. recd. by..................	Checked by

CHARGES ... For twelve words (including address and signature) ... 6d. For every additional word ... ½d. "Urgents," double above rates.

This Telegram is presented for transmission by the undersigned, subject to the authorized conditions.

TO

I deeply regret to learn of the death of

Please accept my sincerest sympathy with you in the loss which you

and New Zealand have sustained.

J. ALLEN,

Minister of Defence.

Note.—When it is not intended or desired that the sender's signature should be telegraphed it must be written on the back of the message.

No. 171A. S.L.—30 Z.] [250/5/15—7608

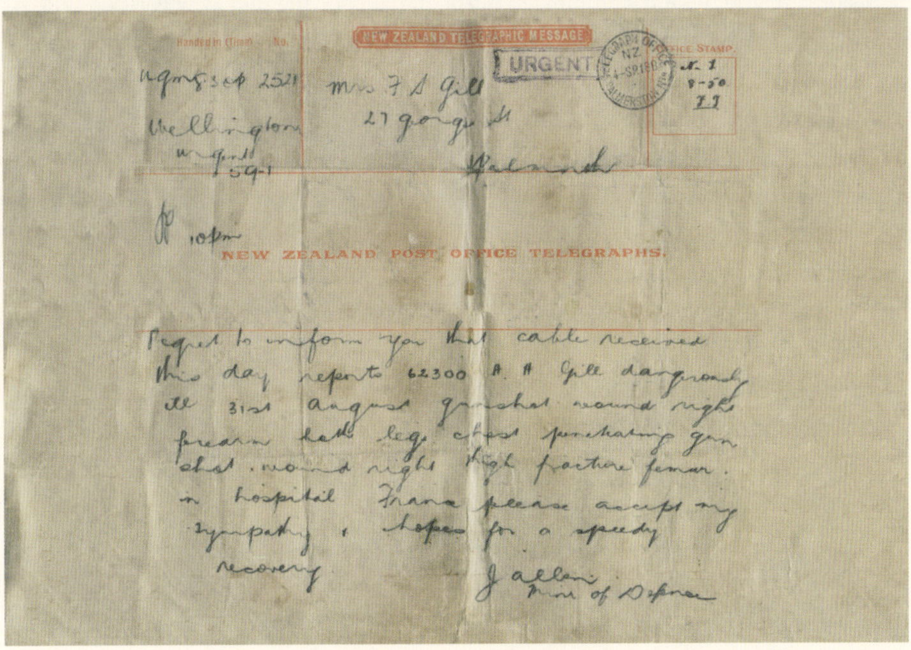

NEW ZEALAND TELEGRAPHIC MESSAGE

Handed in (Time) No.

URGENT

Office Stamp.

Mrs F S Gill

27 George St

NEW ZEALAND POST OFFICE TELEGRAPHS.

Regret to inform you that cable received this day reports 62300 A. H Gill dangerously ill 31st August gunshot wound right forearm both legs chest penetrating gun shot wound right thigh fracture femur. in hospital France please accept my sympathy & hopes for a speedy recovery

J Allen

Min of Defence

above A template for official telegraph notices informing next of kin of a death at the front. ARCHIVES NEW ZEALAND, R22429095

below An official telegram, dated 4 September 1918, informs Frances Gill that her husband, Private Henry Gill, has been wounded in action and is 'dangerously ill'. Henry Gill died from his wounds weeks later. NZ HISTORY

MP for Taranaki, had responded to news of the death of two of his three sons by saying 'a higher Power had called them, and he was ready to submit'. However, a colleague remarked, 'I saw the father's great grief when news was handed him of the death of his second son. He never appeared to be the same after.'[31] Some coped with their loss by withdrawing completely or by denying the truth. Others relied on alcohol or tried desperately to keep busy. When Kate Commons learnt that her son was reported missing, she continued, in an act of hope or denial, to write to him as usual 'because we are clinging fast to the hope that you may still be spared to us & be a prisoner in Constantinople . . . We hear too that the prisoners are being well treated & know that you will charm even the heart of a Turk with your usual courtesy.'[32]

When Eliza Holt visited a bereaved mother, she 'found her in the garden looking sad & bent; I can't believe it she said, they tell me its [sic] my Harry, it must be H. Walker, they had the two telegrams together'.[33] Many were desperate to learn more details of the death. For example, Laurence Holt, in Featherston Camp, wrote to his brother Frank, who was serving overseas: 'Am sending you a short note to ask you if you know anything whatever of a soldier who was killed or believed killed in action . . . His parents are friends of the Pres[byterian] Chaplain here and are very anxious to hear from anyone who knew their boy and especially anyone who may have seen him on the day he was lost.'[34]

After his son John was killed at Gallipoli in June 1915, James Allen sought relief in work. As one study notes, 'after the first shock and grief of the morning hours [he] endeavoured to put aside his private grief by burying himself in the drafting of the first War Pension Bill'. As he wrote in a letter to Godley, 18 months later, 'we grieve over our losses and simply have to bottle up our grief'.[35] Allen was not the only parliamentarian with a loved one in uniform; between them, the 80 MPs ultimately had 76 sons at the front.[36] These included Massey's youngest son, Frank, two of Joseph Ward's sons and three of legislative councillor Sir Francis Bell's. Labour politicians, too, had loved ones at risk and both Alfred Hindmarsh and Harry Holland had boys at the front. At least 15 sons of parliamentarians were killed or died of wounds.[37]

The return of sick and wounded men also confronted those at home with some of the reality of war. On the afternoon of 15 July 1915, the *Willochra* arrived at Wellington's Glasgow Wharf. On board was the first large group of wounded troops from Gallipoli. Over the following days, many of these men travelled, usually by train, to their homes and communities, where they were feted at sometimes lavish official receptions and received gifts. However, as one *New Zealand Herald* reporter noted, seeing the more severely wounded men had an impact on the crowds:

> The exuberance of Auckland's welcome yesterday to those of her sick and wounded soldiers who were passengers by the Red Cross train from Wellington was tempered by a sadness which would not be shaken off . . . The people cheered those men who were able to hobble to the motor-cars provided for them, but when the sick men on the stretchers were carried past, it was too sad. The cheering broke off suddenly, and in the absolute silence which followed, women sobbed openly, and men's faces hardened in the effort of self-control.[38]

One woman was appalled that the soldiers she had farewelled just a few months before had returned 'all mutilated'.[39] Another wrote, 'One's heart aches thinking of all the sorrow this dreadful war is causing it comes home to one now.'[40] Even those who had not seen wounded men may have encountered shocking newspaper photographs. In its April 1916 coverage of the recent arrival in Dunedin of the hospital ship *Maheno*, the *Otago Witness* included a photograph of a man, on crutches, with an amputated leg and a heavily bandaged head. The caption described him as 'a wounded soldier who has faithfully served his King and country'.[41] By September 1916 around 5515 wounded soldiers had returned to New Zealand.[42]

Romantic conceptions of combat were viciously challenged by newspapers reproducing frontline correspondence, which could include graphic accounts. For example, a letter from Egypt by Chaplain Charles Bush-King, written shortly after the initial Gallipoli landings, was widely published: 'Horace Braithwaite is seriously wounded in the head. A bullet entered the top of his head, traversed the curve of his skull, and is now lodged in the temple. Poor boy, he is almost unconscious, screams with pain, but when I go to him he holds my hand tight and usually goes off to sleep or else lies quiet. He is entered on the notice board as "dangerously ill".'[43] Braithwaite came home on the *Willochra* in October 1915 but died in Dunedin Hospital in January 1916. Another soldier gave a detailed account of his wounds to a relative in Invercargill: 'I was struck on the foot, with an explosion, and had a number of my toes blown off and the remainder of the foot badly shattered. I jumped up again to have another go at the Turks . . . when I received a second bullet in the shoulder, but this did not stop me long.'[44] This kind of minimising bravado was common. Others gave more blunt accounts of their experiences. One Southland soldier noted:

> What do I think of war? Well, it is kill, kill, kill. No one cares if you are the next to be shot. Sentiment dies the moment one sets foot in the trenches . . . Your mate may be shot alongside of you, and you will simply remark 'Jack's dead', and that is all . . . There is, however, something fascinating in the game. It grips one, and when it gets hold of you it causes you to become utterly indifferent to anything else. A man reverts to the primitive and takes fiendish delight in dealing out trouble to the other fellow. Your one desire is to get him in front of your rifle or bayonet, and end his worldly career, taking every possible care that he gets no chance to end yours. That is war.[45]

Although censorship, official and self-imposed, restricted such information, the pattern continued as New Zealand's efforts were redeployed to the Western Front. In early 1917, several newspapers printed a letter said to accurately capture conditions in the trenches:

> To form an idea of what one feels like, after a few days wet weather fighting on the Somme, just think of a Taranaki cowyard at its worst, after, say, six weeks' rain. Multiply the result eleven times, then roll in it, taking special care to rub it well into your hair, eyes, mouth, ears, and also rifle. Take a day's rations and stamp them well into the mixture, and use a newly-emptied benzine tin for drinking purposes. Carry a nice hefty load — for instance,

A Wellington crowd greets returned wounded soldiers disembarking from the *Willochra* in July 1915.
ALEXANDER TURNBULL LIBRARY, 1/1-008355-G

a bag of potatoes — through it all day, being sure to fall down every minute and a half, and consider yourself buried several times by shells that are too close for comfort. Continue treatment for some days, being careful not to wash or shave during the period. You can then realise what the cablegram means when it is reported that 'the weather interfered with the operations.'[46]

Enemy actions provoked more volatile emotions in May 1915. When Germany torpedoed the passenger liner *Lusitania* off the southern coast of Ireland on 7 May it generated outrage around the world. Massey described the resulting loss of 1198 lives, including many women and children, as 'one of the foulest crimes ever recorded in history . . . the Kaiser, who was directly responsible, will be looked upon for all time as an inhuman monster'.[47] In that month, too, Lord Bryce's report on German atrocities in Belgium was released, and there were reports of the German use of poison gas, at what became known as the Second Battle of Ypres. All were readily used for propaganda against German militarism.

There was more to come. In October 1915, the German military executed British Red Cross nurse Edith Cavell for helping British servicemen escape occupied Belgium. Along with Captain Charles Fryatt, a British mariner who was executed for attempting to ram his vessel into a U-boat, Cavell became a martyr figure, whose death was offered as proof of the nature of the enemy and the heroism of those resisting him. New Zealand was among those countries to name civic sites in her honour: the Edith Cavell Bridge, completed in 1919, spans Otago's Shotover River.[48]

Just 11 days after Cavell's execution, New

Zealand experienced its own tragedy, and scandal, when, on 23 October, 10 New Zealand nurses and 22 mostly New Zealand Medical Corps men were among the 167 killed when the British transport SS *Marquette* was torpedoed in the Aegean Sea. The dead were members of No. 1 New Zealand Stationary Hospital, which was en route to Salonika. Alongside a scandal that medical staff had been exposed by being transported on a troopship, instead of a marked hospital ship protected under The Hague Conventions, the nurses conduct was lauded. The *Dominion*'s reaction was typical of the considerable press coverage:

> No country in the world could show finer courage in its women, no greater devotion to duty, no greater self-sacrifice: The example set by Nurse Cavell was no finer, and surely if women in New Zealand intend to create a memorial of Nurse Cavell they cannot pass by the example set by the women of their own country, women who knew that when they left New Zealand they left with their lives in their hands, willing to sacrifice them so that they might do what they could in helping to stem the awful-horror and wreckage of war.[49]

The shocks New Zealand society experienced during and after May 1915 had a major impact on its attitude towards the war. The idea of a quick war or a cheap victory, already in decline, rapidly faded. A May editorial in the *Evening Post* stated:

> In August and September [1914] New Zealand had a very vivid perception of the gravity of the peril. But the sense of relief which came with the heading off of the German legions from Paris was followed by an easy optimism which assumed that the complete victory of the Allies was assured and could not be long delayed. This comfortable feeling survived the assurance of Lord Kitchener that the war would really begin in May. Even now it is probable that New Zealand would not have realised the significance of Lord Kitchener's words but for the brilliant gallantry of her troops at the Dardanelles and the heavy toll of casualties that it has cost them.[50]

Similar sentiments appeared in private accounts. On 31 December 1915 Harrold Ennor wrote in his diary: 'And thus ends another year. What a year it has been to [sic]. Never before has the world seen so many broken hearts. Never before have such numbers of heroic deeds been recorded. Even now the end of the struggle is not even on the horizon of our mental vision, but that end is sure and certain. The forces of evil cannot win, since God is God.'[51] By May 1916 Massey was publicly stating that 'the outlook in the way of bringing the war to a close is not good. I don't think it will end for a long time to come . . . the outlook today is not so good for the conclusion of the war as it appeared to be a year ago.'[52]

The continuing casualties and increasing demands of the war did not, however, signal a diminished resolve. The same was true of other nations from 1914 to 1917; casualties alone did not destroy commitment. Indeed, as long as the war's legitimacy remained intact then loss could be understood as a sacrifice towards a greater cause. Before enlisting to serve as

above Stratford school pupils involved in patriotic pageantry. The girl in the centre is dressed as Britannia. ARCHIVES NEW ZEALAND, 1/1-012483-G

below Some of the senior members of the Defence Department. From left: Colonel H. R. Potter (Commander of Trentham Reinforcement Camp); Surgeon General R. S. F. Henderson (Director General of Medical Services in New Zealand); Colonel C. M. Gibbon (Chief of the General Staff in New Zealand); James Allen (Minister of Defence); Colonel N. P. Adams (Commander of Featherston Camp); General Sir A. W. Robin (Commandant of New Zealand Military Forces in New Zealand); Colonel R. C. MacDonald (Chief Instructor at Trentham). ARCHIVES NEW ZEALAND, R24184728 a chaplain in Flanders during the bitterly cold winter of 1916–17, Bishop Henry Cleary noted privately, 'I would gladly give my life for the success of what I conscientiously believe to be the cause of justice.'[53] This sense that something great or necessary was being secured by the sacrifices of war was common and also highly adaptable, and its expression by trusted figures, who made reference to heartfelt creeds, gave it a potentially enormous influence. On the evening of 8 August 1915, for example, the Reverend James Gibb preached at a service in Wellington's town hall held 'to commemorate the anniversary of the war, to mourn the heroic dead, to steel our hearts for the work that yet falls to be done . . . We are pledged to this conflict, to see that the insensate pride, the strong ambition, the merciless cruelty, in one word the militarism of Germany, shall be brought reeling and crashing to the dust. To this task we have put our hand, and we shall not withdraw our hand until this work is done, or we perish in the endeavour to do it. That is our purpose, so help us God.'[54]

Māui Pōmare made a comparable point, claiming in the House that the shared sacrifices of the war had improved race relations: 'I think the misunderstandings which were between the pakeha and the Maori . . . have been swept away forever . . . their blood has commingled in the trenches of Gallipoli.'[55]

From late 1915, such emotional responses were encouraged in more professional and coordinated official national propaganda campaigns. Entirely typographical government war posters encouraging recruitment and donations to patriotic causes were supplemented by colourful and emotive British and Australian material.[56] By 1916 over 70 per cent of the content of the *School Journal*, the textbook used in all schools, was devoted to the war, king and empire.[57] Although both British and New Zealand propaganda was 'generally more persuasive and encouraging, than coercive, restrictive, and manipulative', much of it also carried frank prescriptions about how the war should be faced.[58] One 1916 school text, for example, noted that 'In ancient Greece mothers rejoiced that they had sons who could fight for their country, and, when they went to battle, told them that it was better to die than be beaten. This is the spirit that should move the women of the Empire.'[59] And in order to improve New Zealand representation in news reports from the front, an official war correspondent, Malcolm Ross, was appointed and sent overseas. He reached Gallipoli in June 1915, and later went to the Western Front with the New Zealand troops.[60]

Most propaganda efforts, though, relied greatly on volunteer efforts and private enterprise.[61] Newspaper proprietors blatantly tendered for commissions to carry official war notices, emphasising the value of an established network of readers. In May 1916 the Christchurch Press Co. pitched the value of its advertising services in a letter to the prime minister:

> The Home authorities now realise as never before what a power newspaper advertising is . . . those responsible have good reason to be encouraged by the fact that in response to newspaper advertising, the amount of subscriptions received for the second War Loan was DOUBLE WHAT WAS REQUIRED . . . never before has such a phenomenal return been known . . . we feel sure the wisdom of following the example of the Mother of Parliaments will appeal to you. Especially at this trying period in the history of our Empire it is necessary

An advertisement for Zam-Buk, a patented balm and antiseptic ointment, with endorsements from Australian and British soldiers. A great variety of products was advertised in this fashion. NEW ZEALAND HERALD, 22 JANUARY 1916, P. 8

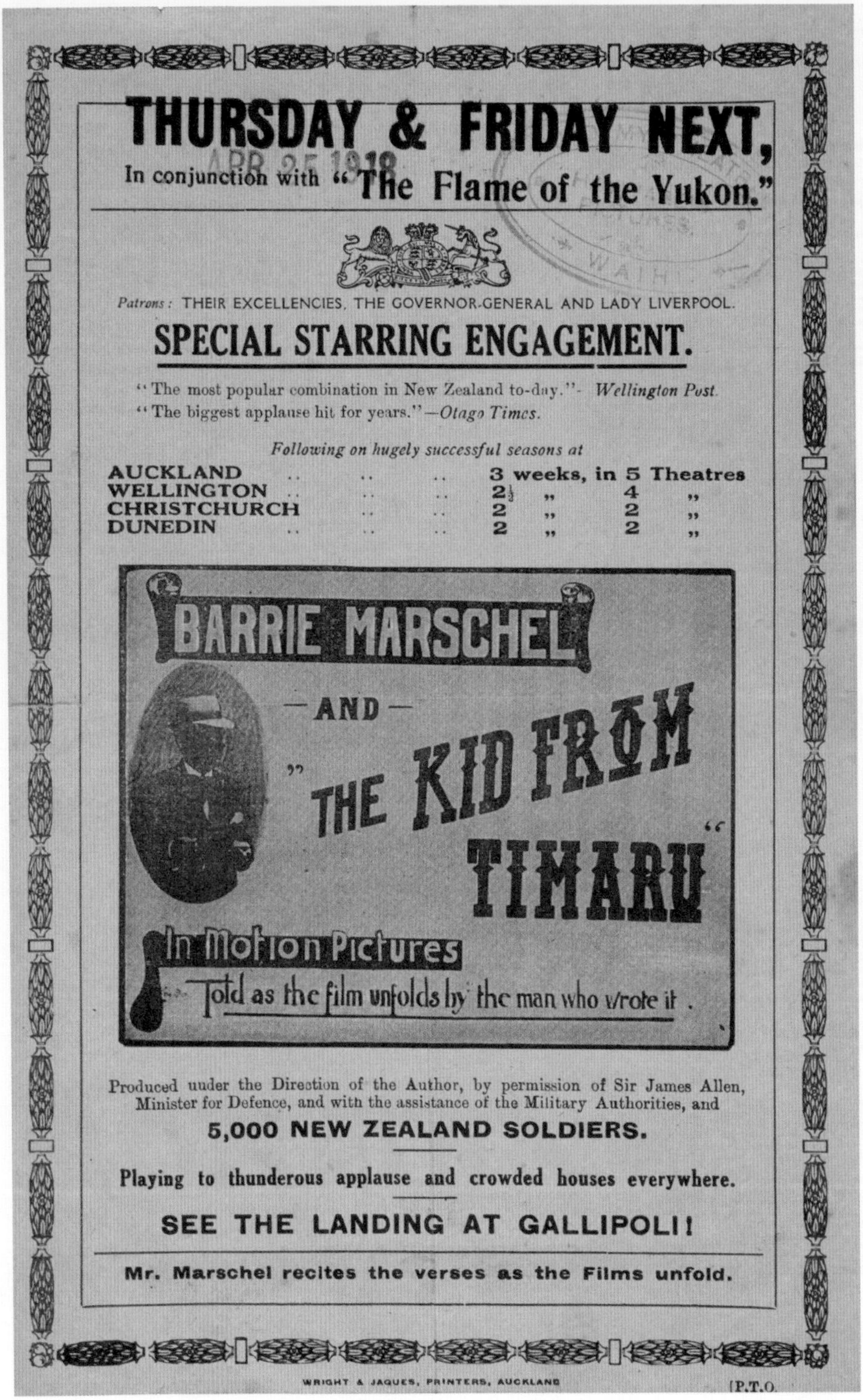

An advertisement for a screening of *The Kid from Timaru* at the Waihī Academy Theatre on Anzac Day 1918. ALEXANDER TURNBULL LIBRARY, EPH-A-CINEMA-1918-01

> for our rulers to keep in constant touch with their people — and the best way to do that obviously is to use those mediums handled daily by the people.[62]

Likewise, business interests advocating economic protectionism argued that the strength Germany was misusing was the result of its exploitation of Britain's markets and that the war represented an opportunity to safeguard British power by transforming the empire into an economic bloc.[63]

Popular culture, too, proved an enormously productive means of addressing the war. Gramophone companies produced records of patriotic songs, as well as locally written and published sheet music, usually promising a percentage of the sale price to such organisations as the War Relief Fund.[64] Cigarettes were sold with patriotic themed collectable cards, and toy manufacturers were soon producing items like the Wellington-based A. W. Moran & Son Company's 'inflatable dying Kaiser', available for 1s 1d each:

> FUN FOR EVERYBODY.
> THE DYING KAISER OR THE EMPEROR OF AUSTRIA.
> WHEN blown up look full of importance. They die down and look dejected and comical.[65]

Easily out-producing official propaganda, private advertising marketed an astounding range of products and services associated with the war. Some were promoted as necessary or desirable items for enlisted men; Dawson, among other jewellers, impressed the 'absolute necessity of the soldier having a reliable watch'; Whitcombe & Tombs proclaimed that '[t]he Soldiers' Diary is the handiest book ever put together for a soldier. Its 365 perforated pages make letter-writing easy'; in Dunedin H. W. Trotman financial services noted the importance of 'Soldier's Life Assurance'.[66]

Women were urged to support Belgium '[i]n every possible way, however small it may seem' and were informed that they might do so 'by buying P. D. Corsets — made in Belgium, designed in Paris. There's nothing German in P. D. Corsets.'[67] Others exploited patriotic or martial word play in advertisements: 'We're at war with the balance of the season's left-overs'; Christchurch biscuit makers Aulsebrook & Co. pledged to 'make war on antiquated methods'; Dunlop promised that there was 'nothing Neutral' about their tyres; Gerstena porridge was proclaimed as '[t]he "Big Gun" in cereal foods'.[68]

The relatively new medium of film proved a highly successful means of dramatising the war for mass audiences; by early 1916 an estimated 320,000 New Zealanders were attending the movies every week — more than went to church.[69] Among the imported films were Australian films 'full of Anzac achievement and topical dramas based on the war', including *It's a Long Way to Tipperary*, *Will They Never Come?* and *A Hero of the Dardanelles*, all screened in 1915.[70] The 74-minute British film *The Battle of the Somme* reached New Zealand by October 1916. The *Free Lance* heralded it as 'the latest and most realistic official war picture to date': 'Every branch of the service that took part in the "great push" is shown at work, especially interesting being the tank fighting and the infantry rushes, as well the aerial fleet in action. The camera man has managed to get wonderfully close, the result being the most realistic battle picture yet seen.'[71]

Some New Zealand war films were also produced, among them, in 1917, the 15-minute *The Kid from Timaru*, 'the verse epic in film of a "sunny-faced youngster from Timaru" who left his "scrumptious" girl with "Irish eyes" and went to war with the Turk for king and country and Timaru'.[72] Many of these films intended to impart moral lessons and were evidently viewed this way. As one reviewer of *The Martyrdom of Nurse Cavell*, billed as 'An inspiring War Drama . . . written around the great and glorious sacrifice of England's Joan of Arc', put it, 'The picture will still more vividly impress upon us the heroic sacrifice this noble woman made for her King and country, for those whom she so dearly loved. It will also show the depths of degradation to which the Bosches [sic] have sunk in taking the life of one who had engaged in a mission of mercy.'[73] Of *Armies of Europe at War* the *Evening Post* critic noted: 'These pictures were terrible in their truthfulness. Nevertheless they should prove powerful agents for recruiting, inasmuch as they show the enormity of the crimes of those responsible for the war and the necessity even at such tremendous sacrifices as the allied nations are making to prevent the perpetuation of such horrors for the sake of the lust for ambition and power.'[74]

Taking advantage of the popularity of cinema, the government distributed magic lantern slides (stills) giving details on enlistment, to be shown at movie screenings. 'It is well known,' stated an official memo, 'that picture theatres are largely patronised by the public at the present time, and particularly by many eligible men who probably would never see the ordinary posters or attend recruiting meetings . . . the exhibition of these slides will provide perhaps the only means of bringing home to many people the duty they owe to their country in the present great crisis.'[75]

After May 1915 there was a stronger sense that the country's war effort should be expanded and that passive patriotism, or apathy, should be turned into active engagement. By the middle of the year prominent newspapers and politicians had latched on to an ambition that the NZEF be expanded to 50,000 men so that volunteers could enlist immediately.[76] Even Allen seemed willing to reassess the degree of commitment that might be required: 'I think the urgency is so great now that even a married man must make sacrifices for the defence of the Empire, which means he should remember the defence of his own home, his wife and children.'[77]

Fundraising drives also embraced the ideal of a total effort, and mutual obligation. A Queen Carnival brochure, for example, noted: 'They are protecting our homes from the tyranny of the sword. *We will protect their homes from the wolf of want.* They are guarding our liberties from invasion. *We will guard their children from hunger.* They are shielding our women from dishonour. *We will shield their wives from privation.* They are spending the resources of their bodies. *We will spend the resources of our wealth.*'[78]

Alongside declining tolerance towards anyone considered a 'shirker' were the first calls for conscription. Often drawing on similar arguments being made in Britain, these calls presented conscription as a means of calmly, efficiently and fairly maintaining the country's commitment. As one letter to the editor in May asked, '[D]o you not think the time has arrived when something should be done to shake up the shirkers? As it appears to be impossible to shame this class into volunteering, why not try conscription? It would be much the fairer system.'[79]

above In 1915 this poster was imported from Britain and distributed in New Zealand with the country's coat of arms added to the lower right corner. It presented the war, and enlistment, as a defence of British honour and territory, and freedom from German aggression. ARCHIVES NEW ZEALAND, R22444093

below A Christchurch tram in 1915 adorned with patriotic decorations and propaganda promoting enlistment. They include references to the execution of the British nurse Edith Cavell and the *Marquette* tragedy, imported posters, a British flag and a portrait of Queen Alexandra. ALEXANDER TURNBULL LIBRARY, 1/1-007697-G

Some challenged this view, arguing that voluntary enlistment was producing a sufficient, indeed magnificent, response and that improving the conditions of service could sustain volunteer rates.[80] Such approaches often presented voluntary service as most consistent with notions of self-reliance and dutiful idealism and associated conscription with the militarism the war was said to be opposing. The cultural forces that would condemn shirkers and demand conscription were emerging.

An enormous expansion in the country's military contribution in the five months following May 1915 also renewed the sense that New Zealand was at war. In August the government agreed to raise and maintain two further battalions, and in October the reinforcement rate rose from 15 to 20 per cent for infantry and mounted rifles.[81] Put another way, the annual requirements to maintain the strength of the NZEF ballooned from 18,500 in May to 23,500 in August, and then to 30,000 in October.[82] Initially, these rising demands were met with record levels of recruiting, fired by strong reactions to the events of May. Recruiting had been, in Allen's words, 'considerably stimulated' since the publication of the casualty lists. As he noted days after learning of his son's death, 'As every troopship goes away I cannot help feeling sad that I have to remain behind and now that I have lost my soldier son I would that I could take his place.'[83]

He was not alone. Reporting on the sinking of the *Lusitania*, the *Evening Post* proclaimed that 'this is the day for a manly resolution by those who have not yet registered; this is the day for an answer to Germany's hate'.[84] The surge in recruiting occurred despite volunteers now being far less ignorant of the reality of the front line. As Labour MP John Payne said in an October 1915 speech, '[t]he men who are volunteering to-day know the hard and terrible phase this war has assumed; and while I do not wish to detract one iota from the spirit of those brave fellows who first volunteered, the men who volunteered to-day in the face of what we now know, with all the glamour of romance out of the situation, must be given credit for an ultra-bravery such as no ordinary situation could have called forth'.[85]

Accommodating this surge in commitments proved a monumental organisational task, which clashed disastrously with the decision to centralise training at Trentham. Built to accommodate a maximum of 2000 men, the camp housed 4000 troops at the end of 1914; by June 1915 the figure was over 7000.[86] The crowded conditions entirely overwhelmed sanitary arrangements and an outbreak of respiratory diseases, measles and cerebrospinal meningitis caused the deaths of 33 men and left thousands severely ill.[87] In early June details of the epidemic began to emerge in the country's media, stirring public outrage. The camp was evacuated in July and temporarily closed. Four new camps were established at Rangiotū and Hīmatangi (both near Foxton), Waikanae and Tauherenīkau in the Wairarapa. A royal commission was organised to investigate the situation and reforms set in train.[88] By the end of July Trentham was reopened, and by late 1915 the camp had been expanded to accommodate 4500 men in huts and a further 1200 under canvas. A second permanent camp was opened at Featherston in January 1916, with huts for 4500 men and tents for 3000.

Wellington Queen Carnival, winner MISS KITTY DOUGHTY (photo, W. H. Bartlett), representing Travellers, Warehousemen, Merchants and Central Club, contributed over £80,000 to N.Z. Patriotic Fund for wounded soldiers, sailors and dependants.

Christchurch Queen Carnival, winner NURSE MAUDE (photo, Steffano Webb), representing Tramway Employees, contributed about £12,000 to the Poor of Belgium Fund.

Ashburton Queen Carnival, winner MISS MAY HARRISON (photo, Halma), representing Rakaia district, contributed over £8,000 to the Belgian Relief Fund.

Dunedin Queen Carnival, winner MISS RUTH HERBERT SMITH (photo, Guy), contributed over £127,000 to the fund for the relief of N.Z. wounded soldiers.

South Canterbury Queen Carnival (Timaru), winner MISS KATHLEEN CASKEY (photo, Havelock Williams) representing Mackenzie Country, contributed about £6,000 to the Belgian Relief Fund.

Queen Carnivals were a popular means of raising money during the first years of the war. Pictured here are some successful carnival queens from 1915 who raised thousands, and in some cases tens of thousands, of pounds for relief funds. A. W. SHRIMPTON (ED.), COUNTESS OF LIVERPOOL'S GIFT BOOK OF ART AND LITERATURE. COURTESY NZ HISTORY

The expanding commitment to the war had similar effects on social organisation, and by late 1915 public financial support for the war became better organised and more businesslike.[89] A War Funds Act, passed in October, aimed to better coordinate and oversee charity efforts by establishing a National War Funds Council that would administer the money raised by registered patriotic societies. No one could collect funds without authorisation.[90] This did not always stop shady behaviour: in February 1916 a former inmate of Burnham Industrial School was sentenced to six months' hard labour after extracting significant sums of money from Christchurch citizens by impersonating a sergeant-major and claiming to be collecting for patriotic causes.[91]

Alongside such formal channels, there was a craze for Queen Carnivals, which combined fundraising with elaborate patriotic pageantry as women competed to raise funds and be crowned Queen. The carnivals reached a peak in 1915.[92] So much money was funnelled into wartime charities that retailers noticed their takings were down. In Invercargill, for example, shopkeepers remarked that the September 1915 Queen Carnival 'has been and is still absorbing a lot of ready cash'.[93]

Many found working for charitable causes a way to turn emotion into action; the grief-stricken and anxious found solace or distraction in pouring immense energy into such initiatives. Writing to her daughter Frances in England, Annis Hamerton, from New Plymouth, described her meeting with a recently bereaved mother: 'I saw Mrs H. Lepper dear brave woman. She is bearing up wonderfully, finds much to do Patriotic Socy, says it helps her.'[94] One Ashburton mother was 'so angry that she took after them [the Germans] in the only way she knew how. She cast about for a weapon. She couldn't find anything deadly that she could wield, but she could and did find something that demanded all her zeal. She flung herself into Red Cross work.'[95]

Local recruiting committees also became more extensive and better coordinated with official efforts. From October, plans were made to work more efficiently with the Defence Department and a recruiting board was established in February 1916.[96] Although the number and organisation of voluntary recruitment committees varied across regions, many were operating by the end of 1915. In October that year, for example, socially active citizens founded the Wellington War League, voluntarily staffing a recruiting office at the town hall, holding patriotic meetings, making their presence felt in the suburbs and issuing recruitment films to be played in picture theatres.[97]

The North Canterbury Recruiting Board stressed the importance of feminine influence in securing enlistments: 'Young men won't come to be talked at. Music can do much, speeches perhaps more, but girls can do most.' A Defence Department survey of training camp officers querying their assessments of recruits' motivations concurred on this point: 'A factor not to be underestimated also, is the stand taken by the women of the Dominion. This is a tremendous lever, and they used their influence unsparingly in [t]he cause of their Country.'[98]

Shame continued to be one means of wielding this influence, and over May and June 1915 giving white feathers (a symbol of cowardice) became much more widespread than in the previous year, with reports from Northland to Southland and many places in between.[99] Both

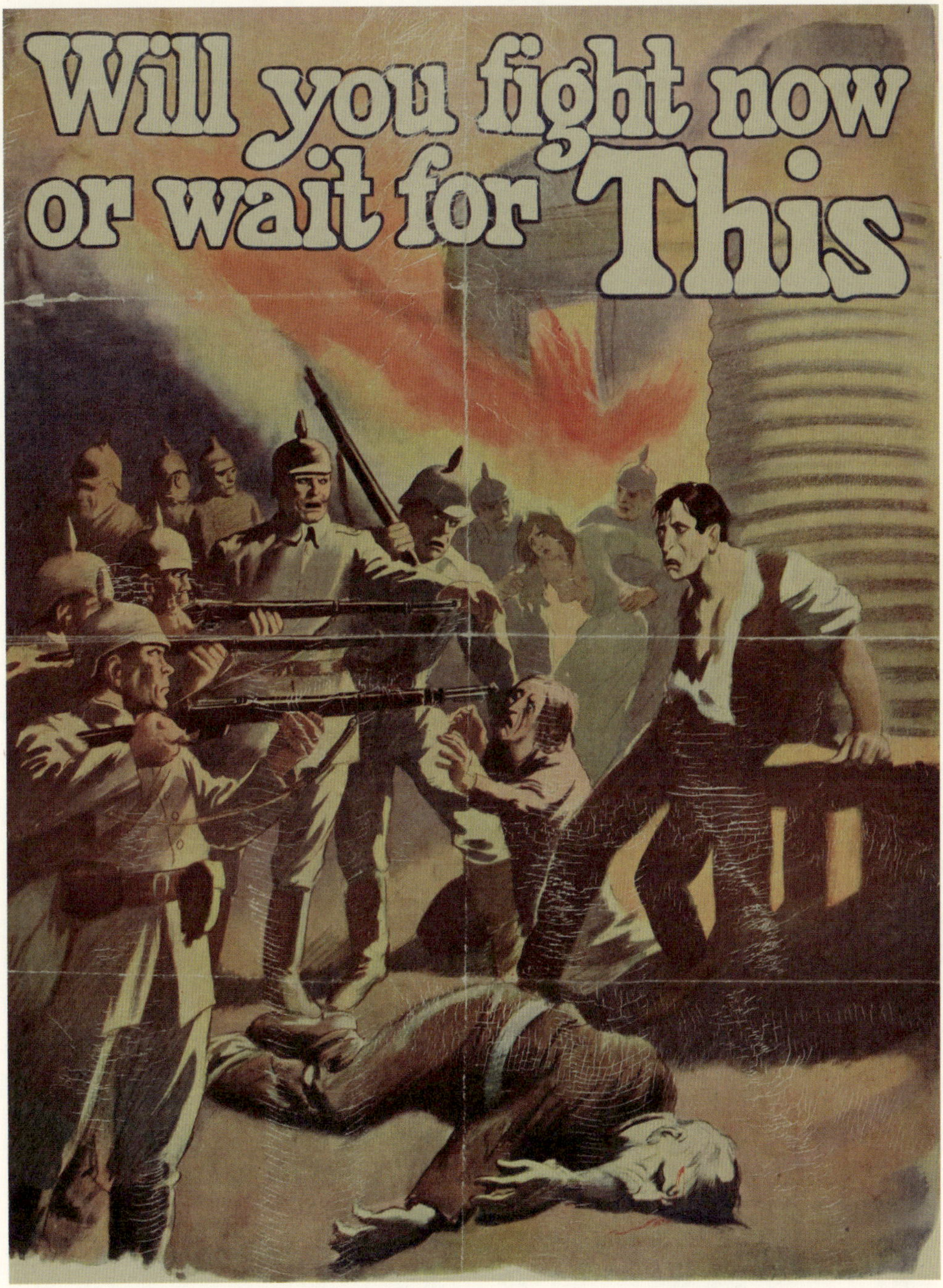

This Australian poster, drawn by Norman Lindsay, played to fears that a failure to stop the German Army in Europe could result in devastation in the South Pacific. It was one of several posters imported for use in New Zealand. ARCHIVES NEW ZEALAND, R22444226

editorials and letters to newspapers condemned the practice, citing instances where feathers had been given to returned soldiers or to men either under or over military age, including a 73-year-old veteran of the South African War.[100] In May 1915, members of the Christchurch White Feather League were chased off the streets by other women.[101] For some commentators, however, it was poor targeting, not the tactic, that was criticised:

> By all means let us encourage the patriotically spirited young New Zealander. By all means, also — but by sensible, decent methods — let the shirker, the coward be brought to book. But, girls — and boys — be sure of your marks! In any case remember that the writer of anonymous letters is one of the meanest persons on earth. And to send, anonymously, a white feather to a young fellow is the very quintessence of meanness unless you are sure of your facts.[102]

Lastly, as more and more men were sent to war, officials increasingly recognised the need to balance the needs of the military against those of industry and the community. A major concern in Britain was that volunteering had taken men employed in vital work, particularly in engineering, to the front. In New Zealand, Allen pointed out that so many doctors, medical students and nurses had departed that hospitals and general practices were short of staff. There was widespread concern, too, that there would be insufficient labour for the upcoming harvest. One possible response was the creation of a national register to best organise the country's resources. In July 1915 Allen said he was 'entirely in sympathy' with the idea, though he felt it would be 'of comparatively little value unless it covered not merely the men who are fit for the firing line but the whole of the labour of the country . . . I believe that before very long New Zealand will have to compile a register that will include everybody capable of serving either with the fighting forces or in connection with the industries.'

He also proposed that all male citizens between the ages of 17 and 55 be registered and an effort made to 'allot to every citizen his share in the national effort, either in the field or at home'.[103] Denying that such a step represented progress towards conscription, he said, in September, 'We have no idea of conscription in our minds, and I hope we shall never give it a thought.'[104] The resulting National Registration Act, passed on 1 October 1915, required men aged between 17 and 60 to register and those between 19 and 45 to signal their preparedness or otherwise to serve in a military or civil capacity.[105]

By now, many of the economic uncertainties of the early months of the war had faded in the face of an economic boom and a general, if uneven, prosperity. Food security improved as 'record weather-conditions' across much of the country made 1915 'an exceptional year', the commandeer system gave much desired stability and labour concerns were less about unemployment and more about shortages.[106] By early 1916, Allen could observe that 'the country is wonderfully prosperous'.[107] The situation in Wellington and the Wairarapa region was particularly positive: 'All skilled trades were very busy, and few, if any, skilled operatives were out of employment.' Textile workers, especially, had earned plenty of overtime thanks to 'the rush of work' and many shopkeepers were reporting record business. 'The large number of troops present in the city during the holidays caused something of a mild panic to restaurant and boarding-house keepers, and these, together with fancy-goods dealers and tobacconists, have had an exceptionally busy time.'[108]

Conditions in Auckland, too, were 'very much better than the corresponding period of last year', and in Dunedin trade had been good, with 'employment in practically every skilled industry plentiful'. There had been so much overtime that 'the Christmas and New Year holidays were very welcome, if only for the relaxation they afforded'.[109] Things were just as buoyant in the provinces, with money being freely spent. Even some export industries hit by trade disruptions were recovering: at the end of 1915 flaxmilling was 'in a flourishing condition' and the kauri gum market was 'much stronger than it has been since the war began'.[110]

There were many signs of greater disposable income. The consumption of relative luxuries, such as sugar, tobacco and beer, stayed largely around pre-war levels, gambling at racecourses steadily increased, cinema attendance swelled and Wellington Zoo reported a record attendance on Christmas Day 1915. The number of motorcars and bicycles grew rapidly during the war, with imports from the United States increasing as British manufacturers devoted much of their output to war production.[111] One furniture manufacturer noted unprecedented orders, often from working people, and often for 'astonishing costly articles such as chesterfields'.[112]

And people appeared to be saving: bank deposits rose from £25.2 million at the end of 1914 to over £36 million at the end of 1917.[113] A substantial proportion of the funds swelling Post Office Savings Bank accounts likely came from small farmers, but this was unlikely in the case of the Auckland Savings Bank, which had been established 'to encourage thrift among the industrial classes'. At the end of 1915, over half of its 56,500 customers, plus around 15,000 children in its 'penny bank', had less than £20 in their accounts, suggesting that it was not an institution greatly used by the better off.[114] Yet the net increase in the total amount deposited that year was £160,000. This was more than double the average figure in the previous decade, despite a drop in the number of depositors, 'probably to be accounted for by the number of young men who have gone to the war'. A further £263,000 accumulated during the 1916–17 year and there was modest growth in the number of depositors.[115]

Wellington and Wairarapa, the epicentres of military activity, became especially prosperous because of the war. The capital benefited from a massive expansion of state employment, particularly in the Defence Department but also in such areas as the Department of Imperial Supplies. The Public Works Department employed several hundred men for many months — the peak was over 1000 in December 1915 — to construct Featherston Camp.[116] Many were skilled tradesmen, who were paid higher rates than the labourers who tended to predominate on Public Works projects. Then there was the business generated by drafts of recruits moving through the camps — 3000 recruits through Tauherenīkau, 500 through Pāpāwai and the 7500 at Featherston, which represented by far the largest population centre in Wairarapa.[117]

Featherston consumed over 393 tons of meat and 33,000 gallons of fresh milk every four months, and most supplies came from local businesses.[118] The soldiers spent money at stores, laundries, watchmakers/jewellers, photographers and private hairdressers both inside and outside the camp. During local leaves, which lasted a day and allowed a late return, soldiers often took taxis to other Wairarapa towns. As Harry Hall wrote in October 1915, 'Last night we three shoreboys got leave and went to Greytown. We motored both ways and had a ripping change. We dined at the pub and afterwards had ham and eggs for supper with a small bowl of English ale . . . Our motor should only have held six but we had 15 aboard. The fare was 2/- per head and so the driver made 20/- each way out of it.'[119] Increased business in the Wairarapa was also due to family members sometimes staying in the district while their loved ones were being trained; many stayed at the Salvation Army's hostel in Featherston, which expanded to 130 rooms.

Another source of economic health was investment in the meat industry, much of it by farmers, who frequently had shares in meatworks. As a Labour Department officer remarked, 'Throughout the Wairarapa there is continued evidence of general prosperity in nearly all branches of trade: this is largely due to the high prices and good returns received by the farmer for almost everything he produces.'[120] Although ongoing problems with securing enough shipping, particularly refrigerated shipping for frozen meat, caused some freezing works to close early or to temporarily suspend killing, the principal response — the construction of new works and greater storage capacity — created many jobs over an extended period. In September 1916 the Masterton freezing works, despite being closed for the season, was 'employing 194 men on improvements and alterations'.[121]

The massive increase in government spending was another major contributor to the boom: the £300,000 a month being spent in March 1915 had shot up to £1 million a month by June 1916.[122]

Featherston Camp, officially opened on 24 January 1916, was New Zealand's largest training camp. In addition to 90 barracks, it had religious institutes, a canteen, a soldiers' club, hospital facilities, stables and shops. ARCHIVES NEW ZEALAND, R18288348

Equipping the thousands of NZEF reinforcements brought business to the textile, clothing and leather industries, while the preparation of transport vessels to take them overseas kept the ports occupied. Soldiers' dependants were also now receiving allotments of pay, separation allowances (for wives while husbands were away) and pensions and, in many cases, payouts on life insurance policies taken out by the men before they departed. Much of this money would have been spent, especially as the cost of living climbed, and retailers did well as a result. Allotments could be made to people other than a wife or a relation, and it appears to have been not uncommon for an allotment to be made to a woman as part of an engagement to marry. Sergeant Dick Travers VC made such an arrangement with Lettie Murray and named her the beneficiary of his will, drawn up a few months before he was killed in 1918, without telling his parents. His family, who had been unaware of Lettie's existence, made determined though unsuccessful attempts to have Travers's medals given to them.[123]

Besides high production demands and the removal of labour through military recruitment, war conditions also restricted the pre-war flow of immigrating British and Australian workers. Along with efforts to stretch the workforce with overtime came a greater level of participation, which included children and 'elderly men who would not be engaged in normal times'. It seems otherwise unlikely, for example, that James Cox, 70 years old and not in good health, would have been given a job at the Belvedere Cheese Factory in Wairarapa in April 1917.[124] Ideas of a dramatic rise in female employment and new uses of the female workforce also became common.[125]

Some businesses and some middle-class women, apparently drawing inspiration from what was happening in Britain, showed considerable enthusiasm for replacing male with female labour. According to one June 1916 advertisement, '"Women and more Women!" is the slogan in business circles to-day. Men are wanted at the front to save their country. Women are wanted here, to take up the duties of men who are fighting — to help the wheels of commerce to run smoothly.'[126]

Women were originally to be included in national registration — Allen claimed 'I certainly think it should include women' — but this ambition disappeared from the 1915 legislation.[127] Massey announced that women would not be included, as they 'had already done so much excellent service voluntarily that the Government felt they could be depended upon in future without registration'.[128] An unofficial Women's National Reserve emerged in mid-1915, chiefly driven by pioneering doctor Daisy Platt-Mills. The reserve sought to prepare registers of women willing to work in war-related fields, although female 'tram conductors, lift attendants, letter carriers, etc.' were also envisaged, to free men for military service and provide relevant training. Regional branches were founded, with some attracting hundreds of volunteers.[129] However, the enthusiasm of some women appears to have been met by official disinterest or reluctance. Liberal MP Thomas Wilford urged the government to use the reserve and another politician considered that 'many of New Zealand's best women were chafing at the bit'.[130]

Ultimately, the movement of women into the workforce, and particularly into industrial jobs previously done by men, was relatively modest. Although census figures showed that the female workforce grew from 75,244 in 1906 to 114,152 in 1921, the rate of growth was faster between 1906 and 1911 than through the war years. (It cannot be overstressed that being outside the workforce did not mean that women 'did not work'. Families were relatively large, the overwhelming majority of households did not have servants and home appliances were few and quite rudimentary.)[131] Most women continued to leave paid employment once they married and generally did not return unless they were widowed, separated or under strong financial pressure. Even among largely unmarried women aged between 15 and 25, the participation rate had risen by only 3.3 per cent by 1916. In that year New Zealand had only two female letter carriers, one female tram conductor and no female 'liftman' at all.[132]

Further, in contrast to the situation in Britain and Europe, where the massive expansion of armament and engineering industries opened new avenues for female employment, most New Zealand manufacturers that experienced wartime expansion were already major employers of women; big examples included the textile and leather industries but also less obvious trades such as confectionery and biscuit-making.[133] There were some exceptions to this pattern. The 1916 census revealed that a small number of women were working in cheese factories and a female cheesemaker gained a 'very satisfactory' score in the dairy factory cheese classes at Taranaki's 1916 Winter Show, apparently the first time a woman had competed at any show in those classes.[134] When, in January 1917, a Bay of Plenty cheese factory was faced with a serious labour problem, 'two ladies in the district volunteered their assistance, and have rendered yeoman service. Though the assistance in this case is only to be temporary, it is apparent that before long many of the factories will have to depend upon female help.'[135]

Likewise, many more women than before the war were doing a wide range of farm work, despite some arguing that they were unsuited to such labours.[136] In September 1916, a farmer in Auckland's St Heliers Bay Road, whose son and a farm hand had both enlisted, turned to his 16-year-old daughter, who proved 'equal to the occasion. She has taken in hand the management of her father's plough team, and last week might have been seen driving two horses harnessed to the plough. At the end of the week she had 3½ acres of ground turned over, and now she is busy discing the same paddock with a three-horse team.'[137] There were also substantial rises in the relatively small numbers of women describing themselves as 'milkers' or 'assistants' on farms, and a significant increase in the number calling themselves 'farmers', particularly, 'farmers, dairy'. This mirrored the continued expansion of the dairy industry, though while the total number of male farmers rose by 42 per cent over the 1911–16 period, the comparable figure for women stood at 416 per cent, from 1487 to 7667.[138]

More striking than an expansion of the female workforce, or its assumption of 'men's work', was its reconstitution across sectors. In 1911 domestic and industrial work were the largest sectors of the female workforce — 37 and 22 per cent respectively.[139] By 1916 female domestic workers had fallen to 32 per cent while the number of women in industry had increased minutely, thanks to a rise in female clerical workers; the number running machines fell. The greatest expansion, from 14 per cent in 1911 to 17 per cent in 1916, was in the 'professional' sector, which essentially meant office work. As early as the winter of 1915 the Secretary for

Labour, F. W. Rowley, noted that 'a good deal of female labour' was being employed in clerical work to replace 'the men who had gone abroad' and that some 'banks and legal offices were employing women clerks now'.[140]

Wellington, home of the head offices of government departments and large private enterprises, led the way. 'Before the war,' noted a November 1915 report, 'the Wellington branch of the Bank of New Zealand had no female employees. To-day the bank is employing some 30 women as shorthand writers and typists, and in other subordinate capacities. These women — the bank still hesitates to employ the mere girl — are doing work that previously was done by men, and the young men whose places they are taking are at the front.'[141] By the end of 1916 that figure had grown to 200 female clerks.[142] After public service exams were extended to women in mid-1916, the 1914 female public servant total of 1826 rose to 4153 by 1917.[143]

In the 'commercial' sector, principally employment in shops, increased consumer spending helped to ensure that the percentage of women grew from 14 per cent in 1911 to 17 per cent in 1916. As one newspaper reported in 1917, Auckland was emulating the capital: 'A legal firm here which employed two lady clerks in pre-war days now employs six. A local warehouse which at one time had 22 female clerks now finds work for 40. A mercantile firm used to find employment for nine ladies. It now employs 21. Some of the Auckland chemists now employ saleswomen.'[144] The number of women working in agriculture, and as mining clerks and accountants, also grew, from 8.3 per cent in 1911 to 10 per cent in 1916. The rural women were mostly female members of farm families, who in many cases would have been paid little or nothing for their labour. Many wives, daughters and sisters had probably been working beyond the traditional areas of garden and poultry before 1914; only when their menfolk left for war did it became undeniable that they were doing more than 'domestic duties'.[145]

Proportionately the greatest increase was in the comparatively small number of women engaged in 'transport and communication', which nearly doubled, although this dramatic jump was off a very small base — only 1.4 per cent of the female workforce in 1911 — and hid the fact that the increase was almost entirely in office work. Comparatively few women became conductors or taxi drivers, though in August 1917 Wellington's *Dominion* was advertising: 'For hire, on Ladies' Taxi Stand, opposite the Government Printing Office, 8-seater Hupmobile Car, No. 15. Mrs Percy Withers, Proprietress.'[146]

The Railway Department briefly employed limited numbers of women to clean carriages, not to drive trains. Asked why men for whom he was seeking exemption from military service could not be replaced by women, a railway official pointed out that female staff 'could not very well be employed on shift work at [isolated] country stations, and they could hardly be employed in shunting operations'. The Post and Telegraph Department did employ many women when its male staff enlisted, but later reduced some of its services because females could not work 'late at night'.[147]

The changing composition of the female workforce reflected women's employment preferences, especially when it came to the domestic sector. The reluctance of working women to take up domestic work in private households, where by far the largest number of jobs were available, was long established.[148] As a female Labour Department officer noted in 1916, women

above Outfitting New Zealand's soldiers required enormous labour. Here female workers operate masses of sewing machines in an unidentified garment factory. ALEXANDER TURNBULL LIBRARY, 1/1-008228-G

below Women workers at the Colonial Ammunition Company in Mount Eden, Auckland, in 1915. AUCKLAND WAR MEMORIAL MUSEUM TĀMAKI PAENGA HIRA, PH–CNEG–C17675 wanted defined work, reasonable hours and assured time off: 'I find these three factors are more important to a maid than high wages.'[149]

These reasons were partially responsible for the popularity of industrial work, which was controlled by awards: 'A good many women who formerly followed domestic work have now gone to work in the factories, and like the change. It usually only takes them a short time to get into the new work, and owing to the war bonus now being paid they earn better money than at the domestic work, and are not subjected to the restrictions usually imposed in connection with private domestic work — their life is more free.'[150]

Work preferences were also significant in explaining the static number of female factory workers. In February 1916 Christchurch employers were experiencing 'great difficulty' in finding 'adequate supplies of female labour, less being available than last year for tailoring, blouse and shirt making, some large firms being fully 15 per cent shorter-staffed'.[151] A Wellington newspaper, also reporting the 'dearth' of women in clothing factories, tailoring establishments, dressmaking rooms and laundries, pinpointed the reason: 'the ease with which girls are finding employment in offices, and especially Government offices. Even where wages and hours are equal the girls prefer the office employment, rightly or wrongly considering it, as one employer said, "more genteel." The principal inducement, however, is the much-increased money which the girls are able to earn at office work, the amount being, one employer stated, more than double the award rates ruling in factories.'[152] Writing to the *Auckland Star* in 1919, a correspondent styling herself 'Staunch N.Z. Woman' put it clearly: 'I myself began as a factory girl, but am now a successful business woman and I say all honour to those girls who instead of being content to remain at the same old thing for years, perhaps with an advancement of 2/6 or 5/- per annum, endeavour to reach the top of the ladder.'[153]

These developments stirred some angst from the male-as-breadwinner ethos that held men as the sole or major economic provider and was backed by state legislation.[154] Some employers openly stated their reluctance to take on female employees or stressed the temporary nature of their positions; one manager noted that his female employees should 'regard themselves as typists and shorthand writers, not as cadets in the banking business'.[155] Extensive training was often perceived as a wasted investment, given that many employers had promised to hold jobs for enlisted men and expected that female employees would marry and resign.

In one bank manager's view, a woman did not, 'as a rule', have a 'mentality . . . suited to ledger work', and was 'always more inclined to worry when she finds that her work is not yielding the proper result — to worry herself into a state in which she really makes her work harder'. Also, 'a woman's health is more liable to change than that of a man, so that the average woman is both temperamentally and physically unfitted for responsible ledger work'.[156] Another explained that as well as lifting a 'good many heavy bags of silver and gold in the course of a day', there was 'the physical labour of handling money across the counter all day long . . . Of course, if it were only a matter of handling clean, new bank notes a girl could do the work very well, because of the natural dexterity of her fingers. But the handling of large quantities of mixed change . . . would soon have a girl "tied up". The responsibility involves a strain for which a girl is physically and mentally unfitted.'[157]

But the war years somewhat eroded the male-breadwinner culture, particularly in a white-collar sector.[158] In October 1915, the secretary of the Auckland United Furniture Trades Union explained that he could only secure two signatures opposing the use of female labour amongst wire mattress makers and that '[t]his may mean that I will have to allow them to come into the business'.[159] A couple of months later, a large Auckland firm was reported to have 'made an innovation which, although at present not regarded at all favourably by the rest of the trade, promises to become inevitable. This is the introduction of women assistants in the Manchester department, where men have formerly held undisputed sway.'[160]

Many sectors proved keen to take on female workers, and the press frequently reported success stories.[161] At the end of March 1916, for example, two Auckland bank managers had only positive responses to 'girl clerks', especially compared with their London counterparts, who, the *Herald* explained, were unpunctual and required women inspectors 'to supervise their comings and goings'. In Auckland, said one manager, the women had proved 'an unqualified success [and] more than justified their appointment. We have 17 girls on our staff now, and have never had the slightest cause for complaint, either in their work or in their observance of office conditions.'

He spoke of 'the readiness with which the girls have adapted themselves to their new work', and their presence also seemed to have put the junior boys 'on their mettle' as 'they have no intention whatever of letting the girls get ahead of them'. The other manager mentioned 'the difficulty of getting the girls to stop coming before nine o'clock and to leave at five!'[162] When Wellington lawyer Heinrich von Haast was searching for 20 to 30 clerks from legal and commercial offices to work a voluntary afternoon shift at Army Base Records, he 'eventually found the office staffs so depleted as to render it impossible to get enough men, and, through my friends, got together a staff of women, who have been enthusiastic and efficient'.[163]

War may have upended conventional mourning practices, but those whose loved ones were killed overseas longed to make sense of their losses, to commemorate the dead and to offer solace to the living.[164] Condolence for the bereaved was often expressed in letters, many filled not only with comfort but also with assurances that the death of a son, husband or brother was meaningful, in both religious and patriotic terms: 'Your comfort is that long before he became a soldier of the Earthly King he had enlisted in the army of the King of Kings', 'your son was a gallant lad indeed he died a gallant death', 'I almost envy you the pride you must feel in the honour gained from the sacrifice he made and that you made for duty' were all frequently expressed sentiments.[165]

Other letters came from the front: commanding officers were required to write to and tell next of kin what had happened, and soldier comrades also sent accounts. These letters typically gave assurances that a loved one had suffered little or not at all, that he had not died alone and that he had been popular. Following the deaths of each of their sons, George, Herbert and William, the Knight family of Dannevirke received such letters from fellow soldiers: 'I had seen him shortly before [an attack], he was so bright & keen to carry out his task and his men had the greatest confidence in him'; 'Believe me lady he was a N.Z.er through and through and a boy that any parent can be proud of'; 'I can assure you he had a good burial and that we tidied up his grave very well'.[166]

In the public sphere, death notices carried the same messages of sacrifice and heroism: 'for Christ, King and country', 'For Christ and Humanity', 'He answered the call', 'He died for our liberty'.[167] The wider community also took up commemoration efforts: town halls, churches, lodges, sporting clubs and municipal institutions held ceremonies and recognised the dead. Despite the relatively low level of adult church attendance, the war spurred many New Zealanders to go to church.[168] In March 1915, Edgar Cruttwell, a former Royal Navy officer and acting vicar in the Canterbury resort township of Hanmer Springs, noted in his diary that '[p]eople in the Dominion show such scanty interest & mostly have no idea yet seemingly that the Empire's existence is at stake'. By May, however, he could report a congregation of 'fully 50 & considering there are hardly any visitors left it meant half the population of Hanmer were there & it did cheer one's heart. Imagine my surprise to see Dr & Mrs Duncan there, Mr Christiansen who has never entered the church door, Mr Stewart the same, & several others had come miles & never before put in an appearance.'[169]

All denominations faced the task of consoling those in mourning and sanctifying the dead. Throughout the country, clergy spoke of soldiers who had acted in an exemplary fashion, with allusions to Christ-like sacrifice. John 15:13 was often quoted: 'Greater love hath no man than this, that he lay down his life for his friends.'[170] Assurances that the dead were at peace and that loved ones would be reunited with them in the afterlife were also universal. In 1915 the editor of *Church News* asked readers to 'think of our brave soldiers marching on, in advance of us, mustering in the greater world that comes next to this . . . They are not sadly looking back, unless it may be that we make them sad. And if your very best and dearest is among them, how would he like you to pity him now?'[171]

The sacrifice made by women, especially mothers, when they lost their men, became another common motif.[172] As Bishop Averill claimed, 'what greater joy can a mother experience . . . than the knowledge that her life and example have helped her boy to live a noble life, and, if need be, to die a noble death?'[173] When the mother of 24-year-old Wilf Knight from Waipori, who was fighting with the Australian Light Horse, heard that he had been killed at Gallipoli, she is reported to have said, in public at least, 'Well, I have no regrets, because he died for a just cause, and if I had a dozen sons I would not object to every one of them going to fight for their King and country and the flag of liberty.'[174]

The impulse for communal recognition also produced some of the first war memorials. Three months after the Gallipoli landings, a number of schools were following the suggestion of the Auckland Education Board to plant trees in memory of former students, and in mid-December 1915 the Auckland Harbour Board lit a memorial beacon to commemorate former employees who had departed for war service.[175] Public demand soon grew for a day of remembrance, and throughout February and March 1916 proposals were submitted and town and council meetings held to plan a ceremony marking the anniversary of the Gallipoli landings.[176] Proposals, including, among other things, a half-holiday, united memorial services,

THE AUCKLAND WEEKLY NEWS

With which is Incorporated "THE WEEKLY GRAPHIC AND NEW ZEALAND MAIL."

AUCKLAND, N.Z., THURSDAY, JULY 27, 1916.

THE CASUALTY LIST.

This composite image links the fighting at the front with a woman grieving in New Zealand. She is holding a newspaper carrying the latest casualty list.
AUCKLAND WEEKLY NEWS, 27 JULY 1916, P. 35

above A Feilding crowd gathers for a public service on Anzac Day 1916. FEILDING PUBLIC LIBRARY

below Nelson's first Anzac Day service on the Cawthron Steps. NELSON PROVINCIAL MUSEUM, F. N. JONES COLLECTION 311332 military parades and patriotic concerts, were forwarded to the prime minister. Much thought went into the desired tone and, consistent with establishment conceptions of a holy day, it was argued that commercial activities and sporting events should be suspended; as a meeting of the Wellington region's mayors stated, 'there should be nothing of a pantomime character about the day's proceedings'.[177]

On 6 April 1916, the 25th was gazetted as a half-holiday, starting at 1 p.m., to commemorate 'Anzac Day'. Massey backed the concept of united services: 'It is specially fitting that on this occasion special services of public worship be held by all religious denominations, and I therefore appeal to all ministers of religion and all congregations to hold such services on behalf of the people of the Dominion at such hours during the forenoon or afternoon as are found convenient.' He also agreed with calls for a sober ambience — 'the day should not be marked by the holding of sports or similar forms of entertainment' — and for practical patriotism: 'opportunity should be taken for all recruiting bodies and others to arrange patriotic meetings for the evening, not only to commemorate the anniversary, but also with a view to assisting the recruiting campaign'.[178]

Not all were persuaded. On 22 April H. B. Goertz of Port Chalmers wrote angrily to the *Otago Daily Times*, asking how Massey's 'right worthy' intention that Anzac Day should not be 'devoted to festivity, pleasure-seeking, and junketing [was] to be reconciled with the action of the Government in issuing "holiday excursion tickets" on that day?' He feared it was 'only too likely — taking Good Friday as a precedent' that the excursions would be popular, 'though the callous dancing on a new-made grave would not be more ghastly in my humble judgment'.[179] And although many denominational leaders saw Anzac Day as a chance for the church to join the wider community, some were reluctant. The Anglican Bishop of Waiapu, for example, forbade a united service in Napier's cathedral on Anzac Day, though his attitude led to 'an indignation meeting' in town. 'Ministers of other Churches are greatly incensed at the bishop's action, and the local papers contain many inspired letters.'[180]

Some of the more broad-minded of the clergy used their discretion and ignored such instructions. Many Anglicans were present at a united service in Rotorua and a prominent supporter of the Napier cathedral maintained that 90 per cent of 'the thinking adherents of our church . . . do not coincide with the course taken'.[181] Smaller towns tended to hold combined services whereas city dwellers had more denominational options. Some very small settlements appear to have celebrated Anzac Day on the last day of the school term because of its proximity to Easter. Many schools, too, held a service on 20 April. As well as holding events and major church services on 25 April, Christchurch hosted a fundraising military demonstration in Hagley Park and on the streets of the city on 11 March, which the local papers referred to as 'Anzac Day'.[182] Some organising committees went with half-day celebrations, while others opted for a full day.

The first Anzac Day took a broadly similar form throughout the country. Crowds gathered to witness processions of returned soldiers and attend ceremonies presided over by officials and religious leaders held at civic centres or, in smaller communities, in local parks. There were speeches and sermons; people sang the National Anthem and hymns that would become standards for future ceremonies: 'Abide with Me', 'O God Our Help in Ages Past' and 'All People that on Earth do Dwell'. Rudyard Kipling's poem 'Recessional', with its refrain of 'Lest we forget', was widely read. Hāwera's service quoted Laurence Binyon's 'Ode of Remembrance', though the pledge 'we will remember them' was not a customary part of national proceedings.[183] Other features that would become conventional in future Anzac ceremonies — dawn parades, the two minutes' silence, poppies — were absent.

Speeches, sermons and newspaper articles all expressed similar themes: veneration of the dead; pride in the conduct of New Zealand soldiers; the sense that their deeds demonstrated a new national standing (typically as a nation within the British Empire); the country's moral obligation to recognise the sacrifices made by individuals, families and communities; and a call for renewed devotion to secure a victorious end to the war. Averill's applauded Anzac Day speech at Auckland's town hall concisely hit all of these points:

> [W]e know enough to refute the foolish idea that our boys died in vain . . . They represented New Zealand's sense of honour and gratitude, New Zealand's loyalty to King and Empire, and by giving their lives they have helped to weld the Empire in imperishable bonds. They have proved the worthiness of the nation to take its place in the great family of free nations in the Empire . . . It remains for us to carry on the work that has been commenced so nobly and keep the sword unsheathed until tyranny has been overcome.[184]

Massey's message described the 'heroic self-sacrifice and endurance displayed by New Zealanders and their Australian comrades at Gallipoli . . . as one of the finest and most memorable feats of arms ever accomplished by men of the British race'. Their 'gallant deeds and magnificent courage appeal for further national effort, so that the lives so freely surrendered in the cause of Liberty may not have been spent in vain. But with all its memories, and its inspiration, Anzac Day brings its responsibilities, and reminds us that we must at all costs continue to do our full share in the present Empire crisis.'

Ward expressed similar sentiments: 'New Zealand does well to hold in proud and grateful remembrance the historic day on which her sons affirmed with their devotion and their blood her right to stand beside the Mother Country . . . Let us then resolve to-day, each for himself, with the hallowed graves on the hillsides of Gallipoli as our witnesses, that the judgement [of posterity] shall be one we can face without misgivings, without regrets, and with the full and certain knowledge of duty well and faithfully done.'[185]

Recruiting efforts were part of 25 April 1916, and of subsequent wartime Anzac Days. In a public statement James Allen bluntly noted, 'There can be no better celebration of Anzac Day by New Zealanders of military age who remain in New Zealand than by their following the steps of Anzac heroes.'[186] This had some effect. On 26 April the *New Zealand Herald* could report that 'The parade of the Anzac heroes evidently stirred a number of eligible men, and there was a mild recruiting boom in the city yesterday.'[187]

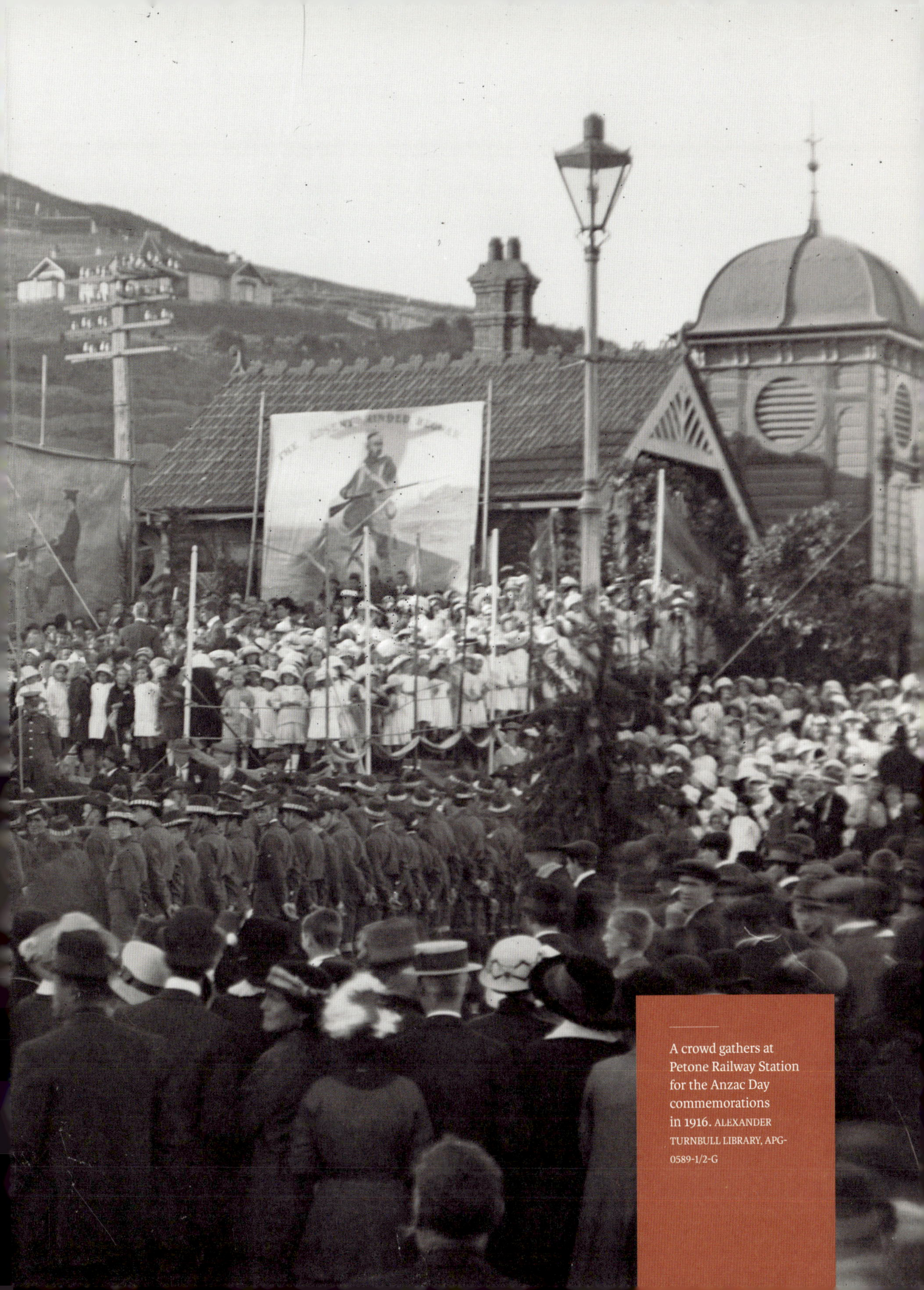

A crowd gathers at Petone Railway Station for the Anzac Day commemorations in 1916. ALEXANDER TURNBULL LIBRARY, APG-0589-1/2-G

THE EVENING NEWS WAR MAP
GERMANY
THE EVENING NEWS WAR MAP
EVENING NEWS
RUSSIA'S
RISING TIDE

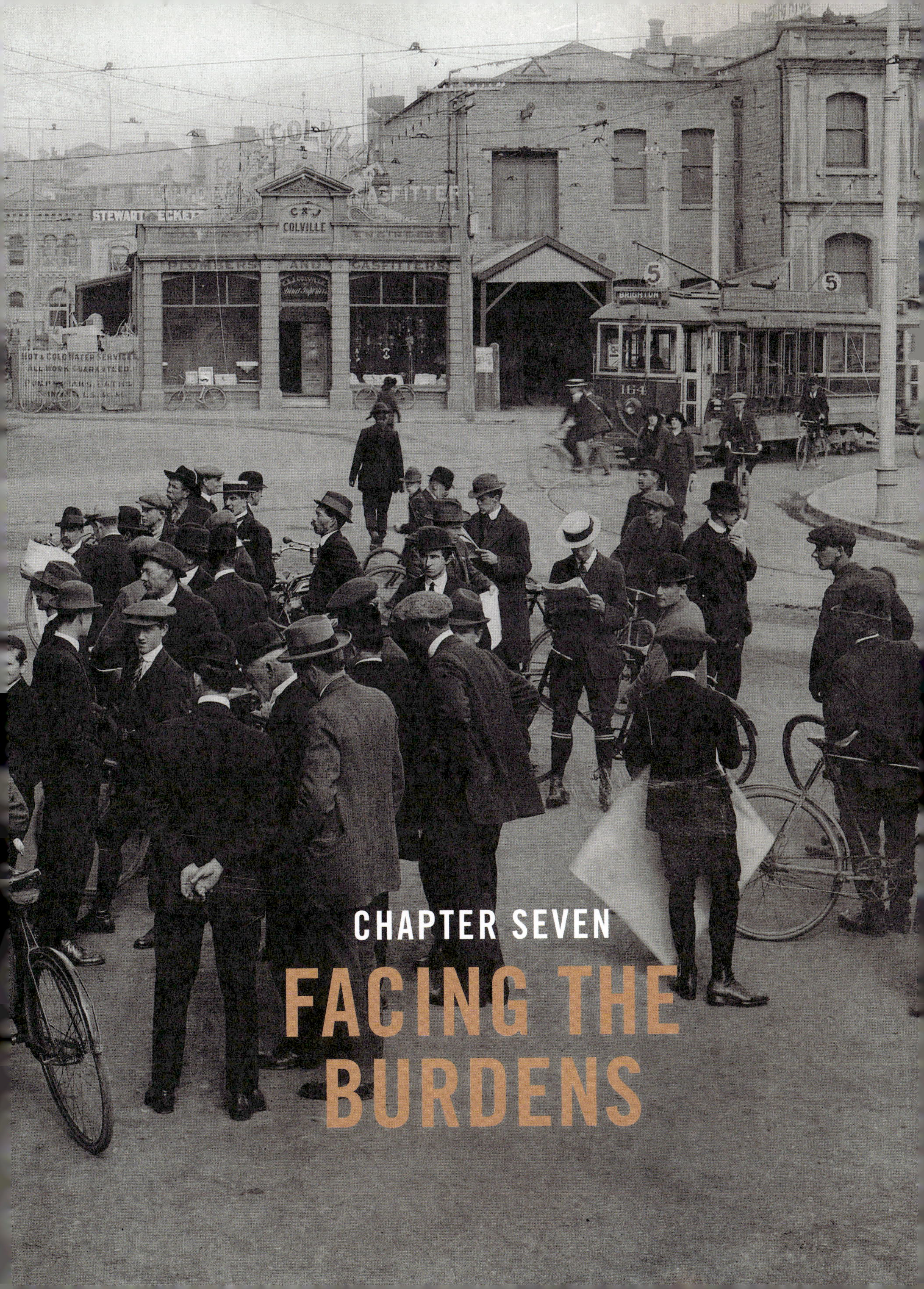

CHAPTER SEVEN

FACING THE BURDENS

previous pages
Men gathered in Cathedral Square, Christchurch, to read the latest war news and look at maps of the positions of armies in Europe. ALEXANDER TURNBULL LIBRARY, 1/1-008414-G

In an almost paradoxical fashion, intensifying mobilisation both rallied and destabilised New Zealand society. The enormous community efforts made over 1915–16 occurred as society's moral and material bonds were frayed by the disappearance of thousands of men from households, communities and the economy, and disagreement over how New Zealanders should fairly bear the growing burdens imposed by the war. Polarisation, weary disengagement and protests resulted in some challenging the legitimacy of the war itself. Some of the most notable divisions appeared along ethnic, religious and political lines, but frustration was apparent even on the part of those entirely committed to the war. In April 1916 Allen, writing to Sir Thomas Mackenzie (New Zealand's high commissioner in London), described the Gallipoli campaign as '[s]o ill-conceived and mad a proposition it is difficult to believe it could have come from British brains . . . I know from correspondence with men whose judgement I thoroughly trust that they agree with me.'[1] The social–political consensus backing the war held, but its conditional nature became more apparent as positions asserted in August 1914 were renegotiated in the face of new expectations.

Compared with other nations, mobilisation was less disruptive to New Zealand — a consequence of recruitment being directed towards young, unmarried men and the relatively limited opening of male work to women — but there was some relaxing of established modes of social control and some growth in female economic independence. Anxieties about deteriorating standards were sparked by the sight of drunken soldiers misbehaving when on leave. Some, like Wellington's Anglican bishop Thomas Sprott, were willing to blame 'foolish civilians for luring the young soldiers into bars and "shouting" for them, excessively' but others saw only young men, away from home and under the influence of alcohol, making thorough nuisances of themselves.[2] In September 1915, for example, four intoxicated soldiers on the night express train from Wellington to Auckland climbed onto the roof of their carriage, ending up 'black with soot from head to foot' after going through tunnels. They were eventually dislodged by railway staff at Taumarunui, a town which, reportedly much to their disgust, they found to be 'dry'.[3]

Prostitution and a general loosening of sexual propriety also caused concern. As *Truth* insinuated, 'War brings many horrors and loosens the social rein in such a way that the unwary one in search of heaps of daring excitement must come a cropper.'[4] There was a sharp increase in the number of illegitimate children, whose fathers registered their paternity after marrying their mothers — 167 in 1915, 281 in 1916 and 309 in 1917.[5] In May 1916 *Truth* reported on the evidence given in the Wellington magistrate's court of Constable Joseph Gunn concerning Emily Thomas, who had a shop and a house in Cambridge Terrace. He had seen 'soldiers and civilians there by the score. The King's army was so well represented in the locality that it had become known as "Gallipoli".' Sergeant James Fitzpatrick agreed. He had observed 'what appeared to be an army corps or two marching in and out . . . and they all seemed to bivouac at Emily's house'.[6] Women who boarded together to cope with rising costs (especially Wellington's soaring rents) and to enjoy some congenial and socially acceptable company were also ensnared by concerns about moral standards. Such households inevitably attracted the attention of young men, and the suspicions of moral guardians.

A concerted effort to reassert moral codes and reinforce boundaries created an atmosphere of moral revivalism.[7] Illiberal restriction became pronounced during the war years, further fuelled by war-related passions — outrage, righteousness and sorrow. In a reaffirmation of bold-hearted, dutiful masculinity, 'shirkers' were denounced as 'cowardly undesirable specimens of manhood'.[8] The traditional women's roles of reproduction, mothering and supporting men overseas by maintaining a warm (yet faithful) hearth were also reinforced.[9] Prominent preachers presented the war as a crucible that would purify and redeem society or argued that society must reform itself to be capable or worthy of victory. A Methodist's description of the war as 'the fiery ordeal that the world will pass to a finer and gentler civilisation if only spiritually-minded men and women will be steadfast in their testimony, while they are valiant in their sacrifice' was typical.[10] Others conveyed a similar message in more secular tones, calling for individuals to curtail unnecessary consumption and cast off vices.

Many social activities were denounced as frivolous and/or irreverent distractions from the serious and solemn duties of the war. Gambling and alcohol were damned as stealing time, energy and money from the war effort and there were repeated claims that if sportsmen were 'able to play football they were able to go to the war'.[11] Speaking on the need for a crackdown on prostitution, police superintendent John Ellison remarked that 'one need not wonder at the number of young people wearing glasses, artificial teeth, and other evidences of constitutional weakness when female vultures are able to fatten and become wealthy while they disseminate disease in a wholesale manner'.[12]

There was anxiety, too, that commercial exploitation might defile sacred shibboleths. In June 1916 the *Free Lance* was noticing 'an inclination on the part of the pushful shopkeeper to make business capital out of this war. It is bad enough to have Gallipoli and Dardanelles [sic] used in this way, but for goodness sake, for the sake of common decency, do not let us have the noble name of Anzac so degraded . . .' The paper feared the country would soon be 'deluged with advertisements of Anzac Tooth Powder, Anzac Antibilious Pills, Anzackilla, the Infallible Rat Poison, or such abominations as "Try Our Best Anzac Tea — Double Strength," or "Step Right In and Inspect Our Anzac Silk Nighties at three and elevenpence three farthings — Just the thing For the Soldier's Best Girlie."'[13] Even some findraising methods were challenged.

The WCTU argued against raffles and criticised the inappropriately festive nature of Queen Carnivals. In Wellington, the Reverend Dr James Gibb asked how many more dead and wounded men were required 'before the people of this country will awake to the seriousness of the situation and the hatefulness of carnivals . . . Hateful indeed must all this frivolity and gambling be to every thoughtful mind in the community.'

A correspondent to *Truth*, writing under the pseudonym 'Common Sense', complained of being 'bailed up by strong young men dressed in the garb of a first prize idiot, their faces daubed with grease paint and their general appearance consistent with a lunatic's masquerade. Now, while I do not doubt the ardor, nor the idiocy, of these proceedings, I do protest that this is not the correct way of raising the necessary funds to provide for the brave boys at the front.'[14]

Although such reactions did not go unchallenged, with some arguing, for example, that sport was an important means of maintaining morale, they clearly had an impact. In May 1916, the Auckland Rugby Union announced that no player aged over 20 on 1 April would be permitted to play in the union's competition during the war.[15] That year specific powers were introduced under war regulations to suppress drinking, prostitution and venereal disease by, among other initiatives, banning women from entering or remaining near bars after 6 p.m. and the practice of 'shouting' alcoholic drinks for soldiers.[16]

Tensions also developed around the war's inequitable social impacts. Although the rise in grocery prices slowed during the second half of 1915, and was even briefly reversed in the early months of 1916, the cost of meat and dairy products, and staples such as bread, continued to increase.[17] There was further austerity as shipping constraints reduced most imported commodities. For example, stocks of imported 'apparel and ready-made clothing' dropped by a fifth between 1914 and 1918, while the largest category of footwear fell by a quarter, hats and caps by a third and imported woollen blankets virtually disappeared.[18] What was available also became less affordable: clothing prices rose an alarming 140 per cent over the course of the war.[19] Residential rents levelled out, and in many instances fell, throughout most of the country, benefiting tenants but not their landlords. The notable exception was Wellington, where rates rose steeply, partly because the nearby military camps drew more people to the city.[20]

By the winter of 1916, wartime strains on working conditions were increasingly obvious. Seasonal unemployment and underemployment had largely disappeared and the conse-quences of a tightened labour market were apparent especially in sectors depleted by recruitment.[21] Coal mining was among those industries suffering labour shortages. At the end of May 1915, the Blackball mine was 'still in urgent need of truckers', at the beginning of July it was claimed that 'a hundred experienced miners could be placed' in Auckland province, and by November Wellington factories were 'depleted of operatives very considerably, and this has caused many employers to readjust their staffs, and in many cases to refuse orders'.[22] By the end of the year, the nation's freezing works were reporting a shortage of butchers, and at the beginning of 1916 Dunedinites were struggling to secure carpenters, painters and other tradesmen involved in outfitting troopships.[23] Later that year, 'several industries, principally in the retail trades' had lost so many staff that it was 'difficult to supply orders punctually and regularly'.[24]

The other side of the wartime boom was an economy with marked disparities and constraints. One clothing manufacturer, for instance, noted the 'satisfactory' impact of import restrictions, but consumers were more likely to notice restricted goods and rising costs.[25] Likewise, the prosperity of this period largely bypassed those reliant on fixed incomes and static returns from investments and pensions. The moratorium on pre-war mortgages made it extremely difficult for those dependent on that common form of retirement income to enforce payment of interest, to foreclose or to sell their investment. Returns from rental properties, another common source of retirement income, generally lagged far behind the ascending cost of living. In the winter of 1916 Miss Morrison of the Auckland Women's Branch of the Labour Department reported:

> The special feature about the last few months' operations has been the number of old-age pensioners who have applied for some kind of light employment for a few hours per day, to help them to eke out a living. Many of these have only their pension to exist upon, and they find even by practising the strictest economy, with the present high cost of living, and having to pay for a room, that they are unable to exist upon 10s. per week, and necessity drives them to the Department for help. These old people are not suitable for employment, yet their need is sincere.[26]

Those living on returns from investments (whose returns improved), professionals (who often benefited from the enlistment of their competition) and those paid hourly (who gained higher wages, 'considerable overtime earnings' and the leverage of labour shortages) were the major economic winners; those on fixed pay were the most severely affected.[27]

To many New Zealanders it seemed that some were making record profits while others were making sacrifices. Pre-war labour polemics attributing price rises to market manipulation by business rings intensified, with condemnation of 'mutton magnates', 'wool kings', 'butter brigands' and 'beef barons', and with caricatures of the capitalist 'Mr Fat' repurposed to damn war profiteers.[28] In an example of the naming and shaming similar to that some proposed for shirkers, in December 1915 the *Maoriland Worker* printed the names and incomes of those 'rich men made richer by the war'.[29] Unease about profiteering also played out within the business community. Indeed, the initial description of war-related profits as 'blood money' appears to have come from a prominent Manawatū farmer, Peter McHardy.[30] Weeks later, the chairman of the Whangarei Co-operative Dairy Company, Henry Wakelin, also 'declared that the high prices for butter-fat were like blood money. They knew what was the cause of the high prices to their sorrow. He hoped the shareholders would show their gratitude.'[31]

Labour shortages and the need to maintain production proved ideal grounds to boost union power and reorganise militant labour, in the aftermath of 1913.[32] At the end of 1915 the membership of unions registered under the Industrial Conciliation and Arbitration Act stood at 67,661 and steadily climbed to reach 82,553 by 1919.[33] In the face of rising discontent and increasing union leverage, the trend of industrial truces begin to erode. The 20 industrial disputes of 1914, involving 4089 workers, had fallen to eight in 1915 involving 295 workers, but the pattern started to reverse in 1916, with 899 workers taking part in 15 disputes.[34] Some industrial action was clearly related to war production: for example, complaints that industries were using sweated female labour became a political concern.[35] In March 1916 the female employees at the Wellington Woollen Manufacturing Company went on strike, demanding a 10 per cent pay rise. They were working 60-hour weeks and were paid 60 per cent less than male employees. They won their increase, but the union was fined £50 for participating in an illegal strike.[36]

As the war dragged on, there were increasing arguments that the costs of the war should be spread as evenly as possible and that all sectors of society should make, or should be forced to make, fair contributions. By late 1915, tensions over 'equality of sacrifice' were perhaps most evident regarding recruitment; the system's long-term viability, and even its ultimate desirability, were being questioned. Champions of the volunteer system noted the pleasing congruence of volunteer soldiers with ideas of dutiful, self-reliant masculinity and the struggle of free societies against tyrannical militarism. They could also point to an impressive record: by 31 October 1915 around 54,155 men had registered for military service, a figure that continued to exceed requirements or capacities to train and field men. At that stage 35,638 men had been or were being trained and the strength of the NZEF overseas was nearly 24,000, including a reserve force in Egypt. They might also have noted that the volunteer system was continuing to deliver remarkable results and volunteer totals were higher in 1916 than in 1915.[37]

There was growing anxiety, however, that volunteering was sparing 'shirkers' at the expense of the dutiful. Social and political commentary about degenerate, lazy, immoral or irresponsible men avoiding service abounded, and was typically accompanied by insistence on corrective measures.[38] Traditional social divisions were also discernible in shirker hunting, with commentators homing in on what they saw as Catholic apathy or workers' over-representation in enlistments.[39]

The results of volunteering were also increasingly being weighed against rapidly escalating demands: 12,000 men were sent to camp in the first eight months of 1915, and 12,500 in the last four months.[40] Moreover, the ambition to expand British forces on the Western Front for a great mid-1916 offensive promised no respite. As part of this strategy, the NZEF, stationed in Egypt after evacuation from Gallipoli, was reorganised into the New Zealand Division, which officially came into being in March 1916. The division was shipped to France in early April while the Mounted Rifles were deployed, as part of the Anzac Mounted Division, to the Sinai. Compared with the 8000-strong Main Body deployed some 15 months before, New Zealand's major contribution was now an 18,000-strong infantry division with artillery, engineering and pioneer elements bringing the total force to over 25,000.[41] This reorganisation consumed the reserve, and reduced the infantry's reinforcement rate from 20 to 15 per cent.

Although the government accepted these new commitments, Allen, Massey and Robin were all anxious about the finite nature of the country's manpower and the reinforcement-hungry nature of infantry commitments.[42] On 15 February 1916, Allen wrote to Godley noting that providing and maintaining a division would prove a large task: 'I do hope that you will not without the very gravest consideration suggest that more be done by New Zealand. We have supplied considerably more than our share of soldiers as compared with the Commonwealth [of Australia] or with Canada and the willing horse cannot be worked until it drops.'[43]

A system of voluntary enlistment was inevitably going to face difficulties as the pool of young, adventure-seeking, relatively unattached men who had manned the NZEF through the early part of the war grew smaller. Meeting ongoing demands would increasingly mean appealing to a wider cross-section, including older men with more obligations and those who had less interest in fighting. The tensions of some potential soldiers is captured in Harrold Ennor's diary: 'I should like ever so much to be at the Front. I'm not a fighter but I don't like to think of the fellows "out there" doing all the work. I can't see my way clear to go I feel that the office work is so very important. Perhaps I am helping that way. I hope so.'[44]

In October 1915, even before the end of the Gallipoli campaign, Allen made a public appeal for married men to consider themselves as potential recruits: 'Recruiting has proceeded very well in the past, but the strain is now becoming more severe. I am making a special appeal now to the unmarried men of military age who have not yet registered . . . We are not exempting the married men from the appeal for recruits. The married man who feels that his responsibilities will let him enlist now is wanted.'[45] Changes were also made to boost the supply of eligible men. After the departure of the Seventh Reinforcements, in October 1915, the equal quotas system was replaced with a proportional system in an effort to balance demands against each military district's capabilities.[46] In November, the physical requirements for enlistment were reduced — height and chest measurements were both

Māori soldiers gathered outside Auckland's town hall for a departure ceremony, which included a traditional farewell, in September 1915. AUCKLAND WEEKLY NEWS, 23 SEPTEMBER 1915, PP. 43, 46

decreased and the previous weight limit of 12 stone was abolished — and the maximum age was raised from 40 to 45.[47]

Various incidents illustrate heightened sensitivities over shirking in late 1915 and almost certainly affected public confidence in voluntary recruitment. There were suspicions about the noticeable jump in marriage rates in the latter part of 1915 and the first quarter of 1916 and allegations that eligible men were attempting 'evasion by matrimony'.[48] Allen warned women 'not to marry a man who is going to hide behind you and so escape his duty . . . If any man does not think you are worth fighting for, then he is not worth being your husband.'[49] Although men continued to marry before they embarked — there were 51 weddings at Featherston in 1916 following the opening of the military camp, more than double the number in previous years — many suggested that the looming national registration had brought many wedding dates forward.[50]

As the *Official Year-book* noted, 'The large number of marriages in 1915 included many that in the ordinary course of events would have been celebrated in 1916, but were hastened by the operation of the National Registration Act, and the desire of many men to be shown in the register as married men and to obtain certain anticipated advantages or escape certain obligations.'[51] These 'anticipated advantages' referred to the almost universal belief that single men should enlist before married men and especially before married fathers. Even at the beginning of 1916, two married men were removed from the West Coast quota for the Twelfth Reinforcements 'on account of objections by their wives'; one had six children.[52] The prospect of family men taking up the slack while single men avoided enlistment would remain a major issue. As the *Evening Post*'s editor proclaimed in late 1915, 'New Zealand cannot afford to be sacrificing husbands and fathers on the unholy altar of single men's selfishness.'[53]

There was more direct evasion, too, with reports of eligible men leaving New Zealand to avoid service. On 12 November 1915, the *New Zealand Herald* reported that firemen on the San Francisco-bound *Moana*, docked in Wellington Harbour, were refusing to work 'because among her passengers were some 58 young men of military age, alleged to be fleeing for safety to the shelter of neutral America'. In the 'expectant crowd', all eyes 'were on a knot of very undemonstrative, sullen, anxious-looking young and middle-aged men hanging over the rail in the steerage section of the deck'. Eventually, the *Moana* did depart: 'At the first motion of the ship all sign of anxiety vanished from the men's faces. They cheered and waved their hats for joy, and there was a distinct note of triumph and defiance in their shouts.' The paper also noted that Massey had been told about 'the exceptional number of young men leaving the Dominion by each boat for America. This matter was now receiving attention.'[54]

There was further angst when the results of the National Registration in December were published. These revealed that, of the 303,704 respondents, 193,341 were eligible for service; the remainder included men over the eligible age, returned soldiers, those unfit for service and foreign subjects. Of those eligible, 112,778 (58 per cent) were willing to enlist; 44,838 (23 per cent) were not but would willingly serve in a civil capacity; and 35,725 (18 per cent) were unwilling to serve in either capacity.[55]

In the considerable discussion that followed, there was a particular focus on the 8821

THE DIRTY SNEAK.

PETTICOAT COVER.

The Shirker: "Ye cannot harm me now!"

above The *Observer* derides the 'shirker' who abandons New Zealand for neutral America.

NEW ZEALAND OBSERVER, 20 NOVEMBER 1915, P. 13

below The *Observer* references wider suspicions over the rising marriage rate in 1915 and shows a 'shirker' hiding behind a timely marriage to avoid serving.

NEW ZEALAND OBSERVER, 11 DECEMBER 1915, P. 13

single men and widowers without dependants within the 35,725 stating they were unwilling to serve. Their reasons were compiled and published in January 1916. The five most common explanations were business obligations (2237), health (2692), religious or conscientious objections (819), family reasons (215) and favouring the introduction of conscription (210). Eleven respondents simply noted that they were afraid.[56]

Doubts over the ability of volunteering to meet future manpower requirements came to the fore in December 1915 when the Eleventh Reinforcements experienced an unusually slow rate of enlistment. This was attributed to the demands of the harvest and the imminence of the Christmas holidays, which few potential recruits wanted to spend in camp. Newspapers spoke of a 'recruiting crisis' and 'urgent appeals' for men. Massey was among those urging men not to delay their enlistment:

> I ask our boys to remember their comrades who are spending their holiday season in the fighting line, where along with other brave men and trained soldiers they are doing their duty to the Empire, their country and fellow citizens. I ask them to remember how thorough training has enabled our soldiers to distinguish themselves, and to do credit to the land to which they belong. If they remember these facts and act accordingly, if they give up the fleeting pleasure of a few days for the more lasting pleasure of having done right things at the right time, I am quite sure that in later life they will always look back with satisfaction to the Christmas holiday of 1915 spent by them in Trentham training camp.[57]

Such appeals ultimately fell flat: by mid-December recruitment was over a quarter short of requirements. In another first, all districts failed to meet their quotas: Auckland was short by 119, Wellington by 153, Canterbury by 231 and Otago by 150.[58] Although vacancies in the Eleventh Reinforcements were filled in the new year, and the Twelfth Reinforcements had a slight surplus, the episode appears to have left a marked impression on public confidence.[59] It also signalled the start of a semi-regular pattern of enlistments falling short of recruitment deadlines: in January and April 1916, the Thirteenth, the Fourteenth, the Fifteen and the Sixteenth Reinforcements mobilised at under full strength. Although these shortages were of varying severity, and were soon filled, they fuelled arguments that volunteering could not meet the country's larger commitments.[60]

For a growing number of New Zealanders, the obvious solution to such inequality of sacrifice was compulsion. Paul Baker's landmark study of New Zealand's experience of conscription noted that although many New Zealanders wanted conscription before October 1915, most wanted it by December, estimating that between 60 and 70 per cent were in favour of conscription and no more than 20 per cent were opposed.[61]

Some arguments for conscription had a largely pragmatic basis. The Liberal MP James Craigie, for example, argued that '[t]he only way to end this war is to keep on sending troops, and the only way to get to Berlin is to provide men to increase and maintain our battalions.

The only thing that matters at present is to speedily end this awful war with victory to us.'[62] Conscription advocates typically went beyond expediency, though, and emphasised the need to counter the inequalities inherent in the voluntary system. Leonard Isitt, the Liberal MP for Christchurch North, denounced the voluntary system as possessing a 'most unfair, most unequal, most cruel, blind and idiotic nature':

> If I have to choose between a system that takes three sons of a widow, leaving five sons of her neighbour untouched; that seizes on a patriotic poor man with a wife and four children and sends him to the war leaving untouched a selfish man with 6000 acres and an abundant income, single, 25 years of age who spends his time between his motor car and the golf links, then I choose legitimate conscription every time. If I have to choose between moral conscription that seizes on a workman who does the hard dirty work of this world at a low wage, and is often exploited, but loves his country and forgets his disabilities as soon as it is in peril, while a shirker blatherskite remains behind to govern the country . . . then I choose conscription by Act of Parliament. The only free agents under moral conscription are thick-skinned men with no conscience.[63]

Such thinking was not confined to parliamentary speeches. By late 1915, around 40,000 men had enlisted, and their families, neighbours, workmates, fellow parishioners and other social connections constituted a potent faction. Letters addressed to the defence minister contained numerous variations on reports of a local figure or family failing to enlist, invariably noting the sacrifices their own loved ones had made, and calling for state action. In Gisborne, 'Patriotic Mother' supplied the name and address of a young man in her neighbourhood: 'I would very much like this one to be made to go soon . . . he is in the territorials, and a good bit over twenty, he just helps his father about the place . . . my own two sons are gone, one is in Egypt, and the other one has just come home on final leave, as I am a pure English woman myself, I think it is every young man's place to go.'[64]

Such attitudes were even common among those eligible for service. When Allen made a recruiting speech at a railway workshop, he was bluntly asked why the government did not simply introduce conscription and was told that the men had no intention of giving up their positions if it meant they would be taken by others equally capable of military service.[65] In January 1916, the socialist James Thorn noted, with frustrated astuteness, that '[w]henever a worker in New Zealand agrees with conscription it is because, to use his own words, "it will make the cockies' sons go". What justifies conscription in his mind is the illusion that it compels equal service and equal sacrifice all round.'[66]

Conscription was also presented as a solution to the level of spite now being used by those pursuing 'shirkers'. By late 1915, previous opponents of white feather giving had begun to adopt strategies of shame and ostracism. *Truth*'s 'Lady Dot', who decried white feather giving as 'a cowardly act', was keen to use the 'columns of the newspaper' to expose the rich farmers' sons who were not doing their bit: 'There is only one way to bring the wealthy shirkers into the ranks, and that is for the Womens' [sic] National Reserve in each district [to] make a list of such

The Unmarried Man's Dilemma

The Government is still dropping gentle hints (or are they threats) that if the single men do not come forward voluntarily, Conscription will be invoked.

Says Bill to the single young man,
"Comerlong o' me, peaceful and quiet,
To the recruiting booth,
Like a sensible youth,
Without any shirking or riot."

"It's plainly your duty to join,
In fact, I'm determined to take you;
If you offer resistance
I'll call for assistance
From this bloke, and he'll jolly soon make you."

above *Truth* observes the 'unmarried man's dilemma', noting the government's 'gentle hints' that a failure to volunteer would result in conscription being introduced and compulsion applied. NZ TRUTH, 26 FEBRUARY 1916, P. 1

right The interior of an Auckland recruitment office in 1917. AUCKLAND LIBRARIES HERITAGE COLLECTIONS, 1-W1597 families . . . and have them published.'[67] Ward, who had previously condemned white feather giving, told a meeting that the 'Maidens of New Zealand' should disown those men who were fit but would not go to the front.[68]

The pressure placed on eligible men also extended to restricting their employment prospects. In September 1915, Allen had urged the country's employers 'to arrange that medically fit unmarried men in your employment may be free to register for service'. Many perceived it as encouraging employers to fire eligible employees.[69] Certainly, a range of employers signalled that they would not hire eligible men. A Wellington manager, for example, advertised for a 'male or female Bookkeeper for Shipping Office . . . No man fit for military service need apply.' The public service commissioner also stated that applications from single eligible men would not be considered 'during the present crisis'. In December came an announcement that eligible men were to be excluded from ballots for government land.[70] Under such moral suasion, it is not surprising that some seemed to welcome conscription as a more civil means of meeting the military commitment.

As a general consensus formed around conscription, the government elected to proceed with caution and Allen, in a letter to Godley dated 4 January 1916, expressed both his confidence and his concerns: 'there can be no doubt about it that the bulk of opinion in the Country is in favour of compulsion, and has been for some time. As far as one can judge, this appears to the bulk of the people, the fairest way to deal with the problem.' This feeling seemed particularly strong among returned soldiers 'and the relatives and kith and kin of those who have gone'. If, as seemed likely, conscription was 'adopted even partially in England, I have no hesitation in my own mind in coming to the conclusion that it will be adopted here. For we are right for it and it is only the fear of what might happen in Labour circles, [which] prevents it being adopted here, with also a desire not to embarrass the Home authorities by doing so before they are right for it there.'[71]

The possibility of 'embarrassing England' was soon inconsequential; a conscription bill was introduced into the British Parliament in January 1916 and came into force in March. This left the issue of 'what might happen in Labour circles' as a key concern.

Conscription divided the labour movement as wider arguments around equality, pragmatism and principle played out. Some moderates, often those with past Liberal associations, were willing to accept conscription or even to approve of it as enacting socialist principles of modern organisation and equity by ensuring that all classes would serve.[72] Others argued conscription's merits on pragmatic grounds. The moderate socialist David McLaren, for example, asked workers to consider the consequences a British defeat would have on the labour movement and workers' rights:

> If Germany should win, or even be able to force a peace to her advantage, democracy throughout the world will suffer for a hundred years to come. The working class of all Europe will come under the same iron rule of Germanic despotism as the workers of Germany are enthralled with and curse most bitterly . . . Labour has got to fight and win the war against Germany because, only by so doing can the humane principles of the Labour movement be sustained.[73]

Other labour figures inverted those priorities, presenting conscription as the greater threat to workers' interests. In December 1915, Peter Fraser, as organising secretary of the Social Democratic Party, stated, 'Wars come and wars go. The working class struggle for economic freedom always goes on . . . Conscription, if imposed upon us, will make our work harder. We must fight it.'[74] Likewise, the *Maoriland Worker* urged its readers to 'resist this atrocious attempt to estrange you from your liberty': 'We must never permit this glorious Empire, engendered in the sanctity of freedom — brought forth in the nobility of patriotism, cherished and nourished by the red rivers of voluntary sacrifice, and reared to its present glorious state under the sun of universal emancipation, to be foully struck down in its hour of trial by the Juggernaut of military despotism and buried in the Conscript's grave.'[75]

Some elements within the labour movement even began questioning the worth of continuing the war. Conferences in 1915 discussed proposals for a negotiated peace, and in 1916 the Social Democratic Party issued a peace manifesto, stating that 'the time for a free and frank discussion of Peace Terms is long overdue'.[76] For such activists conscription was one more sign of the war's illegitimacy. The Canterbury Women's Institute, for example, wrote to the government that there was 'vast reason to believe that the sinister power of the Armament Kings of the world is attempting the complete domination of the world through control of press and parliament, and that we in New Zealand are now in imminent peril from reactionary statecraft and its attendant officialism'.[77]

Others avoided questions of the essential legitimacy of conscription and focused on the conditions under which it might be accepted. As MP Alfred Hindmarsh told the House, 'I hold on the one side it is the duty of men, if necessary, to die for the State; and I do not object to conscription, because there may be a time when conscription is absolutely necessary. But while it is the duty of the individual to serve the State in this way, I say the State has a duty to the individual.' Typically this approach reasoned, as the *Maoriland Worker* suggested, that improving soldiers' pay from 'a shockingly sweated rate' and social reforms would result in more extensive volunteering. Such efforts would, argued Hindmarsh, attract 'probably considerable numbers of men' who were currently repulsed by the idea of enlisting to preserve the economic status quo.[78]

Webb went further, declaring that 'no socialist in the whole land would not willingly go out to fight and die, if necessary, for a country owned by and worked in the interests of the whole of the people'.[79] Throughout the second half of 1915, labour MPs, with their radical Liberal allies, called for improved soldiers' pay and pensions to be funded by increased taxation on upper incomes and an export tax, arguing that equality of sacrifice was lost when the financially fit shirked their part and reminding the government of its promise to fight 'to the last shilling'.[80]

Such initiatives also provided the labour movement with a unifying cause, just as conscription threatened to divide it. Indeed — possibly to forestall potential divisions over conscription — many gravitated to the common ground that conscription, regardless of whether it represented equitable efficiency or encroaching militarism, must be preceded by a 'conscription of wealth'. 'I would not,' stated one activist, 'think of asking a man to give his life for his country until wealth comes within the scope of conscription.'[81] What exactly a

THE SHIRKER: "NO!"

A *Maoriland Worker* cartoon suggests a 'conscription of wealth' and depicts 'Mr Fat' as a financial shirker.
MAORILAND WORKER, 12 JANUARY 1916, P. 1

'conscription of wealth' might entail prompted various proposals that involved ideas of state confiscation of wealth, or the means of production, to reduce profiteering and bring about a more equitable distribution of resources.

The possibility of an anti-conscription faction emerging from within a divided labour movement was clear. Suspecting that the National Registration Bill was a precursor of conscription, Hiram Hunter, the secretary of the United Federation of Labour — and the man who had declared 'my country right or wrong' 11 months before — forwarded a resolution from his organisation to the prime minister.

> During the currency of the present war those people who have been most strenuously opposed to militarism in every shape and form have preserved a dignified neutrality. They adopted this course because they did not want to cause any embarrassment whilst the war lasted, believing that the Empire was engaged in a supreme struggle to uphold the principles of Democracy . . . why should this country be used as a lever for the introduction of a system of militarism which aims at placing the whole burden upon the industrial classes in the community, by making them fight the battles of the Empire, foot the bill, and at the same time rob them of the freedom which they consider they are fighting and paying to uphold?[82]

Other labour elements issued explicit warnings about the consequences of conscription. In early December 1915, the Point Elizabeth and Liverpool State Collieries Employees Industrial Union of Workers, on the West Coast, printed a resolution expressing strong resentment of those promoting conscription of men without an accompanying conscription of wealth and private property, adding that they were 'determined to meet such a calamity as conscription by industrial revolt'.[83] Various newspapers returned fire, denouncing miners as pro-German, influenced by IWW ideology and as 'the enemy in our midst'.[84] Others added further prophecies of 'industrial and political revolt', 'disastrous upheavals', insurrections that would 'imperil the whole social order' and 'civil war'.[85]

A more considerable warning was signalled at a conference organised by the United Federation of Labour in Wellington from 25 to 27 January 1916 with attendees representing 82 organisations and 18,449 union members.[86] Anti-conscription positions dominated proceedings, as those favouring conscription shunned attendance, and a manifesto committee comprising James McCombs, James Thorn, Holland, Fraser, Semple, William Parry and E. Hunter produced a summary of the positions discussed. This document emphasised that conscription was a class weapon ('The clamour for conscription simply resolves itself into the demand of private enterprise for more weapons for its entrenchment and aggrandisement') and that it might be justified only after a 'conscription of wealth', which meant that 'the land, mines, mills, factories, ships, banks, and all the collectively-used means of wealth production shall be seized, and operated for the collective benefit of the people during the war, and shall remain the property of the people after the war'. The manifesto concluded with a call for a negotiated end to the war: 'This conference is strongly of the opinion that the time has arrived when the Allied Governments should publicly

THE FUSION'S "NATIONAL SERVICE"

THE ONE SHALL GIVE-----THE OTHER LEND

Labour (to Fat): "Before I will consent to even consider Conscription of Life, your wealth must be conscripted for national service."

Mr. Massey (to Labour): "You idea of the Conscription of Wealth is not only preposterous but ludicrous."

—Apologies to the "Australian Worker."

A *Maoriland Worker* cartoon depicts the inequality between those making sacrifices and those making profits. MAORILAND WORKER, 8 MARCH 1916, P. 1

state the terms upon which they are prepared to bring the conflict to an end.'[87]

Months later, at Wellington's Alexandra Hall in Abel Smith Street over 7–8 July, a conference was held to form a national Labour Party to which unions and branches of the Social Democratic Party could affiliate. This vision of an independent party able to operate at a national level reflected both earlier dreams of political independence and lessons drawn from the 1913 strike about the value of political power. Agreement that conscription was unacceptable, at least without a radical transformation of social conditions, also provided an immediate and unifying issue.[88] The conference also reflected a pragmatic concern that some Liberals might establish a pro-conscription Labour Party: as John Paul observed a week before, 'it was dangerous to leave the name "Labour" lying about'.[89]

Five MPs — Paul, Hindmarsh, Andrew Walker, McCombs and Webb — attended the conference, which has been described as a quiet 'backroom' meeting in a 'smoke-filled' room, alongside representatives from the Social Democratic Party, the United Federation of Labour and the Labour Representation Committees.[90] The platform decided on closely resembled that of the Social Democratic Party and Labour's objective was stated as 'the socialisation of the means of production, distribution and exchange'.[91] The party structure was based on labour representation committees, comprising unions, trades councils, Social Democratic Party branches 'and other properly constituted Progressive organisations which subscribe to the constitution and platform of the Party'.[92] Although some hoped that the Social Democratic Party might carry on as an affiliated but parallel institution, with propagandist and educational duties, it ultimately withered away. Moderates held several key positions — Hindmarsh was chosen as party leader, McCombs as president and Paul as a member of the committee — but 'the bulk of effective leadership was provided by old "Red Feds" and militants' and Holland, Semple and Fraser were all elected to the new party's national executive.[93]

Media reactions to the new party were generally lacklustre. The *Auckland Star* claimed: 'So far the reconstruction has not attracted much attention even in the ranks of Labour and many level-headed workers are frankly sceptical over the ability of Mr. J. McCombs and his committee to arouse more than half-hearted interest in social questions while the war is engrossing public attention.'[94] *Truth* printed a less than reverent poem about what was seen as just another iteration of a Labour/Socialist party. The final stanza read:

> But fourteen years have vanished
> Since that auspicious day,
> And the workers' Ship of Promise Sails not upon her way.
> The captains and the crew, in turn,
> Have changed her name with much concern,
> Till now they're back to Number One.
> She's still in port. What's to be done?[95]

Even the *Maoriland Worker* gave little prominence to the launch, and emphasised the ongoing importance of the Social Democratic Party.[96]

With both pro- and anti-conscription factions emerging and signalling their demands, a showdown appeared to be looming. Some papers damned the Red Feds for displaying indifference to German rapacity, betraying the empire in its time of need and turning their backs on the men at the front.[97] Unsurprisingly, the government was hostile to the anti-conscription manifesto. Massey claimed that it did not represent the views of New Zealand workers and he could not 'believe that it accurately represents the views of those who were present'. Besides suggesting that those wishing to avoid conscription should help to make the voluntary system work, he made it clear that the government would not be swayed by threats: 'If the manifesto is intended in any way to influence the New Zealand Government it will not have the slightest effect. We know our duty, and will do it to the best of our ability. We are giving the voluntary system a good trial; if it fails — and it has not failed yet — then to do our duty as a community there is only one alternative — compulsion, and the latter must be adopted when that time comes.'[98]

Despite the tough talk, the possibility of industrial disruption or civil unrest bred caution and an instinct to introduce conscription only under the strongest possible consensus: Massey's stated indifference to threats of industrial unrest has been described as 'lying through his teeth'.[99] No doubt with memories of the 1913 strike in mind, Allen privately noted that 'there are some members of the community who would seize any attempt to introduce compulsion as an opportunity to create industrial trouble. We have to avoid this if we possibly can.'[100]

The loudest rumblings came from those debating how the demands of the war effort should be borne while generally accepting the war's legitimacy, but a smaller yet still concerted effort came from those who resolutely rejected both the war's cause and its conduct. Given the public mood in 1914, and because the conflict was expected to be brief, anti-war activists had initially elected to maintain a low profile. However, as the fighting became protracted they began to re-emerge.

They remained a philosophically eclectic mix, citing workers' rights, pacifist positions, liberal traditions, socialist theories, feminist beliefs, non-conformist theology and ethnic identities opposed to involvement in a 'British war'. As Holland later noted, Irish and Māori dissent stemmed less from an unconditional commitment to non-violence than from a desire to pick their fight, and that while 'The Christian Objector is always a Pacifist', 'Sometimes the Socialist is a Pacifist; often he isn't.'[101] This comment was borne out by a letter to the *Dominion* from Walter Nash, a pacifist and a future Labour prime minister, writing under the pseudonym 'Socratus', asking whether Christians should fight: 'How much love is there in a bayonet charge?'[102] Other socialists touted labour's fighting spirit, if not always in a manner comforting to conservatives. In a September 1915 parliamentary debate Webb declared that '[t]he Labour men and Socialists do not want peace at any price either in the industrial field or in the international field. We do not want peace so long as Prussian militarism is over-running Flanders, or Belgium, or any part of France; nor can there be any peace so long as the capitalist forces, the monopolists, the rings and combines, and the land-sharks hold sway in this country.'[103]

New Zealand anti-war activists maintained the international nature of pre-war activism by corresponding with like-minded individuals and organisations in Australia, Britain and the United States.[104] These connections also allowed them to import literature, which would become increasingly proscribed, and receive reports of overseas peace events. By March 1915 Egerton Gill and the Freedom League had resumed their activities and ordered 2000 copies of H. G. Wells's *End of Armament Rings* and the same number of Dr Alfred Salter's *Christianity and War*.

Although there were no New Zealanders among the 1200-plus women who attended an International Congress of Women held in The Hague to discuss proposals for a negotiated peace over April–May 1915, the *Maoriland Worker* provided full coverage. 'In April women of all lands met at The Hague in the sisterhood of sorrow. British women were there, Belgian women were there, German women were there, Austrian women were there. Women were there from nearly all the neutral countries. They sought the way of peace.'[105] This conference became a touchstone, and the Wellington branch of the Women's International League proclaimed later in 1915, 'we dedicate our organisation to the task of encouraging in ourselves and others this ceaseless effort, and of helping to mould institutions in accordance with the vital policy laid down by the International Congress of Women at The Hague . . .'.[106]

The international dimension of the movement was also demonstrated in the North and South Island lecture tour by Adela Pankhurst from May to July 1916. A member of the renowned British family, Adela, along with her mother, Emmeline, and sisters, Christabel and Sylvia, had been heavily involved in the militant wing of the pre-war suffrage movement. Believing in deeds not words, they had endorsed civil unrest, including vandalism, arson, assaulting police officers and hunger strikes; critics spoke of 'the notorious Crankhurst family'.[107] In 1914, Emmeline and Christabel became ardent supporters of Britain's war effort, the white feather movement, conscription and, ultimately, anti-Bolshevism.[108] Adela, however, committed herself to advocating pacifism through radical social reform and, for a time, communism. She arrived in Auckland after a volatile reception in Australia in which patriots had disrupted lectures and she had been hit in the face with a missile thrown by 'a cowardly ruffian'.[109] Her numerous talks over the following weeks proved to be calmer affairs and were well attended; large numbers of women were in the audiences. Her lectures emphasised the destructiveness of the war, the need for social reform and the importance of women's roles in the peace and reform movements.[110]

The increasing discussion of conscription in late 1915 brought a new sense of urgency and a unifying cause for anti-war activists. In September 1915 the Freedom League wrote an open letter to the government, explaining that it had not taken any action while the war was 'carried out professedly upon a voluntary basis of recruiting' but warning that the introduction 'of any measure of compulsion' would 'entirely alter the position so far as the League is concerned'.[111] The Christchurch WCTU and Canterbury's Women's Institute also actively opposed conscription. The latter issued a memorandum stressing 'That the withdrawal of able bodied men from their daily avocations must eventually mean great hardship to a very large number of women who eventually will be left without their natural supporters and bread winners' and 'That the sorrow and mental suffering . . . entailed by all war, falls most heavily upon the women because by this most sinister form of slavery they are deprived of their husbands, fathers and sons.'[112]

The possibility of conscription also encouraged the formation of new organisations, including the Women's Anti-Conscription League and the Women's International League for Peace and Freedom (in Christchurch initially, and then more widely), the Conscription Repeal League (Auckland, Wellington, Christchurch and seven West Coast branches) and the Fellowship of Reconciliation (Auckland).

Political and philosophical divides left little room for constructive exchange, however. When one delegate at a meeting between Massey and a delegation of the Women's Anti-Conscription League asserted that the prime minister was driving 'men to the trenches at the point of the bayonet', he retorted, 'Well, if men won't go of their own free will they will have to be driven!'[113] Public antagonism and expanding war regulations also served as a strong check on some activities. In August 1915, Harry Urquhart, an Auckland-based member of the Fellowship of Reconciliation, wrote and distributed *Christianity and War: A Challenge to the Churches*. The pamphlet questioned Christian support for the war and nearly lost him his job at Seddon Memorial Technical College.[114] Backlash was especially fierce in rural and small-town New Zealand, where 'opposition to conscription was dangerous, and rare'.[115] For example, in late May 1915, Timaru's Unitarian minister James Chapple was confronted by an angry crowd of 200 men. He was known to preach messages held as anti-militarist, mixed with doses of socialism and anti-monarchism, and had been warned that his sermons could provoke public disorder.[116] The following month he announced his intention to leave New Zealand, with his wife and 13 children, for the neutral United States and later vowed not to return until 'democracy crushes militarism'.[117]

Dargaville's Alfred Gregory, a Quaker, a socialist and draper whom the *Maoriland Worker* dubbed 'the lone outpost of socialism in the Far North', was similarly embattled.[118] Early in 1915 Gregory attracted an angry protest when he expressed anti-militarist views, and when he won a seat on the local borough council in September that year his opponents requested that he display a National Reserve enrolment poster in his shop window, knowing that he would refuse on principle. When he did so he was convicted of violating war regulations, fined and relieved of his council seat. When he would not pay the fine, he experienced further public vilification, his children were bullied at school, the windows of his shop were smashed and his walls graffitied — 'From Kiser [sic] to Alfred' and 'Gregory's Recruiting Centre. Boys Enlist Today' — and excrement was left outside the front door. The visitors' book of the Workers' Library Gregory hosted began to include such comments as 'May the Germans drop a bomb on this hellish den'.[119]

He eventually lost so much custom that he had to lease the shop to another draper and he and his family remained outcasts, living on charity from fellow Quakers for the rest of the war.[120] It is no wonder that many anti-militarists privately noted sentiments similar to Christchurch's Sarah Saunders Page, who observed, 'New Zealand as a whole seems so absolutely obsessed by the idea of fighting evil with the devil's weapons that I must confess to a feeling of hopelessness.'[121]

Members of the New Zealand branch of the Women's International League for Peace and Freedom with the visiting Adela Pankhurst (centre, holding flowers). ALEXANDER TURNBULL LIBRARY, 1/2-067533-F

By late 1915 the measure of harmony that had marked Catholic–Protestant relations early in the war was under threat. The Catholic Federation was undertaking renewed, and often assertive, campaigning for state funding for private schools, calling for bans on literature and films it deemed offensive and protesting that the government was 'Sectarian and anti-Catholic'.[122] Part of Protestant opinion was antagonised by what it saw as untimely politicking, sometimes adding suspicions over the Vatican's claimed impartiality in the conflict. According to the editor of the *Sun*, for example: 'The Vatican has clearly shown itself as not neutral . . . [its] attitude of condonation towards Germany, in face of the admitted brutalities which have shocked the civilised world outside the Holy See, and the unveiled antagonism towards England, have made a lasting impression on those who looked to the Vicar of Christ either to preserve a strict and sealed neutrality, or to join in the condemnation of tactics barbarian in their savagery and coldbloodedness.'[123]

In early 1916 Father W. van Westeinde became the first of many Catholic clergymen reported to the Defence Department for disloyalty, in this case for a sermon criticising the organisation of the country's war effort. Informed of the incident, Bishop Cleary wrote to van Westeinde urging the need to avoid potential provocation: 'I have already impressed upon others the pressing need of exercising extreme caution and of keeping to yourself any views which may be out of harmony with those of the body of the people among whom you live.'[124] General anxiety about equality of sacrifice also had a sectarian dimension, seen in doubts about Catholic participation in the war.

Such attitudes were guaranteed to foster

ill-will. 'We are no shirkers,' said one Catholic principal in January 1916. 'We do not wish to side-step our responsibilities. We are ready to bear the burdens of the State equally with others. Our sons have responded to the call of King and Empire in the present struggle and have poured out their blood freely on the battlefields of Europe.'[125] As one historian puts it, 'New Zealand Catholics did not need reminding of the price of their loyalty, as the faces of their dead sons stared out of each weekly issue of the *Tablet*.'[126]

Into these developing sectarian antagonisms stepped the Reverend Howard Leslie Elliott, pastor at Mount Eden's Baptist church in Auckland. Born in Victoria in 1877, and with a history of social activism concerning propriety, Elliott had, since the outbreak of war, delivered numerous sermons on vivid Romanist plots to subvert cherished Protestant liberties. By early 1916 he had become a leading personality in New Zealand's Orange Lodge network, and he and his associates actively attacked papal neutrality, claimed that Catholic Ireland was 'seething with sedition', alleged that Catholic schools in New Zealand were 'seedbeds of disloyalty' and, entirely contrary to evidence, asserted that Catholic clergy were discouraging recruitment and fundraising.[127] Perhaps most fantastical, however, were the conspiratorial views that the war had arisen from the 'political chicanery' of the Catholic Church and that the Vatican was 'an equally guilty party'.[128]

Reactions to this campaigning were mixed. Various newspaper columns denounced both the claims and their fevered delivery; *Truth* emerged as one of the most vocal critics of 'Yelliot', the 'bilious bigot'. The Auckland City Council, too, expressed 'in the strongest terms its disgust at the bigotry and intolerance evidenced'.[129] However, expressions of approval from Presbyterian and Methodist elements led to suggestions that a Protestant association 'representative of all the churches' might be formed. Proponents presented this as playing an equivalent role to organised Catholicism and advancing Protestant political interests.

Plans for the launch of a Protestant Political Association were discussed over Easter 1916, with resolutions including the establishment of a Wellington-based presence to monitor politicians and public servants and increased propaganda efforts. Although they shared the militants' anti-Catholic sentiments, the traditional Orange Lodge leaders were hesitant about political campaigning during wartime, and so the task of heading the militant movement went to the Vigilance Committee, an informal Auckland-based Orange group. Elliott, despite having been a lodge member for less than nine months, was recognised as a primary political spokesman.[130]

Tensions rose after news arrived of an armed insurrection, largely centred in Dublin, by Irish republicans on 24 April. What became known as the Easter Rising involved six days of fighting. The British Army was deployed, the rebels were defeated, parts of inner-city Dublin were ruined, thousands were taken prisoner, martial law was declared and the rising's leaders were court-martialled and executed the following month.

New Zealanders learnt of the Rising the day after many had commemorated the first Anzac Day. The predominant initial response, from Catholics and Protestants alike, was shock and anger that Irish rebels had taken up German aid and attempted, as the *Evening Star* put it, a 'villainous stab in the back'.[131] Much commentary brooded on their low motives. The

New Zealand Herald, for example, claimed that those involved were 'manifestly without any idealistic inspiration. It was destructive, not constructive; the craving for "loot," and not the love of freedom, evidently sustained its instigators and inflamed its dupes . . . The abuse of power which promptly marked the Dublin rising, the wholesale robberies, the callous murders, shows us what sort of men were engaged in this mad outbreak.'[132]

Mainstream coverage also tended to differentiate between the general Irish public and an extreme Sinn Féin element, which the *Otago Daily Times* described as representing a 'small and isolated section of the Irish community' in sharp contrast to 'that far greater band of Irishmen, faithful to their traditions, gallantly serving the Empire in the thick of the fighting in Flanders, France, and elsewhere'.[133] Germany's role in supplying weapons to the rebels, and its possible machinations in causing the rising, were also presented as instrumental. The *Evening Post*, for example, claimed: 'There is ample evidence to show that the rebellion in Ireland, which broke out on Easter Monday, was hatched in Germany.'[134]

New Zealand's Catholic leaders voiced comparable sentiments, swiftly denouncing the 'made in Germany' rebellion, censuring deluded Sinn Féiners, affirming Irish loyalty to the empire and reminding the public that the real Irish patriots were at the front.[135] The *Tablet* reported the various statements made by local Catholic associations condemning the rebellion. One Dunedin meeting, for example, felt sure that 'when history looks at present events in true perspective, the leaders of the outbreak will be found to be men of no standing in their country, and the whole thing will appear but an insignificant, though ugly speck on the face of that magnificent pile of patriotism which the true Irish nation has built up during this war', adding that, as a 'practical means of showing our condemnation of the rebellion in Dublin, we call on every one of our fellow countrymen of an age and fit who have not yet enrolled to offer their services at once to their country'.[136]

However, these initial reactions to the events of Easter 1916 soon shifted under the growing ill-will between Catholics and Protestants. As the *Maoriland Worker* noted: 'It is not going outside of fact to say that the summary executions of the Irish leaders, after trial by court-martial have shocked many thousands of people in N.Z. who were quite out of sympathy with the rebellion.'[137] Moreover, if some commentators were willing to snipe that the Irish had 'something to wipe off the slate', others countered by noting the 'havoc wrought by English Huns in Dublin' and by referring to a 'rising' rather than a 'rebellion'.[138]

By late 1916, influential Protestant voices were calling attention to 'the open rebellion in Ireland, in which priests figured as leaders of disaffection, to the fact that the South of Ireland is far behind Ulster in the proportion of volunteers for service, and to the further fact that the Clerical Party in Canada openly counsels the French-Canadians against enlistment, and . . . is openly fomenting rebellious sentiments . . . Popery is pro-German and anti-British at the present crisis.'[139] Catholic priest Dr James Kelly proved more than willing to return fire and began to earn his description as 'the chief means whereby Catholic indignation over the treatment of Ireland was communicated to the New Zealand public'.[140] In 1915, Kelly had been asked to assist in editing the *New Zealand Tablet* and he claimed that by February 1916 he was doing much of the editorial work. While he had initially dismissed the rising as 'mad, bad

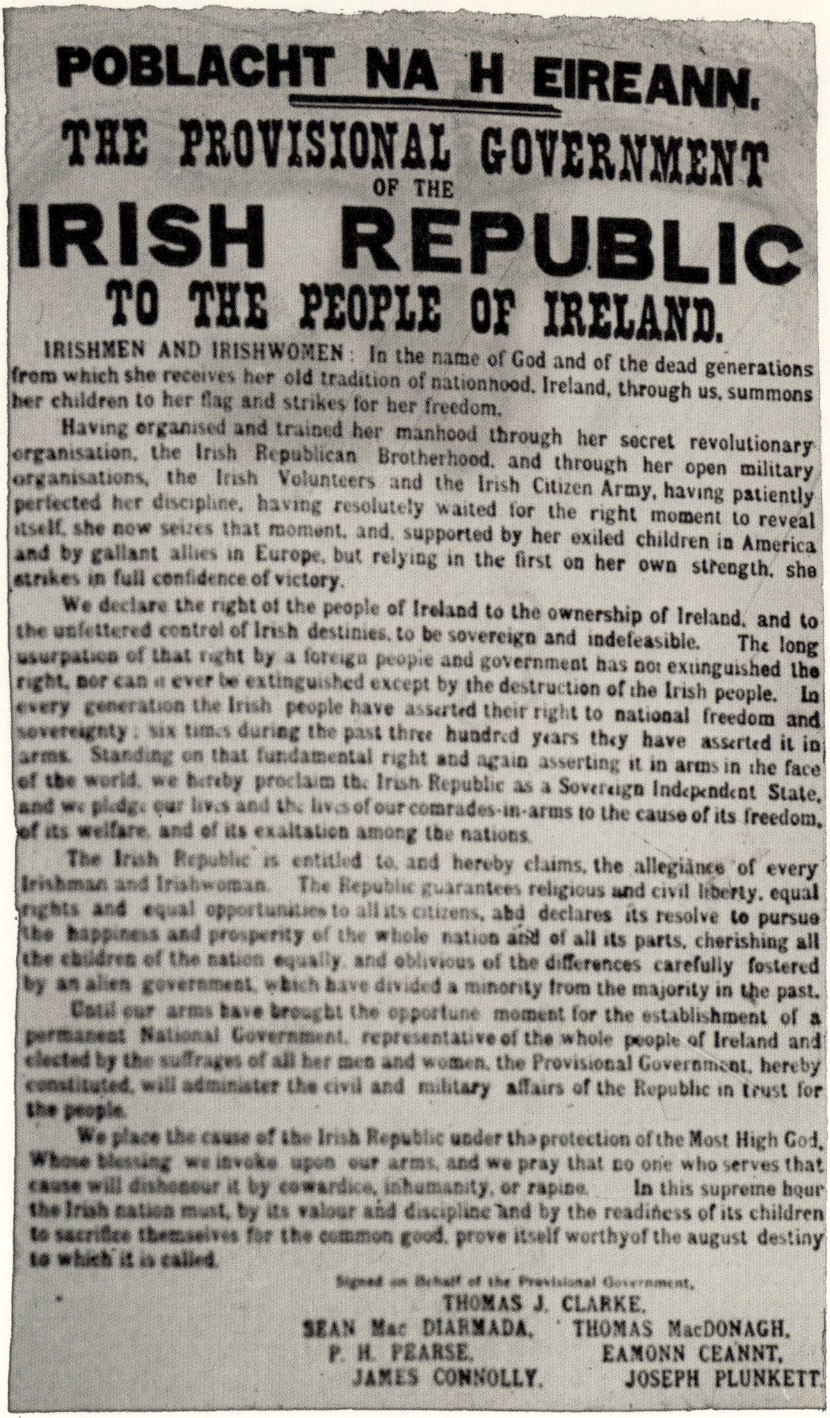

POBLACHT NA H EIREANN.

THE PROVISIONAL GOVERNMENT OF THE IRISH REPUBLIC TO THE PEOPLE OF IRELAND.

IRISHMEN AND IRISHWOMEN: In the name of God and of the dead generations from which she receives her old tradition of nationhood, Ireland, through us, summons her children to her flag and strikes for her freedom.

Having organised and trained her manhood through her secret revolutionary organisation, the Irish Republican Brotherhood, and through her open military organisations, the Irish Volunteers and the Irish Citizen Army, having patiently perfected her discipline, having resolutely waited for the right moment to reveal itself, she now seizes that moment, and, supported by her exiled children in America and by gallant allies in Europe, but relying in the first on her own strength, she strikes in full confidence of victory.

We declare the right of the people of Ireland to the ownership of Ireland, and to the unfettered control of Irish destinies, to be sovereign and indefeasible. The long usurpation of that right by a foreign people and government has not extinguished the right, nor can it ever be extinguished except by the destruction of the Irish people. In every generation the Irish people have asserted their right to national freedom and sovereignty; six times during the past three hundred years they have asserted it in arms. Standing on that fundamental right and again asserting it in arms in the face of the world, we hereby proclaim the Irish Republic as a Sovereign Independent State, and we pledge our lives and the lives of our comrades-in-arms to the cause of its freedom, of its welfare, and of its exaltation among the nations.

The Irish Republic is entitled to, and hereby claims, the allegiance of every Irishman and Irishwoman. The Republic guarantees religious and civil liberty, equal rights and equal opportunities to all its citizens, and declares its resolve to pursue the happiness and prosperity of the whole nation and of all its parts, cherishing all the children of the nation equally, and oblivious of the differences carefully fostered by an alien government, which have divided a minority from the majority in the past.

Until our arms have brought the opportune moment for the establishment of a permanent National Government, representative of the whole people of Ireland and elected by the suffrages of all her men and women, the Provisional Government, hereby constituted, will administer the civil and military affairs of the Republic in trust for the people.

We place the cause of the Irish Republic under the protection of the Most High God, Whose blessing we invoke upon our arms, and we pray that no one who serves that cause will dishonour it by cowardice, inhumanity, or rapine. In this supreme hour the Irish nation must, by its valour and discipline and by the readiness of its children to sacrifice themselves for the common good, prove itself worthy of the august destiny to which it is called.

Signed on Behalf of the Provisional Government,

THOMAS J. CLARKE.

SEAN Mac DIARMADA. THOMAS MacDONAGH.

P. H. PEARSE. EAMONN CEANNT.

JAMES CONNOLLY. JOSEPH PLUNKETT.

A copy of the 1916 proclamation issued by the rebels during the Easter Rising that declared Ireland to be a sovereign republic. This copy was used by Harry Holland to illustrate his lectures on the Irish question. ALEXANDER TURNBULL LIBRARY, PA11-019-01 and sad', his commentary would become increasingly marked by anti-British diatribes and sympathy for Sinn Féin.[141]

Another complication resulted from militant labour's increasing interest in the Irish question.[142] The *Maoriland Worker* was one of the few periodicals that refused to unconditionally condemn the Irish rebels, noting that the situation could have been avoided by wiser policies, and Holland provided sympathetic editorials and lectures regarding Irish history and republican aspirations, asserting that this had been a workers' rebellion.[143] Despite some tension between Catholic conservatism and atheistic socialism, a degree of liaison developed between political labour and Irish associations, which found common ground in spurning Britain's claim to be fighting for the rights of small nations and a common enemy in figures like Elliott, who hurled accusations of Catholic and socialist plots being hatched against Protestant New Zealand.

At a broader level, the episode poisoned general expectations in New Zealand of peaceful progress on the Irish question. 'If a growing number of Catholics were coming to the view that Home Rule would no longer be enough,' some Protestants were beginning to voice 'strong doubts' about its wisdom.[144] Sectarian tensions were clearly growing in the second year of war, and there would be no easy reprieve.

As with other forces at Gallipoli, the Native Contingent's deployment came with significant casualties; of the 477 Māori deployed on the peninsula on 3 July 1915 only 134 remained to be withdrawn in December. Māori felt increased pressure for more recruits, with requirements rising from a May 1915 rate of 250 Māori every three months to 340 every two months by August.[145] Questions were raised about Māori commitment, and many iwi, including some who had previously produced many volunteers, became more conditional in their support. In June 1915, for example, Allen received a resolution signed by 62 leading Ngāti Maniapoto calling for the Native Contingent to be assigned to garrison duties in Sāmoa or Egypt.[146] In February 1916, another petition, with 262 signatures, called for an end to Māori recruitment, noting it was contrary to the intent of the Treaty of Waitangi to protect tangata whenua and was hastening their extinction. The message ended with reference to the original Māori volunteers: 'That was sufficient to evidence their good faith and the proportion was equally sufficient in the circumstances.'[147] Comparing such positions to earlier rhetoric, Āpirana Ngata wearily remarked that the pledges of August 1914 seemed 'all wind and words'.[148]

By the beginning of July 1915 the shortfall in Māori enlistment numbers was becoming evident and Allen was expressing doubt over 'whether we shall be able to keep up the Maori Reinforcements'.[149] Recruiting turned to territories in the Pacific, which had previously offered assistance. Niue and the Cook Islands, for example, had offered money and men when news of the war arrived.[150] There had been little will to take on such recruits, possibly spurred by the resident commissioner's caution that Niueans 'could not possibly provide or pay for the equipment, and, further, they do not understand any language but their own'.[151]

In the context of escalating commitments and troubled Māori recruitment, the government reassessed these earlier offers. The first Niueans and Cook Islanders to serve within the Native Contingent arrived at Devonport in October 1915 and were soon training at Narrow Neck, or Nalo Neke as the Niueans called it.[152] Although the training programme faced teething problems — especially about language, dietary changes and footwear — by February 1916 the first draft was ready to depart.[153] The 203 Niueans and Cook Islanders at the farewell parade held in Auckland on 4 February actually outnumbered the 111 Māori soldiers.[154] Ultimately, some 500 Pacific Islanders served in New Zealand forces during the war, most coming from the Cook Islands and Niue, and smaller numbers from Tahiti, Fiji, Sāmoa, Tonga and Kiribati.[155]

Policies that transgressed tribal sensibilities also revealed the conditional nature of Māori commitment to the war effort. This was most clearly demonstrated in August 1915, when several Māori officers were dismissed on charges of incompetence and plans were announced to distribute the men of the Native Contingent across other battalions.[156] This had a decidedly negative effect on the Native Contingent Committee's willingness to cooperate: in November 1915, Pōmare told Allen that 'it will no longer be possible to raise further contingents unless the race can be satisfied that no injustice has been done'. On 15 February the following year, Allen noted that Pōmare 'intimated that no more recruiting would take place with the Maoris until the Contingent was put back together again', and in March he pronounced Māori recruiting 'absolutely dead'.[157]

The stalemate was overcome the same month, however, as post-Gallipoli reorganisation agreed to keep Māori soldiers together; the Native Contingent was reformed into a Pioneer Battalion. A relieved Allen wrote to Godley, 'Impasse over.' Renewed recruitment efforts were soon under way, with Pōmare 'on his way up North to recruit and a special NCO visiting Tauranga and Urewera' for the same reason.[158]

However, the broader stalemate between the government and those iwi who remained stubbornly disengaged from the war endured. During Allen's inspection of the men of the second Māori contingent at the end of August 1915, he said, 'Some of the Maoris, I understand, are holding back. I cannot realise why difficulties, and even the injustices of the past should stand in the way of their coming forward freely to join their Maori and pakeha brothers in upholding the flag which has done so much for them.'[159] A few days later, in a letter to the editor of the *Otago Daily Times*, Ōtākou woman Erihapeti Karetai offered a response:

> Shall I tell the Hon. James Allen their reasons for holding back[?] The Maori understands that England has gone to war for honour's sake — that Germany violated a 'scrap of paper', which her representative had signed for the protection of a small country. So far so good. But the mere Maori mind cannot help asking, where is Britain's honour? What about the 'scrap of paper' Britain signed for the protection of a small people, and the promises contained therein? Why has Britain allowed the New Zealand Government to violate that 'scrap of paper', called the Treaty of Waitangi? Did I hear the Minister say those injustices were past? No; they live to-day, and will live for ever, a blot on New Zealand's history, and — shall I say it? — on Britain's honour and her much-vaunted fairplay.[160]

Although recruitment had been low in Taranaki and Maniapoto, official attention increasingly focused on Tūhoe, Waikato and the King Country. Rua Kēnana discouraged, if not forbade, enlistment and, more broadly, Ngāi Tūhoe appeared largely ambivalent. The Kīngitanga maintained a public response of 'Waiho ma te hiahia' (Leave it to individual choice), which most appear to have interpreted as 'do not go'; despite the Waikato–Maniapoto region possessing some 1306 eligible men, the Waikato presence in the first contingent was low and only 1.8 per cent were from the King Country.[161] Waikato indifference, fuelled by grievances over land confiscations, placed authorities, and especially Pōmare, as the MP for Western Māori, in an awkward position. Hui also cited King Tāwhiao's 1881 symbolic laying down of arms as marking the end of warfare in New Zealand. In a meeting with Allen in May 1916, Te Heuheu Tūkino, the paramount chief of Ngāti Tūwharetoa, claimed that Waikato were adhering to prophecies made by Tāwhiao: 'As to war, I will leave it to you — the white man', 'Take war with you to your own land — to England.'[162]

By October 1915 signs of possible confrontation were apparent. That month, when an apprehended deserter claimed he had been given sanctuary by King Te Rata, Colonel G. W. H. Patterson of the Auckland Military District advocated a prosecution for a breach of the Army Act. His superior, General Robin, however, doubted that such a case would succeed and the matter was dropped.[163] Another round of posturing came in February 1916 when the army decided to prosecute a number of Waikato Māori in the Huntly district who had failed to comply with territorial training requirements.

The men of whom they chose to make examples included Tonga Mahuta, Te Rata's younger brother, who had previously been prosecuted for the same reason. Because Mahuta's defence was able to argue that a satisfactory scheme for training territorials in Huntly was imminent, the magistrate imposed a minimal 5s fine. However, a battle of wills was developing. Writing to Godley, Allen complained that 'we cannot get the Waikato tribe to encourage their young men to enlist' and noted that the clash with Mahuta had left some question 'as to whether the mana of Mahuta or the mana of the Government is to prevail. There can be no question about it that the Government's mana must prevail.'[164]

Such matters of state sovereignty also lay at the heart of attitudes to Rua Kēnana and his settlement at Maungapōhatu.[165] Compounding the pre-war clashes between Rua and authorities, in the first years of the war there were additional charges of unlicensed trading in alcohol and Rua's non-appearance in court. Newspaper reports noted his incorporation of the war into his millennial prophecies in a manner certain to raise disquiet. 'It was stated,' said the *Star* in January 1916, 'that Rua had assumed the title of "Kaiser," and had promised the Natives a great time when the country was in the hands of the Germans, with the result that it was practically impossible to get the Maoris within his influence to enlist.'[166]

In an interview with the paper a couple of months later, Englishman E. F. Bressy, a former teacher at a native school near Maungapōhatu, summarised many of the rumours about Rua. He apparently had 'a fair store of arms', including a Maxim gun; Bressy had not laid eyes on this, but claimed to have seen the Mauser pistol Rua carried. 'It is suspected very strongly,' he pronounced, 'that German influence has crept into even the Urewera country' and that Rua had spread tales that the Germans were going to take New Zealand and give the land back to the Māori. Bressy considered that a confrontation over authority and the rule of law was looming: 'To a great extent [Rua] has gone out of the Messiah business. He is the Maori Kaiser now.'[167]

On 12 February 1916 Sergeant D. J. Cummings, accompanied by two constables, was dispatched to arrest Rua on the outstanding charges. According to Cummings, he explained the charges to Rua, who was accompanied by 100 followers, and told him that he was under arrest. Rua apparently responded, 'I die first, I'll die on my land before the Government will take me' and warned that 'you touch me and all my people tackle you'. When the officers prepared to leave, Rua added that the governor should be sent to negotiate, that he would not let his people volunteer for service and that, 'When the Germans win, I'm going to be King here. I'll be King of the Maori and the Pakeha.'[168] After travelling to Maungapōhatu in March, Ngata urged the minister of justice, A. L. Herdman, to visit in search of a peaceful solution. Herdman travelled to meet Rua, but when the latter learnt that Police Commissioner John Cullen was also to be present, he refused to attend, saying that he wanted nothing to do with the police. Under a sense that efforts at conciliation were exhausted, arrangements for a police expedition were made.

On 27 March, 67 police assembled in Rotorua.[169] The expedition was 'conducted like a military operation', with the force armed with .303 rifles and service revolvers and using packhorses to carry their baggage on the rugged trek into the Ureweras. The men arrived at Maungapōhatu on Sunday, 2 April; this timing would subsequently raise legal technicalities as no warrants, barring those relating to treason, felony or a breach of the peace, could be served on a Sunday. Cullen, who had elected to head the operation, was at first

above The police expedition to arrest Rua Kēnana being issued with guns and ammunition. AUCKLAND LIBRARIES HERITAGE COLLECTIONS, 7-A3319

below The community at Maungapōhatu. The meeting house is visible at centre right. AUCKLAND LIBRARIES HERITAGE COLLECTIONS, 7-A3328; 7-A3328A welcomed into the settlement, but an attempt to apprehend Rua caused a confused scuffle to break out and there were several arrests. In the police account, as Rua was being led away he called out 'Patua! Patua!', meaning to strike, assault or kill, and a shot was fired. There would be arguments later over his exact meaning and intention and whether he was actually calling to be killed himself, in accordance with his earlier promise that he would die before being taken. Later proceedings also failed to determine from which side the first shot came. In the half-hour shootout that followed, two of Rua's followers, one of them his son, were killed and five policemen and three Māori wounded.[170]

In the trial that began on 9 June 1916, Rua was charged with the use of seditious language, obstructing police duties on 12 February and advocating violence against police on 2 April. He pleaded not guilty on all counts. After 47 days of court proceedings, a national record not surpassed until 1977, the jury returned a verdict of not guilty on the charge of sedition and was divided on the charges relating to the raid on Maungapōhatu.

Despite this, the presiding judge, Frederick Chapman, returned a sentence of 12 months' hard labour followed by 18 months of imprisonment. The cost of the expedition and trial, £2000, was charged to Maungapōhatu, devastating the community.[171] The jury was reported to be shocked by the punitive nature of the sentence and eight members subsequently petitioned Parliament that their verdict had been misinterpreted. Chapman's summary of the case and his verdict were a clear assertion of authority: 'What we have heard has been a long story of defiance of the law, and now you have learned that the law has a long arm, and that it can reach you, however far back into the recesses of the forest you may travel; and that in every corner of the great Empire to which we belong the King's law can reach anyone who offends against him. That is the lesson that your people should learn from this trial and from the verdict of this jury.'[172]

The sense that the war was not simply against an enemy army or regime, but rather against a people and their culture, was intensified from mid-1915. Although the idea that Prussian militarists had driven a generally decent German nation to war endured, it was regularly and passionately contested. As one newspaper noted in August 1915, 'There was a time when many of us believed that the war was the result of the unscrupulous ambitions of German royalty and German statesmen. To-day we know that the Anglophobia of the Kaiser and the Prussian military bureaucracy is shared by the Germans as a nation and as individuals. The whole German race, as a race, and as a conglomeration of individuals, is now consumed by a bitter and deadly hatred of Britain and the British.'[173] This logic of collective guilt carried ugly implications for local residents who might be associated with enemy powers.

Building on previous ideas of spies and saboteurs, rumours of hidden German influences became a new subject of threat and outrage. *Truth*, adding pro-German machinations to its populist arsenal, argued to its largely working-class readership that elements within the upper classes and even within the government tolerated disloyalty. In her 'Sassiety Spice' column on 1 April 1916 'Lady Dot' declared:

> There is altogether too much leniency being shown to Germans and other aliens just now by certain people. Strong comment is being made of the fact that one of our high officials allowed his daughter to marry a German — since the war began, too. Another thing, it does not always follow because a German is naturalised and gives handsome patriotic contributions that he is loyal. The wife of such a man was recently overheard on the telephone making use of the most disloyal expressions.[174]

Some of the most outlandish conspiracy theories came from the Women's Anti-German League. Established on 10 January 1916 and led by a group of socially elite women, the league soon built a membership of around 1500 and began circulating fevered claims.[175] It insisted that there were some 21,000 enemy aliens in the country, rather than about 6000, and that Germans or pro-German elements had significant sway in high places.[176] German agents were said to be responsible for an epidemic of infantile paralysis in Auckland, outbreaks of paralysis among livestock in Canterbury and a mysterious fire in Auckland that destroyed 200 horses and had 'never been explained'.[177]

The sinking of the *Lusitania* on 7 May 1915 had also brought renewed calls for mass internments. Just days later, on 11 May, feelings were running high in Dunedin, with a number of citizens discussing efforts to pressure 'the Government to intern every German, not only in Otago, but throughout New Zealand'.[178] The executive of the New Zealand Patriotic Society declared that 'the time has arrived when Germans and Austrians not naturalised . . . [and] in some cases occupying good positions in the public service, should be immediately interned and held as prisoners of war, and that the Government be asked to scrutinise carefully the conduct of naturalised British subjects'.[179]

In this atmosphere, the tensions surrounding Professor von Zedlitz at Victoria College escalated. Various colleagues rallied to von Zedlitz's defence — Professor Thomas Hunter, for example, argued that 'as we are fighting in this war on the basis of justice, we ought to be just' — and current and former students, some of whom had enlisted, provided glowing testimonials.[180] By mid-1915, however, the affair was becoming a national issue and a political controversy. As one well-travelled letter-writer to the *New Zealand Times* noted in July, 'the employment of Professor von Zedlitz is a topic of discussion in many places' and the conclusion was 'invariably against the professor's continued employment, and anything but complimentary toward the Government'. If von Zedlitz were 'allowed to remain in his exalted position regardless of the fact that his countrymen and ours are engaged in a fight to the death, the responsible parties do not deserve much consideration at the hands of the people of this Dominion'.[181]

The affair was exacerbated by a sense that von Zedlitz was protected by class bias. Thomas Wilford, the Liberal MP for the Hutt, which had a large working-class population, questioned the inconsistent results of internment policies in Parliament, stating that he knew 'a man who worked in one of the Government Departments in New Zealand for forty years — an ordinary working-man — and he is now on Somes Island. That is the discrimination I refer to.'[182]

In 1916 another furore arose around Lieutenant Alexander Hugh Grierson, who had

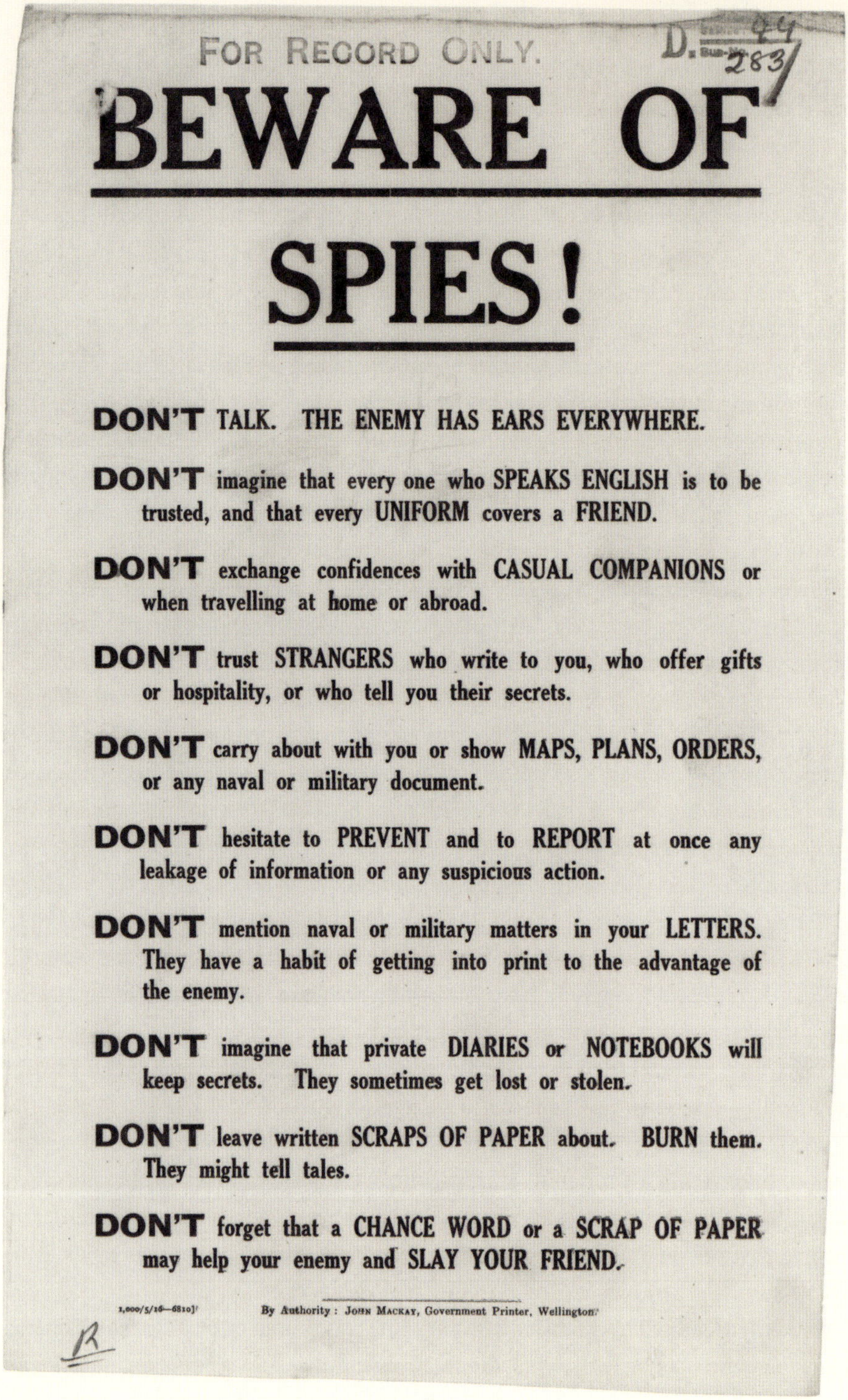
FOR RECORD ONLY.

D. 44/283

BEWARE OF SPIES!

DON'T TALK. THE ENEMY HAS EARS EVERYWHERE.

DON'T imagine that every one who SPEAKS ENGLISH is to be trusted, and that every UNIFORM covers a FRIEND.

DON'T exchange confidences with CASUAL COMPANIONS or when travelling at home or abroad.

DON'T trust STRANGERS who write to you, who offer gifts or hospitality, or who tell you their secrets.

DON'T carry about with you or show MAPS, PLANS, ORDERS, or any naval or military document.

DON'T hesitate to PREVENT and to REPORT at once any leakage of information or any suspicious action.

DON'T mention naval or military matters in your LETTERS. They have a habit of getting into print to the advantage of the enemy.

DON'T imagine that private DIARIES or NOTEBOOKS will keep secrets. They sometimes get lost or stolen.

DON'T leave written SCRAPS OF PAPER about. BURN them. They might tell tales.

DON'T forget that a CHANCE WORD or a SCRAP OF PAPER may help your enemy and SLAY YOUR FRIEND.

1,000/5/16—6810] By Authority: John Mackay, Government Printer, Wellington.

R

In an effort to improve security, 5000 copies of this poster were printed in May 1916 to be distributed at the country's ports and on government transports.
ARCHIVES NEW ZEALAND, R22432787

enlisted for the Twelfth Reinforcements. Allegations that he was a German agent exploded after a dispute over a bill led his former landlady to inspect his room, where she discovered German books and writing in German script that looked suspiciously like code. Memories of Grierson stating some admiration for German 'thoroughness' and, shortly after the outbreak of war, some disbelief at reports of German atrocities in Belgium were recalled and added to the gossip. Then there was the fact that the English-born Grierson had spent some time in Germany before the war, was fluent in German and had worked in the German consulate until the war. Class also played a part again: Grierson was well off and well educated.

A commission of inquiry subsequently declared him to be innocent of all charges and also of 'purely' British descent from prominent families in Hampshire and Cheshire.[183] The Women's Anti-German League refused to accept the verdict and continued to petition for Grierson to be removed from the army. According to John Payne, who had taken up the role of parliamentary spokesman for the league, Allen's unwillingness to recognise the necessity of 'purging the NZ Army of all whose presence in the ranks . . . is a danger to the successful prosecution of the war' indicated his unfitness for office.[184]

Suspicions were also stirring about the 1800–2000 Dalmatians, mostly young, mostly male and mostly single, who were largely concentrated on the gumfields north of Auckland. Rumours that Dalmatians were flying Austrian flags, drilling with rifles supplied by a German submarine and preparing a beachhead for a German invasion led to petitions calling for mass internment.[185] In the House on 10 June 1916 Charles Poole, MP for Auckland West, referred to a newspaper account of an alleged police raid on an 'Austrian' gumfield camp near Whangarei in which a substantial cache of firearms had been seized, and asked what steps were being taken to deal with the threat posed by enemy aliens. In response Allen raised doubts about the 'raid' and Massey said that the government was considering measures which would 'prove satisfactory to the whole of the people of New Zealand and especially to the settlers of North Auckland'.[186] It was subsequently reported that the police were merely enacting policy that Austrians should turn their firearms over: only half a dozen guns and very little ammunition had been taken.[187]

The ugliest episode of New Zealand anti-Germanism occurred on 15 May 1915 in Whanganui, as part of a transnational outbreak of '*Lusitania* riots' across the English-speaking world. New Zealand's experience was less extreme than elsewhere: there were acts of arson, mass destruction and looting in Johannesburg, and London suffered 'the most widespread domestic disturbances in modern British history'.[188] However, the same pattern of mob violence against a surrogate target was clear. Whanganui's riot occurred on a Saturday night a week after the news of the sinking. A crowd gathered outside a pork butchery owned by Conrad Heinold, a naturalised citizen of German origin, who was widely acknowledged as 'a reputable citizen . . . loyal subject, and highly respected in the Wanganui community'.[189] Some advance warning, in the form of several threatening letters to Heinold, meant that the premises were unoccupied, though defended by the police.

The authorities were, however, completely overwhelmed by the 3000 estimated to have gathered outside the shop that night. There were shouts of 'Remember the *Lusitania*!' and the mayor's attempt to defuse the situation by calling for civility and noting that patriotism could be better expressed by attending the recruiting meeting in the local drill hall was greeted by groans and a thrown stone. The mood darkened after 10 p.m. as the hotels closed and 'a leaven of more or less inebriated men joined the throng . . . The stone-throwing increased, and the tinkling sound of breaking glass was proof that in many cases the aim was true.'[190] Constable W. Cooper recalled shouted incitements to violence, including 'come, lets rush them, let us Britishers have our rights, fuck them'.[191]

The mob proceeded to vandalise and loot Heinold's shop as well as other businesses that were German-owned or associated with Germany, including the local branch of Hallenstein's and the Bristol Piano Company, resulting in an estimated £3100 of damages.[192] Days later Hallenstein's representatives held a press interview to 'clear up any idea that the firm was a pro-German one' and stressing their British credentials.[193] The Dunedin-based Bristol Piano Company had already tried to impress this point, having changed its name from the Dresden Piano Company the previous January, advertising the rebranding and insisting that the old name was 'no longer acceptable for an ALL BRITISH COMPANY'.[194]

Although both of Whanganui's newspapers condemned the disorder and the destruction of property, they diverged in their wider assessments. The *Chronicle* was unequivocal in denouncing the riot, describing it as 'at once contemptible and cowardly' and declaring it 'futile to appeal to "patriots" who needed the infusion of "Dutch courage" and the cover of darkness to enable them to display their valour'.[195] It referred to the famous 'scrap of paper, attested in the King's name, by which we have promised liberty and protection, and the full rights of British citizenship to Conrad Heinold and every other naturalised German in the Dominion. In the light of what happened on Saturday night, what is that scrap of paper worth?'

The *Wanganui Herald*, on the other hand, mixed condemnation of the destruction with criticism of the government's failure to intern more Germans, coming perilously close to justifying the rioters' behaviour: '. . . regrettable though [the riot] was as showing that some Britishers are prepared to descend even to the German level, [it] nevertheless had its lesson as evidencing that, when the authorities neglect the obviously right course, the public are apt to take the law into their own hands'.[196]

Throughout May there were other examples of anti-German violence in other parts of the country. In Hokitika, the windows of local businesses suspected of being German were smashed under cover of darkness.[197] And although those congregating outside 'German' businesses in Wellington dispersed without incident, a bottle was thrown through the window of a firm partly owned by the former German consul. There were also acts of individual violence towards those seen to be disloyal, particularly if they could be identified as 'German'.

A widely published story claimed to demonstrate that it was 'unsafe for a man to insult the British flag even in the presence of his hired servant'. It alleged that, during harvesting on a Marlborough farm, a driver decorated his dray with small Union Jacks and took exception when the farmer, who was 'of German blood and German sympathies, which he had never troubled very much to disguise', damned the flags and demanded their removal. Thereupon 'the harvester made the farmer pay dearly for the insult . . . dealing with him so energetically, it is said, that but for the interference of the other men in the field the result would have been serious'.[198]

German names and signs of German culture were also increasingly targeted. Before May 1915 efforts to expunge German heritage were limited and proposals to do so encountered considerable opposition.[199] For example, a January 1915 call, endorsed by the Ngāruawāhia town board, for certain 'German' street names to be changed was generally mocked: 'We can thrash the fighting school of modern Germans without putting mean affronts upon the memory of the peaceful old Germans, Copernicus and Kepler, Handel and Beethoven and the others.'[200] A few months later, however, the *New Zealand Herald* could declare that the man in the street was 'moved to anger at the mention of anything German, particularly German pianos, of which so many thousand have been sold in Australasia in recent years . . . It is all a myth about the German piano being the best. The British piano has always been the best, and, moreover, the birthplace of the piano was England, in the 13th century.'[201]

By mid-June the Greymouth Liedertafel had become the Orpheus Society, its counterpart in Wellington became the Wellington Male Voice Choir shortly thereafter, and the Auckland and Dunedin Liedertafel were male choirs by the end of the year.[202] In October 1915 the *Free Lance* was suggesting to the government that 'the map of New Zealand should be carefully overhauled and purged of each and every German name. Let a start be made with the nomenclature of the Southern Alps. The Franz Josef Glacier, the Hochstetter Dome, the Lendenfeld Saddle, the Silberhorn, Mount Hardinger should one and all be divested of their Teuton names and re-christened.'[203] In January 1916, the residents of German Bay, outside of Akaroa, requested that the existing name be 'wiped from the map' and changed to Takamātua, allegedly out of a hope that goods being delivered would be handled less roughly on the wharves; the minister of internal affairs supported the motion.[204] In July 1916 it was announced that Auckland's Coburg Street was to be renamed Kitchener Street in honour of the recently killed imperial icon. Even a homophone could be a problem: by the end of the year, nearby Jermyn Street, named after the New Zealand Wars veteran Captain John Jermyn Symonds, was renamed Anzac Avenue.[205]

In 1917 some local bodies carried out further renaming. Although Christchurch's Haast Street was saved, thanks to a strong majority on the council pointing out the prominent role Julius von Haast had played in the local community and the patriotic work of his descendants in the war, two other streets were less fortunate. Goethe Street became Domett Street, as the colonial poet and politician Alfred Domett displaced the rather more distinguished German writer; and Spohr Street, named for the violin virtuoso and composer Louis Spohr, became Fielding Street, in honour of the English novelist Henry Fielding. James McCombs had made a spirited protest, noting that Goethe and Spohr dated to a time when Prussia was an ally in Britain's struggle against French militarism.[206]

In Palmerston North the borough council changed Fritz Street, a name the mayor described as 'a little German', to Russell Street after local residents objected to the original choice of Hinemoa Street, and Schlager Street became Maire Street.[207] Ironically the desire of the Wellington City Council to commemorate local war heroes when changing duplicated street names led to Tainui Terrace becoming Freyberg Street.[208]

Important Announcement.

Although the Dresden Piano Company's name has become a household word throughout the Dominion, it has been decided to relinquish this familiar title and to adopt in its place that of

The Bristol Piano Co. Ld

When the business started, over 32 years ago, the name "The Dresden," being honorably associated with all that was best in Music and Art, was chosen as a good trading title, but, despite its well-earned popularity, there can be no doubt it is no longer acceptable for an

ALL-BRITISH

COMPANY

The Shareholders and Directors are, without exception, British born and bred, and are all resident under the British flag; there is not, nor has there ever been, one single shilling of anything but British Capital used or invested in the business; and as Bristol is the birth place of the Founder and present Chairman of Directors of the Company, the Public will fully appreciate the change of title to that of

The Bristol Piano Co. Ld

In early 1915 the Bristol Piano Company took out newspaper advertisements to announce its rebranding from the Dresden Piano Company, and to affirm the British nature of its directors and capital.
EVENING STAR, 2 JANUARY 1915, P. 11

Individuals, too, tried to distance themselves from any enemy associations by changing their names. Some went to the expense of formalising the change by deed poll though it is unclear how many individuals did, since it was illegal, under war regulations, for enemy aliens to do so. In December 1915, Max Adolph Hirschberg and Richard Carl Zimmerman tried to alter their names to, respectively, Max Adolph Hartmont and Richard Charles Vernon. After their arrest they were each fined £2 and costs, and assured the magistrate that they would 'go back to their own names'.[209] Although there was no legal impediment to anyone else, including those with German names after naturalisation or by descent, changing them, it is impossible to know how many did so.

CHAPTER EIGHT

MANAGING MOBILISATION

previous pages
The 1915 Trentham Army Camp rugby team. NEW ZEALAND RUGBY MUSEUM

Past May 1915 the war continued to alter the political landscape, most dramatically in August that year, with the formation of a coalition government. The growing scale and complexity of New Zealand's war effort was putting great pressure on the government and led to extraordinary management measures. By September 1917, in Massey's reckoning, the business of Cabinet, 'especially with respect to industrial and commercial matters', had been multiplied by six.[1] The country's leaders proceeded with cautious pragmatism, maintaining consensus and 'marching in step with [public mood] rather than trying to force the pace'.[2] Nothing demonstrated that approach more than the careful, steady attitude towards conscription. As Massey declared at the beginning of 1916: 'A majority of the nation is certainly in favour of universal service, but it has been tacitly agreed that voluntaryism must be fairly tested, and retained if it is adequate to the country's needs.'[3]

At the beginning of the war, neither the government nor the opposition had considered forming a coalition. Expectations of a short conflict and the mutual antagonism between Massey and Ward made such a move seem unnecessary and undesirable. Furthermore, both sides believed that the 1914 election might strengthen their positions. As the demands of the war grew, however, the idea of a coalition with a strong parliamentary majority became increasingly attractive.

In January 1915, Allen privately conceded in a letter to Godley that a coalition 'is the proper thing to do during the war time. It is, however, hard to bring it about. Ward is a very difficult person to deal with.'[4] Ward doubtless felt the same. The following month Godley wrote to Ward, 'I rather hope that you may have been able to arrange with Mr Massey for some sort of coalition till the end of the War.'[5]

Others were more public in their support. In the uncertain aftermath of the 1914 election, Richard McCallum, the Liberal MP for Wairau, openly called for a 'composite cabinet' with equal Reform and Liberal representation. However, his suggestion that 'the position of Prime Minister should be filled by the leader whose followers obtained the greatest aggregate of votes throughout the Dominion' clearly favoured Ward, assuming that 'followers' included his labour allies.[6] The Reform-supporting *Otago Daily Times* also broached the subject, suggesting that, at least until the end of the war, 'representation should be given in the Government to that section of the Opposition which is more largely in sympathy with the Reform party than with the extremists'. This would, it thought, 'hasten the day when the party lines in New Zealand would be drawn as, in Australia, between the members who are Moderates or Liberals . . . and the members whose views have a distinct flavour of Socialism'.[7]

The idea got a boost from 25 May 1915 when the British Liberal government felt obliged to invite other parties to enter Cabinet in the wake of setbacks and scandals over the Dardanelles campaign, the resignation of First Sea Lord John Fisher and allegations of a shell shortage. Massey insisted that speculation about New Zealand following suit was 'premature and inopportune', presumably because two pending by-elections meant the relative strength of the parties had not yet emerged.[8] However, it appears that arm's-length talks had already taken place, probably before the British announcement. As the *Evening Star* reported on 21 May,

> It is an open secret that third parties have had certain negotiations with the two Leaders with the object of discovering a basis of arrangement. One gathers that up to a certain point the negotiations made progress, and that then came delay, due not to the discovery of any insuperable obstacle to agreement, but simply to the lack of a bold initiative from some responsible quarter . . . Naturally these proceedings were entirely unofficial and non-committal, and nobody outside the inner circle can say just how far they proceeded.[9]

There was also more open signalling that month. C. J. Parr, who in 1914 had traded his role as an exceptionally able and energetic mayor of Auckland for the seat of Eden, was a powerful voice in the Reform Party calling for a coalition. He believed that the public would clearly favour Massey inviting Ward 'and, say, two of his strongest men to fill important positions in a National Ministry'.[10] Arthur Myers, Auckland's leading Liberal politician, and another very able recent mayor, seconded Parr's declaration. The call, however, was predicated on the two sides each having 40 seats, in other words Reform losing both impending by-elections.

News, in early June, that Reform had retained the Bay of Islands and that the Liberals kept Taumarunui clarified both the parliamentary situation and the negotiating positions. Despite Liberal hopes, the support of 'two guesses' Henare for the government seemed secure. Yet the calls for a coalition, from both Reform and the Liberals, grew louder from late May. As one historian puts it, the continuation of party-political bickering against the background of dire news from Gallipoli seemed not unlike 'flatulence in church'.[11] The *Sun* made the same point, if less colourfully:

> Hundreds of families are mourning the loss of brave men who have died for the Empire; hundreds more are anxiously waiting for tidings of sick, wounded, and missing soldiers whose fate is uncertain, and thousands are thinking only of those on active service . . . The last thing anyone wishes to hear is the chatter of politicians over the ordinary bones of party contention, and, except where it touches the war, the political game now interests nobody but the politicians themselves.[12]

The newspaper renewed its call for a 'National Ministry', adopting the widespread view that three Liberal leaders should enter the Cabinet.[13] Significantly, it made Allen's performance a major additional argument. 'It is absurd that Mr Allen should be loaded up with the portfolios of Finance and Defence, to say nothing of Education. How can he prepare a war budget and do justice to the all-important matter of defence at the same time.'[14]

However, neither the narrowness of Reform's final majority nor patriotic pressure made a coalition inevitable. The government seems to have hoped that it would endure without one. On 21 June, Allen said that he envisaged a 'very short' parliamentary session lasting only six weeks or two months and that 'only absolutely necessary legislation would be introduced, such as pensions and other matters arising out of the war'.[15] Liverpool's speech at the opening of Parliament on 24 June repeated the assurance that 'no legislation the discussion of which would involve party strife should be submitted to you'.[16]

The government also hoped to weather a short session by establishing a Secret Defence Committee 'to consider matters relating to defence and the conduct of the war that may be referred to it by the House or the Minister of Defence'. The committee would comprise six Reformers, four Liberals and one labour member, including the recognised leaders of those factions.[17] Although Reform had a narrow majority on the committee, the fact that its deliberations were to be held in secret meant that both the government and the opposition could compromise behind closed doors without losing face. Former Liberal ministers could also once again participate in important decision-making, something they, and not least Ward, undoubtedly desired.

On 28 June the Reform caucus discussed how to approach the session. As one parliamentary journalist remarked, 'The rank and file of both parties in the House are finding themselves more closely consulted by their leaders than they have been for many a long year past.'[18] Massey raised the possibility of a coalition, giving recently elected and technically junior MPs, such as Parr and William Downie Stewart, who were free of the political scars some of their colleagues bore, a chance to have their say.[19] Allen, who had been in opposition for 20 years and who regarded Ward as a recklessly irresponsible mountebank, would likely have preferred Reform to rely on its slender majority. Massey later glossed over any disagreement by saying simply that 'after discussion it was decided that I should offer Cabinet rank for the war period to three Opposition members'.[20] Given that he did not mention this when Parliament met the following afternoon, it seems likely that caucus left the timing of any announcement, and possibly the decision, to the prime minister.

However, any hopes Reform diehards may have had of getting through the session unscathed were soon dashed. The next day the government exceeded the limits of opposition cooperation by attempting to rush through a whole Public Revenue Amendment Bill, arguing that the war loan of £10 million it contained was urgently required. When Ward pointed out that the opposition had not yet seen the bill, Massey told him that it would be circulated forthwith and MPs could read it while the business of the day continued. After reviewing the text, Ward and Russell maintained that it went well beyond the approval of a war loan, proposing that the clause dealing with the loan should be approved and the rest postponed. An informal debate broke out and continued until Massey stated that the bill would be deferred until the next day. Reviewing the exchange, the *Evening Post*'s parliamentary journalist observed a feeling that 'the parties had just escaped a clash' and noted the incident as giving 'a fairly definite indication of the Opposition's attitude — the consciousness of its numerical and debating strength'. Consequently, he added, 'some shrewd readers of the political barometer were not completely surprised by the premier's words in the evening about the possibility of a National Cabinet'.[21]

A further factor was the fallout from the epidemic at Trentham Camp, which was becoming a political crisis by the time of the session. The pro-Liberal *New Zealand Times* had published a damning description by Dr Henry Thacker, the Liberal MP for Christchurch East, of conditions at the camp and their relationship to recent deaths.[22] Probably more troubling for Massey, though, was the level of criticism coming from his support base, with the staunchly Reform *New Zealand Herald* alleging that the episode reflected serious mismanagement and targeting Allen: 'The *Herald* has repeatedly pointed out that, since August last, either Defence or Finance would strain the energies of the ablest and strongest of our statesmen, yet Mr Allen still holds the two . . . This attempt to do what no individual could possibly do satisfactorily has led to many complaints, and has not redounded to the credit of the Government or to the reputation of an administration of the overburdened minister.'[23] Even the *Dominion*, which had been established to support Reform, considered that '[m]uch of the criticism which has been directed against the medical side of the Defence Department, we fear, has not been received by the Ministers concerned in the right spirit'.[24]

The possibility that less committed Reformers might withdraw their support threatened the government's precarious majority. Ōtaki MP Willie Field, who had crossed the floor in 1911 when Ward endorsed the sitting Social Democratic Party member and asked Field to stand in another seat, raised 'critical questions' in Parliament about the camp epidemic.[25] Massey also had reason to be anxious about Henare's vote since one of the soldiers who had died in the epidemic was a prominent Northern Māori constituent. The *Star* reported that there had been 'high words . . . between the Minister of Defence and two of the rank and file of his party' over 'the Trentham scandal'.[26] Far from hopes of a brief and uncontroversial session, the government was facing a potential crisis over a deeply felt issue. Exploring coalition possibilities with Ward may well have seemed preferable, if still undesirable, to trying to tough things out.[27]

On 29 June, in a 'surprise of the first magnitude', Massey announced that he was ready 'to consider any reasonable proposal to establish a National Cabinet in this country, thus following in a small way what has been done in the United Kingdom'. Ward replied that the matter would have to be considered 'by myself and those associated with me'.[28] Negotiations began on 1 July, with Massey extending a proposal, agreed to by the Reform caucus, offering Ward three out of the nine Cabinet places with Reform to retain finance and defence.[29] This was not an attractive proposition, especially as Ward coveted the finance portfolio and the Liberals' bargaining position was strengthened by Reform's limited options: labour MPs had already made it clear that they were 'absolutely against association with the Massey Administration'.[30] On 6 July the proposal was rejected.

A renewed proposal was discussed on 10 and 12 July.[31] Massey now offered four Cabinet posts, with Reform to retain finance and defence. An apparently well-informed journalist later said that this proposal was approved 'by only a reluctant majority of the party', representing 'the most the Prime Minister could wring from his followers'.[32] Even if Ward had been prepared to accept, he was answerable to radical Liberals antagonistic to Massey and Allen and extremely reluctant to sacrifice the Lib-Lab alliance. Besides their ideological affinities with parts of the labour grouping, they typically represented strongly working-class electorates vulnerable to inroads by labour. Moreover, the radicals preferred expanding the powers of the Secret Defence Committee, which contained Hindmarsh and would therefore not involve a divorce between Liberals and labour.[33] Having campaigned particularly strongly over alleged profiteering and increases in living costs, the radicals also required assurances of strong action on that front. On 21 July the opposition caucus rejected the offer.

Before facing another round of negotiations, Massey attempted to sideline Allen, who was especially unpopular with parts of the opposition. Moreover, his association with the Trentham crisis made him a target for public frustration. 'I am told I am the most hated man in the country,' said Allen in one letter, and editorials claimed that '[i]f the people of New Zealand could be asked what is the gravest political necessity of the moment they would be justified in saying "that Allen must go"'. Such sentiments even extended to the Reform caucus.[34] Moreover, Allen was clearly overburdened and mourning the loss of his son; by his private secretary's account he 'was working to the point of mental and physical exhaustion day in, day out'.[35]

However, although Allen was prepared to surrender his education and finance responsibilities, he made it clear that 'he would not under any circumstances remain a member of a Ministry if both [defence and finance] were taken from him'. A meeting between Massey and Allen reportedly resulted in a slammed door and Allen threatening to topple the government by resigning.[36] This brinkmanship rested on the astute calculation that Massey would not want to lose a parliamentary majority while awaiting the outcome of the resulting by-election. Dropping the idea of ousting Allen, Massey now attempted to persuade Ward into accepting him in a coalition Cabinet.

Meanwhile, the degree of discontent among MPs about the decisions their leaders were reaching behind closed doors was revealed in the House. On 9 July, 13 Liberals, five out of six labourites and half a dozen Reform MPs spoke out against the War Pensions Bill introduced by the government and seemingly unanimously endorsed by the Secret Defence Committee.[37] Discipline crumbled on all sides. When Ward declared that a defeat for the bill would be tantamount to calling for the committee's resignation, the Liberal backbencher John Hornsby shouted 'Rubbish!'[38]

A subsequent attack by Hindmarsh on dissident Liberals was interrupted by a point of order from Webb that indicated disagreement with his leader.[39] On 21 and 22 July, the Reform and Liberal leaders met again, as did the Reform MPs on the following two days. 'At this stage,' a journalist remembered, 'feeling in the Reform caucus was so high that a serious split seemed inevitable. One member after another got up and relieved himself of opinions which lost nothing in candour and intensity from the fact that they had been pent up in the

House.' Once Massey finally 'managed to bring his followers to a more amenable frame of mind and to satisfy them that the position was an extremely precarious one', the coalition negotiations accelerated, though 'the Reform caucus would not listen to the proposal for equal representation'.[40]

After a meeting with Ward on 26 July, Massey offered five Liberal Cabinet places to Reform's six, but not finance or defence. This third offer was turned down two days later, and there was a demand for equal representation in Cabinet; the Reform caucus rejected that proposal the same evening. At this stage the governor, who privately held Reform responsible for the breakdown of talks, set up a conference at Government House on 2 August.[41] Liverpool opened by stating that unless a coalition was formed he would dissolve Parliament and call an election.[42] He then withdrew. In light of the Trentham crisis and a precarious majority, the prospect of an election was highly undesirable to Massey, and the Liberal representatives were able to drive an extremely hard bargain.[43]

The resulting agreement was announced in Parliament, to 'pained and ominous silence', on 4 August, the first anniversary of Britain's declaration of war.[44] Ward's quest for equality in Cabinet positions had been successful, with five (later increased to six) ministers from each side plus Pōmare as the Māori member of the Executive Council. Ward took over finance, Allen retained defence, but a new Department of Munitions and Supplies was created for the Liberal Arthur Myers (munitions denoted all military-related supplies). Rather than voting on issues, both leaders talked of making decisions 'by agreement', which appeared to require at least acquiescence by all ministers.

Two other stipulations made in response to Liberal requests soon emerged in the press.[45] First, the operation of the Legislative Council Act, which would have made that body elective, was to be suspended in order to maintain the current balance of parties in the upper house. Second, 'a board shall be set up to investigate merchants' profits, and make recommendations to the Government to prevent merchants from charging exorbitant profits'.[46] Apparently, there was also a secret agreement that Ward would 'share the Prime Minister's duties in Cabinet, at functions and deputations' and that there should be no general election until at least six months after the war.[47] Certainly, this last point was later enacted in August 1916 under the Parliamentary Elections Postponement Act.

The manner in which a coalition altered some of the rhythms of parliamentary politics soon became apparent. A minor example was the enlistment of several MPs who had expressed a wish to volunteer but had been dissuaded, given the tenuous political balance. Thomas Seddon (Liberal) and William Downie Stewart (Reform) had managed to preserve this balance by enlisting as a pair in July 1915 and, before their embarkation, presented the 'unusual spectacle of soldier members of Parliament in uniform': 'They have followed the custom of many soldiers on active service by moustaches, and in appearance they are bronzed and bear evident signs of the spell of active outdoor life.'[48] After the formation of the coalition, Reform politicians John Bird Hine, Gordon Coates and William Henry Dillon Bell all volunteered. More significant was the reception of the royal commission's report on the Trentham crisis in late August. The most damning finding was the military authorities' decision to bring almost 4000 soldiers into an already overcrowded camp after they knew disease had broken out.[49] The report, however, roused little politicking; one newspaper commented that 'not a flicker was aroused in Parliament yesterday by the presentation of the Commission's report'.[50]

The coalition effectively left a labour caucus, consisting of the Social Democratic and labour members, as the sole parliamentary faction outside the government. Some Reform MPs and militant socialists welcomed this new alignment as clarifying what they saw as the fundamental divide in the political landscape.[51] While Ward had toyed with preserving the Lib-Lab alliance by offering Hindmarsh one of the allocated Cabinet positions, the labour caucus rejected the offer. On 29 August, John Payne and Holland publicly debated this decision; the two were increasingly at odds and Payne, styling himself as 'Independent Labour', was offering conditional support to the government.[52]

Payne argued that accepting a Cabinet seat would have advanced labour's political influence and increased its public support. Holland countered by arguing the need to preserve labour's independence and bluntly expressed his doubt over the government's, and specifically Massey's, willingness to advance labour policies.[53] However, this rejection, and disparaging references to the coalition as a 'fusion' government and Massey and Ward as 'the Siamese twins', did not represent any formal rejection of the war. In response to the coalition, the labour caucus issued a 'manifesto' noting that 'the Liberal Party and the Labour Party had loyally supported the Government in all its defence proposals'. Labour, while maintaining its independence, would 'assist the Coalition Government in every effort to help the Mother Country to maintain and uphold the highest ideals of liberty and justice'.[54]

The formation of the coalition in no way ended parliamentary criticism of the government beyond labour. On the contrary, backbenchers on both sides tended to take the government to task and even to vote against it, confident that a defeat would not lead to any change of administration, let alone an election. Some ambitious Liberal and Reform members outside the Cabinet may well have perceived that antagonism could enhance their prospects of a ministerial appointment to make them subject to collective Cabinet responsibility. Downie Stewart later described the coalition as 'cumbersome in action and perpetually agitated by intrigues and dissension', and in September 1915 Allen wrote to Mackenzie in London that 'the House is somewhat out of control as the Party organisation is somewhat superseded. Many of them look upon themselves as free lances.'[55]

As the demands and impacts of the war escalated, the government found itself facing the political reality that the public expected action on living costs. In July 1915, Liberal MP Josiah Hanan noted that, aside from the war, 'the subject which engages on the part of the wage-earning class the most attention and interest in this country is that of the increasing cost of living'.[56] The government's approach to this issue over 1915–16 was largely one of piecemeal experimentation, guided by pragmatism and compromise. The result continued a tradition of market capitalism meshed with significant state involvement, though the government's managerial role was considerably enhanced.[57] Philosophically, the Liberals, more disposed to see the state as an instrument for social and economic betterment, were inclined to accept bolder measures and interventions, especially as labour MPs threatened to attract support from Liberal sections of the public. Conversely, Reform MPs often argued the relatively constrained nature of the state to shape economic realities and often urged thrift as a means of cutting living costs.[58]

Massey, for example, repeatedly argued that price increases in wartime were inevitable, that 'food-prices have advanced . . . to a lesser extent in this Dominion than in any other part of the British Empire' and that 'there were certain fixed economic laws, which it would be as foolish to tamper with as to try to interfere with the rotation of the earth'.[59] Against ideas of a 'conscription of wealth', he bluntly noted that 'the effect would be such a depression, such a slump in this country . . . [that it] would not recover from in half a century'.[60] He continued to stress, though, that 'exploitation' would be punished and that the government was ready to purchase commodities overseas in order to dampen the market.

Indeed, beyond its 1914 cap on prices for wheat and flour and its intervention in the sugar market, Reform proved willing to enact further price control initiatives around staple goods during the first half of 1915. On 2 May, for instance, the government bowed to popular pressure and restricted 'the indiscriminate export of butter . . . in view of an insufficient quantity for New Zealand consumption being in sight'.[61] The approach became more systematic in October 1915 with the passage of the Cost of Living Act, which established a Board of Trade with broad powers of investigation and the authority to regulate prices, a major concession in winning Liberal support for a coalition.[62] The board remained a central mechanism in wartime price control, and by 1919 it had established price controls for 57 major grocery items as well as a range of commodities, including soap, sugar, candles, jams and matches.[63]

Further attempts to meet increases in the cost of living came from the Arbitration Court. In April 1916, a year after it resumed wartime operations, the court began granting 'war bonuses' in acknowledgement that wages in some sectors were being outpaced by living costs. That month, Justice Stringer noted that the present minimum rate for builders' labourers in the northern district was 'insufficient to provide them with a reasonable living-wage'. The court granted them a war bonus of 10 per cent, set to run until three months after the end of the war. A memorandum attached to this award suggested that employers in other industries might 'consider whether workers in their employ should not be granted a war bonus on the same lines'.[64] Like price controls, this bonus system would become a key mechanism in managing industrial relations, especially as falling real wages, a tight labour market and discontent helped to revive union militancy.

State management of the economy was also spurred by impulses to improve national organisation and efficiency, impulses that had also endorsed National Registration. The new minister of munitions and supplies, Arthur Myers, had a reputation as a keen administrator and an 'organising genius'.[65] The son of German-Jewish immigrants, which brought some rancorous accusations from anti-German quarters, Myers had inherited a position in his family's extensive brewing operations before pursuing a political career, both as mayor of Auckland and then in Parliament.[66] Setting out to assess the most practical application

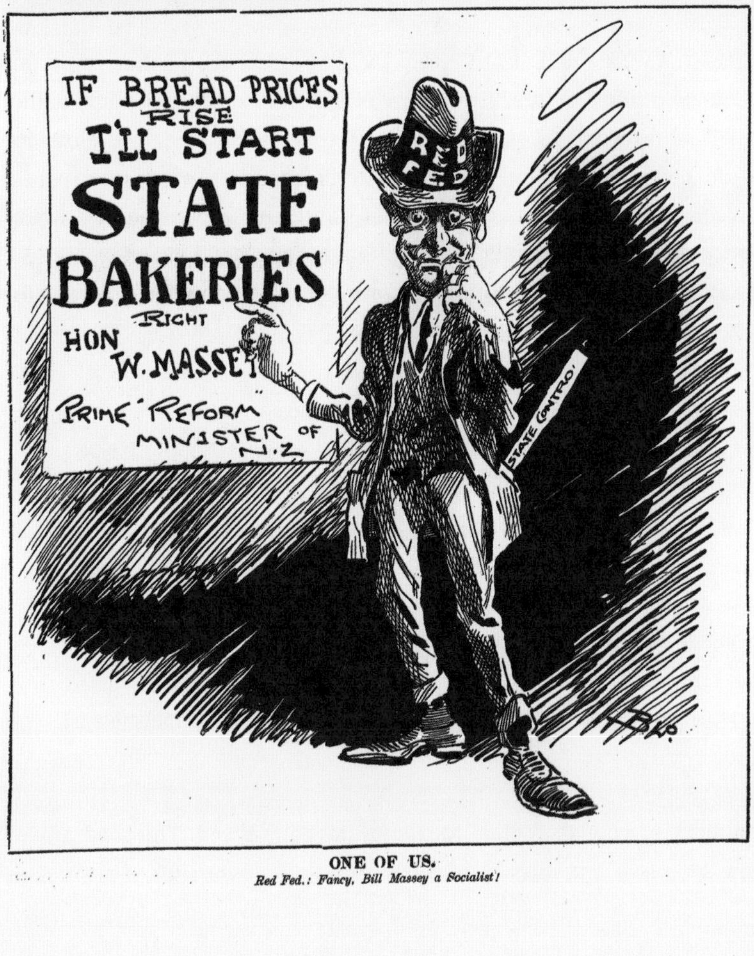

ONE OF US.
Red Fed.: Fancy, Bill Massey a Socialist!

above Members of the National Ministry. Back row from left: William Fraser, Alexander Herdman, Francis Dillon Bell, Josiah Hanan, Robert McNab, Māui Pōmare, Arthur Myers, William MacDonald, George Russell. Front row: James Allen, William Massey, Arthur Liverpool, Joseph Ward, William Herries. ALEXANDER TURNBULL LIBRARY, 1/1-013626-G

left The *Observer* depicts a socialist pondering the wartime peculiarity of a conservative government proposing state bakeries as a means to combat bread prices. NEW ZEALAND OBSERVER, 27 MARCH 1915, P. 1

of New Zealand's resources and capabilities, Myers soon reviewed proposals for the creation of an armaments industry capable of manufacturing munitions beyond small-arms ammunition.

Although initial investigations into the feasibility of securing necessary supplies and engineering skills were satisfactory, as were test grenades and machine guns,[67] the ambition was ultimately rejected because the necessary machinery was unavailable and local engineers and experts returned an unfavourable report on the project.[68] Instead, New Zealand forces were supplied with British munitions and the department focused on coordinating New Zealand manufactures with the needs of the empire.[69]

To this end a government survey between August and September 1915 assessed the capacities of New Zealand's manufacturers. Far from indulging in profiteering, most saw government orders as a problem rather than an opportunity, either because of unsuitable or insufficient facilities, stocks and workers or because of existing civilian demands. The secretary of the Kaiapoi Woollen Manufacturing Company, for example, emphasised that the staff capable of making military overcoats lacked the skills to make tunics and it was 'out of the question to expect interchangeable work — Trousers to Tunics'. The firm's 'special desire [was] that the Government should take care that every Woollen Mill and Clothing Factory is called upon to make its fair quota'. It wished to 'do its full share to meet urgent demands, [but] it should not be called upon to supply more than its fair share, every mill and factory in the Dominion also doing its share'.[70]

Makers of female garments were reluctant to retool their operations, and they could not see themselves making male uniform items.[71] In other cases industrialists proved unwilling to demand more of their workforces; as one Auckland factory owner said, 'We close for holidays so could not do much in January.'[72] The ministry responded by seeking to best assign work across the country's capacities and began an impressive expansion of primary and manufactured goods. In its three and a half years of operation the department oversaw the purchase of almost £4,500,000 of goods, produced or manufactured in New Zealand for military use. The final itemisation noted:

> Foodstuffs — Fresh meat, 10,840,000 lb; bread, 2,187,000 lb; sugar, 6,030,000 lb; flour, 9,020,000 lb; butter, 4,150,000 lb; jam, 3,469,000 lb; cheese, 1,867,600 lb; oatmeal, 1,255,000 lb; fresh milk, 764,700 gallons; candles, 252,000 lb
>
> Forage — Oats, 170,000 sacks; chaff, 2,975 tons; straw, 2,396 tons; hay, 1,368 tons; bran, 396 tons
>
> Equipment — Socks, 364,000 tons; undershirts, 294,200; underpants, 287,000; blankets, 274,000; working-shirts, 249,000; boots, 232,000; trousers, 216,000; jackets, 213,400; puttees, 139,600; hats, 133,700; greatcoats, 120,000; jerseys, 106,000; cholera-belts, 100,000; 'housewives', 99,000; shoes, 97,200; puggarees, 88,000; forage-caps, 83,000; pantaloons, 27,500; jerkins, 13,400.[73]

Under Myers, quality control of goods supplied to the military improved. The government empowered itself to fine suppliers who missed deadlines and took possession of businesses that breached contractual obligations or acted fraudulently. Ultimately, six manufacturers were prosecuted, though only three were thought to have acted fraudulently.[74] The first case to come to public attention was that of Abraham Levy, the Wellington clothing manufacturer whose success in monopolising uniform orders had raised suspicions in early 1915. In August 1916, the New Zealand Military Supplies Office alleged that Levy's factory and his subcontractors had been using cotton thread rather than the more expensive linen thread specified in the contract. It had informed Levy of the breach at the end of April 1916, but he persuaded a Defence Department examiner that linen was in fact being used. When it was revealed in July that Levy was using a particularly cheap form of cotton thread, he admitted the breach of contract, but pleaded that cotton was just as durable and linen thread had been unobtainable. Evidence was produced that the latter claim was untrue, and that Levy had saved £140 by using cotton thread on 11,132 of the 53,303 garments supplied.[75]

Levy's £50 fine was small compared to the cost of bringing the contracted goods up to specification, the loss of reputation and the public humiliation to which he was exposed. *Truth* exulted that at least one of the war profiteers it claimed were legion in New Zealand had been punished: 'Abraham Levy: "Patriot": A Corrupt Army Clothing Contractor: His Mean, Miserable Money-Making Machinations: Whines and Whimpers and Squeals for Consideration.'[76] Making obnoxious reference to Levy's Jewish heritage, the paper suggested that he had got the contract by undercutting a local 'ring' of clothing manufacturers to which he had belonged and that, following the cancellation of Levy's contracts, the 'ring' had secured the orders at the price they had originally proposed.[77]

Beyond organising goods, questions of better organising New Zealand's workforce raised potentially explosive issues which the government decided to approach with caution and generally delay. Ideas of state control over workers raised accusations of 'industrial conscription' from the labour movement. According to the *Maoriland Worker*, such schemes would signal a capitalist coup d'état that would roll back workers' rights. Forced labour would be introduced, unions would be eliminated, conditions would be determined by employers and workers would be court-martialled and executed if they resisted.[78]

Pricking this angst, some papers voiced support for ideas of directing the workforce. The *Otago Daily Times* suggested that there were 'a considerable number of persons who, although they are not rural workers, may under direction perform useful work on the farms', likely disturbing many town workers, who had little enthusiasm for the generally lower wages, poorer conditions and greater isolation involved in such work.[79] However, though some rural interests favoured ideas of channelling much-needed labour on to the farms, they mirrored the labour movement's concerns that wartime changes might negate past gains, specifically freehold control of land. Again, such fears were pricked as some Liberal newspapers asked 'whether the principle of nationalisation of effort that has been applied to certain British industries cannot be applied to our primary industries'. One suggested that now was the time 'to carry out Sir Joseph Ward's plan of setting the land boards throughout the Dominion to inquire and report as to the big areas of good land near our railways and our big centres of population either held absolutely idle or only very inadequately used. Now is the time to force such land into full use.'[80] It was probably not coincidental that Massey took personal responsibility for the national review of agriculture, despite effectively acknowledging that Myers was the obvious candidate. Massey likely preferred not to have the able, ambitious and Liberal Myers driving a vehicle with such potential, which he himself rapidly steered onto a more conservative path.

Similar patterns of expanding roles played out in relation to state welfare. The country had gone to war with state support for disabled soldiers and the dependants of deceased soldiers laid out under the 1909 Defence Act; regulations largely the same as those 'laid down in 1866 after the Maori War'.[81] Disability payments were based on a soldier's rank and the degree of disablement, subject to a unanimous recommendation by a board of three doctors. Privates whose disability was classified as 'first degree . . . losing two limbs or both eyes from wounds or injuries, or being so severely wounded or injured as to be totally incapable of earning a livelihood and to require the assistance and care of some other person', could be paid between 1s 6d and 3s per day.[82]

This was decidedly ungenerous compared with the 5s a day a private was paid, plus lodging, food and clothing. Pensions for soldiers' widows were also graded by rank. The widow of a non-commissioned officer or private was eligible for £36 a year, reduced to £30 in certain circumstances.[83] In addition, an annual allowance of between £6 and £10 (reducible to £4–8 depending on cause of death) was possible for each dependent child.[84] A year's pay (plus a third of a year's pay to each child) could also be awarded to the widow of a soldier killed in action or dying of wounds within 12 months.[85] Although modest when compared with wage levels, these allowances were significantly better than most existing levels of state support for civilians and their relatives. The means-tested old age pension was £26 a year and widows with one dependent child under 14 received a mere £12, increasing to £30 for those with more than three children. Widows without dependent children got no pension.

Pre-war social welfare provisions for dependants also rested on assistance from local charitable aid boards. Elected officials entrusted with distributing funds partly provided by ratepayers questioned those asking for help. Largely because of this vetting the process was often seen as the resort of the shiftless and improvident and regarded as shameful by respectable working people. The war, though, created many more 'respectable' dependants. During the 1914 election campaign, Massey had intimated that the pension rates might be increased.[86] But the long delay in calling the new Parliament meant that no fresh legislation was introduced until well after the Gallipoli campaign was under way and as the country faced unprecedented numbers of casualties. Also, the Reform government was divided over whether pensions should be means-tested, with Allen, as minister of finance and defence, emphasising economy.

In late May, a deputation of local body leaders and representatives of patriotic societies urged Massey not only to make the pension scheme more liberal, but also to remove means-testing and allow additional payments from patriotic funds. After pointing out that his government had recently removed means-testing from the few remaining New Zealand Wars pensions, Massey said he 'would like to make the other war pensions irrespective of private means'. Apparently unhappy with this ambition, Allen asked patriotic societies to consider the prudence of paying pensions to people who did not need them: 'If the man of means was to receive a war pension, then there would be a smaller pension for the man who had no means, since the amount of money that the Dominion could provide for this purpose was necessarily limited.'[87]

The delay in calling Parliament also meant that countries to which New Zealand was most accustomed to comparing itself moved first. In December 1914 the Australian government instituted more liberal pension rates than New Zealand's, including £52 a year for 'total incapacity'. In some circumstances the New Zealand rates were now lower and more subject to means-testing than those in Britain. The *Evening Post* considered the new Australian rates 'quite inadequate' and hoped 'that no such provisions will ever find their way to the New Zealand Statute Book'.[88] Even where the New Zealand scale was more generous, the Reform-supporting *New Zealand Herald* thought that 'in view of the difference in cost of living and wages standards a comparison of the two is decidedly in favour of the new scale fixed by the British Government'.[89] Some, however, argued that pension costs should not be so inflated as to encourage masses of husbands and fathers to enlist. 'There is a great difference,' said the *Star*,

> in a single man enlisting and a married man doing the same thing . . . The fighting qualities of the two men may be equal, but one is a more important economic factor to the Dominion than the other . . . To send married men to the front before making efforts to enlist every single man available would be a costly business for the Dominion. Already we know of cases where married men have been killed, and now the State must keep a widow and three or four children.[90]

Authorities agreed, and kept allowances for soldiers' dependants low to discourage family men from enlisting.[91] At the end of May, though, the government announced that it would pay an additional 7s a week 'separation allowance' directly to the wives of privates and non-commissioned officers, effectively making a married private's pay 6s a day.[92] Together with a typical allocation of 17s 6d from the regular pay of a serving private soldier, his wife would receive 24s 6d a week. Unlike in Britain, giving half a soldier's pay to his wife was not compulsory, but Allen noted that 'New Zealand had made provision largely to carry this out'.[93]

A War Pensions Act passed in August 1915 set a private's pension at £65 for his widow, plus £13 per child; £65 for a totally disabled single man; and £120 for a totally disabled married man, plus £13 per child. The first pension was granted on 2 September 1915.[94] Although some compared the rates favourably with those in other dominions, backbenchers from all parties denounced them as inadequate, particularly for disabled men. Further criticisms developed over shaken assumptions that the three-man War Pensions Board would interpret the legislation generously in awarding pensions; the rates were described as 'proposed' rather than 'maximum'.[95]

The board, in fact, proved less liberal than expected. Clauses within the act directed it to judge how dependent the applicant had been on the deceased soldier before he enlisted and to take into account the applicant's income and property, whether they received the old age pension and what property they had been left by the deceased, including the proceeds of life insurance policies. There was criticism, too, of the board's power to discontinue a pension if the recipient was convicted of an offence punishable by imprisonment. In the words of the *Observer*, this created 'a complete system of espionage and of research into the family, social and business life of the applicant'. The legislation 'might easily have been passed by the Prussian Diet, and approved by the Reichstag and the Bundersat [sic]'.[96]

There were several publicised cases of the treatment of dependants and disabled soldiers, including that of Captain Alto Frandi. Before his death at Gallipoli, Frandi had supplemented the pensions of his father and mother, aged 82 and 66 respectively, with half of his pay. His parents' application for a war pension was turned down, possibly because there was no proof that Frandi had been supporting them before his enlistment — they had not mentioned such support when applying for the old age pension — but also perhaps because he left a small property or because he had a married sister who might be able to provide support. The board subsequently relented, granting the parents £26 a year each.[97] Even the pro-Reform *Dominion* criticised the operation of the war pensions system: 'A man going out to risk his life should at least be given . . . a definite assurance that his dependents [sic] can look forward with certainty to a State pension of a reasonable amount.'[98] In response to the outcry, and possibly some political direction, by late 1915 the board had considerably softened its approach and instances of its new largesse were publicised in early 1916.[99]

Nevertheless, newspapers continued to report cases where mothers and siblings were left in poverty by the deaths of soldiers. In April 1916 there was a considerable outcry about the case of the 65-year-old mother of Henry 'Norke' Dewar, a popular rugby player from Stratford who had been killed at Gallipoli on 9 August 1915. Mrs Dewar had been receiving 20s a week from her son in addition to her 10s old age pension, but the board awarded her only 15s, effectively halving her previous modest income. The Taranaki Rugby Union strongly protested 'against the inhuman treatment of the Pensions Board in failing to make an adequate allowance to Mrs Dewar' and called for her to be 'placed at least in the position of comfort that she was in prior to the death of her son'.[100] Allen pointed out that Mrs Dewar had not listed her son's support when applying for the old age pension, but a New Plymouth editor was undoubtedly expressing widespread sentiments in stating that

> the maximum pension should be fixed on a generous scale; that the pensions should be given as a matter of right — not as a charity — and become payable within the Empire. It is also necessary that the minimum pension should be fixed by law and not by the Board, and that the administration of the Act should be carried out sympathetically, even if a few abuses do creep in, it being above everything desirable that no case of injustice shall mar the scheme and reflect on the Dominion's honor.[101]

The *Marlborough Express* also lambasted Allen's 'obstinate opposition' to the principle of pensions by right, as 'certainly not in accordance with public feeling on the matter'.[102]

A July 1916 amendment adjusted the legislation to provide pensions to widows and disabled soldiers as of right, removing income and property considerations. It also removed the limit on how many children in a family could qualify for support and allowed the parents of disabled and dead soldiers to apply for a pension.[103] MPs of all stripes, and several newspapers, however, still considered this inadequate. The *Evening Post* declared that 'the honest critics of the Act, whose numbers are legion, are far from agreeing that the rates provided are even fairly liberal . . . We trust members will take the earliest opportunity of forcing the Government's hands.'[104]

There were suggestions that Australia's recent increase of payments — 10s per week for the first child, 7s 6d for the second and 5s per additional child — might attract New Zealand men to enlist in Australia.[105] A Liberal MP also questioned the linking of pension rates to rank, an argument strengthened by general awareness that a low rank did not necessarily reflect a soldier's standing in civilian life.[106] As one newspaper declared, 'there are in the New Zealand forces hundreds upon hundreds of men in the rank-and-file who have left well-paid positions to go the front. Many of them have occupied better paid positions than those held by men who are officers.'[107]

In a further concession, the allowance for a private's family was increased to 7s 6d per child, regardless of the number of children. However, in a sign of things to come, this in turn led to calls for an increase in the allowances to the wives of serving soldiers.

> The admission that a child whose father has been killed requires at least 7s 6d for support involves the logical conclusion that 3s 6d is too little for it while its father lives, but is absent at the Front. No sacrifices are being made as yet by the great bulk of the community which would make it just that soldiers' wives, assuming they are capable of so doing, should go out to work as if they were unmarried, or give up their homes to live in squalid lodgings.[108]

Ultimately, the number of deaths, disabilities and dependants resulting from the war left the government facing calls for a level of state provision unthinkable in peacetime, and they were forced to make concessions in the face of near unanimous public feeling that those who had served should receive 'proof of gratitude'.[109]

On 21 June 1915, Allen confirmed that the £2,000,000 loan from the British government had now been spent, along with another £800,000.[110] A further war loan, and the imposition of a war tax, were inevitable. The government subsequently requested a £10 million loan which Parliament passed on 30 June without opposition. Coalition negotiations delayed thornier questions of how the funds needed to service the loan, and meet the ongoing costs of the war, were to be found.

The Liberals tended to favour progressive taxation, especially on the war-related profits of wealthier farmers, which vexed Reform. Conversely, the possibility of more extensive income tax or higher customs duties, which would further raise the cost of living, made Liberals anxious about potential losses of their working-class support. In the 1915 Budget debate, Robert Fletcher, the Liberal MP for Wellington Central, argued that the extra £2 million required from taxation should have come mostly from higher land taxation rather than from increased customs duty.

Unsurprisingly, given his party's rural support base among dairy farmers, Fletcher did not think that sector should be targeted, though 'I certainly think the wool-kings should be called upon to pay an extra tax on their wool'.[111] John Payne let fly, in typical fashion, regarding the £4 million in increased export returns since the outbreak of war: 'It has gone into the pockets of the farming community mainly; and owing to the operation of rings by those pseudo-patriots who always take advantage of a country when it is in trouble, and who would do the same if it were in its death-throes, the people I represent have been bled by an increase in the necessaries of life.'[112]

The 1915 Budget, presented less than a month after the formation of the coalition, had the hallmarks of a compromise. The prospect of the mostly Reform MPs, who believed that farmers were being unduly burdened by a kerosene and petrol tax, uniting with Liberal and labour MPs who saw it hitting the working class (who typically used kerosene for lighting), led the government to replace it with a 1 per cent duty on all imports. A Liberal newspaper still maintained that, despite Ward's claims, merchants would pass this on to consumers: 'The ordinary family will be very well aware of it.'[113]

The biggest increases in revenue were projected to come from higher postal and rail charges, capturing a further £380,000 and £360,000 respectively, while £285,000 was to come from extra customs duties. There were also major adjustments to income tax, with rates rising 3 per cent at the bottom and 13.3 per cent at the top, which were supposed to bring in an extra £300,000.[114] There were also tax increases directed at farmers, and the rate of the graduated tax on country, but not town, land was increased by 50 per cent. For the first time, too, income from farming was made liable for income tax. It was estimated that an additional £250,000 would be derived from this extension. All these changes took taxation rates, particularly income tax, to unprecedented levels. In 1914 some 14,000 taxpayers paid income tax that generated 9 per cent of government revenue; by 1918 the tax base had expanded to 38,000 and constituted 58 per cent of government revenue.[115]

Most of the revenue generated, however, was not earmarked for spending on the war — that came from the £10 million loan — but to meet revenue loss at home due to the war's flow-on effects, principally in customs and railways. Continuing to borrow to finance the war may well have been the only way to preserve political unanimity after both sides had exhausted relatively uncontroversial compromises. Consistent with the broader habit of delaying contentious decisions if possible, the approach seems to have been to borrow and hope that the war would end before the country acquired a massive amount of debt. There was concern, though. As the *Free Lance* noted in September 1915, 'We are piling up war debt at the rate of £400,000 a month; and the end of the war is not yet in sight.'[116]

By early 1916 the consensus was shaken by renewed calls for a tax that targeted war profits. Dunedin's Liberal *Evening Star* described such policies enacted in Britain as 'much superior to the Income Tax imposed by our National Government'.[117] The Australian government's announcement that it, too, would tax war profits added further pressure. The *Manawatu Standard* linked the need for such a tax to the daunting level of war debt, pointing out that 'while we are obtaining the money on loan from the Mother Country, we should be making substantial provision for the reduction of debt. When the war ends war profits will no longer be possible as a source of revenue. The time for taxing them is now.'[118]

Although the 1916 Budget, introduced in June, introduced a 45 per cent 'excess profits tax' intended to capture war-related profits, many of those hoping that farmers would be obliged to part with substantially more of their record profits were disappointed. The tax was seen as modest in comparison with the 60 per cent figure in Britain. The *Evening Post* thought it 'obviously inadequate', the *Taranaki Herald* said it could not 'be regarded as excessive' and the *Marlborough Express* claimed that those who had been 'simply coining money out of the war may congratulate themselves that they have got off very easily indeed'; the paper suggested a 75 per cent figure and retrospective taxation as appropriate.[119] Even the *Southland Times*, which had supported Reform in the 1914 election, realised that the tax would draw little from farmers.[120]

Remarkably, Ward's report of the country's finances, which accompanied the 1916 Budget, announced that the government had achieved a surplus on its revenue over expenditure (not including expenditure from borrowed money) of over £2 million over the previous year. Rather than proposing that such a sum could be used to reduce the debt now piling up, he announced that it was being invested in Treasury notes in London as a reserve to meet 'possible sudden claims in the future'.[121] There could be problems if Post Office Savings Bank depositors, as seemed likely, withdrew large sums when the war ended, because much of that money was invested in New Zealand government securities. He also invoked imperial patriotic sentiment by claiming that investing the surplus with the British government was helping it in a time of need.[122] Although the high commissioner in London augmented the reserve by investing it at higher interest rates there, the long-term cost of the war loans greatly outweighed these short-term profits, especially as the interest on the loans was exempt from income tax for the life of the loan.

The government also turned to local investors to raise £2 million for public works, given that the London market was considered unfavourable towards loans not related to war expenditure. Wellington had been told by the authorities in London that it should borrow no more than £300,000 a month and Ward privately anticipated that 'before long the contributions from the Imperial Government for [our] war purposes will diminish very considerably'.[123] The interest offered to New Zealanders with capital to invest was 4.5 per cent, made significantly more attractive to wealthier investors by being free of income tax. This concession had been offered by the British government for its war loans and Ward presumably felt that his public works issue might fail unless he provided the same terms. New Zealand also followed recent precedent in London by making it possible to invest in the loan in small amounts, encouraging a wider section of the community to participate.

In July 1915, the War Regulations Act, originally set to expire the following month, was extended: it would now remain in operation 'during the present war with Germany, and no longer'.[124] Many new powers and provisions were also put in place as mobilisation escalated over 1915–16. On 11 October 1915, for example, the minister of defence was empowered to requisition 'any military supplies from the owner or occupier of any factory or workshop which is adapted, or which may by reasonable expenditure be adapted, for the manufacture or production of the military supplies so demanded'.[125] On 15 November, any male over 18 years was forbidden from leaving the country without official documentation. This development sprang from increased regulation over movement, especially of those eligible for military service, and the introduction of passport systems.[126] In August 1916, to calm concerns over irreverent exploitation of Anzac Day, regulations prohibited 'the use of the word "Anzac" in connection with any trade or business'.[127]

Provisions to suppress social and political activities deemed injurious to the war effort were also considerably widened. The activities initially prohibited by the War Regulations Act were directly, or relatively, related to the war effort — banning the publication of information of military value to the enemy, outlawing obstructions of military orders, forbidding the circulation of false reports likely to cause panic — but regulations enacted between July 1915 and July 1916 proved less restrained and indicative of increasing psychological mobilisation.

Over those 12 months authorities were empowered to ban the sale or possession of any book considered 'injurious to the public interest in respect of the present war'; prohibit any moving picture that represented or related to the war; ban the printed expression of 'any information likely to interfere with the recruiting, training, discipline or administration' of troops; and forbid incitements, 'by word, writing or otherwise', expressing violence, lawlessness, disorder or any seditious intention.[128] This development is indicative of the extent to which securing concord and suppressing dissent had become a consideration of the war effort; the passage of regulations tailored to suppress opposition to the war effort has been described as constituting 'a small industry'.[129]

The effects of these powers soon became apparent. A particularly controversial case of 'disloyal utterances' occurred in March 1916, when 70-year-old Ellen Fuller, who was of Norwegian birth but had lived in New Zealand for 40 years, lost her temper at the Palmerston North Railway Station when she discovered that troops were being given priority on trains and, consequently, there might not be room for some of her luggage. Witnesses to the resulting scene, which police maintained could have resulted in violence, reported Fuller proclaiming, 'It is always the same with you [redacted] Britishers; your King George is a [redacted], and when the Kaiser comes out he will have a lot of you slaughtered. The Kaiser is my lord and master.'[130] The presiding magistrate judged such remarks as inexcusable and sentenced Fuller to two months with hard labour, subsequently reduced to imprisonment alone, and noted that the accused would not be afforded such leniency had she made comparably disloyal remarks in Germany.

The sentence caused controversy. Many ascribed Fuller's remarks to a customary temper and poor mental health rather than to perfidious resolve, and the adjudicating magistrate was roundly criticised. As the *Manawatu Daily Times* wrote:

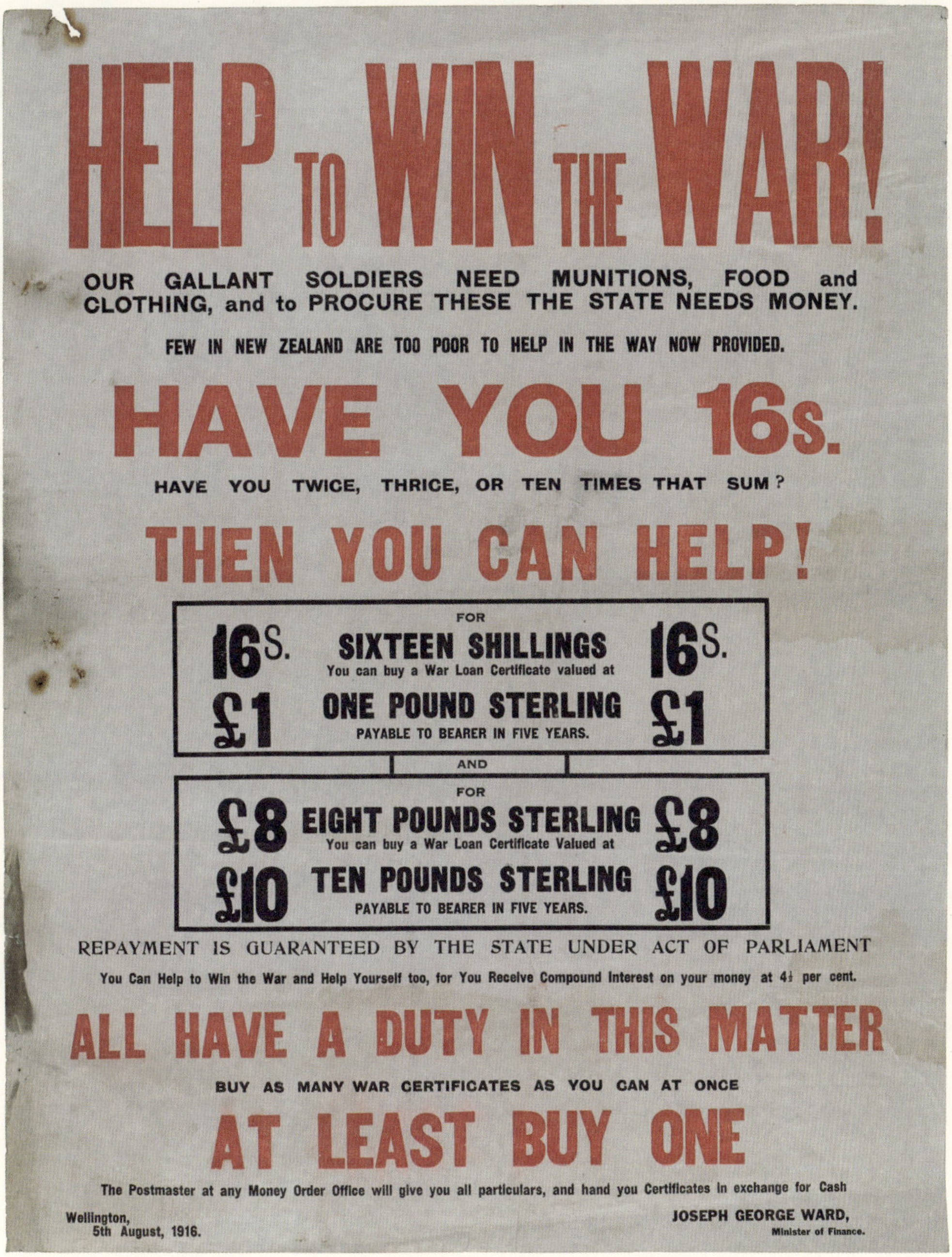

In the effort to raise capital the government sought to encourage citizens to invest in war loan certificates. This poster presents the loan both as a means to aid the war effort and as a sound investment. ALEXANDER TURNBULL LIBRARY, EPH-D-WAR-WI-1916-02

> It is nothing to the point that in a less civilised era this ancient mentally-unbalanced foreigner might have been hung, drawn and quartered, or torn to pieces by wild horses for making invidious references to the reigning monarch. It is nothing to the point that the Germans might have shot her for lese majeste. It is nothing to the point that she has resided in our midst for forty years without being able to subdue the violent aberrations which render her irresponsible when in a tantrum. It is nothing to the point that people of her peculiar disposition were burnt at the stake as witches in the good old days of long ago. A sentence till the rising of the Court and a bond for good behaviour would have amply answered the purposes of justice in this case.[131]

Truth concluded that Fuller would be better placed in a mental hospital than a jail, but added that '[t]here are plenty of instances of Germans in our midst whose utterances and actions call for severe penalties', adding its hope that such powers would be turned on those targets.[132] By the end of the war 287 people had been charged for seditious remarks, 208 convicted and 71 imprisoned.[133]

Other public 'utterances' were more systematically monitored. Political and industrial meetings came under police observation as constables, and in some cases stenographers, were sent to attend and report.[134] During Adela Pankhurst's 1916 lecture tour, for example, Police Commissioner John Cullen instructed various districts to 'please arrange to have all lectures delivered in your district by Miss Adela Pankhurst attended by the police, preferably in plain clothes, and if she makes any disloyal or seditious statements, or statements calculated to interfere with recruiting, the facts are to be immediately reported'.[135] Some constables considered that the lectures might have a negative impact on recruiting, but others expressed variations on statements that 'she said nothing in my opinion which would amount to a Breach of War Regulations' and 'her language was fairly moderate and I do not think that she committed herself in any way'.[136]

As it was, authorities seem to have confined themselves to petty legalism, and when Pankhurst addressed the overflow of a meeting on Wellington's Abel Smith Street, she, alongside Paddy Webb and Harry Holland, was prosecuted on a charge of obstructing traffic on a street 'positively devoid' of traffic. Pankhurst was ultimately acquitted and the two men fined.[137]

Published writings, too, were increasingly managed, monitored and restricted. On 1 April 1916 censorship regulations over the press were tightened. Newly prohibited material included publication of statements about or allusions to casualties, including the army and unit a man had served in or his location, and any casualty figures that had not been officially sanctioned. The publication of uncensored soldiers' letters was also banned.[138] Growing concerns with 'subversive' literature also date to this period. On 20 September 1915, for instance, gazetted regulations prohibited 'the importation into New Zealand of the newspapers called *Direct Action* and *Solidarity*, and all other printed matter published or printed by or on behalf of the society known as "The Industrial Workers of the World."'[139]

Material thought to be interfering with recruiting was also pursued, although the boundaries of what constituted such material could be hazy. When Liberal MP John Hornsby sought the punishment of the Society of Friends for issuing pamphlets that discouraged recruiting, Allen voiced doubt that such literature would threaten New Zealanders' convictions.[140] In October 1915, though, police raided the Freedom League offices in Auckland and a prosecution was lodged about material that breached regulations.[141] The subsequent court case against Egerton Gill focused on pamphlets the league had produced for its members suggesting that when they completed their National Registration cards they wrote: 'Whilst registering as a citizen, in conformity with the Government's demand, I could not for conscientious reasons take part in military service, in employment necessitating the taking of the military oath, or in the production of materials the purpose of which is the taking of human life.'[142]

The Crown Prosecutor claimed that this discouraged enlistment and breached regulations. The magistrate decided that it was 'not a time to deal gently with offences of this description . . . On this occasion a heavy fine [£50] will sufficiently punish the defendant, and will at the same time draw public attention to the necessity for strict compliance with the war regulations.'[143] The case may have had an effect: in the aftermath of the raid, eight Freedom League members resigned and attendance at meetings in early 1916 was about half that of 1915.[144]

By 1915–16 postal censorship was providing authorities with information gleaned by reviewing vast quantities of private mail — over 20,000 letters a month by one estimate.[145] Although this surveillance was principally directed at correspondence to enemy and neutral countries, prisoners of war in Europe and internees in New Zealand, it clearly informed state suppression of those opposing the war effort.[146] This was apparent in the case of Christchurch peace activist Charles Mackie, whom censors were identifying as a '"peace-at-any-price" individual' by the end of November 1915; the solicitor-general soon noted that examination of his correspondence was 'fully justified'. A carton of 'probably 500' leaflets addressed to Mackie from the [British] Stop the War Committee was intercepted and by December 1915 even his Christmas cards were being stamped as being reviewed by censors.[147]

Tougher state powers also targeted enemy aliens, a consequence of the general increase in ethnocentric attitudes. Generally, the government continued with cautious pragmatism. Calls to rename Germanic geographical features, for example, were quietly resisted; although the Tourist Department considered renaming peaks in the Southern Alps, and removed them from a publicity film.[148] Calls for mass internment were also opposed. This, Massey argued, would entail not only seizing and guarding thousands of people but also taking responsibility for their, and their dependants', welfare. He also maintained that New Zealand needed to heed 'instructions' from London advising against needless arrests.[149] Allen, too, challenged activism he saw as illegitimate. When the mayor of Dunedin told him about a deputation protesting about the son of a German consul being given a commission in the NZEF, Allen countered that the man in question was 'a thoroughly loyal citizen' and expressed disappointment with his fellow Dunedinites:

> I cannot conceive that the spirit which has actuated this deputation is the spirit prevalent in New Zealand, because it is so contrary to all that is best in British traditions. What has

> made our Nation great, to a very large extent, has been our fairness and justice, and even our generosity towards our opponents. But to turn upon those who happen to have some German blood in their veins, though they are thoroughly loyal to us, is quite contrary to the best British principles that I am acquainted with.[150]

Allen also responded to the Women's Anti-German League's continued campaign against Lieutenant Grierson, denouncing it as 'entirely wrong and savours of persecution . . . you are at liberty to impugn my own loyalty to the very full, but whilst I am satisfied as to the loyalty of my officers I shall do nothing to injure them or their reputations'.[151]

However, anti-German sentiment clearly had some influence on politics. The fevered and conspiratorial quality of wartime anti-Germanism was most notably brought into parliamentary political theatre via Payne, in his de facto role as parliamentary spokesman for the Women's Anti-German League. In August 1915, as rumours circulated over why von Zedlitz had retained his teaching position, he proclaimed that 'the public are beginning to wonder whether or not we have Germans in the cabinet'. He then singled out Attorney-General Herdman: 'I have been told that the Minister of Justice is of German extraction — that he had a German mother . . . if that rumour was correct, then there was certainly a German sitting in the Cabinet.'[152]

Officials sought to manage these challenges to legitimacy. On 14 June 1915 the government established an Alien Enemies Commission, which travelled to hear cases against enemy aliens 'where concerns for their continued liberty arose'. In July it sat to consider the von Zedlitz case and decided that he should keep his job and his liberty. Intended to defuse public concerns, this judgment only added to claims of class bias.[153] Alongside wild claims that the professor was building a platform for a gun emplacement on his property and was signalling secret messages, there were uncomfortable questions about why he appeared to be receiving preferential treatment. In August the issue was debated in Parliament and resulted in the passing, in September 1915, of legislation that prohibited 'the Employment of Alien Enemies as Teachers in Public Educational Institutions'. This was clearly intended to force von Zedlitz from his position; he was the only individual in the country affected by it.[154] In von Zedlitz's words, 'the Government have done their best to protect me, but they are mostly a knock-kneed crowd . . . the trouble is due to members of Parliament wanting to pose before their constituents as democrats and patriots'.[155]

The Croatian community, often specified as Dalmatians or more generically referred to as Austrians or Yugoslavs, faced similar pressure. There were allegations of a Dalmatian fifth column in the Far North and a proposal was sketched out to 'segregate' Dalmatian gum diggers on the remote gumfield at Pārengarenga. In June 1916, Herdman noted that the government intended to send 'unnaturalized Austrian subjects to a place called Parenga . . . They will be permitted to earn their living by digging for gum, an occupation in which they are experienced.'[156] However, many leading officials doubted the claims of Croatian disloyalty, noting the intense anti-Austrian sentiments among that population.[157]

Protests over the Pārengarenga scheme led to a two-man commission of inquiry which took evidence in Auckland and at numerous places in the north in July and August 1916. It concluded, 'decidedly', that 'the existence of large bodies of Austrian subjects in the North Auckland district is not attended with any danger to the community'. The only instance of intercommunal violence the commissioners discovered had involved a 'Servian boarding-house keeper' on his own premises. 'A number of British and Maoris under the influence of drink rushed in and asked him what he and his countrymen would do to their people when they (his questioners) had gone to the war.' The attackers were prosecuted for assault and each fined £10.[158]

The commission believed that economic competition was the main cause of so many baseless claims. One witness's grievance was 'not that they were arming or drilling, but that they sometimes tendered for contracts at a lower figure than he did'. The commission argued strongly against internment, both because it considered the Yugoslavs were overwhelmingly loyal to the Allied cause, and also because local businesses would be ruined by the loss of customers. The proposed internment in the Pārengarenga district would also damage the Māori community by competing for gum. In July 1916 the commission's report was widely publicised in newspapers, though local resentments continued to simmer.[159] The government accepted the commission's findings, and ideas of a wholesale internment of non-naturalised Yugoslavs and their employment as a segregated labour force were, for the moment, shelved.

Other fronts on the 'enemy alien' question were less secure. In May 1916, shortly after the parliamentary session opened, Payne and a posse of Liberal MPs levelled various pro-German charges at the government. Payne declared that a hidden hand was at work: 'We have in this country a very deplorable pro-German feeling. We have it on the one side from the extreme Socialists, and we have it on the other side from certain sections of the wealthy classes of this country.'[160] Charges over the following weeks included claims that Germans had been allowed to enlist in the expeditionary force, putting the lives of the country's soldiers at risk; that public celebrations of German military actions were taking place in parts of the country; and that class privileges explained the government's internment policies, specifically that wealthy Germans were 'having a high old time at the expense of the country' on Motuihe rather than on Matiu Somes Island.[161]

In a final piece of vindictive political theatre, Payne introduced the 'von Zedlitz Grant Restitution Bill', aimed at retrieving the £700 that Victoria College had awarded him on his forced dismissal. Payne declared this 'robbery of public funds' was both 'a contribution to the Kaiser's espionage system' and 'a manifestation of that sloppy pro-German sentiment which has unfortunately permeated a certain section of society in New Zealand'.[162] Although a second reading was fixed for the following week, the bill disappeared from subsequent debate as parliamentary procedure was adjusted to give preference to war legislation.[163]

Other legislation did not disappear, and attempted to delineate and define the sometimes blurred boundaries of enemy aliens. From 2 May 1916 the wives of enemy aliens, regardless of whether they were British-born citizens, were categorised as enemy aliens.[164] Naturalised individuals from enemy territory, and in some cases their sons, were not treated on the same basis as other citizens in recruiting for the armed forces. According to instructions dated 21 August 1916, sons born in New Zealand of parents naturalised before their birth could be accepted on normal terms; those born after their parents' naturalisation could be accepted on the recommendation of a commanding officer and subject to Defence Department approval; sons with German, i.e. unnaturalised, fathers were not acceptable in any circumstances.[165] Sons born in New Zealand before the naturalisation of their father, regardless of the mother's nationality, were apparently excluded. Michael Kulinski, a farmer from Kaimata, stated that he had been dismissed from camp after enlisting and he believed it was because his father was a German Pole.[166]

Into 1916 the government was caught between balancing its military commitments, louder public demands for conscription and potential opposition from pro-voluntarists and anti-conscriptionists. In order to delay that challenge, and blunt any charge that conscription had been unnecessarily forced on the country, the government embarked on a final attempt to revitalise the voluntary system. At the start of the year Massey issued a 'manifesto', reaffirming the war's cause and pledging that conscription would be introduced only if voluntary recruitment had obviously failed: 'while men are forthcoming in sufficient numbers to fulfil the engagements, which New Zealand has made with the Imperial authorities, there is no desire on the Government's part to depart from that system'.[167]

To demonstrate that it was willing to try to work with volunteering, the government announced a new recruiting scheme, modelled on Britain's Derby scheme, to begin in February. Its key feature was a national Recruiting Board, to coordinate volunteers who would canvass local men and ask them to enlist; this surveying was also intended to test and improve the national register. The scheme's advocates were confident that it could revive voluntary enlistment.[168] Those in favour of conscription refused to believe that a hitherto unenlisted man would go into khaki 'because a borough councillor says he ought to' and wished that the government would simply introduce conscription.[169] Although six local bodies and a Farmers' Union branch initially refused to support the scheme, against 180 promising to support it, detractors generally chose to comply under the belief that this was the final trial of the voluntary system — Allen had publicly pledged that he would resign if the scheme failed and conscription was not introduced — and because active opposition might be seen as sabotage.[170]

Problems soon arose. Many regions had trouble finding people willing to canvass and many canvassers appeared embarrassed to confront potentially hostile strangers, especially when they appeared to be asking others to enlist when they had not. Some returned soldiers proved overly confrontational; a Defence Department official noted that veterans should not be asked to approach unwilling men — 'I know of many instances already where, when this has been attempted, assaults have invariably occurred.'[171] Partially in an effort to avoid possible confrontations, certificates, armbands and badges had been introduced to identify enlisted men, returned soldiers, those who had been medically rejected and those in select occupations.

Of the four main centres, only Dunedin and Christchurch actually completed the canvass. Auckland elected to abandon it, instead focusing on manning a recruiting station that was

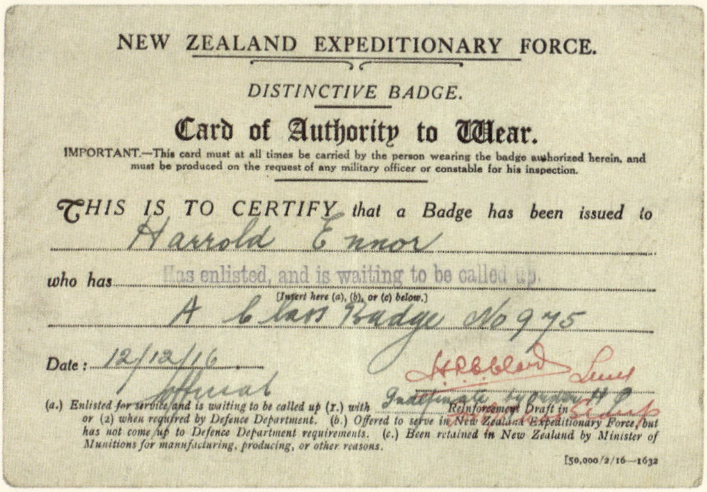

NEW ZEALAND EXPEDITIONARY FORCE.

DISTINCTIVE BADGE.

Card of Authority to Wear.

IMPORTANT.—This card must at all times be carried by the person wearing the badge authorized herein, and must be produced on the request of any military officer or constable for his inspection.

THIS IS TO CERTIFY that a Badge has been issued to Harrold Ennor

who has Has enlisted, and is waiting to be called up.

[Insert here (a), (b), or (c) below.]

A Class Badge No 975

Date: 12/12/16

(a.) Enlisted for service and is waiting to be called up (1.) with .... Reinforcement Draft in .... or (2) when required by Defence Department. (b.) Offered to serve in New Zealand Expeditionary Force, but has not come up to Defence Department requirements. (c.) Been retained in New Zealand by Minister of Munitions for manufacturing, producing, or other reasons.

[50,000/2/16—1632

THE CALL TO THE FLAG

The National Recruiting Board, comprising Mr. Massey, Sir Joseph Ward and Mr. Allen, have initiated a great National recruiting compaign, only the success of which can ward off Conscription.

Hear ye the call to the flag,
It's resounding o'er valley and crag.
If ye heed not the call
'Tis Conscription for all,
So this be your fate if ye lag.

So list to the call of the flag,
Ye lads of the bush drop your swag.
Ye who toil with the pen,
Hear the call and be men,
Or what of the Freedom we brag?

above A ribbon indicating the wearer had enlisted, and the accompanying certificate. This example was issued to Harrold Ennor, an Auckland clerk. ALEXANDER TURNBULL LIBRARY, QMS-0682

left *Truth* depicts the new recruitment campaign to boost voluntary enlistment as a 'call to the flag', urging eligible men to enlist and warning that 'If ye heed not the call 'Tis conscription for all'. NZ TRUTH, 12 FEBRUARY 1916, P. 1

open 12 hours a day, six days a week. While this brought censure from Allen, it appears to have notably boosted local recruitment.[172] There was negativity towards canvassing in Wellington also; some meetings held to recruit canvassers elected instead to vote for an immediate introduction of conscription.[173]

Measuring the success of the scheme was, and remains, a matter of perspective. Those calling for conscription could note that reinforcement quotas continued to fall short by their deadlines. Just before the scheme was launched in February, the Thirteenth Reinforcements had mobilised 120 short, the Fourteenth, mobilised in early March, were 200 short and the Fifteenth, early April, 279 short.[174] Voluntarists could, correctly, argue that these gaps were soon filled and, therefore, that volunteering had not failed. Later assessments are similarly conditional in their judgements. One described the scheme as 'a qualified success', when 'measured in terms of the original justification for its introduction, as an attempt to see whether sufficient recruits could be obtained by voluntary enlistment so as to make conscription unnecessary'; another notes that 'the scheme had neither saved nor killed voluntarism'.[175]

Within this limbo the government elected to move towards conscription. On 27 March 1916, Massey publicly announced that 'a bill providing for some measure of compulsion' would be submitted when Parliament opened in May.[176] The Military Service Bill was indeed introduced on 24 May, Empire Day. Allen began the first reading by noting that the bill had one object: 'to win the war and to secure a lasting peace'. His speech continued by praising the spirit and record of the voluntary effort:

> There have been enlisted and sent from New Zealand — and I include in this total some 240 men who enlisted with the British section and were enrolled in the Mother-country, some reservists, and a few Imperial ranks and ratings, also the men on the 'Philomel' — this country has enrolled, equipped, and despatched over 46,000 men. In addition to that, we have sent away some 351 nurses belonging to the New Zealand Army Nursing Service. It is a pleasure to place on record the fact that 1,010 of our Maori fellow-citizens have left New Zealand for service at the front, and some 230 further Maoris are in training now. It is interesting also to know that 148 Niue Islanders and fifty Rarotongans have left this country for service alongside the pakeha at the front. We have in training in the camps — I include in this total the Seventeenth Reinforcements, who are now mobilizing — 11,309 men, or a total of men sent to the front and in training, of 57,592.[177]

A fuller audit of efforts might have added the 26,951 who, by June 1916, had volunteered but had failed medicals and the thousands of New Zealand-born men and women who enlisted in overseas armies: nearly 12,000 by the end of the war.[178] Nevertheless, Allen emphasised the scale of the task the country faced and stated that conscription represented the fairest and most efficient means of organising the country's reinforcements: 'In my own judgment, the most just, the most democratic — and I emphasize the word "democratic" — the most scientific, and the surest way to secure the necessary men and to win the war would have been compulsory national service right from the start.'[179]

The legislation was intended to be a compromise between those demanding an immediate introduction of conscription and those who stated they would accept it if volunteering had demonstrably failed; 14 members took the former position and 16 non-labour members the latter.[180] The proposed system would continue accepting volunteers, with balloting enacted to make up a shortfall in a military district's enlistment quota. By continuing volunteering and making any application of conscription dependent on its success, the bill circumvented a potential clash, leaving the labour MPs, minus John Payne and William Veitch, as unconditional opponents.

The method of balloting also attempted to take account of concerns about equality of sacrifice, such as the belief that single men should serve before husbands and fathers. Registered men were split into two divisions, the first consisting of unmarried men without children and the second of all other reservists.[181] No second division reservist would be balloted until a district's first division men had been processed and either enlisted or exempted. Also, in order to pacify worries about 'evasion through marriage', men married after 1 May 1915 were categorised as first division. Likewise, section 35, popularly dubbed the 'family shirkers clause', was an active measure to promote equality of sacrifice, allowing the minister of defence to issue immediate call-ups to families containing two or more first division brothers; ultimately 2876 men were investigated under the section with 880 sent to camp.[182] On the other side of the balance, section 18 introduced a 'sole surviving son' clause in which a reservist who had at least one brother killed in action and was the only son left in the family was automatically eligible for exemption.

The appeal process took account of the need to prevent 'shirkers' from escaping but also to allow for reasonable exemptions. After being balloted and medically examined, men could appeal for exemption on the grounds that their service would be contrary to the public interest or that it would result in undue hardship to themselves or others. Each case would be heard and assessed by a Military Service Board. If the government wished someone to be exempted, a certificate would be provided from the minister for munitions and supplies, which the board would be obliged to accept unless it saw any reason not to.

To promote public confidence, much of the machinery of the scheme rested on civil bodies and government departments other than Defence, which would have no authority over civilians until they were soldiers. The balloting process was assigned to the government statistician, working under the minister of internal affairs. The police were given the responsibility of locating defaulters who did not respond to their call-up as well as deserters who failed to mobilise or fled from camp. Military Service Boards would be independent of political and military power, and the Liberal MP George Forbes asked the government 'to see that they do not have too much of the military element on it, because if they do the people of the Dominion will not have the confidence in it, which is most necessary. We must have men on that Board who will do their duty fearlessly, independent of the standing of the men whose cases they have to consider . . .'[183]

Initially there were no provisions for conscience-based appeals or exemptions, and some argued against making such allowances; as one typical remark said, 'it does not seem advisable to allow an appeal on account of religious tenets and doctrines'.[184] Noting the absence of provisions for conscientious objectors, in contrast to the British legislation, Labour MP Tom Paul asked:

> [W]hat is going to happen when you force a man to the front. You cannot make him fight. You can shoot him, but you cannot make him fight; and you are going to force a number of men — possibly a small number — to the front, and amongst them you may force the best citizen this country has, the most moral citizen, the man whose conscience is more delicately attuned than that of his fellows. You are going to force such a man to go into the firing-line.[185]

In seeking consensus, the House debated some liberalising measures. For example, Allen proposed an amendment offering appeals that a balloted man 'objects in good faith to military service on the ground that such service is contrary to his religious belief'. However, this was rejected by eight votes.[186] A similar clause was subsequently introduced by the legislative councillor Sir Francis Bell allowing appeals to be made on the grounds that a man was on 4 August 1914, and had been continuously since, a member of a religious body whose tenets declared 'the bearing of arms and the performance of combatant service to be contrary to divine revelation'.[187]

In order to achieve consensus for this clause, conditions for the appellant were toughened: 'legitimate objectors' had to declare a willingness to perform non-combatant service within or beyond New Zealand, if need be within the Medical Corps or the Army Service Corps.[188] There was little scope for recognising legitimate conscientious objection beyond religious grounds; in Allen's words, 'You can test religious beliefs, but you cannot test conscientious beliefs.'[189]

Another consideration was whether conscription would be applied to Māori. Parliamentary debate saw some divergence between the Māori MPs. Rather circumspectly, Tau Henare affirmed support for the war and the bill but suggested it was better applied to Pākehā shirkers, noting that the Māori population might be fatally depleted if drawn on too heavily.[190] Āpirana Ngata and Māui Pōmare, on the other hand, asserted that Māori could play an equal role to Pākehā. Ngata, rejecting ideas that the small size of the Māori population favoured exemption, asserted that fighting would stimulate racial renewal and advised that 'the Maori should not be excluded'.[191]

Pōmare also leveraged conceptions of a martial spirit: 'The Maoris won their spurs on the fields of Gallipoli — fields made sacred not only to the pakehas but also to the Maoris of this country by spilling their blood there. That blood cries out to us for utu, and utu it shall have; and if by conscription utu is to be extracted, then, Sir, let it be conscription.'[192] Some Pākehā MPs argued along similar lines, but most stayed silent.[193]

Official uncertainty ultimately prevailed. The issue was shelved, with section 50 of the Act stating that '[t]he Governor may, by Proclamation, extend the provisions of this Act, with such modifications as he thinks necessary, so as to provide for the compulsory calling-up of Natives for military service with the Expeditionary Force'.[194]

On 9 June 1916 the Military Service Bill underwent its third reading and was put to a vote with 44 MPs voting (two were paired). The bill passed, with 44 ayes and 4 noes, and the National Anthem was sung. Following some delays in the House, the bill became law on 1 August. A point raised by Forbes would prove prescient: 'It will be easy, I believe, to pass this Bill, but everything will depend upon its administration. I admit that it will be a difficult Act to administer, but we will have to face that, as well as many other difficult problems, before this war is over.'[195]

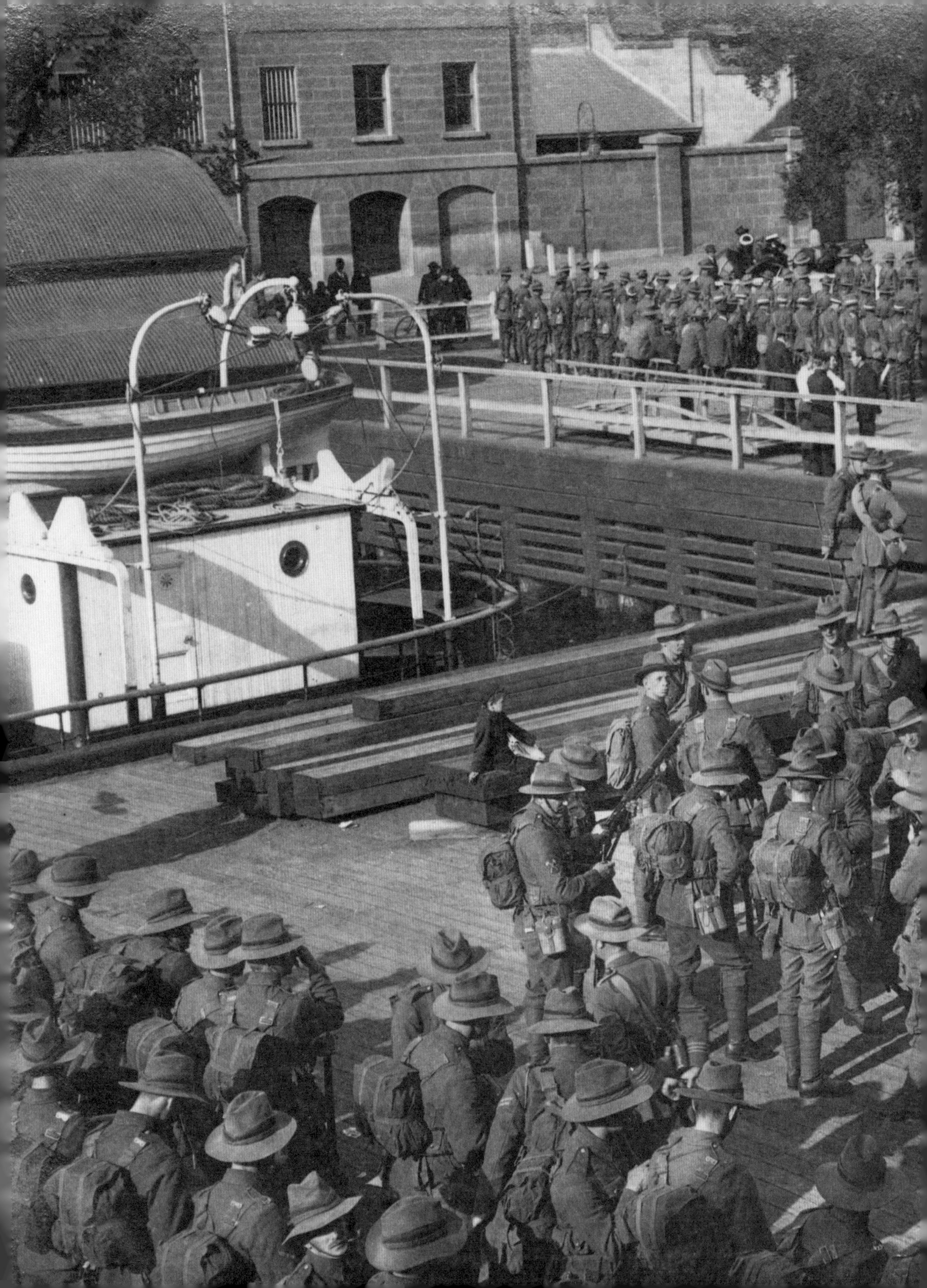

CHAPTER NINE

A BETTER COURSE TOWARDS VICTORY

previous pages
Troops assembling in Wellington and forming up for a march through the city. NATIONAL ARMY MUSEUM, 1993.1223

By the time of the second anniversary of the outbreak of war in August 1916, many aspects of wartime life had become routine. For those living near military camps the sound of rifle ranges and grenade explosions had become a familiar background noise. Farewell parades of men leaving for overseas had become customary. Casualty lists and returned wounded men had become a terrible regularity and the commitment of the bulk of the country's reinforcements to the notoriously lethal Western Front foretold more to come. Against these constants, however, the dynamics of social commitment were shifting. Most wartime societies demonstrated remarkable unity over the first two years of the war. From then on, most became keenly aware that unity and commitment could no longer be taken for granted as protracted mobilisation frayed societies' moral and material bonds. In response, all governments and societies sought to 'remobilise' their efforts by making concessions and suppressing dissent.[1] The early months of 1917 clearly showed, too, that the course of the war was altering radically as Russia's Tsarist regime tottered under the strain and as the United States moved to declare war on Germany.

Almost 320 town halls across New Zealand marked 4 August 1916 with conspicuous affirmations of a commitment to victory. Wellington's resolution was fairly typical: '[O]n this, the second anniversary, of the declaration of a righteous war, this meeting of the citizens of Wellington records its inflexible determination to continue to a victorious end the struggle in maintenance of those ideals of liberty and justice which are the common, and sacred cause of the Allies.'[2] However, while a public consensus remained set on continuing the war towards a decisive victory, a general frustration with the progress and management of the war was clearly apparent. The failure at Gallipoli, the stalemate on the Western Front and the Easter Rising fuelled patriotic discontent over the course the war was taking. Much of this frustration was directed at the civil and military authorities in Britain. Tellingly, the release of some initial findings of a British inquiry into the Gallipoli campaign had a damning reception in many New Zealand papers.[3] The *Press* commented that while the campaign will 'long stand out as one of the most heroic feats of arms in the military annals of our Empire', the report 'proves what most of us have long suspected, namely, that it will also be remembered as one of the most shocking examples of official blundering and malfeasance on the part of British politicians aspiring to the name and rank of statesmen'.[4]

A sense of mismanagement was affirmed as the New Zealand Division took part in its first major engagement on the Western Front. Retrained, reorganised and re-equipped, the division had been deployed in Flanders from April 1916 and spent three months guarding a 'quiet' sector of the line at Armentières, gaining familiarity with new conditions and the tactics that had developed on the front since the start of the war. In late August, the entire division moved south to become one of 55 British divisions that took part in the Somme offensive. Deployed in early September, 18,000 members of the division went into action. When it was withdrawn from the line 45 days later, the division had suffered around 6700 casualties, of whom 2000 had been killed; over half had no known grave.[5] This was the division's mostly costly action on the Western Front and it effectively doubled the total casualties built up over the eight-month Gallipoli campaign.

Cable reports of the 'big push' emphasised the size and significance of the offensive. The dispatches of New Zealand's official war correspondent, Malcolm Ross, impressed that the action was 'the greatest trial yet experienced', and presented the New Zealand soldier in action as formidable, displaying 'splendid courage' in enduring hardships and playing an important role in advancing the war: 'Those whose sons and brothers were killed here, can well be proud. It was a glorious death.'[6] Photographs and cartoons also depicted the scale of the offensive, stressing the sheer number of men and amount of materiel the British were now deploying against the German position.

However, the scale of the casualties and the evident truth that the action had not brought any decisive end to the war was processed alongside growing frustration, and unlike the losses from the Gallipoli landings, the Somme did not stimulate recruiting.[7] Even before the offensive, many who were unquestionably committed to the war regarded the cable news reports of the war with disbelief and exasperation. The reports were portrayed in an *Observer* cartoon as tripe being crammed into the public.[8] Liberal MP Thomas Wilford complained in Parliament of the 'nauseating piffle being cabled out regarding the Anzacs'; Malcolm Ross's name was mentioned. Massey, whose own son would be seriously wounded during the Somme offensive, replied by stating his frank sympathy with the assessment.[9] In private, New Zealanders noted the casualties, and while Harrold Ennor recorded 'New Zealanders in the big push doing great work', his diary entries over the following days also marked acquaintances who had been killed and noted the 'largest casualty list yet published'.[10]

However, popular opinion met these frustrations, as well as hints of a diplomatic end to the war, with a resolve that a better course towards victory should be charted. On 12 December, Berlin issued a 'peace note' stating a willingness for a negotiated end to the war, though no specific conditions were included. Berlin fully expected that Britain, France and Russia — who correctly assumed that Germany intended to retain its occupied territories — would reject this initiative; their refusal of the German offer could then buttress domestic support, given that the Allies could be presented as prolonging the war. Such sympathy was especially significant, given plans for a renewed U-boat campaign against merchant shipping.[11]

Days later, on 18 December, Woodrow Wilson, the recently re-elected American president,

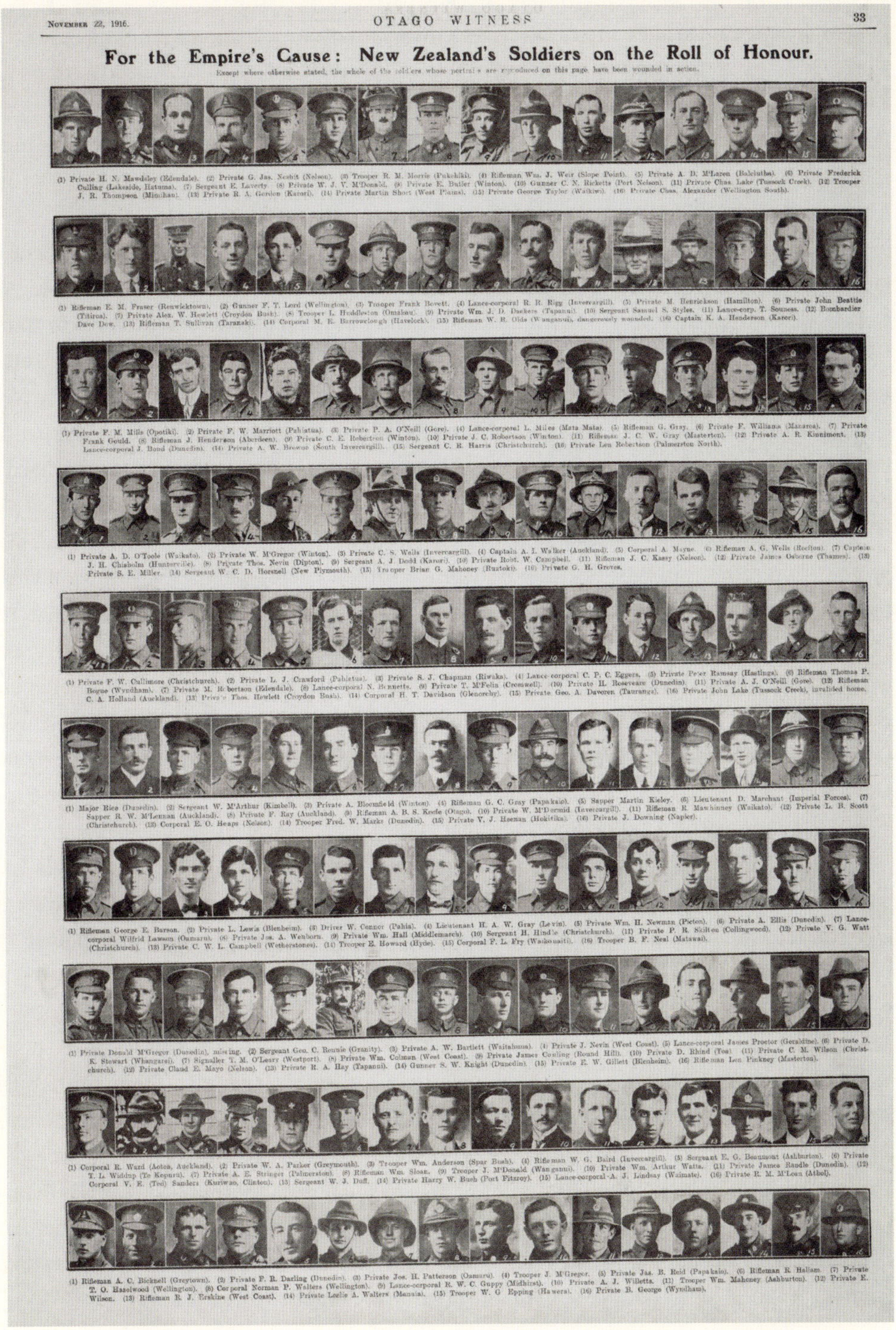

November 22, 1916. OTAGO WITNESS 33

For the Empire's Cause: New Zealand's Soldiers on the Roll of Honour.

Except where otherwise stated, the whole of the soldiers whose portraits are reproduced on this page have been wounded in action.

(1) Private H. N. Mawdsley (Edendale). (2) Private G. Jas. Nesbit (Nelson). (3) Trooper R. M. Morris (Pukehiki). (4) Rifleman Wm. J. Weir (Slope Point). (5) Private A. D. M'Laren (Balclutha). (6) Private Frederick Culling (Lakeside, Hatuma). (7) Sergeant E. Laverty. (8) Private W. J. V. M'Donald. (9) Private E. Butler (Winton). (10) Gunner C. N. Ricketts (Port Nelson). (11) Private Chas. Lake (Tussock Creek). (12) Trooper J. R. Thompson (Minihau). (13) Private R. A. Gordon (Karori). (14) Private Martin Short (West Plains). (15) Private George Taylor (Waikiwi). (16) Private Chas. Alexander (Wellington South).

(1) Rifleman E. M. Fraser (Renwicktown). (2) Gunner F. T. Lord (Wellington). (3) Trooper Frank Bovett. (4) Lance-corporal R. R. Rigg (Invercargill). (5) Private M. Henrickson (Hamilton). (6) Private John Beattie (Titirua). (7) Private Alex. W. Hewlett (Croydon Bush). (8) Trooper L. Huddleston (Omakau). (9) Private Wm. J. D. Dackers (Tapanui). (10) Sergeant Samuel S. Styles. (11) Lance-corp. T. Souness. (12) Bombardier Dave Dow. (13) Rifleman T. Sullivan (Taranaki). (14) Corporal M. E. Barrowclough (Havelock). (15) Rifleman W. R. Olds (Wanganui), dangerously wounded. (16) Captain K. A. Henderson (Karori).

(1) Private F. M. Mills (Opotiki). (2) Private F. W. Marriott (Pahiatua). (3) Private P. A. O'Neill (Gore). (4) Lance-corporal L. Miles (Mata Mata). (5) Rifleman G. Gray. (6) Private F. Williams (Manaroa). (7) Private Frank Gould. (8) Rifleman J. Henderson (Aberdeen). (9) Private C. E. Robertson (Winton). (10) Private J. C. Robertson (Winton). (11) Rifleman J. C. W. Gray (Masterton). (12) Private A. R. Kinnimont. (13) Lance-corporal J. Bond (Dunedin). (14) Private A. W. Browne (South Invercargill). (15) Sergeant C. R. Harris (Christchurch). (16) Private Len Robertson (Palmerston North).

(1) Private A. D. O'Toole (Waikato). (2) Private W. M'Gregor (Winton). (3) Private C. S. Wells (Invercargill). (4) Captain A. I. Walker (Auckland). (5) Corporal A. Mayne. (6) Rifleman A. G. Wells (Reefton). (7) Captain J. H. Chisholm (Hunterville). (8) Private Thos. Nevin (Dipton). (9) Sergeant A. J. Dodd (Karori). (10) Private Robt. W. Campbell. (11) Rifleman J. C. Kasey (Nelson). (12) Private James Osborne (Thames). (13) Private S. E. Miller. (14) Sergeant W. C. D. Horsnell (New Plymouth). (15) Trooper Brian G. Mahoney (Ruatoki). (16) Private G. H. Greves.

(1) Private F. W. Cullimore (Christchurch). (2) Private L. J. Crawford (Pahiatua). (3) Private S. J. Chapman (Riwaka). (4) Lance-corporal C. P. C. Eggers. (5) Private Peter Ramsay (Hastings). (6) Rifleman Thomas P. Bogue (Wyndham). (7) Private M. Robertson (Edendale). (8) Lance-corporal N. Bennetts. (9) Private T. M'Felia (Cromwell). (10) Private H. Roseveare (Dunedin). (11) Private A. J. O'Neill (Gore). (12) Rifleman C. A. Holland (Auckland). (13) Private Thos. Hewlett (Croydon Bush). (14) Corporal H. T. Davidson (Glenorchy). (15) Private Geo. A. Davoren (Tauranga). (16) Private John Lake (Tussock Creek), invalided home.

(1) Major Rice (Dunedin). (2) Sergeant W. M'Arthur (Kimbell). (3) Private A. Bloomfield (Winton). (4) Rifleman G. C. Gray (Papakaio). (5) Sapper Martin Kieley. (6) Lieutenant D. Marchant (Imperial Forces). (7) Sapper R. W. M'Lennan (Auckland). (8) Private F. Ray (Auckland). (9) Rifleman A. B. S. Keefe (Otago). (10) Private W. M'Dermid (Invercargill). (11) Rifleman R. Mawhinney (Waikato). (12) Private L. B. Scott (Christchurch). (13) Corporal E. O. Heaps (Nelson). (14) Trooper Fred. W. Marks (Dunedin). (15) Private V. J. Heenan (Hokitika). (16) Private J. Downing (Napier).

(1) Rifleman George E. Barson. (2) Private L. Lewis (Blenheim). (3) Driver W. Connor (Pahia). (4) Lieutenant H. A. W. Gray (Levin). (5) Private Wm. H. Newman (Picton). (6) Private A. Ellis (Dunedin). (7) Lance-corporal Wilfrid Lawson (Oamaru). (8) Private Jos. A. Wenborn. (9) Private Wm. Hall (Middlemarch). (10) Sergeant H. Hindle (Christchurch). (11) Private P. R. Skilton (Collingwood). (12) Private V. G. Watt (Christchurch). (13) Private C. W. L. Campbell (Wetherstones). (14) Trooper E. Howard (Hyde). (15) Corporal F. L. Fry (Waikouaiti). (16) Trooper B. F. Neal (Matawai).

(1) Private Donald M'Gregor (Dunedin), missing. (2) Sergeant Geo. C. Rennie (Granity). (3) Private A. W. Bartlett (Waitahuna). (4) Private J. Nevin (West Coast). (5) Lance-corporal James Proctor (Geraldine). (6) Private D. K. Stewart (Whangarei). (7) Signaller T. M. O'Leary (Westport). (8) Private Wm. Colman (West Coast). (9) Private James Cowling (Round Hill). (10) Private D. Rhind (Tea). (11) Private C. M. Wilson (Christchurch). (12) Private Claud E. Mayo (Nelson). (13) Private R. A. Hay (Tapanui). (14) Gunner S. W. Knight (Dunedin). (15) Private E. W. Gillett (Blenheim). (16) Rifleman Len Pinkney (Masterton).

(1) Corporal R. Ward (Aotea, Auckland). (2) Private W. A. Parker (Greymouth). (3) Trooper Wm. Anderson (Spar Bush). (4) Rifleman W. G. Baird (Invercargill). (5) Sergeant E. G. Beaumont (Ashburton). (6) Private T. L. Widdup (Te Kopuru). (7) Private A. E. Stringer (Palmerston). (8) Rifleman Wm. Sloan. (9) Trooper J. M'Donald (Wanganui). (10) Private Wm. Arthur Watts. (11) Private James Randle (Dunedin). (12) Corporal V. E. (Ted) Sanders (Kuriwao, Clinton). (13) Sergeant W. J. Duff. (14) Private Harry W. Bush (Port Fitzroy). (15) Lance-corporal A. J. Lindsay (Waimate). (16) Private R. M. M'Lean (Athol).

(1) Rifleman A. C. Bicknell (Greytown). (2) Private F. R. Darling (Dunedin). (3) Private Jos. H. Patterson (Oamaru). (4) Trooper J. M'Gregor. (5) Private Jas. B. Reid (Papakaio). (6) Rifleman R. Hallam. (7) Private T. O. Hazelwood (Wellington). (8) Corporal Norman P. Walters (Wellington). (9) Lance-corporal R. W. C. Guppy (Midhirst). (10) Private A. J. Willetts. (11) Trooper Wm. Mahoney (Ashburton). (12) Private E. Wilson. (13) Rifleman R. J. Erskine (West Coast). (14) Private Leslie A. Walters (Manaia). (15) Trooper W. G. Epping (Hawera). (16) Private B. George (Wyndham).

A page from the *Otago Witness* in November 1916 depicting the latest New Zealand casualties. The casualty rate spiked as the New Zealand Division was committed to major offensives on the Western Front.

OTAGO WITNESS, 22 NOVEMBER 1916, P. 33

invited belligerents to state their 'views as to the terms on which the war might be ended' as a potential first step towards a mediated peace.[12] Some were offended by Wilson's suggestion that the 'objects which the statesmen of the belligerents on both sides have in mind in this war are virtually the same', but even so, the Allies seized the opportunity to present terms that included the restitution of Belgian and Serbian autonomy and the evacuation of German troops from French and Russian territory.

In New Zealand, Germany's offer was regarded as an attempt to achieve a conqueror's peace and to escape a just reckoning. There would be no negotiations, Massey declared, until 'the Germans were driven beyond the Rhine and expelled from all occupied territory'. He added, 'If the Kaiser thinks we are going to make peace on his terms it is another of the Kaiser's many mistakes. We shall carry on until Germany atones her crimes.'[13] The *Southland Daily News* thought Germany's peace initiative sought to exploit the fact that '[t]here are in every allied country an increasing number of people who are sick of the war and would be pleased to countenance any dignified way out of the struggle'.[14]

If Berlin's diplomacy was read as duplicity, Washington's was read as naivety. The most prominent responses to Wilson's proposed 'peace without victory' argued that it would leave unresolved hostilities for posterity, that such an action would be a betrayal of the lives lost in the pursuit of a decisive victory and that, again, a just peace required Germany to be held accountable. More abrasive reactions characterised the president as effete and ineffectual. Such sentiments built on an ongoing criticism that the United States' neutrality represented a failure to recognise the moral issues involved in the war. The *Sun*, for example, noted:

> Mr Wilson is either a fool or is suffering from swelled head consequent on his re-election, if he imagines the Allies will stand for any such thing . . . The President should be told formally and in plain terms to mind his own business, as the Allies are ready and able to manage theirs — which is to hammer Germany into submission, and pave the way for enduring peace. America has no rights connected with peace except what the Allies grant her.[15]

Massey agreed: 'America ought to be firmly but courteously told that as we have carried on the war without her assistance we shall carry on without it now.'[16] Later, and less than courteously, he added that 'if [Wilson] had used a more effective weapon than the typewriter in defence of American interests, when American citizens were drowned and property destroyed, we would have had more respect for his opinions now'.[17] The record profits the United States was making from the Allied demand for materiel was another source of resentment. One commentator decried 'peace without victory' as taking 'the bun for pure flap-doodle' while suggesting a counter-proposal for the 'dollar-worshipping nation: Business without Profit'.[18]

Towards and into 1917, the effects of the economic boom were still evident. The country's producers continued to experience 'a period of phenomenal prosperity' based on high prices for staple products and 'a very substantial increase in the values of the Dominion's exports'.[19] This prosperity continued to underpin a broader affluence. In the first six months of 1916, £150,000 more was spent on alcohol and tobacco, £40,000 more was spent on silk clothing and 371,965 more gallons of beer were brewed than over the same period in 1915.[20] Through 1917, however, the boom appeared to slow and, in places, recede. The annual report of the Auckland Savings Bank registered that the net increase in its deposits was £216,000 in the 1917–18 year, almost 21 per cent less than the £263,000 of 1916–17.[21] Economic indicators were also of concern as costs rose, labour shortages loomed and tax burdens hit record highs. The Oamaru Woollen Factory Company, for example, paid £80 in taxes in 1913 and £6707 in 1916.[22] Moreover, issues that would soon become intractable were developing, including some in vital sectors of the economy. For the Bank of New Zealand, 'the greatest difficulty' was the contraction of New Zealand's access to the British market as the shipping situation became markedly more serious in 1917.[23]

A major contributor to this situation was enemy action, as the Imperial German Navy began to re-evaluate its approach and responded to the Royal Navy's blockade of Germany by targeting British seaborne trade. In part it had turned to U-boats and a policy of sinking merchant shipping, but, this, and especially the sinking of the *Lusitania*, had stoked international outrage and seriously threatened relations with the United States. Another approach had been to outfit ordinary freighters as commerce raiders. By late 1916 these missions were reaching the South Pacific.[24]

In November, SMS *Wolf* set out on what became a 15-month voyage across the Atlantic, Indian and Pacific oceans, during which it sank some 140,000 tons of shipping and laid minefields off various coasts before returning to Kiel in early 1918.[25] In June 1917 the *Wolf* plundered and sank the cargo ship *Wairuna*, en route from Auckland to San Francisco, and laid mines in New Zealand sea lanes, 25 off North Cape and 35 off Cape Farewell.[26] The first victim of these mines was the *Port Kembla*, a British freighter which struck a mine near Farewell Spit on 18 September 1917.[27] On 26 June 1918, the passenger liner *Wimmera*, travelling between Auckland and Sydney and carrying 76 passengers and 75 crew, struck one of the remaining mines and sank within 15 minutes with 26 or 27 lives lost.[28]

The Women's Anti-German League's Anna Stout, who accused the government of being negligent about internment, asked: 'What was there to prevent [local] aliens from laying mines?'[29] During a heated correspondence with James Allen, Stout continued to express 'her doubts' over whether the mines had been laid by the *Wolf*.[30]

Another German raider, SMS *Seeadler*, had made its way into the Pacific by April 1917, having established a pattern of locating merchant ships, boarding and then scuttling them while striving to leave the crews unharmed. After the *Seeadler* was wrecked on a reef at the coral atoll of Mopelia (Maupihaa) in the Society Islands in August, its captain, Count Felix von Luckner, set sail in a 32-foot open boat and captured a ship so he could resume raiding. By September the boat reached Fiji, where it was apprehended. The crew was transported to New Zealand, where von Luckner was interned on Motuihe Island in the Hauraki Gulf.[31]

The German High Command's announcement, on 1 February 1917, of a campaign of unrestricted U-boat warfare constituted a much larger threat to shipping. Berlin was now willing to accept the risk of outraging the United States and provoking American intervention in the confidence that Britain could be starved of supplies and forced to sue for peace within six months. In the short term this seemed frighteningly possible, as U-boats destroyed nearly 500,000 tons of shipping in February, over 550,000 tons in March and over 860,000 tons in April.[32] This represented a devastating assault on New Zealand's trade lifeline: 37 of the 99 ships sunk by U-boats in 1917 were engaged in British–New Zealand trade.[33]

The attacks also led British authorities to tighten shipping controls and increasingly favour transatlantic trade given that a ship could return twice to Britain fully laden in the time it took to make one round trip to New Zealand. By April 1917 the shipping controller had withdrawn 17 ships from New Zealand trading routes. By the end of the year the total insulated carrying capacity (measured in 60-pound carcasses) of ships servicing New Zealand had shrunk to 5.6 million; a dramatic decline from the 8.8 million of 1914.[34]

Consequently, masses of unshipped commodities began to accumulate and producers and exporters became desperate to secure passage for stockpiled goods that would not keep indefinitely. By mid-1917 there were over 250,000 boxes of butter in storage — a third of annual exports and more than five times the quantity stored the year before.[35] The country depended on clearing these exports, given that producers were not paid until their exports had been loaded. In June the head of the Bank of New Zealand solemnly noted that the amount borrowed by producers awaiting payment for stored goods had 'run into large figures', and although extra storage capacity was urgently needed, the construction of new cool stores was hampered by the difficulties of importing equipment. It also required freezing companies to borrow large sums. In its report for the 1917–18 year, the Bank of New Zealand noted that this issue was causing companies to lean heavily on the banks.[36]

Reduced imports also threatened production as raw materials, fuel, machine parts and increasingly necessary labour-saving plant became both less available and affordable. In 1914, for example, most phosphatic fertiliser came from Britain and Germany and was supplemented by guano and rock phosphates, principally from territories in the Indian and Pacific oceans, and some blood and/or bone manures from Australia and India.[37] The war severed supplies from Germany and greatly diminished those from Britain, leaving New Zealand more reliant on superphosphates from Australia and Japan. Although the potential for importing phosphate from Nauru, an Australian-occupied ex-German Pacific possession, was discussed from early 1917, it was not an immediate solution.[38]

Shipping shortages also meant that imported consumer goods became less available and more expensive. By mid-1917, for example, local drapery wholesalers who had bought up considerable quantities of goods from Britain earlier in the war after learning that production was ceasing, and who had been able to hold prices, warned of major price increases if the war continued for another six months. Not only would the goods themselves be more expensive, so would the cost of getting them to New Zealand. As one Christchurch draper pointed out early in July 1917, 'Ordinarily freight cost 40s a ton, now it is 120s; insurance that used to be 6s 8d per cent is now £3 2s 6d.' In the last few days he had heard from the Port of London Authority that 'dock and warehouse charges and rents on goods have advanced from 15 per cent to 30 per cent, and dock dues on overseas vessels will be 27½ per cent instead of 12½ per cent'.[39] The diverse impacts of the shipping shortage were made evident in July 1918 when the manager of Gisborne's Everybody's Theatre announced that, owing to 'prolonged shipping delays . . . Mandeno's performing dogs' would be unable to appear.[40]

Wartime conditions also affected the quantity and quality of some locally produced consumer goods. Early in 1917 one Wellington report claimed that local housewives were receiving 'meagre pints' in place of 'anticipated quarts' and sometimes no milk at all. And what they did get was 'probably . . . the worst milk sold in New Zealand'. Largely brought in, some distance, by rail, much of the milk was more than 24 hours old, and sometimes 48 hours old, before it reached consumers.[41] Suppliers were probably calculating that, given the fixing of the wholesale milk price by the Board of Trade, they could obtain better returns by selling their milk to cheese factories.

By 1917, production was also being pinched by labour shortages in various sectors. After November 1916 the rural workforce was depleted by nearly 18 per cent and the area of land under cultivation was restricted partly by the difficulty of obtaining labour.[42] This hit grain-growers particularly hard at harvest. At the beginning of January 1917, farmers in Ashburton County were obliged to stack their crops rather than thresh them from stooks in the field because the threshing mill owners could not find enough workers.[43] Farmers were advised to pool the available labour, including, presumably, their own families.

The rising cost of labour in rural areas was highlighted late in the winter of 1918 when storms devastated many roads in the west of the North Island. The government announced that it would only pay subsidies to the level of 11s a day for roadmen when '[l]ocal bodies find that with the heavy and increasing cost of living it is absolutely impossible under 14s or 15s a day'.[44] Moreover, the country's military commitment now had to be carefully weighed against the necessity of retaining key parts of the workforce. For example, when William Webb was balloted, his employer, the Wanganui Spiral Steel Pipe Company, appealed, noting that its workforce had been greatly reduced and that Webb's knowledge of how 'to control the manufacture of pipes' was irreplaceable.[45] He was granted an indefinite postponement.

There were problems, too, with coal, the country's chief energy source and essential for heating and to power shipping, rail and electricity generation. Before the war, New Zealand mines produced the lion's share of the average annual consumption of 2.25 million tons, though nearly 15 per cent of the total was imported, largely from Australia.[46] From 1916, however, coal production declined, falling from 2,257,135 tons that year to 2,034,250 in 1918.[47] One factor was fewer miners. As with other muscular industries, enlistment had both poached labour and reduced the supply of new miners: 4734 employees in 1914 fell to 3983 in 1917.[48] Growing unrest was also an issue, with strikes and go-slows at some mines, caused mainly by dissatisfaction over wages and hours but also by opposition to conscription. Between November 1916 and February 1919, strikes against conscription lost an estimated 181 working days and go-slows reduced the coal output by an estimated 5800 tons per week.[49] Moreover, importing Australian coal, the traditional means of relief, was also complicated by industrial unrest across the Tasman. On 23 May 1917 Allen admitted that 'we are trying to import about thirty thousand tons of coal per month from Australia but there is some difficulty about bottoms to carry it'.[50]

The government remained unable to halt, let alone mediate, price rises. Economic analysts note that the burden fell on 'those least able to bear it', including those with 'fixed or comparatively fixed incomes, many wage-earners, a large portion of the small-salaried classes, many of the dependants of those at the front'.[51] These increases threatened the government's legitimacy; out of the many challenges he might have chosen from, Allen thought the rising cost of living was the 'chief difficulty' and 'the handle that can be used against the Government'.[52]

The perception that some were profiting unduly made the situation more volatile and Holland readily accused the government of facilitating racketeering, though reports of the high prices received by farmers were likely just as effective in heightening resentment.[53] In April 1917 a Taranaki farmer noted that he was now receiving 24s 6d for his lambs whereas nine years before he had received 9s 4d. His highest pre-war wool price had been 10½d in London. He had since received 17½d in London, and 'this year 15d and 15½d in Waitara'.[54]

Even staunch supporters of the war effort protested. For example, in May 1917 W. H. Herries, the minister of railways, met with the executive of the Amalgamated Society of Railway Servants to thank members for working so many additional hours. While the union's president replied that they were only doing their duty, his goodwill dissipated when he turned to living costs and profiteering: 'We want you to impress upon Cabinet the necessity for the Government giving some definite public announcement that you are going to take hold of anybody who is seeking to take advantage of present conditions to feather his own nest at the expense of other people.'[55] Such sentiments extended to individuals who could by no means be categorised as 'anti-war'. The treasurer of the Hamilton Red Cross claimed that 'undoubtedly there were many people in the community, especially farmers, who did not realise their responsibilities in regard to giving . . . They must realise that many of the townspeople were much worse off owing to the war, while 80 per cent of the farmers were much better off.'[56]

Even those sympathetic to rural interests and sceptical about state intervention raised criticisms. The editor of the *Ashburton Guardian*, while agreeing that 'the farcical Board of Trade' and the government's attempts to fix wheat and flour prices were misguided, was disappointed by the dominance of self-interest in many speeches at a local farmers' meeting in March 1917, observing that some regarded every proposal 'from a frankly sordid viewpoint':

> It is disconcerting to find wealthy men, whose wealth is being preserved for them by the blood of our gallant soldiers, quibbling over the possibility of losing a few pounds through the Government's efforts to distribute more equitably the sacrifices that the war conditions have made inevitable . . . The soldier completely effaces his personality when he enlists; he places at the disposal of the State his life — something stupendously more valuable than all the farms and wealth in the country . . . If a farmer whose annual profit is £100, or £1000, sells his produce next season that does not realise that profit, is he any worse off than the workers who have been selling their labour for nearly three years at a serious loss?[57]

Against charges of exploitation, many farmers pointed out that the agricultural prices received on the commandeer were now consistently below prices on the open market, and that this advantaged producers in non-British and neutral countries.[58] At the end of April 1917, the chairman of the Invercargill Farmers' Union claimed that '[o]ther organisations had the Government make them concessions, but it was the farmers who had to bear the burden in all cases. Therefore they should unite and concentrate their energies upon meeting the attacks of the other bodies.'[59] The national president complained of 'biased writers' who 'flung contumely on the farmers for being unpatriotic; for not feeding the people with bread at less than cost price, and for asking a reasonable price for their produce'. He closed by arguing that farmers deserved respect for their part in sustaining the Allies' armies and cause.[60]

In an effort to resolve some of the economic and diplomatic friction that had developed in relations with Britain, a New Zealand delegation departed for London in the second half of 1916. This approach had already been used by other dominion representatives; Australian prime minister William (Billy) Hughes had garnered significant publicity earlier in 1916 for his vigorous criticism of the management of the empire's war.[61] A New Zealand delegation had been considered for some time but, in light of the delicate domestic situation over the previous year, had been delayed.

However, with the Military Service Act entered into law, the prospect was revived and an official party left Wellington on the *Rotorua* on 24 August 1916. It consisted of Massey, his wife Christina and their daughter Marian, Ward and his wife Theresa, and two private secretaries. The presence of both Massey and Ward reflected both the latter's determination to present himself as Massey's equal and the former's ambition not to have his political rival pulling rank in New Zealand during his absence. Allen became acting prime minister, while Myers accepted responsibility for Ward's ministerial duties, and the Liberal MP and minister of agriculture William MacDonald assumed control from Massey over the day-to-day business of the Board of Trade.

On 7 October the delegation reached London, described as 'the real capital of the New Zealand war effort'.[62] The delegation's often aggressive efforts to secure New Zealand's interests were certainly a testament to this claim. One of the first tasks was securing an improved contract for farmers, who had grown increasingly bitter that non-British competitors, notably Argentina and the United States, were consistently receiving better prices for meat on the open market than they could get under the commandeer.[63] The party successfully renegotiated an additional £1 million profit per annum, along with an agreement to subsidise the cost of storing meat awaiting shipment, and signed a contract for New Zealand's entire crossbred wool clip; in a cable to Allen, Massey mused, 'Believe this is better than 1916 prices.'[64]

Shipping was another major concern, and Massey and Ward would fight an ongoing battle to direct more shipping to New Zealand. Protesting to the shipping controller about the removal of five more ships from the New Zealand route, Massey demonstrated that he was willing to use New Zealand's loyalty and sacrifices as leverage. This decision would make

> very sad news for the patriotic New Zealand settlers, who have, since the outbreak of war, been doing everything that is possible for good citizens to do in the crisis through which the Empire is passing. I am proud of the fact that New Zealand, in proportion to its population, led the other dominions in the assistance she has been able to render during the war, but am afraid that what is happening now is a somewhat poor return for her loyalty and enthusiasm.[65]

During November, Massey and Ward attended various social functions and it is noted that 'while the pomp and ceremony were familiar to Ward, the visit proved an invaluable education for Massey'.[66] The prime minister was awarded honorary degrees by Cambridge University and Edinburgh University, and received the freedom of London, York, Edinburgh, Manchester and Londonderry. He was also sworn in as a Member of the Privy Council. This contact with British officialdom is thought to have been instrumental in some changing titles within New Zealand politics, with Allen knighted in the 1917 New Year's honours and Lord Liverpool's title changed from governor to governor-general in June. Although this entailed no constitutional change, it brought New Zealand in line with the other dominions and partly recognised 'the services rendered by New Zealand since the outbreak of war'.[67]

The delegation also visited Ireland, where Ward travelled to Dublin to see his seriously injured enlisted son, Gladstone, and the Ulsterman Massey visited his birthplace, Limavady, where he was given an enthusiastic public reception. Priority, though, went to seeing the New Zealand troops. Visits in Britain included time with wounded soldiers at the Royal Hospital Chelsea and No. 1 New Zealand General Hospital at Brockenhurst. At the beginning of November, Massey and Ward sailed for France and spent five days on the Western Front, speaking to New Zealand troops and lunching with General Douglas Haig, who had commanded British forces on the Western Front since late 1915.[68]

In December 1916 Massey and Ward witnessed the collapse of Prime Minister Asquith's coalition government. Facing a divided Cabinet and a public perception that his leadership was inadequate, Asquith resigned on 5 December. His successor, David Lloyd George, presented himself as a dynamic and tough-minded departure from his predecessor's cautious and conventional approach. Born into humble circumstances and orphaned at a young age, Lloyd George had trained as a law clerk before moving into politics and building a record as a firebrand reformer.[69] During the July Crisis he had been a leading opponent of British intervention until the German invasion of Belgium radically shifted his thinking. His political rise reflected a combination of deft, if not ruthless, political manoeuvring and a personal magnetism hinted at in his nickname of the 'Welsh Wizard'. Rejecting any outcome less than a military victory, he called for a total commitment, avowing, 'The one predominant task of the Government will be the vigorous prosecution of the war to a triumphant conclusion.'[70]

Many New Zealand commentators approved of the change, arguing that Asquith was incapable of leading the empire to victory. The *Otago Witness*, for example, thought Asquith, 'who by birth and breeding belongs to the cultured and conservative class', was failing to seize the initiative. Lloyd George, said the *New Zealand Herald*, promised a strenuous effort

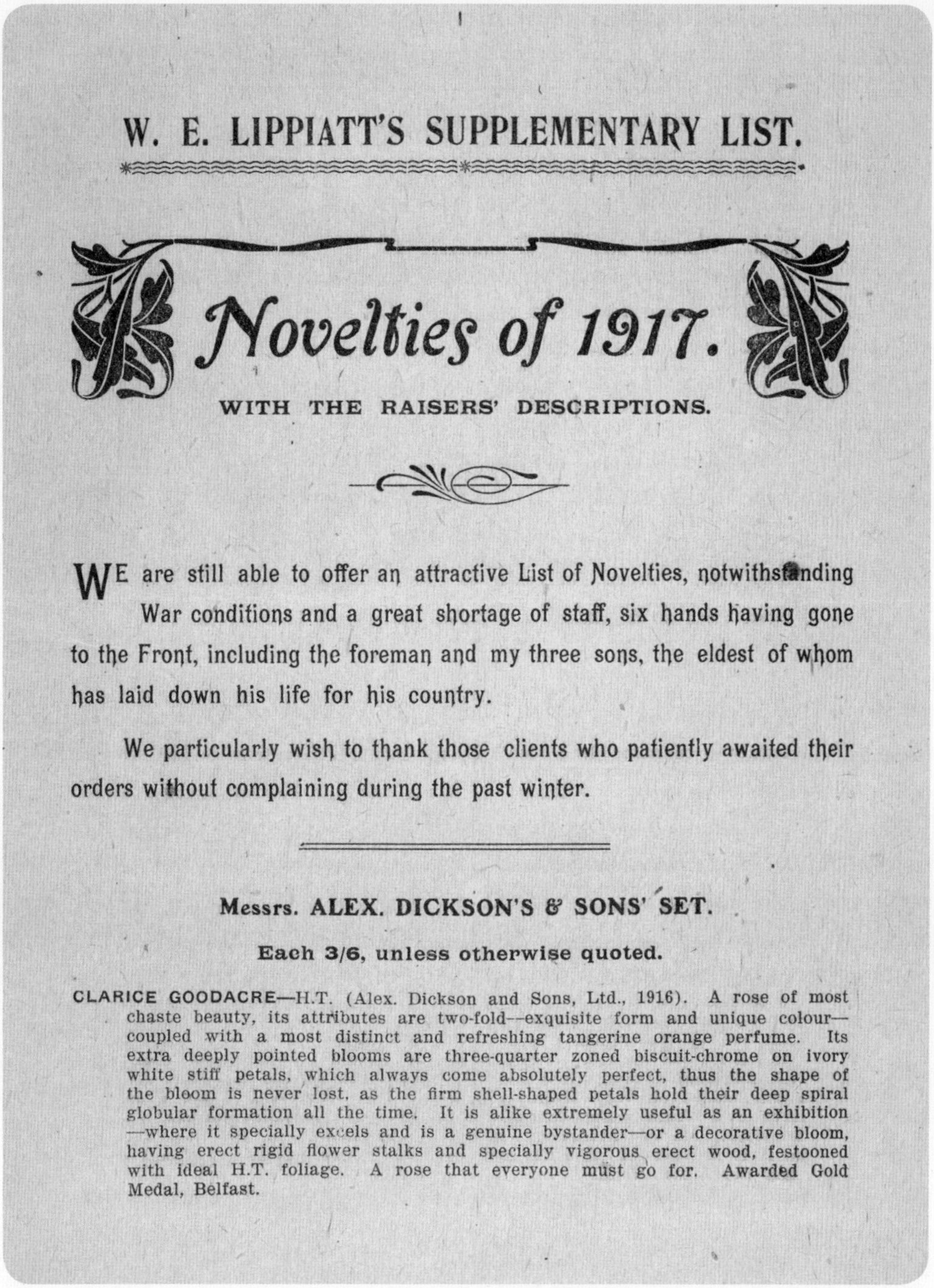

W. E. LIPPIATT'S SUPPLEMENTARY LIST.

Novelties of 1917.

WITH THE RAISERS' DESCRIPTIONS.

WE are still able to offer an attractive List of Novelties, notwithstanding War conditions and a great shortage of staff, six hands having gone to the Front, including the foreman and my three sons, the eldest of whom has laid down his life for his country.

We particularly wish to thank those clients who patiently awaited their orders without complaining during the past winter.

Messrs. ALEX. DICKSON'S & SONS' SET.

Each 3/6, unless otherwise quoted.

CLARICE GOODACRE—H.T. (Alex. Dickson and Sons, Ltd., 1916). A rose of most chaste beauty, its attributes are two-fold—exquisite form and unique colour—coupled with a most distinct and refreshing tangerine orange perfume. Its extra deeply pointed blooms are three-quarter zoned biscuit-chrome on ivory white stiff petals, which always come absolutely perfect, thus the shape of the bloom is never lost, as the firm shell-shaped petals hold their deep spiral globular formation all the time. It is alike extremely useful as an exhibition—where it specially excels and is a genuine bystander—or a decorative bloom, having erect rigid flower stalks and specially vigorous erect wood, festooned with ideal H.T. foliage. A rose that everyone must go for. Awarded Gold Medal, Belfast.

The front page of Otahuhu-based horticultural goods supplier W. E. Lippiatt and Family's 1917 catalogue, advertising its 'attractive List of Novelties'. By the war's end a second Lippiatt son had been killed and a third had lost a limb. ALEXANDER TURNBULL LIBRARY, EPH-A-HORTICULTURE-1917-01-FRONT 'to organise war administration on sound and energetic lines'.[71] *Truth*, however speculated that Asquith's downfall was brought about by vested interests to scotch press intrigues. The *Maoriland Worker*, too, argued that Asquith had been brought down by a cabal.[72]

On 11 December, Massey and Ward endorsed the new prime minister in an address to the Luncheon Club at Leeds University, praising his commitment to victory and affirming that New Zealand would 'provide all the assistance and co-operation in its power to win the war'.[73] Privately Massey wrote that he had met Lloyd George 'once or twice', 'but cannot make my mind up about him'. He also seemed suspicious of his links with the powerful press baron Lord Northcliffe and his papers, which he regarded as 'a real danger' because of their political influence and as 'no friend to New Zealand'.[74] Ward publicly stated that Lloyd George was 'no doubt the strongest figure on the political horizon or in the political hemisphere at the present moment'.[75]

The new prime minister's preference for a small executive did not portend that he would prove exceptionally attentive to New Zealand perspectives, nor did his frank admission that he did not realise that New Zealand lay to the east of Australia.[76] However, Lloyd George's ambition to expand the empire's war effort for a 'fight to the finish' inclined him to a more consultative policy with the dominions. On 12 December he outlined his intentions to Colonial Secretary Walter Long: 'As we must receive even more substantial support from them before we can hope to pull through, it is important that they should feel that they have a share in our councils as well as in our burdens. We want more men from them. We can hardly ask them to make another great recruiting effort unless it is accompanied by an invitation to come over to discuss the situation with us.'[77]

Days later, he announced his government's intention to hold a conference to establish an Imperial War Cabinet that would better coordinate the empire's plan for victory. Although this was precisely the sort of consultation that Massey and Ward had sought, it did commit them to staying much longer in Britain. They had originally intended to leave before the end of the year but now it appeared they would remain in Britain for a significant amount of 1917.

Better management of the economic situation was a major part of the government's campaign to remobilise the war effort. Where the cost of living was concerned, the primary instrument remained the Board of Trade, though some controls were introduced through separate legislation, such as the War Legislation Amendment Bill, passed in August 1916, which strengthened regulations over rent prices.[78] Many operations in this period followed the established pattern of the board's approach, such as fixing the prices of more essential grocery items.[79] The board was also involved in another major management of wheat and flour prices when the 1916–17 wheat crop looked certain to fall well short of the country's needs. On 18 December 1916 the board recommended immediate steps to purchase a million bushels of Australian wheat and, in February 1917, new maximum wheat prices were set ranging from 5s 7d to 5s 9d a bushel, depending on the variety. The price for the Australian purchase was negotiated to 5s 6d per bushel, and though the first shipments arrived over June and July

WHAT WE'D ALL LIKE TO SEE

A National Campaign to Exterminate the Food Manipulator.

When Mrs. Brown goes down the town
To buy the family grub,
The prices make her poor brain ache.
Why should they?—that's the rub!

The Board of Trade by Bill was made
To keep food prices cheap.
But still they're high, so people sigh,
"Maybe it's gone to sleep."

We haven't yet seen Cabinet
Get right upon the scent;
And in the law's remorseless maw
Grip the food-exploiting gent.

If this boodling chap was off the map
The land would happier be.
Why hesitate, exterminate
This incubus, say we.

Mr E. Somerville, of the Farmers' Union, said if H.M.S. New Zealand had been sunk instead of H.M.S. Queen Mary all of them would have put their hands in their pockets. While they were prepared to act loyally it was to a certain extent an insult to the British Government to force charity on them.

N.Z. Farmer: Widows and orphans? Bah! Let's get on with the Harvest!

above As efforts to address the cost of living continued to fall short of expectations, *Truth* envisioned a concerted effort to 'exterminate' the food manipulators it believed were responsible. NZ TRUTH, 3 FEBRUARY 1917, P. 5

below The *Observer* sharply rebukes Mr Somerville of the Farmers' Union for comments that seemed indifferent to Royal Navy casualties during the Battle of Jutland. A rapacious farmer favouring personal enrichment over British welfare is shown stuffing his pockets with pounds, and stating 'Widows and orphans? Bah! Let's get on with the Harvest!' NEW ZEALAND OBSERVER, 1 JULY 1916, P. 13

1917, further deliveries were disrupted by Australian industrial unrest and transportation was not resumed until after October.[80]

Other interventions became more experimental as the board pursued an active regulatory approach under the stewardship of William MacDonald, 'more sensitive than Massey to the complaints of his Liberal colleagues'.[81] An example is evident in the board's approach to butter, where high export prices had led producers to favour the overseas market. By August 1916 the retail price had risen to 1s 8d per pound in the main centres, and as high as 1s 10d in more remote areas.[82] The board established an equalisation fund and in October 1916 introduced a butter-fat levy so that 'the sellers of butter for local consumption could be compensated in order to bring their returns to a parity with the price obtained by factories exporting on private account'.[83] Between that date and June 1917, dairy exports were charged between 2.5d and 3.9d per pound of butter-fat in exported butter and cheese.

Rural producers denounced the scheme as a 'class tax' and deemed it 'cruel and unjust' for targeting the 'hardest worked portion of the community'.[84] In October 1916 the Farmers' Union sent a telegram to Massey protesting against the imposition of an 'export tax' without the sanction of Parliament — the levy had been enacted by order in council when Parliament was not sitting — and entreating him to 'prevent this injustice'. Two dairy companies went further and took legal action, arguing that without Parliament's approval the levy constituted taxation without representation. On 8 November 1916, the Supreme Court upheld the validity of the scheme.[85] The levy remained controversial, however, and was abolished in August 1917, shortly after Massey's return. One newspaper noted, 'it is understood, [Massey] disapproves the butter-fat levy imposed, in his absence, by the Board of Trade'.[86]

Into 1917 the Board of Trade also tried to check prices by opening publicly owned enterprises to offer competition with private business. New Zealand already had some examples of state industries in other enterprises and MacDonald was amenable to such experiments. An initial venture was launched in January 1917 with the opening of two state-owned butcheries in Auckland which agreed to sell meat at prices dictated by the board for a 12-month trial run.[87] The butcheries would effectively operate at cost and, therefore, offer consumers affordable goods. When Massey, who appeared generally concerned about the board's operations, wrote to Allen seeking information on the initiative, he replied, 'I must confess I have been somewhat anxious about this procedure myself, but you know the difficulties, and how essential it is something [sic] to let the public see that we are making an honest endeavour to control the rise in food prices.'[88] By mid-1917 it was claimed these stores were saving customers a total of some £104,000 per annum.[89] Privately owned butcheries were less impressed at being undercut and in January 1917, as wholesale prices continued to rise, told the board that it was 'impossible to continue retailing at prices then ruling'.[90]

The government also hoped to improve economic performance via the creation of the National Efficiency Board.[91] Allen's brainchild, it was established in February 1917 to 'protect and advance the industries of the Dominion' and advise on matters in which the country could be better organised.[92] Its members — all volunteers — were Allen, representing the government, four prominent businessmen and a farmer. Taking to its task with gusto, within weeks the board had submitted a plan for the administration of farms and industries, and by May 1917 it had recommended the compulsory direction of labour under a scheme of industrial service. To this end it offered recommendations for the classification of industry and the registration of labour in what could have amounted to, and what certainly would have been denounced by some as, industrial conscription. However, few in Cabinet wanted to pursue this step unless it proved absolutely necessary. For the moment any such prospect was shelved.

The National Efficiency Board also revived schemes for some manner of war service for Yugoslavs, building on the rejected Pārengarenga plan. In February 1917, a Dalmatian delegation met with government representatives to discuss Yugoslav enlistment. The concept of a Slav contingent to be sent to Salonika had been floated in November 1915 after the Allies had opened a front there in support of Serbia, but had been rejected. Now, however, Allen seemed open to the idea and it was decided that the Defence Department would investigate. Six weeks later it became clear that service would be offered under much lower Serbian rates of pay, with no allowances for dependants, though the Serbian government did pledge an allotment of land to each volunteer.

The delegation thought few men would volunteer under these conditions and the matter was dropped.[93] In its first months, however, the National Efficiency Board examined the subject. By this stage many considered that Dalmatians were unfairly profiting from labour shortages and the land sales many enlistees concluded before departing. The introduction of conscription also greatly embittered local opinion; critics pointed out that Dalmatians, exempted or excluded from military service, were benefiting from the sacrifices of the British population. There were demands for the government to place them on the same footing as most of the rest of the population and various bodies passed resolutions favouring a labour conscription scheme.[94] Auckland returned servicemen, for example, called for a ban on 'the Austrian population' buying land during the war and for all aliens to be compelled to do government work.[95] Still lingering, too, were ideas that enemy aliens might endanger communities denuded of British men. On 31 May 1917, the board reported that it was essential to register all Dalmatians, requiring them to declare whether they were Yugoslavs or Teutons, and that those of military age should state whether they were prepared to take an oath of allegiance to the Allies' cause. Those who complied should be left alone, on the understanding that if they were needed for essential work they might be asked to do it 'at the current rate of wages', while those who refused should be given a choice between performing essential work at soldiers' pay rates or internment.[96]

The board also persistently called for the greater employment of women to address labour shortages and maintain production. It regretted a 'certain amount of reluctance upon the part of employers (other than commercial offices) to make provision beforehand by the training of female assistants to take the place of their male employees who may be called up for active service'. It considered that the issue would become ever more necessary as the war continued.[97] The expansion and recomposition of the female workforce certainly continued throughout this period. In April 1917 the Greymouth Borough Council actually advertised two temporary clerical positions as 'open to females only'.[98]

above Workers, including several women, clearing land on a farm in the King Country. AUCKLAND WEEKLY NEWS, 23 MAY 1918, P. 38

left Two women help with the harvest on a Canterbury farm. AUCKLAND WEEKLY NEWS, 12 APRIL 1917, P. 44

Although women doing farm work unrelated to family seems to have been relatively rare, there were accounts of women taking up the muscular and technical aspects of farming. In May 1917 a visitor to a Waikato farm witnessed 'a girl clad in serviceable overalls . . . learning how to run the oil engine which supplied the power for the milking machines and this was to enable her to take her brother's place who had enlisted and was shortly to leave for camp'.[99] Over the summer of 1916–17 a group of young Whanganui women, 'daughters of well-to-do people', were regarded as 'pioneers of female farm labour':

> They weeded an area of five acres, and also thinned out three or four acres of soft turnips . . . Mr. Wilson was so pleased with the result of their work that he took them on again for haymaking, and they raked and stoked [sic] eight acres of hay and assisted in building the stack. The same team of girls is now working for Mr. Allan Cameron at Marangi, and here their work is stacking and carting fifty acres of oats . . . They are now working for 1s an hour, and doing a nine-hour day . . . They realise that what English girls have done for the Empire, New Zealand girls can also do, and, having the time on their hands, they have set about doing it.[100]

Other experiments included employing girls to deliver telegrams; in July 1918, the superintendent of the Wellington telegraph office declared this had proven 'highly satisfactory'. By July 1918, 40 were working locally for 15s a week and, as well as a dress, each was provided with an 'overcoat, macintosh, cloth hat, sou'-wester and leggings' in recognition of the capital's winter weather.[101]

However, as the board observed, a scepticism and reluctance about mass utilisation of female labour endured. As Minister of Internal Affairs George Russell noted in April 1918, 'New Zealand is a pastoral country, and the employment of women as shepherds, musterers and general farm hands is impractical, and this is even more evident, regarding the coal mining and shipping industries . . . The need of female labour to take the places of conscripted men has not become directly apparent. The employment of Second Division men and men beyond military age has so far enabled the country to be carried on.'[102] And women were not necessarily heading to sectors most suffering labour shortages. Indeed, during the summer of 1917, fruit-growers in Nelson were unable to hire the seasonal women workers they had previously employed.[103] It seems likely that many of those who had previously travelled to Nelson from Wellington to undertake such work had secured more desirable, regular and lucrative jobs.

The National Efficiency Board also had the restriction of alcohol in its sights as another easy means of encouraging fiscal prudence and boosting production. There had been a notable revival of prohibition campaigning and some 'dries' clearly saw the war, and the board, as a means to strengthen their cause. By mid-February 1917 the WCTU was campaigning for prohibition to be introduced for the rest of the war and for six months afterwards.[104] Other campaigners fell short of demanding full prohibition but called for restrictions on opening hours for bars. In May 1917 Allen wrote to Massey, 'I must warn you about the feeling which is strong in the country, about public houses. There will be a big attempt to secure a provision that hotels shall be open only from 8 am to 6 pm.'[105] After investigating the 'liquor question', the board was 'convinced that it would be beneficial to the nation and conducive to the well-being of the people that the importation, manufacture, and sale of wines, beer, and spirituous liquors (including medicinal preparations containing alcohol) should be prohibited', and recommended a national referendum on prohibition.[106]

Beyond the Board of Trade and the National Efficiency Board, a series of measures were introduced to address the worsening coal situation. In February 1917 Myers introduced austerity measures to conserve supplies, explaining that coal usage would have to be restricted and prioritised for rail and shipping needs. Domestic use was to be restricted to 5 tons at any one time, and 20 tons in a period of 28 days. By mid-April 1917 rail services were cut back and restrictions of gas and electricity use were introduced in June.[107]

Coordinating schedules across various countries meant the first meeting of the Imperial War Cabinet did not take place until 20 March 1917. Besides Massey and Ward, there were representatives from Canada, South Africa, India and Newfoundland. Australia, in the midst of a contentious federal election, was not represented. Over the following weeks, the War Cabinet, and an associated Imperial War Conference, addressed both urgent matters of wartime policy and post-war considerations. Lloyd George had stated a preference to keep attendee numbers small and proceedings nimble, and while Massey was automatically afforded a seat in the Cabinet, Ward's entitlements proved a point of uncertainty and, when his attendance was brought into question, sensitivity.

As a British observer recorded, 'Massey has insisted that Ward is to be invited to all meetings attended by himself; otherwise Ward will go home, and if he does so Massey will have to go too; otherwise Ward will upset him. In fact they are a set of political Siamese twins, who hate each other. So both had to be invited.'[108] This accommodation had the consequence of other participants also being afforded additional representatives.

The meetings took place in a heady atmosphere of rhetoric and expectation. Claiming that 'Peace will come in 1917', Lloyd George had already presented the Imperial War Cabinet as part of his government's plan to remobilise Britain's war effort and oversee the emergence of a new social and global compact.[109] The New Zealanders, too, appreciated what was at stake. Ward claimed that the conference was 'next in importance from the point of view to the future of the Empire to the immediate work of the proper conduct of the War'.[110] Massey and Ward's agenda revolved around an established tradition of calling for a strong and united empire that could guarantee New Zealand's interests. In doing so they were readily willing to evoke the sacrifices made and the reciprocal obligations expected.

A priority in discussions of war aims was a promise that former German territories in the Pacific would not be returned. As Massey warned, 'if we have to give back Samoa and allow the Germans to re-establish themselves in the South Pacific it will be the bitterest pill that the New Zealanders ever had to swallow.' Ward agreed, claiming that the restoration of German control over Sāmoa would be as dangerous to New Zealand as a German control of Ireland would be to Britain. Massey also raised interests in assuring that Ocean Island and Nauru, and its 'very import phosphate deposits', would remain in British control after the war.[111] However, the British government was conflicted on the issue of territorial spoils. While it wanted to maintain dominion commitment, and was willing to make concessions in order to do this, it also wished to court the neutral United States and be seen as sympathetic to President Woodrow Wilson's principle of 'peace without annexations'. In attempts to balance these interests, the unconditional guarantee Massey and Ward were angling for was side-stepped and it remained to be seen whether the British government could develop an approach acceptable to both the United States and the dominions or whether it would be forced to choose a side.

Concerns about regional security also led the New Zealanders to raise the issue of the Royal Navy's presence in the Pacific and Japan's expansion in the region. Under the February 1917 Anglo-Japanese agreement, the British government was pledged to support Japanese claims to German territories it had seized in China and in the Pacific north of the equator in exchange for Japanese support for British claims to German colonies in the South Pacific. Although suspicion of Japanese expansion had certainly not been quelled, both New Zealand and Australia supported this agreement. Massey may have seen both that Japan's assistance in providing naval escorts must be recognised — he noted the Japanese Navy had been of great service and that Japan had 'played the game' — and that Japan's capture of German territory could not be easily reversed.[112]

Massey and Ward were less conciliatory, however, in stating a grievance against the Admiralty for failing to provide New Zealand with sufficient naval protection in general and specifically during the escort crisis in the early part of the war. Their point was taken and Ward was heavily involved in securing Resolution IV, which committed the Admiralty to a review of its imperial naval defence strategy.[113]

The meetings also became another forum in which to push New Zealand's concerns about securing adequate shipping. At the Imperial War Cabinet Massey bluntly stated that the shipping controller's reduction of ships assigned to New Zealand was as damaging as the German submarine campaign. When the controller countered by noting that it was only 21 days to Argentina compared with 42 to New Zealand, Massey described the situation as 'a sorry requital for all New Zealand's sacrifices in the common cause'.[114] The recent sinking of the New Zealand Shipping Company's SS *Rotorua* also became part of the argument. After disembarking its 264 passengers at Plymouth, the ship was en route to London when it was torpedoed in the English Channel. All but one crew member were saved but the vessel, and its cargo of frozen meat, worth nearly £1 million, were lost.

When Massey asked why the *Rotorua* had not been permitted to discharge its cargo at Plymouth, and why the Admiralty had not provided protection, he was told that Plymouth lacked the facilities to unload frozen meat and that the Royal Navy could not protect every merchant ship. The episode ended in Mackenzie lodging a protest with the Colonial Office: 'the High Commissioner trusts that more intelligent action in the handling of vessels trading with New Zealand will be taken by the responsible authorities'.[115]

The constitutional arrangements of the British Empire were also on the agenda. Although it was decided that this subject would be properly discussed after the war,[116] it was acknowledged that the dominions should be fully recognised 'as autonomous nations of an Imperial Commonwealth' and that there should be 'continuous consultation in all important matters of common Imperial concern'. Massey considered the war a watershed moment. Previously the 'Dominions had been willing to share the burden of Empire, but had no voice. That would not occur again.' Both New Zealanders squared this with a traditional view that a strong, united and enduring empire was essential to New Zealand's interests, and it was unambiguously stated that 'New Zealand should remain part of the Empire throughout all time, and . . . [it was] hoped that the Empire would last until the day of judgement'.[117]

The two men disagreed, however, on the best way to achieve that. As he had before the war, Ward supported the concept of an imperial parliament to determine collective policy,[118] but Massey, keen to preserve dominion autonomy, favoured an arrangement in which the dominions and Britain would remain self-governing entities in close and free cooperation.[119] Massey also pushed for the adoption of a system of imperial preference in trade and an immigration scheme that would maintain 'the British character in the Dominions'. With support from the Canadian prime minister, Sir Robert Borden, and after a number of revisions, Massey's draft became the basis for Resolution XXI, which adopted the principle that 'each part of the Empire, having due regard to the interests of our Allies, shall give special treatment and facilities to the produce and manufactures of other parts of the Empire'. Moreover, the resolution pledged that emigrants from Great Britain would be encouraged 'to settle in countries under the British flag'.[120] When it came to discussions about war graves and the creation of an Imperial War Graves Commission, Massey tabled what would become another recurring matter: to have part of the Gallipoli Peninsula, 'where lie the remains of so many British and Oversea Dominion soldiers', placed under British authority after the war.[121]

When discussions were adjourned in early May 1917, Massey noted that he had initially felt some doubt about the practicality of the affair, but that the Imperial War Cabinet had been 'an unqualified success' and he hoped it would become a permanent institution.[122] Moreover, despite observations that they were 'Siamese twins who hate each other', it is noted that the Cabinet saw Massey and Ward demonstrate 'an effective working relationship with Ward's institutional knowledge complementing Massey's strong personality'.[123] With their business completed, Massey and Ward set out for New Zealand. They arrived home on 25 June 1917, 10 months after their departure.

In early February 1917, in the hope of bringing the war to a conclusion that year, the British government assessed the empire's manpower potential, and asked the dominions for more troops — in New Zealand's case, a second division.[124]

Massey was open to the proposal, and instructed Allen that the reply to the British request 'should be couched in generally favourable terms', but the Cabinet, especially Allen, Liverpool and Robin, were hesitant or opposed.[125] A second division would exacerbate industrial problems and generally strain public goodwill. There was also a rankling sense that New Zealand was being asked to do more than Canada and Australia, neither of which had

January 17, 1917. OTAGO WITNESS. 33

VISIT OF MR WM. MASSEY (PRIME MINISTER OF NEW ZEALAND) AND SIR J. G. WARD TO THE BATTLE-FRONT IN FRANCE.

Mr Massey is seen coming out of a captured German dug-out, and to the left, immediately behind the man carrying the lantern, is Sir Joseph Ward.

NEW ZEALAND'S REPRESENTATIVES, IN COMPANY WITH GENERAL HAIG, ON THE WESTERN FRONT.

From left to right: Sir Joseph Ward, General Sir Douglas Haig, and Mr Massey.

(Photos by Newspaper Illustrations.)

above These scenes from Massey and Ward's visit to France were published in January 1917 and included a visit to a captured German dugout and a meeting with General Douglas Haig, who had commanded British forces on the Western Front since late 1915. OTAGO WITNESS, 17 JANUARY 1917, P. 33. ALEXANDER TURNBULL LIBRARY, N-P-2131-33

below Members of the Imperial War Cabinet in May 1917. Joseph Ward is in the middle row, fourth from right; William Massey is in the front row, second from right; Canadian prime minister Robert Borden is in the front row, third from right; and British prime minister David Lloyd George sits in the front row, fourth from right. ALEXANDER TURNBULL LIBRARY, 1/1-015312-G introduced conscription. As Liverpool reported to the Colonial Office, 'New Zealand considers that she has already contributed a larger quota in proportion to our population than any of the other dominions and it is questionable whether it would be in the interests of the Empire for New Zealand to suffer disproportionally to other dominions because they had not applied compulsion to maintain their obligations.'[126] On 15 February, after a detailed review of New Zealand's manpower, Cabinet's objections were cabled to London. These noted that, although New Zealand was 'most anxious to support the Empire with all her resources in men as well as produce', the country had to preserve its workforce and agricultural production and had arranged its priorities in order to maintain the New Zealand Division at full strength.[127]

Despite subsequent pressure from London, various military commanders and Massey, Allen continued to argue against the proposal. The request was then scaled down to the creation of a Fourth Brigade for the New Zealand Division, which would be raised out of the existing reinforcements in Britain. Allen reluctantly agreed but insisted that the new brigade would be given no further reinforcements. In a notable reversal of his push for steady reinforcements, he seems to have believed that a burst of effort now, even if unsustainable, could prove decisive.

On 27 March, Allen announced the Fourth Brigade. Some comfort was taken from the arguments that this new unit could be considered a temporary creation, that it would be disbanded if required and that it would not poach reinforcements needed to maintain the New Zealand Division. As Allen explained to Parliament, 'We are not sending reinforcements to that brigade . . . If the Division for some reason becomes depleted then the brigade will be used to reinforce it.'[128] In this sense the new brigade could be presented, as Godley put it, as simply a 'more satisfactory way of collecting and employing the reinforcements, as long as they are of sufficient numbers, than letting them accumulate at Sling or Etaples' (Sling was the New Zealand training camp in England, Étaples its French base).[129] The public reception was one of general reluctance to take on this new commitment and doubts about Allen's assurances that the brigade would not require additional reinforcements. For some, creating the brigade from reserves in England was evidence that the country had been sending too many men overseas; a stark contrast to earlier accusations that Allen was failing to maximise the country's effort.[130]

The creation of the Fourth Brigade represented the height of the NZEF's expansion and around 60,000 men were deployed overseas by mid-1917. The country's training camps were now in high gear. Trentham was 'alive with waggons delivering every day and rail waggons were shunted down the camp siding to deliver coal, meat vegetables and fodder'. In an average month of 1917, the camp was consuming 66 tons of meat, 66 of groceries, 130 of vegetables, 140 of coal, 200 of firewood, 20 of forage and 9510 gallons of milk. The camp bakeries produced 3200 loaves a day. Before a draft was due to leave, when letter writing and parcel sending reached a peak, almost 27,000 letters would arrive and 30,000 letters and 2 tons of parcels leave.[131] By 1917 the Public Works had added or improved roads and water and sewage pipes and provided additional street lighting. From October that year over 120 acres of nearby marshland was drained to give an extra manoeuvring area.[132] To match the type of war the troops were now fighting, the camps trained recruits in trench construction and the use of new weapons, including rifle grenades.

In the first months of 1917 there were two revolutionary events in global affairs. In March the Tsarist regime in Russia collapsed after it failed to quell the popular uprising dubbed the 'February Revolution' (Russia used the Julian calendar). On 15 March, Tsar Nicholas II abdicated, naming his brother Michael as his successor. When Michael refused the crown, the 300-year-old Romanov dynasty came to an end. Two rival centres of power emerged: the Temporary Committee of the Duma, dominated by the lawyer and politician Alexander Kerensky, which had 'the closest thing to formal power but no authority in the streets', and the Petrograd Soviet, made up of deputies from the army and the workers, which had 'the closest thing to power in the streets but no formal authority'.[133] The situation was uneasy but both elected to continue the war, both out of patriotic spirit and as a condition for the British and French aid the country desperately needed.

Weeks later, the United States declared war on Germany. As predicted, the resumption of unrestricted submarine warfare in February had had immediate repercussions on relations between Washington and Berlin, and calls for American action had become more strident as hundreds of thousands of tons of ships, and their crews, were destroyed. Although diplomatic relations with Germany were soon cut and the president's Cabinet was almost unanimously in favour of war, Wilson, who had been re-elected in November 1916 on the slogan 'He kept us out of war', remained reluctant to declare it. In the Senate many Republicans called for intervention, as did numerous business interests who had invested heavily in an Allied victory. Many farmers, manufacturers, shippers and labourer unions also called for action as merchant ships refused to travel the Atlantic, prices rose and perishable goods rotted. Much of this outcry, though, was undirected, and anti-German expressions were balanced by anti-English and anti-war voices. Some called for 'armed neutrality', in which the United States would protect its shipping without declaring war. In March, however, came stunning news that Germany had sought an alliance with Mexico and Japan for a possible war on the North American continent in which Berlin promised to recognise a transfer of territory to Mexico. On 2 April 1917, Wilson delivered a speech to Congress, arguing that '[t]he world must be made safe for democracy'. The House of Representatives approved a resolution for war with 373 members in favour and 50 opposed. In the Senate the same resolution passed 82 to 6, and on 6 April the United States declared war on Germany.[134] A New Zealand cartoon entitled 'No More Notes' depicted Wilson's fountain pen listed as 'For Sale Owner Enlisted'.[135]

Besides their influence on the course of the war, and what would follow, both these developments acted to redefine the conflict. With the collapse of the Romanov dynasty, some acknowledged the anomaly of Tsarist autocracy within the Allied narrative of fighting for liberty. As one letter to the editor of the *Sun* put it: 'From the outbreak of the war until shortly before the abdication of the Tsar there was scarcely a day on which some fulsome eulogy of that autocrat did not appear in our papers. The people of the Allied countries were asked to believe that he was a god — worshipped by the trusting Russians as their little father. All this, of course, was done for diplomatic reasons — and it failed.' As the revolution raised hopes of a Russian democracy, the notion of the war as a confrontation between democratic and autocratic regimes was renewed. The correspondent continued: 'what we have to do is readjust our forces, take our bearings once more and put our democratic soul into the fight, and we will do it. The forces on our side are now all democratic, and omens are good.' The *New Zealand Herald* cited Washington officials describing the Russian revolution as the 'greatest democratic victory of the century', bringing Russia 'into the ranks of the western democracies' and emphasising 'more than ever the political character of Prussianised Germany'.[136]

It was unclear how the regime change in Russia would affect the Eastern Front. Much revolved around rumours that the Tsarist household had not been fully committed to a war against Germany. A local Russian interviewed by the *Auckland Star* voiced a common rumour that the Tsar was 'pro-German in his sympathies, and practically all the officials in high places held similar sympathies'.[137] MP Thomas Wilford told Parliament that such sympathies had even risked German and Russian autocrats signing a separate peace. This would have been a disaster, as Germany would have been freed to better fight in other theatres. Wilford predicted that Kerensky would rise as 'a man of destiny' who would bring new energy to the Russian effort.[138]

This gave sense to why earlier predictions that the Russian steamroller would simply flatten its opponents had not come to pass, and offered some hope that both the conflict on the Eastern Front, and the wider war, would soon turn. Mr J. Zeekul, 'a Russian gentleman, who finds himself in Christchurch', agreed, claiming 'The Russian revolution was the best thing that could have happened in Europe', and he hoped that democratic revolution against autocracy might spread to Germany: 'He was inclined to think that the Russian revolt would be an encouragement to Germany, where the Socialist party had been even stronger than in Russia. A revolution in Germany was quite a possibility.'[139]

The United States' entry into the war was also loaded with greater meanings. The declaration of the chief neutral power for the Allies added further volume to the argument that Germany was on the wrong side of global opinion. Many also hoped that American resources would soon have a decisive impact on the course of the war. As the first American troops arrived in France in mid-1917, the *New Zealand Herald* praised the dynamism of the United States: 'Her population, her resources, her national energy, are so immense that the Central Powers must feel deeply concerned as to the use she will make of them.'[140]

But there was also some unease about what expanding American power might mean for the British world. More specifically, some considered that the American Meat Trust represented a serious threat to New Zealand's economic interests on the London market. In a November 1916 letter to Massey, Allen outlined his concerns: 'I venture to predict that the great danger of the future, if not to the Empire at least to us in these Southern seas, is the domination that will be secured over our trade by America or Japan, or both . . . Just now we are asked to sit down and submit to almost anything that America wishes to do with us because we do not wish to offend them. As far as I can judge they have Australia in their grip with regard to the meat trade, and they are getting their grips into New Zealand in the same trade . . . There is no mercy in the American; he is out for money, and I am firmly of the belief that the Japanese is not only out for money, but out to rule the Pacific as well.'[141]

Massey, too, denounced the British government's practice of making profits by selling surplus New Zealand meat on the open market to subsidise a purchase of American meat: 'The New Zealand producers have not complained of the prices paid to them, but they will complain bitterly when they know that the profit on their meat is really benefiting those whom they consider as being the worst type of exploiters.'[142] Such sentiments endured after the United States entered the war. In July 1917 C. J. Talbot, the Liberal MP for Temuka, pulled no punches in denouncing the American Meat Trust as an enemy 'doing as great harm as the Huns'.[143]

However, even those suspicious of American power made much of the sense that the United States was a fellow Anglo-Saxon power animated by common values. After his return from Britain, Massey told Parliament, 'Some of us did think and say harsh things about the United States prior to her declaration of war.' When an interjector noted that he might include himself in that category, he agreed, but continued: 'I believe the coming-together of the two great branches of the Anglo-Saxon race is one of the greatest events in the history of the world.' Although the two nations would 'probably never be under the same flag, because there is neither necessity nor inclination for that on either side . . . I think it is a splendid thing to know that we can unite and work together in the interests of civilization and humanity.'[144]

Such sentiments were felt more widely, and on 4 July 1917 some New Zealanders marked Independence Day by flying the Stars and Stripes alongside the Union Jack on public buildings and private businesses, and various formal respects were sent to the United States consul-general A. A. Winslow. 'I am quite certain,' he responded, 'that the peoples of the two great English-speaking races will stand firm and united until the object for which they entered the struggle is achieved and a victory won that will free the world of a hideous menace. From the news that is now coming to hand it looks as if Russia is with us, not only for democracy, but for a speedy victory . . . [i]t is my opinion that a final victory will be achieved before the close of 1917.'[145]

CHAPTER TEN
CONSCRIPTION

previous pages
Rotoaira Prison in the central North Island was originally built for criminals but held objectors during the war. ARCHIVES NEW ZEALAND, R3195153

In the 10-month period that Massey and Ward were overseas, conscription was enforced with a heavy-handedness that underscored just how sensitive regulations around dissent had become. Behind state power, however, public approval or at least acceptance of conscription endured. Indeed, many of the biggest challenges around conscription came from factions within the patriotic consensus as controversies arose over how equality of sacrifice was to be achieved.[1] Although the challenges to conscription and tensions were managed, by mid-1917 the patriotic consensus had grown increasingly strained; much was invested in the hope that forthcoming efforts on the Western Front would bring decisive results.

After the Military Service Act was passed in August 1916 came the major task of preparing conscription's balloting system. Rather than undertake another registration of eligible men, the government decided to reuse the returns collected under the 1915 National Registration Act. This introduced a degree of error as a number of men had changed their addresses or left the country since late 1915. Although those who had since come of age, and those wishing to amend details, could do so by a postal registration, an estimated 3500 to 5000 avoided registering and slipped the administrative net. Only one act of official corruption was discovered: a clerk had removed her sweetheart's details.[2]

Although voluntary enlistment continued — and over 26,000 men volunteered over 1917–18 — the rates remained consistently short of quotas and Allen announced, on 28 October 1916, that the first conscription ballot would be held in mid-November.[3] Balloting involved drawing two numbered marbles from a barrel. The first of these referred to one of 233 drawers and the second to one of the 500 cards within these, each listing a man's details. At first this process took two and a half days to produce a full allotment of balloted men, but it was later reduced to one.[4] The first ballot, on 16 November, was attended by Allen, the mayor of Wellington and a number of journalists. Holland, appearing on behalf of the *Maoriland Worker*, 'almost precipitated a debate by informing the Minister that he did not approve of the principles of Conscription'. Having witnessed the first use of the system, the female clerks organising the ballot, 'who it is quite possible will draw their sweethearts' cards as time goes on', and the newspaper representatives were invited to join the mayor for tea.[5] Ultimately, some 134,632 men would be balloted over the following two years.[6]

If he was selected, a balloted man's details were gazetted for official notification and he was sent a telegram. He then had a month in which to undergo a medical examination by a board of two doctors acting under military observation to assess his fitness for military service. There were five possible assessments: A: fit for active service; B: able to be made fit with medical attention; C1: likely to become fit for active service after special training; C2: permanently unfit for active service but fit to serve in New Zealand; and D: permanently unfit for any kind of service. A degree of deception had been anticipated and the Medical Service Boards soon began to recognise a number of techniques intended to thwart medical checks. There were cases of 'men injecting their knees with fluid, or "knuckling" their eyes, to cause pain and swelling; chewing tobacco to destabilize the heart; or even deliberately contracting venereal disease'.[7]

Perhaps more concerning to officials was the quantity of poor physiques, deformities and defects that showed up in the examiners' reports.[8] Between November 1916 and November 1918 some 15,396 balloted men were rejected for heart disease (17.3 per cent of all those rejected), another 7888 (8.9 per cent) for failing army standards, and another 11,239 (12.7 per cent) for 'defects'.[9] Problems with feet alone led medial officers to call for reforms in public policy and the introduction of legislation 'prohibiting the manufacture of boots so constructed as to cause deformities of the feet'.[10] By the end of the war around 121,519 balloted men had undergone medical exams and some 62 per cent had been classed as unfit for military service.[11]

Every balloted man also had the right to appeal for exemption to a Military Service Board. These travelled throughout their military districts, generally including remote localities, and hearings were typically open to the public. The original four boards were soon overwhelmed and increased to 10. To make them as palatable as possible to the public, the boards included respected men with backgrounds in law, unions and farming, with the military representative typically a solicitor with territorial experience.[12] Appellants, or employers acting on their behalf, could make their cases on grounds of public interest, undue hardship or conscience (i.e. religious grounds). Boards could dismiss appeals, adjourn them for rehearing at a set date, adjourn them *sine die* (indefinitely) or allow them.[13]

Most appeals (51.73 per cent) were entered on grounds of public interest, often noting negative consequences for the economy, and 38.98 per cent were based on undue hardship, usually citing financial or physical support being given to relatives. The rarest category, just 4.76 per cent, were appeals based on conscientious objection to military service.[14] The boards faced a difficult task in assessing men's circumstances and balancing their interests against community expectations of equality of sacrifice. Examples included men such as George Cook, who maintained that his mother was in a weak state of health and requested exemption while she recovered; James Bennett, who requested a three-month delay to dispose of his property; and Harrold Ennor, who had earlier noted that he was 'no fighter', who entered an appeal that he was indispensable at the Stamp Department.[15]

By the end of the war the boards had heard tens of thousands of cases: estimates range between 32,445 and 43,544. This means that, even at the highest count, less than one-third of balloted men appealed for exemptions. New Zealanders were, apparently, less likely than

Australians or Canadians to appeal — despite the fact that Australians were appealing for exemptions to military training within Australia, rather than for frontline service. Some 2461 appeals were accepted, another 11,343 were offered provisional exemptions and 1769 cases were not determined.[16] In total this potentially means nearly half of the appeals heard were granted in the appellant's favour.

After the first ballot in November 1916, the first balloted men were soon moving through the system of medical checks and Military Service Boards, and New Zealand's first conscript soldiers were in training camps by January 1917. By the end of the war, 32,270 of the 91,941 men who served would be conscripts.[17]

By coincidence, Allen announced the first ballot on the same day, 28 October 1916, that New Zealanders learnt the result of an Australian referendum that rejected conscription, by a narrow margin. Although Allen wrote to Massey, 'Thank goodness we have avoided that blunder', New Zealand's anti-conscription movement took new heart from the Australian decision and proposed a second anti-conscription conference in Wellington to call for a repeal of the Military Service Act.[18] With that legislation now about to be applied, the phoney war between the government and the anti-conscription movement was entering its last stages.

The government certainly intended to act from a position of strength. Noting a recent Labour manifesto which declared that 'the organised workers of New Zealand are opposed to conscription', Allen privately wrote that it was 'our bounden duty to protect ourselves against it [the anti-conscription movement] as far as possible'.[19] This protection came partly in the form of a series of additional war regulations tightening restrictions on expression. On 4 December the definition of 'seditious utterance' was greatly expanded, so that utterance covered 'words, writing, pictures, or any other significant expression or representation whatever'.[20]

The scope of such utterance was extensive, including exciting 'disaffection against His Majesty or the Government of the United Kingdom, or of New Zealand, or of any other part of His Majesty's Dominions'; inciting 'violence, lawlessness, or disorder whether in New Zealand or in any other part of His Majesty's Dominions'; inciting class ill-will; any interference with recruiting or war production; and any discouragement of the prosecution of the war to a victorious conclusion.[21] Hearings for those charged under the regulations were to be restricted to a magistrate, removing the option of trial by jury. Penalties for seditious utterances were a £100 fine or 12 months' imprisonment.

Industrial unrest over conscription was also looming. On 23 November 1916, a leading Liberal minister warned Allen that 'I have heard from a reliable source that the whole of the Waterside workers, coal miners, and kindred industries, are ready to step out on word from Australia'.[22] On the West Coast, coal miners at Blackball and nearby Roa soon went on strike, ostensibly over conscription, though a demand for a 17.5 per cent increase in wages was also stated. Although this action proved short-lived, and the miners resumed work on 11 December, it alarmed a government desperate to avoid coal shortages. There was also the risk that unrest in one sector could lead to solidarity strikes and, most alarmingly, a coordinated 1913-style

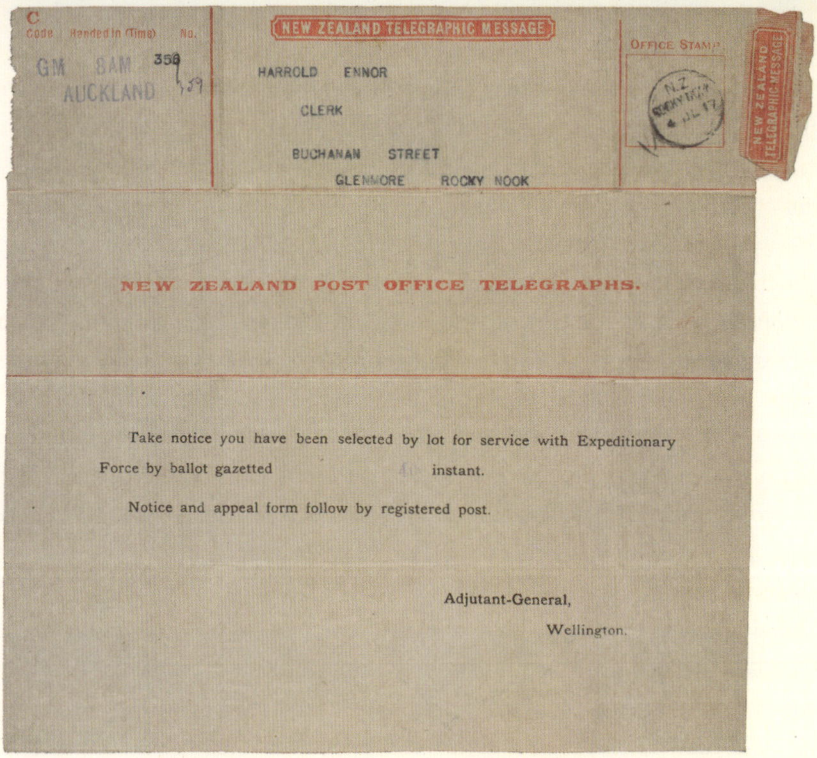

C
Code Handed in (Time) No.
GM 8AM 356
AUCKLAND 59

NEW ZEALAND TELEGRAPHIC MESSAGE

HARROLD ENNOR

CLERK

BUCHANAN STREET

GLENMORE ROCKY NOOK

OFFICE STAMP

N.Z. ROCKY NOOK 4 JL 17

NEW ZEALAND TELEGRAPHIC MESSAGE

NEW ZEALAND POST OFFICE TELEGRAPHS.

Take notice you have been selected by lot for service with Expeditionary Force by ballot gazetted 4th instant.

Notice and appeal form follow by registered post.

Adjutant-General,

Wellington.

above Clerks in Routh's building in Wellington attend drawers holding registered men's details. STATISTICS NEW ZEALAND, COURTESY NZ HISTORY

below An official telegraph notifying Harrold Ennor that he had been balloted and that further instructions would follow. ALEXANDER TURNBULL LIBRARY, QMS-0683 action by miners and waterfront workers. In November 1916, Allen urged the employers in the drivers' dispute 'to be very careful in coming to their conclusions as the Government were especially anxious to avoid any industrial trouble at the present moment'.[23]

Again the government flexed some muscle. Belying Massey's earlier claims that the government did not take threats of industrial unrest over conscription seriously, Herdman had, by June 1916, secretly drawn up plans to deal with major strikes, especially given that enlistment had reduced the pool of men who might act as specials.[24] Allen wrote to Massey at the end of December:

> We have arranged for horses and forage, and at very short notice we could secure a fair number of special constables. We have also erected a barricade near Taranaki Street Wharf, which will be useful for us to embark horses and also, in case of trouble, to paddock horses. I heard today from a labour man that it had been realised what the enclosure might be used for, and that they are beginning to see we have made a good deal of preparations to meet a strike, should it come. We are hopeful that preparations and a knowledge of them will make the labour people see that they had better remain quiet . . . For my part I am very hopeful that we shall avoid a strike altogether. The conferences, however, may lead to a different conclusion.[25]

More regulations the following February empowered the government to exercise management over any wharf or wharves and determine matters including employment, conditions and payment.[26]

The anti-conscriptionist position was less secure. Conscription may have helped to create a unified Labour Party, but it had not unified the labour movement. Several union leaders in Dunedin, supportive of or willing to accept conscription, refused to support the new party.[27] To the disappointment of trade unionist Jack McCullough,

> A number of Unions & Trades Councils have protested, but then strange to say one Union The Greymouth Watersiders have carried a motion in favour & I was present when a majority of the Otago Trades Council prevented any protest being raised against it or to assist in convening a meeting to discuss it. I concluded that this was done because a majority at the meeting favoured the [Military Service] Bill, & did not desire that their attitude should be known.[28]

Otago's Kaitangata mine decided, on the ludicrously small poll of 14/14 plus the chairman's casting vote, not to even participate in the anti-conscription conference.[29]

A particularly public demonstration of the movement's split over conscription developed around the figure of Victor Grayson, a British socialist who had arrived in New Zealand in early 1916, accompanying his wife, who was a member of a touring Shakespearean company. By late August he was giving public lectures on Christianity, labour and the war, which he argued would be to socialism's advantage as mass enlistment cultivated class consciousness and impulses for reform. In response, the *Maoriland Worker* declared Grayson 'was only fit to occupy Labor's platform as an enemy of Labor', and Social Democrat activist Tom Brindle denounced him as an 'ex-socialist' writing 'capitalist claptrap'.[30] In response Grayson enlisted in the New Zealand Expeditionary Force and fired back, in a published tract, that Australia and New Zealand had reminded him of Bernard Shaw's gibe that 'the most formidable obstacle to the attainment of Socialism was the Socialists'. He accused the Labour Party of

> bleating harmlessly, well behind the fighting line, about matters which cannot and will not be settled, or even touched, until this gigantic world war is terminated . . . I have enlisted because I am sick of the cant of antimilitarism. I have accepted the khaki of the fighting democracy because the flamboyant red tie of the mouthing stand-backs has made me weary of a traitor-stained cause . . . I am a Socialist, and will wear the uniform of the warrior with good logic and a bright spirit. I hate war and I hate killing. Yet if I account for one of the vassals of the world's mad-dog I shall have 'done my bit' towards the world's regeneration.[31]

Regardless of internal divisions and animosities, the second anti-conscription conference opened in the capital on 20 December 1916. Seeking to counter police surveillance — detectives had been trying to gain admittance — delegates decided to forgo a memorial photograph lest it later be used by the authorities for identification purposes.[32] The conference sessions continued into the new year, with the major points of discussion being conscription, the cost of living and civil liberties. The conference concluded with a series of resolutions including the repeal of the Military Service Act, or at least a referendum on the issue; the removal of restrictions on free speech; and the release of 'political prisoners'.[33] More significantly, a secret meeting of several union representatives at the conference had sought to harden resolve for a general strike planned to begin in early February 1917. Conscription was the central issue, but negotiations over pay and employment conditions were also clear considerations.[34]

Government confrontation with anti-conscriptionists started over the same time. Robert Semple, drawing energy from his recent lecture tour in Australia, was the first arrested. Official attention fastened on speeches he made in November and December, praising Australia's rejection of conscription, urging a comparable rejection in New Zealand and arguing that conscription was a plot to set back workers' rights: 'It is the one forged chain that can be applied to the legs and minds of men and women. Conscription was not intended to fight the Kaiser, but to fight trades unionism and the working classes.'[35]

On 12 December he was charged with sedition and sentenced to 12 months' imprisonment. The solicitor-general, who considered Semple 'one of the most dangerous and mischievous men in New Zealand', privately stated to the Crown solicitor that there should be 'as long a term of imprisonment as practicable, and there should be no question of a mere fine'.[36] With this first skirmish, Allen wrote to Massey: 'There can be no doubt about it, that there is to be a fight about the Military Service Act, and I am only too pleased to tell you that every member of the Cabinet is solid and loyal over the question that the Act must be enforced.'[37]

Within weeks several more leading figures within the Labour Party — Peter Fraser, Tom Brindle, James Thorn and Fred Cooke — were arrested on charges of seditious utterances and each was sentenced to 12 months' hard labour.[38] Although Holland was spared, he claimed that a Hansard stenographer and detectives were present and took notes at every meeting he addressed.[39] On 19 December, the offices of the *Maoriland Worker* were raided by the police, who seized some 3000 copies of the Labour Party's peace manifesto and issued a court summons against the paper.[40] As 1916 ended, Allen noted that anti-conscription activists 'are all pretty well muzzled by the new regulations with regard to seditious utterances'.[41]

The militant industrial scene, however, was far from defused. Word of Semple's arrest had threatened to trigger industrial action and a warning came from Rūnanga, where 'unions resolved that if Semple refused bail today they will strike tomorrow'.[42] However, when Allen refused to intervene, and bail was denied, Semple sent a message to Paddy Webb, urging 'no drastic action to be taken', and the resolution was not put to the test.[43] This drawing back appears to reflect the Federation of Labour's assessment of its vulnerable situation, not simply because the government might conscript and arrest strikers, but also because of limited worker support for striking. By one historian's assessment, 'The vast majority of workers were not sufficiently opposed to conscription to sacrifice their wages, jobs and even freedom, and perhaps to sabotage the nation's war effort, in order to fight it.'[44]

Plans for a general strike action were downgraded to a go-slow in the mines and on the waterfront, which became apparent at ports around the country in January 1917. In Wellington watersiders began to refuse to work after 5 p.m. and to reduce the number of boxes of butter lifted in a hoist from 48 to 30. A mining go-slow began at the Waipā mine in Waikato by 2 February and had spread to most West Coast mines by the middle of the month. Despite mines outside the Federation of Labour continuing normal operations, the campaign reduced total coal production by an estimated 5800 tons per week.[45] Allen was now in a delicate situation. Attempting to force an end to industrial action risked a retaliatory strike and an even more drastic fall in productivity, but he had no desire to follow the British example of a punitive conscription of miners, which would exacerbate the manpower shortages and reduce coal production. Doing nothing, and hoping the miners and employers might settle the dispute themselves, risked exhausting coal supplies and causing hardship and frustration.[46]

Ultimately, the government approached the issue with a mix of concession and coercion.[47] Electing to pressure employers to negotiate over pay and conditions, which Allen suspected was more of an issue than conscription, the watersiders ended their go-slow in early March and voted to accept an agreement.[48] Meanwhile, negotiations with the miners stalled and Allen ordered a show of strength. On 16 February, he instructed Military Service Boards to defer appeals from balloted miners, who would typically be given exemptions through their involvement in a crucial industry, until coal production returned to normal.[49] On 3 April the police raided union offices at Huntly and two West Coast mines, taking nine union leaders into custody. Within days all the West Coast mines and all but one in the Waikato went on a retaliatory strike. As one historian notes, 'the arrests succeeded where the Federation of Labour had failed and had united the miners'.[50]

Changing tack, Allen chose to negotiate directly with delegates of the striking unions and travelled to the West Coast, accompanied by MacDonald, as minister of mines. By Allen's account, 'We had a great fight with the delegates all the way through, and some half a dozen times were on the brink of separating',[51] but a deal was brokered: in return for the miners resuming work by 25 April, and an unwritten assurance of no further strikes throughout the war, the government promised not to press for penalties in the case of the arrested miners and to make it clear to Military Service Boards that miners were to be exempted.

However, a day after the agreement came into effect, further strikes broke out at two West Coast mines, dragging out a smaller industrial action, which ended on 30 April. Angry at this breach of agreements, Cabinet elected to conscript the striking miners and the Military Service Boards were requested not to allow exemptions for the 200 or so strikers involved. In the face of threats of further industrial unrest and petitions from mine owners, Allen backed down and promised that any miners who had entered training camps 'could, when a short period had elapsed and the law been satisfied, be permitted to return to the mines'.[52]

Besides a ready use of state power and divisions within labour, the confrontation with the anti-conscriptionists was buttressed by popular support and public frustration with industrial unrest. Although the Parliamentary Elections Postponement Act of August 1916 prevented a national test of public feeling on conscription, it did become a major issue in the April 1917 municipal elections, which also represented the start of the new Labour Party's political career. In Christchurch, the heartland of anti-militarism and labour causes, the local Labour Representation Committee made a repeal of the Military Service Act the first plank in its platform.[53] The rest of the party's platform centred on the high cost of living, blaming it largely on exploitation by farmers and merchants. Labour made specific proposals to extend the use of municipal enterprise to outflank the exploiters and hold prices down. Repealing the Military Service Act was also raised in elections in the overwhelmingly working-class Christchurch borough of Woolston, and in Greymouth, a port town in a coal-mining region with a well-earned reputation for radicalism.

Labour's campaigning appeared to go well, with strong fundraising and a public meeting on the cost of living packing the town hall to overflowing. Some Labour leaders' decisions to associate the party with the continuing industrial actions were less politically useful. Webb, who had so far proved more circumspect than some of his arrested colleagues, publicly praised the striking miners in their struggle against conscription: 'It is up to the men and women to rise and say to the Government: "you will not take one man."'[54] For this he was arrested, charged with making a seditious utterance on 1 May. He served three months in prison.

Much public opinion, including moderate labour, was decidedly cool, if not openly outraged, towards the strikers' actions during a war and a coal shortage. Sensitive to the allegation that profiteers were exploiting the nation during its time of trial, businessmen wielded a comparable charge against labour unrest, damning them as 'pro-German', 'law breakers', 'traitors', 'vipers', 'enemy in our midst' and aspiring dictators.[55] In hindsight, MP Dan Sullivan considered that 'Labour must have lost thousands of votes as a result of the coal strike'.[56]

Similar tensions were apparent at an April 1917 meeting called by the Canterbury branch of the Women's National Reserve. A motion calling for women to influence their husbands to end the strike caused a clash along class and patriotic divides, with feelings running high. Jane Bean, a daughter of the late Richard Seddon, supported the motion, urging that there must be a united effort to win the war and that workers 'should be anti-German, not anti-conscriptionist', but Elizabeth McCombs, the wife of James McCombs, stated her surprise at 'the amazing effrontery of a group of wealthy women in the city'. Speaking against conscription, Louisa Nuttall, mother of conscientious objector Thomas Nuttall, asserted that women did not raise their boys to be soldiers. To this Bean fired back, 'I wonder what the women of Belgium brought their girls up for?' The motion was ultimately carried 'by a large majority', though 'the disaffected portion of the audience remained seated' during the final singing of the National Anthem.[57]

The election results were a bitter disappointment for Labour and the anti-conscriptionist cause.[58] In Christchurch, Labour's mayoral candidate, McCombs, faced a crushing defeat at the hands of the rather lacklustre Reform aligned incumbent, Henry Holland (no relation to Harry Holland), by a margin of two to one. The Social Democratic Party had held six seats in 1915; Labour now had only five.[59] Labour representation on the Christchurch City Council, though, had increased, by one, to a total of five, including Ada Wells, who became the first woman on the council.[60] The results were worse in Woolston, where the Social Democratic Party had won both the mayoralty and all but one council seat in 1915. The sitting mayor was heavily defeated by his pro-conscription opponent and Labour was left with only one councillor. In Greymouth the Labour ticket for the borough council was opposed by a pro-conscription grouping. In a heavy poll the 'patriotic ticket' swept the field by a substantial margin.[61]

Although militants continued to insist that New Zealanders were opposed to conscription, these defeats in an environment that should have been favourable to the cause led to a resigned acceptance that the masses either approved of conscription or had come to accept it. As the *Maoriland Worker*'s columnist, 'The Vag', sadly acknowledged, 'It is no use our blinking our eyes and wondering what has hit us, it is no use our putting up this, that, and the other excuse . . . [i]f the fight was coming again to-morrow we could not do better . . . two-thirds, and more than two-thirds, voted in favour of the Government; in favour of Conscription; in favour of cheap soldiers and in favour of continuing the war.'[62] The anti-conscriptionist president of the Lyttelton Waterside Workers' Union, E. E. Langley, similarly noted that Labour leaders 'put up a fight against Conscription and were turned down by 50 per cent of their own class . . . That the people want conscription has been proved beyond a shadow of a doubt.'[63]

By mid-1917 the forces that had pledged to meet an introduction of conscription with major disruptions had been laid low. Almost half of the Labour Party's most effective speakers were incarcerated, its remaining leaders were exercising caution and the party was struggling to function.[64] In Herdman's words, the campaign had been 'calculated to revive again the spirit of disaffection and unrest that had been beginning to exhibit itself in formidable shape in the Dominion after the anti-conscription triumph in Australia', but the steady use of regulations 'had enabled New Zealand, during months of grave difficulty, to present a well-ordered and respectable front to the rest of the world and had prevented ill-advised and ill-intentioned members of the community dragging the fair name of New Zealand in the mud'.[65]

The relatively limited extent of the industrial action against conscription, in an economy that gifted workers enhanced bargaining power, spoke of considerable ambivalence. The most militant part of the labour force now appeared to accede to conscription and to working within the arbitration system. As one study notes, 'By late July the coalfields were quiet. Miner militancy had been bought off.'[66] Although negotiations had stressed the economy and public patience, the government's combination of concession and coercion had successfully contained unrest and avoided serious disruptions.

Pacifists, too, had felt the bite of suppressive regulations. In April 1917, for example, Auckland Freedom League member Harry Urquhart was summoned to court for a pamphlet entitled *Men and Marbles*, which reproduced a speech he had given months earlier in Auckland's Globe Theatre, condemning conscription and calling for a negotiated peace.[67] The magistrate judged the pamphlet seditious and said that Urquhart possessed a 'good character' but an 'unbalanced mind'. Sentenced to 11 months, the habitually amicable Urquhart thanked the magistrate for a 'very kind, courteous and patient hearing'; the two men would later form a lifelong friendship.[68]

A more concealed power was flexed as police and the censorship system worked to quietly neutralise anti-conscription and pacifist material.[69] In what censor Walter Tanner described as a particularly successful operation, an entire mailing campaign, believed to have been undertaken by a group affiliated with the Women's International League for Peace and Freedom, appealing to Christian ministers to support a peace without annexations, had been intercepted and suppressed. As a result, 'the appeal never gained any publicity whatever'.[70]

While an organised opposition to conscription stalled, more individual efforts to evade or resist the system were taken up. The question of what to do with men who might refuse to comply had been considered when the Military Service Act was designed, with conventional responses arguing that 'shirkers' would fall into line under sufficient moral and physical pressure. This was optimistic, given the pre-war problems with deserters and objectors to compulsory military training, but some were perhaps convinced that the state of war would bring a higher level of compliance.

Those intending to refuse or avoid military service were motivated by a variety of philosophies, values and dispositions. High-minded theological and political objections to war, or this particular war, stood beside less principled desires to avoid military life and the risks of combat. Holland would later conclude that objectors could be divided into four major categories: religious, socialist, Irish and Māori.[71] However, many of these categories overlapped and one study notes just how eclectic some pacifists' reading and influences could be: in one case, Edward Bellamy, Jonathan Swift and Leo Tolstoy; in another, Tolstoy, George Bernard Shaw and Sidney and Beatrice Webb; and a third, Mohandas 'Mahatma' Gandhi and Bertrand Russell.[72] In his refusal to serve, John Rogers claimed to be a citizen of heaven, not earth. Tim Brosnan 'would not shame my good parents [sic] name or become a traitor to my country, by donning a uniform and taking an oath of allegiance to fight and die for my greatest enemy the oppressor & tyrant of my native land'. Another man said simply that he would not under any circumstances leave New Zealand and that he preferred to be shot.[73]

There was variety, too, in the way the non-compliant responded when they were called up.

The Free Man (to the Man behind the Bars): Take this Key and let yourself out. There's no sense in remaining caged up like that.

IN THE SHIRKERS' CAMP.

Deserter from Conscription: Yer know, Tom, the public "hooray" for the soldiers in the trenches, but they chase and howl at us and don't know the horrible sufferings we go through for our conscience sake—eh?

above The *Maoriland Worker* presents Australia's rejection of conscription in an October 1916 referendum as exemplary. MAORILAND WORKER, 15 NOVEMBER 1916, P. 1

left The *Observer* offers a sardonic depiction of military defaulters. NEW ZEALAND OBSERVER, 20 APRIL 1918, P. 17

When a balloted man failed to report, an investigation was carried out to determine whether his call-up notice had been correctly delivered and that there were no extenuating circumstances preventing his appearance. If this investigation did not rectify the situation, he would be gazetted as a defaulter and the police informed. Some non-compliance was well-impressed. Palmerston North flax worker Mark Briggs, drawn in the third ballot, was proudly defiant before he was arrested on 23 March 1917. After he ignored his call-up notice, an army major appeared at his workplace with an order to parade in Duke Street at 9.30 the following morning.

> I replied: 'I will not'. The Major then said: 'Will later in the day suit you?' I said: 'No,' He then asked: 'You are the Mark Briggs who was drawn in the ballot, are you not?' I replied: 'I have had sufficient notifications from the military authorities to lead me to believe I am.' The Major then wanted to know when it would suit me to appear for examination. I told him that it would never suit me. He then said: 'All right; I'll send you a registered notice in the morning.'

Briggs ignored this when it arrived, as well as a further card summoning him to parade in town before proceeding to camp. 'Then, after all these interviews and notices, I found my name gazetted as "Missing and cannot be found." When this Gazette notice appeared in the Palmerston North papers it was the source of much amusement.'[74]

Others used their right of appeal and argued their objections before Military Service Boards. While many based their appeals on conscience, the legislation only recognised appeals from a member of a religious body whose tenets declared 'the bearing of arms and the performance of combatant service to be contrary to divine revelation'. Only Quakers or Christadelphians were deemed eligible under this provision, though Seventh-day Adventists were later recognised in July 1917.[75] The recognition of conscientious objection was also conditional on the appellant being willing to serve in a non-combatant role, which soon became a point of contention, since such roles remained under military authority and some objected to taking oaths or to assisting the army to kill. By the end of 1917 some 28 men had accepted offers of non-combatant work and by the end of the war this had grown to 60.[76]

Other balloted objectors forwent their right to appeal. As Archibald Baxter, a Christian pacifist farmer, later stated, 'Even if it had been possible to obtain exemption I would never have gone before an Appeal Board to plead my case, for I did not consider that any Board had the right to be judge of a man's sincerity.' Proceeding through this induction, a balloted man was deemed as subject to military law and a refusal of orders resulted in a month's jail time followed by a full court martial. If he still refused, he faced a prison sentence of between 11 months and two years.[77]

Some balloted men took active, even exceptional, measures to avoid authorities. Some tried to lay low with relatives, one lived in a boat in the Waitematā Harbour, another joined a circus, some signed on as seamen before disappearing when they reached foreign ports. Rumours, then and since, suggest some organised measures, including an illicit 'underground railway' network that smuggled men out of the country.[78] Others headed for remote locations and sought work on the backblocks, in mines, in mills, on road or railway gangs, often under assumed identities. Some men eked out an existence in the bush, with intermittent runs for supplies, news and company.[79] Despite a penalty of £50–100 for knowingly employing defaulters, some were evidently willing to turn a blind eye to mysterious employees, either to exploit desperate men or to help out of sympathy. Reports came in of farmers supposedly hiring defaulters as cheap labour for scrub-cutting, and sympathetic West Coasters were said to have devised a system of signals to warn local fugitives when police searches were imminent. Some defaulters living in the bush had, said one newspaper, clearly 'been assisted by civilians in their food supplies'.[80]

Given the amount of bureaucracy involved, it was some time before the government and the public could get any sense of the extent of resistance. In late February 1917 only four men had been listed as defaulters and though Allen could 'scarcely believe this to be true', he hoped that defaulting might prove minimal: 'If it is true, it is a most remarkable performance.'[81] By September 1917, however, official figures revealed that, to 31 August, 5505 had defaulted: of these, 2705 remained under investigation and 349 warrants remained outstanding. This was approaching 10 per cent of the 49,588 men balloted thus far.[82] But these numbers were not reliable, thanks to significant administrative errors. Some men had already been gazetted or were found to be already serving; some had left the country; some were hospitalised, imprisoned or dead. Hundreds of men were located without the need for a warrant, suggesting their 'default' status was in error. The most reliable estimate is that, by the end of the war, between 3900 and 8500 men deliberately tried to evade conscription — around 2.8 to 6.2 per cent of all balloted men.[83] By November 1917, 103 balloted men had been incarcerated for refusing to serve under the Military Service Act; by the end of the war this number has been calculated as 286.[84] This meant imprisoned objectors represented a sizeable proportion of a prison population gauged at a daily average of 981.95 in 1918.[85]

Managing this issue became one more task for the authorities. There was an attempt to deter potential deserters, and a widely circulated Defence Department advertisement warned of long-term repercussions: 'The future life of a deserter in New Zealand, accordingly, does not promise to be a happy one.' In October 1917 Parliament discussed initial ideas for a scheme of stripping defaulters of civil rights for 10 years, under a philosophy that civil liberties and civil duties were reciprocal.[86]

The arduous task of searching for missing men became an ongoing duty. Police occasionally searched such venues including racecourses, cinemas and workplaces for defaulters. One such check in Christchurch turned up a deserter from Trentham Camp, seeking to avoid suspicion by wearing an Australian uniform. After trying to shield him from the police, his female companion 'used physical violence' in an attempt to free him. After a 'strenuous fight', the man, who had been under observation for several days, was arrested. In other cases, targeted raids were facilitated by information supplied by locals, who almost invariably said that they had a loved one in uniform.[87]

Searching for men hiding in the wilderness was more difficult still. For one pursuit in remote Fiordland, a police expedition ended up tramping over 250 miles in challenging conditions over three weeks to hunt down a group of deserters who had been securing supplies by impersonating surveyors. Confrontations could carry the threat of violence. One cornered man threatened the police with an axe and another, discovered largely by accident in a lonely bush clearing in Te Awamutu, brandished a rifle before being arrested.[88] Searches eventually located hundreds of men, and by November 1918 the number missing had fallen to 2047.[89]

Deciding what to do with men who refused orders proved more contentious. Seeking to classify these men, an official memorandum advised that the law 'recognises only one class of objector for any measure of exceptional treatment, and this person may be classed as the "religious objector"'. Besides this legally recognised class, the memorandum noted two further categories. The first was the 'conscientious objector', namely those 'whose objections are founded on religious grounds but who do not come within the statute' and those who objected to service on 'conscientious grounds apart from religion'. The second was the 'defiant objectors', understood as those who based their opposition 'on a defiance of the law or a disinclination to serve in the Forces'.[90]

However, the Defence Department became uneasy about its task of sorting and processing 'defiant' and 'conscientious' objectors. An official report claimed that various imprisoned 'conscientious objectors' deserved 'consideration just as much as the religious objectors who have passed the test of the statute'. Conversely, it was reckoned that 'defiant objectors', 'whose case merits no consideration', were being given gratuitously lenient treatment: 'the rebel and the coward are removed from any danger to their persons and remain in security, while the sons of loyal people go abroad to risk wounds and death'.[91] Allen made comparable distinctions and stated a support to accommodate the 'real conscientious objector' while punishing 'shirkers'. For example, when Henry Such, the secretary of the Auckland Fraternity of the Christadelphians, assured Allen that the sect's members were not shirkers and that they would gladly do non-military duties, the minister replied that he would be pleased to do what he could to help.[92] He proved less sympathetic to those refusing any role: 'Can it be assumed for a moment that any man's conscience should excuse him from the saving of life, and is it fair to suggest that a man who develops such a conscience is to enjoy all the privileges which belong to the State without undertaking the duties that pertain to the citizens of the State in its defence?'[93]

Moreover, training camp authorities had no wish to be saddled with objectors who might challenge the discipline they were trying to instil.[94] Writer and future publisher A. H. Reed remembered one such clash of protocols in Featherston Camp:

> Private B., a sincere and determined pacifist, was under open arrest. He was strolling about the camp in a grotesque attitude, with bent shoulders and hands clashed behind his back. The Provost-Marshal happened to approach, but Private B. let him pass without notice. An order had been issued to the camp police to be more strict in enforcing the rules about saluting, and the Provost-Marshal turned back, touched B. on the shoulder and asked 'Don't you –'

> but before he could finish his question, B. anticipating him, cut him short, and straightening himself, said rapidly and decisively, 'No! I never salute anyone; it is not my custom,' and strolled dreamily away, with bent shoulders as before. The Provost very sensibly saw the humour of the situation and took no further notice.[95]

The commandant at Trentham had a different attitude to 15 objectors stationed under his jurisdiction, who had to be guarded to protect them against the soldiers 'amongst whom feeling runs very high'. In his view, 'the example of these fat loafers, and rabid anti-militarists living in the lines, doing nothing, and priding themselves on their conduct is having a bad effect on the discipline of some men in Camp, especially on raw recruits'.[96] He asked for some way to dispose of these men.

For the rest of the war there were various answers to the question of what to do with these objectors, as officials understood and judged them. In March 1917 a plan was drafted in which the National Efficiency Board would assign successful appellants to report for 'employment which should be of a purely non-military character to avoid the resistance which any employment with a military connection invites'.[97] While noting there was no legal provision for industrial conscription, Solicitor-General Salmond observed that the Defence Department might assign men to another government department.[98] Tree planting for the Lands Department emerged as a favoured scheme and new regulations were gazetted on 24 April 1917. The men would not be compelled to wear uniforms and were entitled to the rate of pay and allowances of a private soldier.[99] This would effectively allow the Defence Department to quietly rid itself of 'conscientious objectors' and 'religious objectors' who would not accept non-combat roles within the military.

Not long into its introduction, conscription became embroiled in sectarian politics, which were developing an increasingly bitter and volatile fringe. The trigger was the question of whether Catholic clergy should be exempt from conscription. Catholics urged that their priests, religious teachers and theological students should not be conscripted; the more vocal among them promised repercussions if this were to happen. Priests, it was declared, were essential to the community's welfare and its institutions; certainly the 47 Marist Brothers who staffed Catholic schools could not readily be replaced. Advocates warned of a future Catholic community dispossessed of its religious customs, where members would be 'left to live and die without sacraments, and be buried like cattle'.[100] Those raising this warning pointed out that their priests' celibacy, and therefore their first division status, meant those of military age would be selected before the clergy of the other denominations. Further sensitivities revolved around the fact that priests who had taken their vows were forbidden by ecclesiastical law to fight and, as the *Tablet* put it, dragooning the clergy 'into abandoning their ministry of peace and reconciliation' and coercing them into 'imbruing their hands in human blood' would be regarded as a very serious matter.[101]

For many non-Catholics, however, such an automatic exemption would represent an unacceptable breach of equality of sacrifice. Some considered it a hypocritical expectation that other men should make the sacrifice Catholic clergymen would not. One correspondent thought it 'astounding' and 'monstrous' that a physically fit and military eligible clergyman should seek to claim exemption:

> Can a clergyman, under any conceivable circumstance, ask or expect a layman to do what he is not prepared to do himself? If it is wrong for a clergyman to shed blood or take life in a just cause, it cannot be right for a layman to do so . . . A truly conscientious follower of Jesus (one cannot help suggesting) would be among the very first to offer his services voluntarily in a truly just and righteous cause — such as is the present war.[102]

Truth took aim at the 'jingoistic curate' who had supported the war from the pulpit but wished for others to fight in his stead:

> He'll address empty benches,
> But bars digging trenches,
> He'll preach while the other blokes bleed.
> The spirit is willing,
> Till it comes to killing.
> The poor flesh is then weak indeed.[103]

Some Protestants added that Catholics were asking for a privilege that no other denomination was granted. This especially rankled given that Protestant theological students had volunteered to an extent that teaching institutes had been closed. These frustrations would only be sharpened when prospects of balloting second division men were raised: men with wives and families, it was argued, should not have to 'take the places which the single men of the Marist and Christian Brothers ought to fill'.[104]

For its part, the government was caught between respecting the principle of equality of sacrifice and a desire to preserve social unity in an increasingly toxic sectarian environment. When the question of conscripting Catholic clergy had arisen earlier, with National Registration, Massey and Allen had made a carefully worded promise to favourably consider the exemption of Catholic clergymen, while Ward had made a more unconditional pledge, noting that he had already sought to exclude them from registration.[105] The issue had resurfaced when the Military Service Act was being drafted and Archbishop Thomas O'Shea led a delegation seeking a provision for the exemption of Catholic clergy. The government had urged the delegation not to endanger the passage of the legislation by pushing for a specific exemption and O'Shea subsequently claimed that the government had assured him that 'means would be provided by the Government to have clergy of all denominations exempted'.[106]

Catholics therefore had what the *Tablet* called a 'decidedly unpleasant shock' when a number of Catholic priests appeared in the first ballot. At a meeting with a delegation from the Catholic hierarchy a few days later, Allen confirmed that Catholic clergy would be balloted but

THE REASON WHY.

Judge (to Conscientious Objector): Objection granted. Here is your certificate.

The *Observer* dismisses conscientious objection with an unsympathetic citation from *Hamlet*.
NEW ZEALAND OBSERVER, 15 JULY 1916, P. 16

noted that the authorities of every church would have the right of appeal on behalf of a priest or minister whose name was drawn. The government could also supply recommendations for exemptions in such cases. Although the *Tablet* was satisfied that the matter had been 'definitely straightened out', it seems both the editor and the bishops were unaware that Military Service Boards were not obliged to act on government recommendations.[107]

This was driven home in February 1917, when the third Wellington Military Service Board chafed over government recommendations to exempt clergymen. It agreed, under Allen's persuasion, to exempt them, on the condition that those cases be reviewed when the first division was exhausted, but it refused to cooperate regarding theological students. On 11 February it rejected the appeals of two theological students, made by the church and supported by government recommendations. The result was a surge of Catholic outrage and threats of civil disobedience. O'Shea told Allen that the situation was 'nothing less than religious persecution' when 'all should be working in harmony for Victory', and threatened that New Zealand's Catholics would 'fight it by every means at their disposal'.[108] He privately issued instructions that students should ignore call-up notices and publicly warned of 'the organised attempt by sectarian bigots to injure the Church'.[109] O'Shea was not alone in his bellicose stance. 'The priests will not go; and our people have a habit of defending their priests', said one letter to the *Tablet*, and a correspondent to the *Evening Post* wrote, 'when you are challenging the religious convictions of a determined body of men you are opening a road that leads to infinite trouble'.[110] On 15 March two more students' appeals were turned down, this time by the Otago Military Service Board, and the *Tablet* claimed that 'it is well known that the Minister of Defence would enforce conscription of priests if he could do so safely . . . It is our duty as Catholics, and also as patriots to see that he does not do so.'[111]

The episode exacerbated the ugly posturing of the previous year, now maturing into a new militancy on both the Catholic and Protestant extremes. In late 1916 a number of Irish clubs had federated as the Maoriland Irish Society and launched a newspaper, the *Green Ray*, on 1 December.[112] The paper took a pugilistic stance in denouncing the perceived enemies of the church and Ireland and, in vivid contrast to earlier denouncements of the actions and leadership of the Easter Rising, voiced praise for republicanism and its political party, Sinn Féin. On the second anniversary of the Easter Rising, the *Green Ray*'s editorial read: 'Once again it is our privilege to commemorate the men and deeds that made Easter week 1916 the most glorious pages in the annals of our race . . . Precious to us should be the memories of the brave who gave up everything that the soul of Erin might be saved.'[113]

Another voice of Catholic militancy emerged from February 1917 when James Kelly was officially made editor of the *Tablet*. He shifted the paper's editorial line from the earlier focus on the Catholic contribution to the country's war effort, to fiery assertions of Irish grievances.[114] Kelly also specialised in rancorous jabs intended to antagonise patriotic Anglo-Protestant sensibilities. These included gibes that 'for possession of German blood our Sovereign beats the Kaiser by a short head'; that Protestantism was 'a made-in-Germany religion'; and that Queen Victoria was 'a fat old German woman'.[115] In seeking to delegitimise the Allies, he gave succour to Germany: 'there may be some truth in their claim that they are fighting a war of self-defence; that for 44 years, from 1870 to 1914, they had never done any act of aggression against any country, a claim which neither England, nor France, nor Russia can claim for itself'. He protested that New Zealanders were expected to surrender themselves to a bureaucracy which 'bids fair to rival Prussian despotism without the saving grace of Prussian efficiency'.[116]

Protestant sectarianism was similarly on the rise, a reaction to the sense that the government and Catholics were conspiring to arrange undue exemptions. This appeared to be precisely the kind of special privilege and hidden influence some Protestants had warned of. The Christchurch Ministers' Association, for example, declared, 'It had fallen as a bombshell amongst us that there was a secret understanding between the Government and the Roman Catholic Church.'[117] Moreover, Howard Elliott had continued to tour the country, spreading a message of Vatican duplicity and warning that Protestants must waken to the need to guard their liberties.

A dramatic indication of how explosive this campaigning was becoming came on 28 February 1917 in a meeting in Hamilton, where around 900 people crowded into the hall and Elliott denounced an alleged 'secret deal' over clergy conscription. The meeting soon descended into 'fierce' heckling, with audience members 'standing, shouting and arguing violently'. The argument spilled out on to the streets, and only firm police intervention and arrests prevented physical violence.[118] Some Protestants perhaps saw the disruption as confirming rumours that Catholics would attempt to break up the meeting. Conversely, the government's inaction in a volatile situation — it did nothing beyond requesting that Elliott be cautioned by the police — likely encouraged some Catholics to see an official sympathy with Elliott's campaigning.[119]

Allen was now in an unenviable position. Uncertain of the consequences of a show of force, he attempted to offer concessions to the Catholic hierarchy without stirring Protestant outrage. On 27 April 1917, Cabinet tried to persuaded the Military Service Boards to accept a ministerial certificate for priests or theological students in the last four years of their training who had taken their vows, and to exempt religious teachers who could not be replaced.[120] With an agreement reached, a hopeful Allen wrote to Massey, 'I think we have straightened this thing up now.'[121] The arrangement, however, provided ammunition for Protestant ire.

On 11 July, coinciding with Protestant recognition of the anniversary of the Battle of the Boyne (1690), Howard Elliott presided over the formal launch of the long-planned Protestant Political Association (PPA) at the Auckland Town Hall. Over 3500 packed the hall and large crowds gathered outside.[122] Elliott declared that the Catholic Federation was 'a challenge to every Protestant man and woman to defend their rights' and warned that it aimed 'to control national and civic life in this Dominion'. Implying that Catholics were avoiding enlistment in the hope of swaying an election that would be bereft of patriotic Protestants, he declared that Catholic power was on the march. In fact, at the end of July 1917, Catholics made up 12.6 per cent of enlisted men, only marginally under the Catholic proportion of the New Zealand population (almost 13 per cent).[123]

Referring to the compromises made over the conscription of clergy, he declared that Catholics had been able to 'bring the New Zealand Government to its knees, and to obtain concessions no Protestant could get'. At the height of the address he introduced a new charge, asserting that mail intended for the Orange Order had been suppressed by politically motivated surveillance brought about by Catholic 'corruption in the Postal Service'. He claimed that, to test the scope of the censorship, various test letters, with no war-related content, had been mailed to the order's postal box and several had not been delivered.[124] Elliott also read accounts, purportedly from anxious Protestants, of Catholic machinations around the country. One example, which would have later repercussions, implied that a nun who had drowned at Taumarunui the previous year may have been pregnant. Although these allegations were soon proved to be fabrications, they guaranteed the PPA a windfall of publicity.[125]

Clearly, conscription, with its promise of equal sacrifice, had not ended sectarianism. Indeed the government now faced a delicate task in assessing exactly what 'equality' entailed and to convince increasingly divided and militant elements to abide by its assessment. Pondering the divisive nature of sectarian material in print, Salmond urged the introduction of prior restraint censorship, in which listed publications would have to submit proofs to a censor before they could go to print.[126] The government, uncertain of what antagonisms this might aggravate, was reluctant to enact such a system and the measure was shelved. This hesitancy 'effectively handed over the initiative to the sectarians', and by mid-1917 prospects for the future on this front looked bleak.[127]

Alongside managing the issues arising from the implementation of conscription, potential controversy also loomed around those the Military Service Act had defined as potential conscripts. The first of these groups were the country's husbands and fathers. In January 1917, Allen announced that the first balloting of second division men would possibly occur in July, though the date was later pushed back to November or December.[128] This was a scenario many had hoped to avoid. Calling up husbands and fathers assured increased disruption to families and communities. The threat to household economies alone was dire. Although half of a private soldier's weekly pay of 42s could be deducted to support his family, this represented a significant decline for the wife of a skilled worker or businessman turned conscript, especially given the inflated costs of 1917. Neither was she likely to be impressed by the prospect of a weekly pension of 20s if her husband were to be killed.

There would also be a wider economic upheaval. In a February letter to the Defence Department, the Wellington Chamber of Commerce warned that 'the business of the Dominion (both farming and commercial) is largely in the hands of men eligible for service under the second division classification'.[129] Breaking up families also promised to raise the temperature around the politics of sacrifice on issues like exemptions for the Catholic clergy, the existence of defaulters and objectors, and the extent of New Zealand's military commitment. Lastly, angst over how the welfare of second division dependants would be secured risked damaging an underlying philosophical tenet within the war effort, namely that enlistment represented the protection of both a man's loved ones and his country.

Public reaction varied. There was some more light-hearted and recurrent comment about family men staring down the coming trials of military life, and commercial interests saw business opportunities as a new group of men faced enlistment. The Guardian Trust and Executors Company of New Zealand, for example, was ready to help the 'many business men and responsible heads of families' who were 'concerned for the safe administration of their affairs while away on service'.[130]

More serious, and worrying to the government, were protests coming from those who were unimpeachably loyal and supporters of conscription. Agitation over second division interests began in Dunedin, far from a hotbed of radicalism, and the initiative appears to have come from the *Otago Daily Times*, generally known for its conservatism.[131] The Second Division League was launched there in February 1917 and its inaugural public meeting attracted an audience able 'to fill the larger part' of the Early Settlers' Hall.[132] The league quickly developed a nationwide mass membership, becoming 'by far the most extensive of any patriotic organisation' beyond war relief associations. Although detailed figures for the league's membership remain unknown, Auckland initially had 400 members and there were over 6500 in the Otago region. Some 91 branch delegates, said to represent every town and city in the country, were present at the first national conference in July 1917.[133]

Thankfully, from the government's perspective, the Second Division League committed itself to cooperative lobbying rather than militant dissent and Allen privately noted, 'I have no doubt about their loyalty and about their willingness in general to serve.'[134] The league presented itself as a model of respectable civic engagement, its goal of representing second division interests conspicuously shown to be wholly compatible with loyalty to the war effort. The initial Dunedin meeting was chaired and endorsed by Mayor J. J. Clark, who, after the singing of the National Anthem, was cheered for his statement that 'the great Imperial British Empire . . . was saving the world today, and without the hearty cooperation of every single unit in the Empire it would be impossible for us to contend against the savage and brutal hordes arrayed in battle against us'. The gathering's purpose was, Clark declared, not for 'harassing the Government, the military authorities, or anyone else, but to assist in organising the man-power of New Zealand, to try to arrange matters so that a man could go with an easy conscience knowing that his loved ones would be cared for if anything should happen to him'.[135]

The league hinted, however, at potential discord if their interests were not respected. For example, the first resolution at the July conference, 'carried unanimously with acclaim', affirmed 'the principle of carrying on New Zealand's part in the war to the end, provided the principle of equality of sacrifice be applied by legislation to the whole community'. Likewise, President Rupert Ashley Armstrong signalled the conditional nature of the league's compliance in the published proceedings of the conference:

> The first clause of our constitution is to the effect that we are organised to demonstrate our loyalty to His Majesty the King, and his government in New Zealand, by assisting in every way possible to carry this war to a victorious conclusion. I may say that in a few words addressed to the Minister of Defence at our conference the other day, I added 'consistent to the duty to our dependants'; for the first law of nature is the protection a father gives to his children, and to the woman he married.[136]

The league's support of the war was also threatened by anti-war elements who joined the organisation. For example, discussing the importance of 'taking up active work in other organisations', the Southland District Labor Council specifically mentioned the Second Division League as 'an opportune body to attempt capturing'.[137] Such infiltration was also at work in Christchurch, during the preliminary meeting of the league there. A motion that the league should endeavour to carry out the provisions of the Defence Act and the Military Service Act led to objections and an eventual rejection by 16 votes to 13. Other motions affirming loyalty led to similar 'wrangling' and an eventual recess.[138] The *Evening Star* considered, however, that this result represented, not a failure of the league's purpose, but rather the presence, among the 35 attendees, of 'a sort peculiar to Christchurch — anti-militarists, peace-at-any-price fools, conscientious objectors, soap-box Socialists, and heaven only knows what else'.[139]

While such scenes hinted at potential dissent, the league's foundation generally tapped a broad reserve of goodwill. Its sheer numerical strength gave it a sense of legitimacy, and media coverage characterised league representatives as respectable family men compared to unmarried 'shirkers' thumbing their noses while families were broken up.[140] Even the *Evening Star*'s denouncement of Christchurch 'cranks' urged a sympathetic hearing for the organisation: 'There is a wide gulf between sense and sedition, and only fools may fall into it.'[141] In Parliament, too, many praised the league as representing right-minded citizens. In the view of Liberal MP Charles Talbot, for example, 'the Second Division League is thoroughly loyal, and . . . all its members are willing to go to the front if need be. They have assured us that such is the case. They have not formed their league in order to shirk their duty.'[142]

The league's priorities also suggested grounds for fruitful negotiation. The diverse issues raised at the first conference included various minute and practical considerations relating to departures from family and business life, such as provisions for overseas voting and the supply of official signs to signal that business owners had been called up. Three broad areas, however, emerged as central concerns. First, the league wanted all second division men to be medically examined as soon as possible to give them, on account of their greater business and social obligations, more certainty about whether they were eligible for service. Second, they wanted efforts to ensure that first division men were not unduly exempted before married men were balloted. Third, they called for state financial support for married conscripts to be increased.[143]

These areas formed fertile grounds for concessions. The business community welcomed measures to provide increased certainty over the impact on the workforce of second division conscription.[144] Authorities were content to continue the general principle of delaying any balloting of second division men for as long as possible. This was certainly Allen's position and in private correspondence, dated 7 May 1917, he noted that 'it will be a great blessing if we can get the war over without calling on Second Division at all'. Publicly he told the league that 'the Department would use its best efforts to secure all of them [first division men] before the Second Division was called on'.[145] There was general acceptance, too, of the league's call for increased financial support, and the government promised to review state support for soldiers' dependants, which had been kept low to discourage family men from enlisting.

The result was a series of concessions and initiatives. Although a shortage of doctors, and a wish to avoid possibly inaccurate outdated medical diagnoses, derailed calls to examine all second division reservists before balloting began, the Defence Department calculated that it could give balloted men a three-month window between their medical examination and entering camp.[146] Furthermore, several initiatives to scrape the bottom of the first division barrel and delay a balloting of second division men were enacted up to September 1917. In August the Military Service Boards agreed to begin reviews of the then 2300 adjourned cases; by May 1918, 5771 cases had been reassessed and 900 formerly exempted men sent to camp.[147]

Marginally unfit men were re-examined, and a C1 camp that opened at Tauherenīkau in September 1917 claimed a 49.1 per cent success rate in raising fitness through exercise, fresh air and clean thinking.[148] The Defence Department also adjusted the reinforcement system to prioritise first division men, with any shortfall in a district's volunteering filled by balloting first division men from across the country.[149] The government also committed itself to re-evaluated rates for soldiers' dependants, with results to be announced later in the year.

Proposals raised during these negotiations did reveal, though, that official and public goodwill towards the league was not limitless and that second division men were not inevitably on the right side of the politics of sacrifice. A late July 1917 proposition to inflate the first division by lowering the enlistment age to 19 split the military authorities and was poorly received.[150] 'A Soldier's Mother' wrote to the *Evening Post* in August 1917:

> We parents with our unmarried sons have kept this terrible war going nobly and uncomplainingly: we have done what we considered our duty, and now the Government proposes lowering the age limit. Is this fair? Will the married men sit quietly down and allow this? . . . Now, as a wife and mother of fighting sons, I contend that every man who has a wife has a greater right to go to the front than any lad of nineteen. This is the feeling of most of the mothers.[151]

Many Second Division League members rejected the idea that they were, as the *Maoriland Worker* put it, 'Abraham clamouring to be allowed to offer up Isaac'.[152] Although the proposal was dropped, it was partially resurrected in the decision, made months later, to allow 19-year-olds to volunteer with parental consent.[153]

In a signal that second division conscription was coming, and as a strategy to limit disruption, regulations were gazetted in July 1917 to subdivide the second division into classes to be balloted in sequence: A (married men without children), B (married men with one child), C (married men with two children), D (married men with three children), E (married men with four children) and F (married men with more than four children).[154]

Māori, too, faced an extension of conscription. Following Gallipoli, the reformed Pioneer Battalion had faced its first major action as part of the Somme offensive, suffering a casualty rate of 20 per cent.[155] This caused increasing disquiet at home and Māori MPs noted that some parents were dissuading their sons from enlisting.[156] Māori leaders urged renewed commitment to the war effort. At a hui held at Waiōmatatini, north of Gisborne, over 17–19 February 1917, Ngāti Porou, which had already sent twice as many men on active service as any other iwi, called for a special recruiting drive.

Āpirana Ngata called for fundraising to help returned Māori soldiers, and by the end of 1917 this Maori Soldiers' Fund had raised nearly £20,000, almost all on the East Coast of the North Island. Māori landowners also gifted tens of thousands of acres to be set aside for veterans.[157] However, Māori enlistment rates remained somewhat anaemic; the 2227 Māori soldiers deployed at the end of the war constituted close to 4.33 per cent of the Māori population, proportionally about half the effort of the Pākehā population.[158]

Many contrasted the high rates of volunteering from Ngāpuhi, Ngāti Porou and Arawa, and the significant numbers from Ngāti Kahungunu and South Island iwi, to the negligible recruitment from others, particularly in Waikato. As with Pākehā, conscription was upheld as a means of ensuring efficient and equitable enlistments. At the end of October 1916, nearly three months after the passage of the Military Service Act, Pōmare and Allen met to discuss a mission to the Waikato to boost recruiting and the defence minister called for proposals to be drafted to extend conscription to Māori, as envisioned under section 50 of the Military Service Act.[159]

On 24 November Allen travelled to Waikato, accompanied by a number of politicians, including Ngata, and 75 recruits from the Māori training camp. Speaking at Te Rata's annual coronation hui, Allen appealed to tribal pride: 'the Maoris of old . . . were noted for their chivalry and their devotion to duty and he believed the same spirit remained in their descendants. Indeed, had it not already been well proven by all the tribes except the Waikatos?' He also urged his audience to resist German militarism, lest New Zealand suffer the 'cruel fate of Belgium': 'Your women and children and babies might become the sport for German bayonets, your country ravaged by enemies who know not the meaning of mercy, and your strong men compelled at the point of the bayonet to work in the factories and mines of cruel foes . . . If you fail now you and your tribes can never rest in honour in the days that are coming.'[160]

This speech, which King Te Rata and most men eligible for conscription had not attended, was reportedly met with a 'murmur of applause' and Allen was informed that no one was stopping men from enlisting. In a later meeting with Tupu Taingākawa, the uncle and tumuaki (a position comparable to a prime minister) of the king, Allen's call for unity was met with the response: 'Who will suffer? My people cannot suffer more than they have done in the loss of their lands and of their mana.'[161]

'I am afraid,' Allen wrote to Godley after the mission, 'it will take pressure, not talk, to bring them in.' However, he also noted, 'We do not want to apply conscription to the Natives until we have the pakehas into working order'; a prescient comment given that he would, over the following months, be faced with the anti-conscription protest, industrial unrest and sectarian outrage.[162] By the following March, the government was prepared to begin planning an extension of the Military Service Act to Māori. Although all males of military age were potentially eligible to be balloted, conscription would, initially at least, be applied only to 'the Waikato tribe who had not answered the call to enlist voluntarily'.[163]

above In late 1916 James Allen travelled to the Waikato to urge local Māori to enlist. To Allen's left are Āpirana Ngata and Māui Pōmare. To his right are Colonel Patterson and Richard Bollard, MP for Raglan. AUCKLAND WEEKLY NEWS, 30 NOVEMBER 1916, P. 38

left A staged photograph of a man representing the unflattering stereotype of a C1 recruit. C1 was the designation given to those deemed unfit for service but likely to be made fit with special training. MATT POMEROY COLLECTION

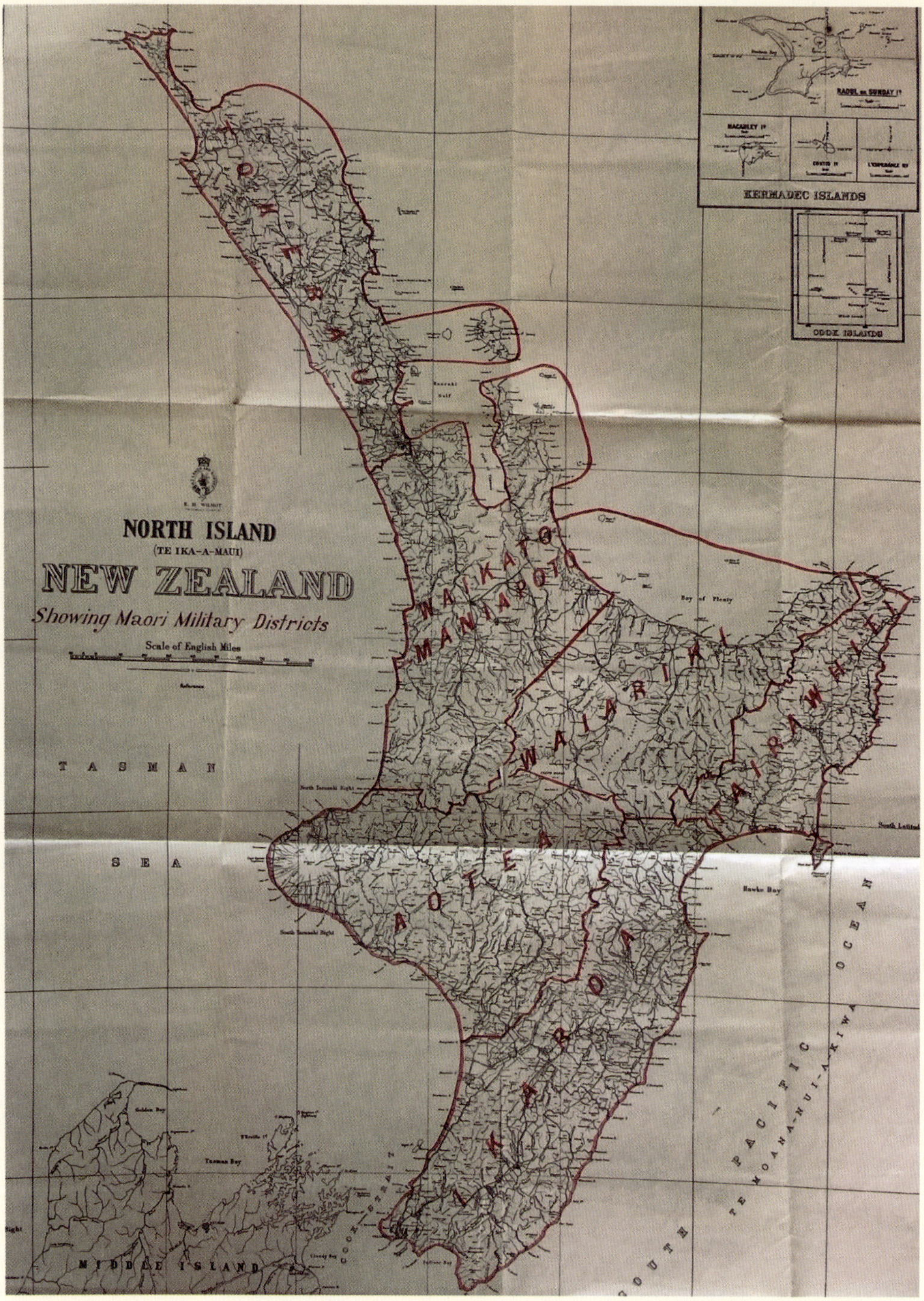

A mark-up of the established boundaries for Māori military districts. Determining these was a key step in plans to extend conscription to Māori. ARCHIVES NEW ZEALAND, R18874766

Māori military districts were established for the North Island; South Island Maori were considered more integrated and able to enrol on European lines. The six districts followed Māori land district, rather than county, boundaries. This was done presumably because the Waikato–Maniapoto Maori Land District captured the recalcitrant tribes of that area and excluded the willing more neatly than county boundaries would have. The solution was less than perfect, however. Hauraki, noting the proportion of their men who had enlisted, forwarded a petition calling for their exemption from the Waikato–Maniapoto military district.[164]

Compiling a roll for balloting was a more trying task. Before 1913 Māori were not required to register births and official records were fragmented. Because a survey would certainly encounter significant non-compliance, the initial solution was to use confidential information collected in the 1916 Māori census to create a ballot register.[165] This information, however, was supposed to be exclusively used for census purposes, and the government was aware that it was breaching the law; as the Secretary of the Recruiting Board, James Gray, wrote to Allen, 'the information in the census is confidential and it is very undesirable that any indication should be given that the census is being used for this purpose'.[166]

As with the rest of the eligible population, Māori ballots were initially to be drawn from the first division. However, the Māori census had not dealt with individuals' marital status and clarifying who was actually in the first division would require further information. This was to be gathered by calling for all eligible men to register with the local policeman who, it was hoped, could then note the marital status of those registering on a printed roll compiled from the census. Names not appearing on the roll would be added from the personal knowledge of the policeman or from other informants when men registered. The same approach could be used to note any eligible, unmarried men who were neither on the printed roll nor registering.

A new recruiting campaign was also launched, spearheaded by the elderly Colonel Thomas Porter, a famous Māori-speaking veteran of the New Zealand Wars, and Captain Cossgrove, director of recruiting. Posters outlining the provisions of the Military Service Act were printed in Māori, registration cards distributed and local police briefed.[167] On 26 June, the Military Service Act was extended by gazette to include Māori.[168] Over the first six months of 1917 conscription had survived a succession of logistical, political, social, industrial and electoral challenges. Its application to Waikato Māori promised to produce the most obstinate resistance yet.

TOILET ROOMS
HOWEY WALKER
HOWEY WALKER
DENTIST
RS, ALL TRAVELLING REQUISITES
CITY CHAMBERS
CITY
RECRUIT
STAT
ENLIST N
It's Our Flag
Fight for it
Work for it
Come
Lads
Give us a spel
CITY RECRUITING OFFICE
YMCA

CHAPTER ELEVEN

NADIR

previous pages
A recruiting station in the centre of Victoria Street West, Auckland. A portrait of Lord Kitchener sits at the top of the stairs. AUCKLAND LIBRARIES HERITAGE COLLECTIONS, 1-W1594

By mid-1917, the war seemed to be turning in the Allies' favour. The British were preparing for another push on the Western Front, the entry of the United States promised to bring new strength to bear, and some spoke of Russia remobilising under a democratic regime. The Battle of Messines, fought between 7 and 14 June and a prelude to a larger offensive on the Western Front, was regarded as indicative of the changing tide of the war. In one widely quoted Australian officer's assessment, 'On the whole the great German fighting machine is not so good as it was, while the Empire's fighting machine is better than ever.'[1]

By August there were reports of steady progress. The *New Zealand Times* claimed that 'Twice before have great battles been fought in this war over nearly the same ground that saw the Allied triumph at Ypres and Messines early in June, but nothing could be more impressive than the difference between the Allies' prospects . . . Things are changing now.'[2] The New Zealand Division's role in the effort to capture Messines Ridge was held as a particular, though costly, mark of distinction; by the time it was withdrawn on 9 June, the division had suffered 3633 casualties, 700 of whom were killed.[3] The effort was headlined a 'New Zealand Victory' and 'one of the shining feats of the war', and Godley wrote to Allen, 'You may tell the people of New Zealand with authority that there is no division in the British armies in France which has a higher reputation.'[4] Ōtaki MP Willie Field considered his soldier son 'very brave over the whole awful business. I cannot think it will last much longer. There seems to be a growing feeling that it will soon be over.'[5]

Such hopes were cruelly dashed, however, as the Allies suffered a period of desperate setbacks from late 1917 to the early months of 1918.[6] After the cumulative strains of the last three years, these reversals damaged social commitment to the war, fuelling weariness and unrest, aggravating frustrations over the conduct of the fighting while reviving some suppressed dissent. The extension of conscription to Māori and to second division men promised new controversies.

When Massey and Ward departed for London in August 1916, divergence from a wholehearted commitment to the war was confined to isolated elements. By the time they disembarked in Auckland on 25 June 1917, however, the resolution that the war would be pursued to a final victory, and to the 'last man and the last shilling', was being more widely questioned.

At the Labour Party's July 1917 conference a committee drew up peace proposals, inspired by the New South Wales Labor Party's commitment to a position of 'no annexations or no indemnities'; by early 1918, the party was 'opposed to wars of aggrandisement', and favoured 'peace by negotiation'.[7] On 1 August 1917 Pope Benedict XV issued an initiative for a mediated peace. This became another piece of ammunition for those who questioned Catholic commitment to the war effort. While some Catholics rebutted by pointing to their record in the war, others tellingly noted the prudence of the Pope's initiative.[8]

On 29 November the *Daily Telegraph* published a 'peace letter' written by Lord Lansdowne that called for a statement of Britain's war aims as a means to stimulate moderation in Germany and promote a compromise peace.[9] Coming from an establishment figure such as Lansdowne, with a record as a former governor-general of Canada, viceroy of India, secretary of state for war and secretary of state for foreign affairs, this departure from a principle that the war would be fought to the finish caused a minor scandal in Britain.

In New Zealand, commentary was generally derisive. In a speech to mark the opening of a railway at Raetihi, Massey voiced his contempt for Lansdowne, and the editor of the *Grey River Argus* questioned the qualities of a man who would counsel covenants with those who had demonstrated such scorn for law and civility. In criticism similar to that levelled at Asquith, the paper's editor speculated that 'the prestige of heredity' had more to do with his position than competence: 'Is it any wonder, in view of such happenings, that serious mistakes have been made and golden opportunities lost in the matter of war organisation and equipment.'[10]

More significantly, a diminishing resolve about the war was detectable in the second half of 1917, as a range of voices called for a review of New Zealand's military commitment and for it to be balanced against social and economic needs. In a July parliamentary debate, Reform MP Dr A. K. Newman declared that 'until Canada and Australia have done an equal part as to the number of people they send away we should slacken off, and I hope we will slacken off'.[11]

Moreover, news from the United States made the sheer scale of mobilisation there clear — seven million men were reported to be eligible for the newly introduced draft, a $7 billion bond bill required to cover initial war expenses had been requested, and there were plans to begin sending 1000 aviators a month to France. As the *Evening Star*'s San Francisco correspondent suggested, 'Evidence accumulates to cause the German historian of the future to lament the day that America entered the war.'[12]

This spurred both hope of a changing tide for the Allies and arguments that New Zealand might now reassess its commitments. Wairarapa MP John Hornsby pointed out, 'Since the United States has come in, that country with her great population and the enormous number of men that it is possible for her to send to the fighting front, I do think that we might review our position and see whether it is not possible to content ourselves up to the point of, say, the men in the Second Division who are widowers without children, or childless married men.' A similar point was made by J. D. Ormond, one of the Legislative Council's oldest and most experienced members, who asked whether the country's manpower would now be better occupied in producing food for the Allies.[13]

Some called for a limit or review at 100,000 men, with the implication that the New Zealand Division might not then be reinforced, and an Otago organisation called the National Welfare League was established to advocate for reducing reinforcements to the minimum needed to maintain the division.[14] Even Massey and Ward, while in London, had flirted with ideas of placing a ceiling on New Zealand's commitment and statements on the matter were reported at home.[15] Back in New Zealand, Ward told a deputation, 'The only thing that passes through my mind is that we will have to consider how much further this country can go in sending men at all . . . This country has done remarkably well, better than any of the other Overseas Dominions, and the time will come — I can't say when — when it may not be possible to let any more men go.'

Massey, also present, hardly seemed to disagree: 'we shall have to take into consideration something of what Sir Joseph Ward mentioned just now'. As the *Evening Post* pointed out in its editorial, 'Coming from the two leading members of the Government, who have just returned from the inner War Councils of the Empire, and who, therefore, have the fullest information at their disposal, their remarks cannot be regarded other than as possessing a special significance.'[16]

But it was soon evident that Massey's position had not shifted. He warned that notions of sending food instead of soldiers were at odds with the view in London and 'it must be clearly understood that men were wanted more than supplies'. He also argued that only total victory for the Allies would eliminate the threat posed by the German colonial system in the Pacific.[17] Ward, too, noted that relying on the power of the United States would mean yielding influence: 'the longer the war the greater must be America's part in it and the more profound will be our obligations to the loyal people of the United States'.[18]

Allen declared that the country would be false to its pledges if it failed to keep the Expeditionary Force at full strength: 'New Zealand wanted to be there so that we may say that we have done our part right up to the end, we have never shirked, we have never grown weary, never been faint or downhearted at the last moment.' To those who measured New Zealand's effort against Canada or Australia, he countered that 'New Zealand has not done so much in proportion as Great Britain and France, and the people who make comparisons between us and Australia and Canada are, to my mind, only seeking an escape, instead of trying to do their duty.'[19]

This perspective was being discussed outside Parliament, too. In June the *New Zealand Herald* printed a cable message sent to New Zealand media by Captain Samuel Atkinson, recently killed while saving a fellow officer:

> Until New Zealand does as France has done, putting into the field every fit man except the minimum required for the essential industries, and putting into the allies' common pot her

wealth and the united work of her people, for so long will New Zealand continue to play with her freedom and sponge on others for her defence. There are a hundred good reasons why New Zealand has not yet done more, but if we mean to keep our freedom and self-respect, we must overcome each of these reasons, which obviously are useless for defeating the enemy.[20]

Legislative Councillor Francis Bell perhaps went furthest in denouncing any reduction in the country's commitment.[21] Recalling the pledges made at the outbreak of war and repeated on each anniversary for an 'inflexible determination' to make 'any sacrifice', he chastened those whose 'determination became flexible . . . when the point has arrived that something of our convenience and comfort is to be sacrificed'.

> How can the entry of America into this quarrel make any difference to the obligation of New Zealand? If any part of the Empire was in danger more than another, New Zealand was that part. It is our New Zealand soil we are defending, and the enemy is at the gates of one New Zealand avenue which stretches to the other side of the seas . . . Are we to sit behind a rampart of Americans or of any nation?

Referring to the Napoleonic Wars, he called on 'the descendants of men who in the last century bore privation and suffering, almost starvation, rather than give way to a military despotism', to not let it be said that their heritage was to be 'calculated in money, and to be defended not to the utmost limit of physical endurance, but only until our pockets begin to be affected'.[22]

Though publicly pledging that the country should maintain a wholehearted commitment, Allen remained acutely aware of the limits of New Zealand's capacities and still wished to delay the call-up of second division men for as long as possible. Seeking to relieve pressure and circumvent a debate on the matter, he sought a reduction in the 20 per cent rate for infantry reinforcements and waited for an opportunity to disband the Fourth Brigade. Some negotiating leverage came in July as Australia announced that its reinforcement rate was to drop to 8 per cent. Liverpool telegraphed the Colonial Office to ask for a similar modification in New Zealand.[23] On 4 August, London agreed and monthly reinforcements for the infantry were reduced to 12 per cent and, after further negotiation, to 10 per cent on 7 September.[24] Allen presented this change as the result of instructions from the War Council, and of fewer casualties.[25]

Another palliative was a proposed furlough system, announced in August 1917, that would give 250 personnel a month two months' leave in New Zealand, plus four months' travelling time, or two months in Britain.[26] Concerns were raised over the willingness of men to return to the front once they were back in New Zealand, but these became irrelevant when the War Council scuttled the scheme in late September, worried that Canada and Australia would follow suit.[27] Lastly, on 11 October, Allen informed Godley that he did not plan to reinforce the Fourth Brigade.[28] In justifying his decision, he warned the general of a 'growing feeling in New Zealand that the willing horse is being worked to death': 'The strain is coming on New Zealand fairly severely and I daresay you realise how weak-kneed some men become under strain. I have a difficulty in Cabinet keeping things going and if there is weakness there you can imagine what it is among some of the Members of the House.'[29] The events unfolding on the Western Front would certainly add to the mounting disillusionment.

Messines had been a prelude for the much larger Third Battle of Ypres, fought from July to November. Actions in October, which sought to take ground around the village of Passchendaele, subsequently came to dominate the public view of the entire offensive and arguably the war in general. The division's first action to capture Gravenstafel Spur in the Battle of Broodseinde on 4 October was a notable success. However, a second major action, launched on 12 October to assault Bellevue Spur, faced deteriorating weather, worsening mud, uncut wire and German defences that had not been adequately shelled. On 13 October, General Haig ordered the offensive to be halted in the face of heavy rain.[30]

The New Zealand Division's losses in the Third Battle of Ypres were slightly lower than at the Somme the previous year, with more than 6000 casualties, of whom at least 1900 were killed. The toll spiked on 12 October with nearly 2700 casualties, of whom 843 were killed; when those who died of injuries over the subsequent three months are included, the figure reaches 957.[31] In terms of lives lost on a single day, this was the bloodiest incident in New Zealand's history as a modern nation.[32]

Public awareness of these events grew over October as newspaper bulletins arrived, followed, over subsequent days, by correspondents' accounts and, towards the end of the month, by Godley's official report, which was read in Parliament and published in the press.[33] A major theme of the reporting was the sense of achievement, that this was the anticipated big push: 'a smashing blow and a complete victory'; 'this may well be the turning point of the war'; 'Ypres Advance Likely To Break The German Line'.[34]

Several correspondents suggested that German morale was eroding and that this was the last phase of the war. British war correspondent Philip Gibbs claimed that the enemy's spirits had fallen so low that Tommies 'only need to make a grimace at the Hun to make him "hands-up"'.[35] The New Zealanders had 'fought magnificently' and had 'every reason to rejoice at their victory on the Gravenstafel Ridge', where 'they dealt the enemy a smashing blow on this part of the battleground'.[36] Also mentioned was 'dogged determination' that was 'peculiarly characteristic of the colonial temperament' and 'which carried them on in spite of the difficulties confronting them'.[37] Their heroic efforts 'will in future be told wherever Australasians gather'.[38]

Although Godley's official report and various correspondents noted that 'New Zealanders had been held up by uncut wire and a nest of machine-guns and strong redoubts called Bellevue', emphasis was placed on the terrible conditions responsible for robbing the Allies of a greater success.[39] The mud was 'the soldiers' worst enemy'; it was 'the deep quagmire of the battlefield which really ruined the attack' and '[t]he weather in the last attack undoubtedly saved the Germans from a big defeat'.[40]

Some were privy to less absolving accounts. In early November, Allen was receiving correspondence from Major-General Andrew Russell that gave some sense of the scale of the disaster at Bellevue Spur. Noting that '[t]he Artillery Barrage was quite inadequate' and '[u]ncut wire was the cause of our failure', Russell bluntly assessed the assault as a futile loss of life: 'You cannot fight machine guns, plus wire, with human bodies. Without the wire to check them the men would have tackled machine guns in spite of their losses. As it was, they tried heroically to tackle both. This was humanly impossible.'[41] Such assessments may have been kept from the public, but many were clearly coming to similar conclusions, especially as the casualty lists began to arrive. Annis Hamerton wrote to her daughter on 21 October: 'we have had a sad time, with awful casualty lists. Our brave N.Z. lads facing fearful odds, & doing wonders but oh the cost — George Duffill & Parkin from Inglewood & Mrs H. Arden's only son such a fine bright lad (Neville) & Mrs G. Kelly's older son a fine promising lad it is heart-breaking & no end in sight.'[42] Despite Massey's urging, on 1 November, that 'whatever happens, there is only one thing for us to do, and that is to set our teeth and carry on to the end', in the months after Third Ypres public attitudes hardened. There was a growing recognition of the loss of life and an acknowledgement that the action had not been a decisive one.[43] As Paul Baker points out, 'A year or two earlier such losses would have prompted calls to send more men; now they caused anger and disillusionment.'[44]

By early 1918 Allen detected public 'uneasiness', describing to Godley 'a very uncomfortable feeling spreading throughout New Zealand that men's lives have been sacrificed unnecessarily, not only at Gallipoli but on the Western Front also'. With regard to Passchendaele, he observed, 'Rumours have been circulating through parts of New Zealand that the situation was not properly appreciated' and that the episode had stirred 'a feeling of unrest, and I have it myself. There is no use denying it.'[45]

The aftermath of the offensive also had implications for New Zealand's military commitment. On 28 November, the British Army Council approved a drastic reduction in the infantry reinforcement rate, to just 6.5 per cent. From 2000 men a month in the previous year, to the more recent 1266, the country now faced the lighter burden of 831.[46] The matter of the Fourth Brigade's tentative future was also settled, and after the New Zealand Division was withdrawn from the salient in February 1918 it was disbanded to boost the reserves.

Deteriorating economic issues compounded the discontent. Globally, Britain's shipping situation remained grave, though losses to U-boats declined as counter-measures were introduced. For New Zealand the crisis was increasingly acute: in July, Massey dubbed it the 'greatest difficulty' facing the economy.[47] That same month, the British authorities noted that 'beyond occasional palliatives', it was not possible 'to hold out any hope of the situation in regards to Australasian trade improving'.[48] Consequently, the value of New Zealand exports declined from £33.3 million in 1916 to £31.6 million in 1917 and would fall to £28.5 million in 1918.[49] Following the inaugural meeting of the Gore Farmers' Union in the winter of 1917, John McQueen, manager of the Southland Frozen Meat Company, noted that there were fewer available ships than last year and that the 1918 season would start 'with nearly half the storage capacity filled, notwithstanding the fact that new space for 65,000 additional carcasses had been provided'.[50]

There was one concession at the end of November when, after months of negotiation, it was announced that shipping would be made available for butter, which was added to the commandeer. Although the set price was far above the pre-war price, it was significantly below that paid on the London market for European and American butter and some producers argued that they were effectively subsidising the price of butter for British consumers.[51] Others may simply have been grateful for the opportunity to release pressure on stockpiled goods. By the end of March 1918, the stored goods awaiting shipping included 350,315 boxes of butter, 363,790 crates of cheese and 3,398,364 60-pound frozen meat carcasses.[52]

Access to coal remained a major concern. Australian industrial action, beginning in early August 1917, paralysed trans-Tasman shipping and coal imports, with local stocks soon low enough to make 'conservation measures absolutely imperative'.[53] Moreover, a degree of distrust remained around the truce won on the coal fields towards the start of the year. In October 1917, following his release from jail, Bob Semple toured the coal fields, attracting large audiences. His speeches, observed as 'liberally interspersed with pithy humour and caustic criticism', damned the government for allowing profiteers to bleed the empire for millions while living costs rose, and for regulations that denied trial by jury to 'the Labor man, but [extended it] to the murderer and the sexual pervert'.[54] Renewed militancy seemed certain and the winter of 1918 promised to be chilly.

Living costs were hit as the prices of various imported goods rose, thanks both to shipping problems and the enormous demands for supplies and transport created by United States mobilisation. In July, 'the entry of Uncle Sam into the war' was affecting the cost of soap, 'for caustic soda supplies were coming from that country', as well as the cost of kerosene 'on account of the commandeering of steamers by the American Government'.[55] Imports from Japan also declined as Japanese freighters were diverted to more remunerative routes and cut services to Australasia.[56]

Massey returned from London professing a new concern over the shipping controller's priorities in relation to New Zealand interests. He expressed some support for the idea of a state-owned shipping fleet, an ambition also recommended by the Cost of Living Committee set up to inquire into and report on the subject.[57] It was left to Ward to torpedo the idea: 'the suggestion will not bear examination . . . for the simple reason that we could neither buy nor build steamers for delivery until long after the war is over'.[58]

The 1917 Budget, presented in August, continued the policy of financing the war effort by paying direct costs through borrowing and using increased taxation, which rose to an unprecedented one-third for higher incomes, to service interest payments, cover reductions in revenue sources and pay military pensions. The government approached the problem of securing the £24 million investment in the war loan in two ways. First, rather than increasing the rate of interest, it made the loan free from income tax. Second, it laid the groundwork to make investment in the loan compulsory for taxpayers who earned more than £700. They could be required to contribute to the loan by three times the amount they had paid in income or land tax the previous year. This could be increased to 4.5 times if they had not subscribed to the 1916 loan, and the legislation even included provision for taxpayers to borrow from banks in order to invest.[59]

This 'special war tax' was considered a replacement for the 45 per cent 'excess profits tax', introduced in 1916 to target war-related profits, which was now abandoned as Ward conceded the difficulties in isolating such revenues.[60] He agreed with critics that it was unfair to enterprises that were only a few years old and whose profits would increase as they got established regardless of the war. He also noted that the measure had fallen short of the £2 million revenue he had projected for it.[61]

Although most editorial commentary, including *Truth*, supported the decision to drop the 'excess profits tax', the conservative *Otago Daily Times*, demonstrating the breadth of feeling against war profiteering, regretted its abandonment: 'It is not the existence of high prices during war time that is the glaring evil. The mischief consists in the fact that the proceeds of these high prices, due entirely to the war, have been pocketed by individuals. War profits should rightly be diverted to the service of the State.'[62] Conservative opinion objected to the borrowing policy, with the Reform-supporting *Press* laying the blame on Ward: 'Not only is this [policy] piling up our load of indebtedness unnecessarily, but the large surplus will probably be used as an argument against the increased taxation which is proposed, and which, we believe, is really necessary if New Zealand is to do her duty in the crisis.'[63] The *Otago Daily Times* considered that the government had not 'recognised the advisability of throwing on taxation a substantial share of the expenses of the war. The country can better afford to pay taxes now than it will be in the years following the war when it may be suffering from reaction.'[64]

There was equally strong criticism from the Liberal press. The *Star* accused the government of showing 'far too much consideration for the present generation, and far too little for our successors by piling up the national debt of the country in a quite unjustifiable manner'. It had 'only tinkered' with taxation, 'apparently for fear of offending a section of the community'.[65]

A number of Liberal papers, and many of the party's backbenchers, also protested the tax changes on the grounds that they weighed unduly heavily on people with modest incomes already struggling with a higher cost of living. Shortly after the Budget was presented, it was reported that 'a section of the Liberal Party is on the verge of revolt against the National Government' with a group, largely consisting of urban MPs, determined to oppose the increased duty on tea and to promote what they saw as true Liberal policies.[66] The *Star* attacked Ward's increase in the duty on a pound of tea from 2d to 5d, arguing that it was 'unjust' because 'in the colonies it is the accepted drink of the people, and has become a necessity, just in the same sense as bread'.[67]

There were growing murmurs, too, that New Zealand's capacity to bear economic burdens was approaching a hard limit. Early in August 1917, Christchurch's *Sun*, which generally backed Reform but also catered for a large working-class readership, attacked the government for expecting too much:

> It was no doubt very fine and very patriotic to determine that we at this distance should give as large a proportion of our manhood as Great Britain and pay our soldiers six times the rate that Tommies receive, but it could only be done on the assumption that proportionately we were six times as rich as Great Britain, and that our citizens had six times the wealth-earning capacity

of the British taxpayer. No one is fool enough to argue that this is actually the case, and as a result we have undertaken responsibilities that are quite beyond our abilities to maintain.[68]

The *Sun* was further vexed about how the call-up of the second division would further strain the country: 'if Sir James Allen persists in his policy of getting the £4 a week Second Division men away in a little more than a year he is merely hastening a financial collapse'.[69]

New measures were also introduced to promote equity and boost productivity and efficiency. In September a cost of living bonus, intended to compensate for the effects of wartime inflation on pensions, was introduced. Widows' pensions, for example, were increased by £6 per child, raising the allowance for one child to £18.[70] To improve oversight of flour and bread prices, new September regulations prohibited private purchase of wheat from the 1917–18 harvest and a scheme gazetted on 22 December, and headed by MacDonald as wheat controller, allowed the state to purchase and distribute wheat among millers.[71] In late October, the Statute Law Amendment Act empowered the Board of Trade to further address price increases for commodities by enabling the governor-general to fix maximum prices.[72] More coal regulations were also gazetted that month, with committees established in Auckland, Christchurch and Wellington and to control regional distribution.[73]

From 1 November, entertainment ventures, including exhibitions, games and sports that charged admissions, had to pay an 'amusement tax', and in late October the Sale of Liquor Restriction Act proclaimed that public houses had to remain closed between 6 p.m. Saturday and 9 a.m. Monday, and between those hours every other week day until six months, 'and no longer', after the war ended.[74] *Truth*, probably speaking for a good proportion of the population, was far from impressed: 'in the end the wowsers and the people (who did not want it), got six o'clock closing, and as the hotels will close at six o'clock commencing on December 1 next, we must look forward to the war being won from that date'.[75] Also in October, Russell, as minister of health, introduced a Social Hygiene Bill intended to improve national efficiency by protecting against venereal disease.[76] Providing for compulsory detention and inspection for prostitutes and suspected prostitutes, the bill revived controversies around similar provisions in the Contagious Diseases Act, overturned in 1910, which had been a focus of feminist activism. Although protests and criticism brought some modification of the legislation, it was passed into law in late October. It notably contrasted with the more progressive, and clandestine, measures authorities took to manage venereal disease within the New Zealand Division.[77]

In late September, hoping to prepare the way for a smooth mobilisation of second division men, the government announced its re-evaluated rates for soldiers' dependants. As well as increasing the disability and widows' pensions, these raised the separation allowance for a soldier's wife from 1s to 3s a day, the daily rate per child from 9d to 1s and the special financial assistance provision from £1 to £3 per week.[78] Various commentators congratulated the government on 'having solved a difficult issue both boldly and satisfactorily . . . they must be unreasonable persons indeed who find room for serious complaint in the increased separation and special allowances'.[79] One cartoon depicted a family man pocketing a 'big pensions' cheque, shaking hands with Allen and saying, 'Thanks; the war for me now my pension's right.' To this the minister replies, 'And may you never get it.'[80]

However, anticipation of mutual concord was premature. A day after the new rates were announced, a Second Division League deputation met Massey, Ward and Allen to request additional concessions. These included further increases to the separation rates for wives and children (6s for the former and 1s 6d for the latter), an increased age limit for the daughter's pension from 17 to when she was 'of marriage age, say, 20 years' and recognition that second division men required a 'nest egg' for a potentially unstable future.[81] The responses of the three ministers were a mixture of touting the concessions already made, warnings about financial constraints and uncommitted acknowledgements that the adjusted rates were not perfect.

Just days later, however, the first class A second division men were balloted and soon began their progress through medical exams. By December 1917 Military Service Boards were hearing appeals from second division men, and the first reinforcement draft to include married men was set to mobilise on Monday, 29 April 1918.[82] Throughout the war, other second division gradations were similarly called up, with the first class B men balloted from mid-April 1918 and class C men from June.

As this process began, the rhetoric became more charged and sometimes radical. Second division men continued to emphasise that they were willing to fight but that it was unfair for husbands and fathers to go while those who should have enlisted remained free. It was 'not right', said a Second Division League conference in October, 'that British men should be sent away to fight while aliens were left to enjoy all the

A well-attended public meeting at Christchurch's Colosseum hall. The turnout was estimated at 2600. HOCKEN COLLECTIONS TE UARE TAOKA O HĀKENA, 7931

privileges of citizenship of the Dominion ... The root of the evil lay at the door of Parliament.'[83]

Others pointed out that an estimated 3637 deserters remained at large, more than enough to make up a reinforcement draft, and urged the Defence Department to make more of an effort to find these men: 'Before members of the Second Division are called up, the deserters should be accounted for as far as is humanly possible.'[84] Tensions also endured over possible exemptions for Catholic clergymen: one Baptist commentator darkly hinted that 'a strike of the 2nd Division would be a natural answer to the clerical strike which has cowed Sir James'.[85]

In December the Wellington branch of the Second Division League was rumoured to be considering the formation of a political organisation to contest an upcoming local by-election, though it ultimately decided to continue lobbying for public and political support rather than compete for power.[86] The situation in Christchurch went much further. By February 1918, the Christchurch branch had 'developed into a very lively and aggressive body, with a penchant for passing lengthy, comprehensive and strongly-worded resolutions'.[87] On 4 February, for example, a public and 'lively meeting' for married reservists highlighted the growing discontent towards and within the Christchurch branch. Charges hurled at the branch president, M. J. Gresson, included accusations that he 'was not a worker', that he was 'in the Government [sic] pay' or that he had been 'put into the League by the military people'. Various motions called for campaigning on more radical positions.[88]

On 26 April, the Christchurch executive passed a resolution recommending the National Executive declare that league members were 'released from all obligations' if the government did not grant their demands by 31 May.[89] A meeting of class A and B reservists held on 27 April was advertised as having 'no connection whatsoever with the Second Division League', which was accused of having 'hopelessly failed to obtain a fair deal for the wives and children of conscripted men'. The principal motion 'to enter an emphatic protest against any more reinforcements being sent from New Zealand until a referendum of the people is taken, and ... that there be no industrial conscription of the wives and children of reservists' was among the far-reaching resolutions raised. It was 'carried unanimously, midst scenes of tremendous enthusiasm'.[90]

On the night of Sunday, 28 April, the eve of mobilisation, around 1600 citizens packed the Christchurch Opera House for a public meeting organised by the league and chaired by the mayor. Called to discuss the social impacts of the war, the meeting took a radical turn when Lyttelton watersiders John Flood and Ernest Langley moved an amendment from the floor that 'the first line of the Second Division shall not be broken and no Second Division man shall leave for camp until the demands of the League are acceded to'. The amendment soon found a seconder in Hiram Hunter. Further discussion resulted in a slightly rephrased adaptation, which added the demand for a general election, seconded and voted on, apparently with only two dissenters.[91] An open statement that government policy would be resisted had been declared and endorsed. The following day's mobilisation seemed sure to promise a confrontation.

After the June 1917 decision to extend the Military Service Act to Māori, the task of preparing a balloting register involved months of administrative work, forestalling any easy solution to the manpower needs of the Pioneer Battalion, officially renamed the Māori Battalion in September 1917. Registration proved arduous, given the more remote and less documented areas where most Māori lived. Isolation from postal services meant a number of requests for extensions ran beyond the fortnight provided for registration.[92] Adding to official headaches was the often non-standardised spelling of Māori names and the fact that some men went by both a European and a Māori name. Although regulations decreed that a customary marriage, contracted before 1 May 1915, placed a man in the second division, authorities with sufficient local knowledge to verify such details were scarce.[93]

Various forms of recalcitrance added to frustrations. In the Blenheim subdistrict, a constable reported that only three Māori had registered, and the majority had no intention of joining them.[94] A Hāwera officer claimed that local Māori 'absolutely refused to have anything to do with the signing of the enrolment card'.[95] Many exploited the lack of familiarity with the Māori community and gave false addresses and names such as 'Henuwera Harry' (roughly translating as 'hot stuff').[96] Another officer noted that 'quite a large section of Maoris in these parts cannot read English, or speak it very much, and at the present time they make it convenient not to understand what I try to tell them'.[97] A Te Awamutu constable concluded that the existing records were 'useless as a guide to the number of Natives, their ages and addresses in any of the Maori settlements in the Waipa, Waitoma [sic] and West Taupo Counties'. A third of the young Taupō men were not on the register.[98] A police inspector recommended that 'to properly complete this work of registration with any degree of accuracy it will be necessary to employ a capable reliable Interpreter to visit each of the Settlements . . .'.[99]

The government also failed to anticipate the reaction to compulsory registration among tribes that had already provided substantial numbers of volunteers. Even Arawa, with its strong history of cooperation, protested. In June 1917, an Arawa petition beseeched Allen not to impose conscription on them 'because our youths are proceeding to the front in every contingent . . . The Arawa is the Maori Tribe that absolutely encourage the going forward to the war.'[100] South Island Māori were similarly concerned.

Anxieties appeared to grow with registration efforts in February 1918. Henare Parata, the government's candidate for the approaching by-election in Southern Māori, sent Allen a telegram: 'all South Island Maori boys gone volunteering not necessary to register reply at one [sic] matter urgent',[101] At this stage Allen was notably ambiguous over whether conscription would be confined to Waikato–Maniapoto: he stated, for example, in a marginal note on an internal memorandum that conscription would be applied there 'to commence with'.[102] His reply to Parata also avoided a guarantee on the matter: 'It is not likely that any ballot will be taken in the South Island as Maoris there have enlisted so well voluntarily.'[103]

However, the threat of a political crisis obliged Allen to make a commitment on whether conscription might be applied to other Māori. On 7 February 1918 Nau Paraone Kawiti, 'authorised by the natives of North Auckland', cabled Allen to inquire whether the compulsory registration was to be for home or foreign service.[104] There were signs of strain in the region.

The previous December, Tau Henare, MP for Northern Māori, had offered another platoon on behalf of his people, with the caveat that this should be considered the last: 'I believe they have sent somewhere about 600 from my electorate.'[105]

In response to Kawiti, Allen offered the familiar reply that the purpose of registration was to draw up a roll but that the government had no current plans to apply conscription in Northland: 'It is not proposed to take any ballot in your district at present as the Maoris there have enlisted so well.' The following day Henare telegraphed Allen, restating the matter: 'Do you mean the conscription does not apply to my electorate great alarm amongst my people.' Keeping his loophole open, Allen responded: 'Your district has recruited so splendidly there is no intention of applying conscription to your people at the present time.'[106] A week later it was clear that concerns in the north had escalated. Matiu Tawhai of Waimā cabled Allen to say that '[s]everal telegrams from the Ngapuhi district have reached me asking that my tribe should not go to register for the war'. He had called a meeting of 'all the people' in the area: 'The attitude taken up here is that they should not register for fear lest they be conscripted by that Act . . . We are desirous that we should be left in the old way under which our sons went to war (voluntaryism).'[107]

Allen, at home in Dunedin, received an urgent telegram from Massey: 'Tau Henare has notified Speaker that he intends to resign as protest against Maori conscription proposals.' Then came a cable from Henare: 'My people overcome me on regarding conscription to the Maori I have already told you my position I agree upon to send my resignation.'[108] This prospect galvanised Allen. Henare's resignation carried a risk that Ward might dispute Massey's claim to be prime minister since the numbers of government and opposition MPs would then be equal, and a by-election might tip the balance in Ward's direction.

Before hurriedly boarding a train north, Allen cabled reassurances to Massey — 'Maori conscription proposals are intended for Waikatos there is no intention to apply conscription to Tau Henares [sic] people' — and to Henare himself: 'Please explain to your people that conscription is intended for the Waikato maories who have not voluntarily enlisted and who are not doing their part with other maories [sic] in the war your people have behaved so splendidly that there is no intention to apply conscription to them tell them also from me that they must not allow you to resign.'[109] He also sent an urgent telegram to Matiu Tawhai, promising that there was 'no intention to apply conscription to the North Auckland tribes because we know how well your young men have enlisted voluntarily. You can assure your people that their sons will be left to volunteer in the old way to go to the war.'[110]

While on the train Allen composed a memo to Robin, telling him of Henare's threat to resign and asking him to tell Cossgrove and Porter immediately that they must not use the threat of conscription during their recruiting, especially with the 'northern Maoris'. In fact, he added, 'it might be best to leave Maori recruiting generally to the Maoris themselves until we have time to talk the matter over'.[111] Finally, on 18 February, Allen assured Kawiti that only Waikato were to be conscripted, adding his hope that 'you will assist me in ensuring that the Waikatos take their share in helping to protect our Country and King in this time of National peril'.[112]

The flurry of telegrams ultimately had a good outcome for the government. On 19 February

Tawhai told Allen that Ngāpuhi had agreed to register 'as your explanation by wire was so clear that the law will not be applied to the North of Auckland . . . but if the assurance in your telegram is departed from, then we will again consider the matter'. Allen answered, 'you may rely upon it that any promise given by me will be kept'.[113]

Unsurprisingly, the strongest opposition came from Waikato. After the legal extension of conscription, there had been further efforts to drum up commitment. In early July 1917, at a hui involving Waikato, Ngāti Maru, Ngāpuhi and Ngāti Paoa iwi, Te Heuheu asserted that 'many of the best warriors had sprung from the Waikato tribe; let them, therefore, put all past grievances aside for the present and fight for the Empire of which they formed a part'.[114] When this attempt was unfruitful James Carroll told Allen in November, 'afraid our friends are only playing for time, though a pity still conscription must be employed'.[115]

Te Heuheu's call was countered with the increasingly common claim that under the Treaty of Waitangi the government could not conscript Māori.[116] Other arguments against conscription presented it as a threat to Māori autonomy and mana, dubbing the Military Service Act Te Ture Puruma, literally the Broom or Sweeping Act. The Māori newspaper *Te Kopara* elaborated on this theme:

> Listen to the voice of Allen who cries, Sweep! Sweep! Sweep the Maori people from the face of the earth . . . Why should I be taken by this broom, so that I may sit within the heat of battle? Maori people, is it correct that we should come under this law? . . . Each iwi has its own mana, its own tikanga and its own way of doing things. Therefore I shall not thoughtlessly tramp the heel of my foot on someone else's turangawaewae . . .

Such commentary also evoked tribal pride as a case against conscription: 'The Maori are a chiefly people, a people admired by Pakeha for fighting in the wars. A people who have developed expertise, at the arts of war, a brave and strong people when faced with battle. It is not appropriate to leave it to conscription to fetch them. I say to the iwi, my way of looking is that this belittles us the Maori people.'[117]

Tensions in Waikato rose as registration proceeded. Even previously 'friendly' Māori were described as hostile or insulting, sometimes calling for a German victory, and employers who had previously offered seasonal work to Māori withdrew it.[118] In February, Kāwhia resident J. C. Jack wrote to Allen warning of his concerns that a rebellion of Waikato Māori, possibly linked to German intrigue, was possible. He recommended distributing rifles to local Europeans: a police assessment politely considered that this evaluation was hyperbolic.[119] The *Huntly Press* blamed the government for its unwillingness to enforce the law: 'The average Maori has now imbibed the idea that he is above the Government and some think that they are above any power on earth.'[120] What exactly would happen were conscription to be enforced in the district remained a matter of debate. On 19 February, Allen informed Pōmare that 'large gatherings of Natives men women and children have assembled at Morrinsville and Huntly in anticipation of close of enrolment period tomorrow. They are showing no aggressiveness but they [intimated] to constable that if he leads they will follow whether to camp or to gaol is not quite clear.'[121]

Towards the end of April 1918, the government statistician was finally able to report that the roll for the first division of Waikato–Maniapoto was serviceable. For those in charge of reinforcements for the Māori Battalion this came none too soon; by mid-March there were fewer than 30 men in training.[122]

In the months after its mid-1917 founding, the membership of the Protestant Political Association mushroomed. By the end of the year it claimed almost 20,000 members in more than 40 branches. Predictions that this figure would reach 100,000 by the end of 1918 seemed wildly optimistic, though they actually underestimated the PPA's growth to 200,000 members in 225 branches by April 1919.[123]

This rapid growth owed much to Elliott's recruitment drives across the country, with significant turnouts at public meetings that focused on the association's standard allegations of undue Catholic influence. Indeed, PPA proponents emphasised that the association was a defensive reaction to the Catholic Federation's agenda. Prominent Auckland member Dr J. S. Reekie argued that the PPA was established 'because of the efforts of a sectarian organisation to press claims and operations distinctly against the national well-being, and inimical to the national prosecution of the war . . . Our attention is wholly given to the civic aggressions already made, and being attempted, upon our national education system; the over-riding of the New Zealand law, and against a system which injures our civic unity.'[124]

PPA campaigning also began to associate political labour with Catholics, and Elliott claimed there was a Catholic conspiracy to capture the Labour Party and that the Australian Labor Party had aready been subverted. He contended that Labour representatives 'got into Parliament on the votes of the Roman Catholics', and that this was 'true in every electorate', that Irish names had been predominant at recent Labour conferences, that priests were acting as organisers and that not a single Labour MP would hold his seat 'in the face of Roman opposition'.[125] In order to represent 'sane' labour and save workers from 'ruin and disintegration', Elliott pronounced that the PPA would wield its influence within the political process.[126] By September 1917 Elliott was speaking of 'nominating' candidates for every seat in the next general election.[127]

The rise of the PPA also owed something to allegations that a Catholic influence within the government was suppressing mail directed to its post office box. In July 1917, Ward, as postmaster-general, initiated a full inquiry, headed by Magistrate H. W. Bishop.[128] The commission examined 65 witnesses over eight days in August and, despite wartime restrictions on its inquiries, it soon became clear that censors had indeed been monitoring the PPA's post office box for months.[129]

As Solicitor-General John Salmond explained, official attention had been stirred from December 1916 after various complaints about a pamphlet titled *The Hideous Guilt of Rome in the European Carnage.*[130] He had advised censors to review mail to PO Box 912, the address the literature directed readers towards, under the rationale that such publications 'would have a considerable effect on the recruiting of Roman Catholics' and because of a possible breach of war regulations.[131] Hubert Ostler, the counsel for the PPA and Salmond's former subordinate, questioned the legality of censorship, noted its threat to civil liberties, and challenged the impartiality of its application.[132]

The results of Bishop's inquiry were announced in early September. The commissioner found that mail not delivered was of a 'trifling' quantity and 'there was in no degree satisfactory evidence of any impropriety or corruption on the part of the Auckland Postal officials'.[133] As far as censorship was concerned, Bishop agreed with Salmond that 'matter connected with this box was distinctly mischievous in tendency and was likely to very seriously interfere with the proper conduct of the war, and . . . the Post Office should not be allowed to be the medium made for its circulation to the public'.[134]

Although Elliott's allegations of a Catholic plot were entirely rejected, the acknowledgement that mail had been interfered with likely boosted public sympathy for the PPA's cause. It also added to the association's notoriety. When some of the material raised in the inquiry was read in Parliament, Massey said that in all his years in the House he had never encountered statements more calculated to stir religious hatred.[135]

However, the issue that afforded the PPA the most traction was the conscription of clergy. Under the motto 'equal rights for all; special privileges for none', the association was able to tap into the strength of public feeling about equality of sacrifice, and each new branch of the PPA was launched with resolutions to oppose Catholic privileges.[136] This occurred as the exhaustion of the first division loomed and as Cabinet, aware of the extreme fragility of its 'solution' of deferring the call-up of Catholic clergy, considered legislation to exempt the Marist Brothers and remaining teachers in state schools.[137]

Ward's return to domestic politics after his return from London may also have been a factor. His biographer notes that, for almost the only time in his career, he proved willing to openly make a special case for Catholic interests.[138] The Military Service Amendment Bill, introduced into Parliament on 11 September and debated over the following weeks, initially provided only for the exemption of ministers and those in holy orders, though Ward had successfully moved an amendment to extend exemption to all teachers, thereby exempting the Marist brothers and moving the legislation away from a purely Catholic concern.[139] Regardless, public commentary around the legislation remained blighted by sectarian posturing. The Catholic hierarchy continued to campaign for Catholic solidarity on the issue backed by threats of resistance. One priest requested churchgoers to stand, raise their right hands and promise before the Blessed Sacrament that they would back up and stand by their clergy; the congregation were noted as doing so with a 'mighty will'.[140] Simultaneously, Elliott warned Massey that 'If that Bill becomes law you are going to create a revolution in this country: and although we don't want to do it, if necessary we will call the Protestants of this dominion to fight and turn your Government out of office.'[141]

By late October the bill had been narrowly passed in the House of Representatives (36 to 32) and had moved to the Legislative Council.[142] However, in an extraordinary development, the council decisively rejected the legislation (11 to four), leading a Liberal newspaper to declare that it possessed 'as little respect for democracy as the Huns'.[143] 'Again we find,' said the *Tablet*, 'that at the nod of the bigots Messrs. Massey and Allen are ready to take a stand against their colleagues of the Coalition'.[144] The majority of the press, however, and probably the public, opposed the bill, and the PPA staged a thanksgiving celebration in the Auckland Town Hall.

More pressingly, the council's actions threatened a constitutional crisis and Cabinet was clearly divided. Rumours swept the country that Ward would lead the Liberals out of the coalition and force an election, and on 28 October absent MPs were ordered to return to Wellington. On 30 October, with the parliamentary session due to end that night, there was no agreement between representatives of the House and the council and Massey declared the bill would be dropped.[145]

With its legislative solution stymied, the government resumed its policy of quietly encouraging Military Service Boards to exempt priests, teachers and students, not calling up any who were not exempted, and taking no action against those who had already been called up and had not responded. Catholics were generally reasonably satisfied with this unofficial policy, but more militant elements continued to target Allen as persecuting the Catholic community and the *Tablet* beseeched Ward to save Catholics from 'the tyranny of Sir James Allen K.C.B.'.[146] The PPA continued to condemn a clandestine deal between Catholics and the government. Ward was already well within the PPA's crosshairs, and Allen was targeted for his perceived role in accommodating Catholic privileges.

Coinciding with these episodes was a souring of civil restraints. On 15 October 1917, three men assaulted Elliott outside his Mount Eden home, one of the assailants making liberal use of a rawhide horsewhip while a gathering crowd cheered on the attackers.[147] One of the attackers was Christopher Clements, a returned soldier and the brother of the drowned nun Elliott had defamed at the PPA's launch. At the subsequent court hearing Clements was met by a large, cheering crowd.[148] The magistrate evidently shared some of this sense of natural justice and discharged Clements without penalty, stating that Elliott had 'cast aside all considerations and pretence of ordinary decency'.[149] In mid-February 1918, when Elliott spoke at a well-attended Feilding meeting to form a PPA branch, local organisers, receiving word of possible trouble, secured an exit for him. However, two attending clergymen were viciously set upon by up to a dozen men, thought to be employees of the local freezing works, who had mistakenly identified one cleric as Elliott.[150]

The public was clearly unimpressed with the degree to which disharmony had grown. *Truth* saw sectarian divisions as deprioritising workers' interests and denounced Elliott as 'a slimy sectarian skunk'. The Labour Party, too, continually confronted PPA charges of a Red–Roman conspiracy; ironically, Elliott's attacks probably helped to align those groups.[151] Party officials noted that Labour did not favour any sect; that, contrary to the Catholic Federation's campaigning, it supported secular education; and that there was not a single Catholic on the party executive.[152]

Others emphasised the need for wartime unity and an Auckland journalist pleaded for the community to recognise 'the evil of the religious strife, which, although we are fighting for our own and the world's freedom, is more acute in New Zealand today than at any time for many years'.[153] An *Observer* cartoon depicted sectarians squaring off over the grave of a New Zealand soldier above the caption 'There's a War on!'[154]

Catholic leaders also sought to remind their congregations and the wider public of their shared identity, interests and moral bonds. In September 1917, Father Ainsworth of Auckland's St Patrick's Cathedral preached that 'the blood of Catholic and Protestant soldiers, a common family of loyal Britishers, was at present running in a common stream'.[155] When Bishop Cleary returned to New Zealand in October 1917 after his service as a military chaplain, he felt that he had waded into 'a conflict almost as bitter as the one he had left in Flanders'.[156] As he had before the war, he tried to disarm criticism and acrimony against Catholics by emphasising reason, interdenominational harmony and integration. He refused to allow advocacy for Sinn Féin in his diocese and banned symbols that might be associated with Irish republicanism, including Irish flags and emblems.[157]

At the same time he publicly warned the government that 'we are not going to take this filth-bombardment lying down' and urged a move to address anti-Catholic propaganda. For his own part he took up a direct challenge to the PPA and pledged £500 to the Red Cross if it could prove its assertions on Catholic positions in an open court.[158]

The general hardening of attitudes over these months exacerbated the situation around enemy aliens. On 30 July 1917, the secretary of the Women's Anti-German League, E. J. Moore, forwarded a resolution to Attorney-General Alexander Herdman, proclaiming that 'the time has come when in the interest of the welfare of the Nation it is imperative to eliminate all traces of enemy interest from our social, political and economic life'.[159] This translated into calls for more extensive internment and the passage of legislation to prevent naturalised British subjects who possessed enemy parentage from holding civic positions. League president Anna Stout wanted a review of denaturalisation policies, claiming they currently 'did not go far enough'.[160]

At the end of July, a bill allowing for a revocation of naturalisation in 'cases where it was considered that such a course was essential in the public interest' was being read and Russell signalled his intent to introduce legislation calling for the registration of aliens.[161] By September the government had passed the Revocation of Naturalization Act, which allowed the governor-general to order the revocation of a naturalised alien's citizenship, and the Registration of Aliens Act, which required every alien to register with the police within 28 days.[162] In October, in response to concerns that the recent sinking of the *Port Kembla* had been caused by a bomb smuggled aboard, regulations banned aliens and naturalised aliens from working on wharves or ships without a licence and prevented enemy aliens from voting in local elections.[163] Others took matters into their own hands. In July 1917, Lutheran churches at Rongotea and Halcombe were destroyed by arsonists while Marton parishioners elected to keep a watch to guard their church from a similar fate.[164]

Official suspicions lingered. In late 1917 the German population of Pūhoi became the focus of a number of official inquiries. Using a week's leave to investigate the town, a military policeman stated he was 'absolutely convinced that some serious business is afoot' and credited the community with 'a system of espionage which was perfect'.[165] A military officer

THERE'S A WAR ON!

THE REV HOWARD ELLIOTT GIVES AN ITEM AT GORE.

above The *Observer* denounces religious infighting as an affront to wartime sacrifices. The figure on the left bears Howard Elliott's likeness. NEW ZEALAND OBSERVER, 17 NOVEMBER 1917, P. 13

right Nearly a month later the paper offered a less than reverent take on Elliott's campaigning. NEW ZEALAND OBSERVER, 22 DECEMBER 1917, P. 5

who led a mounted patrol on a 300-mile trek around the district to search for suspicious activity concluded that 'the general bearing of a number of the inhabitants leaves me convinced that the Puhoi district could be quickly organized (if it is not already so) as a "jumping off place" for any operations which circumstances might enable the German navy to undertake in this country'.[166] Constable Lambert undertook a plain-clothes investigation to 'make inquiries whether any Germans there are displaying symptoms of disloyalty and whether any of them should be interned'.[167] He determined that the only 'feeling' that he could detect in the community was 'on account of a young man who is employed by Schischka Bros in their store and who obtained *sine die* exemption from the Military Board at Auckland through placing before the Board facts that were not considered to be genuine and also the fact that none of the sons of the Schischka families have gone to the front'.[168]

The imminent mobilisation of the second division helped to feed these tensions. Earlier in the war there had been concerns that men of enemy descent might enlist; now the focus was the exemption of unnaturalised men. In September 1917 an enthusiastic meeting of 500 people in the small Northland town of Dargaville, clearly with the local Yugoslav population in mind, unanimously called on the government 'to take immediately such action as will effectually ensure equal sacrifice being made by all aliens in some form of war work before calling upon the first class of the Second Division to go into camp'.[169]

Suspicions were also inflamed when some balloted men cited ancestral claims as their reason for objecting to service. In April 1917, for example, Waihī miner F. L. Groshinski appealed, unsuccessfully, on the grounds that he 'objected to taking up arms against his blood relatives'. He was prepared to serve in New Zealand but not abroad, even against the Turks, Austrians or Bulgarians.[170]

The leaders of targeted communities responded by seeking to emphasise their loyalty and willingness to cooperate with authorities. On the third anniversary of the declaration of war, a Pūhoi meeting, led by John Schollum, the chairman of the local road board, noted that aspersions had been cast on the loyalty of the locals and that certain reservists had sought to evade their obligations via ancestral claims. The meeting decided that such claims were 'merely a pretext to shirk their responsibilities' and issued a further statement noting that 'now, at the time of our country's need, those who claim to be British should do their duty, and those who fail should be treated as Germans'.[171]

Meetings of Yugoslavs similarly sought to impress their commitment to New Zealand and revived many previously raised ideas that they should have a means of service. One 30 October meeting asked the government 'to remove the restrictions placed upon Jugoslavs in the matter of enlistment with the New Zealand Expeditionary Force' and to 'devise ways and means whereby Jugoslavs desiring to do so may be despatched to join the Servians at Salonika to fight their direct national foes'. It also stated that Yugoslavs were 'prepared and willing to devote all their energies to such essential industries, or other works, in the Dominion as the Minister for Internal Affairs may direct, and so help the Government and the country to bear the burden of war easier'.[172] However, such resolutions were beset by a degree of community division and officials received competing messages from individuals claiming to truly represent their fellow Yugoslavs while denouncing others.[173]

By this time the government was taking action. From 31 October 1917 a section within the War Legislation Act allowed provisions 'for regulating, controlling, and enforcing the labour of alien enemies'.[174] At the end of November, it was finally announced that naturalised Yugoslavs of verified loyalty would be accepted for service in the New Zealand Expeditionary Force. Non-naturalised men could enlist in the Serbian Army, at Serbian rates of pay.

Plans for some kind of labour service also came to fruition: recently retired police commissioner John Cullen, who had led the 1916 raid on Maungapōhatu, was invited to oversee a home service work scheme.[175] The government could not legally force enemy aliens to volunteer for this scheme, but they could be legally interned if they would not perform labour service at soldiers' rate of pay, and threats to close the gumfields, a major means of livelihood for many, loomed.

After mid-1917, authorities began to introduce more possibilities for balloted objectors who refused to serve. With regard to men categorised as 'conscientious' objectors, camp commandants quietly allowed those who would accept a uniform and obey orders to take on a non-combatant role in the Medical Corps.[176] Plans to use conscientious objectors in labour projects were also enacted and in December, for example, 32 men were assigned to the Weraroa state farm in Levin and others were sent to various areas to plant trees.[177]

Many in such camps endured isolated, rugged conditions — one internee called Rotoaira the Siberia of New Zealand[178] — and often suffered from cold and hunger. Some struggled with unfamiliar work and one man, distressed at being arrested but noted by authorities as isolated and 'very sullen', attempted suicide. However, discipline was more relaxed compared with civilian prisons and military camps, and communities formed among the men, though some camps reported tension between fundamentalist Christians and socialists.[179] At least in letters received by the Women's International League, which ran a writing campaign in support of objectors and their dependants, those in the camps seemed relatively content and still determined: 'We are glad to report that we are all in good health, and in so far as we have tried to do our duty in accordance with our light, contented with our lot'; 'We are all happy, notwithstanding a big sentence lurking ahead. We are satisfied we have done the right thing, and are more pleased to know that persecution has not cowed us down with its tyranny, but rather has consolidated our determination and the cause for which we stand.'[180]

The fact that, after mid-1917, some men were being released after completing their sentences only to continue to refuse orders and face a second conviction added to the Defence Department's sense that the current system was too lenient on 'defiant objectors'. With prison and detention space under strain, and questions remaining over Catholic clergy, Māori and the second division, and under a rationale that reoffenders had spurned opportunities for accommodation, a harsher system of deterrence and correction was proposed. Those who refused orders would follow the sequence of summary punishments, court martial and imprisonment and, when their sentence expired, would be shipped abroad without training.

In theory they would be treated like soldiers and would be held to the same consequences faced by soldiers who refused orders.

In July 1917, 14 men were taken on board the transport *Waitemata* to be sent to Europe with the Twenty-eighth Reinforcements. They were Lewis Penwright, Thomas Harland, Albert Sanderson, Garth Ballantyne, Henry Patton, Fredrick Adin, Daniel Maguire, David Gray, Lawrence Kirwin, William Little, Mark Briggs and three brothers — Alexander, John and Archibald Baxter. All were classed as 'defiant objectors' except David Gray, who appears to have been included in error. Trentham commander Colonel H. R. Potter took this action on his own initiative, apparently to clear accommodation at Trentham before the *Waitemata* departed and from a wish to dispose of men he regarded as wasters.

A letter sent to General George Richardson in Britain, under whose authority the men would soon fall, shows the ad hoc nature of the scheme: 'if we retain in New Zealand these people who manufacture conscientious objection, the practice would so grow that it would get beyond our control. How you will deal with them is left to your discretion, but I hope you will realise that they are all men who have been given opportunities here, have refused orders, and have proved particularly troublesome.'[181] Richardson decided on a regimen intended to inculcate military discipline and noted that continued defiance would see the men separated, court-martialled, awarded detention, sent to France 'at the first available opportunity', given field punishments, sent to their units, given further field punishments, and then sent into the trenches 'even if they had to be carried on stretchers'. He believed that 'if this system were adopted it would cure them and save a lot of future trouble'.[182]

This was effectively the policy carried out in an episode that played out into 1918.[183] After the men reached Britain, they were placed in solitary confinement in Sling Camp, handcuffed for extended periods and placed on a bread and water diet. Penwright, Adin and Sanderson agreed to take on military work and Gray was also permitted to remain at Sling, but the other 10 were sent to France in October. They were warned that disobedience would result in execution by firing squad, but this was a bluff: Godley had stated that the creation of martyrs would be 'the very worst thing that could possibly happen'.[184] Harland, John Baxter, Maguire and Kirwin submitted and the remaining six men were subjected to increased intimidation. Ballantyne, Little and Alexander Baxter were court-martialled and given death sentences, which were commuted at the last minute to two years' hard labour to be served at No. 10 military prison, Dunkirk. Faced with the harsh conditions there, they eventually agreed to stretcher-bearing.

The remaining three objectors, Patton, Briggs and Archibald Baxter, were sent to the front in late November, to be joined by Kirwin, who had recanted. Here, after refusing orders, they were sentenced to No. 1 field punishment. This involved a man being bound to a pole, with his hands tied behind his back, for a fixed period.[185] The method of tying, however, could make the experience torturous, and Baxter claimed that when he was taken down his hands were 'always black with congested blood'.[186] On 1 January 1918 Patton agreed to take on non-combative work. In March the three remaining objectors were sent to the trenches, where less official measures were deployed. When Briggs would not march he was dragged by a piece of cable wire, which tore his back open. He was hospitalised and then sent back to New Zealand. In consequence of Briggs' treatment, Kirwin agreed to become a stretcher-bearer.

Baxter, the last of the 14, endured beatings, was denied food, and appears to have been deliberately sent to a part of the line under bombardment. Suffering from physical and mental exhaustion, he collapsed at the end of March and, after a period of hospitalisation, was shipped to New Zealand, arriving in August 1918, almost a year after the experiment began.

Although a message was smuggled off the *Waitemata* before the objectors departed and was reported in the *Maoriland Worker* soon after, public awareness of these events remained semi-obscured for some time.[187] Sympathetic activists, often from unions and pacifist groups, began writing campaigns in support of objectors and attended appeal board hearings.[188] Allen may have expected letters from the United Federation of Labour and the National Peace Council, but he also began receiving entreaties from bishops, the Christchurch Ministers' Association and the WCTU, questioning the transportation of the 14 men or protesting it as un-British.[189]

Still, other commentators declared they held no sympathy for men they described as shirkers: 'The average conscientious objector of our acquaintance is a bilious youth to which a free ocean voyage should come as a pick me up of the highest value . . . we should have imagined that any ordinary, sensible and loyal citizen would be only too glad to see the back of a degenerate offspring, who, soured by I.W.W. sedition, refused to do his duty to his country.'[190]

Somewhat in the dark, and seeking information on a policy he had not enacted, Allen now had to decide whether the initiative should be defended and/or continued; in October 1917 the Trentham commandant had another batch of 29 'defiant' objectors ready to be sent away.[191] Allen delayed, wanting to know about the status of the men already transported. In November, letters written to relatives and subsequently detailed in newspapers were giving the public some idea of the objectors' treatment thus far, noting forced dressing and punishments and that men were being taken to France. When Allen received a report about the degree of resistance encountered he decided to restrict future transportation of objectors to those not refusing military service; nearly 100 were subsequently sent.[192]

On 7 November 1917, a deteriorating situation in Russia came to a head. In the 'October Revolution', Vladimir Lenin's revolutionary Bolshevik Party launched an armed insurrection against the increasingly isolated Provisional Government and seized power in Petrograd while Kerensky fled into exile. This act signalled the beginning of the end of the war on the Eastern Front and the beginning of a civil war that would continue into the 1920s, killing perhaps 10 million Russians, many times more than the 1.7 million who died between 1914 and 1917.[193] Bolshevik rule also saw the rise of a totalitarian project which brought the deaths of further millions subjected to its power.

The episode became a subject of intense interest in New Zealand politics as the Bolsheviks claimed to be leading a global revolution. For many, and anti-socialist conservatives in particular, the Bolsheviks seemed to perfectly embody a radical threat to the civil, political and economic order. 'Bolshies' increasingly trumped the IWW 'Wobblies' and the 'Red Feds' for the chief position within conservative demonology. As with German atrocities in Belgium, plentiful reports — real, exaggerated and fictional — of the 'Red Terror' campaign focused on barbaric breaches of civilised restraints and the slide into chaos. These included plundering private property; the despoliation of churches and other hallowed heritage; the execution of the former royal family; indiscriminate massacres; victims being impaled, buried alive and having their noses and ears cut off; the emergence of deprivation and famine; and episodes of cannibalism.

Another focus was the society the Bolsheviks appeared to be building, with reports noting mass internment in concentration camps, the designing of an electric guillotine that could decapitate 500 people simultaneously, the abolition of the family and the 'nationalisation' of women in a bureau of free love. Early in 1918 a report summarised that the situation in Russia was 'worse than in the darkest time of the old regime'.[194]

The labour movement faced another division over the situation in Russia.[195] Many moderates broadly accepted accounts of atrocities and denounced those who associated labour with the Bolsheviks. Christchurch city councillor Dan Sullivan, for example, noted that Bolshevism was held to mean 'murder, anarchy and pillage and it is abominable that people in respectable positions should accuse the Labour Party of sympathising with these things'.[196] MP John Paul noted that Bolshevism had become 'the bogey-man of the hour', which flowed off the tongue with the same ease as 'I.W.W.' or 'Red Fed', and damned Labour's enemies for attempting to 'fasten this term on to New Zealand labour': 'Our opponents know very well that the people of this country read the newspapers, and they are told of the crimes committed by the Bolsheviks . . . These critics know very well that if they can use that criticism in connection with the New Zealand leaders of labour it must retard and hurt the future growth of the Labour party, and that is the reason why this method of criticism is indulged in.'[197]

However, there was also scepticism about the news from Russia, with voices from the left — moderate and radical — arguing that they were not receiving the whole truth. Noting that 'revolutions are generally accompanied by bloodshed', unionist Tom Bloodworth thought the press wrong 'for saying that the Bolsheviks have given Russia nothing but crime, anarchy, and chaos. Russia had all those in abundance long before we heard of the Bolsheviks.' When 'the full truth of the matter' was known, he argued, it would be clear that the Bolsheviks had made 'noble efforts' to wipe out previous evils, and 'then we shall marvel not that they made some mistakes, but that they made so few'.[198]

In mid-1918 Peter Fraser thought the press reports were biased and 'at present there is no means of knowing with absolute certainty what the exact condition of Russia is'. 'On the one hand,' he pointed out, 'we have from the interventionist camp stories of incompetency, chaos, anarchy, starvation, rapine, bloodshed, and . . . great natural resources lying unexploited by international capitalists.' On the other were reports that 'while disorder is still prevalent in many parts, owing to the struggle of the adherents of Tsardom and autocracy against the revolution, and owing to the unscrupulous machinations of German militarism, vast and unprecedented improvements have already been made in the social life of Russia'. Fraser resolved that 'there is sufficient material available to justify the conclusion that things in

Transported objectors being forced into uniforms. The man in the front centre having his shirt buttoned is Thomas Harland. Behind him (facing away from the camera) is Garth Ballantyne. Sitting to the left is David Gray. ARCHIVES NEW ZEALAND, R22429763

Russia are not nearly so bad as they are painted by the enemies of the Bolsheviks, and not nearly so good as their friends would desire'.[199]

Radical members in the Labour Party also did much to aid red-baiters in associating Labour and Bolshevism with comments that more than suggested approval of the Bolshevik project, or their sense of what that was. Holland, for example, told a Wellington meeting that the Bolsheviks were the leading example of standing true to working-class principles and had created 'the keenest democracy that had ever been established in the world'.[200] Fraser described the effort of the Bolsheviks to overthrow 'the bloodiest autocracy the world has ever known', and to establish 'the foundations of a . . . civilisation and social justice such as the world has hitherto only known in the dreaming of its thinkers', as 'a marvellous achievement'.[201]

By December, the Bolsheviks had initiated armistice proceedings with Berlin, clearly signalling an intent to exit the war. This revived the fears raised during the February Revolution that Tsarist Russia might abandon the Allies, leaving them to face a Germany better able to concentrate its strength. However, the Russian exit was now being organised not by like-minded autocrats but rather by German militarists and revolutionary socialists. Negotiations at Brest-Litvosk occurred as Russian resistance collapsed and as Germany used its regional dominance to leverage enormous concessions which appeared to destine Russia, as one commentator put it, to become a 'mere appanage of Germany'. For those committed to the war this development was a clear warning of the consequences of a German peace: 'The Kaiser proclaims that everyone wants peace. True, but not the peace he has in view, and not any peace that can be evolved in such a farce as the Brest-Litvosk conference.'[202]

On 3 March 1918, the Treaty of Brest-Litosvk ended Russia's participation in the conflict and determined a new political order across a swath of Eastern Europe. Under the treaty's terms, Russia ceded 34 per cent of its population, 32 per cent of its agricultural land, 54 per cent of its industry and 89 per cent of its coal mines.[203] New Zealand commentators regarded the treaty as a signal of the nature of German ambitions. Russians, said the *Auckland Star*, have 'awakened to the appalling truth that the acceptance of a "German peace" has condemned their country to dismemberment and servitude'.[204]

It was known that the German government had provided financial support to the Bolsheviks in an effort to destabilise Russia. This fact was added to the anti-Bolshevik case, with the revolutionaries denounced as useful idiots for German ambitions: 'The Brest-Litvosk treaty furnished the evidence of Germany's designs and Lenin's treachery . . . The Bolsheviks, though helped by German gold and German organisers, have not succeeded as they imagined.'[205]

In the first weeks of December 1917, British troops captured Jerusalem from the Ottoman Turks. It was received as good news in what had become a period of setback and tension for the Allies. The historical and religious significance gave the city added importance. The victorious soldiers were described as 'the New Crusaders', and Massey, the British Israelist, cast the taking of the city as adding to British prestige, if not destiny: 'the capture of Jerusalem is one of the great events of the war. May the Holy City now and for always remain under British control and so be part of a nation whose Sovereign is descended from David's Royal House.'[206]

A smaller wartime epic broke around the same time, though far removed from the changing balance of power in the Middle East and hardly adding to British prestige. On 13 December, Felix von Luckner, the former captain of the SMS *Seeadler*, and 10 other internees escaped from Motuihe Island by stealing the commandant's motor boat. In a further act of audacity, von Luckner managed to appropriate the commandant's sword and even had his photo taken while escaping. Using handmade nautical instruments and a map copied from a school atlas, the escapees set a course for the Mercury Islands, where they intended to capture an ocean-going vessel capable of reaching South America.[207]

After seizing the scow *Moa*, which was en route from Auckland to Tauranga, von Luckner headed for the Kermadec Islands, planning to resupply from emergency stores maintained there. He was, however, intercepted on 21 December, and imprisoned for the duration of the war. The incompetence that facilitated his escape attracted serious criticism of the Defence Department and an official inquiry was called. As Allen wrote to Godley at the end of January 1918, the Motuihe commandant was being court-martialled and he 'failed to see how he can escape getting into serious trouble over the matter'. In von Luckner's own words, 'You left the door open, you cannot blame me for walking out.'[208]

Massey's New Year message, printed in newspapers throughout the country, claimed that 1917 would be remembered as 'one of the most eventful which the British people have ever experienced' as they took 'the leading part in a struggle which dwarfs into insignificance all the wars in which at any time they have been engaged'.

> There have been times when victory appeared to be almost in sight; there have been other times when the very foundations of the Empire seemed to be shaken. They have seen one of their most powerful Allies broken by internal dissensions and cease to be a factor of any importance in carrying on the war. They have seen another nation, a people kindred to themselves, take up arms and make the necessary preparations for coming into the war, and for what may still be a protracted contest. They have seen British troops take possession of Jerusalem — the Sacred City — and the Cross once again triumphant over the Crescent.

Predicting that 1918 would prove decisive, he urged continued commitment: 'We know there is only one course to follow, and that is to carry on until victory comes — to carry on as British citizens, not in any half-hearted manner, but with a strong and steadfast determination which will overcome all difficulties and remove all obstacles to our progress.' He touched on controversies over the handling of conscientious objectors and calls for a negotiated peace: 'We know perfectly well that within our Imperial gates we have a proportion of pacifists and anti-militarists and others whose national sympathies are doubtful; some of them dangerous, some harmless, but all of them people who in a time like this are a hindrance rather than of any service. Such people have to be taken care of, and, if necessary, dealt with by a strong hand . . .'

He also warned that 'unless this war is fought to a finish and Germany is forced to acknowledge defeat it will be a victory for the Central Powers, and any peace that may be arranged will be temporary rather than permanent, lasting only long enough to allow Germany time to renew her strength and prepare to attack the liberty-loving nations of the world again. That is what we are up against, and in our inmost souls we know it.'[209]

SOLDIERS' CLUB.
TE. IKA. A. MAUI
Swimming Sports

CHAPTER TWELVE

ENDURANCE

previous pages
Part of the procession in Palmerston North's 'Final Battle Campaign for Sick and Wounded Soldiers' fundraiser, outside the Soldier's Club on the corner of Cuba and George streets. This fundraiser ran for around four weeks in early 1918 and raised nearly £20,000.
MANAWATŪ HERITAGE, 2007N_CHAR7_WAR_0019

The crises of the previous year lingered in early 1918. The failure to strike a decisive blow brought disenchantment, while Germany, having won the war in the east, instigated a series of critical offensives on the Western Front. In the first, which began on 21 March, German troops broke through the British line, captured hundreds of guns and, in a few days, made easily the greatest advance in the west since the first six weeks of the war.[1] By the end of May, German soldiers stood on the banks of the Marne River, not far from Paris. The strained mood in New Zealand fuelled demands that the country must do more as well as grumbling that it had done enough. This atmosphere informed the ongoing debates on the conscription of the second division and Waikato Māori, sectarian feuding and objectors. It also coloured a series of by-elections in 1918.

The first of these, in February, was triggered by the retirement of Alexander Herdman, the Reform member for Wellington North, to take a position on the Supreme Court. The government endorsed Wellington mayor John Pearce Luke, widely known as 'Peanut', after his diminutive stature, for the safely conservative seat. Holland, who had stood as the Social Democratic Party candidate in the electorate in 1914, was selected to stand for Labour. Fraser, who had been released from prison on 22 December, was his campaign organiser.[2] Alfred Brandon, a former Wellington mayor, and Angus Polson stood, respectively, as Liberal and an Independent Liberal, and threatened to split the vote.

The war was a central issue in what has been described as a 'frontal conflict between Massey and Holland'.[3] Holland opened his campaign by dubbing himself the 'Crown Prosecutor' against the government, saying he would call for its death sentence, if it would not be 'a waste of good hemp'. Labour challenged the government on conscription, which 'jettisoned Christ, and enthroned Mars' and which, he claimed, the people had never supported. Labour also challenged the government on 'withholding information about their war policy, on their War Regulations and the administration of them, on their treatment of the soldiers after they returned to New Zealand, on their policy with regard to conscientious objectors, on their muddled finance, on their ineptitude with regard to the increasing cost of living, and on their using the war to hold down wages while prices were rising all the time'.[4]

Massey warned the electors of Wellington North of potential chaos. He cited the Russian situation, Australia's shunning of conscription in a second referendum in December 1917, disaffection in Ireland and sedition in India as 'influences which, if they were sufficiently powerful, would wreck the Empire. It is our duty to guard against them, and to put them down at every possible opportunity.' He asked the electors 'not to play Germany's game by vote-splitting, but to make sure of the return of a candidate who will be loyal to those principles which British citizens hold sacred and dearer even than life itself'.[5]

The growing awareness of the fate of the 14 objectors sent abroad was also a notable touchstone. Holland publicised the case in the *Maoriland Worker* and condemned the government's failure to take a more liberal view of conscience:

> For the first three centuries of the Christian era the Christians generally held similar views to those held by the Christian conscientious objectors of today and the ruler of that period took the same view that Mr. Massey and his Government take to-day. Then the conscience men (and women) were flung to the lions or nailed to the cross. Mr. Massey makes a law which refuses to the Catholic, the Anglican, the Presbyterian, the Methodist, the Salvationist, or the Socialist, the right to hold a conscientious objection to military service; and, having made his law, he then pronounces its victims 'conscienceless'.[6]

Allen's riposte was that the transported objectors were not 'conscientious objectors' as understood under the law: rather, they had refused orders and were considered to be soldiers undergoing punishment. He claimed that forced dressing was a consequence of a refusal to cooperate. 'If responsible authority is to knuckle under to insubordination the whole fabric of the British Empire would crumble into chaos.' Moreover, he claimed, the method was achieving results, since all but Briggs and Baxter had agreed to serve.[7]

Massey agreed, arguing that the government was simply performing its duty to uphold the law and that the 14 men were 'soldiers of the Expeditionary Force who have been called up with their fellow citizens by ballot to take their share in the defence of the country of whose privileges and protection they have taken full advantage'.[8] He also quoted extracts from a letter purporting to be from the parent of an objector 'whose conscience only developed after his appeal on all other grounds had failed':

> I'm sick of the Union Jack. For thirty years it has been bloodsoaked without cessation. We English are played out. There's no good in us. We are a set of brutal thieves . . . By heaven, the whole country is rotten — absolutely rotten . . . The idea of fighting for such filth makes one sick . . . Wriggle out if possible, and don't be particular. Once you get away from them you can manage till we can leave them to the Japs; May the Japs mutilate every cursed man and rape every woman.[9]

Claims that the treatment of the 14 was judicious and effective left some unconvinced. On 3 February 1918 activist Sarah Saunders Page delivered a speech in Christchurch's Victoria Square:

> I am not accepting the report of the men's conversion as necessarily true. Sir James Allen has made — mistakes, shall we call them — before, and this report, unfortunately offers no reliable evidence that our brave lads are not still suffering the tortures of the damned, but let us for the moment accept it — and out of their own mouths condemn them. Do you realise what this report means? Twelve men bludgeoned into violating their consciences, and you and I and the rest of New Zealand silently acquiescing.[10]

On 28 February, a crowd gathered outside the *Evening Post* building in Wellington to hear the poll results. Thanks to the absence of so many men, over 1000 fewer votes had been cast than in 1914. Luke won with 42 per cent of the vote, followed by Holland (36 per cent), Brandon (11 per cent) and Polson (10 per cent). The narrowness of Luke's victory — a mere 420 votes separated him from Holland — and the surge in Labour's share of the vote, which had more than doubled from 15 per cent, rattled Reform supporters. The *Dominion* attributed the result to the unpopularity of all wartime governments and the *New Zealand Herald* insinuated that the Labour Party had arranged to cram workers into boarding houses to entitle them to enrolment.[11] Fraser had certainly proved himself a savvy organiser. As well as claiming to have added 1000 names to the roll, he made an institution of street-corner meetings, used the *Maoriland Worker* effectively and sent canvassers door to door.[12]

A boisterous element at the victory event reflected the ugly mood stewing in 1918. Luke was booed and Massey's appearance was 'the signal for the utmost uproar', as he was 'assailed with missiles varying from crumbs of bread to oranges, lemons and eggs'. A witness noted that one egg narrowly missed the prime minister, striking a bystander, but he 'got the full benefit of a banana skin right on the forehead'. Turning to the reporters, he remarked, 'They take their licking badly',[13] and before departing thumbed his nose at the crowd. A cartoon depicting the event was much reproduced in Labour circles in subsequent years.[14]

On 20 March 1918, came cable news that the expected German attack in the west appeared to have been delayed, and that German artillery had failed to gain ascendancy over British gunnery.[15] Within hours, however, the first of Germany's Spring Offensives began with a barrage of some 3.2 million shells. On 30 March, Massey told the British that 'though the furthest of the Dominions from the scene of operations — and one of the smallest — in this hour of the nation's trial New Zealand is heart and soul with Britain and the other dependencies of the Crown'.[16] Days later Massey would feel the impact personally when he received word that his son had been seriously wounded by a bullet to the chest.[17]

The rapid German advance over the following weeks was the focus of intense attention. Cabinet was described as 'watching carefully almost hour by hour for news'; some despaired that 'the darkest hour of the war' had arrived and that 'absolute defeat seemed probable'.[18] In June, Allen also privately observed that many around him found it 'disturbing that the [German] success has been so great', and that word of the British retreat had raised questions about the fighting spirit of the British: many were said to readily run or surrender.[19] Declaring that 'the fate of the Empire may be trembling in the balance', Massey suggested that New Zealand might have to follow Britain's lead in raising the maximum age of military service.[20] Others were more hopeful, considering Germany's move a gamble. A verse, titled 'The Challenge Accepted', appeared on the front page of *Truth* on 6 April:

> In blood-thirsty fashion
> The Germ-huns now smash on,
> Attempting our armies to break.
> Their great drive has started,
> But 'are we downhearted?'
> Our 'NO' makes the universe shake.
>
> Near four years our fighters
> Have hammered the biighters [sic],
> Invariably giving 'em hell.
> To back our contention,
> Permit us to mention
> Mons, Somme, The Marne, Neuve Chapelle.
>
> So while they attack us,
> Attempting to hack us
> Right clean off the face of the map.
> We give 'neath the pressure
> (Exacting full measure
> Of casualties every lap).
>
> In manner elastic,
> Our tactics are plastic,
> Our motto is 'Bend, but not Break.'
> Till, when they're exhausted,
> Well-winded and worsted,
> A turn at attacking we'll take.[21]

In recognition of the critical period the war had entered, and in a notable reverse of the pattern of previous months, New Zealand's infantry reinforcements rates were doubled, on 6 April, from 800 to 1600 per draft. Also, four reinforcement drafts were dispatched early, the use of New Zealand troops stationed in Britain was authorised and Cabinet approved the formation of a New Zealand tank battalion, though this never eventuated.[22] By October the 7000 NZEF reinforcements in Britain at the beginning of 1918 would become 15,000 across Britain and France.[23]

On 2 May, in the midst of this changing situation, Massey and Ward departed for another meeting of the Imperial War Cabinet in London. Allen was again made acting prime minister. This second meeting had been approved the previous November and was set for June 1918 to suit the schedules of those involved. Because of the U-boat threat, the leaders' wives remained at home. Travelling via the United States, Ward and Massey arrived in London on 7 June.

In April another by-election was announced, this time in Grey, where the seat had been left vacant by Paddy Webb's arrest. After being balloted for military service the previous October, he had appealed to a Military Service Board, but his rejection of a non-combatant role resulted in his arrest on 11 March. When he refused to wear a uniform, he was court-martialled, sentenced to two years' imprisonment and sent to a tree-planting camp in Kāingaroa.[24]

With Webb's blessing, Holland chose to stand and headed for the West Coast to contest the election, set for 29 May. Once again Fraser was on hand to help organise the campaign. Thomas Coates, a former mayor of Greymouth, stood as an independent candidate. Suspecting that endorsement might aid Holland, the government decided to distance itself from Coates, though some Labourites suspected Coates had government backing nonetheless.[25] James Kerr was originally slated as a Liberal candidate but withdrew to prevent potential vote-splitting. Even more than Wellington North, this by-election promised to be a showdown over the social impacts of the war, with Holland repeating his arguments about the enthronement of Mars, and Coates declaring himself a pro-conscription 'win the war' candidate.[26]

Although conscription was a major issue, there was some deviation from party lines; many prominent Labour supporters with enlisted sons ardently supported Coates. Conversely, many traditionally Reform and Liberal voters in the second division evidently regarded Holland as a better means by which to protest their dissatisfaction.[27] Coates proclaimed himself a trenchant critic of the government's domestic agenda, announcing that he would push for more favourable railways and land policies and, in a nod to second division electors, declaring that all single men must be sent before husbands and fathers.[28]

The 'austere Holland', lacking Webb's gregarious character, 'was not completely at home with his West Coast audiences, accustomed to ready warmth and bluff geniality'.[29] His opponents and critics readily exploited his outsider status in an often clannish community; the *Greymouth Star*, for example, denounced him as 'an absolutely rank outsider'. But the *Grey River Argus* vouched for him, printing letters from both Holland and Webb and reminding readers that 'every vote for Holland is a vote for Webb'. Holland also benefited from his support of Irish independence. The *Green Ray* endorsed him: 'We sincerely hope that every man and woman of Irish blood, irrespective of class or creed, shall unite in returning the labour candidate for Grey . . . [and] give the militarist, capitalist and shoneen [a pejorative for Irish Anglophiles] cliques a smashing defeat.'[30] In Allen's later assessment, the Irish situation significantly assisted Holland's campaign.[31]

Holland secured a narrow victory, with 51 per cent of the vote. This was a significant decrease on Webb's large majority, of 980 to just over 200 votes, and the turnout was down, seemingly because the Liberal voters who had previously supported Webb stayed home.[32]

This photograph, taken from Paddy Webb's album, is captioned: 'on way to Kaingaroa'. Webb spent two years there planting trees.
ALEXANDER TURNBULL LIBRARY, PA1-O-646

Holland was delighted with the result: 'the whole Labor movement is agreed that the victory is the greatest ever won by Labor in New Zealand — because it was the first time that Labor had ever succeeded in defeating the Tories & Liberals in a straight out fight'.[33] He also proclaimed his election a condemnation of the government and conscription, though the cost of living and profiteering were more likely the decisive issues. Regardless, one of the government's most trenchant and committed critics now had a seat in Parliament.

To free up accommodation in training camps and civilian prisons, and in line with its belief that defiant objectors could be converted into soldiers, in March 1918 the Defence Department decided to send men serving initial sentences to the Whanganui detention barracks, used to punish soldiers found guilty of disobedience and other disciplinary offences. The first men arrived on 8 April and found themselves under the authority of the commanding officer, Lieutenant J. L. Crampton. Thoroughly embodying the notion that a sufficient application of discipline and the removal of choice would make soldiers of 'shirkers', Crampton informed his new charges that they would be 'broken in by main force'.[34] Days later he was reporting that all but three of his charges were now willing to accept service and he subsequently requested more objectors, pledging they would be 'disciplined and ready within a month to embark for service abroad'.[35]

In late May, however, a letter from Harry Wilson, and signed by other Whanganui inmates, was put before Holland and, subsequently, various newspaper editors. It claimed that Crampton was forcing men to wear uniforms and subjecting them to severe physical and psychological abuse. 'If these outrages were perpetrated by Germans,' Wilson noted, 'they would be condemned as brutal atrocities: but . . . I am sure the people of New Zealand do not know what is going on in Wanganui, and it is up to those of us that do know to expose it as much as possible and also demand an enquiry into the treatment of Objectors in that hell, otherwise they will go just a little too far one of these days and kill somebody.'[36]

When Allen was contacted about the allegations, the press was asked to delay publication to allow for an investigation. In mid-June a departmental court of inquiry confirmed the use of some force, though nothing like the amount alleged. Not satisfied, on 19 June, Allen commissioned an inquiry headed by magistrate J. G. Hewitt. Although this was to be held in camera, several newspapers broke the story and reported 'serious allegations of ill-treatment'.[37] In early July, *Truth* printed more specific details of Wilson's letter, painting a picture of brutal sadism. One objector, for example, was reported to have been 'forcibly dressed in denims, handcuffed and then dragged round the yard by means of pull through ropes, round his neck, which nearly choked him. He was kicked and punched at the same time, and also pushed against the wall with sickening thuds, until his face on both sides was like a piece of raw steak and drops of blood were to be seen all round the yard and also on the walls.'[38]

There were similar accounts of sanctioned beatings of objectors at Featherston Camp and further controversy concerning Archibald Baxter; in early May copies of a letter he had posted to his parents in March were circulated in sympathetic circles. They were printed in several papers by June.[39] Baxter wrote that he had been sentenced to No. 1 field punishment, that he was about to be sent into the lines, and that although he had suffered 'to the limit of my endurance' he was resolute: 'If you hear that I have served in the Army or that I have taken my own life, do not believe that I did it in my sound mind. I never will.'[40] Many copies were circulated alongside an official communication, dated 14 May, to Baxter's father noting that Archibald had been admitted to hospital with a mental condition, leaving readers to draw the conclusion that he had been tormented into insanity.[41]

These cases brought renewed protests from labour, pacifist, church and women's groups.[42] Again, however, many others stated they had no sympathy for 'shirkers' and sometimes openly supported harsh treatment: 'One observes in reading Sir James Allen's official reply to the ladies who hate to have C.O.s disciplined (but who weekly read casualty lists of soldiers who have suffered Hell for them), that the official mind and heart are hardening against all frauds.'[43] The Defence Department considered the allegations about Baxter to be exaggerated but, as with the Whanganui inquiry, sought further details. An August request noted it was desirable to know 'what degree of mental derangement the man is suffering from as this will affect the nature of the public statements the Minister must make'.[44]

Actions taken against several prominent peace activists added to the tension. Egerton Gill, who had recently been fined £20 for publishing a pamphlet regarded as discouraging military training, was balloted for military service on 3 May.[45] He entered an unsuccessful appeal, on conscience grounds, was deemed 'insincere' and sent to Mount Eden Prison with a nine-month sentence, despite the magistrate's comments that he was 'reluctant' to convict Gill as there was no doubt of his honesty of purpose. He was permitted a light in his cell so that he could study until 9 p.m.[46] Harry Urquhart, recently released from his sentence, was also balloted in May. When he refused to submit to a medical examination, he was court-martialled and sentenced to another 11 months' imprisonment. He spent much of this time growing strawberries in Waikeria Prison.[47]

Other Freedom League members were also jailed for sedition or objection. By mid-1918 attendance at meetings averaged only seven, and in October they were suspended unless something important occurred. James Chapple, having returned from the United States, was charged with sedition in May, owing to speeches in which he claimed that those who fought went 'to die for the profiteer', that the churches were acting as 'the recruiting agent for the world's greatest tragedies' and that 'If Jesus Christ was now on earth he would be tried for sedition'. At a second lecture, entitled 'the glorious Bolsheviks of Russia', Chapple said the Bolsheviks were being misrepresented in the news, praised the revolution and added, 'I hope before I die to see a similar movement in New Zealand.' In his sentencing the magistrate assessed Chapple as a 'dangerous man to be at large', noting that anyone calling for an equivalent of the chaos wrought by the Bolshevik revolution in New Zealand was mad. He was sentenced to 11 months' imprisonment.[48]

On 21 September 1918 Baxter returned to New Zealand on the hospital ship *Marama* and a specialist was sent to assess his mental state. An official report soon announced that although he was of 'a surly and morose disposition' and melancholic he was perfectly rational.

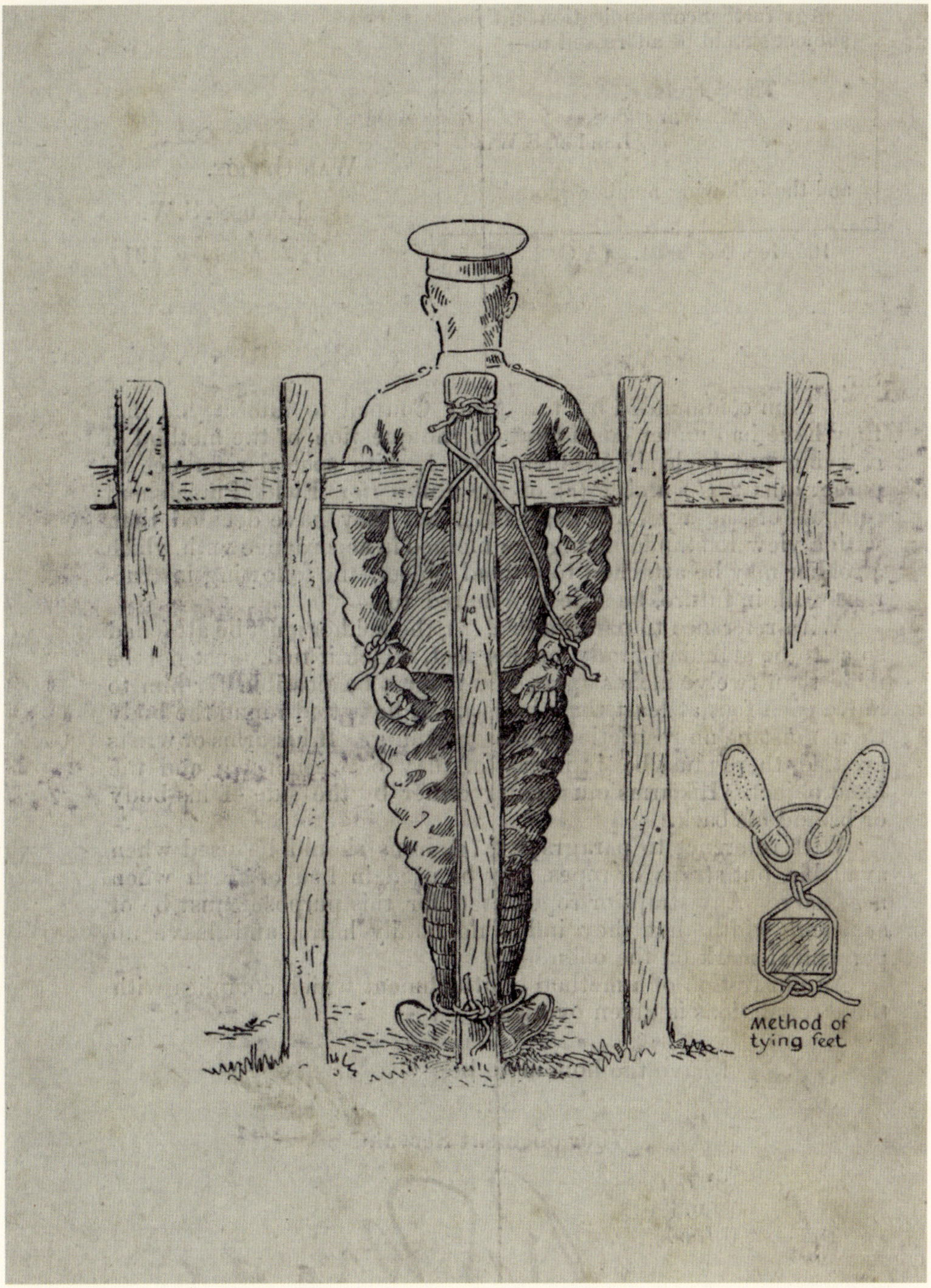

Military regulations illustrating the correct method to apply No. 1 field punishment.
ARCHIVES NEW ZEALAND, WA78 3/15

Hedging its bets, however, the report added, 'If he has suffered any disability involving mental derangement be it great or small, the disability is the natural outcome of his consistently setting up his will in opposition to the will of the community.'[49] Perhaps wanting a second opinion, Allen decided to visit Baxter himself.[50] Baxter would subsequently return to labouring in Brighton, outside Dunedin, and, decades later, wrote an account of his experiences entitled *We Will Not Cease*.[51]

On the day Baxter disembarked, Hewitt also reported to Allen that there was substance behind the Whanganui allegations and that 'severe punishment' had been used. The investigation included further testimony of the methods applied. Thomas Moynihan, for example, recounted being punched, kicked and pulled by his hair, and having his head pushed into a wall and struck by a rifle: 'the sergeant banged the barrel of it against the side of my face saying "will you hold it?" I did not answer. He banged me several times till blood was streaming down the uniform.' These accounts also presented Crampton as having a sadistic disposition; it was claimed that during beatings he said, 'Ah, the sight of blood does my eyes good', and, 'I've got power to bury you here', while having photographs taken of the proceedings.[52]

Hewitt recommended restricting the facility to military offenders, replacing the staff of the barracks and appointing civilian inspectors. The Defence Department's Adjutant-General Tate accepted the idea of inspectors and that no more objectors should be sent, citing the difficulty of distinguishing between 'conscientious' objectors, 'who should definitely not be sent to Wanganui', and 'defiant' objectors, 'for whom no treatment is too severe'. Although he generally agreed that the staff should be removed, he argued that Crampton should retain his position, noting that he had acted in a difficult situation and in the belief 'that he was within his rights'.[53] The army's director of personnel services, Major James Osborne-Lilly, argued that Crampton had committed an error of judgement in departing from the regulations for dealing with 'growsers', whom he thought had made exaggerated complaints, but that he had ultimately 'done good service at Wanganui'.[54] Hewitt's recommendations were accepted piecemeal: no more objectors were sent to Whanganui and Crampton remained in command.[55]

The Spring Offensives, the growing strength of sectarian factions and the active conscription of second division men increased the possibility of a further exacerbating situation around Catholic clergy and conscription. All this was ahead of a deepening crisis in Anglo-Irish relations in April, as Lloyd George tried to apply conscription to Ireland, offering Home Rule in exchange. The result was a unification of various nationalist factions against his government. Events escalated in May as the British government ordered the internment of the Sinn Féin leadership, alleging that they were engaged in a conspiracy to launch a German-backed insurrection in Ireland.

In New Zealand the Maoriland Irish Society passed a resolution protesting the proposed introduction of conscription in Ireland.[56] The notion of a 'German plot' was greeted with considerable scepticism and, tellingly, there was 'no repeat of the loyal protestations and denunciations of Irish political radicalism by leading New Zealand Catholics which had marked the aftermath of the 1916 Rising'.[57] Meanwhile, the PPA continued to grow and Elliott declared that married men were being made to take the places of Catholic priests because of a 'wretched bargain' which Archbishop O'Shea had 'openly thrown in Sir James's face, and defied him to alter'.

Speaking on the need to safeguard Protestant freedoms against Catholic conspiracies, Elliott promised that 'The spirit of Cromwell, which had been slumbering, was about to awake.'[58] The Irish conscription crisis only added to the climate of anxiety and restless suspicion and, in *Truth*'s judgement, the PPA took 'a wicked advantage of a nerve-wracked and anxious community'.[59] The government continued to respond cautiously, not wanting to favour or punish one denomination. Allen had already felt obliged to provide the Christchurch Ministers' Association with a detailed account of all his dealings with the Catholic hierarchy over the exemption of clergy.[60]

With sectarian tensions appearing worse than ever, Bishop Cleary continued his mission to rebuild moderate relations and interdenominational cooperation. Given his time at the front, he was well placed to reject claims that New Zealand's Catholics were disloyal to the empire or beholden to any political party — in Ireland or New Zealand. Rather they were, he asserted, being unjustly maligned by a handful of disreputable and bigoted cranks. Cleary also tried to calm or isolate Catholic militants. In mid-July 1918, he launched the measured and scholarly *Month* as a moderate rival to Kelly's *Tablet*. Behind closed doors, he continued to debate with the Catholic hierarchy to rein in Kelly's antagonism to Protestants and his association of the church with party politics and the Irish question. In response, Kelly accused Cleary of being an unpatriotic Irishman in league with the Protestant establishment.[61]

Cleary also demanded government action to suppress anti-Catholic propaganda and was soon corresponding with Allen on the matter. Unimpressed by the minister's observation that Catholic publications had produced their own sectarian propaganda, he also refuted Allen's claim that regulations permitted action only if public safety was endangered. Countering that he was 'one who is strongly out to win this war', Cleary argued that sectarian turmoil represented a clear threat to the war effort. Allen assured him that the government was considering the matter.[62] This was borne out in June, with new regulations enacted to restrict literature likely to cause religious offence, and a broad interpretation of public safety:

> Literature attacking any religious doctrine or political principle is only objectionable if the language used is outrageous in its insolence. Again, the attribution to a religious sect of objects distinct from the advancement of religion is not of itself sufficient to justify intervention by us. But the attribution of habitual immorality to classes of persons who have taken a vow of celibacy is beyond the line of permissible controversy during the war. Members of one of such classes cannot defend themselves, and the public peace and safety would be endangered if the circulation of such matter were permitted.[63]

General restrictions on literature were further strengthened in July 1918, when Cabinet acceded to the solicitor-general's earlier requests for prior restraint censorship. Martin Chapman, a well-known lawyer, was appointed to work with the attorney-general and the minister of customs as a preliminary censor. The attorney-general could now prevent the publication of any nominated periodical until it had been given official approval.[64]

Whether out of consistency or to avoid accusations of bias, the new regulations listed, among their initial targets, both the *Green Ray* and *The Black Prophet*, a book being circulated by the PPA. A growing list of anti-Catholic titles — *Convent Life Unveiled, The Vatican, the Kaiser, and the World War, Priestly Celibacy Exposed* — were also banned over subsequent months.[65]

At the request of the minister of justice, the police had been monitoring the *Green Ray* since March, and on 8 July, Dunedin detectives descended on the paper's office once its suppression had been ordered.[66] A few days later a sedition case was brought against *Green Ray* writer Thomas Cummins and publisher Albert Ryan (sometimes O'Ryan) for a May article praising the martyrs of the Easter Rising, though the presiding judge noted that it 'seemed to him that on every page there was a seditious utterance'.[67]

When an appeal for defence funds for the case described the Easter Rising's leaders as 'a gallant band of heroes', David Griffin and John Troy, respectively the president and the secretary of the Wellington Maoriland Irish Society, were also charged.[68] Indicative of the Labour Party's increasing interest in Irish issues, the *Maoriland Worker* helped to raise money. Kelly declared that Irishmen would not forget this.[69] On 24 July, in a packed courtroom where 'on more than one occasion those whose sympathies apparently lay with the accused, gave vent to them by applauding, and by stamping their feet', and after defence lawyer B. J. Dolan's two-and-a-half-hour speech, which 'manifested a knowledge of Irish history which was doubtless envied by many of his countrymen present', Cummins and Ryan were each sentenced to 11 months' imprisonment, with hard labour.[70]

Although the destabilising and protracted conflict continued to fuel sectarian angst, the reassertion of moderates and strengthened censorship pushed back against militancy. As one historian has noted, 'the thought of suppression, whether by the authorities of Church or State, was a restraining influence on Kelly'.[71] However, a greater restoration of domestic harmony appeared impossible while the war, and the volatile politics that came with it, continued.

On Monday, 29 April, the Christchurch and North Canterbury drafts of the Forty-first Reinforcements were marshalled. Among them, for the first time, were balloted members of the second division — married men without children.[72] The previous evening, the Second Division League had passed a resolution that 'the first line of the Second Division shall not be broken and no Second Division man shall leave for camp until the demands of the League are acceded to'. On the morning of 29 April the *Press* gave a lengthy account of that meeting, followed by a letter from the league's Christchurch branch president, Maurice Gresson, announcing his resignation; he could not agree with the threat to refuse to mobilise.[73]

That morning the league's executive and local MPs met for a conference. Harry Ell, the Liberal MP for Christchurch South, had not attended the Sunday night meeting 'because he did not think any good purpose would be served', and he would not, 'either directly or indirectly', be party 'to a counsel of revolt as a means to gain what you are after'. George Witty, the Liberal MP for Riccarton, supported fair allowances for dependants but counselled the league not to prevent any men going to the barracks that night.

At 1 p.m., MPs Witty, Ell, James McCombs and Henry Thacker sent a telegram to Allen: 'very strong and anxious feeling here among Second Division men about the allowances to wives and children. Kindly state definitely, and make public, what Cabinet intends to do in regard to allowances to soldiers' dependants.'[74] Allen's response, which came through late that night, explained that the matter had been 'finally disposed of in Cabinet today'.[75] The new rate increased the separation allowance for a soldier's child to 1s 6d (up from 1s) per child per day, offered additional provisions for widowed mothers and extended government support for life insurance policies.[76] The *Evening Post* considered these further concessions made the New Zealand soldier 'the envy of all others who fight under less paternal Governments' and hoped that the league would now 'cease making further exorbitant demands'.[77]

But all this came too late for Christchurch, which was, according to *Truth*, 'agog with excitement'.[78] Towards 3.30 p.m., when the draft was scheduled to assemble at the King Edward Barracks, the footpaths of Cashel Street 'were congested for the distance of a quarter of a mile or more'. 'Women were everywhere,' wrote the *Truth* reporter. 'In fact, the whole of the crowd seemed to consist of women . . .' On all sides he heard 'the query "Do you think they will go?" And the chorus of "Leave it to us." The day was beautifully fine, and the atmosphere was electric. In that array of five thousand women were all the elements of a raging storm.' Many pushed into the barracks and surged past the rope that marked off the area set aside for the roll-call of the departing soldiers. As the roll was called the mood darkened: 'the mob, thinking it had full control of the situation, vented its feelings in full-blooded hoots whilst the feminine portion spoke its opinion of the Defence staff officers present in very uncomplimentary terms'.

Events quickly escalated as the authorities attempted to carry on and keep to the transport schedule. When the 28 men of the North Canterbury draft marched outside, accompanied by women shouting 'Don't go!', pandemonium broke out as police struggled to clear the area. There was a 'particularly exciting bout' between a returned soldier and a burly opponent; a policeman trying to detain an 'unduly obstreperous' youth in knickerbockers was promptly attacked by a woman armed with an umbrella; a young man assaulted a policeman and when an attempt was made to arrest him the crowd rushed to his rescue and the arresting officers had 'a distinctly bad quarter of an hour'. Fists were raised and threats shouted at the mayor, who was spied on the balcony from which the farewell speech was customarily given. A mounted policeman appeared and for a moment seemed to consider riding into the crowd, but he evidently reconsidered and disappeared, 'much to the relief of many of the spectators'. By five o'clock, things had quietened down and the building was cleared, but in the chaos it seemed that some 50 of the approximately 140 men due to depart had not left for the railway station to head to Lyttelton.

This episode, described by the Christchurch mayor as 'a disgraceful exhibition', vividly demonstrated how politicised and radicalised the second division question had become since the expressed goodwill of early 1917. The immediate disruptions were temporary, however, and by 1 May only 18 men in the Christchurch draft, only six of whom were second division, were unaccounted for.[79] And, as one historian notes, there were not enough second division men 'in any given reinforcement to create much impact. Conscription was safe.'[80]

Efforts to isolate radical dissent and re-engage social commitment to the war were soon employed. In Christchurch, the mood after 29 April was volatile. The following day a speaker at a Christchurch women's meeting demanding better treatment for soldiers' dependants declared, 'There is a strong undercurrent of feeling. It requires only you to set a match to the flame.'[81] Christchurch North MP Leonard Isitt, writing to Allen, also on the 30th, warned the minister that 'we are on the edge of very serious trouble'.[82] A *Press* editorial on 3 May appealed for tough measures, proclaiming that 'the Bolsheviks must not be allowed to bring the rest of the city into disgrace. We call upon the Government to take vigorous steps to put down anything in the shape of sedition.'[83]

As it was, the only identifiable targets were those who, at the 28 April meeting, had written, proposed and seconded the motion not to comply with conscription unless the league's demands were met. Consequently, on 8 May, John Flood, Ernest Langley and Hiram Hunter were found guilty of sedition, with Flood and Langley sentenced to six months' imprisonment and Hunter to three. However, on 21 May, as part of an effort to mend industrial relations, a Cabinet meeting voted to suspend these sentences in exchange for promises of good behaviour.[84]

On 9 May, the *Free Lance* felt it was 'quite clear that the "Red Feds" ever on the watch for an opportunity of fomenting contempt for and defiance of constituted authority are hoping to utilise Second Division discontent for their own revolutionary ends'. It called on the Second Division League leadership to 'weed out the skulking, shirking, disloyalist element without delay'. This process was already under way in an internal battle between radicals and loyalists within the Christchurch branch. The outcome was a national executive intervention to reconstitute the branch and elect new officers from which, as the *New Zealand Herald* put it, 'extremists are missing'.[85]

The league then recommitted itself to renewed lobbying. On 25 May it again petitioned the government for an increase in separation allowances. It also raised new proposals to stretch the first division, including reassessing exempted men under stricter criteria, removing exemptions for essential work and reorganising agriculture to 'comb out' more first division farm workers. In some districts, league branches formed committees to 'assist the military representative on the Military Service Board' and 'review the bona-fides of every exempted reservist'.[86]

By now, though, both the government and the public had a harder attitude to the second division question. Allen proved unyielding on ambitions to renegotiate allowances. On 14 May, in a letter to Massey, he considered the government had 'acted liberally. My opinion is that it is best to make a straight out statement to them that we have done all we deem it desirable to do, except that we will make an honest attempt to provide for the soldier on return who has no billet to go into during the time between his discharge and securing employment.' This became the basis of the Cabinet position announced at the end of May.[87] The league's demand for

A staged photograph, printed in the *Auckland Weekly News* and captioned 'final leave', idealises the call-up of second division men.
AUCKLAND WEEKLY NEWS, 20 JUNE 1918, P. 31

ever-tougher exemption standards for first division men was also unsympathetically received; its store of public goodwill was much reduced. This was especially the case among returned soldiers and the relatives of soldiers. Such comments as 'we object to going while there are so many exempted first division men' now drew hostile ripostes. As 'Returned Soldier' noted:

> These are the men who made an unfit single man's life scarcely worth living with jeers of 'Shirker!' and questions such as 'What did you do in the great war, daddy?' And now that the ranks of the single men are so depleted, what do we find when the time comes for the married men to help the boys in the trenches to fight their own battles? . . . It is a pity that more of the babies whom these shirkers are hiding behind are not old enough to shame their fathers by asking, 'What are you doing in the great war, daddy?'[88]

Likewise, declarations of the willingness of second division men to do their part were now mocked as cases of protesting too much, and 'another returned soldier' noted that 'the married men are willing to make great sacrifices — of other men's blood. Their wives and children are so dear to them . . . But they won't go and fight for them. They talk, they wrangle, they clamour while real men do and die.'[89] 'Mother of a married returned man' agreed: 'Why will the Second Division men haggle over a few shillings when, if they don't help crush Germany, Germany will have no hesitation in crushing them?'[90]

The absence of state and social backing and an unwillingness to take direct action slowed the league's momentum. Some acceptance of the status quo potentially drew on the high exemption rates for balloted second division men. Indeed, while 54,549 second division men were balloted between October 1917 and November 1918, exemptions meant that 68 per cent of these ballots did not translate into military service. By November 1918, only 832 second division conscripts had embarked, and they all seem to have been in England at the end of the war.[91] According to one historian, 'by luck and judgement the Government and the Second Division League had actually managed to keep all married conscripts out of the firing line. Potentially the greatest financial and social traumas of the war had been avoided.'[92] By contrast, the consequences of sending thousands of conscripted family men into combat were not hypothetical for many European belligerents.[93]

Days before the disturbance on Cashel Street, another threatened defiance of conscription was looming when, on 26 April, 209 names were drawn on the Māori roll. All the effort put into registering Māori and seeking to build cooperation was now put to the test. The result has been described as 'increasingly embarrassing and farcical': just 68 reported.[94]

A major factor was the influence of King Te Rata's elder sister, the 34-year-old Te Puea Hērangi, popularly known to Pākehā as Princess Te Puea. She had taken up a leading opposing role when registration began and emerged as a key figure of Waikato resistance when conscription was enacted.[95] Her objection to Waikato involvement in the war evoked King Tāwhiao's 1881 statement of pacifism and was accented with historical grievances over land confiscations: 'They tell us to fight for king and country,' she noted with regard to recruiting posters, 'well that's all right. We've got a king. But we haven't got a country. That's been taken off us. Let them give us back our land and then maybe we'll think about it again.'[96]

The government now faced the issue of how to handle this blatant non-compliance with the law it had enacted. Dispatching police to locate defaulters might well result in a confrontation. On 7 June, Pōmare advised Allen, 'Send one or two policemen at the very most,' and 'do not make any demonstration . . . There is plenty of time for that later if they resist.'[97] On 11 July, eight constables arrived at Te Paina, a pā Te Puea had rebuilt at Mangatāwhiri in Waikato, to apprehend balloted men. The police were formally welcomed and led to the meeting house, where around 400 people were gathered. Sergeant Waterman proceeded to explain that they were there to execute warrants but 'desired to do their duty in a friendly manner'.[98]

Stating that he would read the list of wanted men, he urged those called to come forward and asked the community to cooperate in locating any who did not comply. Te Puea then replied: 'These people are mine. My voice is their voice . . . I will not agree to my children going to shed blood. Though your words be strong, you will not move me to help you. The young men who have been balloted will not go . . . You can fight your own fight until the end.'[99] Waterman read the list and, when no one came forward, the constables sought to identify and apprehend the listed men. They were met with passive resistance; those arrested had to be carried to the waiting cars. One man, described as 'enormously fat', proved a particular trouble. 'He just lay on the ground,' said one witness. 'The police had much difficulty in carrying him to the motorcar. Of course no one would help them. We had to laugh, despite our tears.'[100] In a final exchange, Waterman thanked Te Puea and the crowd for their peaceful behaviour and stated his hope that they might cooperate in future; Te Puea promised peaceful defiance.

Unsurprisingly, this approach to finding defaulters was problematic: men were mistaken for fathers, sons and brothers, and some deliberately claimed balloted men's identities in order to travel to Auckland before the error was discovered.[101] The commandant of the Narrow Neck training camp subsequently complained that many of those sent to camp were ineligible because they had dependants or were under age.[102] Even when men were located and taken to Narrow Neck, resistance could continue as some refused uniforms.[103] Among those balloted and arrested was Te Rata's younger brother, Te Rauangaanga. Authorities attempted to cultivate his support, believing that his compliance would convince others to follow; that he was 16, and thus ineligible for military service, seems to have been ignored. Singled out and offered promotion, Te Rauangaanga was successfully persuaded to cooperate, accept a uniform and begin training. By 2 July, eight other previously resisting men did indeed follow his example, leaving seven still refusing service.

In August another batch of defaulters was arrested, including Tonga Mahuta, another of Te Rata's brothers. He told the 44 men taken with him to accompany him to camp without resistance and by September he, too, had agreed to wear uniform and to train. However, despite some acquiescence, 34 men remained uncooperative and were punished with a bread and water regimen and periodic imprisonment. Six were court-martialled and given the standard sentence of two years' hard labour.

Other attempts to alter the Waikato stance used persuasion, shaming and coercion. As Te Puea captured official and media attention, rumours spread that she was pro-German, particularly when it was realised her grandfather's name was Searancke.[104] Other pressure came from tribal rivalries and a Wairoa resolution was sent to Allen: 'all the tribes throughout the East Coast are responding to the call of our King and Empire, registering with enthusiasm, being noble of a fighting race, determined to carry out this war to a victorious conclusion'. The message ended with the request that it be published to 'show Waikato the Patriotism of the East Coast tribes'.[105]

The Reverend Wī Paraire Rangihuna, the editor of *Te Kopara*, an East Coast-based newspaper with a Church of England and Ngāti Porou focus, published an article entitled 'The obdurate refusal of Waikato': 'Waikato, do not let our people, the chiefly Maori people, a people held up high by the nations of the world, be brought low by you.' Further stoking tribal rivalries, the article compared Waikato and Tūhoe enlistments and challenged the assumption that Tūhoe was the least 'civilised' iwi: 'It can be seen now that Waikato has sent less people than Tuhoe.'[106]

Indeed the situation among Tūhoe had developed as Rua Kēnana was released from prison in April, some 10 months early, apparently in exchange for a pledge to encourage recruitment. Although local authorities were concerned that Rua's presence might strengthen Tūhoe defiance, he did produce some volunteers. 'You will be interested to hear,' Allen told Massey, 'that Rua has become a convert to military service, and has agreed to find forty men at once to go into camp.'[107] *Te Kopara* suggested that around 150 Tūhoe had volunteered by September 1918, though contemporary research suggests the figure may be closer to 50. The probable explanation for this discrepancy is that many volunteers were obviously unfit, very old or too young. Some suspect Rua was engaging in malicious compliance; he is reported as stating 'the government won't take them . . . It won't be long. No more war; all the people will come back.'[108] Indeed, none of these volunteers saw service before the war ended.

Officials also tried to persuade cooperation from Waikato. Copies of a letter typed, or at least signed, by Te Rauangaanga and urging Te Rata and Waikato Māori to accept the law were distributed across the Waikato. In July, Pōmare, accompanied by Te Heuheu, undertook one more official mission. The pair were met by abusive haka interspersed with the whakapohane (ritual baring of buttocks) followed by a poi dancer, who approached and exposed herself, in another ritualised form of contempt. She also asked what use her genitals were if Pōmare was going to take her husband away. Besides the broader opposition to conscription, some of this enmity reflected rumours that Pōmare was using his influence to seek revenge for nineteenth-century Waikato–Maniapoto defeats of Taranaki. That Maniapoto had supplied six times as many recruits as Taranaki, on a per capita basis, hardly helped to quell such speculation.[109]

Invited to speak, Pōmare first challenged the idea that conscription was against the Treaty of Waitangi and interpreted the royal protection it bestowed as a compact obliging compliance with the Crown's law, including conscription. Claiming that equal standing under the law necessitated equal compliance, he cited the coronation oath of the first Māori king, Pōtatau, that 'There is but one eye to the needle, through which the white, the black, and the red threads must pass', and continued: 'You tell me to-day that Potatau's needle must have more than one

TURE WHAKARITE MAHI HOIA, 1916.
MILITARY SERVICE ACT, 1916.

REHITATANGA I NGA MAORI HEI HOIA.
ENROLMENT OF MAORIS.

PANUITANGA.
NOTICE.

KO nga tane Maori katoa kei waenganui i te 20 me te 46 tau te pakeke tenei ka whakahaua kia haere atu ki te teihana pirihimana tutata ki o ratou kainga kia tuhituhia ratou ki roto ki te rehita o te Rahui Ope Hoia o Niu Tireni mo te Pakanga i mua mai o te 20 o nga ra o Pepuere, 1918.

Ko te whiu—E rima tekau pauna, e toru marama ranei ki te herehere.

Kua whakaturia nga Apiha Pirihimana katoa hei Apiha Rehita, a kua whakamanaia ratou hei tuhituhi ki roto ki te rehita i nga Maori katoa e noho ana i roto i o ratou takiwa kua rite nga tau mo te mahi hoia.

Ki te nuku tetahi Maori Tangata Rahui ki tetahi atu kainga noho ai me tere tonu tana whakaatu ki te Kaitatau a te Kawanatanga (Government Statistician), Poneke, kei te nuku ia ki tetahi atu kainga; ko nga whooma (forms) mo taua mahi kei nga poutapeta katoa e takoto ana.

Ko te whiu—E rua tekau pauna.

He mea whakahau.

MALCOLM FRASER,
Kai-tatau a te Kawanatanga.
(Government Statistician.)

Poneke,
31 o Hanuere, 1918.

ALL male Maoris between the ages of 20 and 46 are required to attend at the nearest police-station and make application for enrolment in the New Zealand Expeditionary Force Reserve on or before 20th February, 1918.

Penalty—Fifty pounds or three months imprisonment.

All Police Officers have been appointed Registration Officers, and are empowered to enrol all Maoris of military age in their respective districts.

Any Maori Reservist changing his place of abode is required to immediately notify the Government Statistician, Wellington, thereof. Forms for this purpose are provided at all post-offices.

Penalty—Twenty pounds.

By order.

MALCOLM FRASER,
Government Statistician.

Wellington,
31st January, 1918.

A te reo Māori translation of legal obligations under the Military Service Act. These were printed and distributed from early 1918. ARCHIVES NEW ZEALAND, R18874766

In organising resistance to the conscription of Waikato Māori, Te Puea Hērangi emerged as a leading figure in the Kīngitanga. ALEXANDER TURNBULL LIBRARY, 1/2-001920-G eye; for you contend that there should be a different law for the Maoris . . . that conscription should not apply to them.'

Pōmare then argued that Tāwhiao's banishment of warfare from New Zealand was intended to bring peace between Māori and Pākehā and in fact justified enlistment, rather than pacifism: 'in order to keep his words sacred, in order to keep the fighting across the seas, you must enlist, you must see that your sons fight across the waters, and not allow the foe to fight here'. He cited Christian doctrine as commanding righteous deeds rather than non-violence: 'It is our Christian duty to root out all evil, and the greatest evil of the age is the German evil.' He concluded by acknowledging grievances over land confiscations, but urging that the war should take precedence: 'That is a family quarrel. Put aside the petty quarrels of the family, and take hold of the battles of the Nation.'[110]

But Pōmare's entreaties failed to alter sentiment. A harder approach was suggested. In September, Colonel G. W. H. Patterson, commander of the Auckland Military District, prepared a proposal in which Te Puea might be incited into calling for men not to enlist in the presence of reliable witnesses and, therefore, prosecuted under war regulations. This plan was rejected, however, since it risked enhancing her prestige and it was 'doubtful whether a prosecution against the so-called Princess Te Puea will result'.[111]

Accordingly, a degree of resistance continued, with further balloting bringing further defaulters and arrests. By November 1918, 552 Māori from the Waikato–Maniapoto military district had been balloted. Of these, 139 had not been located, 76 had been found ineligible, 161 had proved unfit, 17 had been exempted, 74 were being processed, another 74 were training and 11 had been imprisoned for refusing orders. Ngata later reflected that 'as a device for securing men for the Maori contingent conscription was a dismal failure'. Between the mid-1917 extension of conscription to Māori and the end of the war, the system failed to place a single Māori conscript at the front.[112]

The long-considered national service scheme for enemy aliens in the Far North became a reality in 1918. Registration began from December 1917, and in June 1918 regulations were gazetted providing that enemy aliens could be required to report for national service. In order to encourage registrations, all gumfields were closed and around 1800 men were ultimately registered. They were then called up and offered either national service or internment. A number defaulted but almost 600 were soon reporting for national service on government works. Retired police commissioner John Cullen would oversee the scheme as commissioner of aliens.[113]

Given the physical demands and rugged conditions his charges typically endured, Cullen considered they would be well suited to the work, which included swamp clearing, building roads and railway construction as well as labour on private farms. Many, however, resented the compulsory aspect of the scheme, and a degree of tension, exacerbated by language barriers, was soon evident. Elements within the Dalmatian community protested that men were being treated as if they were enemies or prisoners of war. In June some 40 men, working at Mātīere near Taumarunui on the main trunk line, briefly went on strike to protest conditions; 34 were prosecuted and two were interned on Matiu Somes Island in Wellington Harbour. Soon after, another strike broke out when 60 men at the swamp drainage works near Kaitāia downed tools after a worker was discharged.[114] Other men simply absconded. Cullen complained that he was receiving up to 60 letters a day from Yugoslavs who, he claimed, were doing all they could to hamper him in his work.

Never a lenient man, Cullen grew progressively negative about his charges. After the war he privately admitted that Yugoslavs were 'not desirable persons to be allowed to remain in this Country; and I feel convinced that if serious industrial troubles should arise, they would band themselves with the disloyal element'.[115]

The last year of the war also brought an inquiry into internment facilities on Matiu Somes Island. This owed much to a letter written to the governor-general by von Luckner who, though never interned on the island, had heard of substandard conditions there from a former *Seeadler* crewman.[116] The complaints listed poor food and sanitation, men not being paid for their labour, and allegations that the commandant, Major Dugald Matheson, 'administered ill treatment for its own sake . . . for the mere love of indulging in such conduct'.[117] There had been previous protests. In March 1915, in a 'bleak southerly', two young German internees, Edwin Balke and Paul Wolf, swam the mile and a half separating Somes from Petone. When they surrendered to police they explained that 'the object of their escapade was to draw attention to the treatment of Germans on the Island. They had been employed on road work, which they declared was fit for convicts, not prisoners of war.'[118]

Security would be a problem again in 1918, when there was another escape on the bitterly cold night of 30 July. Karl Mertin, Wilhelm Knab, Alfred Kraut and Hugo Kosel managed to get away to Ngāūranga, on the western side of Wellington Harbour, using a raft constructed from kerosene boxes and oil drums. They then intended to seize a boat and make for South America, but Kosel died from exposure and the remaining men were soon recaptured.[119]

The inquiry that began on 12 March 1918 was headed by Supreme Court Judge Frederick Chapman, who had presided over the case of Rua Kēnana two years earlier. After hearing from 113 witnesses, Chapman completed his report in June. It painted a scene of mutual enmity between the internees and guards. 'In all my career,' he concluded, 'I do not think I have seen so much evidence of bitterness and animosity.' Karl Joosten, the former German consul, who had become a spokesman about abuses on the island, prophesied that 'dispassionate historians' would judge wartime internment as a 'black page in the book of this dominion's history'.[120] Brutalities and indecencies administered by the guards, many of whom were former convicts, ranged from the destruction of personal belongings to vicious beatings. Interviewed internees complained that Matheson was willing to respond to minor infractions with punishments intended to humiliate internees and/or to assert his authority, such as the withdrawal of visiting and letter-writing privileges and corporal punishment that included forcing an internee to sleep for 26 nights on a concrete floor.[121]

These conditions likely informed the escape attempts alongside seven instances of mental breakdown and two suicide attempts.[122] Chapman noted poor conduct by some guards, but

above A procession of internees on Matiu Somes Island. The leading man holds a standard bearing a Reichsadler, the heraldic symbol of Imperial Germany. ALEXANDER TURNBULL LIBRARY, PACOLL-5523

below A Bavarian band formed by internees on Matiu Somes Island. ALEXANDER TURNBULL LIBRARY, 1/2-112230-F decided Matheson lacked 'the malevolent character implied' and judged that he had done 'everything within his power' to 'preserve the health, comfort, and well-being of the men committed to his charge', including securing 'a more liberal scale' of rations. He deemed that the allegations were exaggerated and partially reflected the degree of resentment that had developed. He recommended the establishment of a board of visitors to better oversee conditions and improve harmony on the island. A recent assessment summarises internment on Matiu Somes Island as 'a macabre mix of freedom, boredom and insidious repression'.[123]

In July 1918, in contrast to some earlier restraints, there was an extraordinary destruction of German heritage in Christchurch. In the 1870s, the German Lutheran community in Christchurch had asked German chancellor Otto von Bismarck to supply metal from French guns captured in the Franco-Prussian War to make bells for their new church. Soon thereafter, John Ruddenklau, a prominent German businessman who was active in Christchurch municipal politics, had received iron from Kaiser Wilhelm I, which became the three bells — named Kaiser, Crown Prince and Bismarck — that were subsequently installed in the church. In August 1915 a letter to the *Sun* called for the peal to be gifted to France or melted down for ammunition or sold for patriotic fundraising. The paper responded with a level-headed retelling of the bells' history.[124]

By July 1918, however, the bells were, in the *Sun*'s words, 'offensive to the French nation', an 'abhorred trinity [whose] very names are offensive'. On Bastille Day, 14 July, Allen, noting the wish 'to remove everything that might be offensive to the French people', announced that the bells were to be removed and melted down, 'unless the French Consul wished them devoted to some other purpose'.[125] Two days later, George Humphreys, the French consul in Christchurch, and a French resident, Mr Malaquin, told the *Press* that they proposed to send the bells back to France and had written to the chief French consul in Auckland.

But no time was allowed for a reply from France, and on 6 August the bells were taken to a foundry, smashed, melted down, cast into ingots and shipped to France. The *Sun* proclaimed this 'execution' to be a proud act, but one workman commented, 'To an engineer, this is just an act of vandalism.' The foundry owner seemed to agree.[126] The *Press* seethed about the 'gruesome performance', finding it 'deplorable that nobody in authority could think of any better way of expressing our abhorrence of Germany than the destruction of some excellent pieces of craftsmanship' and suspecting that 'as people of taste the French people will privately feel that the episode was astonishingly barbarous and Hun-like'.[127]

The destruction of the bells apparently elicited some cheers from a nearby factory. *Truth* pointed out that the Lutheran church in Marton retained 'its bells, its service in the German language, and all the other privileges it possessed when the war started', which 'illustrates admirably the public contention that a stricter and less lenient attitude on the part of the authorities is imperative'. Upon being melted down, the bells were found to contain no gun metal.[128]

above The bells of Christchurch's Lutheran church being smashed to pieces. They were subsequently melted down. WEEKLY PRESS, 14 AUGUST 1918, P. 32. HOCKEN COLLECTIONS TE UARE TAOKA O HĀKENA, S19-570a

below A gum diggers' camp north of Auckland. ALEXANDER TURNBULL LIBRARY, 1/1-006374-G

Increasing, and seemingly irresolvable, economic constraints further strained the public mood throughout 1918. Access to shipping remained critical and in March producers were dismayed to learn that the British authorities were further reprioritising shipping towards North America, with Australia and New Zealand now assigned a lower priority than South America.[129] By the winter of 1918, Taranaki farmer W. A. McCutcheon noted that only 30,000 carcasses might be moved by his local co-operative freezing works in the 1918–19 season and only 600,000 by the whole country, and 'unless something was done to increase storage, four out of every five fat sheep and cattle would have to remain in the paddocks'.[130] A new processing method that increased storage by up to a third gave some relief and the British government advanced £3 million against the value of stored meat to help cover the increased cost of storage. This sum was distributed across the freezing companies in proportion to their stocks.[131]

Fertiliser shortages threatened another strategic bottleneck. During the winter of 1918, a Department of Agriculture officer noted that potash, widely used in the cultivation of winter feed crops, was 'unprocurable except by the collection of wood ashes'.[132] Some attempted to find substitutes, and several farmers purchased meatworks waste to use as manure, one claiming that 'the land was becoming poorer every day, and that unless it was replenished the supply of stock for the works would very soon cease'.[133] The cost of fertiliser meant only half the usual crops were being sown and wheat production was falling.[134] Rising costs were not helping. Early in the 1918 season, growers were warning the government that they would be unable to afford to plant wheat for the following season unless it 'substantially increased' its maximum price.[135]

Shrinking coal supplies caused more discontent. Over April and May, several centres reported shortages as the country prepared for what would prove a particularly harsh winter and some railed that miners had deliberately run down the supply in order to achieve bargaining leverage.[136] Militant union activity was reviving and in January 1918 the Miners' Federation renewed its campaign for a 20 per cent pay increase. The mine owners refused, reiterating that wages returns showed 'the capable miner is probably the best-paid skilled worker in the Dominion', with the best hewers able to earn more than £1 per day.[137] Also indicative of the fraught situation was an internal union dispute among Rūnanga miners in March, which featured arson and violence against miners who ignored union policy.[138] By May, Allen, Myers and MacDonald were meeting with representatives of the coal miners, including Semple. Noting that they were only months into the agreement brokered between miners and employers in 1917, Allen privately considered that Semple appeared to be carrying out the Red Fed policy of 'to hell with agreements'.[139]

Towards the end of July, it was claimed that 'hundreds of homes' in the capital were without coal and one commentator dammed the scandalous management of Wellington's supplies: 'the coal supply has been lamentably inadequate and the price simply exorbitant'.[140] In late July, Pat Tooker, a miner living in Reefton, thought Christchurch had a four-day supply of coal and noted the country was 'in a hell of a state industrially', with the coal miners on the 'verge of a strike again'.[141]

In the last week of August many of the mines went on strike and the government tried to bring the owners to the negotiating table to enact a further wage increase. By mid-September the mines reopened.[142] Although the government was determined to maintain coal production, its circumvention of the Arbitration Court was arguably undermining the broader willingness to work within the system. One labour historian notes that 'as a result of direct action [the miners] obtained wage increases of up to 27 per cent while unions remaining loyal to the Court received increases of between only 10 and 15 per cent. Such developments were calculated to undermine the arbitration system, to discourage and embitter the moderates and to give a fillip to militant labour.'[143]

This incentive for direct action was apparent in strikes in October, as tramwaymen in Wellington and Christchurch, 'emboldened by the success of the miners', initiated go-slows alongside demands for wage increases. The government had to intervene and agreed to the requests.[144] Dissatisfaction was mounting, too, over the Arbitration Court's capacity to secure wage raises against living costs, and over the failure to address 'profiteering'. In August 1918 the editor of the largely middle-class *Free Lance* felt that the government had 'dismally failed to do its duty with regard to the cost of living'. In his view, 'Neither that mysterious body, the National Efficiency Board, nor its understudy, the equally mysterious Board of Trade, has ever succeeded, even if either has ever seriously tried to succeed, in coping with the greedy exploitation of the public.' It was a 'remarkably hard time' for the average worker, and 'the small-salaried clerk and shop assistant'.[145]

Discontent led even those unions with a distinctly moderate history to form national organisations, previously a feature of the more militant unions. By July 1918 there were determined efforts to establish a national federation of shop assistants. Some of this activity reflected concerns about further mobilisation. Tailors, for instance, were discussing how to resist schemes that would see 'the ultimate replacing of men by women operatives'.[146] Unions found a major unifying issue in April 1918 as the National Efficiency Board's previous industrial service proposals were suddenly revived. A clause inserted into the Finance Bill enabled the government to regulate for the direction of labour, the prohibition of any business and the placement of either under 'National Service', although businesses would still be privately owned and controlled.[147]

There was little political will to exercise these powers; they were perhaps more indicative of alarm at the apparent successes of the Spring Offensives. But union anxiety about industrial conscription was high and trust of government restraint low. In Dunedin, a well-attended meeting of the hardly militant Hillside branch of the Amalgamated Society of Railway Servants unanimously condemned industrial conscription. Auckland's most prominent revolutionary socialist, Michael Joseph Savage, also seized the issue. Speaking for 50 Auckland unions, he called for the complete rejection of industrial conscription and the introduction of public ownership.[148]

Official remedies displayed some willingness to adjust existing schemes but non-controversial solutions were conspicuous by their absence. Rather than fix a maximum price for wheat, the Board of Trade elected to pay a minimum of 6s 4d per bushel and to leave the market open so that growers would be free to ask more if the harvest price exceeded the price floor.[149] Many growers reacted favourably to the new policy. As one commented, 'the Government has at last put the wheat-grower in a fair position'.[150] But the move angered those who believed that rising costs were being unfairly pushed on to consumers. The Board of Trade's experiment with state butcheries was discontinued in early 1918, to be replaced by the sale of frozen meat through regular butcheries, with the government effectively taking the role of a middleman.[151] Under the scheme, run through the livestock division of the Department of Agriculture, butchers obtained a permit from the Board of Trade to draw supplies at requisition prices. In return they undertook to retail meat at prices approved by the board. This initiative copied a similar system the board had run in Gisborne, New Plymouth, Whanganui, Palmerston North, Masterton and Christchurch in 1917. Only in Gisborne was there any noticeable reduction in retail prices.[152]

Another experimental state enterprise to address constrained imports and rising prices was announced in mid-April. Massey noted that the Board of Trade was considering a scheme for controlling 'the prices of standard qualities of clothing and boots'. Boots 'of certain sizes made of New Zealand leather and in New Zealand factories' would be sold at prices the board deemed 'reasonable', with preference for such production 'given to apparel and boots worn by the working classes'.[153] Proposals were soon drawn up for standardised shoes that would be produced by manufacturers and branded with a mark reading 'New Zealand Board of Trade' as a guarantee of quality. They would be distributed to retailers with a maximum price to be set by the board.

However, numerous delays meant it was not until late 1919 that state 'standardised boots' were available. A report claimed that 'large numbers' were made and sold between the end of 1919 and mid-1921, though it acknowledged that the scheme had not achieved the 'anticipated success'.[154] The scheme was never officially abandoned but was allowed to lapse as the post-war economy and rising imports lowered the price and increased the availability of footwear.

The financing of the war in 1918 largely continued within the established, and somewhat frayed, dynamics. In January 1918 Ward decided to raise £8 million of a proposed £12 million war loan locally, offering it at 4.5 per cent free of income tax in a move designed both to attract subscribers and avoid an increase in interest rates.[155] He still felt it was necessary to strengthen compulsory provisions when the time came for the third loan to be raised, in April 1918. The emphasis on financing so much of the war effort through lending was again questioned during 1918 given that Britain aimed to meet 28 per cent of its war expenditure from taxation and the United States set a target of a third.[156] Although regrets were expressed that Ward had pledged the government not to increase income tax further, one critic admitted that he was 'hampered by the original error of financing the war on loans, and he would have difficulty in enforcing increased taxation while the Consolidated Fund shows an unusually large credit balance'.[157]

The 1918 Imperial War Cabinet gathered for the first time at noon on 11 June at 10 Downing Street and continued to meet over the following months alongside further sessions of the Imperial War Conference. One of the first topics raised was the management of the war. New Zealand's uneasiness was mirrored by the other dominions and Canada's Sir Robert Borden led the charge. In a speech that lasted almost an hour, he inveighed against the 'almost indescribable confusion' of Passchendaele, which had cost 16,000 Canadian casualties, for a gain 'not worth a candle'. It was, he said, the result of military incompetence caused by a lack of meritocracy.[158] Massey appreciated the 'frankness' of Borden's comments and added his own thoughts:

> I was told last night by a reliable man — a man I knew years ago, before he joined the Army — that the New Zealanders (he was one of them) were asked to do the impossible. He said they were sent to Passchendaele, to a swampy locality where they found themselves up against particularly strong wire entanglements which it was impossible for them to cut. They were, he said, simply shot down like rabbits. These are the sort of things that are going to lead to serious trouble.

He warned the Cabinet that Passchendaele had undermined public morale in New Zealand and that 'a great deal of uneasiness' was evident in the country.[159] Australia's prime minister, Billy Hughes, contributed his own blunt criticisms after his arrival on 15 June.[160] Faced with this outcry, Lloyd George proposed a Committee of Prime Ministers to better involve the dominions in discussions of military strategy. Assessments have seen this manoeuvre as an effort to deflect criticism and to co-opt it for his feud with General Haig.[161]

What might happen after the successful conclusion of the war, including to Germany's former colonies, emerged as a major topic. The issue had been notably complicated by President Wilson's public announcement, in January 1918, of a 14-point statement of principles intended to inform a peace settlement and the post-war order. His call for a liberal international system, with a League of Nations to guarantee collective security, made territorial annexation a more sensitive issue. For his part, Borden noted that Canada had no wish to extend the territory or responsibilities of the British Empire and, believing it would be the means to maintain American engagement in world affairs, observed that he was 'perfectly ready to let any of these [former German] Colonies pass under the direct protectorate or even the actual ownership and control of the United States'.[162] This outlook differed greatly from Massey's and Ward's, who again pushed for a firm commitment that Germany's former Pacific territories would not revert to German control and stated that direct annexation was preferable.

The New Zealanders' consideration of post-war security continued to turn on perceptions that Japan was a growing concern. In briefings, Allen had warned of 'the prospective danger to British Possessions in the Pacific if the Japanese are allowed after the war to continue in occupation of the Marshall Islands', which had been captured from Germany in September 1914. Favouring a forward defence, he had urged Massey to seek a British commitment to incorporate Tonga and Sāmoa into the British Empire.[163] In pursuing this agenda, Massey and Ward emphasised the strategic importance of the Pacific to the Empire, questioned encouraging American control in the region and forged a common front with Hughes, who was equally committed to securing a guarantee over New Guinea, the former German territory which Australia had occupied early in the war. Indeed, the arrival of the Australian entourage had been delayed by Hughes' mission to the US in an unsuccessful effort to win President Wilson over to an 'Australian Monroe Doctrine' in the South Pacific.

The volatile Hughes made Massey's lobbying look relatively mild. When Wilson's sensitivity about annexations was raised, Hughes exclaimed, 'If you want to shift us, come and do it.'[164] Lloyd George remained determinedly uncommitted, not unwilling to alienate Wilson over territories far from Britain. He did confirm it as 'essential that Germany should be deprived of her colonies', though he preferred a trusteeship system.[165] Unpacified, Massey could not 'agree to the idea that America should be given any of the Pacific Islands which we had conquered' or see why the United States, which had been slow to realise 'its duty to civilisation', should be accommodated.[166]

Also discussed were British–dominion relations, constitutional arrangements, trade and the administration of the empire. Both the Australian and New Zealand representatives favoured a self-sufficient and united empire, but they diverged in some key areas. Hughes called for greater levels of consultation, a 'real recognition of the fact that the Dominions were participants in the councils of the Empire on a footing of equality'. He wanted the dominions to be able to appoint their own governors-general and to have direct relations with the British prime minister's office. Borden, interested in greater Canadian autonomy, supported the proposal.[167] Colonial Secretary Walter Long countered by claiming that such direct contact might overburden the prime minister's office and make the British government less alert to dominion interests and priorities.

Massey and Ward proved receptive to Long's point and favoured reforms that made the empire more responsive to New Zealand's interests, rather than increased autonomy that could see them marginalised. Massey made it clear that he would not support initiatives that weakened the colonial secretary's position and proposed, instead, that the dominions appoint a 'resident Minister' in London to sit at a permanent Imperial War Cabinet. The final outcome was a resolution that dominion and British prime ministers could communicate directly with each other on questions of Cabinet importance, with the Colonial Office to remain the conventional channel for less urgent manners, and the adoption of Massey's proposal for a representative in London.[168]

The New Zealand leaders proved more in favour of local autonomy when it came to discussing the Admiralty's review of imperial naval defence, which restated the traditional belief in a single imperial navy. Ward displayed some sympathy for the report, but the general dominion consensus, based on the wartime experiences of the Royal Australian Navy, favoured having local navies. Massey, perhaps with the escort crisis in mind, believed a local navy would offer flexibility for regional contingencies.[169] The Admiralty agreed to re-evaluate its position; Admiral John Jellicoe would head planning for an acceptable imperial naval strategy.

Massey also used his time in London to continue lobbying about shipping costs. His direct

above Massey and Ward arrive in Boulogne, France, in late June 1918. ARCHIVES NEW ZEALAND, R24204010

below Massey and Ward address New Zealand soldiers from a carriage in France. ALEXANDER TURNBULL LIBRARY, 1/2-013319-G contact with British officials initially appears to have been relatively ineffective and frustrated letters to Allen gloomily noted that New Zealand's economic interests were not considered a high priority.[170] On 11 July, however, he introduced a motion to the conference calling for the establishment of an Inter-Imperial Commission to regulate shipping and protect the trading interests of the distant dominions. On 26 July, the establishment of an Inter-Imperial Board to review shipping relations was passed unanimously.

Massey, the economic non-interventionist, had successfully led the establishment of a regulatory body on the imperial stage.[171] This offered a long-term answer to inflated shipping costs but could not ease the immediate shortage. On 14 August, he warned that unless immediate steps were taken, Australia and New Zealand's financial position 'would be so seriously affected that their capacity for carrying on the war would be materially hampered'.[172] By the end of August, Massey's persistence produced results. The Shipping Ministry allocated more shipping to the Australasian trade route and the Ministry of Food offered a contract to purchase all of New Zealand's butter and cheese for a year after the war. Massey's cable to Allen captured some of the elated relief: 'I have done more for Dairying Industry than any other man could have done and propose to lay whole correspondence and papers before Parliament.'[173]

As with their previous visit, Massey and Ward visited France to meet New Zealand's troops and to attend a meeting of the Allied Supreme Council. After arriving on 1 July at the headquarters of the New Zealand Division, the two men addressed as many soldiers as time allowed — by Massey's reckoning 'not less than 20,000'.[174] An English observer was struck by 'the heartiness and informality of the proceedings'. Some of this reflected an ugly mood; the men were war-weary and homesick. By some accounts the politicians received 'a universally unfriendly welcome' and 'no favourable comment can be found'.[175] 'Regret to say,' Massey wrote to Allen, 'I have found feeling among troops in France very unsatisfactory. This applies to all ranks. Defence Department and our side of Government being serious [sic] blamed.'[176]

Both men tried to lift morale. Ward spoke of the optimistic mood abroad in Britain and predicted that the war would come to a satisfactory end in the next few months, and both politicians claimed the men would return to a 'land fit for heroes'. Massey also held audiences, dealing with 'over 100 deputations with grievances'.[177] There has been some questioning of claims of a 'universal' poor reception for the leaders, and soldiers' accounts support their views.[178] Decades after the war, Labour MP and veteran John A. Lee sought to explain why the soldiers had supported Massey, to the extent they had, and recounted his visit to a military hospital:

> 'I want to go through a ward,' he says. 'Which ward?' he is asked. 'The worst.' He doesn't know what he has let himself in for . . . a chamber of war horrors. They take the old man down one side and at the end of the ward he is trembling with shock, on the verge of collapse. They take him away and give him a deep whisky. 'You've had enough', the medical officer in command tells him. 'Take me back to that ward,' says Old Bill, 'I'm going down the other side.' And down the other side he goes. 'Nothing much in that' you might say, but the men in the hospital think differently.[179]

By early September, Massey and Ward had completed their business in London and they departed for New Zealand. The results of the second trip were mixed. The delegation had been assured that former German colonies would not be returned, but their future remained unresolved and Wilson's ideas of international control left Massey nervous. Before leaving, he wrote to Lloyd George expressing his opposition 'to handing over any of the German colonies or Palestine to the United States either in trust or in any other way'. Claiming that 'anything of this nature would be exceedingly unpopular with British citizens all over the Empire and would be looked upon by neutrals as an indication of weakness', he stated his intention to fight for New Zealand's interests at the expected future peace settlement: 'We may not get on as well as we expect and deserve at the Peace Conference but if we lose there, it will not be looked on as a surrender which would certainly be the case if we made arrangements beforehand, such as have been suggested.'[180]

Massey and Ward's partnership had also begun to show some signs of strain. Ward had been excluded from four meetings restricted to dominion prime ministers, a move guaranteed to injure his ego. As he told Liverpool, 'I feel that I am labouring under such a sense of injustice, humiliation and indignity that to go on as I have been both in London and here is scarcely possible.'[181] Some of this tension had been evident in the meetings. During discussions over the meat trade the pair slipped into their opposition roles, as Ward disparaged Massey's ambition to restrict American trading opportunities with the British Empire as 'fatuous stupidity'.[182]

The best news the ministers would be able to relate was that the balance of power on the Western Front was now far more favourable than when they left New Zealand in May. By the end of July 1918, Germany's Spring Offensives were being revealed as a failed gamble. The German Army had failed to defeat the French or the British and had suffered almost a million casualties since March. Moreover, the number of American troops in France, 287,000 in March, ballooned as 250,000 fresh reinforcements arrived every month.[183] In August the Allies seized the initiative, launching a continuous series of attacks that became known as the Hundred Days Offensive; German morale began to display serious weakness as soldiers surrendered en masse. The German High Command soon privately acknowledged that it could not end the war by forcing terms on the enemy and began efforts to secure the most favourable terms for Germany.[184]

The sense that the tide was turning and that American strength was rising revived previous calls that New Zealand's efforts might now be reduced or redirected. Even Mackenzie, speaking at a patriotic rally in London in July, proposed that New Zealand now work to 'supply a superabundance of foodstuffs and raw material, while America — Thank God for America — had men in plenty willing to go'.[185] Allen, frustrated by this indiscretion, which was widely printed in New Zealand media, protested to Massey that such statements undermined public support of New Zealand's military commitment; indeed when Parliament opened in October, various MPs, both Liberal and Reform, asked that no more married men be sent overseas.[186]

Some prominent editorials came to Allen's aid, arguing, 'The patriotism of New Zealand has hitherto been equally unwilling to shirk its obligations under the pretext that others are better able to discharge them, and we do not believe it is going to fail now'.[187] As he had done before, Allen publicly pledged that New Zealand would play its part until the end while seeking a means to pre-empt unrest.[188] Given the large reserve of New Zealand troops built up in England, the reinforcement rate was reduced to 6.5 per cent on 29 July. Altogether New Zealand's military commitment had been enormously decreased from the previous year: just over 9600 men were sent in 1918, compared with more than 27,000 in 1917.[189]

Another palliative was the previously curtailed furlough scheme, instituted early in 1918 on a smaller scale: each month 50 men with at least three years of service were selected to return to New Zealand for 28 days' leave; Military Service Boards would consider applications for men with shorter service records.[190] By August some 300 men had been returned. However, Allen, who had once favoured the idea, soon noted problems in managing men who clearly had no wish to return to the front: only 10 of the 300 re-embarked, and he predicted that a wider furlough would have become a major problem, and that 'there would have been the greatest difficulty in getting the majority of them back to the front again'.[191]

On 4 September the death of the Liberal MP Robert Fletcher triggered a by-election for Wellington Central to be held on 3 October. Liberal city councillor William Hildreth stood as the coalition's candidate, and the Labour Party, keen to contest a seat and build on its previous showing in Wellington, selected Peter Fraser as its candidate. Four independent contenders also entered the race. The most prominent, and likely to split the vote, was Matthew Joseph (Joe) Mack, secretary of the Amalgamated Society of Railway Servants, who stood as Independent Labour. He had opposed the Labour Party's anti-conscription stance and had taken a seat on a Military Service Board.

The PPA also tested its clout in the by-election. With Hildreth considered a lukewarm contender, it agreed to sponsor Mack's campaign. In many ways he was an ideal candidate for the association, presenting himself as a 'sane' Labourite with impeccable Protestant credentials and a record of refusing exemptions to seminarians during his service on a Military Service Board.[192] Mack's campaigning emphasised that he was a moderate who would push for efficiency, equal service and equal sacrifice. He denounced Hildreth as standing for a government that had placed itself beyond criticism 'and now wants you to vacate your right of judgment and vote blindly for its candidate'.

Embracing the developing 'red scare' and PPA demonology, Mack habitually referred to Fraser as 'an anti-conscription Bolshevik', and claimed that a vote for him was a vote for 'the Bolsheviks, their programme and methods (made in Germany)'. A variation on this, adapting a slogan used in Lloyd George's campaigning, was that a vote for Fraser was a vote for the Kaiser.[193]

Hildreth presented himself as a 'win the war' candidate with unswerving loyalty to king and country. He offered a Liberal platform for addressing living costs: the acquisition of state-owned steamers, increased pensions, the cutting up of larger estates and a referendum on the liquor trade. His campaign warned that Mack was a potential vote-splitter who would advantage Fraser: 'Remember! Every vote cast for Mack means a vote for Fraser.'[194] Both the government and the Liberal press endorsed Hildreth.

Fraser's campaign, with Semple as election secretary, repeated the style of canvassing undertaken during the Wellington North campaign earlier in the year, as organisers worked to enrol voters living in boarding houses around Newtown, Aro Valley and Upper Willis Street.[195] As usual the high cost of living was a central topic, though Fraser proved willing to be more partisan, condemning the Reform Party as plutocrats and the press as controlled by capital.[196] His response to charges of support for the Bolsheviks contained a degree of ambiguity: 'They will tell you . . . that the Labor candidate is a revolutionary Socialist and a Bolshevik. That translated into English means a majority. Well, if I am to be the majority candidate, I will be quite satisfied.' He was more direct in refuting accusations that Labour was biased towards Catholic interests: Labour 'have not, and do not, and will not encroach one iota upon the private religious opinions of any person in the community'.[197]

On election night a crowd gathered outside the *Evening Post* building to hear the results. Turnout was down — 4719 votes compared with 8087 in 1914 — but the results surprised even optimistic Fraser supporters. He won 57 per cent of the vote, with Mack a distant second at 22 per cent and Hildreth at 17 per cent.[198] Many political commentators spluttered that the result was 'A Bolshevik win at Wellington Central' and described Fraser as a 'self-proclaimed Bolshevik'.[199]

The PPA attributed the result to the 'sectarian and self-seeking interests of extreme Red Fedism, Liquor and Roman Catholicism'.[200] As with the Wellington North by-election, a rowdy element was present at the post-election addresses with hoots and produce hurled at the losing candidates.[201] Fraser told the crowd that 'he could assure his constituents and the other people of New Zealand that his return would be a good thing neither for the Kaiser nor for the infamous principles and institutions for which the Kaiser stood'.[202]

Less than a year after his release from prison, Fraser joined Holland in Parliament when it opened in October. In the words of his biographer, Holland, in his maiden speech, presented himself and Fraser as 'the militant socialist vanguard in parliament'.

> We do not come merely to make a change to individuals on the Government benches. We of the Labour Party come to endeavour to effect a change of classes at the fountain of power. We come proclaiming boldly and fearlessly the Socialist objective of the labour movement throughout New Zealand; and we make no secret of the fact that we seek to rebuild society on a basis in which work and not wealth will be the measure of a man's worth . . . We shall often shock the unthinking members of this House, and . . . often infuriate the intolerant members. But one thing is certain: we shall in the end succeed in converting the intelligent.[203]

Labour Party leader Alfred Hindmarsh confessed that he found his two new colleagues wild-eyed.[204]

28 OTAGO WITNESS. November 6, 1918.

The Surrender of Turkey: Enthusiastic Demonstrations in Dunedin.

THE LARGE CROWD IN PRINCES STREET.

THE MAYOR OF DUNEDIN (MR J. J. CLARK) ADDRESSING THE CROWD FROM THE TOWN HALL.

—Guy, photo

A SNAP OF A SECTION OF THE CROWD IN THE OCTAGON.

Dunedin crowds gather to celebrate the news that Turkey had surrendered through an armistice signed on 30 October 1918. OTAGO WITNESS, 6 NOVEMBER 1918, P. 28. ALEXANDER TURNBULL LIBRARY, N-P-2135-28

On 12 October, after 10 months away, Massey and Ward arrived in Auckland aboard the *Niagara*. They gave positive accounts of their meetings, their visit to the front and the direction of the war. Massey claimed that the end was in sight and that the victory of the Allies was assured.[205] There was in fact a general sense that the war's climax was approaching. Even those tired of war news could not doubt photographs showing masses of German troops surrendering, or the collapse of Germany's allies.[206] Bulgaria capitulated on 29 September, followed by the Ottoman Empire on 30 October and Austria–Hungary on 3 November.

Each surrender was met with spontaneous celebrations and official ceremonies. Newspaper extras were rushed out, anything that could make noise — school, fire and church bells, factory and train whistles — was put to use, flags were flown and half-holidays were declared. Formal occasions mixed themes of thanksgiving for the efforts made, calls for no slackening of commitment until final victory, relieved anticipation of the end of the war and speculation about the nature of the coming peace.

News of the Turkish surrender in particular recalled New Zealand's role in the Gallipoli and Sinai and Palestine campaigns. Gallipoli, Massey told Parliament, 'will never be forgotten: it will remain for all time throughout the world as a standard of heroism, gallantry, discipline, and endurance'. At the Wellington celebration of the surrender, Massey was heartily cheered when he announced that he had 'requested the Imperial authorities garrison Turkish forts with Anzac troops'. This was both 'an honour that is due to the Anzacs . . . to the boys brought up under the Southern Cross', and in line with his calls for the British Empire to retain control of the Gallipoli Peninsula.[207]

Some commentators saw the result as emotional closure or as a strategic vindication of the Gallipoli campaign. An editorial from the *Dominion* sought to do both:

> There is joy in the thought that representatives of the Anzacs will see Gallipoli once more; possess the strongholds they formerly failed to enter, and gaze on the narrow sea (as rich in historic associations as any sea in the world). Doing so they will in the fullest sense reap what they have sown, for their assaults had a great place in the weakening of Turkey that led to her downfall. In the downfall of a stronghold of iniquity the first blows are as valuable as the last.[208]

Alexander Malcolm, the MP for Clutha, sought to sketch the mood of Wellington crowds reacting to Turkey's surrender: 'There was scarcely a dry eye . . . Opposite me was a constable, standing stiff and straight, with the tears rolling down his cheeks. Did the people feel more joy or sorrow? Did they feel joy at victory or sorrow at what it had cost?' 'Both,' Malcolm concluded, but 'still this was a day of rejoicing'.[209]

H. Gibson FOUNTAIN
DENTIST
CY DRAPERS MILLINERS DAVID MEIKLE
AND COMPANY

CHAPTER THIRTEEN

PEACE IS DECLARED

previous pages
Celebrations to mark the formal end of the war on Auckland's Queen Street. AUCKLAND LIBRARIES HERITAGE COLLECTIONS, 1370-U079-10

The eleventh hour of the eleventh day of the eleventh month of 1918 marked an end to the fighting on the Western Front at least: in other regions, revolutionary, counter-revolutionary and civil conflict would continue for years. New Zealand was spared this kind of political violence, but it did share in the chaos of the worldwide influenza pandemic that was beginning even before the armistice was signed.

Towards the end of October, Auckland was reporting cases of, and then deaths from, a lethal strain of influenza. It is now considered that this was introduced to New Zealand by three troopships coming into Auckland that month carrying infected soldiers. They demobilised across the country, rapidly disseminating the virus.[1] Further cases were soon reported, first in port cities and main centres and then in more isolated areas. There was some regional variation across the country, but generally the epidemic rapidly escalated in early November and peaked mid-month before subsiding by mid-December. Cruelly, the disease was often spread at mass gatherings held to celebrate the surrender of the Central Powers and later the armistice.

As Stratford doctor Doris Gordon recalled, 'The joy bells for the peace with Turkey rang out when we probably had twelve to twenty severe influenza cases in our region of ten thousand people. But no one had authority to stride down the street shouting "do not foregather, do not celebrate — death is around the corner". So collectively we celebrated, and danced in the Town Hall on a warm November night, and within twenty-four hours nearly a third of the revellers were rigoring.'[2]

Ultimately, the national infection rate was somewhere between a third and half of the entire population and in some regions reached 80 per cent. The virus was characterised by a sudden onset of symptoms — including chills, fevers, sneezing, sore throats, headaches and acute weakness — and apparently healthy individuals could collapse within hours. Pneumonia was a common secondary complication; often called 'the real killer', it was also responsible for, in what was an impressed memory, the bodies of the dead turning a vivid purple-black as the lungs failed to oxygenate blood.[3] All parts of society were vulnerable and could rapidly succumb. On 1 November, Alfred Hindmarsh was speaking in parliamentary debates about the surrender of Turkey; urging an ethos of humility and citing Shakespeare, he called for a commitment to 'make war breed peace: make peace stint war'. On 12 November he was reported to be suffering from complications from influenza: 'it will probably be two or three weeks before he will be about again'.[4] He died the following day.

The swift and widespread diffusion of the disease closed businesses, restricted or suspended public services and halted shipping. Schools, banks, hotels, theatres and hairdressers were shut by official decree.[5] Fears of a breakdown in morale led to a ban on the publication of death tolls. Rumours of mass graves and burials at sea filled the silence and were apparently accepted by many.[6] Various procedures and remedies were proclaimed and there were dedicated efforts to improve public sanitation. As the *Manawatu Standard* noted, it was 'safe to say that at no time in its history has [Palmerston North] received such a thorough disinfecting. Buildings, public and private, outside and in, simply reek with the pungent smell of germ-killers.'[7]

Although such initiatives opened some eyes to the slum conditions in some cities, no effective cure was available. Best practice entailed isolating the infected and keeping them warm, rested and supplied with meals and fluids. In this, the volunteering spirit, networks and expertise that had marked the war effort were invaluable. As early as 5 November the Auckland branch of the Women's National Reserve had established a food depot which, at the height of the epidemic, was feeding some 2000 people. These efforts were especially vital considering that almost a third of the country's doctors and hundreds of its nurses were still serving overseas.[8]

Ultimately the influenza pandemic, which caused untold millions of deaths worldwide, killed an estimated 8573 New Zealanders in under two months, approaching half the dead the war had brought in 52 months. In some smaller centres, 'the number of influenza victims almost equalled the war dead'. Mortality rates demonstrated some remarkable patterns. For reasons that are still debated, males, often in their prime, were disproportionally affected; 63 per cent of Pākehā dead were male and the death rate for men aged 30–34 was twice that of women in the same age group.

The virus was especially deadly for Māori: the estimated 2160 killed represented a per capita mortality rate more than seven times higher than that for Pākehā.[9] A catastrophic situation also developed in New Zealand-administered Western Sāmoa as quarantine regulations proved ineffective, relief efforts were overwhelmed and offers of medical aid from American Sāmoa were refused, seemingly because of the administrator's anti-American prejudice. The result was a mortality rate between 20 and 25 per cent with around 8500 Samoans killed.[10]

In and around the course of the pandemic, the public continued to anticipate Germany's surrender and the end of the war. By 7 November, newspapers were reporting that a German delegation was making its way to Compiègne in northern France to discuss an armistice, and editorials contemplated how much longer Germany could last before accepting terms. Out of the public eye, the governor-general was receiving telegrams marking the progress of the armistice talks.[11] On 6 November, Massey pledged in Parliament that news of the war's end 'would be given to the public at the earliest possible moment' and various communities announced how they would mark the longed-for occasion.[12] Businesses exploited the expected

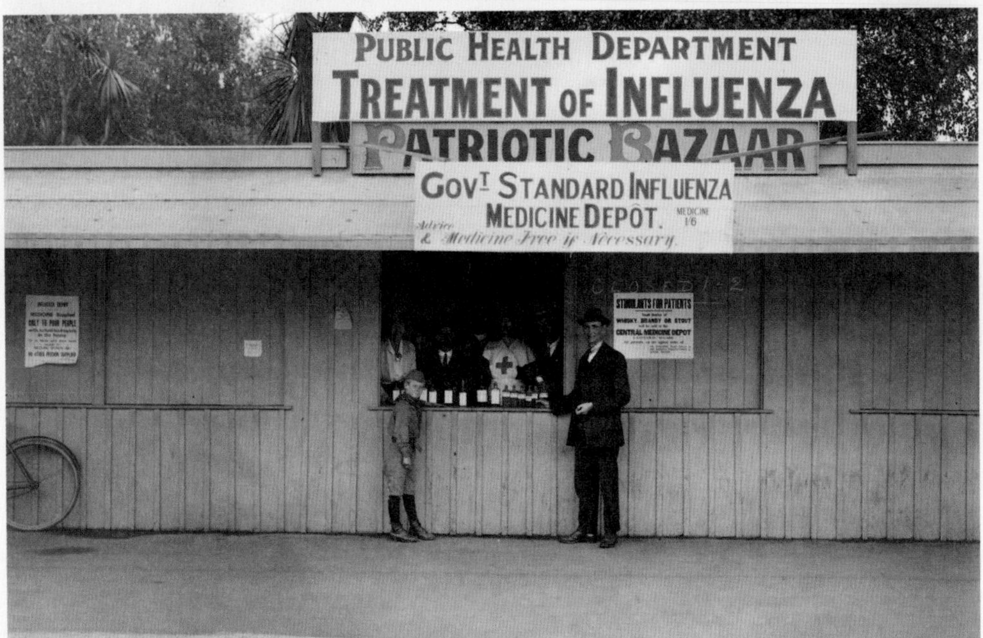

above Ambulances, including private vehicles being employed as ambulances, outside the Wellington Town Hall during the 1918 influenza pandemic. ALEXANDER TURNBULL LIBRARY, PACOLL-7489-6

below A Christchurch medical station in December 1918. The poster on the building's front notes that the station will only supply medicine to 'poor people with actual bad cases in the house or those who have been unable to secure other aid'. ALEXANDER TURNBULL LIBRARY, 1/1-008542-G peace. 'Every day brings peace nearer', said H. H. Cook & Co. in the *Press* on 7 November. 'There's no doubt how the war will finish, and there's no doubt that land prices will soon be rising. Write for our complete list of farms for sale.' On the same day, in Timaru, Miss H. C. Strachan in Stafford Street reminded readers that '[p]eace is near and you want to join wholeheartedly in the celebrations'. Fortunately, she was ready with 'large stocks of entente flags and fireworks'. On the 9th Wellington department store Kirkcaldie & Stains encouraged customers to 'Fly a flag for victory!' and to do so as quickly as possible: 'only a limited quantity now left on account of the tremendous demand yesterday'.[13]

Shortly before nine o'clock on 8 November, newspapers received a cable report from the United Press agency at Paris that an armistice with Germany had been signed and that hostilities on the Western Front had ceased at 2 p.m. the previous day. Many newspaper offices posted the news on their publicity boards in the early morning and telephone exchanges were overloaded for hours.[14] The *New Zealand Herald* reported a 'veritable pandemonium of rejoicing' down Queen Street: 'Elderly citizens swathed their hats with Union Jacks, matrons draped them across their shoulders and even infants in arms waved the flag of victory. Motor cars, lorries, delivery wagons, everything on wheels passed in unceasing procession, crowded with cheering girls and men, and small boys trailing and beating tin-cans.'[15]

'Happily,' said Wellington's *Evening Post*, 'the weather enemy had declared an armistice. It was a good blue-and-white day for fun and frolic . . . There was never such a fluttering of flags, such a wild welter of bright colour on men and women, boys and girls, horses and carts, motor-cars, and anything else that happened to be handy. From a height the streets were like an animated moving garden of summer flowers.' There were schoolchildren blowing paper trumpets, plus 'sundry hootings and tootings of motor-cars, snatches of song from merrymakers in various vehicles, skirlings of bagpipes, blasts of bugles and other instruments, and a wonderfully exhilarating chatter of conversation . . . Care and anxiety fled, as darkness does at the touch of an electric switch.'[16]

Further south, as if 'to contradict the allegation that Christchurch people are lethargic and unenthusiastic, the spirit of unrestrained jollification was indulged in, and for an hour or so Cathedral square was the scene of spontaneous outbursts of rejoicing that have been rarely, if ever, exceeded'.[17] Dunedin's *Evening Star* similarly declared, 'What a sight! What a crowd! Jumping, laughing, clapping, shouting, singing, howling — all merry-mad . . . Never has there been such wild excitement and such spontaneous enthusiasm in this notoriously staid and sober City.'

In Dunedin, as elsewhere, anti-German feeling was evident: 'Further along another lot of flag-waving stragglers followed, cheering the Kaiser in effigy, "the cause of all the trouble" being shown hanging dismally from the gallows. One motor load of celebrants bore aloft an ancient German sausage liberally "stuck" with miniature flags of the Allies.' It was all too much for some: in Tapanui the mayor, overwhelmed, collapsed in a fainting fit.[18]

Within two hours of the initial announcement, however, word arrived that the news was incorrect. In some regions this brought a disheartened end to festivities; in others, it 'failed to qualify, much less extinguish, the wild rejoicings'. As the *Evening Star* suggested, 'A tension of four years' duration had snapped in a moment, and in the torsion of the wrench people's emotions swung in a dizzying arc.'[19] In the aftermath of the 'fake armistice', the *Wanganui Chronicle* resoundingly condemned the censor. Of the 'many foolish things' he had done 'he certainly excelled himself yesterday by allowing the cable announcing the signing of an armistice to be despatched. Words fail to properly condemn such crass folly.'[20] An embarrassed government said news of the surrender would be announced by official proclamation and the firing of a signal gun.[21]

Days later, minutes before 11 a.m. on 11 November, telegraphic instructions arrived from the Colonial Office. The decoded details read: 'MOST URGENT Armistice signed 5 AM this morning.'[22] Since the armistice was to come into effect at 11 a.m. Western European time, hostilities would officially end at 10.30 p.m. New Zealand time, and the government decided to make the announcement the following day. As Massey noted, however, there was a leak, 'because young men came to his gate about two o'clock in the morning and raised cheers and sang songs'.[23]

Shortly before 9 a.m. on 12 November, every postal station in the country received a note reading 'Armistice signed' and, on the hour, Wellington's signal gun was fired. By 10.30 a crowd had gathered at Parliament grounds to hear Lord Liverpool formally announce the armistice from the spot where he had, years earlier, read the declaration of war. Parliament was adjourned and a national holiday was declared. Across the country bells were rung and, despite the worsening influenza pandemic, large crowds gathered in many civic centres. The *Stratford Evening Post* summed up the mixed emotions of the day:

> The pent up feeling of years could not be expressed in words all at once. Perhaps it was the thought of a dear one forever gone, of the empty sleeve, maimed limb, or disfigured feature of a relative or close friend; maybe the thought of the Hell of the past four years welled up in the heart and made all else matter nothing for the time being. It almost seemed good to be sad for a moment, and then Joy won, and the rest of the day was spent with the spirit of thankfulness uppermost, and an exuberance of pleasure, tempered with the remembrance of the dignity of Victory.[24]

In some regions influenza stifled public celebration. Kaponga, in Taranaki, postponed events indefinitely, while the scene in Auckland was one of decorated buildings and empty streets; the city's death toll peaked on 12 November, with 83 deaths, and Chief Medical Officer Dr Joseph Frengley had advised people not to congregate.[25] Some Aucklanders marked their rejoicing in private. Harrold Ennor's diary entry for 12 November read, 'The long looked for peace has come. May it be for all time.'[26]

In anticipation of the end of the war, arrangements had been drawn up regarding British and Allied positions at an expected peace conference. Lloyd George had cabled Massey on 27 October informing him that should Germany accept the terms being proposed he 'ought to be prepared to start for Europe without any delay'.[27] Some significant domestic issues, however, postponed any immediate departure. Most serious were popular rumours linking the influenza epidemic with Massey and Ward's return on the *Niagara* in October. It had been reported that the ship carried sick passengers and a crewman had died of pneumonia shortly before arrival, and there were claims in Parliament that the ministers had overridden quarantine procedures.[28] Massey announced a royal commission would investigate the matter.[29]

After hearing evidence in each of the four centres from February 1919, the commission exonerated Massey and Ward and noted that quarantine regulations had not been breached. However, the accusation remains apocryphal. In the words of historian Geoffrey Rice, 'Many at the end of 1918 would have shared the bitterness of an unknown individual who scrawled across a document now preserved in Auckland's Catholic Diocesan archives: "Make Bill Massey pay for what he brought here!"'[30]

In early December, after only five weeks back in New Zealand, Massey and Ward were again planning their departure for London to discuss aspects of British policy before attending a conference in Versailles to determine peace terms and formally end the war. The party of nine comprised Massey, his wife Christina, his daughter Marian and his private secretary F. D. Thomson; Ward, his wife Theresa, his son Pat and his private secretary, Alice Saunders; and Dunedin parliamentary correspondent Robert Riley as the official journalist. Before boarding the *Remuera* on 11 December, Massey wished his fellow citizens 'a Merry Christmas and a Bright and Prosperous New Year. Let us hope that when peace is finally and definitely arranged it will be worthy of all it has cost in the lives of our brave men and the sacrifices that have been made by our citizens. Kia-ora to all.'[31]

When the party arrived in London five weeks later, it was informed that New Zealand, like the other dominions, had been allocated one delegate at the conference. This again raised the sensitive matter of Ward's position, and a potential political crisis as he threatened to return to New Zealand. After Massey complained that New Zealand's sacrifices were not being properly recognised, a solution was found by appointing Ward as New Zealand's representative for the rotating dominions' slot on the British Empire panel, though this gave him little real influence.[32]

Leaving Christina and Marian Massey and Theresa Ward in London, on the evening of 21 January the New Zealand delegation arrived in Paris, where they stayed in the Hotel Majestic, near the Arc de Triomphe. Over the next six months the Versailles conference, which had opened on the 18th, would seek to settle terms and establish a post-war order. It undertook this task in the face of the enormous instabilities and outright chaos resulting from the collapse of the Russian, German, Austro-Hungarian and Ottoman empires and the diplomatic complexities created by competing visions and interests.

The New Zealand delegation arrived at Versailles with a clear set of concerns and interests.[33] Foremost was a sense that German militarism must be held accountable and disarmed. Massey argued that a harsh peace was necessary to punish transgression and to prevent a future threat. He openly stated that it was delegates' duty 'to see that there was no possibility of such a condition of affairs again arising as had been seen under Germanism. Those responsible for

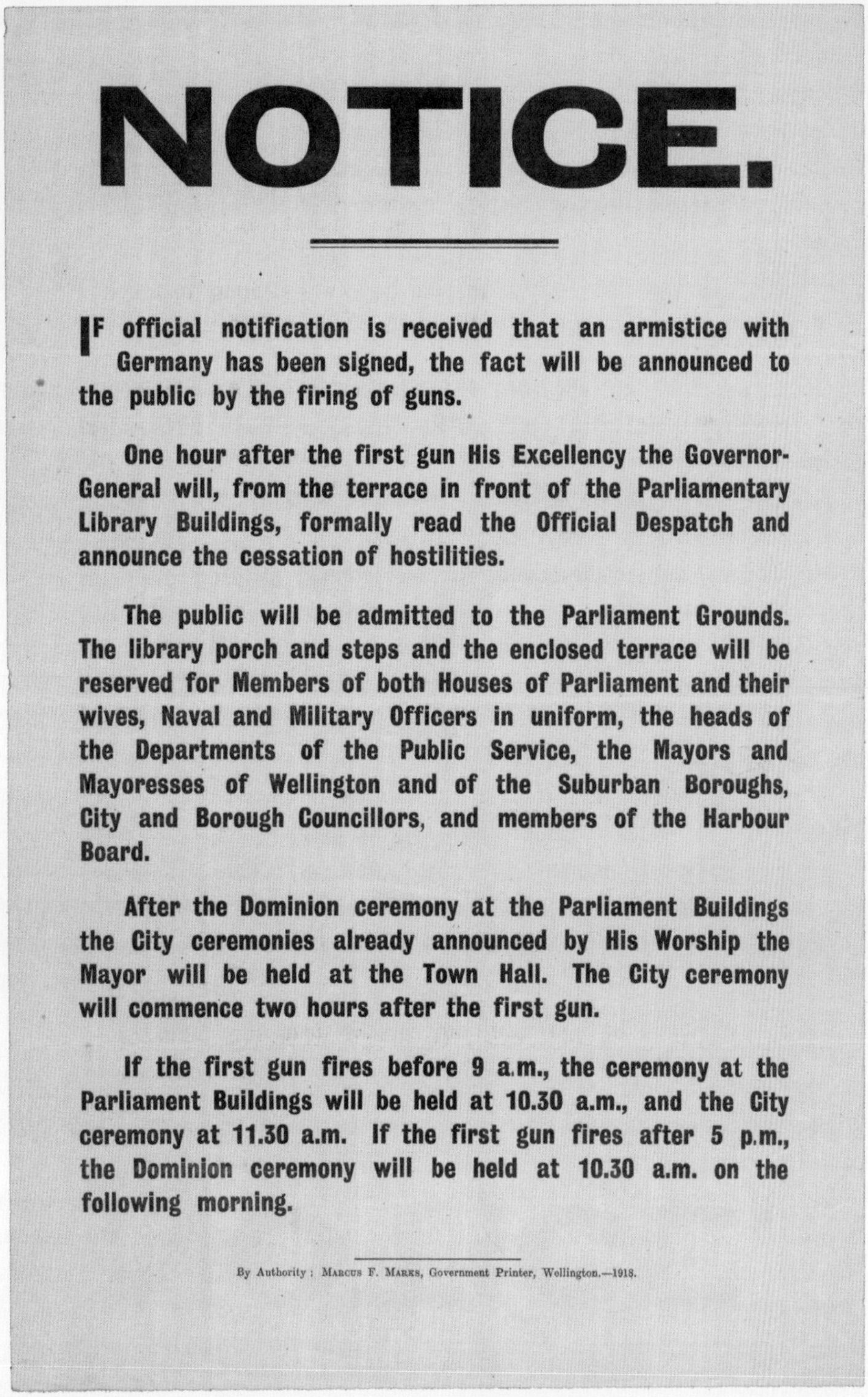

NOTICE.

IF official notification is received that an armistice with Germany has been signed, the fact will be announced to the public by the firing of guns.

One hour after the first gun His Excellency the Governor-General will, from the terrace in front of the Parliamentary Library Buildings, formally read the Official Despatch and announce the cessation of hostilities.

The public will be admitted to the Parliament Grounds. The library porch and steps and the enclosed terrace will be reserved for Members of both Houses of Parliament and their wives, Naval and Military Officers in uniform, the heads of the Departments of the Public Service, the Mayors and Mayoresses of Wellington and of the Suburban Boroughs, City and Borough Councillors, and members of the Harbour Board.

After the Dominion ceremony at the Parliament Buildings the City ceremonies already announced by His Worship the Mayor will be held at the Town Hall. The City ceremony will commence two hours after the first gun.

If the first gun fires before 9 a.m., the ceremony at the Parliament Buildings will be held at 10.30 a.m., and the City ceremony at 11.30 a.m. If the first gun fires after 5 p.m., the Dominion ceremony will be held at 10.30 a.m. on the following morning.

By Authority: Marcus F. Marks, Government Printer, Wellington.—1918.

A poster advising procedures for the anticipated news of an armistice with Germany. ALEXANDER TURNBULL LIBRARY, EPH-B-WAR-WI-PEACE-1918-01 war crimes must be made to pay the penalty.'[34] In part, this penalty meant reparations. Massey claimed that the war had cost New Zealand £100 million, though he acknowledged before the conference that he had 'not the faintest idea of what we shall be able to get from Germany in the way of indemnities'.[35] Summarising his opinion, he noted 'Germany caused the war, Germany lost the war, and Germany should be compelled to pay as far as possible.'[36]

Ward could appear more conciliatory, saying he wished normal relations to be restored, but his leniency was by degree: he anticipated that Germany would be disarmed and publicly stated that 'it would be only justice if the ex-Kaiser were lynched'. He also had a keen sense of restorative justice: 'it is our duty to see those responsible for the wholesale butchery and murder that have characterized this altogether barbarous and never to be forgotten war shall be made to pay their tribute for years to come to the people all over our Empire against whom they have been in arms'. Ward estimated that Germany and Austria would pay an annual bill of £1.25 billion for the next 20 years.[37]

The future of the Pacific remained a central concern; as Massey bluntly put it, 'Never again; no more Germans in the Pacific.'[38] They also aimed to formalise New Zealand's claim to Sāmoa. This, Massey claimed, was a matter of strategic interest and national prestige, and in accordance with the welfare and wishes of the Samoan people. Meanwhile, on 28 January a delegation of Samoan chiefs, unimpressed by New Zealand's administrative record, petitioned for political union and rule from American Sāmoa or, if that was not possible, governance from the British Colonial Office.[39] The New Zealand delegation also stated its interests in Nauru, specifically its phosphate deposits.

Pre-war anxieties about Japanese expansion had not gone either. As Allen told Massey, 'Jaluit [part of the Marshall Island chain] is a good harbour and can be easily fortified, and as a submarine base in the hands of the Japanese I fear that British shipping would have a very bad time should we at any time come into conflict with that Nation. I cannot understand any argument in favour of the Japanese remaining in the Marshals [sic]. They cannot progress further eastwards. It seems clear to me that it is meant as an indication that the Japanese intend to rule the Pacific Seas . . . I am perfectly satisfied in my own mind that we shall live to regret even more the conditions in the Pacific if we allow the Japanese to remain where they are.'[40] He had stated a similar sense of foreboding in Parliament: 'I have always had a feeling, and I have it to-day, that in years to come we may have a contest nearer our own door than the contest of to-day.'[41]

In securing these interests, the New Zealanders continued to regard a strong and united British Empire as critical, but in the wake of the war both Massey and Ward were well aware that New Zealand's and Britain's outlooks could not always be assumed to be the same. Although Lloyd George and his colleagues were willing to support New Zealand's interests, they had multiple and competing objectives at Versailles — protecting British interests, shaping a new balance of power in Europe, honouring obligations to France, Japan and Italy, and appeasing Wilson's insistence that the conference was not a 'division of spoils' but rather the beginning of a new liberal world order. Australia may have shared many of New Zealand's objectives, such as securing British power in the Pacific, the wish to check Japanese expansion and scepticism about Wilson's idealism, but Massey found Hughes 'most unreliable' and doing 'practically nothing to assist me in anything where the interests of New Zealand have been concerned'.[42]

Massey was willing to take independent, and sometimes aggressive, action in pushing his sense of New Zealand's interests; it was likely this quality that saw one Canadian observer describe Massey 'as thick headed and John Bullish as his appearance would lead one to expect'.[43] His stance also put him in the centre of a 'David and Goliath' confrontation with Wilson over the status of former German territories in the Pacific.[44] The confrontation began when Lloyd George opened a meeting by stating that 'he saw no insuperable difficulties in reconciling the views of Great Britain with those expressed by President Wilson'.[45] However, Massey called for a special exemption for the dominions and argued that New Zealand governance was necessary to secure the welfare and security of New Zealanders and Samoans. Drawing comparisons with the American Revolution, he expressed scepticism about the viability of the League of Nations, citing historical failures to frame a universal peace and noting that while 'he hoped that this Congress would not end the same way', 'it was well to remember that history repeated itself'.

By Lloyd George's account, Massey's comments left the president 'perceptibly nettled'.[46] Wilson, a former history professor, responded by denying that there was any 'historical precedent for the work now at hand' and claiming that 'under the regime of the League of Nations there was little chance that any power would be able to play in Samoa the part played by Germany without attracting the attention of the United States'.[47] Wilson was further nettled when his question of whether Australia and New Zealand were presenting an ultimatum to the conference was answered by Hughes' quip 'that's about the size of it Mr President. That puts it very well'. Massey was observed as grunting his assent.[48]

The confrontation was largely resolved as Lloyd George continued his efforts to mediate between Massey, Hughes and Wilson, and when a mandate system was accepted as a compromise. New Zealand was granted a mandate over Sāmoa, Australia one for territories south of the equator, Japan one for islands north of the equator and the British Empire one for Nauru. This arrangement allowed Wilson to save some face by giving the League of Nations some oversight power in mandate territories while persuading Australia and New Zealand to accept the mandate system 'without compromising their annexationist desires'.[49]

Massey would also clash with the Americans on the question of prosecuting Germany for war crimes and the fate of the ex-Kaiser, who had fled to the Netherlands. Under his stated philosophy that 'immunity from punishment encouraged crime', Massey called for Wilhelm Hohenzollern to be extradited and put on trial. As chairman of the Sub-Commission on Criminal Acts, Massey catalogued 32 criminal acts and concluded that the Central Powers had waged war 'by barbarous or illegitimate methods'.[50] However, although delegates agreed that Germany and the Central Powers had initiated a premeditated plan of aggression, there was fierce debate over judicial proceedings as 'the European delegates ranged against the Americans and the Japanese, whose imperial government did not want to call into question the inviolability of any monarchs'.

Ultimately, no consensus could be reached on designs for an international tribunal to assess and judge war crimes, and the scope of any punitive action was greatly curtailed. Massey was left disappointed: 'such a proceeding will not do justice to the millions who have suffered miseries from the crimes committed during the war period, nor will it give satisfaction to the citizens of the Allied countries'.[51] As he said, 'Evidently the legal view of the sanctity of the heads of States had prevailed. The display of aggressive arrogance of Germany's military caste yesterday at Versailles should be regarded as a warning.'[52]

Anglo-Japanese relations became another point of tension. Besides formalising its seizure of German assets in the Pacific and China, Japan's major aspiration at Versailles was to secure a clause on racial equality within the covenant of the League of Nations. When this proposal was raised on 13 February, general support was lukewarm at best, though 'the loudest opposition' came from Hughes, with Massey following in his wake.[53] Neither country wished to make concessions that might compromise immigration policies intended to bar or discourage non-European immigration. This, again, left Britain in an awkward position of trying to reconcile the wishes of the Pacific dominions and its desire for good relations with Japan and a continuance of the Anglo-Japanese alliance.

On 28 June 1919, some six months after the conference opened and exactly five years after the assassination at Sarajevo, Massey lined up alongside other representatives in the Hall of Mirrors to sign the Treaty of Versailles. A series of further treaties signed over subsequent months and years settled terms with other former belligerents.[54] Like most attendees, the New Zealand delegation's record was one of compromises and successes, though the latter were notable for a country with little diplomatic weight.

Besides securing a claim to Sāmoa, New Zealand negotiations, in competition with Australia, had obtained 16 per cent of Nauru's superphosphate industry. Cheap fertiliser made an important contribution to the grasslands revolution of the following decades. As Massey said later, 'settlers have told me over and over again that the Nauru purchase was the best bargain the Government ever made'.[55] Massey's hopes that Germany would pay for New Zealand's war effort were not realised: in a scheme that has been described as a 'fiasco', the most New Zealand received was a payment of £500,000 allocated at a 1921 Imperial Conference.[56]

Cable reports to New Zealand papers described the Treaty of Versailles as the foundation of a stable post-war order. 'Not a "Scrap of Paper" this Time', said one of the headlines in the *Otago Daily Times*, which quoted Lloyd George: 'the terms were in many respects terrible, but so were the deeds and the consequences thereof inflicted upon the world. The latter would have been more terrible had Germany succeeded. The terms of the treaty were stern but just.'[57] Media commentary on the treaty expressed gratitude that the war had been formally concluded and stressed that a peaceful world would require continuing work. Vigilance would be needed: 'No one trusts Germany's promise even now she has signed a new treaty of peace, but no one, on the other hand, can imagine Germany able to set the world alight again even if she tears up the new scrap of paper.'[58]

Massey was openly dour about Versailles: 'there were many flaws and defects in the treaty, and too many risky experiments, giving Germany loopholes to evade her responsibilities'. He feared the treaty had failed to defang Germany, that the League of Nations was a dangerous distraction from the need for a strong and united empire to guarantee peace, and that 'the

above A parade on Whanganui's Victoria Avenue to celebrate news of the armistice. OTAGO WITNESS, 27 NOVEMBER 1918, P. 32. ALEXANDER TURNBULL LIBRARY, W-P-2133-32

below Dunedin officials announce news of the armistice on the town hall steps. OTAGO WITNESS, 20 NOVEMBER 1918, P. 31. ALEXANDER TURNBULL LIBRARY, N-P-2134-31 next generation would probably see a still more terrible war'.[59] Ward, by contrast, considered the league 'necessary for the protection of humanity, in order to prevent those horrible wars on such a gigantic scale ever taking place in the years to come'.[60]

The Labour Party denounced the peace terms as the work of the victors, capitalism and imperialism and as failing to reform the global system. The League of Nations was deemed 'representative of Government and not of peoples, and would seem to have been designed for the purpose mainly of protecting the trading interests of the Allied capitalists'.[61] Fraser echoed Massey's scepticism about the league's ability to prevent war: it had already 'told the Poles to stop murdering the Jews, but the Poles have not stopped'. He also argued that another war was probable 'unless labour comes to power in all important countries'.[62]

By the time Massey was signing the treaty, Ward and his entourage had already left Versailles. After Allen urged Massey, in a coded message, not to let Ward come home alone and set the parliamentary timetable, the prime minister hastily departed and, by means of a Royal Navy destroyer, intercepted the passenger liner on which Ward was travelling. The two arrived in New Zealand together in early August.[63]

New Zealand would be involved in a number of peace celebrations in London, Paris, Sydney, Niue and Western Sāmoa. At home the government initially envisaged centralising events to make them more impressive, but coal shortages reduced train services and made transporting large numbers of people to the main centres difficult. In early December 1918, therefore, it was decided that 'each Local Body should have full liberty to make its own arrangements' and

Peace celebrations in Christchurch. The parade of returned servicemen and -women proceeded through arches named for various theatres of war and Christchurch suburbs. Visible here are arches marked 'Falkland Islands' and 'Heligoland Bight'.
ALEXANDER TURNBULL LIBRARY, 1/1-008741-G

the government would announce its plans in due course.[64] Many communities appear to have taken inspiration from the Australian federal government's idea of a three-day, three-theme celebration — a day of thanksgiving, a day of rejoicing and a children's day.

In February 1919 the government officially adopted a similar approach. The three days would, in turn, 'express our gratitude for victory', 'recognise the splendid services of our soldiers' and 'impress the minds of our children with the great event celebrated'.[65] Official recommendations for communal activities included church services, in stated recognition that 'victory has been gained by the blessings of Almighty God', the singing of 'suitable hymns and national songs', public processions, the firing of artillery, the decoration of government buildings with the flags of 'Britain, the Dominions and the Allies being prominently displayed', military reviews, athletic events and picnic lunches. A 'silent bare-headed tribute for one minute' for the dead would be held at noon on soldiers' day. A system of subsidies to assist local events was also announced.[66]

However, efforts to coordinate with London and several alterations confused these plans,[67] and the government finally announced a pan-empire day of thanksgiving on Sunday, 6 July and a soldiers' day celebration on Saturday 19th; Monday the 21st would be a public holiday for communities who wished to proceed with their plans for three days of events. The result was a good deal of regional variation in how communities marked the end of the war.[68] Some began their celebrations on Friday 18th and others, like Raetihi and Ōhakune, ended on Tuesday 22nd. Dunedin held a six-day programme, ending on 24 July, whereas Tauranga decided on a single day of events on the 19th. Some elected to hold a second day of thanksgiving, after the official one on 6 July, and others substituted in a new themed day. Invercargill, for instance, acknowledged the war's impact on rugby with a day for 'fallen footballers' on the 22nd.[69]

Although electric illuminations had featured in many celebration plans, with 'public buildings illuminated and streets festooned with electric lights', ambitions were scaled back in the face of coal shortages, and on 8 July, Allen ordered that 'no peace illuminations involving the consumption of coal were to be allowed'.[70] Regions that generated electricity from hydro-electric power, though, were able to light up.

After a day of celebration, on the night of Saturday, 19 July, Christchurch was transformed. 'It was,' said the *Press*, 'as though a good fairy had lightly touched the city with her wand, such was the brilliant effect of the illuminations'. On two big arches in Cathedral Square, 'Dozens of coloured electric bulbs, red, white, and blue, produced a miraculous effect, giving the white-washed canvas the appearance of beautifully-grained marble', and the utilitarian tramway shelter became 'a thing of beauty and of joy to behold. Festoons of coloured lights gaily adorned the structure, and effectively revealed gracefully-drooping flaxes. In a Grecian temple revolved a globe, at the foot of which were lions couchant. Heralded on placards were the words, "Courage, Resource, Sacrifice, Victory — Peace by thy might of right."'

The *Press*'s building was memorable, too, with the western wall 'a glorious blaze of light. On every minaret was a parti-coloured globe, giving a most novel effect. Underneath glittered a red, white, and blue star. Then came three laurel wreaths in green, dedicated to the Royal Air Force (in yellow), the Navy (in blue), and the Army (in red). A transcendent Union Jack flew over the Prince of Wales's feathers, and underneath this again appeared in huge letters the legend: "Peace with honour, justice, and freedom."' Official buildings, city businesses, shops and theatres pulled out all the stops. Even the band rotunda in Victoria Square 'looked like an eastern pagoda, a creation of the Arabian Nights'.[71] Alternative spectacles were provided by fireworks displays and some communities organised bonfires, sometimes with effigies of the Kaiser thrown in.

Most communities held their soldiers' day on 19 July. When the armistice was signed, some 58,000 New Zealand soldiers were overseas. Although their return to New Zealand began within seven weeks, its completion was delayed by the occupation of Germany and strains on shipping: the last 24 men arrived on the *Ionic*, which left Britain on 31 March 1920.[72] By July 1919, however, the bulk of the NZEF had come home and could be honoured, most often in military parades, sometimes with carnival-style floats, and also at sporting events. The *Otago Witness* described Dunedin's parade as a 'magnificent procession, replete with gorgeous pageantry, tableaux of significant symbolism, handsomely decorated vehicles, a multitude of beautiful displays'.[73]

The day of thanksgiving was generally held on Sunday, 20 July, often with morning services in churches and interdenominational services in the afternoon. Speeches universally impressed recognition and gratitude for the soldiers' sacrifice, alongside the ongoing moral debt, effectively continuing the wartime themes of exemplary sacrifice and social commitment. As Invercargill's souvenir programme put it, 'the thought that comes home is that these great sacrifices will be in vain, and we will be unworthy of them, if the peace now inaugurated is not an abiding peace and if the world is not made a better and happier place to live in'.[74] Children's day commemorations typically included processions, singing, dancing, games and sometimes Christmas-style occasions as a substitute for those cancelled by the influenza pandemic. Many communities announced their plans for memorials or to plant trees.[75]

Some sections of the labour movement could not, in the words of United Federation of Labour president Tom Bloodworth, support 'any celebrations in honour of an event which makes the workers of one nation to be the slaves of the capitalists of another nation, and which does not extend to all nations the right of self-government; and we oppose all wasteful expenditure on such celebration'.[76] Semple refused to attend any occasions, declaring them a sheer waste of public money that could be spent on assisting returned soldiers and workers.[77] The *Maoriland Worker* kicked against some of the proclamations of a better world: 'The peace being celebrated has no surety of permanence; it has not abolished war, or the desire for war, or the causes that make war inevitable.'[78]

Smoke STATE

CHAPTER FOURTEEN

DEMOBILISATION AND LEGACIES

previous pages
A crowd outside the Christchurch Railway Station welcomes returned servicemen.
ALEXANDER TURNBULL LIBRARY, 1/1-017610-G

In one sense, formal declarations and organised celebrations distinctly marked New Zealand's transition from war to peace. In another sense, however, the path out of the war was more intricate. The conflict had 'seeped and stormed into New Zealanders' lives and could not be quickly dislodged at war's end'.[1] The legacies and impacts of the war were varied, sometimes paradoxically so, and rippled through New Zealand's politics, society, culture and populace in equally complex ways.

The scale of New Zealand's mobilisation at the end of the war was staggering. The reinforcement system had successfully kept the New Zealand Division at full strength, despite the distance involved, and at the end of the war the division was arguably the best reinforced on the Western Front.[2] Some 100,444 men had been on active service — in war zones, within staging areas and on troopships. When those in training camps are added, the total figure was 124,211, some 10 per cent of New Zealand's total population or 19.4 per cent of the male population.[3] Britain, by contrast, mobilised 27.4 per cent of its men, Australia 13.5 per cent, Canada 13.5 per cent and South Africa 11.1 per cent.[4]

The Defence Department had faced a huge task. A mid-1918 independent audit into its administration indicated what had been achieved: 'We have looked for failings and recorded them herein but on the way we found admirable work of much greater quantity . . . In all essentials the Administration has succeeded. A few instances: £40,000,000 spent and no frauds. An Army of 100,000 men excellently and fully equipped, and carried to the other end of the world. A declaration by the most responsible public man four years ago that this could be done by New Zealand would have been described as "rhetoric" — or worse.'[5]

Other official, semi-official and volunteer bodies could boast the same kind of success, whether it was the number of medical checks performed or exemption hearings assessed or charity performed. In the course of the war, patriotic societies raised an estimated £5,447,991 — roughly $587 million in contemporary terms. The wealth poured into the war effort is estimated at £81,538,570, at the end of the 1921 financial year, effectively doubling public debt.[6]

More significantly, the human costs of the war were measured in lives cut short, the physical and psychological scars borne by survivors, and the lives diminished by the loss of loved ones. New Zealand's total casualties were registered as 59,483, 16,302 of whom were killed in battle or died of wounds. Subsequent revisions have increased the total killed to about 18,100, a per capita figure of almost 1.6 per cent of the population.[7] This was broadly comparable with Britain's 1.5 per cent, and lower than Austria–Hungary's 2.5 per cent, Germany's 3 per cent, France's 3.5 per cent and Serbia's figure of near 25 per cent. There is no basis to claims that New Zealand had a higher number of dead per capita than any other nation.[8]

The resolve and capacity to bear this effort and its costs is also staggering. Partly this reflects the enduring convictions of New Zealand authorities. Foremost was Sir James Allen, who by the end of the war had won wide recognition for his stewardship of the country's military system, and much else, in his role as acting prime minister for 23 of the war's 52 months. Noting the crowd's reception of Allen at an event to mark the Turkish surrender, his fellow Reform MP Alexander Malcolm reported:

> Two years ago it was often said that Sir James Allen was the most unpopular man in New Zealand. To-day, I am told, that, in the North Island at any rate, he is the most popular, and that the people honour and admire him for his courage, his strength, and his steadfastness. Listening to the long and continued cheers and shouts of welcome that greeted him as he stepped forward, I could believe it.

Truth, no fawning admirer of Massey's lieutenant, stated a qualified respect for Allen's conduct: '"Truth" seldom agreed with his policy. "Truth" often questioned his administration, but "Truth" once again admits that it knows of no man in the House, certainly of no man on the Tory side of the House who could have done as well as, not to say better than, Sir James Allen did . . . It is admitted by friend and foe alike that he had the heaviest burden of all to carry.'[9]

New Zealand's resolve ultimately reflected a broader public consensus that the war should be fought. This commitment was not universal or unconditional, as various instances of absolute and provisional dissent demonstrated, and it was buttressed by coercion. However, the nation's domestic and political consensus remained remarkably intact compared to the extreme cases of Russia, Germany or Ireland and even in comparison to Australia, which experienced far higher levels of industrial unrest, political division and sectarian antagonism, and Canada, where the 1918 Easter riots have been described — with pardonable exaggeration — as taking that country to the 'brink of civil war'. It is noted that Hughes 'must have looked across the Tasman in envy at the relative ease with which conscription was introduced in New Zealand' and New Zealand officials only had to glance across the Tasman to 'remind them of the wisdom of maintaining a tight ship'.[10]

A similar point might be made about the economy. Despite intractable troubles with labour shortages, shipping constraints and tense industrial relations, production was remarkably resilient. As one 1918 assessment noted, 'perhaps the most salient feature of New Zealand agriculture during the year — a period comprising most of the fourth year of the Great War — has been its remarkable ability to "carry on" at a level of production but little below normal'.[11]

To some extent, New Zealand was able to carry on because it had continuous, if constrained, access to trade and a secure food supply, and was largely spared from enemy actions and economic disruption seen elsewhere. Over the 'turnip winter' of 1916–17, for example, official rations in Germany declined towards a July 1917 nadir of 1100 calories a day, some 11,000 ersatz products were on sale, Berlin's food prices had risen 178 to 400 per cent, and the average schoolchild was up to an inch shorter, between 4 and 8 pounds lighter and more susceptible to disease than their 1913 counterpart.[12]

By contrast, the standard weekly expenses for a New Zealand husband, wife and three children in July 1917 included 4 pounds of sirloin steak, 1 pound of bacon and of sausages, 3 pounds of stewing steak and 2 pounds of chops.[13] By 1918, when British consumers were restricted to a weekly meat ration of three-quarters of a pound, a New Zealander on a fixed pre-war budget could, even with inflated costs, afford more than five times as much meat and the country appeared to be consuming more than 5 pounds a head each week.[14] Although rising living costs proved a contentious domestic issue, New Zealand's 34 per cent increase from the outbreak of the war to March 1918 was significantly more bearable than the 107 per cent experienced in Britain over the same period.[15]

The end of the war held a promise that conditions would return to normal. An obvious aspect of demobilisation was the repatriation of an army's worth of servicemen and their re-entry into civilian life.[16] The undertaking was shaped by some competing concerns. On one hand was the sense of moral obligation and ongoing responsibility for returned and especially disabled servicemen's welfare: in the *Evening Star*'s words, 'we still have a great war responsibility'.[17] Efforts to evoke solidarity with veterans also informed various political campaigns. A returned soldier publication, for example, carried opposing political advertisements: 'You who have risked life and limb for your country's sake will not hesitate to banish Liquor for the Common Good' and 'Prohibitionists are like the Huns: They want to compel all to be like them.'[18]

Conversely, the government wanted, as much as possible, to avoid taking on permanent dependants and believed returned men would be best served by taking up conventional masculine roles of productive and self-reliant citizens. As Alexander Herdman had said in 1917, 'While the State will help to the utmost of its ability, it is impossible to supply every one with a Government billet — that way lie disappointment and disaster. Those who have returned in health and strength will best complete their service to their country by resuming as quietly and quickly as possible the duties they have temporarily laid down, and displaying in civil life the same qualities of courage, perseverance, and devotion to duty which have won them such a great reputation on the field of battle.'[19]

There was concern, too, that troops might bring venereal disease back to New Zealand and that many would have been 'brutalised' — left with psychological problems that would now be labelled post-traumatic stress but were typically then described as neurasthenia or shell shock.[20]

Some experience had been won during the war, with over 24,000 servicemen returning before the armistice. In August 1915 the Discharged Soldiers' Information Department was opened to assist the almost 700 who had returned from Gallipoli. In April 1916, a national Returned Soldiers' Association (RSA) had been founded from several local groups. By 1920 it had around 57,000 members and was established as a notable force in political lobbying and as a major social institution.[21] In December 1918, with the imminent prospect of some 58,000 troops returning, the Information Department was expanded into the Repatriation Department, managed by a board comprising the ministers of repatriation, railways, agriculture, education and lands and a journalist to handle publicity.[22] In its major objective of getting returned soldiers into the workforce, the department used several strategies. It issued more than 19,000 cheap loans to help veterans establish and furnish small businesses, but its most ambitious initiative was the soldier-settler scheme.[23] In October 1915 Parliament had passed the Discharged Soldiers' Settlement Act, which granted land and finance to ex-servicemen on generous terms. Over the next 15 years there were around 15,060 applications and 4018 allotments of a total of 1,415,847 acres of land.[24] In the spring of 1916, the Otamakapua Block, at Ōhingaiti south of Taihape, was a 'scene of great activity'.

> Each of the young settlers is rapidly felling the Manuka which covers his frontage, and getting the land nearer to a condition which will give some return for the labour expended. Some have done the work with their own labour, but those whose wounds still keep them from doing heavy work have had to get their work done by contract. Each section is beginning to show a small piece of ploughed ground on which the young farmer hopes to grow his potatoes, and in some cases a small amount of oats.[25]

The department also arranged vocational training for ex-soldiers and soldiers' widows, ranging from agricultural training to industrial trades and clerical work. Similar initiatives for Māori veterans included efforts to offer practical educational lectures and land settlement.[26] In 1921, 7193 returned men — 91.14 per cent of trainees on various courses — had completed their training and were 'absorbed by the industry or calling in which they were trained'. The state also encouraged employers to take on returned soldiers in their training schemes by offering wage subsidies. By August 1921 the department had helped 24,959 men into work. The Labour Department was told to give employment priority to returned servicemen and to favour them when filling public service vacancies. By 1921 some 8000 ex-soldiers were working in the Railway, Postal and Telegraph departments, and the general branches of the public service, and teaching in state schools.[27]

The ambition for self-reliance was most tested by veterans with ongoing or permanent health conditions, and some 'incurable cases' required long-term care. During the New Zealand Division's time on the Western Front, around 1511 had been evacuated as psychiatric casualties — though that figure represented but the tip of the iceberg — and by March 1920, 1007 men had been registered as amputees.[28] The number of war pension applications rose sharply as men returned to New Zealand: between 1918 and 1920 the Pensions Department received 35,524 applications from soldiers and soldiers' dependants.[29] By 1930 the state was paying pensions to around 12,653 permanently and temporarily disabled veterans and 6984

above A crowd gathers outside the Carterton Railway Station to welcome local returned servicemen. ALEXANDER TURNBULL LIBRARY, MSY-3872

below A Rotorua crowd watches a parade to welcome returned Māori servicemen. AUCKLAND WEEKLY NEWS, 17 APRIL 1919, P. 32

above A prostheticist working at Trentham Camp. Castings of artificial arms and feet are visible. AUCKLAND WAR MEMORIAL MUSEUM TĀMAKI PAENGA HIRA, PH-NEG-C34436

below An injured veteran performs rehabilitative leg exercises at Trentham Camp. AUCKLAND WAR MEMORIAL MUSEUM TĀMAKI PAENGA HIRA, PH-NEG-C34445 dependants.[30] Of these pensions the three largest categories were for 'wounds' (48 per cent), respiratory issues (16 per cent) and amputations (7 per cent).[31]

During the war the public hospital system had dealt with returned servicemen, and military hospitals and a series of convalescent homes had been established to aid recuperation.[32] In early 1918, the military increasingly managed and specialised the system.[33] Trentham Camp hospital came to serve as a diagnostic centre for returned soldiers, who were then sent to specialist facilities. Those with orthopaedic problems went to King George V Hospital in Rotorua, as well as to Trentham Camp hospital, Chalmers Hospital in Christchurch or Dunedin Public Hospital (where pioneering reconstructive surgery was carried out by Henry Pickerill).[34] Pulmonary tuberculosis cases were referred to the Pukeora Sanatorium, or to the military ward within Christchurch's Cashmere Sanatorium. Heart problems were addressed at Featherston and Narrow Neck camp hospitals. Psychiatric conditions were treated at Queen Mary Hospital at Hanmer Springs and civilian mental hospitals.[35]

Some camp facilities were used to aid rehabilitation efforts. In June 1919 Trentham Camp hospital was reorganised with facilities including a gym, and a curative and vocational training workshop with a strong focus on rehabilitating ex-soldiers into trades.[36] Hospitals and convalescent homes also offered 'cot cases' activities including leather- and basket-work, wood-carving, spinning and weaving and embroidery. Those less physically incapacitated were offered other vocational activities including farming and carpentry.[37]

By 1922 most returned servicemen had been reintegrated into civilian life, and the need for a specialised repatriation system was greatly reduced. Pension applications fell dramatically after 1920 and still more after 1921.[38] By 1921, the majority of wounded men had been discharged from the hospital system and the Defence Department began to transfer its hospitals back to the Health Department. Between June 1921 and June 1922 the Repatriation Department's staff numbers were effectively halved from 111 to 63 and branches outside the four centres were closed.[39] Six months later, the department closed entirely. Its financial assistance role would, at least in part, be inherited by the State Advances Office.

A historical tradition has firmly impressed the limits of repatriation efforts with claims that the soldier-settler scheme was 'one of the greatest disasters of social planning New Zealand has ever known'; according to one view, 'The story of the World War One veteran in New Zealand is one of betrayal.'[40] These are not baseless charges: many soldier-settler farms did ultimately fail. Whanganui's 'bridge to nowhere', constructed in the abandoned ambition to open up land for cultivation, has remained a symbol of forsaken endeavours.[41] Likewise, the Māori education scheme has been described as 'not very successful' and only 1.8 per cent of Māori veterans, compared with nearly 10 per cent of Pākehā, were helped to acquire land.[42]

However, a revisionist tradition has offered a warmer evaluation, generally emphasising the efforts made and the successes gained and that the economic volatilities of the 1920s and the Great Depression affected society as a whole, not just former soldiers.[43] Perhaps most telling were the results of a 1929 commission established to 'inquire into and report upon the position of physically and economically incapacitated soldiers'. It confirmed a basis for conceptions of veterans suffering in hardship and found that an estimated 5000 — some 6 per cent of returned servicemen — were 'not in a position adequate to maintain themselves and their dependants'.[44] Beyond this, the picture was decidedly more mixed, with large numbers of men having successfully re-established themselves in civilian life.

The political arrangements of the coalition government did not long survive the end of the war. There was talk of a permanent political truce between Reform and Liberal, and such rumours had some basis. At the start of 1919, the *New Zealand Herald* noted that 'there are adherents of both Liberalism and Reform who believe that the coalition should become a fusion in order to safeguard the State against extremists and their Bolshevik doctrines'.[45] However, on 21 August, a fortnight after he and Massey returned from Versailles, Ward signalled the end of the coalition by announcing he was resigning his portfolios.[46] A general election was set for December 1919, near half a decade since the previous contest.

If the war had masked, rather than suspended, party politics, the 1919 election saw them vividly, if not viciously, reasserted. Internally, Massey survived serious division within Reform ranks and an attempted coup.[47] Externally, the party presented the election as a showdown between conservativism and radicalism. In Massey's words, 'We have solved the problems of war, and, if we deal with the problems of peace with the same determination, all will be well.' The most important issue was, he announced, 'Who is going to govern the country for the next three years? Is it to be the law-abiding, responsible, and patriotic elements of the community, or is it to be the political extremists — a combination of Bolsheviks, I.W.W.'s, revolutionary Socialists, and others of the same category?'[48] Ward and the Liberals were presented as insignificant, although Reform claimed that a vote for them was dangerous as they could partner with 'extremists' in the Labour Party. Reform's electoral policy was light: it has been described as 'a shred of socialism, a patch of patriotism, a humanitarian thread, and an imperialist ribbon on the ragged conservative cloak'.[49]

Labour returned fire, pitching the election as a showdown between Tories and workers. Signalling an end of the Lib-Lab alliance, the party campaigned as an independent entity with ambitions to constitute a government in its own right and contested 54 seats, three times more than in 1914.[50] Its advertisements presented the Labour Party as the heirs of Seddon and drove the point home by pronouncing that the Liberals belonged to 'the dead past' and would 'never again be a serious force in the politics of this country'.[51] Labour's election manifesto pledged extensive social reforms including free medical care and education; public ownership of all food industries, banking, shipping and coal mining; and state control of insurance. The Military Service Act and compulsory military training were to be repealed. Proposed electoral reforms included the abolition of the country quota and the introduction of proportional representation.[52]

The Liberals also declared a decidedly radical party programme; Labour's performance in last year's by-elections had demonstrated that the party's left flank was vulnerable. Efforts to rally workers to the Liberal tradition included the nationalisation of the Bank of New Zealand, ferry services, the production of electricity, coal mining, freezing works and flourmills, and massive spending on public works and land settlement. Liberal political advertisements called for workers to 'Stand by Liberalism NOW!', warning that Labour vote-splitting would help Reform, and adding, 'The extremists are blind leaders of the blind! The path they would have you follow descends into the abyss of Revolution, Anarchy and Ruin.'[53]

The election was hard fought, with an ugly undercurrent fed by wartime strains and ideological battle lines reflecting the situations in Russia and Ireland. For the Labour Party, the division between revolutionary socialism and welfare reformism was illuminated with 'a realism, bluntness and urgency never experienced before'.[54] Some militant socialists within the party underwent 'a partial revision towards their traditionally doctrinaire position' and some willingly, if credulously, endorsed revolutionary positions.[55] The increasingly national profile of Bob Semple was a clear example.

In December 1918, a little more than a year after his release from jail, Semple had stood for Wellington South, left vacant by Hindmarsh's death, and won with 56 per cent of the vote; his victory speech had proclaimed that whereas the government had sent him and Fraser to jail, the voters were sending them to Parliament.[56] Semple began to weave revolutionary rhetoric into his speeches and, in February 1919, for example, proclaimed: 'They call us now "Bolsheviks". I accept the term. I glory in the Russian workingmen's pluck, and I am sorry that there is not more of it in New Zealand. If I were in Russia I would be with Trotsky and Lenin. If I were in Ireland I would be a Sinn Feiner and if I were in Germany I would be a Spartacusan.'[57]

Against ongoing reports of the chaos and atrocities in the Russian Civil War, such claims repulsed Labour moderates, who distanced themselves from such rhetoric; poet and social activist Jessie Mackay suggested that Semple be chloroformed if not repudiated. The *Maoriland Worker* directed a similar hint at Holland: 'When he declared that he does not object to being called a Bolshevik, he should bear in mind that many of his followers might.'[58] In Allen's view, the campaigning efforts of Labour moderates such as John Paul had been 'largely discounted by speech delivered by Semple declaring himself in favour of Bolshevism'.

Allen also noted that such rhetoric was causing businessmen to organise, 'to secure good men to stem the tide of Anarchy and Bolshevism'.[59] In July 1919 the New Zealand Welfare League emerged, announcing its purpose of countering 'the activities of extreme and revolutionary Labour' whose 'most prominent leaders had announced approval of the activities of the I.W.W. doctrines and Bolshevism, and of the reign of terror in Russia'.[60] Besides those from the ranks of the Employers' Association, the 'good men' of the league included several formerly prominent Labour figures, notably David McLaren. Commanding considerable financial resources, the league put its support behind anti-Labour candidates and placed virulent anti-Labour Party advertisements in newspapers.

Likewise, the PPA was continuing to grow. According to Elliott, it had some 250,000 members by 1920, just under 20 per cent of the population.[61] Even allowing for considerable embellishment, the organisation clearly had significant influence. Although the results of the 1918 by-elections deterred the PPA from standing its own candidates in 1919, it acted as a pressure group aligned with Reform, though the dynamics of this alignment have been debated. Some have stated that the association worked hand in glove with Reform; others have suggested that 'far from being considered an ally', Massey regarded Elliott and the PPA as 'a menace' and that an open affair with the PPA was an unnecessary risk since 'the "Protestant vote" was Reform's already'.[62] The PPA ran a repeat of its 1918 smear campaign, warning of the unholy alliance of Catholics and radical labour and endorsing every Reform candidate except Allen, whom Elliott had not forgiven for his exemption of Catholic clergy.[63]

Wartime sentiments meant the contest was obviously going to be a khaki election and opponents presented Labour's record as suspect at best. In a speech greeted with 'loud and long applause', the Independent Liberal candidate for Parnell, Rosetta Baume, asked: 'Did extreme Labor, which, now says it was loyal all through the war, ever condemn the sinking of the Lusitania, the murder of Captain Fryatt, the murder of Nurse Cavell and many other things I could mention?'[64]

It was perhaps Massey, though, who was most content to place himself at the heart of such a combative contest and to present himself as embodying patriotic solidarity with returned soldiers and as a bulwark against disloyalty. Replying to a heckler in Papakura, he declared, 'The soldiers have had a "square deal," and I am going to see they continue to get a "square deal," . . . All the "Red Feds," and "I.W.W.'s" and Sinn Feiners in New Zealand can't keep me out.' Amid the applause was a hostile interjection from 'a voice with a brogue', to whom Massey retorted, 'You go back to Ireland. We don't want you here.'[65]

Bellicosity did not, however, always go Massey's way. His campaigning in polarised Christchurch was met with both cheering and counter-demonstrations. On 4 December, the prime minister was due to speak at the 4000-seat Colosseum hall at 8 p.m., but by seven o'clock the seats were full and the doors were shut for an hour. By 7.30, men were 'struggling to approach the doors and scores of people [were] ventilating personal grievances or political convictions'. Some young men 'had climbed up to the corrugated roof and proceeded to storm the skylights'. When Massey rose to speak, 'his voice was drowned by the excited efforts of the battering rams on the side doors', which gave way so that hundreds of men poured into the hall, 'like Niagara Falls', bringing the total to an estimated 6000–7000. In the resulting chaos the event was cancelled and relocated to the rotunda in Victoria Square, but electors heard a band rather than Massey.[66]

The 1919 election was held on 16 and 17 December, with an official turnout of 80.5 per cent. Reform took 35.7 per cent of the vote.[67] Although this was a decrease from its 47.1 per cent in 1914, the idiosyncrasies of a first past the post system with a country quota meant the party gained six seats, ending up with a total of 45. This large majority marked the beginning of Reform's dominance for nearly a decade after the war. The party's post-war domestic policy revolved around what has been called 'the provision of opportunities', particularly home ownership, which continued ideals of a property-owning democracy; secondary schooling, where state investment grew significantly; and modernisation schemes for electrification and development.[68] Massey also headed a pugilist stance against radical politics and continued to see staunch imperial unity as necessary to guarantee security. New Zealand's attitude towards the League of Nations was characterised by degrees of indifference, low-level antagonism, suspicion and resigned acceptance.[69]

The Labour Party's professed sympathy with the Returned Soldiers is a bit touching, but it does not touch the point of how little the Party helped the Soldiers when they were away.

The Labour Party hails Paddy Webb as a hero because he would not fight and praises Jim McKenzie because he did fight. You see, the Party is neutral, quite neutral.

Don't sublet your Thinking to a Party, especially a Party that attacks the rights of free speech and honest representation.

The voter who supports the Labour Candidate because he looks mild, and talks moderate, forgets that his Party is a Tiger for Revolution.

PUBLISHED BY ARRANGEMENT FOR

N.Z. WELFARE LEAGUE.

An example of the Welfare League's political propaganda during the 1919 general election. The Labour candidate is depicted as betraying the New Zealand soldier and is wearing a Phrygian cap, symbolising freedom-fighting or, in this context, revolution. NEW ZEALAND FREE LANCE, 10 DECEMBER 1919, P. 20

Retaining his position as prime minister, Massey demonstrated a longevity in marked contrast to other Allied leaders — including Lloyd George, Georges Clemenceau, Sir Robert Borden and Woodrow Wilson — all of whom either died, retired or were removed from office shortly into the peace. On 10 May 1925, nearly 13 years after Ward's wry toast wishing him as long a time in office as he deserved, Massey died of cancer while still serving as prime minister. In 1927, the newly founded New Zealand Agricultural College was renamed after him and his memorial/tomb, built at Point Halswell, Wellington, was unveiled in September 1930. Its inscription reads 'A Memorial of Loyal Service to King and Country'. When Christina Massey died in April 1932, she, too, was interred there.

Some recent assessment has broken from a historical tradition that has generally portrayed Massey as bigoted, unpleasant and dull and has reconsidered his leadership, skill and popularity. To this end he has been ranked as on par with Richard Seddon as the country's second-greatest prime minister.[70]

By the time of Massey's death, Sir James Allen's career had developed outside the limelight of parliamentary politics. Exhausted by his wartime burdens, he had stood in the 1919 election only on the understanding that he could shortly retire to serve as high commissioner in London. Although he retained his seat, he left New Zealand for his new role on 30 April 1920. In the following years he oversaw arrangements for New Zealand's administration of Western Sāmoa, served as New Zealand's delegate to the League of Nations, and represented the country at the dedication of war memorials in Europe and at Gallipoli. In this last role he was one of the rare interwar New Zealanders able to visit his son's grave.

After returning to New Zealand in 1926, he was prominent in the Institute of Pacific Relations, became a lay reader in the Anglican Church and resumed his association with the Bible-in-Schools League, becoming its vice-president and chairing the Otago branch. In 1927, when he became a legislative councillor, he sat alongside Mark Briggs, one of the 14 objectors forcibly transported to Europe. He is said to have apologised for what Briggs had suffered, claiming he had not known about it at the time.[71] Some years after his wife's death, Allen died on 28 July 1942, 28 years to the day after Austria's declaration of war on Serbia, knowing that his prediction of a 'contest nearer our own door than the contest of to-day' had come to pass as the Second World War raged in the Pacific.

Another major development of the 1919 election was the Liberals' 'quantum leap towards oblivion'.[72] The party's share of the vote dropped from 43.1 to 28.7 per cent and their number of seats from 34 to 19. Prominent casualties included Ward, who lost his Awarua seat to Reform, and his deputy George Russell, who lost his Avon seat to Labour. Portions of the party's traditional voters appear to have migrated to the right and the left, as Reform tightened its rural support base and Labour appealed to urban workers. According to the *New Zealand Herald* the election showed that 'the trend of political development is towards two parties, one extreme the other moderate'.[73] *Truth* agreed on the trend, if valuing it differently, and regretted the end of the Lib-Lab alliance.[74]

In the election's aftermath Sir Joseph Ward resigned as Liberal Party leader and left Parliament. He did, however, have an extraordinary second wind. In the 1925 general election he won Invercargill and re-entered a Parliament now without his rival. In 1928 he led the United Party, formed out of the remnants of the Liberal Party, and, in his seventies, again became prime minister. In his biographer's assessment, Ward's second premiership was marked by failing political vision and declining vitality — during one parliamentary session he was observed sleeping on his seat with his hat over his face.[75] Theresa Ward's death in 1927 also removed an important confidante and source of support.

In May 1930 Ward resigned as prime minister, though he retained a Cabinet position, and seven weeks later he died and was buried with some ceremony in Bluff, where a statue in his likeness stands. In his tribute to Ward, Harry Holland reflected on an almost 40-year career in public office that connected the 'present period with the strenuous past' and said that his death represented 'the breaking of a link of historical significance'.[76] Six years later the United Party merged with Reform to establish the National Party, seemingly fulfilling the realignment of party politics envisioned when the wartime coalition was formed.

In 1919 the Labour Party, in its first general electoral run, secured 24.2 per cent of the vote and eight seats in Parliament, three more than the previous Labour grouping; the remaining eight seats were taken by independent MPs. Those who had believed that wartime discontent and revolutionary examples would fire a decisive rejection of the status quo were disappointed and bitter. For the *Maoriland Worker*, the election,

> on the part of the two great parties which have monopolised the power of misrepresenting the people, was a sordid fight for the sweets of office, in which money, and the power of the Press, vituperation, misrepresentation, and distortion of facts showed to what an extent the political game, as played to-day, can reduce people claiming to be intelligent. A people that tolerates this kind of thing could not be expected to have taken so big a step towards something like real self-government as voting Labor into power.[77]

Those with more cautious, or realistic, expectations appeared pleased with Labour's gains. The election has been cast as a milestone in the rise of the Labour Party towards holding the balance of power after the 1928 election and forming a government in 1935.[78]

This development was entwined with the post-war lives of some major Labour leaders. In 1919 Harry Holland won in Buller — Grey was abolished by boundary changes — and, with Hindmarsh's death, soon secured the leadership of the party. Throughout the 1920s he continued his criticism and activism — championing workers' rights, opposing military training, protesting the situation in Ireland — and emerged as a resolute critic of New Zealand's record in Sāmoa. However, Labour's political thinking shifted over this time: opposition to arbitration faded, plans for land nationalisation were abandoned and praise for Bolshevism soured as antagonism developed between the Labour Party and a domestic Communist Party. Holland has conventionally been regarded as slow to change and it has been questioned whether his doctrinaire Marxism alienated voters.[79] On 8 October 1933, he died of a heart attack at Huntly after attending the funeral of Te Rata. Following a state funeral on 11 October, Holland was buried in Wellington, a short distance from Seddon's tomb.[80]

In the 1919 election Peter Fraser held Wellington Central, a seat that would remain his for the rest of his career. Aged 34, he was positioned for the ever more prominent role he would play in political and national life. This trajectory eventually saw him become a Cabinet minister in the first Labour government, which set out to restore a depressed economy, enact various social reforms and establish itself as a critic of Britain's policy of appeasement in the face of Japanese, Italian and German belligerence. In 1940 he became prime minister of a country at war and found himself facing a series of political, social and economic concerns that would have been familiar to his 1914–18 predecessors. His performance throughout the war and until his political defeat in 1949, and death some 12 months later, has conventionally ranked him among New Zealand's greatest prime ministers, if not the greatest.[81]

The wider apparatus of the war effort underwent an often haphazard demobilisation. Some powers and practices were surrendered relatively quickly; for instance, the 1919 general election obviously signalled the overturn of the Parliamentary Elections Postponement Act. In other cases, the reversion to earlier forms was gradual. For example, customs duties, which constituted 60 per cent of taxation revenues in 1914, had fallen to 29 per cent by 1918 as other forms of taxation were introduced. By 1925, however, they were once again the most significant source of taxation at 50.39 per cent.[82] Some wartime powers remained on the statute books well into peacetime; the 'emergency' measure of six o'clock closing, for example, remained the law of the land until 1967, five decades after its introduction.[83]

The military machinery of balloting, training and supplying soldiers was soon wound down. Within days of the news of the armistice, many Military Service Boards were suspending operations and a number had disbanded by December. The Department of Munitions and Supplies had closed by the end of March 1919. Arthur Myers received numerous letters of commendation; his administration was described as 'probably the only department in the British Empire dealing with munitions that had not been the subject of some scandal'.[84]

On 21 November 1918 London ordered an official halt to reinforcements, making the Forty-third Reinforcements, which had embarked in October, the last in a long chain.[85] Days earlier Allen had pledged that 'we shall not hold any of the men in camp a day longer than we need to'.[86] Although the influenza pandemic and the consequent disruption of transport schedules enormously complicated this, and helped to fuel an 'ugly demonstration' by 5000 troops at Featherston Camp, by early December hundreds of men were being discharged daily.[87] Māori conscripts in training were sent home and Cabinet cancelled the outstanding warrants for Waikato defaulters. An advisory board advocated special treatment and, against advice from the military, Cabinet elected to quietly release Māori prisoners on 20 May 1919.[88]

Cabinet's attitude towards other men imprisoned for refusing or avoiding military service was less forgiving. Ministers considered it unfair to release imprisoned men until the repatriation of servicemen had been completed. The industrial conscription of Yugoslavs continued into 1919, to the surprise and anger of many involved. The government insisted that the underlying rationale, to equalise sacrifice for a population that was exempt from military

THE SOLDIER'S CHAMPION

NAPIER'S POPULAR PARLIAMENTARY REPRESENTATIVE

Who speaks his mind, and speaks it well,
Who does the deed while others dwell;
Who ne'er forgot the soldier boy,
Who changed the tear to heartfelt joy?
Was It Not VIGOR BROWN?

Whose promises have been redeemed,
Does what by him the best is deemed,
Who fought the enemy within
While "Diggers" drove him to Berlin.
Napier's VIGOR BROWN!

Who's patriotic and sincere,
Who's never known to quail or fear,
Who's been the most progressive Mayor,
And with the workers has been fair?
Why, good old VIGOR BROWN!

Various causes continued to court returned soldiers' support. Here Liberal MP Vigor Brown is presented as 'the soldier's champion' during campaigning for the 1919 election. NZ TRUTH, 13 DECEMBER 1919, P. 2

service, remained valid. Cullen met refusals to work with a crackdown on 'ring-leaders' and threats of deportation. The scheme did not formally end until the end of August 1919.[89]

Other machinery and powers of the wartime state lingered, particularly those related to official concerns of global instability and social unrest. At the end of January 1919, Police Commissioner O'Donovan circulated a confidential memorandum to district officers across New Zealand, announcing that since 'considerable industrial and other unrest' in other countries 'may extend to this Dominion', special precautions were needed to 'keep in touch with the movements and actions of persons of revolutionary tendencies who are already here, or who may arrive'. A detective in each of the four main centres was assigned to full-time monitoring of revolutionary activity; in smaller towns and rural areas detectives and constables would report as necessary. In September 1920 the Defence Department observed that Bolshevik-inspired actions would lead to violence and that it was 'reasonable to assume that the authorities would be required to deal with outbreaks of Bolshevism, and strikes on a large scale in New Zealand'.[90]

Critics looked darkly on these enduring regulations. In August 1920, Labour MP William Parry asked, 'Is there any man in the House who can justify a continuation of the war regulations?... It seems to me that this government is bent upon entering into an undignified scuffle with the rank and file of the people.'[91] In this context state management of information also lingered for some time, and after Gibbon left New Zealand in April 1919, Walter Tanner was retained to oversee the system of postal censorship and, later, film censorship.[92] As Allen privately put it, 'we find that a good deal of valuable information comes to the Government through the medium of the Censor, and it was thought wise not to lose this information'. Tanner also defended the practice: 'During the course of the late war [it was necessary] to examine secretly the correspondence of certain persons who were supposed to be disaffected,' and added that censorship 'gave the Police the necessary opening... to break up organisations whilst still in the act of formation'.[93] After mid-1920 the continuation of postal censorship was repeatedly questioned in Parliament, with the government citing technicalities as the reason for delaying its cessation. Systematic operations under military authority appear to have officially concluded on 16 November that year.[94]

The future of state intelligence and surveillance work was also being considered on a wider field. In March 1919, Liverpool wrote to Allen regarding British plans to put intelligence co-operation between Britain and the dominions 'on a permanent footing'. Allen replied, 'I have no hesitation in giving assurance that in the event of the organization of the Imperial Special Intelligence Bureau being placed on a permanent footing the New Zealand Government will be only too pleased to see that the co-operation of the local bureau is continued in the future.'[95] Measures to regulate and suppress subversive literature continued into the 1920s, with day-to-day monitoring of 'revolutionary' material relying on co-operation between the police, customs and the postal and telegraphic services. Others discussed the possibility of turning propaganda efforts towards improving public awareness of military affairs, though this initiative was ultimately rejected.[96]

The transition of the economy to a peacetime footing was marked by both a return to pre-war norms and lasting wartime influences. The commandeer continued to provide a degree of stability and economic buoyancy; by 1921 the arrangement had, since its introduction, earnt some £160 million. However, between June 1920 and March 1921 Britain wound down the initiative and stockpiled goods were dumped on the British market, bringing a collapse of commodity prices during 'the slump' of 1920–21.[97] Likewise, in a heady mix of socialistic ideals and commercial pragmatism, some called for the retention of the principles and practices of centralised management in the post-war economy.[98] Certainly, ongoing tensions over living costs led to an extended mandate for the Board of Trade in 1919, giving it various regulatory powers over prices and industry. The National Efficiency Board, on the other hand, contributed some planning to post-war economic adjustments but was soon disbanded, though elements of its work and rationale were echoed in other state planning endeavours.[99]

Although some restrictions lingered — for example, a nationwide shortage of woollen goods was reported in the winter of 1919 — imports boomed from £24 million in 1918–19 to £61.1 million in 1920: a level not exceeded until 1937.[100] A binge of consumption followed as a war-weary population sought normality and diversion. 'People here,' wrote the *Manawatu Times* in December 1920, 'have never spent more on their amusements . . . The moving picture houses are crowded . . . Money is being thrown about in gambling at the rate of over three-quarters of a million sterling a month . . . We have imported much more wine, spirits and beer, much more tobacco; the number of new motor-cars has doubled — even the figures for millinery and the personal adornment of the female of the species show a tremendous increase.' But it was not mere extravagance: 'we are all replenishing our rather threadbare wardrobes'.[101]

Worsening industrial relations also continued beyond the end of the war. Indeed, the relative calm of 40 industrial disputes, involving 4056 workers, in 1918 contrasts with the 77 disputes, involving 15,138 workers, that broke out in 1920. As during the war, rising living costs and reviving militancy within the labour movement were part of the explanation.[102] Moreover, longer hours and lack of leave during the war had generally been accepted as a contribution to the war effort, but in peacetime pent-up frustrations flared.

The wartime passions and animosities that underwrote public commitment were fuelled by righteous attitudes and many highly personal sentiments, and these did not promise to easily disappear with the armistice. The *Observer*, for example, would not countenance rapprochement with anything German:

> You are not going to shake hands with the brother of the soldier who carved off the hands of little Flemish girls, are you? Will you fall on the neck of the German with a bagful of samples knowing that his cousin spiked octogenarian women to French barn doors? Will you admit to your universities German professors who exonerated Prussian villains from blame by publicly boasting of relationship to them . . . Peace comes with the bitterness of the greatest war still unhealed, and unlikely to be healed in our time. Peace comes without any indication of world fraternity, and without forgiveness.[103]

Actions backed rhetoric: in May 1919 over 400 internees and former residents were deported from New Zealand on the *Willochra*. Indicative of entrenched attitudes, news on the event was headlined 'A Good Riddance'.[104]

Enduring, too, were punitive attitudes towards 'shirkers'. As Archibald Baxter's wife Millicent wrote many years later, 'nowadays people cannot realise the extent of the feeling against conscientious objectors that still existed shortly after the first war'.[105] This was revealed when Hewitt's report of abuses at Whanganui detention barracks was made public in December 1918. Many denounced the methods used as intolerable and decried the idea of using such coercion to make men violate their principles. Headlines noted 'Hun methods', 'Barbarous methods' and 'horrors at Wanganui'. The Christchurch Ministers' Association passed a resolution to register 'its detestation of the ferocity and brutality exhibited by those in charge of the Wanganui Detention Barracks' and its assessment that 'the perpetrators of these barbarities should be brought to trial and severely punished'.[106]

Hewitt's findings were reported alongside the further revelation that Crampton had been court-martialled in December 1916 for assaulting a woman while stationed in Sāmoa. Though cleared of sexual impropriety, he had been found guilty of assault and reprimanded. A letter to the *Sun* thought that this behaviour showed Crampton was clearly unfit to be in charge at Whanganui. Holland requested a guarantee that Crampton would not be retained as an officer and that men would not be placed under his charge.[107]

Many, however, felt differently, and in response to the Christchurch Ministers' Association's protest, a group of Whanganui ministers stated that justice had already been done.[108] Much commentary argued that the treatment of the objectors was mild compared with what

A Masterton crowd gathers for the unveiling of the local war memorial on 16 September 1923.
WAIRARAPA ARCHIVE, 92-128

the soldiers had suffered and that professed sympathy would be better directed towards returned servicemen.[109] Under the heading 'Howls of the Shirker', the *Rangitikei Advocate and Manawatu Argus* proclaimed that shirkers were 'little better than brutes', that pulling 'recalcitrants' around by a rope was 'harder on the puller than the pulled', that 'compliance with the rules of the establishment would at any time have ensured them immunity from corporal punishment' and that '[i]f we have any commiseration to spare it is for those heroes of ours in the firing line who, through hardships and suffering that transcend their own powers of description, have saved the Empire'.[110]

Unrepentant, Crampton demanded a court martial to clear his record, and returned soldiers and some relatives of soldiers urged support for him. He was found not guilty on 11 charges of ill-treating a soldier and honourably acquitted in February 1919. A later assessment notes that this court was 'more impressed than Hewitt with arguments about the military justification and precedent for force' and that it possibly 'came closer to the truth and the force used was not as severe as initially alleged, or as found by Hewitt, but undeniably force was used'.[111]

The passions in play also offer some context for the objections raised against any amnesty towards objectors. The Christchurch branch of the RSA was one of many that passed a resolution protesting 'any remission of sentence being granted to any man, who is undergoing imprisonment for refusal to serve his Country or for sedition' and wanted 'all steps taken' to prosecute deserters. The Rotorua RSA asked for objectors on the medical staff at Rotorua Hospital to be declared ineligible for promotion or duty pay and 'compelled to wear distinguishing armlets' so they would not be confused with returned soldiers. After an investigation set up in January 1919, 'about half' of the 273 in prison were released. The last imprisoned objectors were not freed until November 1920, after the last servicemen had come home.[112]

However, with time, wartime bellicosity faded. Indeed, historian Miles Fairburn considers the 1920s as a decade that successfully checked and absorbed much of the discord of the previous decade: 'From 1912 to 1921, Pakeha New Zealand was wracked by the worst years of collective conflict in its history, but by the end of the period unity and peace prevailed within the framework of a new consensus.'[113]

In March 1919, Katherine Holmes, now president of the Women's Anti-German League, convened a farewell afternoon tea to mark the end of the organisation's activities, although there was a brief reunion in July when the Alliance Française gave members of the original executive medals and bouquets in recognition of their wartime work.[114] Handing out the prizes was Sir Robert Stout, the acting governor-general and husband of Anna Stout. In her view, the league had 'prevented a great deal of harm being done by enemy aliens in our midst'. It had 'been confronted with many difficulties, and had had to fight against powerful influences. It had also had to work very quietly. Had not members dropped away from the society in the way they had much more work could have been accomplished.' It would still be necessary, though, to boycott German goods and to fight for 'restrictive measures against the Germans in our midst', including banning them from becoming magistrates, justices of the peace, entering the civil service or holding parliamentary seats.[115]

Sectarian tensions were more entrenched. While some were eased by the removal of volatile wartime questions around equality of sacrifice, and despite some answer being given to the Irish question by the 1922 formation of the Irish Free State, militant elements endured for some time. In the aftermath of the 1919 election, Howard Elliott held that the PPA was the most powerful political force in the country. Seventy per cent of MPs pledged to uphold the association's principles, and around 40 owed their seats directly to its support.[116] The PPA remained a mass and politically influential organisation throughout another two election cycles, campaigning for various concessions. James Kelly also continued the political style he had honed during the war and met news of the peace conference by writing, 'Now, for an Irishman who sees at the end of the war for the freedom of small nations the heel of John Bull on the neck of Erin it would be natural enough to find no cause to rejoice and to dance to order like any Jingo marionette.'[117] The time and the efforts of moderates, however, ultimately reduced militant posturing. Henry Cleary, for example, continued his work to isolate Kelly. When he died of influenza and exhaustion in December 1929, he was given a large funeral, and tributes from various denominations testified to his success 'in reducing sectarian tensions and in beginning to bring the Catholic Church firmly into the mainstream of New Zealand life'.[118]

Kelly's position as editor of the *Tablet* became 'increasingly fractious and unhappy' and he resigned in December 1931, becoming a parish priest in Pungarehu, Taranaki.[119] By this time the PPA was in its death throes. Elliott resigned shortly after the 1928 election, when Ward, his long-time bogey, again became prime minister, and instead directed his oratorical and organisational skills towards financial journalism. The PPA was finally wound up in 1933.

The wartime veneration of self-sacrifice also underwent a post-war demobilisation. These sentiments were expressed in the wealth of memorials erected during the interwar years.[120] Wellington's cenotaph quotes from Rupert Brooke's 'The Dead': 'These laid the world away; poured out the red sweet wine of youth; gave up the years to be of work and joy, and that unhoped serene, that men call age; and those who would have been, their sons, they gave, their immortality'; the memorial gates of Auckland's Normal Intermediate School proclaims: 'These gates stand in proud memory of teachers of this province who in the hour of national danger took their place in the front line of battle and in the end yielded their lives for the land and people they loved'; Christchurch's Bridge of Remembrance is inscribed with 'Quid non pro patria' ('What will a man not do for his country'); Otago Boys' High School Memorial Archway quotes Horace's *Odes*: 'Dulce et decorum est pro patria mori' ('It is sweet and proper to die for one's country'); Palmerston North's memorial claims, 'On Armistice Day their spirits lined the parapet and cheered for a victory that had been worth the sacrifice'; Waitōtara's memorial quotes from the Gettysburg Address: 'Let us highly resolve that these dead shall not have died in vain'; Feilding's memorial, among many others, cites John 15:13, 'Greater love hath no man'; and the memorial in the small South Canterbury town of Winchester claims, 'We lie dead in many lands so that you might live here in peace.'

However, while themes of exemplary sacrifice and a moral relationship between the living and the dead endured, the wartime lesson that sacrifice was necessary to secure victory was extended into an ongoing obligation. As the mayor of Christchurch said on Anzac Day 1924, 'May we all prove worthy of what has been done for us, by placing the interests of the community before those of self, and making the Dominion a sweeter and better place for those who will come after us.'[121] Moreover, many explicitly demilitarised the nature of this ongoing commitment. At a 1922 memorial unveiling, for example, General Richardson declared, 'The great lesson Anzac had to teach us was sacrifice for the sake of others', but '[t]here were various forms of sacrifice, and a man did not need to wear a uniform to serve his country' and '[t]he service our women had rendered had perhaps been greater than that of the men'.[122]

Along with monuments, ongoing remembrance saw an acquisition of new rituals and symbols. The custom of a two-minute silence was adopted in Britain on the first anniversary of the armistice and instituted throughout the empire on 11 November 1920 to coincide with the interment of an unknown soldier in Westminster Abbey to represent the empire's dead.[123] One description claimed that the heart of the city ceased to beat:

> Prompt at the boom of the gun from Albert Park the traffic stopped in the streets as if stricken into stone. Offices ceased work, and far and wide in home and factory the pause of remembrance was honoured. In Queen Street the hurrying trams and motor cars ceased upon the instant. On the side walks little groups of citizens who had formed awaiting the signal stood with heads bared and bowed . . . Above in the sunshine a few great flags fluttered in the breeze, their life and colour and motion symbolising the victory whose price that great moment of silence was designed to recall in deep and reverent commemoration.[124]

Another pan-British institution was the choice of a poppy as a remembrance symbol; poppy appeals began as a New Zealand fundraising activity in November 1921.[125] In 1939, New Zealand Anzac Day commemorations institutionalised the dawn service — which originated in Australia — though some New Zealand ceremonies had included the ritual before that year. Some other elements of remembrance faded. For example, Armistice Day, later renamed Remembrance Sunday, was an official memorial day through the interwar period but went into terminal decline after 1945.[126]

As much as demobilisation promised, and delivered, some return to normalcy, it was recognised that the consequences of the war included an irreparable disruption of what had been. In the words of one editorial, printed with news of the armistice:

> Some people are troubled because they cannot feel as joyful as the occasion seems to demand, but this is simply because, after more than four years, the war has become a habit. Many children can hardly remember the days before the war and even older persons find it difficult to think back to the time before August, 1914, when suddenly the whole world was plunged in conflict. Our whole mental outlook has changed during the last four years and we cannot simply go back to the old conditions as if the war had never taken place.[127]

A memorial to former students of the Christchuch school Mairehau Boys' High who had served. Such memorials, recognising those who served as well as those who had been killed, became common in schools, churches, businesses and other institutions.
ALEXANDER TURNBULL LIBRARY, 1/1-024009-G

For many these disruptions were highly personal, and the war's legacies include their efforts to resume lives in the face of new conditions — as veterans, widows, fatherless children, mourners, pensioners and invalids. Other legacies occurred at a broader social level and, as with other aspects of the war's impacts, they can appear almost paradoxical. As one study notes, they include 'a mild reforming spirit, tempered by a general yearning for stability; an economic boom and bust which appeared to deliver and then destroy the "land fit for heroes"; an unprecedented Imperial loyalty, sectional rivalry, and social conformity'.[128] The war certainly accelerated many trends, such as the transformation of the political landscape, the population drift to the North Island, the huge boost to rural productivity made possible by technology and scientific management, and the rise of the 'tight society' in which codes of conformity became more rigid under a sense that all social elements should act, or at least appear to act, for the larger social good.[129]

This obligation to the public good also applied to the state. A large body of scholarship has observed a pattern between warfare — most notably the twentieth century's world wars — and the advance of welfare; as one study summarises, 'when governments are desperate for manpower to help them fight more effectively, they may be forced to pay more attention to the common man'.[130] The Great War had a major effect on New Zealand's welfare system, greatly extending some entitlements and vastly increasing expenditure, albeit largely for servicemen and those related to them.[131] In 1914 pensions (including non-military) cost £473,295 (4 per cent of total government spending). By 1918 this had more than doubled to £1.2 million (8.47 per cent) and by 1920 the figures were £2.7 million (11.54 per cent).[132] The war also marked the first removal of means-testing from a substantial social welfare scheme, effectively making payment universal, an approach often associated with legislation passed by the first Labour government.

However, if the war saw some enhancement of the 'tight society's' communitarian ethos, it saw liberal dispositions suffer. Post-war New Zealand has been memorably described as a 'clench-buttocked community, more intolerant of dissent or disunity or diversity than ever before or since'.[133] Some restrictions grew directly from the political directions and emotional strains brought by the war; the 1918 Expeditionary Forces Amendment Act, for example, barred wartime defaulters from holding public employment or office and from voting as electors or as members of any public authority for 10 years after 1918.[134]

Other post-war practices would also seem to reflect the momentum of a wartime mindset and an effort to buttress the social order. Examples include flag saluting in schools, as part of a new push for civic loyalty; the 1919 Undesirable Immigrants Exclusion Act, which Massey considered necessary to prevent the entry of 'people who are disaffected, who favour Bolshevism and IWWism and who have sympathies with revolutionary socialism'; and the 1921 introduction of loyalty pledges for teachers, in an effort to root out radicals from the profession.[135] New Zealand's only prosecution for blasphemous libel, in October 1921 against the *Maoriland Worker*, has been interpreted as reflecting post-war attitudes and tensions, as has the high-profile May 1922 sedition trial of the Auckland Catholic priest James Liston. Liston had praised the 'men and women who in the glorious Easter of 1916 were proud to die for their country — murdered by foreign troops', but the trial ultimately ended in his acquittal.[136]

Building on the wartime promotion of sobriety as efficient and patriotic, in October 1918 a petition signed by more than 240,000 was presented to Parliament, demanding an end to the manufacture and sale of alcohol. When a referendum was held in April 1919, the initial result gave prohibition a narrow majority. When the special votes, largely from servicemen still overseas, were added, the outcome swung to continuance.[137]

By popular account, the war's legacies are entwined with seminal shifts for sections of society, although many demonstrate a much more uneasy mix of change and continuity. For women the war meant both.[138] Kate Sheppard, one of the founders of the New Zealand suffrage movement, asserted, in an address to the National Council of Women, that 'fossilized prejudices crashed' with the upheaval of war and there was a keenness to revive the recessed National Council of Women.[139] Certainly, the debate over the Women's Parliamentary Rights Act, passed on 29 October 1919, which allowed women to be elected to the House of Representatives, often referred to the female war record. Sir William Hall-Jones, for example, stated that 'thousands of women did splendid work during the war-time, and we have our own knowledge of the fine work done by the women of this city [Wellington] during the pneumonic plague'.[140]

In Ward's view, women's part in securing victory had 'altered the whole aspect of the question of what was due to the women of the world'.[141] Three women stood in the 1919 election — Ellen Melville as a Progressive Reform candidate for Grey Lynn, Rosetta Baume as a Liberal candidate for Parnell and Aileen Cooke as an Independent Liberal for Thames.[142]

Many, though, have questioned the extent to which the war was a watershed for New Zealand women. Efforts to reintegrate returned soldiers, and a focus on 'fighting men first', meant that women were encouraged and pressured to give up jobs. As early as July 1916, the *Otago Witness* was writing that after demobilisation women and girls 'must be prepared to put their own interests aside and let the men who have fought for them have first claim. It is the only decent thing to do, though it may not be an easy one.' Many women had worked only temporarily, and others had 'so proved their worth that they will be kept on by their employers in some capacity or another', but 'many girls who have entered occupations which are open to them for the time being . . . must just accept the position with a good grace, and turn to something else, though it may mean sacrificing a year or two of training and experience'.[143] From 9661 in 1916, the number of women employed in agriculture declined to 9167 by 1921 and plummeted to 3497 by 1926. The number of temporary public service workers, most of them women, fell dramatically from 2089 in April 1921 to 583 by November of that year.[144]

Similar dynamics are apparent in the war's impacts on Māori standing within New Zealand society. Wartime experiences have been observed as broadening the horizons of Māori veterans and forging some degree of respect between Māori and Pākehā. Towards the end of the 1920s, Pākehā commentator Ralph H. Ward thought that the Māori race had not only regained its mana, not least because of its participation in the war, but was also destined to play an increasing role in the development of New Zealand as a nation.[145] Some later studies have viewed Māori military commitments as 'an important psychological filip [sic] to advocates of assimilation who sought ways of improving the status of Maori in a Pakeha world'.[146] Certainly

Māui Pōmare continued to espouse his ideal that the war had proved Māori as of equal standing. As he wrote in 1926,

> Our people's voluntary service in the Great War gave a new and glorious tradition to the story of the Maori race. It gave the crowning touch to the sense of citizenship in the British commonwealth; it satisfied in the one fitting fashion the intense desire of the Maori to prove to the world that he was the equal of the pakeha in the fullest sense — physically, mentally and spiritually . . . Henceforth he was the racial peer of any man on earth.[147]

Both Pōmare and Āpirana Ngata cited the Māori war record as leverage for the government to address land grievances. A commission set up in October 1926 ultimately ruled that some confiscations had been excessive and recommended compensation.

However, the scholarship of these dynamics also emphasises that 'The immediate post-war environment offered little succour for those Maori who returned from the front community (where they had fought as equals with Pakeha) only to find their heightened expectations frustrated by the political establishment.'[148] Despite Peter Buck's observations in an April 1919 interview of 'the cordial manner' in which the general public welcomed returning Māori troops, the 'colour bar' continued in various parts of life.[149]

Only a month after Buck made this statement, Captain Edward 'Tip' Broughton of the Māori Battalion wrote a letter of complaint to the *Wanganui Chronicle*. Broughton, in mufti, had gone into a bar with two other returned soldiers, in uniform, only to be 'rudely informed that no Maoris were served in that hotel'. Thinking it likely that when the matter was made public, 'these people would say we were already the worse for liquor and that this was the reason for declining to serve us', the trio asked the nearest policeman 'to note our condition'. Broughton wanted 'to protest against the attitude of any tradesman in endeavouring to draw the colour line, especially so as to prejudicially affect returned Maori soldiers. We fought to give Europeans a fair deal, and we expect in return to get a fair deal from Europeans.'[150]

Furthermore, grievances remained unresolved and, if some Māori leadership worked with the government, others stressed the significance of independent institutions and actions. Te Puea Hērangi, for example, emerged as among the most active Māori leaders in Waikato and her personal charisma and mana forged a friendship and working relationship with Ngata and strengthening relationships among many tribes in Taranaki, in the Whanganui district, on the East Coast and in the Far North.

Although Te Puea became more willing to work with Pākehā officials, she did so very much on her own terms. Rua Kēnana also continued his efforts. Most notably, in 1927 he prophesied the end of the world and gathered his followers at Maungapōhatu, where he ordered houses to be rebuilt with protective tin roofs against the stars that would fall from the sky. However, by the early 1930s, the community had failed economically; its people departed and Rua took up residence at Matahi, a community he had founded on the Waimana River in the eastern Bay of Plenty.

In 1925 Tahupōtiki Wiremu Rātana founded the pan-iwi church that bears his name, which grew into a major political movement. Rātana claimed to have received a vision during the influenza epidemic: 'I am the Holy Spirit, I have visited the scene of the war which has recently raged in Europe. In my travels I have found that the whole world has forgotten me. I have looked all over for some place to establish myself, and to ensure that God will again be truly known and accepted in the hearts of men. That is why I have come to you, the Maori people.'[151] Rātana also looked to the monarchy for a redress of land grievances. In 1924, a decade after Te Rata's journey, he planned to take a 45,000-signature petition to England to present to King George V. This did not eventuate, owing to government opposition.[152]

The war's impacts on Protestant–Catholic relations in New Zealand have also been differently appraised by historians. Jock Phillips has noted that 'if war did bring strains to the question of the Irish Catholic place in New Zealand, it also emphasised how far those of an Irish, and indeed Irish Catholic, background had become an accepted part of New Zealand life'. James Belich has also observed the significance of Anzac Day as a public ritual that was above denomination and could bind sects into a larger community.[153] However, Rory Sweetman makes the grimmer assessment that 'the stresses of world conflict not only ruined the chances of a peaceful resolution to the Anglo-Irish problem but also left those who sympathized with Irish national aspirations in Britain's colonies feeling alienated and deeply aggrieved'.[154]

Other legacies revolve around the changing interpretation of the war past 1918, as the process of layering greater meanings on the conflict continued. In the interwar years there was an international boom in histories, memoirs, novels, theatrical presentations, films and artistic works seeking to exhibit, assess and judge the war. New Zealanders were well connected and exposed to this trend.[155] Many continued conventional wartime interpretations, and in the 1920s 'middle-brow' novels, with themes of heroism, bravery, duty, sacrifice and purpose, were prolific.[156]

For some time, school lessons also presented the war with regard to a greater purpose. For example, *The New Zealand Citizen*, a standard text for schools through the 1920s, presented the conflict as a contest between democracy and autocratic militarism:

> This great struggle, the fiercest and most important in the history of the world . . . was a struggle between forms of government. Although the government of Russia, which was one of Germany's enemies in the first half of the war was despotic, it is broadly true to say that Germany and her allies stood for government by kings, nobles, and soldiers — government by the few in the interests of the few, whereas Britain, France, and their allies stood for government by the people in the interests of the many . . . The real issue of the war was, which of these two ideals of government should prevail and consequently be the dominating system of the world.[157]

Towards the end of the 1920s, however, darker, more graphic and cynical representations and harsher judgements of the war appeared, most famously in Erich Maria Remarque's *All*

Quiet on the Western Front, and these ultimately became the predominant style and then the effectively unquestioned tradition.[158] One New Zealand commentator recognised this shift in 1930: 'During the Great War, and shortly afterwards, we remember war books that were harmless and often humorous, as well as others that showed in a clear light the gallantry and patience of our troops . . . suddenly out of the open sky another very distinct type of book relating to the War appeared. It based its claim to notice on the ground of stark realism.'[159]

In the 1930s counter-cultural interpretations bloomed as peace groups grew, a generational divide opened and global stability was rocked by economic depression and geopolitical volatility. In the broadest sense this reinterpretation inverted the conception of the war as a necessary or principled stand and presented it as a clash between morally bankrupt belligerents driven by ignoble profiteering and base political agendas. As an editorial in the progressive literary journal *Tomorrow* put it, 'During the years 1914–1918 the major capitalist nations were locked in a struggle for a redivision of the world, a struggle which grew out of the "peaceful" competition for markets, spheres of influence and colonies.'[160]

The threat and then the outbreak of the Second World War added further complexities to the legacies of the First. Many framed their expectations of this new conflict against their sense of the last war and it was consequently evoked both as a source of inspiration and as a warning that the present should not repeat the mistakes of the past. The *Evening Post* addressed the outbreak of the war with the view that, 'Whatever the demand, it is certain that New Zealanders will acquit themselves with honour to their country and glory to themselves as they did in the Great War', while anti-war activists argued, 'The young men of this country are being told the same lies that were told them in 1914–1918. They are being told a lot of lies about democracy and fighting for their country. What they are really fighting for is Imperialistic interests.'[161]

The more influential legacy, however, and one apparent throughout the English-speaking world, was that the First World War was assessed and habitually defined as futile and senseless against the necessity and high purpose of the Second. The trend began during the Second World War as some stressed the different nature of the two conflicts while seeking to reconcile their anti-war pasts with contemporary commitments. Thus Prime Minister Fraser found himself overseeing the introduction and exercising of an array of wartime powers including censorship, anti-sedition laws and conscription. His biographers note that he rarely discussed his earlier stance and carefully vetted official summaries of his career for references to it.

They also assert that he operated under a sincere sense that the two wars possessed different natures: 'To his mind . . . World War I had been a conflict between imperial powers; its only relevance to workers had been that they provided the cannon fodder. World War II, on the other hand, had been started by right-wing reactionary forces out to smash the legitimate organisational and political expression of workers' rights.'[162] Semple, who as minister of public works would draw the first conscription ballot in July 1940, selectively remembered that his 1916 arrest had been for protesting war profits and argued that the protests of the past no longer applied: 'during the First World War the working man had nothing to gain but now that the Labour Party was in power New Zealand's new "heritage" had to be defended at all costs, especially against the fascists'.[163]

Webb, who as minister of labour had to manage coal production against unrest, in a dynamic that would have been readily recognised by Allen and MacDonald, rebuked strikers as 'those who persisted in seeing the war in outdated socialist terms, as an "imperialist" or "capitalist" one' and claimed that a worker who did not give his best in wartime was a traitor to the cause.[164]

Another enduring, but evolving, set of legacies revolved around collective identity. A major tradition has perceived the First World War, and especially Gallipoli, as a milestone in shaping a New Zealand national identity, and such sentiments were certainly present in interwar New Zealand.[165] On Anzac Day 1926, for example, *Truth* referred to New Zealanders' 'common citizenship in the world's most beneficent Empire', but also stated, 'The Dominion of New Zealand, eleven years ago, stepped full-fledged into Nationhood . . . As the April dawn burst over the shell-swept crags, cliffs, and ridges of Anzac, the New Zealand nation was born in a baptism of heroic blood.'[166]

Others explicitly stated that wartime legacies included an identity independent from the British tradition, and at the end of the war the veteran Ormond Burton wrote: 'The years of struggle have given us a history of our own, a superb and glorious tradition to pass on to our children . . . By the deeds our men have done, by the victories they have achieved, by the blood they have shed, we have come to the full consciousness of what we are. New Zealand is a nation, distinct, separate, and apart. We have no Home but New Zealand.'[167]

For a significant section of public opinion, however, New Zealand's war record did not represent independence from the British Empire, but rather an affirmation, or an apotheosis, of the country's ongoing identity and renown within it. As George Russell asked towards the end of the war, 'is there one man here whose blood does not flow faster as he thinks of the position that the men from this Dominion will take in the annals of the British Empire?'[168] There was certainly no doubt about the answer as far as the country's leadership was concerned. As Massey said, 'We signed [the Treaty of Versailles] not as independent nations in the ordinary sense of the term. We signed it as the representatives of self-governing nations within the Empire; we signed it as partners in Empire — partners, with everything that name implies.'[169] Allen was even more adamant: 'My opinion is that never has anything been done in the history of the Empire that has brought the various dominions into closer contact with the Mother-country, and tied the bonds tighter, than what was done during the Peace Conference.'[170]

This sense that the war signalled a new standing within the imperial family remained conventional for decades afterwards. In the words of a 1922 *School Journal*, 'The Dominions also paid their share in the cost of the war. Recognising this, the British Ministers took the lead in suggesting that they, as young partners in the Empire, should have a voice in its concerns. It was as if a family of sons had grown to manhood, and the father had recognized their ability by taking them into partnership in his firm.'[171] Interwar Anzac Days and other public occasions also assumed that national identity and destiny were enduringly bound to a wider British tradition. At the 1932 inauguration of New Zealand's National War Memorial, for example, Wellington Mayor T. C. A. Hislop noted that Anzac Day marked 'the first occasion when we as a mature people took part on the fields of Europe in saving the ideals of the British peoples'.[172]

Such sentiments dissipated post-1945 as British power declined and under the influence of an array of social and cultural changes. One result is a modern gulf in understanding the New Zealand society of 1914–18, its commitment to defend what was, but no longer is, and its involvement in what was now sometimes deemed to be 'someone else's war'.[173]

NOTES
SELECT BIBLIOGRAPHY
ACKNOWLEDGEMENTS
ABOUT THE AUTHORS
INDEX

NOTES

INTRODUCTION: TOWARDS 1914

1 *New Zealand Official Year-book*, 1909, p. 637; *New Zealand Official Year-book*, 1911, p. 567; *New Zealand Official Year-book*, 1918, p. 64.

2 Trevor Bentley, 'Musket wars', in Ian McGibbon (ed.), *The Oxford Companion to New Zealand Military History* (Auckland: Oxford University Press, 2000), pp. 340–44.

3 Ian Pool, *Te Iwi Maori: A New Zealand Population, Past, Present & Projected* (Auckland: Auckland University Press, 1991), pp. 29–58, 76.

4 https://nzhistory.govt.nz/war/new-zealand-wars/end; Richard Boast and Richard S. Hill (eds), *Raupatu: The Confiscation of Māori Land* (Wellington: Victoria University Press, 2009).

5 Miles Fairburn, 'The Rural Myth and the New Urban Frontier: An Approach to New Zealand Social History, 1870–1940', *New Zealand Journal of History*, Vol. 9, No. 1 (April 1975), pp. 3–21.

6 *New Zealand Official Year-book*, 1911, pp. 577, 581–82.

7 Ben Schrader, *The Big Smoke: New Zealand Cities, 1840–1920* (Wellington: Bridget Williams Books, 2016).

8 James Belich, *Making Peoples: A History of the New Zealanders from Polynesian Settlement to the End of the Nineteenth Century* (Auckland: Allen Lane, 1996), pp. 437–46.

9 Ian Hunter, *Age of Enterprise: Rediscovering the New Zealand Entrepreneur, 1880–1910* (Auckland: Auckland University Press, 2007), p. 36; *Appendix to the Journals of the House of Representatives (AJHR)*, 1875, F-1a, 'Telegrah [sic] Department', p. 11; Elisabeth Airey, *The Taming of Distance: New Zealand's First International Telecommunications* (Wellington: Dunmore Publishing, 2005).

10 André Siegfried, *Democracy in New Zealand*, translated by E. V. Burns (London: Bell, 1914), p. 323.

11 Belich, *Making Peoples*, pp. 360–67.

12 M. F. Lloyd Prichard, *An Economic History of New Zealand to 1939* (Auckland: Collins, 1970), pp. 113, 209.

13 Melanie Nolan, *Breadwinning: New Zealand Women and the State* (Christchurch: Canterbury University Press, 2000); Erik Olssen, 'Working Gender, Gendering Work: Occupational Change and Continuity in Southern Dunedin', in Barbara Brookes, Annabel Cooper and Robin Law (eds), *Sites of Gender: Women, Men and Modernity in Southern Dunedin, 1890–1939* (Auckland: Auckland University Press, 2003), p. 59.

14 Herbert Roth, *Trade Unions in New Zealand Past and Present* (Wellington: Bridget Williams Books, 1973), p. 169.

15 Erik Olssen, 'Waging War: The Home Front 1914–1918', in Judith Binney, Judith Bassett and Erik Olssen (eds), *The People and the Land: Te Tangata me Te Whenua: An Illustrated History of New Zealand, 1820–1920* (Wellington: Bridget Williams Books, 1990), p. 311.

16 Gavin McLean, *The Governors: New Zealand's Governors and Governors-General* (Dunedin: Otago University Press, 2006), pp. 172–82.

17 John Darwin, *The Unfinished Empire: The Global Expansion of Britain* (New York: Bloomsbury Press, 2012), pp. 194–202.

18 Raymond Miller, *Democracy in New Zealand* (Auckland: Auckland University Press, 2015), p. 1.

19 James Cowan, *Official Record of the New Zealand International Exhibition of Arts and Industries* (Wellington: Government Printer, 1910), pp. 2, 7.

20 Siegfried, *Democracy in New Zealand*, p. 4. Similar observations of developing nationalism were observed by Richard Jebb, see *Studies in Colonial Nationalism* (London: Edward Arnold, 1905). For a modern study, see Ron Palenski, *The Making of New Zealanders* (Auckland: Auckland University Press, 2012).

21 Jane Stafford and Mark Williams, *Maoriland: New Zealand Literature 1872–1914* (Wellington: Victoria University Press, 2006).

22 Jock Phillips, *A Man's Country?: The Image of the Pakeha Male* (Auckland: Penguin, 1987), pp. 38–42; Steven Loveridge, *Calls to Arms: New Zealand Society and Commitment to the Great War* (Wellington: Victoria University Press, 2014), pp. 104–13.

23 *Ashburton Guardian*, 23 December 1904, p. 3; *Oamaru Mail*, 17 December 1912, p. 1; *Evening Post*, 7 January 1911, p. 9.

24 Palenski, *The Making of New Zealanders*, p. 167.

25 James Belich, *Paradise Reforged: A History of the New Zealanders from the 1880s to the Year 2000* (Honolulu: University of Hawai'i Press, 2001), pp. 77–78.

26 Siegfried, *Democracy in New Zealand*, p. 327.

27 For the tightening links between the British metropole and colonial peripheries see James Belich, *Replenishing the Earth: The Settler Revolution and the Rise of the Anglo-World, 1783–1939* (Oxford: Oxford University Press, 2009), pp. 456–78. For news see Simon Potter, *News and the British World: The Emergence of an Imperial Press*

System 1876–1922 (New York: Oxford University Press, 2003). For imports see Prichard, *An Economic History of New Zealand to 1939*, p. 209.

28 Phil Briggs, *Looking at the Numbers: A View of New Zealand's Economic History* (Wellington: New Zealand Institute of Economic Research, 2007), p. 6.

29 For New Zealand's collective identity within the British Empire see Felicity Barnes, *New Zealand's London: A Colony and its Metropolis* (Auckland: Auckland University Press, 2012); Loveridge, *Calls to Arms*, pp. 28–68.

30 Vincent O'Malley, '"Recording the Incident with a Monument": The Waikato War in Historical Memory', *Journal of New Zealand Studies*, 19 (2015), p. 81.

31 Michael Bassett, *The State in New Zealand, 1840–1984: Socialism Without Doctrines?* (Auckland: Auckland University Press, 1998), p. 103. The Young Māori Party's efforts have been described as working 'to *combine* the technological, cultural and other benefits of European civilisation with preserving "the best" of Maori culture'. Richard Hill, *State Authority, Indigenous Autonomy: Crown–Māori Relations in New Zealand/Aotearoa 1900–1950* (Wellington: Victoria University Press, 2004), p. 44. Emphasis in original.

32 Belich, *Making Peoples*, pp. 230–45.

33 Āpirana Ngata and a number of important Ngāti Porou rangatira visited King Te Rata unsuccessfully attempting to convince Te Rata and Taingākawa to halt this plan. *Te Kopara*, April 1914, pp. 5, 8, 9.

34 Peter Webster, *Rua and the Maori Millennium* (Wellington: Price Milburn for Victoria University Press, 1979), p. 82.

35 Judith Binney, Gillian Chaplin and Craig Wallace, *Mihaia: The Prophet Rua Kenana and His Community at Maungapohatu* (New York: Oxford University Press, 1979), p. 17. Webster, *Rua and the Maori Millennium*, pp. 35, 158.

36 Webster, *Rua and the Maori Millennium*, pp. 1, 167, 170, 216; Binney, Chaplin, Wallace, *Mihaia*, p. 57.

37 Webster, *Rua and the Maori Millennium*, pp. 212, 224; Binney, Chaplin, Wallace, *Mihaia*, p. 73.

38 *Poverty Bay Herald*, 25 June 1906, p. 2; *New Zealand Herald*, 6 April 1916, p. 9.

39 *New Zealand Herald*, 20 April 1908, p. 7.

40 Graeme Dunstall, 'Frontier and/or Cultural Fragment? Interpretations of Violence in Colonial New Zealand', *Social History*, Vol. 29, No. 1 (2004), pp. 59–83.

41 Belich, *Paradise Reforged*, pp. 157–80.

42 *Wairarapa Age*, 8 April 1914, p. 4.

43 Richard Newman, 'New Zealand's Vote for Prohibition in 1911', *New Zealand Journal of History*, Vol. 9, No. 1 (April 1975), pp. 52–71.

44 *NZ Truth*, 21 August 1909, p. 1.

45 Rory Sweetman, 'New Zealand Catholicism, War, Politics and the Irish Issue 1912–1922' (PhD thesis, University of Cambridge, 1990), p. 5.

46 Richard P. Davis, *Irish Issues in New Zealand Politics, 1868–1922* (Dunedin: University of Otago Press, 1974), pp. 71–98.

47 Sweetman, 'New Zealand Catholicism', p. 26.

48 *New Zealand Parliamentary Debates* (*NZPD*), Vol. 104, 14 September 1898, p. 69. For further consideration see James Watson, 'Were Catholics Over-Represented in the Public Service during the Early Twentieth Century?', *Political Science*, Vol. 42, No. 2 (1990), pp. 20–34.

49 *Auckland Weekly News*, 14 May 1914, p. 53.

50 Brad Patterson, '"We love one country, one queen, one flag": Loyalism in Early Colonial New Zealand, 1840–1880', in Allan Blackstock and Frank O'Gorman (eds), *Loyalism and the Formation of the British World, 1775–1914* (Woodbridge: Boydell & Brewer, 2014), pp. 255–61.

51 Rory Sweetman, '"Who Fears to Speak of Easter Week?" Antipodean Irish Catholic Responses to the 1916 Rising', in Ruan O'Donnell (ed.), *The Impact of the 1916 Rising: Among the Nations* (Dublin: Irish Academic Press, 2008), p. 72.

52 Seán Brosnahan, '"Shaming the Shoneens": The Green Ray and the Maoriland Irish Society in Dunedin, 1916–1922', in Lyndon Fraser (ed.), *A Distant Shore: Irish Migration and New Zealand Settlement* (Dunedin: Otago University Press, 2000), p. 120; Rory Sweetman, 'Cleary, Henry William', *Dictionary of New Zealand Biography* (*DNZB*), Te Ara — Encyclopedia of New Zealand, https://teara.govt.nz/en/biographies/3c22/cleary-henry-william.

53 Tom Brooking, *Richard Seddon: King of God's Own* (Auckland: Penguin Books, 2014).

54 *Press*, 29 July 1892, p. 5; David Low, *Low's Autobiography* (London: Michael Joseph, 1956), p. 39.

55 Michael Bassett, 'Ward, Joseph George', *DNZB*, Te Ara — Encyclopedia of New Zealand, https://teara.govt.nz/en/biographies/2w9/ward-joseph-george/print.

56 Michael Bassett, *Sir Joseph Ward: A Political Biography* (Auckland: Auckland University Press, 1993), p. 111.

57 Bassett, *Sir Joseph Ward*, p. viii.

58 *Weekly Press*, 9 October 1907, p. 40.

59 Erik Olssen, *The Red Feds: Revolutionary Industrial Unionism and the New Zealand Federation of Labour 1908–1913* (Auckland: Oxford University Press, 1988); Barry Gustafson, *Labour's Path to Political Independence: The Origins and Establishment of the New Zealand Labour Party 1900–19* (Auckland: Auckland University Press, 1980), p. 158.

60 P. J. O'Farrell, *Harry Holland: Militant Socialist* (Canberra: Australian National University, 1964),

p. 211; Patrick Lawlor, *Pat Lawlor's Wellington* (Wellington: Millwood Press, 1976), p. 76.

61 Gustafson, *Labour's Path to Political Independence*, p. 30.

62 Lawlor, *Pat Lawlor's Wellington*, p. 76.

63 Olssen, *Red Feds*, pp. 1–15.

64 Michael Bassett with Michael King, *Tomorrow Comes the Song: A Life of Peter Fraser* (Auckland: Penguin, 2000), p. 41.

65 *Maoriland Worker*, 9 May 1913, p. 4.

66 *Report of Proceedings of the Unity Congress: July 1st to 10th, 1913, Establishing the United Federation of Labor and the Social Democratic Party* (Wellington: Worker Print, 1913), p. 28.

67 Erik Olssen, 'Towards a Reassessment of W. F. Massey: One of New Zealand's Greatest Prime Ministers (Arguably)', in James Watson and Lachy Paterson (eds), *A Great New Zealand Prime Minister?: Reappraising William Ferguson Massey* (Dunedin: Otago University Press, 2011), p. 19.

68 Miles Fairburn and S. J. Haslett, 'Who Voted for Massey, 1908–1914?', in Watson and Paterson, *A Great New Zealand Prime Minister?*, pp. 64–65; Miles Fairburn and Stephen Haslett, 'How Far Did Class Determine Voting in New Zealand General Elections, 1911–1951?', *New Zealand Journal of History*, Vol. 39, No. 2 (October 2005), pp. 215–41.

69 *NZPD*, Vol. 137, 4 September 1906, p. 332.

70 *Evening Post*, 12 February 1909, p. 8.

71 Theresa B. Graham, 'Massey, Christina Allan', *DNZB*, Te Ara — Encyclopedia of New Zealand, https://teara.govt.nz/en/biographies/3m47/massey-christina-allan; Linda Bryder, '"A Worthy Helpmeet": Christina Massey, Plunket and Maternalism', in Watson and Paterson, *A Great New Zealand Prime Minister?*, pp. 39–47.

72 Leicester Chisholm Webb, 'The Rise of the Reform Party: A History of Party Politics in New Zealand between 1910 and 1920' (Honours thesis, University of New Zealand, 1928), pp. 55–56.

73 Dora Christine Massey, *The Life of Rt. Hon. W. F. Massey* (Auckland: D. C. Massey, 1996).

74 James Watson, *WF Massey: New Zealand* (London: Haus, 2010), p. 29.

75 Webb, 'The Rise of the Reform Party', p. 103.

76 *New Zealand Official Year-book*, 1911, p. 507.

77 Bassett, *Sir Joseph Ward*, p. 216.

78 A different interpretation notes, 'The negative feelings between the two men [Massey and Ward] tend to be exaggerated by historians. Those feelings existed, of course, but there is no evidence to suggest that the pair did not respect or support each other as occasion demanded, nor that they were unable to have friendly social contact.' Bruce Farland, *Farmer Bill: William Ferguson Massey and the Reform Party* (Wellington: First Edition Publishers, 2008), p. 398.

79 Bassett, *Sir Joseph Ward*, pp. 216, 224.

80 Massey's time as a grand master has been dated to 1892. Farland, *Farmer Bill*, p. 18. Massey later reflected on his time as an Orangeman. See *NZPD*, Vol. 189, 4 November 1920, p. 651.

81 Donald C. Gordon, *The Dominion Partnership in Imperial Defense, 1870–1914* (Baltimore: John Hopkins Press, 1965), pp. 279–80.

82 Watson, *WF Massey*, p. 70; Farland, *Farmer Bill*, p. 558; Sweetman, 'New Zealand Catholicism', pp. 38–39.

83 H. E. Holland, *The Tragic Story of the Waihi Strike* (Wellington: Worker Printery, 1913), p. 193.

84 Melanie Nolan (ed.), *Revolution: The 1913 Great Strike in New Zealand* (Christchurch: Canterbury University Press in association with the Trade Union History Project, 2006); Olssen, *Red Feds*.

85 Olssen, *Red Feds*, p. 210.

86 Lawlor, *Pat Lawlor's Wellington*, p. 70.

87 Olssen, *Red Feds*, p. 210.

88 Holland is alleged to have said, though he challenged this, 'if they hit you with a baton, hit them with a pick-handle, and have something at the end of it'. Semple declared that if Evans did shoot a policeman, as was alleged, then he was 'doing his duty and should have shot more of them'. Fraser was reported as telling a rally in Newtown Park that 'if [self-preservation] compels the workers to get food, then the workers of Wellington, and of New Zealand, are going to get food, and if a few doors have to be burst . . . all the worse for the doors'. *Evening Post*, 6 December 1913, p. 9; H. E. Holland, *Twelve Months for Sedition: Harry Holland's Speech from the Dock and the Chief Justice's Remarks in Delivering Sentence* (Wellington: Printed at the Worker Printery, 1914), p. 7; Len Richardson, *Coal, Class & Community: The United Mineworkers of New Zealand, 1880–1960* (Auckland: Auckland University Press, 1995), p. 137; Bassett and King, *Tomorrow Comes the Song*, p. 61.

89 For a classic study see Paul Kennedy, *The Rise of Anglo-German Antagonism, 1860–1914* (London: Allen & Unwin, 1980).

90 John Dunmore (ed.), *New Zealand and the French: Two Centuries of Contact* (Waikanae: Heritage Press, 1990); Glynn Barratt, *Russophobia in New Zealand, 1838–1908* (Palmerston North: Dunmore Press, 1981); M. P. Lissington, *New Zealand and Japan, 1900–1941* (Wellington: A. R. Shearer, Government Printer, 1972).

91 Archives New Zealand (ANZ), R3885320, 'Defence scheme, expeditionary action by territorial force, August 1912–June 1913', Godley to Allen, 9 October 1912.

92 *Evening Post*, 8 August 1908, p. 11.

93 *Southland Times*, 27 October 1900, p. 3.

94 Jürgen Tampke (ed.), *'Ruthless Warfare': German Military Planning and Surveillance in the*

Australia–New Zealand Region before the Great War (Canberra: Southern Highlands Publisher, 1998), pp. 14–17, 36, 90, 101.

95 Richard Hill, 'Surveilling the "Enemies" of Colonial New Zealand: Counter-subversion and Counter-espionage, 1840–1907', in Brad Patterson, Richard Hill and Kathryn Patterson (eds), *After the Treaty: The Settler State, Race Relations & the Exercise of Power in Colonial New Zealand* (Wellington: Steele Roberts Aotearoa, 2016), p. 285.

96 Ian McGibbon, *The Path to Gallipoli: Defending New Zealand, 1840–1915* (Wellington: GP Books, 1991), pp. 208–9, 239–43.

97 McGibbon, *The Path to Gallipoli*, pp. 125–36.

98 McGibbon, *The Path to Gallipoli*, pp. 145, 174.

99 McGibbon, *The Path to Gallipoli*, pp. 215–32.

100 'South African War 1899–1902', URL: https://nzhistory.govt.nz/war/south-african-boer-war/introduction, (Ministry for Culture and Heritage), updated 7-Mar-2018.

101 *New Zealand Times*, 13 March 1913, p. 6.

102 *New Zealand Official Year-book*, 1899, pp. 51, 362; *New Zealand Official Year-book*, 1914, pp. 270, 818.

103 Loveridge, *Calls to Arms*, pp. 104–21.

104 Paul Goldstone, 'The Imperialist Movement and National Defence, 1900–1909' (MA thesis, Victoria University of Wellington, 1993), pp. 110–36.

105 Peter Cooke, '"Priceless Worth": The Territorial Force and Senior Cadets in World War One', in Steven Loveridge (ed.), *New Zealand Society at War, 1914–1918* (Wellington: Victoria University Press, 2016), pp. 64–76.

106 *Lyttelton Times*, 5 January 1910, p. 7.

107 For example, in 1897 the National Council of Women passed a resolution calling for 'the women of Australasia to co-operate in promoting permanent and universal peace'. Megan Hutching, '"Mothers of the World": Women, Peace and Arbitration in Early Twentieth-Century New Zealand', *New Zealand Journal of History*, Vol. 27, No. 2 (October 1993), p. 175.

108 David Grant, *Out in the Cold: Pacifists and Conscientious Objectors in New Zealand during World War II* (Auckland: Reed Methuen, 1986), p. 15.

109 *The Great Illusion: A Summary of Norman Angell's Suggestive Book on the Peace Question* (Christchurch: National Peace Council of New Zealand, 1912).

110 Gustafson, *Labour's Path to Political Independence*, p. 106; R. L. Weitzel, 'Pacifists and Anti-Militarists in New Zealand, 1909–1914', *New Zealand Journal of History*, Vol. 7, No. 2 (October 1973), p. 134.

111 David Grant, 'Where Were The Peacemongers?: Pacifists in New Zealand During World War One', in Loveridge, *New Zealand Society at War*, pp. 220–34.

112 Gustafson, *Labour's Path to Political Independence*, p. 107.

113 Hutching, "'Mothers of the World'", pp. 180–81; Alexander Turnbull Library (ATL), 82-213-02, Herbert Otto Roth, Papers, 'Pacifism in New Zealand', 'To the Women of New Zealand: A Plea for the Repeal of the Defence Act'.

114 *New Zealand Times*, 12 December 1912, p. 1; Weitzel, 'Pacifists and Anti-militarists in New Zealand', pp. 130–31, 133, 141; General Sir Alexander Godley, *Life of an Irish Soldier: Reminiscences of General Sir Alexander Godley G.C.B., K.C.M.G.* (London: John Murray, 1939), p. 158.

115 *AJHR*, 1914, H-19, 'Defence Forces of New Zealand', pp. 13–14, 37.

116 Figures calculated from data collected between the inauguration of the defence scheme and 30 April 1914. *AJHR*, 1914, H-19, 'Defence Forces of New Zealand', p. 37.

117 Ian McGibbon, 'Allen, James', *DNZB*, Te Ara — Encyclopedia of New Zealand, https://teara.govt.nz/en/biographies/3a12/allen-james.

118 Paul Baker, *King and Country Call: New Zealanders, Conscription and the Great War* (Auckland: Auckland University Press, 1988), p. 34.

119 Cited in Richard G. H. Kay, 'In Pursuit of Victory: British–New Zealand Relations During the First World War' (PhD thesis, University of Otago, 2001), p. 10.

120 K. R. Adams, 'The Growth and Development of the Society of Friends in New Zealand, 1840–1920' (MA thesis, Canterbury University, 1986), pp. 163–67.

121 Herbert Roth, 'The Prisoners of Ripa Island', *Here & Now* (1954), pp. 16–18; S. V. Bracher, *Ripa Island: A Lesson for Conscriptionists* (London: Peace Committee of the Society of Friends, 1913), p. 2.

122 *AJHR*, 1914, H-19, 'Defence Forces of New Zealand', p. 27.

123 *Marlborough Express*, 7 April 1913, p. 4.

124 *NZPD*, Vol. 161, 15 October 1912, p. 228.

125 *New Zealand Herald*, 8 June 1914, p. 6.

CHAPTER ONE: CRISIS

1 *Auckland Star*, 29 June 1914, p. 4. See also editorials in the *Sun*, 29 June 1914, p. 5, *Marlborough Express*, 30 June 1914, p. 4, *Wanganui Chronicle*, 30 June 1914, p. 4, and *Poverty Bay Herald*, 2 July 1914, p. 2, entitled 'The Foredoomed Hapsburgs', 'The Ill-Fated Hapsburgs', 'The Austrian Tragedy' and 'The Curse on the Hapsburgs' respectively; and commentary on 'A House of Tragedy' in the *Star*, 30 June 1914, p. 4, and 'Romance of Ferdinand' in the *Feilding Star*, 30 June 1914, p. 2.

2 Archives New Zealand (ANZ), R2825280, 'Telegrams to and from the Secretary of State — 30 June 1914–14 May 1915', Liverpool to Emperor of Austria, 30 June 1914.

3 Dunedin's evening newspaper and that of Nelson did likewise. *Evening Star*, 29 June 1914, p. 4; *Nelson Evening Mail*, 3 July 1914, p. 4.

4 *New Zealand Herald*, 30 June 1914, p. 6.

5 *Star*, 29 June 1914, p. 4. The *Hawke's Bay Herald* also perceived 'a position of considerable menace to the peace of Europe'. *Hawke's Bay Herald*, 30 June 1914, p. 4.

6 *Sun*, 29 June 1914, p. 6.

7 *Dominion*, 30 June 1914, p. 6.

8 *Dominion*, 23 July 1914, p. 6. See also *Auckland Star*, 6 July 1914, p. 4; *Wairarapa Daily Times*, 10 July 1914, p. 4.

9 *Waikato Argus*, 27 July 1914, p. 2; *Star*, 27 July 1914, p. 4; *Evening Post*, 27 July 1914, p. 6; *Otago Daily Times*, 27 July 1914, p. 4; *Colonist*, 27 July 1914, p. 4; *Sun*, 27 July 1914, p. 6; *North Otago Times*, 28 July 1914, p. 4; *West Coast Times*, 28 July 1914, p. 2.

10 *Nelson Evening Mail*, 30 July 1914, p. 4.

11 Alexander Turnbull Library (ATL), qMS-0680, 31 July 1914.

12 *Auckland Star*, 27 July 1914, p. 4.

13 *New Zealand Herald*, 28 July 1914, p. 6.

14 *Southland Times*, 31 July 1914, pp. 3–4.

15 *New Zealand Parliamentary Debates* (*NZPD*), Vol. 169, 28 July 1914, p. 208. The telegram from London was in reply to one from Massey himself. *Evening Post*, 28 July 1914, p. 8.

16 *Evening Post*, 28 July 1914, p. 7. Another report of the speech included the statement '[t]hat cloud might burst at any moment, though he sincerely trusted that it would not'. *Dominion*, 29 July 1914, p. 7.

17 Richard G. H. Kay, 'In Pursuit of Victory: British–New Zealand Relations During the First World War' (PhD thesis, University of Otago, 2001), p. 24.

18 Ian McGibbon, *The Path to Gallipoli: Defending New Zealand, 1840–1915* (Wellington: GP Books, 1991), pp. 245–46; ANZ, R22430488, 'Administration and Miscellaneous — Defence schemes — Precautionary — War stages'.

19 *Hawke's Bay Herald*, 1 August 1914, p. 5.

20 *Appendix to the Journals of the House of Representatives* (*AJHR*), 1915, H-19, 'Defence Forces of New Zealand', p. 4.

21 *Evening Star*, 7 August 1914, p. 4; *Colonist*, 20 August 1914, p. 4.

22 Peter Cooke, '"Priceless Worth": The Territorial Force and Senior Cadets in World War One', in Steven Loveridge (ed.), *New Zealand Society at War, 1914–1918* (Wellington: Victoria University Press, 2016), pp. 65–66.

23 *Hawera and Normanby Star*, 4 August 1914, p. 5.

24 *New Zealand Herald*, 28 July 1914, p. 7.

25 *Dominion*, 1 August 1914, p. 5. Dargaville Croatians telegraphed their support and maintained that '[i]t is very necessary for us to show that we are a white people, longing for liberty, and that we are sufferers under an Asiatic race'. The latter claim referred to the Hungarians. *Auckland Star*, 31 July 1914, p. 2.

26 *Star*, 31 July 1914, p. 6. Some names of individuals prepared to serve in the Serbian Army were collected. By 6 August it was reported that 'nearly a hundred' volunteers had put their names forward to go to Europe to fight for Serbia and almost £1000 had been collected. *Auckland Star*, 1 August 1914, p. 6; *Auckland Star*, 6 August 1914, p. 6.

27 *Auckland Star*, 29 July 1914, p. 5. Subsequently, demonstrators are said to have paid to have a flag made for the purpose of burning it outside the Austrian consulate. Some 100 demonstrators were reported to have attended, but the police intervened and the emblem was instead trampled and torn to bits. ANZ, R3794939, 'Ordinary Outwards Despatches to the Secretary of State — 5 October 1916–28 March 1917', Report to Minister of Justice, 21 August 1916, attached to Governor to Colonial Secretary, 9 October 1916.

28 *Auckland Star*, 28 July 1914, p. 4. See also *Hawera and Normanby Star*, 29 July 1914, p. 4; *Oamaru Mail*, 31 July 1914, p. 4. A Dunedin editor looked to 'British and German statesmanship'. *Evening Star*, 30 July 1914, p. 4.

29 *Dominion*, 3 August 1914, p. 8.

30 *Dominion*, 1 August 1914, p. 5.

31 *Evening Post*, 1 August 1914, p. 6.

32 *Wanganui Chronicle*, 3 August 1914, p. 8.

33 *Auckland Star*, 3 August 1914, p. 2. Some of the congregation may have been rather puzzled by the bishop's declaration that '[h]owever much we deplore the murder of the Archduke Ferdinand, it is monstrous to think that such an act should necessitate a resort to war on our part as the price of the Triple Entente'.

34 *Evening Post*, 3 August 1914, p. 8; *Dominion*, 3 August 1914, p. 8.

35 *Evening Post*, 3 August 1914, p. 8.

36 *Evening Post*, 4 August 1914, p. 7.

37 *Auckland Star*, 4 August 1914, p. 6; *Wanganui Chronicle*, 4 August 1914, p. 4.

38 *Sun*, 4 August 1914, p. 7.

39 *Press*, 5 August 1914, p. 8. The *Press* was appreciably more ready than other newspapers to accept that war with the German Empire might be inevitable, given its apparent determination to challenge the British Empire, not least in naval terms. Like other commentators it eschewed 'Jingoism', but somewhat undermined that by citing the jingle from which the term derived in noting that Britain had the ships, men and money to defeat Germany. *Press*, 4 August 1914, p. 8. Curiously, the jingle summed up the predominant mood in New Zealand — a preference not to fight, but a confidence in victory if obliged to do so. 'We don't

want to fight, but by Jingo if we do, We've got the men, we've got the ships, we've got the money too!'

40 *Ashburton Times*, 28 July 1914, p. 4.

41 *Oamaru Mail*, 31 July 1914, p. 4. The *Otago Daily Times*, 31 July 1914, p. 4, simply declared 'if the worst comes to the worst, Great Britain must support the other members of the Triple Entente'.

42 *Poverty Bay Herald*, 3 August 1914, p. 2.

43 *Evening Star*, 28 July 1914, p. 4.

44 *Evening Post*, 31 July 1914, p. 6.

45 *Timaru Herald*, 1 August 1914, p. 8.

46 *Grey River Argus*, 4 August 1914, p. 4.

47 *Hawke's Bay Tribune*, 3 August 1914, p. 4; *Poverty Bay Herald*, 3 August 1914, p. 2; *Bay of Plenty Times*, 3 August 1914, p. 4; *Star*, 4 August 1914, p. 4; *Mataura Ensign*, 4 August 1914, p. 4; *Auckland Star*, 4 August 1914, p. 4; *Otago Daily Times*, 4 August 1914, p. 4.

48 *Evening Star*, 29 June 1914, p. 4.

49 *Evening Post*, 3 August 1914, p. 6.

50 *Evening Post*, 5 August 1914, p. 6. The editorial was clearly written before news of the declaration of war arrived. In a curious about-face the *Wanganui Chronicle* decided at the last minute that the Triple Entente did place on Britain 'a moral obligation which cannot be honourably repudiated'. *Wanganui Chronicle*, 5 August 1914, p. 4.

51 Cited in Graham Hucker, '"The Great Wave of Enthusiasm" New Zealand Reactions to the First World War in August 1914 — A Reassessment', *New Zealand Journal of History*, Vol. 43, No. 1 (April 2009), p. 66.

52 *New Zealand Herald*, 1 August 1914, p. 6.

53 *Evening Star*, 4 August 1914, p. 4.

54 *West Coast Times*, 4 August 1914, p. 2.

55 *Maoriland Worker*, 5 August 1914, p. 4.

56 *Maoriland Worker*, 5 August 1914, p. 6.

57 *NZ Truth*, 1 August 1914, pp. 1, 7.

58 *Wairarapa Age*, 3 August 1914, p. 5.

59 *Press*, 4 August 1914, p. 10.

60 *Evening Post*, 4 August 1914, p. 8.

61 *NZPD*, Vol.169, 4 August 1914, p. 394.

62 News from abroad certainly confirmed this. See, for example, *Ashburton Guardian*, 31 July 1914, p. 5, regarding increases in flour prices in Britain.

63 *Sun*, 1 August 1914, p. 11; *Evening Post*, 5 August 1914, p. 8.

64 *Ashburton Guardian*, 4 August 1914, p. 1. Timaru bakers placed a similar advertisement two days later. *Timaru Herald*, 6 August 1914, p. 3.

65 *Ashburton Guardian*, 4 August 1914, p. 5.

66 Major Fred Waite, *The New Zealanders at Gallipoli* (Auckland: Whitcombe & Tombs, 1919), p. 2.

67 John Horne, 'Introduction: Mobilizing for "Total War", 1914–1918', in John Horne (ed.), *State, Society and Mobilization in Europe during the First World War* (Cambridge: Cambridge University Press, 1997), p. 2. Michael S. Neiberg, *Dance of the Furies: Europe and the Outbreak of World War I* (Cambridge: The Belknap Press of Harvard University Press, 2013). For a further exploration of this scholarship in regard to the New Zealand experience see Hucker, 'The Great Wave of Enthusiasm', pp. 59–75. Christopher Clark, *The Sleepwalkers: How Europe Went to War in 1914* (London: Allen Lane, 2012), p. 553.

68 *New Zealand Herald*, 5 August 1914, p. 8.

69 *Auckland Star*, 5 August 1914, p. 6.

70 *Wanganui Herald*, 5 August 1914, p. 4; *Wanganui Chronicle*, 5 August 1914, p. 4. There was also a very brief cabled report that a patriotic demonstration occurred at Wairoa when the mobilisation of British forces was announced. *Nelson Evening Mail*, 5 August 1914, p. 5.

71 *Otago Daily Times*, 4 August 1914, p. 5.

72 *Dominion*, 5 August 1914, p. 8. *Evening Post*, 5 August 1914, p. 3, estimated the crowd at 200 when it reached Parliament.

73 *Evening Post*, 5 August 1914, p. 3; *Dominion*, 5 August 1914, p. 8; *New Zealand Herald*, 5 August 1914, p. 6. Virtually the same phrase had been used by the Australian leader of the opposition Labor Party, Andrew Fisher, on 31 July and this had been widely reported. See, for example, *Press*, 1 August 1914, p. 10. However, it had been used in speeches in Dunedin and in London during the South African War, so clearly had an earlier provenance. See, for example, *Evening Star*, 10 February 1900, p. 3.

74 *Sun*, 5 August 1914, p. 8.

75 *Maoriland Worker*, 12 August 1914, p. 2. For a description of the sometimes rowdy meeting, in which those who interrupted the speakers were threatened with violence, see *Sun*, 3 August 1914, p. 8; *Press*, 3 August 1914, p. 10.

76 *Evening Post*, 4 August 1914, p. 8.

77 O. E. Burton, *The Auckland Regiment* (Auckland: Whitcombe & Tombs, 1922), p. 1.

CHAPTER TWO: WAR IS DECLARED

1 Cited in Miranda Carter, *Three Emperors: Three Cousins, Three Empires and the Road to World War One* (New York: Fig Tree, 2009), p. 427. Clive Ponting, *Thirteen Days: The Road to the First World War* (London: Chatto & Windus, 2002).

2 *Dominion*, 6 August 1914, p. 6.

3 According to Massey, the cable had arrived just before 1 p.m. and the governor had not told the prime minister what it contained before reading it to the crowd. Official telegram records confirm that the declaration of war was received at 12.15 p.m. *New Zealand Parliamentary Debates* (*NZPD*), Vol. 169, 8 August 1914, p. 480; Archives New Zealand (ANZ), R3796176, 'Inwards and outwards

despatches relating to the European War — 30 July–9 August 1914', message dated 5 August, 12.15 p.m.

4 John Darwin, *The Empire Project: The Rise and Fall of the British World-System, 1830–1970* (Cambridge: Cambridge University Press, 2009), p. 333.

5 *Press*, 6 August 1914, p. 8.

6 *Press*, 6 August 1914, p. 8.

7 *Evening Post*, 6 August 1914, p. 8.

8 *Evening Post*, 6 August 1914, p. 4.

9 *Auckland Star*, 6 August 1914, p. 6.

10 See also the report in *New Zealand Herald*, 6 August 1914, p. 9.

11 *New Zealand Herald*, 7 August 1914, p. 6.

12 *Otago Daily Times*, 7 August 1914, p. 8.

13 *Sun*, 6 August 1914, p. 7; *Sun*, 10 August 1914, p. 7.

14 *Manawatu Times*, 8 August 1914, p. 5.

15 *Southland Times*, 10 August 1914, p. 5; *Wanganui Chronicle*, 10 August 1914, p. 8; *Poverty Bay Herald*, 13 August 1914, p. 6.

16 *Timaru Herald*, 6 August 1914, p. 8; *Timaru Herald*, 7 August 1914, p. 8; *Hawke's Bay Tribune*, 7 August 1914, p. 5.

17 *Hawke's Bay Herald*, 7 August 1914, p. 5.

18 *Colonist*, 11 August 1914, p. 7. There had been a previous demonstration following news of the declaration of war. *Nelson Evening Mail*, 6 August 1914, p. 4. The population of Motueka Borough had been estimated at 1352 earlier in the year. *New Zealand Official Year-book*, 1914, p. 105.

19 *Timaru Herald*, 11 August 1914, p. 2.

20 *Timaru Herald*, 14 August 1914, p. 5.

21 *Wairarapa Age*, 10 August 1914, p. 4; *Feilding Star*, 10 August 1914, p. 4.

22 *Grey River Argus*, 11 August 1914, p. 5.

23 *New Zealand Herald*, 8 August 1914, supplement, p. 1.

24 Paul Baker, 'New Zealanders, the Great War and Conscription' (PhD thesis, University of Auckland, 1986), p. 15.

25 *New Zealand Herald*, 15 August 1914, p. 6.

26 *NZPD*, Vol. 169, 5 August 1914, p. 399.

27 *Evening Post*, 6 August 1914, p. 4.

28 *Evening Post*, 5 August 1914, p. 8.

29 *Otago Daily Times*, 6 August 1914, p. 7. Some of the initial raggedness of the cheering may also have been due to the fact that most of the crowd was out of earshot and the message took some time to reach them. *Wanganui Herald*, 6 August 1914, p. 3.

30 *New Zealand Free Lance*, 8 August 1914, p. 6.

31 Alexander Turnbull Library (ATL), MS-Papers, 5580-08, Coster to Beachamp, 8 August 1914, Lillian Annette Beachamp — Letters from Lewis Edward Coster, Beachamp Family Papers.

32 *Maoriland Worker*, 26 August 1914, p. 1.

33 *North Otago Times*, 10 August 1914, p. 4.

34 ATL, MS-Papers-0259-005, Letters to Algernon Charles Gifford, Sophie to Charles and Lucie, 7 August 1914.

35 *NZPD*, Vol. 169, 6 August 1914, p. 400.

36 Erik Olssen, 'Negotiating Conditions and Commitment: The Union Movement and the First World War', in Steven Loveridge (ed.), *New Zealand Society at War, 1914–1918* (Wellington: Victoria University Press, 2016), p. 143.

37 *Otago Daily Times*, 15 August 1914, p. 7.

38 *NZ Truth*, 15 August 1914, p. 1.

39 *Evening Post*, 10 August 1914, p. 6.

40 Erik Olssen, *The Red Feds: Revolutionary Industrial Unionism and the New Zealand Federation of Labour 1908–13* (Auckland: Oxford University Press, 1988), p. 208.

41 *Press*, 7 August 1914, p. 10.

42 *Evening Post*, 24 October 1914, p. 3.

43 *Auckland Weekly News*, 20 August 1914, p. 19; *NZPD*, Vol. 169, 14 August 1914, p. 566.

44 *New Zealand Herald*, 13 August 1914, p. 8.

45 *Poverty Bay Herald*, 15 September 1914, p. 4.

46 *Wanganui Herald*, 6 August 1914, p. 3.

47 *Northern Advocate*, 21 August 1914, p. 5; *Nelson Evening Mail*, 5 August 1914, p. 5; *Sun*, 14 August 1914, p. 8.

48 *Te Puke Times*, 25 August 1914, p. 2.

49 *Press*, 12 August 1914, p. 11.

50 *Evening Post*, 29 September 1914, p. 3.

51 *New Zealand Herald*, 19 September 1914, p. 8.

52 *Stratford Evening Post*, 11 August 1914, p. 7.

53 *Feilding Star*, 12 August 1914, p. 3.

54 *Nelson Evening Mail*, 13 August 1914, p. 4.

55 *Colonist*, 25 August 1914, p. 7.

56 *Rodney and Otamatea Times*, 19 August 1914, p. 4. John Schollum, who often acted as spokesperson for the Pūhoi community, later wrote to that newspaper to insist 'that 90 per cent of these people are New Zealand born, the remainder being Bohemians, who have been naturalised British subjects for 40 years'. Schollum also claimed that members of the community had served in the South African War. *New Zealand Herald*, 3 September 1914, p. 10; *New Zealand Herald*, 29 August 1914, p. 7.

57 *NZPD*, Vol. 169, 7 August 1914, p. 467; *NZPD*, Vol. 169, 8 August 1914, p. 477; *Evening Post*, 7 August 1914, p. 8.

58 *NZPD*, Vol. 169, 8 August 1914, p. 478.

59 *Evening Post*, 10 August 1914, p. 6.

60 *Auckland Star*, 12 August, p. 6; *Auckland Star*, 14 August 1914, p. 6.

61 *Nelson Evening Mail*, 13 August 1914, p. 4.

62 An abbreviated account of the meeting and statement was published in several other

New Zealand newspapers; see, for example, *Grey River Argus*, 14 August 1914, p. 5; *Colonist*, 14 August 1914, p. 7. Similar resolutions and declarations of loyalty were voiced by other German communities as well as the Lutheran Church. For an example see *Wanganui Chronicle*, 11 August 1914, p. 5; *Nelson Evening Mail*, 17 August 1914, p. 7.

63 *Patea Mail*, 7 September 1914, p. 3; *Wanganui Chronicle*, 8 September 1914, p. 7, though this may have been influenced somewhat by doubts about whether 'native troops' would be accepted for a European war.

64 *Otago Daily Times*, 2 September 1914, p. 6.

65 *Patea Mail*, 7 September 1914, p. 3.

66 *Inglewood Record and Waitara Age*, 14 August 1914, p. 2.

67 *Ashburton Guardian*, 22 August 1914, p. 5.

68 *Grey River Argus*, 24 August 1914, p. 4; 3 September 1914, p. 4. Ironically, O'Brien was later to serve as chairman of directors for the *Grey River Argus* when it became associated with the Labour Party. Barry Gustafson, *Labour's Path to Political Independence: The Origins and Establishment of the New Zealand Labour Party 1900–19* (Auckland: Auckland University Press, 1980), p. 163.

69 *Grey River Argus*, 9 September 1914, p. 5. Ten of the 25 individuals elected to the branch's committee were women.

70 *Evening Post*, 15 September 1914, p. 8.

71 *Press*, 15 August 1914, p. 8.

72 *Maoriland Worker*, 12 August 1914, p. 4.

73 Monty Soutar, 'Te Hokowhitu-A-Tui: A Coming of Age?', in John Crawford and Ian McGibbon (eds), *New Zealand's Great War: New Zealand, the Allies and the First World War* (Auckland: Exisle Publishing, 2007), pp. 99–100.

74 *Evening Post*, 15 September 1914, p. 2.

75 *King Country Chronicle*, 26 September 1914, p. 5.

76 *Southland Times*, 11 August 1914, p. 4.

77 *Star*, 22 August 1914, p. 8.

78 For example, the *Sun*, complaining that it had been led to believe that the British Expeditionary Force had left for the continent when it had not. *Sun*, 19 August 1914, p. 4.

79 *NZPD*, Vol. 169, 8 August 1914, p. 478.

80 *Dominion*, 26 August 1914, p. 6.

81 *NZPD*, Vol. 169, 9 September 1914, p. 806.

82 ATL, MS-Papers-2350, George Bollinger Diary, 28 September 1914.

83 ATL, MS-Papers-5507-12, Annis Bracken Hamerton to Frances Hamerton, 25 October 1914.

84 *Auckland Star*, 6 August 1914, p. 6.

85 *NZPD*, Vol. 169, 5 August 1914, p. 399.

86 *Otago Daily Times*, 6 August 1914, p. 7.

87 *NZPD*, Vol. 169, 5 August 1914, p. 399.

88 The belief that the conflict could last years was apparently not uncommon among European military experts. Hew Strachan, '1915: The Search for Solutions', in John Crawford, David Littlewood and James Watson (eds), *Experience of a Lifetime: People, Personalities and Leaders in the First World War* (Auckland: Massey University Press, 2016), pp. 14–15.

89 *Sun*, 8 October 1914, p. 6.

90 *NZPD*, Vol. 169, 5 August 1914, p. 399.

91 *Otago Daily Times*, 20 August 1914, p. 5; *Dominion*, 19 August 1914, p. 4.

92 *NZPD*, Vol. 169, 27 August 1914, p. 614; *NZPD*, Vol. 169, 3 September 1914, p. 730. There was no clear consensus on what was meant by 'short' or 'long'. In October, Lord Charles Beresford was quoted as saying the war would not be short, that it might last a further six months or a year. *Poverty Bay Herald*, 19 November 1914, p. 6; *NZPD*, Vol.169, 15 September 1914, p. 867. For other arguments by apparently well-informed individuals that the war would be over later in 1914 or early in 1915, see *Southland Times*, 6 October 1914, p. 7; *Oamaru Mail*, 28 October 1914, p. 2.

93 *Poverty Bay Herald*, 4 August 1914, p. 9.

94 *Maoriland Worker*, 12 August 1914, p. 4.

CHAPTER THREE: TO ARMS

1 Paul Baker, *King and Country Call: New Zealanders, Conscription and the Great War* (Auckland: Auckland University Press, 1988), p. 23.

2 For example, Michael King, *The Penguin History of New Zealand* (Auckland: Penguin, 2003), p. 295. Togoland in Africa surrendered days earlier.

3 *Auckland Star*, 20 August 1914, p. 5.

4 John Horne and Alan Kramer, *German Atrocities, 1914: A History of Denial* (New Haven: Yale University Press, 2001), p. 419; Adrian Gregory, *The Last Great War: British Society and the First World War* (Cambridge: Cambridge University Press, 2008), pp. 44–46.

5 'Frightfulness' has been noted as sounding 'rather twee' to the modern ear, with the advice, 'To understand the way it was used at the time, it is useful to substitute the term "terrorism".' Gregory, *The Last Great War*, p. 307.

6 Alan Kramer, *Dynamic of Destruction: Culture and Mass Killing in the First World War* (New York: Oxford University Press, 2007), pp. 6–18.

7 *New Zealand Herald*, 8 December 1914, p. 8. Another direct witness account came from Wellington businessman M. A. Carr, who had been touring Germany before the war. In October, Carr recounted his experience of being imprisoned for a fortnight in insanitary, crowded conditions and badly treated. This experience led him to express anger at the relative comfort in which German

subjects were detained in London. His account was widely published. *Dominion*, 14 October 1914, p. 6.

8 Horne and Kramer, *German Atrocities*, pp. 202–4.

9 *New Zealand Herald*, 31 August 1914, p. 4.

10 *Otago Daily Times*, 7 September 1914, p. 3.

11 For examples of the unofficial production of war culture see Ian F. Grant, 'War a Daily Reminder, But Life Goes On: Newspapers during the First World War', in Steven Loveridge (ed.), *New Zealand Society at War, 1914–1918* (Wellington: Victoria University Press, 2016), pp. 127–41; Peter Lineham, 'First World War Religion', in John Crawford and Ian McGibbon (eds), *New Zealand's Great War: New Zealand, the Allies and the First World War* (Auckland: Exisle Publishing, 2007), pp. 467–92; Chris Bourke, *Good-bye Maoriland: The Songs and Sounds of New Zealand's Great War* (Auckland: Auckland University Press, 2017); Sarah Murray, *A Cartoon War: The Cartoons of the* New Zealand Freelance *and* New Zealand Observer *as Historical Sources, August 1914–November 1918* (Wellington: New Zealand Cartoon Archive, 2012); Steven Loveridge, 'Sketching New Zealand's War: William Blomfield and the *New Zealand Observer*', in James Watson, John Crawford and David Littlewood (eds), *Experience of a Lifetime: People, Personalities and Leaders in the First World War* (Auckland: Massey University Press, 2016), pp. 249–67; Glenn Reddiex, *Just to let You Know I'm Still Alive: Postcards from New Zealanders During the First World War* (Wellington: Grantham House Publishing, 2015); Barbara Lyon, 'World War One at Home: In Ephemera', *Turnbull Library Record*, Vol. 46 (2014), pp. 40–61. For official exports, see E. P. Malone, 'The New Zealand School Journal and the Imperial Ideology', *New Zealand Journal of History*, Vol. 7, No. 1 (April 1973), pp. 12–27; Stephanie Gibson, 'First World War posters at Te Papa', *Tuhinga*, 23 (2012), pp. 69–84; Gregory Hynes, '"We New Zealanders pride ourselves most of all upon loyalty to our Empire, our country, our flag": Internalised Britishness and national character in New Zealand's First World War propaganda', in Michael Walsh and Andrekos Varnava (eds), *The Great War and the British Empire: Culture and Society* (New York: Routledge Ltd, 2017), pp. 81–101; Jenny Haworth, *Behind the Twisted Wire: New Zealand Artists in World War I* (Christchurch: Wily Publications, 2016).

12 *Wanganui Chronicle*, 1 September 1914, p. 7.

13 *New Zealand Tablet*, 20 August 1914, pp. 33–34.

14 *Southland Times*, 28 June 1915, p. 2.

15 *Evening Post*, 19 October 1914, p. 6.

16 *Auckland Star*, 30 July 1915, p. 4.

17 *New Zealand Herald*, 2 January 1915, supplement, p. 1.

18 *Auckland Weekly News*, 21 October 1915, p. 14.

19 *New Zealand Herald*, 2 January 1915, supplement, p. 1.

20 *New Zealand Herald*, 16 February 1916, p. 6.

21 *New Zealand Parliamentary Debates* (*NZPD*), Vol. 175, 1 June 1916, pp. 634–35. These ideas lasted until the end of the war and Ward warned, for example, of Germany's ambition to capture New Zealand in November 1918. *NZPD*, Vol. 183, 1 November 1918, p. 172.

22 Jürgen Tampke (ed.), *'Ruthless Warfare': German Military Planning and Surveillance in the Australia–New Zealand Region before the Great War* (Canberra: Southern Highlands Publisher, 1998).

23 *Evening Star*, 19 October 1914, p. 6.

24 *Manawatu Times*, 31 December 1914, p. 2.

25 Cited in Dickon John Milnes, 'The Church Militant: Dunedin Churches and Society During World War One' (PhD thesis, University of Otago, 2015), p. 75.

26 *The Carnival Book: Cartoons and Sketches of the Queen Carnival, The Taking of Samoa and the Dardanelles*, illustrated by G. P. Hanna, edited by Philip Hereford (Wellington: New Zealand Patriotic Society, Wellington Branch, 1915), p. 44.

27 *Maoriland Worker*, 5 August 1914, p. 3; *Maoriland Worker*, 16 December 1914, p. 1.

28 Michael King, *Te Puea: A Life* (Auckland: Reed, 2003), p. 77.

29 Cited in Steven Loveridge and Basil Keane, 'Turangawaewae: Maori Relationships with the Great War', in Loveridge (ed.), *New Zealand Society at War*, p. 287.

30 *New Zealand Herald*, 14 August 1914, p. 4.

31 Cited in Pierre Purseigle, 'The Reception of Belgian Refugees in Europe: A Litmus Test of Wartime Social Mobilisation', in Crawford and McGibbon (eds), *New Zealand's Great War*, p. 69.

32 This contradistinction is aptly observed in Robert and Isabelle Tombs, *That Sweet Enemy: The French and the British from the Sun King to the Present* (New York: Alfred A. Knopf, 2007), pp. 446–67.

33 L. J. Du Flou-Mestdagh, *Tri-colour Day in New Zealand: Its Meaning, its Aims, its Results* (Auckland: J. Buelens, 1916), p. 18.

34 *Oamaru Mail*, 30 September 1914, p. 7.

35 *Evening Post*, 4 January 1915, p. 3.

36 *Evening Star*, 8 December 1914, p. 4.

37 *Star*, 12 August 1914, p. 4.

38 *New Zealand Herald*, 3 December 1914, p. 6.

39 Cited in Richard G. H. Kay, 'In Pursuit of Victory: British–New Zealand Relations During the First World War' (PhD thesis, University of Otago, 2001), p. 164.

40 Natalie J. Wright, 'Beyond the Pale of Human Recognition: The Image of the Enemy as Portrayed in the Otago/Southland Press during World War One: Attitudes towards British Propaganda and Censorship' (MA thesis, University of Otago, 1996),

pp. 100–1.

41 *Otago Daily Times*, 12 October 1914, p. 6.

42 *Evening Post*, 10 November 1915, p. 11.

43 The contradictions within these depictions are considered in Wright, 'Beyond the Pale of Human Recognition', pp. 86–101.

44 *Colonist*, 25 August 1914, p. 7.

45 *North Otago Times*, 10 August 1914, p. 4.

46 *Maoriland Worker*, 16 December 1914, p. 1.

47 Wright, 'Beyond the Pale of Human Recognition', p. 32.

48 *Auckland Star*, 9 October 1914, p. 4.

49 *Grey River Argus*, 20 March 1915, p. 4.

50 Steven Loveridge, 'A German is *Always* a German?: Representations of Enemies, Germans and Race in New Zealand, c. 1890–1918', *New Zealand Journal of History*, Vol. 48, No. 1 (April 2014), pp. 51–71.

51 *New Zealand Herald*, 24 October 1914, supplement, p. 1. The *Herald*'s editorial line was not fixed on this issue. In January 1915, for example, it published a column by Frank Morton, who had recently returned to Australia after some years as a prominent journalist in New Zealand. Morton refused 'to condemn the whole German people', maintaining that a small number of Prussians 'have dragged a whole great people into war' and that 'the great majority of the German people are merely the victims and bondslaves of this war'. *New Zealand Herald*, 9 January 1915, supplement, p. 1.

52 *Otago Daily Times*, 25 November 1914, p. 8.

53 *Colonist*, 20 August 1914, p. 3.

54 *Evening Post*, 11 December 1914, p. 9. In response 'F Wolter' pointed out 'that King George has German blood in his veins', that '[t]he Angles and Saxons came from the shores of Germany' and that naturalised Germans had renounced their birthplace in order to become British subjects. *Evening Post*, 15 December 1914, p. 2.

55 *Population Census*, 1911, p. xi.

56 Cited in J. W. Pobog-Jaworowski, *Polish Settlers in Taranaki, 1876–1976* (Lower Hutt: the author, 1976), p. 22.

57 *Evening Star*, 18 March 1915, p. 2; *NZ Truth*, 27 March 1915, p. 8.

58 *Colonist*, 19 May 1915, p. 7.

59 *New Zealand Observer*, 29 August 1914, p. 7.

60 *Star*, 26 April 1915, p. 5.

61 *Auckland Star*, 22 August 1914, p. 3. The Syrians of Wellington and Dunedin also raised money for the Patriotic Fund. *Evening Post*, 25 August 1914, p. 8; *Evening Star*, 14 August 1914, p. 3.

62 *Auckland Star*, 12 August 1914, p. 6.

63 Cited in Pobog-Jaworowski, *Polish Settlers in Taranaki*, p. 12.

64 In September 1914, a number of newspapers printed a detailed report of 'a dastardly attempt' to cut the telegraph cable that came ashore in Lyall Bay in Wellington, with shots fired at the saboteurs by a guard and a pursuit through the sandhills. *Manawatu Standard*, 5 September 1914, p. 5; *Feilding Star*, 7 September 1914, p. 2; *Wanganui Chronicle*, 7 September 1914, p. 4. Readers of another paper got the same story, but it was followed by a statement from General Godley that there was no evidence of a sabotage attempt. In the atmosphere of the time, it is likely that many readers failed to accept 'that the individuals at whom the sentries fired were endeavouring to hoax them, or were loafers who got frightened when challenged and ran away'. *Wanganui Herald*, 7 September 1914, p. 3. The other newspapers do not appear to have reported Godley's rebuttal.

65 *Auckland Star*, 15 May 1915, p. 9.

66 *NZPD*, Vol. 171, 20 October 1914, p. 139.

67 *New Zealand Free Lance*, 5 September 1914, p. 8.

68 *Manawatu Times*, 21 September 1914, p. 4; *Mataura Ensign*, 29 September 1914, p. 5. The *Marlborough Express* later headlined the arrested man as 'the Wellington Spy', 29 September 1914, p. 8. Experts disagreed as to how far the equipment could transmit messages, indeed whether it was capable of transmission at all, but it was suggested that with some modification a range of a hundred miles was possible.

69 The man in question, Hugo Sewald, appears to have been under police observation for some months, apparently not because he was a German but because they suspected he was a vagrant and presumably thought he might turn to crime to support himself. He was subsequently interned as a prisoner of war. *NZPD*, Vol. 171, 23 October 1914, p. 309.

70 Tampke, *'Ruthless Warfare'*, pp. 90, 99–102.

71 *Dominion*, 24 February 1916, p. 6. Seegner was subsequently released in June 1916 on grounds of ill-health.

72 Andrew Francis, *'To Be Truly British We Must Be Anti-German': New Zealand, Enemy Aliens and the Great War Experience, 1914–1919* (Oxford; New York: Peter Lang, 2012), pp. 153–54. See also Francis, 'Anti-Alienism in New Zealand during the Great War: The von Zedlitz Affair', *Immigrants & Minorities*, 24/3 (2006), pp. 251–71.

73 *Dominion*, 25 February 1915, p. 4.

74 *Maoriland Worker*, 10 March 1915, p. 4.

75 *Marlborough Express*, 2 March 1915, p. 4.

76 *New Zealand Herald*, 1 December 1914, p. 7. The report estimated that 300 'Croatian and Dalmatian gumdiggers' were seeking such work.

77 *NZ Truth*, 8 August 1914, p. 5.

78 *New Zealand Herald*, 1 December 1914, p. 7.

79 *Colonist*, 30 October 1914, p. 4.

80 *Dominion*, 7 August 1914, p. 4. A provincial editor further declared, 'This is "Jingoism" in its most malevolent aspect, and is equivalent to a shameful insult to a man with his hands tied. Germany is our enemy to-day only because of that nation's leaders' failure to conform to international law or to respect the rights of non-belligerents, but there is no call for Britons to make a personal enemy of every German who, for reasons beyond his control, is compelled to stay on British soil.' *Ashburton Guardian*, 7 August 1914, p. 4.

81 *Wanganui Herald*, 6 August 1914, p. 4; *New Zealand Free Lance*, 15 August 1914, p. 6. The *Evening Post* described the vandals as 'larrikins' and said there was now strict police surveillance 'to see that there was no repetition of the outrage'. *Evening Post*, 10 August 1914, p. 6.

82 *Evening Post*, 8 August 1914, p. 4.

83 A history of mental illness in Rottmann's family was also alleged. Rottmann was sentenced to death on 13 February 1915 and hanged the following month.

84 *Evening Post*, 2 January 1915, p. 3; Archives New Zealand (ANZ), R24209573, 'Naturalisation — Application — Wohnsiedler, Friedrich'.

85 *New Zealand Observer*, 9 January 1915, p. 2.

86 *Poverty Bay Herald*, 2 January 1915, p. 2.

87 Although labour parliamentarians, besides Payne, generally avoided denouncing local Germans, this sense of class bias could create a comparable sense of intuitive in-group and foreigner menace. Webb, for example, asserted the British credentials of his constituents while denouncing foreign influences elsewhere: 'Amongst the miners not 1 per cent have foreign blood; they have all been born in Britain, or New Zealand, or Australia. We have no foreigners in the mines. We have them in the merchants' guilds and Chambers of Commerce, and we have got them fixing up prices.' *NZPD*, Vol. 179, 10 August 1917, p. 157.

88 *Evening Star*, 10 November 1914, p. 5. Shacklock was unsympathetic to the deputation, but admitted that '[s]o far as individual members of German firms were concerned, he knew very well that there was a certain section of the Dunedin public whom nothing would satisfy short of putting the conspicuous leaders in gaol'.

89 *Auckland Star*, 16 January 1915, p. 5. The resolution appears to have been justified by real or imagined slights, hearsay and a desire for retaliation against the alleged mistreatment of British subjects in Germany. *Northern Advocate*, 18 January 1915, p. 5.

90 *Evening Star*, 23 February 1915, p. 3.

91 *Manawatu Times*, 7 January 1915, p. 4.

92 *Colonist*, 21 January 1915, p. 6.

93 *Star*, 18 January 1915, p. 4. Opposition to the JPs' proposal was also expressed by the *Wairarapa Age*, 18 January 1915, p. 4; *Ashburton Guardian*, 20 January 1915, p. 4; *Colonist*, 22 January 1915, p. 4, and 25 January 1915, p. 4; and *Maoriland Worker*, 27 January 1915, p. 4. The *New Zealand Observer*, 23 January 1915, p. 3, pilloried the JPs' arguments. The Masterton petition received similar treatment in the *Ashburton Guardian*, 23 January 1915, p. 4.

94 *Wairarapa Age*, 23 February 1915, p. 2; *Wairarapa Age*, 26 February 1915, p. 4.

95 *NZPD*, Vol. 169, 10 August 1914, p. 498.

96 For the imperial context and implication behind this development see Timothy C. Winegard, *Indigenous Peoples of the British Dominions and the First World War* (New York: Cambridge University Press, 2012), pp. 97–99.

97 *Dominion*, 8 August 1914, p. 6; *NZPD*, Vol. 169, 14 August 1914, p. 566.

98 *Kai Tiaki*, October 1914, p. 147.

99 Anna Rogers, *While You're Away: New Zealand Nurses at War 1899–1948* (Auckland: Auckland University Press, 2003), p. 51; ANZ, R21078971, 'New Zealand Expeditionary Force, its provision and maintenance', p. 44.

100 *Hawera and Normanby Star*, 2 August 1915, p. 4.

101 For a study of these women see Jane Tolerton, *Make Her Praises Heard Afar: New Zealand Women Overseas in World War One* (Wellington: Booklovers Books, 2017). See also Glyn Harper, *For King and Other Countries: The New Zealanders who Fought in Other Services in The First World War* (Auckland: Massey University Press, 2019).

102 John Graham, 'The Voluntary System: Recruiting 1914–16' (MA thesis, University of Auckland, 1971), p. 20.

103 Glyn Harper, *Johnny Enzed: The New Zealand Soldier in the First World War* (Auckland: Exisle Publishing, 2015), p. 45.

104 Graham, 'The Voluntary System', p. 28.

105 *Dominion*, 3 June 1915, p. 6.

106 Christopher Pugsley, *Gallipoli: The New Zealand Story* (Auckland: Sceptre, 1984), pp. 54, 370. The rural slant was doubtless boosted by the substantial proportion of mounted rifles in the Main Body and the requirement that they should bring their own horses.

107 Harper, *Johnny Enzed*, pp. 694–96.

108 Alexander Turnbull Library (ATL), MS-Papers-1794, Diary of Duncan Burrell Stevens, 12 August 1914.

109 Pugsley, *Gallipoli*, p. 36.

110 *New Zealand Herald*, 14 November 1914, supplement, p. 1.

111 George Skerrett, quoted in Pugsley, *Gallipoli*, p. 36.

112 *NZPD*, Vol. 169, 11 August 1914, p. 502; *NZPD*, Vol. 169, 26 August 1914, p. 582.

113 Harper, *Johnny Enzed*, p. 16.

114 Harper, *Johnny Enzed*, p. 16. For further context on income levels see Margaret Nell Galt, 'Wealth and

Income in New Zealand: c. 1870 to c. 1939' (PhD thesis, Victoria University of Wellington, 1985).

115 Baker, *King and Country Call*, p. 37.

116 Mindy Chen, 'Between Two Worlds: A Study of the Letters, Diaries and Reminiscences of some Otago and Southland Soldiers in the Great War' (BA Hons thesis, University of Otago, 1982), p. 3.

117 The rapidly decreasing proportion of single to married men between August and November 1914 among those helped by the Labour Department suggests that many unmarried men out of work due to the dip in economic activity may have volunteered. In August more than twice as many single men as married were assisted; in September the discrepancy was only 70 per cent and in November 28 per cent.

118 Cecil Malthus, *Anzac: A Retrospective* (Auckland: Whitcombe & Tombs, 1965), p. 11.

119 *NZPD*, Vol. 169, 10 August 1914, p. 498.

120 *Evening Post*, 24 August 1914, p. 8.

121 Later that summer the couple agreed he could depart after making further provision of 10 shillings a week for his family. ANZ, R22550061, '[Correspondence re Deserters/Military Defaulters/Detentioners]', Captain W. Thring to Adjutant-General, 17 December; 18 December 1914; 8 January; 5 February 1915.

122 *Star*, 19 February 1915, p. 4.

123 George Knight to Ellen Knight, 13 November 1914, in Nancy Croad (ed.), *My Dear Home: The Letters of Three Knight Brothers Who Gave Their Lives during WWI* (Auckland: The Editor, 1995), p. 26.

124 Chen, 'Between Two Worlds', p. 3.

125 *New Zealand Tablet*, 20 August 1914, p. 34. There was particular satisfaction that the cathedral in Christchurch was full of benches of young men preparing to volunteer. *New Zealand Tablet*, 27 August 1914, p. 23.

126 *Otago Daily Times*, 5 September 1914, p. 12.

127 *Dominion*, 24 August 1914, p. 4.

128 Cited in Rachel Patrick, 'An Unbroken Connection? New Zealand Families, Duty, and the First World War' (PhD thesis, Victoria University of Wellington, 2014), p. 37.

129 *Auckland Star*, 7 August 1914, p. 6. Monty Soutar, 'E te Iwi, Whitiki! Whiti! Whiti! E! Call to Arms: The Formation of the Maori Contingent in the First World War', *Turnbull Library Record*, 46 (2014), p. 13.

130 *Wanganui Chronicle*, 8 September 1914, p. 7.

131 P. S. O'Connor, 'The Recruitment of Maori Soldiers, 1914–18', *Political Science*, Vol. 19, Issue 2 (December 1967), pp. 51–52; Soutar, 'E te Iwi, Whitiki! Whiti! Whiti! E! Call to Arms', p. 12; ANZ, R22429031, 'Expeditionary Force — Maori Contingents N.Z.E.F'.

132 *Hawera and Normanby Star*, 2 September 1914, p. 5.

133 Steven Loveridge, *Calls to Arms: New Zealand Society and Commitment to the First World War* (Wellington: Victoria University Press, 2014), pp. 183–89.

134 See, for instance, *Mataura Ensign*, 19 October 1914, p. 4. The term 'to show the white feather', meaning to display cowardice, was widely used in New Zealand during the early twentieth century. It arose from the sport of cockfighting and was based on the belief that purebred fighting cocks had no white feathers and therefore the appearance of such a feather on a bird indicated that it was a cross-breed and lacked the inherent courage of the true fighting cock.

135 'Here is a hint for the young women of Christchurch to present white feathers to those young men who are liable to territorial service but who pay no heed to their duty.' *Sun*, 19 November 1914, p. 4; *Otago Daily Times*, 5 December 1914, p. 7.

136 Chen, 'Between Two Worlds', p. 3.

137 *Evening Star*, 2 January 1915, p. 10.

138 *Evening Post*, 4 February 1915, p. 6.

139 The *Sun* called the practice 'unworthy and insulting'. *Sun*, 11 January 1915, p. 6.

140 *Star*, 10 February 1915, p. 7. This story was then quoted in a number of other newspapers.

141 Margaret Tennant, 'Of Violets and Poppies: Charities in the Great War', in Loveridge (ed.), *New Zealand Society at War*, p. 211.

142 Katie Pickles, 'A Link in "the Great Chain of Empire Friendship": The Victoria League in New Zealand', *The Journal of Imperial and Commonwealth History*, Vol. 33, No. 1 (2005), pp. 29–50; Margaret Tennant, *Across the Street, Across the World: A History of the Red Cross in New Zealand, 1915–2015* (Wellington: New Zealand Red Cross, 2015), pp. 29–54; Sarah Dalton, 'The Pure in Heart: The New Zealand Women's Christian Temperance Union and Social Purity, 1885–1930' (MA thesis, Victoria University of Wellington, 1993).

143 *New Zealand Herald*, 7 August 1914, p. 9.

144 Annette Liverpool, *Her Excellency's Knitting Book* (Wellington: Ferguson & Osborn, 1915).

145 The fund established by the mayor of Christchurch on 6 August was '[p]rimarily . . . for the benefit of the dependents [sic] of those who volunteer and are called away to the war'. *Evening Star*, 7 August 1914, p. 4.

146 Patrick, 'An Unbroken Connection', pp. 46–47.

147 *Evening Post*, 15 August 1914, p. 3.

148 *Hawke's Bay Tribune*, 24 August 1914, p. 4; *Star*, 29 August 1914, p. 10.

149 *Auckland Star*, 14 November 1914, p. 6. The respective figures were £1593 and something well in excess of £2338.

150 Compared with 11.4 per cent for the Britain and Ireland Fund, 8 per cent for the NZEF and an

ambulance fund, 4.6 per cent for local distress and virtually nothing for unspecified purposes. *Evening Star*, 18 January 1915, p. 6.

151 *Evening Star*, 12 April 1915, p. 6.

152 *Star*, 10 September 1915, p. 8. Of Canterbury's contribution during the war, 10.6 per cent went to Belgian relief. This compared with 6.8 per cent of Auckland's and 3.5 per cent of Wellington's. The executives of the Otago and Westland Patriotic Funds may well have followed the same policy, as the Belgians received 12.8 and 18.7 per cent of their wartime contributions respectively. Calculated from *Appendix to the Journals of the House of Representatives* (*AJHR*), 1919, H-46, 'Patriotic Funds', pp. 2–3.

153 *Taranaki Daily News*, 4 September 1914, p. 3; *King Country Chronicle*, 5 September 1914, p. 5; *Poverty Bay Herald*, 14 September 1914, p. 4. It was said that '[a]ll the leading Urewera chiefs and others interested were present at the meeting, which was presided over by Mr Kereru, and keen enthusiasm was displayed throughout in the object under consideration'. The land involved was apparently 'the Tuararangia block, adjoining Ruatoki No.2 block, and contain[ing] some first-class country'.

154 *Otago Daily Times*, 22 October 1914, p. 6.

155 *Dominion*, 23 February 1915, p. 5.

156 *Otago Daily Times*, 29 March 1915, p. 2. The story wrongly states the monthly grant at £4000.

157 *AJHR*, 1916, H-41, 'Patriotic Society Funds', p. 3; *New Zealand Official Year-book*, 1914, p. 837.

158 *Dominion*, 15 August 1914, p. 8.

159 Imelda Bargas and Tim Shoebridge, *New Zealand's First World War Heritage* (Auckland: Exisle Publishing, 2015), p. 36.

160 *New Zealand Herald*, 1 August 1914, supplement, p. 1. For further assessment see Loveridge, *Calls to Arms*, pp. 101–35.

161 *Evening Post*, 18 August 1914, p. 6; *New Zealand Observer*, 29 August 1914, p. 2.

162 Māori soldiers appear to have been kept separate out of a sense that they were more susceptible to disease. Bargas and Shoebridge, *New Zealand's First World War Heritage*, p. 53.

163 *Evening Post*, 24 August 1914, p. 8.

164 Graham, 'The Voluntary System', p. 27.

165 *Evening Post*, 11 February 1915, p. 8.

166 Neil Frances, *Safe Haven: The Untold Story of New Zealand's Largest Ever Military Camp: Featherston: 1916–1919* (Masterton: Wairarapa Archive/Fraser Books, 2012), pp. 67–68.

167 Herbert Knight to Ellen Knight, 24 January 1915, Croad (ed.), *My Dear Home*, p. 8.

168 *Evening Star*, 7 September 1914, p. 4.

169 *Southland Times*, 23 September 1914, p. 6.

170 *Sun*, 26 September 1914, p. 11.

171 *New Zealand Herald*, 24 September 1914, p. 9.

172 *Evening Post*, 25 September 1914, p. 3; *Sun*, 26 September 1914, p. 11.

173 *Evening Post*, 25 September 1914, p. 3.

174 Kay, 'In Pursuit of Victory', pp. 75–76.

175 W. D. Stewart, *The Right Honourable Sir Francis H.D. Bell, P.C., G.C.M.G., K.C.: His Life and Times* (Wellington: Butterworth, 1937), p. 114. If the minister concerned, F. M. B. Fisher, was correct in his later belief that this encounter happened after midnight, his implication that the telegram was sent to the transports afterwards is incorrect. It was sent shortly after 8 p.m.

176 Full accounts of these crises can be found in Ian McGibbon, *Blue-Water Rationale: The Naval Defence of New Zealand, 1914–1942* (Wellington: Government Printer, 1981), pp. 19–27, and Kay, 'In Pursuit of Victory', pp. 56–85.

177 ATL, MS-Papers-5210-100-113, Paraphrase of telegram from Secretary of State for the Colonies to Governor, 3 October 1914.

178 Cited in Augustus Agar, *Showing the Flag* (London: Evans Brothers, 1962), p. 63. At this time Liverpool's title was 'governor' not 'governor-general'.

179 ATL, MS-Papers-5210-100-113, Paraphrase of telegram from Governor to Secretary of State for the Colonies, 4 October 1914.

180 For accounts see *New Zealand Free Lance*, 28 November 1914, p. 24; *Rangitikei Advocate and Manawatu Argus*, 20 November 1914, p. 8.

181 ANZ, R21078971, 'New Zealand Expeditionary Force, its provision and maintenance', p. 5.

182 Howard Weddell, *Trentham Camp and Upper Hutt's Untold Military History* (Upper Hutt: Howard Weddell, 2018), pp. 45–57.

183 Franchesca Walker, '"Descendants of a Warrior Race": The Maori Contingent, New Zealand Pioneer Battalion, and Martial Race Myth, 1914–19', *War and Society*, Vol. 31, No. 1 (March 2012), pp. 1–21; Christopher Pugsley, 'Images of Te Hokowhitu a Tu in the First World War', in Santanu Das (ed.), *Race, Empire and First World War Writing* (Cambridge: Cambridge University Press, 2011), pp. 194–210.

184 *Dominion*, 15 February 1915, p. 6.

185 *New Zealand Herald*, 7 January 1915, p. 6.

186 *Evening Post*, 20 October 1914, p. 6.

187 Christopher Pugsley, *Te Hokowhitu a Tu: The Maori Pioneer Battalion in the First World War* (Auckland: Reed, 1995), p. 30.

188 *Evening Post*, 8 April 1915, p. 8.

CHAPTER FOUR: THE EMERGING WAR ECONOMY

1 *Grey River Argus*, 20 March 1915, p. 4.

2 *Evening Post*, 9 September 1914, p. 3.

3 *Evening Post*, 28 July 1914, p. 7. This reaction

mirrored the fall in such stocks in Britain and Australia and appears to have reflected the frequently speculative nature of investment and anticipation that credit would become more expensive as British capital was reprioritised.

4 *Feilding Star*, 4 August 1914, p. 2.

5 Alexander Turnbull Library (ATL), MS-Papers-0154-29A, Isaac Ewing to Hector McLeod, 24 August 1914.

6 *Nelson Evening Mail*, 5 August 1914, p. 5.

7 *Press*, 1 August 1914, p. 10.

8 *Mataura Ensign*, 4 August 1914, p. 7.

9 *Evening Post*, 7 August 1914, p. 4.

10 *Evening Post*, 1 August 1914, p. 6.

11 *New Zealand Parliamentary Debates* (*NZPD*), Vol. 169, 11 August 1914, p. 506. There was a report the day after the declaration of war that withdrawals had been 'somewhat heavy, especially on the part of ladies' in Dunedin. *Dominion*, 7 August 1914, p. 6.

12 *Dominion*, 7 August 1914, p. 6.

13 ATL, qMS-0680, Harrold Ennor Diaries, 12 August 1914.

14 *Press*, 8 March 1920, p. 7.

15 *Southland Times*, 5 August 1915, p. 5.

16 *Evening Post*, 9 September 1914, p. 3.

17 *Hawera and Normanby Star*, 11 December 1914, p. 2.

18 *NZPD*, Vol. 169, 10 September 1914, p. 821.

19 *New Zealand Herald*, 19 August 1914, p. 9; *Colonist*, 27 August 1914, p. 4; *Sun*, 14 September 1914, p. 11.

20 *Journal of the Department of Labour*, 22:261 (1914), pp. 811, 828, 832. Dunedin reported that there was little work available from private employers for carpenters or unskilled workers (pp. 830, 832).

21 *NZPD*, Vol. 169, pp. 464–65; *NZPD*, Vol. 170, 8 October 1914, pp. 512–13.

22 *Wairarapa Age*, 28 August 1914, p. 4.

23 *Wanganui Herald*, 10 August 1914, p. 4.

24 *Auckland Star*, 5 November 1914, p. 4.

25 According to Massey, the fact that most of the flax was exported to the west coast of the United States, and the Pacific had been declared unsafe by the British government because of the presence of the German East Asia Squadron, meant that war risks insurance charges on such exports were extremely high. *Manawatu Standard*, 24 August 1914, p. 7.

26 *Manawatu Standard*, 24 August 1914, p. 7.

27 *Dominion*, 9 November 1914, p. 9. W. Ross reported a similar situation in Foxton; *New Zealand Herald*, 5 December 1914, p. 1.

28 *Auckland Star*, 23 March 1915, p. 1.

29 Although one vessel carrying New Zealand meat, the *Kaipara*, was sunk in the Atlantic by a German raider on 16 August.

30 *Evening Post*, 28 October 1914, p. 8.

31 *Auckland Star*, 1 October 1914, p. 4.

32 *Hawke's Bay Herald*, 10 November 1914, p. 3.

33 *Journal of the Department of Labour*, 23:265 (March 1915), pp. 221, 228.

34 *Journal of the Department of Labour*, 23:266 (April 1915), pp. 282, 289, 290, 294; 23:267 (May 1915), p. 377.

35 *Press*, 8 August 1914, p. 14.

36 'Weekly Budgets', *Journal of the Department of Labour*, 23:271 (September 1915), pp. 708–9; Barry Gustafson, *Labour's Path to Political Independence: The Origins and Establishment of the New Zealand Labour Party 1900–19* (Auckland: Auckland University Press, 1980), p. 96.

37 *Sun*, 10 August 1914, p. 7.

38 Malcolm Fraser, *Prices: An Inquiry into Prices in New Zealand 1891–1914* (Wellington: Government Printer, 1920), pp. 116–38.

39 'Weekly Budgets', *Journal of the Department of Labour*, 23:271 (September 1915), pp. 708–9. The composition of the 'basket' of purchases, based upon a pre-war survey, contained 3 pounds of butter and only a quarter of a pound of cheese, indicating that New Zealand families then consumed relatively little of the latter. The increase in the dominion-weighted average retail price for butter was 14.45 per cent, slightly lower than that for the four main centres. Calculated from 'Group II — Dairy-Produce Index Numbers', *Journal of the Department of Labour*, 23:271 (September 1915), p. 705.

40 *Oamaru Mail*, 23 April 1915, p. 4. That the price for cheese exports had risen more sharply than that for butter exports apparently also led some dual-purpose factories to continue producing cheese after they would normally have switched to making butter for the local market in the autumn. *Hawera and Normanby Star*, 1 May 1915, p. 2.

41 *Auckland Star*, 20 April 1915, p. 6.

42 *New Zealand Herald*, 22 April 1915, p. 9.

43 *Sun*, 14 April 1915, p. 6.

44 *Maoriland Worker*, 13 January 1915, p. 8.

45 For a time meat prices were substantially higher in Wellington than in other towns. *Dominion*, 27 August 1914, p. 7. This was possibly because the bulk of the expeditionary force was at Trentham and its transports were to depart from the port.

46 *Wanganui Chronicle*, 25 September 1914, p. 4.

47 *Mataura Ensign*, 23 September 1914, p. 5.

48 *Dunstan Times*, 26 October 1914, p. 5.

49 *Auckland Star*, 12 October 1914, p. 7; 'Weekly Budgets', *Journal of the Department of Labour*, 23:271 (September 1915), pp. 708–9.

50 *Star*, 28 August 1914, p. 4.

51 *Wanganui Chronicle*, 27 August 1914, p. 8.

52 *Auckland Star*, 22 April 1915, p. 6.

53 'House–rent', *Journal of the Department of Labour*, 23:271 (September 1915), p. 710.

54 *Journal of the Department of Labour*, 23:267 (May 1915), p. 394; 23:272 (October, 1915), p. 803.

55 *Journal of the Department of Labour*, 23:267 (May

1915), p. 396; *Otago Daily Times*, 30 December 1914, p. 3.

56 James Holt, *Compulsory Arbitration in New Zealand: The First Forty Years* (Auckland: Auckland University Press, 1986), pp. 119–20.

57 *New Zealand Herald*, 13 January 1915, p. 7; 26 January 1915, p. 8. *Dominion*, 1 March 1915, p. 8.

58 Holt, *Compulsory Arbitration in New Zealand*, pp. 120–21.

59 Archives New Zealand (ANZ), R3898752, 'New Zealand's part in the war, March 1917–September 1919', p. 11.

60 Selwyn Parker, *Wealthmakers: A History of the Northern Employers' and Manufacturers' Associations* (Auckland: Employers' & Manufacturers' Association Northern, 2005), p. 64.

61 *Star*, 4 August 1914, p. 6.

62 *Evening Star*, 29 August 1914, p. 12.

63 *Evening Star*, 2 February 1915, p. 2.

64 *New Zealand Herald*, 26 February 1915, p. 6.

65 *Evening Post*, 26 August 1914, p. 8.

66 *New Zealand Official Year-book*, 1916, p. 633.

67 *Letters from Arthur Lush to his Family in New Zealand: Written during World War I and transcribed by John Challands* (Thames: Alison Williamson, 2003), p. 6.

68 *Wairarapa Daily Times*, 11 August 1914, p. 4.

69 *Wanganui Herald*, 5 November 1914, p. 4; 30 September 1918, p. 7.

70 *Wairarapa Age*, 28 August 1914, p. 4.

71 *Dominion*, 27 August 1914, p. 7.

72 *Evening Post*, 27 January 1915, p. 2.

73 *Northern Advocate*, 2 February 1915, p. 3.

74 *New Zealand Official Year-book*, 1916, p. 644.

75 *Star*, 10 November 1914, p. 4.

76 Consequently, the premium usually commanded by finer wools, merino and half-breeds, was eroded. This was accentuated by the fact that a lot of the market for these finer wools lay in the factories of Germany, Belgium and northern France, now in enemy hands.

77 *Press*, 19 November 1914, p. 3; *Evening Post*, 26 February 1915, p. 10. A fall in prices in December had been attributed to 'pessimistic views from Bradford as to the probable position of the market when their purchases would arrive Home, viz., in March–May'. In other words, there was 'pessimism' that the war would have ended, probably victoriously for the Allies, by then. The story was headlined 'More Khaki' and claimed that 'it has been estimated that in the trenches a month is about the life of a uniform'. *Evening Post*, 26 January 1915, p. 8.

78 *Auckland Star*, 31 July 1915, p. 9.

79 *New Zealand Official Year-book*, 1916, p. 644; *Oamaru Mail*, 23 April 1915, p. 4; *New Zealand Official Year-book*, 1916, p. 644.

80 This mass purchasing was also intended to deny goods to the enemy. Laws against trading with the enemy, whether directly or through neutral countries, had previously been introduced in New Zealand. A royal proclamation to that effect was published two days after the declaration of war and at the beginning of November 1914 exports of wool to countries not within the British Empire or allied to it were banned. *Evening Post*, 7 August 1914, p. 8; *Evening Post*, 4 November 1914, p. 8.

81 *Evening Post*, 3 February 1915, p. 7; *Evening Post*, 18 February 1915, p. 2.

82 *Evening Post*, 18 February 1915, p. 2.

83 *Appendix to the Journal of the House of Representatives* (*AJHR*), 1918, H-38, 'Department of Imperial Government Supplies', pp. 1–23. Vocal protests were briefly raised by beef farmers who maintained that pastoralists had not been represented independently and that the processing companies had been able to secure too great a share of the profits. These were rapidly quelled by news that the producers' share would be increased. *Evening Post*, 30 March 1915, p. 3.

84 *AJHR*, 1919, B-6, 'Financial Statement', pp. xxvi–xxviii; John E. Martin, 'War Economy', in Ian McGibbon (ed.), *The Oxford Companion to New Zealand Military History* (Auckland: Oxford University Press, 2000), p. 582.

85 James Watson, 'Patriotism, Profits and Problems: New Zealand Farming during the Great War', in John Crawford and Ian McGibbon (eds), *New Zealand's Great War: New Zealand, the Allies and the First World War* (Auckland: Exisle Publishing, 2007), pp. 534–49.

86 *Evening Post*, 10 August 1915, p. 8; *Mataura Ensign*, 20 February 1915, p. 4.

87 True, the wartime arrangements were also made with competitors outside the British Empire, but for the moment those competitors were not driving prices for dominion produce down.

88 Will Lawson, *Food-ships for Britain: An Account of the Work of the Department of Imperial Government Supplies in New Zealand to the End of August 1918* (Wellington: Government Printer, 1918), pp. 9–10, 19, 25–29.

89 Steven Loveridge and James Watson, 'Economic Mobilisation: New Zealand Businesses and the Great War', in Steven Loveridge (ed.), *New Zealand Society at War, 1914–1918* (Wellington: Victoria University Press, 2016), p. 163.

90 *Journal of the Department of Labour*, 22:262 (December, 1914), p. 821; 23:263 (January, 1915), p. 71; 23:264 (February 1915), p. 139, 148; 23:267 9 May, 1915), p. 389.

91 *NZPD*, Vol. 169, 10 August 1914, p. 497.

92 *Journal of the Department of Labour*, 22:261 (1914), p. 797.

93 *Poverty Bay Herald*, 24 March 1915, p. 4.

94 *Colonist*, 27 August 1914, p. 4; *Sun*, 14 September 1914, p. 11; *Journal of the Department of Labour*, 23:264 (February, 1915), p. 137.

95 *Poverty Bay Herald*, 24 March 1915, p. 4.

96 Claims made by opposition politicians regarding large stocks being held by farmers were mostly vague and Massey insisted on names being provided before launching investigations. Four Canterbury farmers who were named in January were found to possess only a few bushels of 'seconds'. *Wanganui Chronicle*, 27 January 1915, p. 5.

97 *Manawatu Standard*, 17 March 1915, p. 5. Figure calculated using the Reserve Bank's Inflation Calculator, http://www.rbnz.govt.nz.

98 The Australian government had already made a similar announcement. *Evening Post*, 29 August 1914, p. 2; *New Zealand Herald*, 20 April 1915, p. 9.

99 *Auckland Star*, 29 April 1915, p. 8.

100 *Star*, 21 April 1915, pp. 6, 4.

101 *NZ Truth*, 22 May 1915, p. 5.

102 Fairbairn's only son, William, who had enlisted at the age of 18, served as a gunner at Gallipoli, and was killed in action on the Western Front in November 1916. *Dominion*, 21 November 1916, p. 5.

103 *New Zealand Herald*, 25 August 1914, p. 7; *New Zealand Herald*, 4 September 1914, p. 6. Some unsuitable boots made elsewhere were also discovered. *Wanganui Herald*, 7 September 1914, p. 3.

104 *Star*, 21 April 1915, p. 7.

105 *New Zealand Observer*, 7 November 1914, p. 2.

106 *New Zealand Observer*, 7 November 1914, p. 2; 31 October 1914, p. 2; 7 November 1914, p. 18.

107 *Otago Daily Times*, 11 May 1915, p. 6.

108 *Star*, 14 October 1914, p. 5.

109 *New Zealand Herald*, 15 October 1914, p. 8; *Poverty Bay Herald*, 29 October 1914, p. 4; *Auckland Star*, 26 November 1914, p. 9.

110 *Manawatu Times*, 11 March 1915, p. 4. The previous pattern was bought at 13s 9d.

111 ANZ, R3898751 'Return of expenditure furnished to Defence Stores Commission [Commission of Inquiry re Defence Stores], August 1915'.

112 ANZ, R22430459, 'Courts Martial and Courts of Inquiry — Tenders Board — Formation of for purchase of Defence stores and equipment in NZ', D. Robertson to J. Allen, 24 February 1915.

113 ANZ, R22430459, 'Courts Martial and Courts of Inquiry — Tenders Board — Formation of for purchase of Defence stores and equipment in NZ', A. Robin to J. Allen, 1 March 1915.

114 ANZ, R3885211, 'Commission of enquiry — Defence stores 1915, June–August', A. Robin to J. Allen, 16 June 1915; J. Allen to A. Herdman, 22 June 1915; A. Herdman to J. Allen, 23 June 1915.

CHAPTER FIVE: POLITICS PRESSES ON

1 *New Zealand Parliamentary Debates* (*NZPD*), Vol. 171, 23 October 1914, p. 307; *New Zealand Statutes*, 1914, No. 38, 'War Regulations Act', section 3, p. 128.

2 Tristan Egarr, 'The Dominion State at War' (MA thesis, Victoria University of Wellington, 2018), p. 140.

3 Alex Frame, *Salmond: Southern Jurist* (Wellington: Victoria University Press, 1995), p. 168.

4 *New Zealand Statutes*, 1914, No. 38, 'War Regulations Act', p. 129.

5 *NZPD*, Vol. 169, 6 August 1914, pp. 403, 406.

6 *NZPD*, Vol. 169, 6 August 1914, p. 406. The description of Russell is in Antony Wood, 'The Origins of the First National Government: A Study in New Zealand politics, 1914–15' (MA thesis, Canterbury University, 1963), p. 36.

7 *NZPD*, Vol. 169, 11 August 1914, p. 509.

8 See, for example, the prolonged and rather acerbic debate less than a fortnight after the outbreak of war on whether parties were continuing to hold public meetings. *NZPD*, Vol. 169, 27 August 1914, pp. 626–41.

9 *NZPD*, Vol. 170, 18 September 1914, p. 64.

10 *NZPD*, Vol. 170, 18 September 1914, p. 69.

11 *NZPD*, Vol. 170, 22 September 1914, p. 119. It could have been worse. In Hastings a disagreement between the mayor and a councillor escalated into a physical confrontation in which the former received a severe blow to the face and retaliated. The battle raged fiercely for several minutes, until the rival forces agreed upon an armistice, leaving the floor of the council chamber like a blood-stained battlefield. Accordingly, the office staff observed strict neutrality and the incident was said to be the sole topic of conversation in town that morning, overshadowing the crisis in Europe. *Hawke's Bay Herald*, 7 August 1914, p. 4.

12 Massey argued that the war might well be largely over by December and alternatively that it might last a good deal longer. In the first case the postponement would be unnecessary; in the latter case it would be constitutionally undesirable to postpone consulting the electorate for such a long time, possibly years. Given the prime minister's repeated references to his expectation that the war would be quite short, this seems to have been a convenient rather than a strongly held argument.

13 *NZPD*, Vol. 170, 29 September 1914, pp. 187, 168; Vol. 171, 4 November 1914, p. 873.

14 *NZPD*, Vol. 171, 20 October 1914, p. 139.

15 *NZPD*, Vol. 171, 20 October 1914, pp. 139–40.

16 *Wairarapa Daily Times*, 19 December 1914, p. 4.

17 *Manawatu Standard*, 21 October 1914, p. 6.

18 *Auckland Star*, 10 August 1914, p. 7; *Wairarapa Daily Times*, 19 December 1914, p. 4.

19 *Press*, 10 August 1914, p. 8.

20 *Press*, 10 August 1914, p. 8; *Colonist*, 10 August 1914, p. 3; David McGill, *Island of Secrets: Matiu/Somes Island in Wellington Harbour* (Wellington: Steele Roberts & Silver Owl Press, 2001), p. 44; Samantha Owens, '"Unmistakeable Sauerkrauts": Local Perceptions of Itinerant German Musicians in New Zealand, 1850–1920', *Nineteenth-Century Music Review*, Vol. 15 (2018), pp. 37–49.

21 *Sun*, 10 August 1914, p. 7.

22 *Evening Post*, 13 August 1914, p. 8.

23 McGill, *Island of Secrets*, p. 44.

24 *Evening Post*, 15 August 1914, p. 8. The former German consul was allowed to visit and also made a favourable report. *Evening Post*, 17 August 1914, p. 8.

25 *Dominion*, 25 August 1914, p. 6.

26 Archives New Zealand (ANZ), R21371869, 'Prisoners of war: letters for'.

27 *Evening Post*, 14 August 1914, p. 8. Two of the families were apparently 'in financial straits' at the time. *Evening Post*, 15 August 1914, p. 8.

28 *Evening Post*, 17 August 1914, p. 8.

29 *Dominion*, 20 August 1914, p. 6.

30 *New Zealand Gazette*, 10 November 1914, p. 4022.

31 *Marlborough Express*, 5 December 1914, p. 2.

32 *Dominion*, 27 February 1915, p. 7.

33 *Northern Advocate*, 6 August 1914, p. 2.

34 *Press*, 25 August 1914, p. 8.

35 *NZ Truth*, 8 August 1914, p. 5.

36 *Mt Benger Mail*, 26 August 1914, p. 2.

37 John Anderson, 'Military Censorship in World War I: Its Use and Abuse in New Zealand' (MA thesis, Victoria University College, Wellington, 1952), pp. 168–69.

38 *Marlborough Express*, 6 August 1914, p. 5.

39 Ian F. Grant, 'War a Daily Reminder, But Life Goes On: Newspapers during the First World War', in Steven Loveridge (ed.), *New Zealand Society at War, 1914–1918* (Wellington: Victoria University Press, 2016), p. 127.

40 *Otago Daily Times*, 6 August 1914, p. 8; *Otago Witness*, 12 August 1914, p. 52. Again this was speculation, but it would seem to have been better to avoid saying it in light of the message from the Defence Department.

41 *Evening Star*, 12 August 1914, p. 6.

42 *Star*, 11 August 1914, p. 4. The *Press* obligingly provided the offending details the next day. *Press*, 11 August 1914, p. 8. The incorrect date for the actual departure meant Godley could deny the rumour without lying.

43 *Sun*, 11 August 1914, p. 6. See also *Sun*, 8 August 1914, p. 8.

44 *Star*, 23 September 1914, p. 4.

45 Anderson, 'Military Censorship in World War I', pp. 205–12.

46 Anderson, 'Military Censorship in World War I', pp. 37–42.

47 Anderson, 'Military Censorship in World War I', p. 105; Jared Davidson, *Dead Letters: Censorship and Subversion in New Zealand 1914–1920* (Dunedin: Otago University Press, 2019), p. 35.

48 By 24 August 1914 letters addressed to the Austrian consulate (and presumably other consulates as well) were being intercepted and analysed. ANZ, R3885411, 'Censorship of German messages, August–September 1914'.

49 Davidson, *Dead Letters*, p. 31.

50 ANZ, R22432692, 'Staff, miscellaneous — Deputy Chief Censor Wellington — Appointment of'; ANZ, R22430468, 'Administration and Miscellaneous — Censorship — Regulations postal', W. H. S. Moorhouse to Chief of Staff, 1 August 1914. Operations were given a legal foundation under the terms of the 1908 Post and Telegraph Act and War Regulations prohibiting the delivery of correspondence to persons or firms in New Zealand or elsewhere who had been named in warrants under the postmaster-general's hand, and to require the delivery of such letters to a military authority. *New Zealand Statutes*, 1908, No. 147, 'Post and Telegraph Act', section 27, p. 605; ANZ, R19162367, 'Report on Postal Censorship during the Great War'. For further postal regulations gazetted through war regulations in 1914 see *New Zealand Gazette*, 1914, pp. 4021–23, 4361–63.

51 ANZ, R22430468, 'Administration and Miscellaneous — Censorship — Regulations postal'; ANZ, R19162367, 'Report on Postal Censorship during the Great War'.

52 ANZ, R22430468, 'Administration and Miscellaneous — Censorship — Regulations postal'.

53 Davidson, *Dead Letters*, pp. 24, 35.

54 *Appendix to the Journals of the House of Representatives* (*AJHR*), 1915, H-19e, 'Expeditionary Force: Provision of Reinforcement Drafts for the (memorandum on)', p. 1.

55 For examples of 'knock-out blow' rhetoric see *New Zealand Herald*, 14 November 1914, p. 6; *Evening Post*, 14 November 1914, p. 6; *Evening Post*, 29 December 1914, p. 6; *Press*, 20 February 1915, p. 10.

56 *New Zealand Herald*, 19 January 1915, p. 6.

57 *West Coast Times*, 16 November 1914, p. 2; *Evening Post*, 29 December 1914, p. 6.

58 *Evening Star*, 19 February 1915, p. 4.

59 *Evening Star*, 27 November 1914, p. 3.

60 *Press*, 20 January 1915, p. 7.

61 *Evening Post*, 19 April 1915, p. 6.

62 *Otago Daily Times*, 29 May 1915, p. 5; *New Zealand Herald*, 10 September 1914, p. 7; *New Zealand Herald*, 24 November 1914, p. 6.

63 ANZ, R22429100, 'Expeditionary Force — Recruiting for Expeditionary Force — General'; ANZ, R22429103, 'Expeditionary Force — Recruiting for Expeditionary Force — General'; ANZ, R22429104, 'Expeditionary Force — Recruiting for Expeditionary Force — General'.

64 ANZ, R22429100, 'Expeditionary Force — Recruiting for Expeditionary Force — General'.

65 *New Zealand Herald*, 17 December 1914, p. 8; *Evening Post*, 14 April 1915, p. 6.

66 *New Zealand Herald*, 19 December 1914, p. 8.

67 ANZ, R22431244, 'Establishments and Recruitment — Enlistment — Return showing number from each district'.

68 *New Zealand Herald*, 16 April 1915, p. 6; ANZ, R22431244, 'Establishments and Recruitment — Enlistment — Return showing number from each district'.

69 *Evening Star*, 30 October 1914, p. 4; 23 November 1914, p. 4.

70 ANZ, R22431244, 'Establishments and Recruitment — Enlistment — Return showing number from each district', letter dated 6 August 1915.

71 The bills would be sold to financial institutions rather than floated on the open market and the first £400,000 was advanced by the Bank of England. *New Zealand Herald*, 23 October 1914, p. 7.

72 *Auckland Star*, 13 August 1914, p. 4.

73 In early October Allen told a journalist, 'I cannot issue stock except at [sic] price that would be too high for the country. At least I don't think I can.' *Hawke's Bay Herald*, 8 October 1914, p. 2.

74 *Oamaru Mail*, 22 August 1914, p. 4.

75 *Dominion*, 10 November 1914, p. 4.

76 *Press*, 10 August 1914, p. 9.

77 *Auckland Star*, 10 August 1914, p. 7. The meeting ended up unanimously recommending the government move immediately towards increasing income tax or levying a special war tax.

78 *Hawera and Normanby Star*, 24 August 1914, p. 5.

79 *Poverty Bay Herald*, 24 March 1915, p. 4.

80 *Evening Post*, 8 March 1915, p. 7.

81 *Poverty Bay Herald*, 24 March 1915, p. 4.

82 The coupon rate of interest was 3.5 per cent, but the issue was discounted to 95, thus yielding 4 per cent. *Grey River Argus*, 6 January 1915, p. 6.

83 *Evening Post*, 17 December 1914, p. 2.

84 *Wanganui Chronicle*, 18 March 1915, p. 5; *Poverty Bay Herald*, 24 March 1915, p. 4; *Manawatu Standard*, 16 April 1915, p. 4.

85 *NZPD*, Vol. 169, 5 August 1914, p. 397.

86 *Otago Daily Times*, 8 October 1914, p. 6.

87 Indian wheat was also considered but deemed unsuitable for New Zealand requirements. *New Zealand Herald*, 3 December 1914, p. 8; *Oamaru Mail*, 6 October 1914, p. 4. *Timaru Herald*, 18 November 1914, p. 7.

88 *Nelson Evening Mail*, 14 August 1914, p. 5.

89 According to Massey, the 'wheat and flour census' carried out later in the year revealed that an extra 23,000 acres had been sown. *New Zealand Herald*, 3 December 1914, p. 8. A survey of farmers in Bruce and Clutha counties at the end of August concluded that there might be a 20 per cent increase in wheat and 10 per cent increase in oats sown in the former, but no extra wheat and only 10 per cent more oats in the latter. *Evening Star*, 25 August 1914, p. 7.

90 *Hawera and Normanby Star*, 29 August 1914, p. 4.

91 *Star*, 19 October 1914, p. 3.

92 Similar proclamations had been made in New South Wales on 15 September and Victoria on 23 September. *Otago Daily Times*, 17 October 1914, p. 8; *Press*, 3 October 1914, p. 11.

93 *AJHR*, 1915, H-34, 'Report of Royal Commission Appointed under the Regulation of Trade and Commerce Act, 1914', p. 4.

94 *Otago Daily Times*, 26 January 1915, p. 6; *Maoriland Worker*, 18 November 1914, p. 4.

95 *Otago Daily Times*, 8 October 1914, p. 6. This point had been made earlier by a miller in Ashburton. *Ashburton Guardian*, 1 October 1914, p. 7.

96 *Press*, 8 October 1914, p. 9.

97 *Evening Post*, 3 October 1914, p. 3.

98 *Oamaru Mail*, 5 October 1914, p. 4.

99 *New Zealand Herald*, 3 December 1914, p. 8; *New Zealand Herald*, 8 December 1914, p. 8. The date of the 'census' is given in *Press*, 22 January 1915, p. 8.

100 *Star*, 21 October 1914, p. 2; *Oamaru Mail*, 13 November 1914, p. 4.

101 *Star*, 25 November 1914, p. 2; *New Zealand Herald*, 28 November 1914, p. 8.

102 *New Zealand Herald*, 15 December 1914, p. 9.

103 *Ashburton Guardian*, 28 November 1914, p. 5; *New Zealand Herald*, 8 December 1914, p. 8.

104 *Press*, 22 January 1915, p. 8.

105 Stephen Broadberry and Mark Harrison, 'The Economics of World War I: An Overview', in (eds), *The Economics of World War I* (Cambridge: Cambridge University Press, 2005), p. 19.

106 *Dominion*, 16 December 1914, p. 6.

107 The delivery of Canadian wheat had been delayed by the war's impact on shipping and, on 5 December, Massey cabled the New South Wales government, offering to buy 30,000 bushels of wheat on the assurance that it would be compensated from the forthcoming Canadian purchase. New South Wales agreed and the quantity involved was increased to 100,000 bushels. However, on 12 January, the shipment, aboard the *Kaiapoi*, was detained in Sydney by a claim from Victorian interests that they had

purchased the wheat before it was seized by the New South Wales government. On 20 January the *Kaiapoi* was given permission to depart with the legal battle ongoing.

108 *Star*, 28 November 1914, p. 6; *Manawatu Standard*, 13 January 1915, p. 4.

109 *Sun*, 13 January 1915, p. 11; 2 February 1915, p. 8.

110 A decrease in bread consumption estimated at around a fifth due to its increased price certainly had a significant effect on the conservation of wheat stocks. *Sun*, 2 February 1915, p. 2.

111 *Marlborough Express*, 8 January 1915, p. 8; *Otago Daily Times*, 30 January 1915, p. 13.

112 *North Otago Times*, 10 March 1915, p. 5.

113 *Evening Post*, 13 March 1915, p. 8; *Marlborough Express*, 19 March 1915, p. 4.

114 *Ashburton Guardian*, 1 December 1914, p. 4.

115 *Poverty Bay Herald*, 2 December 1914, p. 2.

116 *Inangahua Times*, 27 November 1914, p. 2.

117 *Sun*, 19 November 1914, p. 2.

118 *Evening Post*, 24 October 1914, p. 3.

119 *Manawatu Standard*, 12 November 1914, p. 7.

120 *Evening Post*, 29 October 1914, p. 4.

121 *New Zealand Times*, 26 November 1914, p. 6.

122 *Evening Post*, 30 October 1914, p. 4.

123 *General Election Campaign 1914, Reform Party Handbook* (Wellington: Wright & Carmar, 1914), pp. 38–39.

124 *Evening Post*, 24 October 1914, p. 3.

125 Fraser would presumably have known this as it was reported in a news story carried in the *Maoriland Worker*. This quoted Emile Vandervelde, the Belgian Socialist leader visiting the United States in a government delegation. *Maoriland Worker*, 28 October 1914, p. 4. The *Worker* truncated the quotation, not printing the portion denouncing German atrocities. *Star*, 31 October 1914, p. 9.

126 *Sun*, 8 December 1914, p. 2.

127 *Maoriland Worker*, 16 December 1914, p. 8.

128 *Taranaki Daily News*, 7 December 1914, p. 4.

129 *Evening Post*, 9 December 1914, p. 3.

130 *Press*, 9 December 1914, p. 10. Massey had made a similar claim about the 1908 election, but on that occasion was referring to 'misleading and scurrilous literature'. *Evening Post*, 19 November 1908, p. 2.

131 *New Zealand Herald*, 8 December 1914, p. 7. The Liberal-supporting *Auckland Star* endeavoured to downplay these events, ascribing the trouble to 'a small mischievous section' of youths. *Auckland Star*, 8 December 1914, p. 2.

132 *Auckland Star*, 8 December 1914, p. 4.

133 *Dominion*, 11 November 1914, p. 7.

134 *Evening Post*, 18 February 1915, p. 8.

135 *Press*, 30 November 1914, p. 10.

136 *Dominion*, 3 November 1914, p. 5.

137 *Evening Star*, 3 November 1914, p. 4.

138 *Wanganui Herald*, 12 November 1914, p. 4.

139 *Press*, 9 December 1914, p. 10.

140 David C. Thorns and Charles P. Sedgewick, *Understanding Aotearoa/New Zealand: Historical Statistics* (Palmerston North: Dunmore Press, 1997), p. 166.

141 A majority of votes for labour went to candidates who were not standing for the Social Democratic Party or not standing for that party alone. The SDP went into the election with three MPs and emerged with two, while the number of non-SDP labour MPs increased from three to four.

142 His reply was first reported in the *Northern Advocate*, 16 December 1914, p. 5; *Evening Star*, 16 June 1915, p. 10.

CHAPTER SIX: COMMITMENTS ESCALATE

1 *Grey River Argus*, 2 September 1914, p. 5.

2 *Poverty Bay Herald*, 22 October 1914, p. 6. Corporal M. Ryan from Otago was reported wounded at the same time. *Thames Star*, 5 November 1914, p. 4. Walker was subsequently killed in April 1915 and his remains have been recently discovered by Belgian archaeologists. Those New Zealanders serving with British forces whose deaths were notified during 1914 included Lieutenant Robert Gee of Wellington (*Waikato Argus*, 30 October 1914, p. 3), Captain Oliver Steele of Auckland (*Evening Post*, 3 November 1914, p. 5), Major Maidlow (*Marlborough Express*, 9 November 1914, p. 4), Dr Angus McNab (*Waikato Argus*, 10 November 1914, p. 3), Lieutenant O. D. M. Garcia of Christchurch and Captain Kenneth Mathieson of Rangitīkei (*Auckland Star*, 11 November 1914, p. 6), Lieutenant Frederick George Andrews (*Poverty Bay Herald*, 17 November 1914, p. 3), Lieutenant E. Wynne Chapman of Canterbury (*Sun*, 24 November 1914, p. 6) and Captain Stewart Richardson (*Poverty Bay Herald*, 1 December 1914, p. 3).

3 Captain Russell's death was reported in Hastings on 28 October. *Dominion*, 29 October 1914, p. 6.

4 Among those who embarked with the Main Body, Cecil Alexander from Lauder died in Wellington Hospital, while Jack Gilchrist, Ernest Webb and Duncan Mackay died on the voyage. Glyn Harper, *Johnny Enzed: The New Zealand Soldier in the First World War* (Auckland: Exisle Publishing, 2015), pp. 92–108.

5 *Poverty Bay Herald*, 24 March 1915, p. 4.

6 *Evening Star*, 28 April 1915, p. 4.

7 *West Coast Times*, 29 March 1915, p. 2.

8 *Feilding Star*, 10 April 1915, p. 2. A similar letter was printed in the *Otago Daily Times*, 15 April 1915, p. 3, but the writer thought on balance that Jaffa was a more likely destination than the

Dardanelles. An editorial in the *Wairarapa Age*, 17 April 1915, p. 4, mentioned that recently received letters had foreshadowed a move, possibly to the Dardanelles. A letter from another New Zealander, Bernard Freyberg, serving with the Royal Naval Division, not the NZEF, informed his mother (who released it to the newspapers) that 'We are on our way again and are off on an expedition into the Mediterranean, perhaps to Constantinople. We are to be a landing party to the fleet that is trying to force the Dardanelles.' *Nelson Evening Mail*, 17 April 1915, p. 5.

9 *New Zealand Herald*, 12 April 1915, p. 7; *Waikato Times*, 12 April 1915, p. 5.

10 *Poverty Bay Herald*, 14 April 1915, p. 3.

11 *Star*, 29 April 1915, p. 1.

12 *Press*, 30 April 1915, p. 6; *New Zealand Herald*, 30 April 1915, p. 6; *Auckland Star*, 13 May 1915, p. 7.

13 Alexander Turnbull Library (ATL), MS-Papers-1582-02, 'Commons Family Papers', Correspondence — Kate Commons to Kenneth Commons, 2 May 1915.

14 Archives New Zealand (ANZ), R22429810, 'Territorial Force — Statistics — Moral, mental and social changes in consequence of war'.

15 *Star*, 29 April 1915, p. 6; *Nelson Evening Mail*, 30 April 1915, p. 5.

16 *Evening Post*, 29 April 1915, p. 8.

17 *Evening Post*, 3 June 1915, p. 7; *Evening Post*, 15 September 1915, p. 8.

18 'First World War by the numbers', URL: https://nzhistory.govt.nz/war/first-world-war-by-numbers, (Ministry for Culture and Heritage), updated 14-Sep-2017.

19 *Southland's Tribute to Belgium* (Invercargill: News Print, 1915), p. 18.

20 ATL, MS-Papers-1582-05, Mrs A. B. Clarkson to Katherine Commons, 18 June 1915.

21 Imelda Bargas and Tim Shoebridge, *New Zealand's First World War Heritage* (Auckland: Exisle Publishing, 2015), p. 120.

22 ANZ, R22429095, 'Expeditionary Force — Casualties — Next of Kin — Method of Notifying re', A. H. Wallace to Allen, 10 October 1917.

23 Unbeknown to Allen, Massey and Ward later resumed the practice, so three telegrams continued to give some families trepidation about other loved ones. The initiative to restart the practice apparently came from Ward's office. The political attraction was presumably that a representative of the Liberal Party got to express condolences to the next of kin and not just Allen, a Reformer. ANZ, R22429095, 'Expeditionary Force — Casualties — Next of Kin — Method of Notifying re', Allen to Lord Liverpool, 19 October 1917, M. Montgomery to Private Secretary, Minister of Defence, 5 February 1918.

24 George Fowlds to D. Orr, 23 June 1915, G. M. Fowlds Papers, quoted Paul Baker, *King and Country Call: New Zealanders, Conscription and the Great War* (Auckland: Auckland University Press, 1988), p. 23.

25 ATL, MS-Papers-1582-02, 'Commons Family Papers', Correspondence — Kate Commons to Kenneth Commons, 2 May 1915, 30 May 1915, 13 June 1915.

26 E. H. McCormick, *An Absurd Ambition: Autobiographical Writings*, ed. Dennis McEldowney (Auckland: Auckland University Press, 2004), p. 13.

27 Pat Jalland, *Death in the Victorian Family* (New York: Oxford University Press, 1996), p. 3.

28 Robert J. Kastenbaum, *Death, Society, and Human Experience*, 11th edn (Boston: Routledge Ltd, 2015), pp. 343–45, 360.

29 Auckland War Memorial Museum Library, MS 1318, Folder 2, Eliza Helen Holt to Laurence Williams Holt, 22 April 1918.

30 *New Zealand Times*, 3 December 1915, p. 4.

31 *New Zealand Parliamentary Debates* (*NZPD*), Vol. 183, 25 October 1918, pp. 12–13.

32 ATL, MS-Papers-1582-02, Kate Commons to Kenneth Commons, 22 June 1915.

33 Auckland War Memorial Museum Library, MS 1318, Folder 2, Eliza Helen Holt to Laurence Williams Holt, 18 September 1918.

34 Auckland War Memorial Museum Library, MS 1318, Folder 4, Laurence Holt to Frank Holt, 5 November 1918.

35 John Crawford, '"I get blamed for everything": Enduring the Burdens of Office, James Allen as Minister of Defence in 1915', in David Monger, Sarah Murray and Katie Pickles (eds), *Endurance and the First World War: Experiences and Legacies in New Zealand and Australia* (Newcastle upon Tyne: Cambridge Scholars Publishing, 2014), p. 23.

36 Baker, *King and Country Call*, p. 73.

37 'Parliamentarians and World War I', updated 6-Nov-2008, URL: http://www.parliament.nz/en-nz/features/00NZPHomeNews061120081/parliamentarians-and-world-war-i; Barry Gustafson, *Labour's Path to Political Independence: The Origins and Establishment of the New Zealand Labour Party 1900–19* (Auckland: Auckland University Press, 1980), p. 112.

38 *New Zealand Herald*, 17 July 1915, p. 4.

39 Baker, *King and Country Call*, p. 27.

40 ATL, MS-Papers-1582-05, Henrietta Armitage to Kate Commons, 17 June 1915.

41 *Otago Witness*, 19 April 1916, p. 39.

42 *Evening Post*, 30 September 1916, p. 4.

43 *Evening Star*, 16 June 1915, p. 4.

44 *Taranaki Herald*, 15 July 1915, p. 2.

45 *New Zealand Herald*, 21 July 1915, p. 9. See also *Taranaki Herald*, 15 July 1915, p. 2.

46 *Evening Post*, 12 February 1917, p. 9.

47 *Press*, 15 May 1915, p. 8.

48 Katie Pickles, *Transnational Outrage: The Death and Commemoration of Edith Cavell* (Basingstoke: Palgrave Macmillan, 2007), pp. 186, 194–95. See also Pickles, 'Mapping Memorials for Edith Cavell on the colonial edge', *New Zealand Geographer*, Vol. 62 (March 2006), pp. 13–24.

49 *Dominion*, 1 December 1915, p. 2. For further details see Anna Rogers, *Stand for All Time: The Marquette Sinking and the Nurses' Memorial Chapel* (Christchurch: Friends of the Nurses' Memorial Chapel, 2018).

50 *Evening Post*, 8 May 1915, p. 4. Some changing awareness of the potential scale and duration of the war is apparent before May with the description of the struggle as a 'war of attrition' becoming commonplace in early 1915. See, for instance, *Southland Times*, 14 January 1915, p. 5; *Otago Daily Times*, 15 January 1915, p. 4.

51 ATL, qMS-0681, Harrold Ennor Diaries, 31 December 1915.

52 *Colonist*, 27 May 1916, p. 4.

53 Cited in Rory Sweetman, 'New Zealand Catholicism, War, Politics and the Irish Issue 1912–1922' (PhD thesis, University of Cambridge, 1990), p. 86.

54 *Dominion*, 9 August 1915, p. 6; L. .H. Barber, *The Very Rev. James Gibb: Patriot into Pacifist* (Dunedin: Presbyterian Historical Society of New Zealand, 1973).

55 *NZPD*, Vol. 177, 8 August 1916, p. 942. Enlisted politician Peter Buck (Te Rangi Hīroa) and historian/journalist James Cowan made similar points of new esteem forged in shared hardship at Gallipoli at this time. See James Cowan, *Maori in the Great War* (Christchurch: Willson Scott Publishing, 2011), pp. 65, 73.

56 Greg Hynes, 'Propaganda, Perspective, and the British World: New Zealand's First World War Propaganda and British Interactions, 1914–1918' (MA thesis, University of Canterbury, 2013), pp. 100–7.

57 D. R. Jenkins, *Social Attitudes in the New Zealand School Journal* (Wellington: New Zealand Council for Educational Research, 1939), p. 4.

58 Hynes, 'Propaganda, Perspective, and the British World', pp. 18–19.

59 *School Journal*, 10, 2 (1916), p. 41.

60 Ron Palenski, 'Malcolm Ross: A New Zealand Failure in the Great War', *Australian Historical Studies*, Vol. 1 (2008), pp. 19–35.

61 For a study of the significance of patriotic organisations in arranging the importation and distribution of material see Greg Hynes, 'Picturing the Empire: Enduring Imperial Perceptions and Perceptions and Depictions in British First World War Photographic Propaganda', in Monger, Murray and Pickles (eds), *Endurance and the First World War*, pp. 215–35.

62 ANZ, R10075019, 'Advertising, February 1916–January 1918', Christchurch *Press* to Massey, 26 May 1916.

63 Anti-German Trade Campaign, *War Pictures and Their Obvious Lesson* (Christchurch: Smith & Anthony, 1915).

64 Chris Bourke, *Good-bye Maoriland: The Songs & Sounds of New Zealand's Great War* (Auckland: Auckland University Press, 2017), pp. 134–35; Kate Hunter and Kirstie Ross, *Holding On to Home: New Zealand Stories and Objects of the First World War* (Wellington: Te Papa Press, 2014), pp. 103–4.

65 *Auckland Weekly News*, 30 May 1918, p. 66; *Dominion*, 1 September 1915, p. 1.

66 *Otago Daily Times*, 30 June 1915, p. 3; *Star*, 9 March 1918, p. 5; *Otago Daily Times*, 14 August 1918, p. 6.

67 *Hawera and Normanby Star*, 12 January 1915, p. 7.

68 *Stratford Evening Post*, 6 August 1914, p. 6; *Press*, 7 May 1915, p. 3; *New Zealand Free Lance*, December 1915 (Christmas annual), p. 17; *NZ Truth*, 7 October 1916, p. 2.

69 *Evening Post*, 12 June 1916, p. 8. By 1917 this figure is estimated to have risen to 550,000. *NZPD*, Vol. 179, 21 August 1917, p. 449.

70 Christopher Pugsley, *The Camera in the Crowd: Filming New Zealand in Peace and War, 1895–1920* (Auckland: Oratia Books, 2017), p. 359.

71 *New Zealand Free Lance*, 13 October 1916, p. 12.

72 Pugsley, *The Camera in the Crowd*, p. 364.

73 *Hastings Standard*, 1 August 1916, p. 3; *Greymouth Evening Star*, 17 June 1916, p. 5.

74 *Evening Post*, 4 October 1915, p. 3.

75 ANZ, R10075029, 'Pictures — May, October 1916'.

76 For examples see *Star*, 14 July 1915, p. 4; *New Zealand Herald*, 12 May 1915, p. 6.

77 *New Zealand Herald*, 25 May 1915, p. 8.

78 Cited in Rachel Patrick, 'An Unbroken Connection? New Zealand Families, Duty, and the First World War' (PhD thesis, Victoria University of Wellington, 2014), p. 30.

79 *Hawera and Normanby Star*, 26 May 1915, p. 4.

80 See, for example, *NZPD*, Vol. 174, 23 September 1915, p. 134; *Maoriland Worker*, 28 July 1915, p. 8.

81 Baker, *King and Country Call*, pp. 26, 45.

82 Baker, *King and Country Call*, pp. 21, 26; John Graham, 'The Voluntary System: Recruiting 1914–16' (MA thesis, University of Auckland, 1971), p. 77.

83 ANZ, R22319697, 'Ministerial Files — Correspondence with General Godley', Allen to Godley, 11 May 1915; Crawford, 'I get blamed for everything', in Monger, Murray and Pickles (eds), *Endurance and the First World War*, p. 23.

84 *Evening Post*, 8 May 1915, p. 4.

85 *NZPD*, Vol. 174, 12 October 1915, p. 961.

86 *Appendix to the Journals of the House of Representatives* (*AJHR*), 1915, H-19b, 'Trentham Camp Commission', pp. i–l.

87 Most of the deaths (17) were classified as from pneumonia. It was determined that while the mortality from meningitis was officially six, it was likely that more of the deaths had been from that cause as it was not until 12 July that the presence of meningococcal bacteria was confirmed. Well over 2000 soldiers were reported as sick in the two worst months, with measles cases peaking at 492 in June, while influenza, colds and sore throats collectively afflicted 707 in June and 736 in July. *AJHR*, 1915, H-19b, 'Trentham Camp Commission', pp. xxiii, xvi–xvii, xxv. See also Howard Weddell, *Trentham Camp and Upper Hutt's Untold Military History* (Upper Hutt: Howard Weddell, 2018), pp. 59–67.

88 *Sun*, 6 July 1915, p. 10. Both Ward and Massey subsequently used the term 'royal commission', as did the newspapers, when strictly speaking the body was a commission of inquiry.

89 Damien Fenton with Caroline Lord, Gavin McLean and Tim Shoebridge, *New Zealand and the First World War: 1914–1919* (Auckland: Penguin, 2013), p. 47.

90 *New Zealand Statutes*, 1915, No. 41, 'War Funds', pp. 285–91.

91 *Sun*, 7 February 1916, p. 11.

92 Margaret Tennant, 'Fun and Fundraising: The Selling of Charity in New Zealand's Past', *Social History*, 38:1 (2013), p. 60.

93 *Journal of the Department of Labour*, 23:272 (October 1915), p. 823.

94 ATL, MS-Papers-5507-14, Annis Bracken Hamerton to Frances Hamerton, 7 May 1916.

95 Graham Hucker, 'The Rural Home Front: A New Zealand Region and the Great War, 1914–1926' (PhD thesis, Massey University, 2006), pp. 80–81.

96 ANZ, R22434777, 'Publications, instructions, etc. — War 1914–1918 — NZEF [New Zealand Expeditionary Force] — Its Provision and Maintenance', p. 10.

97 *Evening Post*, 30 October 1915, p. 9; Graham, 'The Voluntary System', pp. 108–9.

98 *Press*, 11 December 1915, p. 12; ANZ, R22429810, 'Territorial Force — Statistics — Moral, mental and social changes in consequence of war'.

99 *Waimate Daily Advertiser*, 15 May 1915, p. 1; *Wanganui Herald*, 27 May 1915, p. 4; *Otago Daily Times*, 29 May 1915, p. 16; *Ohinemuri Gazette*, 31 May 1915, p. 2; *Taranaki Daily News*, 31 May 1915, p. 4; *North Otago Times*, 3 June 1915, p. 4; *Poverty Bay Herald*, 4 June 1915, p. 6; *Star*, 5 June 1915, p. 4; *Nelson Evening Mail*, 10 June 1915, p. 3; *Inangahua Times*, 12 June 1915, p. 2; *Otago Daily Times*, 12 June 1915, p. 8; *Sun*, 14 June 1915, p. 8; *Rodney and Otamatea Times*, 16 June 1915, p. 5; *Manawatu Standard*, 25 June 1915, p. 4; *Waikato Times*, 29 June 1915, p. 6; *New Zealand Herald*, 30 June 1915, p. 10; *Wairarapa Daily Times*, 8 May 1915, p. 4.

100 *Wairarapa Daily Times*, 11 May 1915, p. 4.

101 *Otago Witness*, 19 May 1915, p. 4.

102 *New Zealand Free Lance*, 2 June 1915, p. 8.

103 *Wanganui Herald*, 28 July 1915, p. 8.

104 *Otago Witness*, 1 September 1915, p. 10. See also his comments in *NZPD*, Vol. 174, 23 September 1915, p. 129.

105 *New Zealand Statutes*, 1915, No. 33, 'National Registration Act', pp. 67–69.

106 *AJHR*, 1916, H-11, 'Department of Labour', p. 1.

107 ANZ, R24048326, '[Correspondence between] General Sir Alexander Godley [Commander New Zealand Expeditionary Force] and Colonel Hon. [Honourable] Sir James Allen, Minister of Defence, 4 January–29 December 1916', Allen to Godley, 4 January 1916.

108 *Journal of the Department of Labour*, 24:275 (January 1916), p. 37.

109 *Journal of the Department of Labour*, 24:275 (January 1916), p. 27; *Journal of the Department of Labour*, 24:275 (January 1916), p. 45.

110 *Journal of the Department of Labour*, 24:275 (January 1916), p. 35; *New Zealand Herald*, 1 January 1916, p. 5.

111 M. F. Lloyd Prichard, *An Economic History of New Zealand to 1939* (Auckland: Collins, 1970), p. 252; *Otago Daily Times*, 3 January 1916, p. 8; *New Zealand Herald*, 1 January 1916, p. 5.

112 Alan Everton, 'Government Intervention in the New Zealand Economy 1914–1918: Its Aims and Effectiveness' (MA thesis, Victoria University of Wellington, 1995), pp. 425–26; G. T. Bloomfield, *New Zealand, A Handbook of Historical Statistics* (Boston: G. K. Hall, 1984), pp. 416–17; ANZ, R22319764, 'Ministerial Files — Cost of living taxation and fixing prices'.

113 Prichard, *An Economic History of New Zealand to 1939*, p. 260.

114 *Evening Star*, 28 April 1916, p. 4.

115 *New Zealand Herald*, 5 May 1917, p. 5.

116 Neil Frances, *Safe Haven: The Untold Story of New Zealand's Largest Ever Military Camp: Featherston: 1916–1919* (Masterton: Wairarapa Archive/Fraser Books, 2012), pp. 19–21.

117 Frances, *Safe Haven*, pp. viii–ix.

118 A camp bakery was opened at Featherston in August 1916 and the canteen was run by the military from November 1917. Frances, *Safe Haven*, p. 64.

119 Cited in Frances, *Safe Haven*, p. 120.

120 *Journal of the Department of Labour*, 24:277 (March 1916), p. 164.

121 *Journal of the Department of Labour*, 24:283 (September 1916), p. 498. Poverty Bay reported a

similar situation. See *Journal of the Department of Labour*, 24:283 (September 1916), p. 492.

122 Fenton and others, *New Zealand and the First World War*, p. 42.

123 Glyn Harper and Colin Richardson, *Acts of Valour: The History of the Victoria Cross and New Zealand* (Auckland: HarperCollins, 2016), p. 150.

124 *Journal of the Department of Labour*, 24:286 (December 1916), p. 673; ATL, MS-Papers-4296-28, James Cox Diary, 3 April 1917. Such engagement could be very taxing and, although the most dogged of workers, he found the work too hard for him and left on the first day.

125 For extended consideration of the issue see Sarah Luxford, 'Passengers for the War: The Involvement of Women in Employment During the Great War 1914–1918' (MA thesis, Massey University, 2005); Melanie Nolan, '"Keeping New Zealand Home Fires Burning": Gender, Welfare and the First World War', in John Crawford and Ian McGibbon (eds), *New Zealand's Great War: New Zealand, the Allies and the First World War* (Auckland: Exisle Publishing, 2007), pp. 493–515.

126 *Southland Times*, 22 June 1916, p. 4.

127 *Otago Witness*, 1 September 1915, p. 10.

128 *Poverty Bay Herald*, 18 August 1915, p. 6.

129 *Dominion*, 19 August 1915, p. 3; *New Zealand Times*, 24 July 1915, p. 5.

130 *Otago Witness*, 20 October 1915, p. 49; Paul Baker, 'New Zealanders, the Great War, and Conscription' (PhD thesis, University of Auckland, 1986), p. 45.

131 Bloomfield, *New Zealand, A Handbook of Historical Statistics*, pp. 134–36.

132 *Census*, 1916, pp. 126, 136.

133 In July 1915 it was noted that the biscuit and confectionery industry in Auckland had 'increased very considerably during the past six months; several firms have increased their shifts, but cannot cope with orders'. *Journal of the Department of Labour*, 23:269 (July 1915), p. 571.

134 Eleven women described themselves as 'cheesemakers', 19 as 'assistant cheesemakers' and four as 'cheesemaker packers'. One 'buttermaker', seven 'butter-factory assistants' and two 'butter-factory packers' were women. *Census*, 1916, pp. 116–17. In 1911 there had been 19 women whose occupations were lumped together under the heading of 'cheese, buttermaker, worker'. The comparable total in 1916 would seem to have been 44 and it is quite possible that none of those in the broad category in 1911 was actually a cheesemaker. *Census*, 1911, p. 495. *New Zealand Herald*, 26 June 1916, p. 6.

135 *Otautau Standard and Wallace County Chronicle*, 23 January 1917, p. 1.

136 *Northern Advocate*, 24 April 1918, p. 3. In February 1917 it was reported from Wairarapa that '[o]n some farms the wives and daughters of the holders are taking the place of the hired help, that cannot be obtained'. *Auckland Star*, 21 February 1917, p. 5.

137 *Fielding Star*, 27 September 1916, p. 2.

138 *Census*, 1921, pp. 33–34. The fall in the number of female relatives assisting was from 6060 to 2992.

139 Bloomfield, *New Zealand, A Handbook of Historical Statistics*, p. 135.

140 *Dominion*, 26 August 1915, p. 2. A little of the clerical work undertaken by women in direct connection with the war was done on a voluntary basis, notably the keeping of the Defence Department's voluminous personnel records. *Ashburton Guardian*, 16 November 1915, p. 7.

141 *Ashburton Guardian*, 16 November 1915, p. 7.

142 *Star*, 8 December 1916, p. 6.

143 Baker, *King and Country Call*, pp. 55–56.

144 Bloomfield, *New Zealand, A Handbook of Historical Statistics*, p. 135; *King Country Chronicle*, 22 September 1917, p. 5.

145 The increase by a quarter in the 'relative assisting' category for females in farming since the 1911 census was an indication of this. Furthermore, whereas in clerical work the greatest increase was in single workers and those under 25, in agriculture it tended to be more among married and older women: while 50.7 per cent of the increase in the professional category was in women under 25, the comparable figure in primary industries was 44.4 per cent.

146 *Dominion*, 2 August 1917, p. 1.

147 *Feilding Star*, 12 April 1916, p. 4; *New Zealand Herald*, 27 January 1917, p. 11; *Press*, 30 January 1917, p. 6; *Dominion*, 28 June 1918, p. 7.

148 The Arbitration Court's decision, in the middle of 1916, to extend award wages and conditions to employees in boarding houses also diverted domestic workers away from employment in private homes. *Journal of the Department of Labour*, 24:282 (August 1916), p. 446.

149 *Journal of the Department of Labour*, 24:285 (November 1916), p. 430.

150 *Journal of the Department of Labour*, 25:288 (February 1917), pp. 94–95.

151 *Journal of the Department of Labour*, 24:277 (March 1916), p. 171.

152 *Evening Post*, 15 January 1917, p. 3. The Auckland Industrial Association similarly suggested that young women considered factory work as 'beneath their social scale'. *Auckland Star*, 17 April 1919, p. 8.

153 *Auckland Star*, 30 April 1919, p. 2.

154 Melanie Nolan, *Breadwinning: New Zealand Women and the State* (Christchurch: Canterbury University Press, 2000).

155 *New Zealand Times*, 13 November 1915, p. 10.

156 *Sun*, 16 November 1915, p. 10.

157 *Sun*, 15 November 1915, p. 10. Regardless of the virtual disappearance of gold coins from regular

circulation, it was unlikely that shifting large bags of them would have been a major task.

158 Erik Olssen, 'Working Gender, Gendering Work: Occupational Change and Continuity in Southern Dunedin', in Barbara Brookes, Annabel Cooper and Robin Law (eds), *Sites of Gender: Women, Men and Modernity in Southern Dunedin, 1890–1939*, (Auckland: Auckland University Press, 2003), p. 83.

159 Melanie Nolan (ed.), *War and Class: The Diary of Jack McCullough* (Wellington: Dunmore Press, 2009), p. 316. McCullough was more successful the following year when his prolonged opposition to the employment by Wardell's of 'a girl packing Grocery's in small parcels' prevailed. Nolan, *War and Class*, pp. 334–35.

160 *New Zealand Herald*, 24 December 1915, p. 8.

161 J. C. McLeod, 'Activities of New Zealand Women during World War I' (BA Hons thesis, University of Otago, 1978), p. 84.

162 *New Zealand Herald*, 29 March 1916, p. 9.

163 *Evening Post*, 2 November 1915, p. 3.

164 For a classic study see Jay Winter, *Sites of Memory, Sites of Mourning: The Great War in European Cultural History* (Cambridge: Cambridge University Press, 1998).

165 ATL, MS-Papers-1582-05, M. C. Cook to Katherine Commons, 18 June 1915. Other collections of condolence letters show similar dynamics. See, for example, ATL-MS-Papers-5548-11, 1915, 1917, 1918, 1919, 'Letters of sympathy'; Knight family: Papers relating to World War One (MS-Group-0462), ATL-MS-Papers-8670-117, 1915, 'Letters from family and friends'; Chapman, Eichelbaum and Rosenberg families: Papers (MS-Group-0754).

166 ATL, MS-Papers-5548-11, Knight Family Papers, G. S. Smith, 18 October 1917; T. W. Hamil, 31 October 1917; Jim Hogan, 25 July 1917. For further details of soldiers' condolence letters see Michael Roper, *The Secret Battle: Emotional Survival in the Great War* (Manchester: Manchester University Press, 2009), pp. 210–18.

167 Kathryn Hunter, '"Sleep on Dear Ernie, Your Battles are O'er": A Glimpse of a Mourning Community, Invercargill, New Zealand, 1914–1925', *War in History*, Vol. 14, Issue 1 (2007), p. 53.

168 For literature outlining the differing notion of the impact of the war on Christianity in New Zealand see Peter Lineham, 'First World War Religion', in Crawford and McGibbon (eds), *New Zealand's Great War*, pp. 447–66, and Tobias Harper, '"Amen, Amen!": Christianity, Society and Visions of the Future in 1920s New Zealand', *New Zealand Journal of History*, Vol. 42, No. 2 (October 2008), pp. 133–53.

169 ATL, MS-0658, Edgar Cruttwell Diary, 22 March 1915, 2 May 1915.

170 For further discussion of the sense of sacrifice within the war see Dickon John Milnes, 'The Church Militant: Dunedin Churches and Society During World War One' (PhD thesis, University of Otago, 2015), pp. 110–29.

171 Allan Davidson, 'New Zealand Churches and Death in the First World War', in Crawford and McGibbon (eds), *New Zealand's Great War*, p. 458.

172 Steven Loveridge, *Calls to Arms: New Zealand Society and Commitment to the Great War* (Wellington: Victoria University Press, 2014), p. 180; Joy Damousi, *The Labour of Loss: Mourning, Memory and Wartime Bereavement in Australia* (Cambridge: Cambridge University Press, 1999), p. 30. For further work on the dynamic see Nicoletta Gullace, *The Blood of Our Sons: Men, Women, and the Renegotiation of British Citizenship During the Great War* (New York: Palgrave, 2002) and Sandra Callister, 'Stabat Mater Dolorosa: Death, Photography and Collective Mourning', *New Zealand Journal of History*, Vol. 41, No. 1 (April 2007), pp. 3–26.

173 Baker, *King and Country*, p. 29.

174 *Otago Witness*, 5 May 1915, p. 27.

175 Jock Phillips, *To the Memory: New Zealand's War Memorials* (Nelson: Potton & Burton, 2016), p. 85. For scholarship on New Zealand's early Anzac Days see Maureen R. Sharpe, 'Anzac Day in New Zealand: 1916 to 1939', *New Zealand Journal of History*, Vol. 15, No. 2 (October 1981), pp. 97–114; Scott Worthy, 'A Debt of Honour: New Zealanders' First Anzac Days', *New Zealand Journal of History*, Vol. 36, No. 2 (October 2002), pp. 185–200.

176 *New Zealand Herald*, 26 February 1916, p. 9; *Evening Post*, 14 March 1916, p. 3; *Timaru Herald*, 4 April 1916, p. 5. This followed similar patterns in Australia. See, for example, *Colonist*, 26 February 1916, p. 5.

177 *Evening Post*, 14 March 1916, p. 3. This insistence on a solemn atmosphere perhaps marks the beginnings of what has been seen as the more funereal quality to Anzac Day in New Zealand, compared with the more celebratory tone in Australia. See, for example, Philippa Mein Smith, 'The "NZ" in Anzac: Different remembrance and meaning', *First World War Studies*, 7, 2 (2016), pp. 193–211.

178 *New Zealand Gazette*, 6 April 1916, p. 977.

179 *Otago Daily Times*, 25 April 1916, p. 2.

180 *Otago Daily Times*, 25 April 1916, p. 10.

181 *New Zealand Herald*, 26 April 1916, p. 4; *Wairarapa Age*, 26 April 1916, p. 4.

182 *Press*, 13 March 1916, p. 3; *Sun*, 13 March 1916, p. 7.

183 *Hawera and Normanby Star*, 25 April 1916, p. 7.

184 *New Zealand Herald*, 26 April 1916, p. 4.

185 Sun, 25 April 1916, p. 6.

186 *Sun*, 25 April 1916, p. 11.

187 *New Zealand Herald*, 26 April 1916, p. 8.

CHAPTER SEVEN: FACING THE BURDENS

1 Archives New Zealand (ANZ), R22319725, 'Ministerial Files — Miscellaneous correspondence with High Commissioner for New Zealand', Allen to Mackenzie, 12 April 1916. He added, 'We must accept our losses, sad as they are, and bottle up our indignation over this folly.'

2 *Evening Post*, 5 October 1914, p. 6.

3 *Manawatu Daily Times*, 1 October 1915, p. 4.

4 *NZ Truth*, 25 May 1918, p. 2. For further reading see Katherine Sanders, '"The Sensational Scandal which has Worried Wellington": The Kelburn Raid, Sex, and the Law in First World War New Zealand', *New Zealand Journal of History*, Vol. 48, No. 2 (October 2014), pp. 91–118; Bronwyn Dalley, 'Lolly Shops "of the Red-Light Kind" and "Soldiers of the King"', *New Zealand Journal of History*, Vol. 30, No. 1 (April 1996), pp. 3–23.

5 It was no doubt mostly the case that, as the *Official Year-book* claimed, '[t]he prospect of a prolonged absence abroad, and the uncertainty as to whether one will ever return, have naturally caused many a Reservist to make proper provision for his illegitimate issue'. *New Zealand Official Year-book*, 1918, p. 110.

6 *NZ Truth*, 20 May 1916, p. 3.

7 Sanders, '"The Sensational Scandal which has Worried Wellington"', p. 103.

8 Cited in Steven Loveridge, '"Soldiers and Shirkers": Modernity and New Zealand Masculinity during the Great War', *New Zealand Journal of History*, Vol. 47, No. 1 (April 2013), p. 72.

9 Sanders, '"The Sensational Scandal which has Worried Wellington"', p. 103. In regard to the continuity of traditionally feminine roles within New Zealand's war effort see Steven Loveridge, *Calls to Arms: New Zealand Society and Commitment to the Great War* (Wellington: Victoria University Press, 2014), pp. 171–204.

10 Ross Malcolm Anderson, 'New Zealand Methodism and World War 1: Crisis in a Liberal Church' (MA thesis, University of Canterbury, 1983), p. 187. See also Peter Lineham, 'First World War Religion', in John Crawford and Ian McGibbon (eds), *New Zealand's Great War: New Zealand, the Allies and the First World War* (Auckland: Exisle Publishing, 2007), pp. 467–92; Allan Davidson, 'New Zealand Churches and Death in the First World War', in Crawford and McGibbon (eds), *New Zealand's Great War*, pp. 447–66.

11 *Evening Post*, 14 May 1915, p. 4. For tensions concerning sport see Greg Ryan, '"The whole question bristles with difficulties": Sport and War', in Steven Loveridge (ed.), *New Zealand Society at War, 1914–1918* (Wellington: Victoria University Press, 2016), pp. 175–89. For tensions about gambling and drinking see Sarah Dalton, 'The Pure in Heart: The New Zealand Women's Christian Temperance Union and Social Purity, 1885–1930' (MA thesis, Victoria University of Wellington, 1993), pp. 31–33.

12 Richard S. Hill, *The Iron Hand in the Velvet Glove: The Modernisation of Policing in New Zealand, 1886–1917* (Palmerston North: Dunmore Press in association with the New Zealand Police and with the assistance of Historical Branch, Department of Internal Affairs, 1995), p. 345.

13 *New Zealand Free Lance*, 1 June 1916, p. 8. For more on the relationship between Anzac and commercial activity see Scott Worthy, 'Communities of Remembrance: The Memory of the Great War in New Zealand 1915–1939' (MA thesis, University of Auckland, 2001) and Maureen R. Sharpe, 'Anzac Day in New Zealand: 1916 to 1939', *New Zealand Journal of History*, Vol. 15, No. 2 (October 1981), pp. 97–114.

14 *Evening Post*, 6 September 1915, p. 8; *NZ Truth*, 5 June 1915, p. 5.

15 *New Zealand Herald*, 6 May 1916, p. 9.

16 *New Zealand Gazette*, 21 August 1916, pp. 2801–4. An amendment to introduce eight o'clock closing for bars was debated, and although there was a large minority in favour, the regulations passed without altering opening hours. *New Zealand Parliamentary Debates* (*NZPD*), Vol. 177, 27 July 1916, pp. 498–99.

17 The cost of a 2-pound loaf of bread (averaged across the centres) rose from 3.57d in 1913, to 3.90d in 1914, to 4.74d in 1915. Malcolm Fraser, *Prices: An Inquiry into Prices in New Zealand, 1891–1919* (Wellington: Government Printer, 1920), p. 20. The main factor in the lower rate of increase in the cost of living was a fall in the prices of wheat, with previous government yield predictions ascertained as far too pessimistic and Australian wheat production recovering spectacularly from the disastrous drought of 1914–15.

18 Imports of 'apparel and ready-made clothing' were valued at £1,169,030 in 1914 and £949,226 in 1918. *Statistics of New Zealand*, Vol. 2, 1914, p. 204; 1918, p. 149. Imports of 'other' footwear was 83,527 dozen pairs in 1914, and 62,251 dozen pairs in 1918. *Statistics of New Zealand*, Vol. 2, 1914, p. 208; 1918, p. 150. 96,780 dozen hats and caps were imported in 1914 and 64,135 dozen in 1918. *Statistics of New Zealand*, Vol. 2, 1914, p. 211; 1918, p. 155. 4651 pairs in 1914; 163 pairs in 1918. *Statistics of New Zealand*, Vol. 2, 1914, p. 215; 1918, p. 158. In regard to the significance of imported drapery in the New Zealand economy see Ian Hunter, *Age of Enterprise: Rediscovering the New Zealand Entrepreneur, 1880–1910* (Auckland: Auckland University Press, 2007), pp. 44–45.

19 Fraser, *Prices: An Inquiry into Prices in New Zealand*, p. 127.

20 Massey announced that 11 more workers' dwellings

were being erected in Kilbirnie and Lyall Bay, and he hoped that Cabinet would approve 20 more because 'such houses were required more urgently in Wellington than elsewhere'. He later claimed that the introduction of a War Legislation Amendment Act with provision to control rents was because of the situation in Wellington: 'Since the camps have been established here a number of people have found it necessary, on account of business or convenience in some way, to take up their residence in Wellington.' *NZPD*, Vol. 177, 25 July 1916, p. 394.

21 *Appendix to the Journals of the House of Representatives* (*AJHR*), 1915, H-11, 'Department of Labour', p. 3. A lack of skilled labour appears to be especially true in regard to those high-skill trades that had expanded rapidly in recent years, such as those in the motor and electrical industries. In June 1915 'a scarcity of wiremen owing to a number having gone to the front' was reported in Christchurch. At the end of that year there was a 'dearth of motor mechanics' in Nelson and by December 1916 coachbuilders and garages in Palmerston North were 'seriously embarrassed for want of mechanics'. *Journal of the Department of Labour*, 23:269 (July 1915), p. 585; 23:274 (December 1915), p. 921; 24:286 (December 1916), p. 271.

22 While some militants in mining settlements such as Runanga opposed enlistment, young miners flocked to the colours. That a number of them came originally from Britain and no doubt saw a chance to visit home may also have contributed to some deciding to join up. *Journal of the Department of Labour*, 23:268 (June 1915), p. 492; 23:269 (July 1915), p. 571; 23:273 (November 1915), p. 872.

23 *Wairarapa Age*, 12 January 1916, p. 2; *Journal of the Department of Labour*, 24:276 (February 1916), p. 109.

24 *Journal of the Department of Labour*, 24:284 (October 1916), p. 537.

25 *Colonist*, 26 February 1919, p. 2.

26 *Journal of the Department of Labour*, 24:283 (September 1916), p. 512.

27 ANZ, R22319764, 'Ministerial Files — Cost of living taxation and fixing prices'.

28 Barry Gustafson, *Labour's Path to Political Independence: The Origins and Establishment of the New Zealand Labour Party 1900–19* (Auckland: Auckland University Press, 1980), pp. 95–104.

29 *Maoriland Worker*, 8 December 1915, p. 1.

30 *NZPD*, Vol. 172, 6 July 1915, pp. 143–44.

31 These remarks were widely reported; *Evening Post*, 30 August 1915, p. 8. See also *Northern Advocate*, 30 August 1915, p. 2; *Auckland Star*, 30 August 1915, p. 6; *Waikato Times*, 30 August 1915, p. 4; *Dominion*, 31 August 1915, p. 7; *Wairarapa Daily Times*, 31 August 1915, p. 4.

32 Erik Olssen, 'Negotiating Conditions and Commitment: The Union Movement and the First World War', in Loveridge (ed.), *New Zealand Society at War*, pp. 142–58.

33 Herbert Roth, *Trade Unions in New Zealand: Past and Present* (Wellington: Reed Education, 1973), Table 2, pp. 169–70.

34 *New Zealand Official Year-book*, 1921–22, p. 529.

35 *NZPD*, Vol. 176, 27 June 1916, p. 206.

36 Kate Hunter and Kirstie Ross, *Holding On to Home: New Zealand Stories and Objects of the First World War* (Wellington: Te Papa Press, 2014), pp. 82–83.

37 ANZ, R22431244, 'Establishments and Recruitment — Enlistment — 'Return showing number from each district', Return of men enlisted and sent to camp by districts and approximate population of district, up to 31st of October, 1915'; Paul Baker, *King and Country Call: New Zealanders, Conscription and the Great War* (Auckland: Auckland University Press, 1988), p. 96.

38 Loveridge, *Calls to Arms*, pp. 136–70.

39 *NZPD*, Vol. 174, 23 September 1915, pp. 140–41; *Evening Star*, 18 October 1915, p. 6.

40 John Graham, 'The Voluntary System: Recruiting 1914–16' (MA thesis, University of Auckland, 1971), p. 85.

41 Ian McGibbon, *New Zealand's Western Front Campaign* (Auckland: Bateman, 2016), pp. 29–30; ANZ, R21078971, 'New Zealand Expeditionary Force, its provision and maintenance', p. 7.

42 John Crawford, '"The Willing Horse is Being Worked To Death": New Zealand's Manpower Problems and Policies during 1917', in Douglas E. Delaney and Nikolas Gardner (eds), *Turning Point 1917: The British Empire at War* (Vancouver: UBS Press, 2017), p. 117. Robin had been promoted to brigadier general in June 1915.

43 ANZ, R22319698, 'Ministerial Files — Correspondence with General Godley', correspondence from Allen to Godley, 15 February 1916.

44 Alexander Turnbull Library (ATL), qMS-0681, Harrold Ennor Diaries, 31 December 1915.

45 *Ashburton Guardian*, 5 October 1915, p. 6.

46 *AJHR*, 1915, H-19e, 'Expeditionary Force: Provision of Reinforcement Drafts for the (memorandum on)', p. 5.

47 The minimum height went from 5 feet 4 inches to 5 feet 2 inches and the minimum chest measurement from 35 to 33 inches. *Southland Times*, 22 November 1915, p. 7.

48 *Auckland Star*, 27 November 1915, p. 4.

49 *Colonist*, 11 May 1916, p. 4.

50 *Statistics of New Zealand*, 1913, p. 38; 1914, p. 34; 1915, p. 34; 1916, p. 32.

51 *New Zealand Official Year-book*, 1918, p. 113.

52 *Evening Star*, 12 January 1916, p. 4.

53 *Evening Post*, 9 December 1915, p. 6.
54 *New Zealand Herald*, 12 November 1915, p. 7.
55 *AJHR*, 1916, H-35, 'National Register', pp. 1–3.
56 *Evening Post*, 27 January 1916, p. 7.
57 *Evening Post*, 11 December 1915, p. 2.
58 Graham, 'The Voluntary System', p. 84.
59 *Evening Post*, 19 January 1916, p. 7; Graham, 'The Voluntary System', pp. 84–85.
60 Graham, 'The Voluntary System', pp. 169–72.
61 Baker, *King and Country Call*, pp. 96, 98.
62 *NZPD*, Vol. 175, 31 May 1916, p. 533.
63 *Auckland Star*, 1 June 1916, p. 7. At the end of 1915 Reform MP James Parr made a similar point claiming 'surely the Government must see by this time that public opinion is dead against the inequality, and injustice of the played out system of voluntarism?' *Evening Star*, 8 December 1915, p. 2.
64 ANZ, R22429657, 'Territorial Force — Shirkers — Gisborne District', letter to Allen, 6 December 1915.
65 Arthur Berriedale Keith, *War Government in the Dominions* (Oxford: Clarendon Press, 1921), p. 97.
66 *Maoriland Worker*, 5 January 1916, p. 3.
67 *NZ Truth*, 1 April 1916, p. 2.
68 *Evening Post*, 1 November 1915, p. 3.
69 *Star*, 1 October 1915, p. 5.
70 *Evening Post*, 5 August 1915, p. 1. See also *Dominion*, 9 November 1915, p. 1; *Otago Daily Times*, 5 April 1916, p. 1; *Auckland Star*, 6 April 1916, p. 1; *Hawke's Bay Herald*, 11 July 1916, p. 1; *Sun*, 3 October 1916, p. 10; *AJHR*, 1916, H-14, 'Public Service Commissioner', p. 11; *Evening Post*, 21 December 1915, p. 2.
71 ANZ, R24048326, '[Correspondence between] General Sir Alexander Godley [Commander New Zealand Expeditionary Force] and Colonel Hon. [Honourable] Sir James Allen, Minister of Defence, 4 January–29 December 1916', Allen to Godley, 4 January 1916.
72 Examples include Ernest Allen, Robert Breen, Edward Kellett, David McLaren, Matthew Mack and William Veitch, who found themselves alienated from the labour movement by their support of conscription. Gustafson, *Labour's Path to Political Independence*, pp. 153, 154–55, 159, 161, 160–61, 168.
73 *Evening Post*, 14 June 1916, p. 2.
74 *Maoriland Worker*, 1 December 1915, p. 4.
75 *Maoriland Worker*, 8 December 1915, p. 2.
76 *Maoriland Worker*, 14 July 1915, p. 5; *Peace Manifesto* (Wellington: Workers Print, 1916).
77 *Maoriland Worker*, 15 September 1915, p. 4.
78 *NZPD*, Vol.175, 31 May 1916, p. 542; *Maoriland Worker*, 3 February 1915, p. 4; *New Zealand Herald*, 9 December 1915, p. 6.
79 *NZPD*, Vol. 174, 23 September 1915, p. 143.
80 For examples see *NZPD*, Vol. 172, 20 July 1915, p. 419; Vol. 173, 8 September 1915, p. 481; Vol. 173, 7 September 1915, p. 432; Vol. 174, 20 September 1915, p. 3.
81 *Ohinemuri Gazette*, 26 January 1916, p. 2.
82 *Maoriland Worker*, 15 September 1915, p. 4.
83 *Grey River Argus*, 3 December 1915, p. 2.
84 Len Richardson, *Coal, Class & Community: The United Mineworkers of New Zealand, 1880–1960* (Auckland: Auckland University Press, 1995), pp. 166–67.
85 *Maoriland Worker*, 8 December 1915, p. 3; *Maoriland Worker*, 15 December 1915, p. 4; *Evening Post*, 2 December 1915, p. 2.
86 *Maoriland Worker*, 2 February 1916, p. 4.
87 The full manifesto was published in *Evening Post* (28 January 1916, p. 4) with a version later produced as a pamphlet. See *Labour and Conscription* (Wellington: Maoriland Workers Print, 1916?).
88 As some historians have noted, it was remarkable that conscription contributed to creating a unified labour party in New Zealand while so bitterly splitting the Labor Party in Australia. Bruce Brown, *The Rise of New Zealand Labour: A History of the New Zealand Labour Party from 1916 to 1940* (Wellington: Price Milburn, 1962), p. 26. The significance of opposition to conscription in the party's formation is further emphasised in Peter Franks and Jim McAloon, *Labour: The New Zealand Labour Party, 1916–2016* (Wellington: Victoria University Press, 2016), p. 69, and Jack Vowles, 'Ideology and the Formation of the New Zealand Labour Party: Some New Evidence', *New Zealand Journal of History*, Vol. 16, No. 1 (April 1982), pp. 39–55.
89 Michael Bassett with Michael King, *Tomorrow Comes the Song: A Life of Peter Fraser* (Auckland: Penguin, 2000), p. 70.
90 Brown, *The Rise of New Zealand Labour*, p. 18; Franks and McAloon, *Labour*, p. 13.
91 Brown, *The Rise of New Zealand Labour*, p. 25.
92 Franks and McAloon, *Labour*, pp. 70–71.
93 Brown, *The Rise of New Zealand Labour*, pp. 20, 25.
94 *Auckland Star*, 12 July 1916, p. 7.
95 *NZ Truth*, 15 July 1916, p. 1.
96 *Maoriland Worker*, 19 July 1916, p. 6.
97 *Press*, 28 January 1916, p. 6; *Hastings Standard*, 2 February 1916, p. 2.
98 *New Zealand Herald*, 29 January 1916, p. 8.
99 Baker, *King and Country Call*, p. 44. For further analysis on official orientation towards caution and placation see Erik Olssen, 'Towards a Reassessment of W. F. Massey: One of New Zealand's Greatest Prime Ministers (Arguably)', in James Watson and Lachy Paterson (eds), *A Great New Zealand Prime Minister?: Reappraising William Ferguson Massey* (Dunedin: Otago University Press, 2011), p. 23.
100 ANZ, R22319723, 'Ministerial Files — Correspondence with WH Triggs (Press Editor)',

James Allen to W. H. Triggs, 8 December 1915.

101 H. E. Holland, *Armageddon or Calvary: The Conscientious Objectors of New Zealand and 'The Process of Their Conversion'* (Wellington: The Maoriland Worker Printing and Publishing Co. Ltd, 1919), pp. 5–6.

102 *Dominion*, 10 March 1915, p. 7. This letter is further discussed in Keith Sinclair, *Walter Nash* (Auckland: Auckland University Press, 1976), p. 40.

103 *NZPD*, Vol. 174, 23 September 1915, p. 146.

104 Megan Hutching, 'The Moloch of War: New Zealand Women Who Opposed the War', in Crawford and McGibbon (eds), *New Zealand's Great War*, pp. 87–88.

105 *Maoriland Worker*, 12 January 1916, p. 3.

106 ANZ, R22434536, 'Publications, instructions, etc. — Women's International League — correspondence', Manifesto (issued by the Conference held on September 30th and October 15th, 1915, to form the British Section of the organisation and endorsed by the Wellington Branch).

107 Martin Pugh, *The Pankhursts: The History of One Radical Family* (London: Vintage, 2008); *New Zealand Free Lance*, 7 January 1916, p. 4.

108 Some of Emmeline's writings advocating the necessity of the war and women's part in the cause were reproduced for New Zealand readers. See, for example, *Star*, 14 July 1915, p. 4.

109 *Maoriland Worker*, 8 November 1916, p. 5.

110 For coverage emphasising high attendance of Pankhurst's lectures see *NZ Truth*, 27 May 1916, p. 4; *Maoriland Worker*, 7 June 1916, p. 2; *NZ Truth*, 3 June 1916, p. 6.

111 *Maoriland Worker*, 15 September 1915, p. 4.

112 *Maoriland Worker*, 15 September 1915, p. 4.

113 *Maoriland Worker*, 21 June 1916, p. 3.

114 David Grant, *Out in the Cold: Pacifists and Conscientious Objectors in New Zealand during World War II* (Auckland: Reed Methuen, 1986), p. 33.

115 Baker, *King and Country Call*, p. 77.

116 ANZ, R22434529, 'Publications, instructions, etc. — Literature (anti-militarist) — Publication of'; *Poverty Bay Herald*, 25 May 1915, p. 7.

117 *Maoriland Worker*, 8 December, 1915, p. 6.

118 *Maoriland Worker*, 11 October 1916, p. 6.

119 *Northern Advocate*, 14 September 1916, p. 2; *Maoriland Worker*, 11 October 1916, p. 6.

120 When Gregory's wife decided to contest his vacant council seat he was further vilified not only as a man who would defend her but also as one who would hide behind her. She lost badly in the by-election. Paul Baker, 'New Zealanders, the Great War and Conscription' (PhD thesis, University of Auckland, 1986), pp. 154–57.

121 Baker, *King and Country Call*, p. 75.

122 Brad Patterson, '"We stand for the Protestant religion, the (Protestant) King and the Empire": The Rise of the Protestant Political Association in World War One', in Loveridge (ed.), *New Zealand Society at War*, p. 239.

123 *Sun*, 28 June 1915, p. 6.

124 Cited in Rory Sweetman, '"Who Fears to Speak of Easter Week?" Antipodean Irish Catholic Responses to the 1916 Rising', in Ruan O'Donnell (ed.), *The Impact of the 1916 Rising: Among the Nations* (Dublin: Irish Academic Press, 2008), p. 90.

125 *New Zealand Tablet*, 20 January 1916, p. 26.

126 Sweetman, '"Who Fears to Speak of Easter Week?"', in O'Donnell, *The Impact of the 1916 Rising*, p. 77.

127 *New Zealand Herald*, 10 April 1916, p. 7; *New Zealand Herald*, 14 April 1916, p. 7; H. S. Moores, 'The Rise of the Protestant Political Association: Sectarianism in New Zealand Politics during World War I' (MA thesis, University of Auckland, 1966), p. 116.

128 *Rome's Hideous Guilt in the European Carnage* (Auckland: Free Press Print, 1915).

129 *NZ Truth*, 22 September 1917, p. 6; *New Zealand Herald*, 20 April 1916, p. 8.

130 Moores, 'The Rise of the Protestant Political Association', pp. 122–23, 124–35.

131 *Evening Star*, 4 May 1916, p. 6.

132 *New Zealand Herald*, 2 May 1916, p. 6.

133 *Otago Daily Times*, 2 May 1916, p. 4.

134 *Evening Post*, 21 June 1916, p. 20.

135 Sweetman, '"Who Fears to Speak of Easter Week?"', in O'Donnell (ed.), *The Impact of the 1916 Rising*, pp. 74–77.

136 *New Zealand Tablet*, 4 May 1916, pp. 25–27.

137 *Maoriland Worker*, 17 May 1916, p. 4.

138 *Taranaki Daily News*, 22 August 1916, p. 3; *Taranaki Daily News*, 23 August 1916, p. 5.

139 Moores, 'The Rise of the Protestant Political Association', p. 139.

140 Sweetman, '"Who Fears to Speak of Easter Week?"', in O'Donnell (ed.), *The Impact of the 1916 Rising*, p. 81.

141 Rory Sweetman, 'New Zealand Catholicism, War, Politics and the Irish Issue 1912–1922' (PhD thesis, University of Cambridge, 1990), p. 89; Sweetman, '"Who Fears to Speak of Easter Week?"', in O'Donnell (ed.), *The Impact of the 1916 Rising*, p. 81.

142 Richard Davis, *Irish Issues in New Zealand Politics, 1868–1922* (Dunedin: University of Otago Press, 1974), pp. 185–212; R. P. Davis, 'The New Zealand Labour Party's "Irish Campaign" 1916–1921', *Political Science*, Vol. 19, Issue 2 (December 1967), pp. 13–23.

143 *Maoriland Worker*, 17 May 1916, p. 4; Sweetman, '"Who Fears to Speak of Easter Week?"', in O'Donnell (ed.), *The Impact of the 1916 Rising*, pp. 79–80.

144 Patterson, '"We stand for the Protestant religion, the (Protestant) King and the Empire"', in Loveridge (ed.), *New Zealand Society at War*, p. 245.

145 Ashley Gould, 'Maori and the First World War', in Ian McGibbon (ed.), *The Oxford Companion to New Zealand Military History* (Auckland: Oxford University Press, 2000), p. 297; P. S. O'Connor, 'The Recruitment of Maori Soldiers, 1914–18', *Political Science*, Vol. 19, Issue 2 (December 1967), p. 53; *Otago Daily Times*, 30 August 1915, p. 2.

146 ANZ, R22429222, 'Expeditionary Force — Maori contingent active service', correspondence to Allen, 14 June 1915.

147 ANZ, R22319740, 'Ministerial Files — Correspondence with Governor General', petition dated 24 February 1916.

148 O'Connor, 'The Recruitment of Maori Soldiers', p. 53.

149 ANZ, R24048325, '[Correspondence between] General Sir Alexander Godley [Commander New Zealand Expeditionary Force] and Colonel Hon. [Honourable] Sir James Allen, Minister of Defence, 2 April–18 December 1915', Allen to Godley, 1 July 1915.

150 The Niuean Island Council's written offer of service was read in the New Zealand Parliament and £164 14s 5d was donated to New Zealand's war fund. *Dominion*, 9 October 1914, p. 6.

151 *Dominion*, 9 October 1914, p. 6.

152 Margaret Pointer, *Niue and the Great War* (Dunedin: Otago University Press, 2018), p. 59.

153 One reporter observed the problems with Pacific Island recruits in training and boots. 'Nearly all the Niueans have lived for 20 years or more without boots. Their feet are huge, covered with masses of muscle and callous, and they can run easily over the coral reefs that wear holes in the footgear of the exasperated European. Those of the recruits who have found boots to fit them in the camp stores have developed sore feet, and are awkward and profoundly unhappy.' *New Zealand Herald*, 30 October 1915, p. 8.

154 Michael King, *Te Puea: A Life* (Auckland: Reed, 2003), p. 81.

155 Figures for the numbers of Pacific Islanders recruited vary across sources and one survey observes a low count of 346 and a high of 650. Kolokesa Mahina-tuai, 'FIA (Forgotten in Action): Pacific Islanders in the New Zealand Armed Forces', in *Tangata o le Moana: New Zealand and the People of the Pacific* (Wellington: Te Papa Press, 2015), p. 349, note 9. An official paper drawn up in 1919 counts 450 in the ranks and 11 officers. ANZ, R21078971, 'New Zealand Expeditionary Force, its provision and maintenance', p. 41. See also Christine Liava'a, *Le Fitafita Mai Samoa: The Force from Samoa: Soldiers from the Samoan Islands in the Great War* (Auckland: Polygraphia Ltd, 2013).

156 Monty Soutar, 'Kua Whewhe Matou! Breaking up the Maori Contingent and the ordering home of its four officers', in Charles Ferrall and Harry Ricketts (eds), *How We Remember: New Zealanders and the First World War* (Wellington: Victoria University Press, 2014), pp. 49–79.

157 O'Connor, 'The Recruitment of Maori Soldiers', p. 57; ANZ, R22319698, 'Ministerial Files — Correspondence with General Godley', Allen to General Godley, 16 February 1916; ANZ, R24048326, '[Correspondence between] General Sir Alexander Godley [Commander New Zealand Expeditionary Force] and Colonel Hon. [Honourable] Sir James Allen, Minister of Defence, 4 January–29 December 1916', Allen to Godley, 6 March 1916.

158 ANZ, R22319698, 'Ministerial Files — Correspondence with General Godley', Allen to Godley, 15 March 1916.

159 *Otago Daily Times*, 30 August 1915, p. 2.

160 *Otago Daily Times*, 6 September 1915, p. 2.

161 ANZ, R18874768, 'Military Service Act, 1916 — Military Service registration and calling up of Maoris in Waikato-Maniapoto district', report of Māori of military age, dated 22 April 1918.

162 King, *Te Puea*, p. 77; *New Zealand Herald*, 8 May 1916, p. 7.

163 O'Connor, 'The Recruitment of Maori Soldiers', p. 62.

164 ANZ, R22319698, 'Ministerial Files — Correspondence with General Godley', Allen to Godley, 15 February 1916.

165 The significance of issues of state sovereignty within escalating tensions has been impressed in numerous accounts. See, for examples, Baker, *King and Country Call*, pp. 214–17; Mark Derby, *The Prophet and the Policeman: The Story of Rua Kenana and John Cullen* (Wellington: Craig Potton, 2009); Richard Hill, *State Authority, Indigenous Autonomy: Crown–Māori Relations in New Zealand/Aotearoa 1900–1950* (Wellington: Victoria University Press, 2004), p. 92; Peter Webster, *Rua and the Maori Millennium* (Wellington: Price Milburn for Victoria University Press, 1979), p. 261; Judith Binney, Gillian Chaplin and Craig Wallace, *Mihaia: The Prophet Rua Kenana and his Community at Maungapohatu* (New York: Oxford University Press, 1979), p. 82.

166 *Star*, 29 January 1916, p. 10.

167 *Auckland Star*, 15 March 1916, p. 6.

168 Webster, *Rua and the Maori Millennium*, pp. 238–39.

169 The most detailed accounts of this episode are in Webster, *Rua and the Maori Millennium*, pp. 243–60, and Binney, Chaplin and Wallace, *Mihaia*, pp. 81–134.

170 Webster, *Rua and the Maori Millennium*, pp. 243, 248, 262–64.

171 Baker, *King and Country Call*, p. 217.

172 The jury's public protest was laid out in *Auckland Star*, 7 August 1916, p. 6. Chapman quoted in *New Zealand Times*, 4 August 1916, p. 5. His conduct throughout the trial has been widely criticised as less than impartial; see Webster, *Rua and the Maori Millennium*, p. 264; Binney, Chaplin and Wallace, *Mihaia*, p. 126.

173 *Marlborough Express*, 30 August 1915, p. 4. Such editorial commentators were very common: 'the average German only needs an opportunity to prove himself a blood brother to the brigands who tortured Belgium and the pirates who sank the Lusitania'; 'Wherever a German is to be found he should be considered an enemy — a bitter, unscrupulous, deadly enemy — and treated as such'; 'Every typical German has the same mania . . . Whether this typical German lives in Auckland or in Berlin, in the palace or in the slum, he is one and the same'; 'Once a Hun Always a Hun'. *New Zealand Herald*, 15 May 1915, p. 6; *Marlborough Express*, 30 August 1915, p. 4; *Auckland Weekly News*, 12 August 1915, p. 14; *NZ Truth*, 31 July 1915, p. 7.

174 *NZ Truth*, 1 April 1916, p. 2.

175 Graham Hucker, '"Bundling out the Hun": The Women's Anti-German League during the First World War', in Loveridge (ed.), *New Zealand Society at War*, pp. 252–65.

176 The 1911 census recorded 4015 Germans and 2131 Austrians. *Population Census*, 1911, p. xi. *New Zealand Times*, 23 June 1916, p. 4.

177 *Otago Witness*, 16 February 1916, p. 66; *New Zealand Times*, 13 March 1916, p. 3.

178 *Otago Daily Times*, 11 May 1915, p. 6.

179 *Colonist*, 13 May 1915, p. 2.

180 Andrew Francis, '*To Be Truly British We Must Be Anti-German': New Zealand, Enemy Aliens and the Great War Experience, 1914–1919* (Oxford; New York: Peter Lang, 2012), p. 178.

181 *New Zealand Times*, 6 July 1915, p. 2.

182 *NZPD*, Vol. 174, 6 October 1915, p. 707. A contemporary examination agrees with the sense of class bias. See Francis, '*To Be Truly British . . .*', p. 151.

183 *NZPD*, Vol. 175, 11 May 1916, p. 39.

184 ANZ, R22319681, 'Minister of Defence-Anti-German League, circulars etc', Re necessity of demanding retirement of the Minister of Defence. Further notions of conspiracy were advanced in *The Truth about the Grierson Inquiry* (Wellington: New Zealand Times Office, 1916?).

185 Judith Bassett, 'Colonial Justice: The Treatment of Dalmatians in New Zealand during the First World War', *New Zealand Journal of History*, Vol. 33, No. 2 (October 1999), pp. 155–79.

186 *Sun*, 8 June 1916, p. 10.

187 *Northern Advocate*, 9 June 1916, p. 3.

188 Tilman Dedering, '"Avenge the Lusitania": The Anti-German Riots in South Africa in 1915', *Immigrants & Minorities*, Vol. 13 (2013), pp. 256–88; Nicola F. Gullace, 'Friends, Aliens, and Enemies: Fictive communities and the Lusitania riots of 1915', *Journal of Social History*, 39:2 (2005), p. 346.

189 *Mataura Ensign*, 19 May 1915, p. 4.

190 *Wanganui Chronicle*, 17 May 1915, p. 5.

191 ANZ, R21371890, 'Riot, Wanganui [with "Disturbances"]', report of Constable W. Cooper, 2 January 1915.

192 *New Zealand Herald*, 17 May 1915, p. 6.

193 *Evening Post*, 21 May 1915, p. 10.

194 *Dominion*, 2 January 1915, p. 9. For further examples of rebranding and denial of German credentials see *Press*, 17 May 1915, p. 2; *Press*, 21 May 1915, p. 4; *Evening Post*, 18 May 1915, p. 6.

195 *Wanganui Chronicle*, 17 May 1915, p. 4.

196 *Wanganui Herald*, 17 May 1915, p. 6.

197 *Dominion*, 18 May 1915, p. 7. The attacks in Hokitika were renewed on a Saturday night or Sunday morning in July, when 'a band of hoodlums, taking advantage, with characteristic courage, of the temporary absence of the police at a fire near the racecourse, proceeded to smash the windows and lamps of various premises in Revell Street'. *West Coast Times*, 12 July 1915, p. 2.

198 *Mataura Ensign*, 11 January 1916, p. 4. The story appeared verbatim in several other newspapers, including the *West Coast Times*, 10 January 1916, p. 2, and *Feilding Star*, 12 January 1916, p. 4.

199 In early 1915 the *Evening Post* claimed that 'German names of places, streets, and businesses are fast disappearing' in New Zealand. However, while this was common in other parts of the British Empire, there was minimal evidence that it was then happening in New Zealand. The *Post* only cited the recent renaming of the Dresden Piano Company. *Evening Post*, 2 January 1915, p. 6.

200 *Northern Advocate*, 23 January 1915, p. 3; *Timaru Herald*, 26 January 1915, p. 6.

201 *New Zealand Herald*, 21 July 1915, p. 10.

202 *Grey River Argus*, 18 June 1915, p. 5; *New Zealand Free Lance*, 22 October 1915, p. 8; *Auckland Star*, 14 December 1915, p. 7; *Press*, 8 January 1916, p. 4. Despite being under pressure to change its name, the Christchurch Liedertafel retained its title throughout the war. It played at patriotic concerts and led the singing at the vast evening gathering in Victoria Square organised by the local Returned Soldiers' Association to celebrate the armistice. *Press*, 13 November 1918, p. 5.

203 *New Zealand Free Lance*, 22 October 1915, p. 8.

204 Imelda Bargas and Tim Shoebridge, *New Zealand's First World War Heritage* (Auckland: Exisle Publishing, 2015), p. 112; *Evening Post*, 5 January 1916, p. 8.

205 *New Zealand Herald*, 14 July 1916, p. 7; *New Zealand Herald*, 1 December 1916, p. 9.

206 *Star*, 26 September 1917, p. 8; *Sun*, 30 January 1917, p. 5.

207 *Manawatu Standard*, 3 October 1917, p. 5; *Manawatu Times*, 3 October 1917, p. 5.

208 *Evening Post*, 20 April 1917, p. 6. The Mount Albert Borough Council altered Hansen Street to Marne Street, and its counterpart in Takapuna changed Katrine Street to Anzac Street, but it is unclear whether there was any objection to the original names. *New Zealand Herald*, 12 April 1916, p. 6; *Auckland Star*, 8 June 1916, p. 7.

209 *Star*, 18 December 1915, p. 4.

CHAPTER EIGHT: MANAGING MOBILISATION

1 *New Zealand Parliamentary Debates* (*NZPD*), Vol. 180, 13 September 1917, p. 134.

2 Hew Strachan, 'Foreword: New Zealand Society in the Great War', in Steven Loveridge (ed.), *New Zealand Society at War, 1914–1918* (Wellington: Victoria University Press, 2016), p. 12; Erik Olssen, *A Great New Zealand Prime Minister?: Reappraising William Ferguson Massey* (Dunedin: Otago University Press, 2011), p. 23; Paul Baker, *King and Country Call: New Zealanders, Conscription and the Great War* (Auckland: Auckland University Press, 1988).

3 *Press*, 14 January 1916, p. 6.

4 Archives New Zealand (ANZ), R24048324, '[Correspondence between] General Sir Alexander Godley [Commander New Zealand Expeditionary Force] and Colonel Hon. [Honourable] Sir James Allen, Minister of Defence, 13 December 1912–31 March 1915', Allen to Godley, 18 January 1915.

5 ANZ, R24048329, 'Semi-personal letters by General Officer Commanding, 5 September 1914–31 October 1916', Godley to Ward, 9 February 1915.

6 *Marlborough Express*, 15 December 1914, p. 5; *Daily News*, 17 December 1914, p. 4.

7 *Otago Daily Times*, 17 December 1914, p. 4.

8 *Poverty Bay Herald*, 21 May 1915, p. 7.

9 *Evening Star*, 21 May 1915, p. 2.

10 *New Zealand Herald*, 22 May 1915, p. 10. Far from advocating a wartime coalition on principle, Parr maintained that if Reform won both by-elections, 'the Government could carry on for three years without being under obligations to anyone'.

11 Michael Bassett, *Three Party Politics in New Zealand, 1911–1931* (Auckland: Historical Publications, 1982), p. 20.

12 *Sun*, 21 June 1915, p. 6.

13 Three seems to have been favoured by other Reform editors seeking a coalition. See *Waikato Times*, 22 June 1915, p. 4.

14 *Sun*, 21 June 1915, p. 6. The fact that the government's majority rested on a Māori MP appeared to add to the discomfort: 'The Government has a majority of one — Mr Tau Henare, a most honourable man, according to Mr Massey, and we are quite ready to take his word for it. A law proposed by the Government and passed with the acquiescence of Mr Tau Henare, may be good or bad, but it will be as valid as an Act put on the Statute Book by Mr Seddon when he had a majority of 50, and the size or colour of the Government's majority will make no difference to the man who gets six months for breaking that law.' An opposition newspaper in Palmerston North was more direct a few days later: 'The great Tau Henare, who can make or unmake Ministries, has taken his seat on the Ministerial side of the House . . . The descendant of aboriginal chiefs has practically become the ruler of the Government, and on his will or caprice hangs the political fate of a Cabinet.' *Manawatu Daily Times*, 28 June 1915, p. 4.

15 *Sun*, 21 June 1915, p. 9.

16 Massey apparently repeated the assurance to Liverpool himself on the evening of 24 June, after the public assurance and the speech at the opening. See Richard G. H. Kay, 'In Pursuit of Victory: British–New Zealand Relations During the First World War' (PhD thesis, University of Otago, 2001), p. 97.

17 *Auckland Star*, 26 June 1915, p. 6. The Reform MPs were Massey, Allen, Herdman and Heaton Rhodes, and David Guthrie (Ōroua) and Ernest Lee (Ōamaru) from outside Cabinet; the Liberals were Ward, McNab, Myers and Russell; Hindmarsh represented the labour grouping. *Wanganui Chronicle*, 7 July 1915, p. 4.

18 *Star*, 26 June 1915, p. 10.

19 Stewart had been mayor of Dunedin in 1913 and tended to emphasise principles rather than party. Stephanie Dale, 'Stewart, William Downie', *Dictionary of New Zealand Biography*, Vol. 3, http://www.teara.govt.nz/en/biographies/3s35/stewart-william-downie.

20 Another Reform MP was more forthcoming: '[t]he feeling may not have been altogether unanimous, though there was ample support of the proposal'. *Evening Post*, 30 June 1915, p. 7.

21 *Evening Post*, 30 June 1915, p. 3.

22 *New Zealand Times*, 29 June 1915, p. 9. The account also appeared in a Christchurch opposition newspaper that afternoon. *Star*, 29 June 1915, p. 8.

23 *New Zealand Herald*, 1 July 1915, p. 6. The pro-Reform newspaper in Palmerston North similarly declared that 'he should either voluntarily resign the portfolio of Defence or the whole of the other portfolios he holds'. *Manawatu Evening Standard*, 2 July 1915, p. 4.

24 *Dominion*, 1 July 1915, p. 4.

25 *Oamaru Mail*, 30 June 1915, p. 4.

26 *Star*, 6 July 1915, p. 1.

27 Richard Kay has suggested that Massey had realised in the five days since Parliament opened that he had effectively relinquished legislative power, by promising Liverpool that the government would not introduce anything controversial, and might, therefore, explore possibilities of a coalition. Kay, 'In Pursuit of Victory', pp. 97–98. However, Massey and Allen had publicly announced some days before the session began that they would not introduce 'party' legislation and had presumably thought about the implications. If Massey had already decided to seek a 'national cabinet' by 29 June, it is a bit puzzling that he did not make the offer immediately the House met in the afternoon.

28 *Evening Post*, 30 June 1915, p. 7.

29 According to an opposition newspaper, Reform MPs knew the details of the initial offer before Massey raised the issue of a possible national government in Parliament because those details had been decided at the caucus on 28 June. *New Zealand Times*, 3 July 1915, p. 8.

30 *Colonist*, 24 June 1915, p. 6.

31 This sequence is taken from Antony Wood, 'The Origins of the First National Government: A Study in New Zealand politics, 1914–15' (MA thesis, Canterbury University, 1963), pp. 192–202.

32 *Star*, 14 August 1915, p. 11.

33 In practice, however, the existence of the committee, far from reducing dissension in the House, appears to have led backbenchers on all sides to feel that they were free to criticise its decisions. Wood, 'The Origins of the First National Government', pp. 190–92.

34 ANZ, R24048325, '[Correspondence between] General Sir Alexander Godley [Commander New Zealand Expeditionary Force] and Colonel Hon. [Honourable] Sir James Allen, Minister of Defence, 2 April–18 December 1915', 17 July 1915; *New Zealand Observer*, 14 August 1915, p. 3. On 3 August a parliamentary reporter remarked that '[i]t is an open secret that Reform members are not anxious that Defence should be retained absolutely by Mr Allen'. *Poverty Bay Herald*, 3 August 1915, p. 4.

35 Cited in Kay, 'In Pursuit of Victory', p. 101.

36 Cited in Kay, 'In Pursuit of Victory', p. 102.

37 *NZPD*, Vol. 172, 9 July 1915, pp. 228–71.

38 *NZPD*, Vol. 172, 20 July 1915, p. 440.

39 *NZPD*, Vol. 172, 20 July 1915, pp. 449–50.

40 *Star*, 14 August 1915, p. 11.

41 The *Star* journalist claimed that '[t]here was rejoicing among a large section of the rank and file on both sides when it was supposed the negotiations had finally failed, and the Governor's intervention was not welcomed by a dozen members'. *Star*, 14 August 1915, p. 11.

42 Kay, 'In Pursuit of Victory', p. 102.

43 It is possible that bad news from the Eastern Front affected feeling on the government's side. The Russian retreat since early May now appeared likely to include the abandonment of Warsaw. In the context of the coalition talks, one MP remarked the day before the meeting, 'We have to face the fact that the war is not progressing favourably . . . The Russians are suffering a very severe reverse, and probably they will be unable to resume the offensive for months to come . . . Soon the German offensive will be transferred to the west. What then? We have to face the possibility — perhaps the probability — that the war will not be ended this year or next year, and that the Empire will require all its men and all its resources before the end is reached. The thing is bigger than we thought.' *New Zealand Times*, 2 August 1915, p. 4. See also *Dominion*, 2 August 1915, p. 5.

44 *Star*, 14 August 1915, p. 11.

45 *New Zealand Herald*, 6 August 1915, p. 9.

46 *Dominion*, 7 August 1915, p. 6.

47 Wood, 'The Origins of the First National Government', p. 204; Kay, 'In Pursuit of Victory', p. 104. It is unclear whether all the publicised and secret conditions were agreed at the outset or in subsequent negotiations.

48 *Wanganui Chronicle*, 25 August 1915, p. 5.

49 *Appendix to the Journals of the House of Representatives* (*AJHR*), 1915, H-19b, p. xviii.

50 *Evening Star*, 28 August 1915, p. 6.

51 For example, W. Downie Stuart had already noted, 'I believe it is only a question of time till, to a large extent, these two parties [Liberal and Reform] merge, and we shall then get for the first time for some years a proper alignment of parties in this House.' *NZPD*, Vol. 172, 29 June 1915, pp. 67–68.

52 Some of Holland's bitterness towards Payne was later expressed in an Auckland speech, reported as bringing 'down the House', where he claimed Payne's attitude was 'violently anti-Labour' and declared, 'Labour's clear duty in Grey Lynn is to put Mr. Payne out of political business next election.' *Maoriland Worker*, 22 March 1916, p. 4.

53 *Labour and the Fusion: Should Labour Have Joined the National cabinet? Debated by John Payne and H. E. Holland* (Wellington: Maoriland Worker Printery, 1915).

54 *Dominion*, 7 August 1915, p. 6.

55 W. Downie Stewart, *The Rt Hon Sir Francis Bell, P.C., G.C.M.G., K.C.: His Life and Times* (Wellington: Butterworth & Co., 1937), p. 120; Michael Bassett, *Sir Joseph Ward: A Political Biography* (Auckland: Auckland University Press, 1993), p. 227.

56 *NZPD*, Vol. 172, 27 July 1915, p. 547.

57 Later assessments have both considered state

intervention in the economy as potentially preventing worse conditions and as economically counter-productive. M. F. Lloyd Prichard, *An Economic History of New Zealand to 1939* (Auckland: Collins, 1970), p. 264; Alan Everton, 'Government Intervention in the New Zealand Economy 1914–1918: Its Aims and Effectiveness' (MA thesis, Victoria University of Wellington, 1995).

58 For example, A. K. Newman (the Reform MP for Wellington East) noted in a debate in the House, 'I do not want to see everything done by the State, but I do believe that in this country by exercising economy in various ways we should find it possible to very materially cut down the cost of living.' *NZPD*, Vol. 174, 7 October 1915, p. 766.

59 *Wanganui Chronicle*, 23 June 1915, p. 8. For further examples see *NZPD*, Vol. 181, 15 October 1917, p. 167; *NZPD*, Vol. 182, 15 April 1918, p. 251.

60 *NZPD*, Vol. 175, 18 May 1916, p. 253.

61 *Wanganui Chronicle*, 3 May 1915, p. 8. Some days later the prime minister received a report of the Foodstuffs Commission recommending the action he had already taken, which suggests that he was depending more on his own judgement than the commission's. *Evening Post*, 7 May 1915, p. 8.

62 *New Zealand Statutes*, 1915, No. 69, 'Cost of Living Act', pp. 444–47. For further assessment of the board see Michael Bassett, *The State in New Zealand: Socialism Without Doctrines?* (Auckland: Auckland University Press, 1998), pp. 130–32.

63 *AJHR*, 1919, H-44, 'Board of Trade', p. 1.

64 James Holt, *Compulsory Arbitration in New Zealand: The First Forty Years* (Auckland: Auckland University Press, 1986), pp. 121–22. In present conditions the court estimated that a reasonable living wage was 1s 3d per hour or £2 12s a week.

65 *New Zealand Free Lance*, 13 August 1915, p. 5.

66 For the Women's Anti-German League accusations see Graham Hucker, '"Bundling out the Hun": The Women's Anti-German League during the First World War', in Loveridge (ed.), *New Zealand Society at War*, p. 263. For further background on the Myers family see Paul Goldsmith and Michael Bassett, *The Myers* (Auckland: David Ling, 2007).

67 Arrangements were made for the supply of small-arms ammunition through the Auckland Colonial Ammunition Company. For the supply contract see *AJHR*, 1915, H-19d, 'The Ammunition Contract 1915', pp. 1–4; *NZPD*, Vol. 174, 11 October 1915, pp. 883–84.

68 ANZ, R22428909, 'Ammunition and Explosives — Munitions manufacture in New Zealand — 4/5/1915 — September 1915'.

69 H. T. B. Drew, 'War Finance', in Drew (ed.), *The War Effort of New Zealand: A Popular History of Minor Campaigns in which New Zealanders took Part, Services not Dealt with in the Campaign Volumes, the Work at the Bases* (Auckland: Whitcombe & Tombs, 1923), p. 242.

70 ANZ, R3898721, 'Register of factory output, August 1915–August 1920', Secretary Kaiapoi Woollen Manufacturing Company to Minister of Munitions, 7 October 1915.

71 ANZ, R3898721, 'Register of factory output, August 1915–August 1920', Manager, F. M. King Ltd to Minister of Munitions, 8 September 1915.

72 ANZ, R3898721, 'Register of factory output, August 1915–August 1920', Manager, Archibald Clark and Sons, to Minister of Munitions, 11 September 1915.

73 *AJHR*, 1919, H-24, 'Munitions and Supplies Department', p. 1.

74 ANZ, R3898752, 'New Zealand's part in the war, March 1917–September 1919'.

75 It was also agreed by both sides that cotton ran more freely through the sewing machines, which presumably saved time and therefore money on fixing breakages of thread. Levy's contract involved supplying 3500 tunics, 1700 trousers, 1740 pants and 2000 greatcoats a month.

76 *NZ Truth*, 23 September 1916, p. 5.

77 In October another Wellington firm, Scoullar and Company, was prosecuted for supplying the Defence Department with mattresses below specification. They were significantly underweight and 'more than half' were filled, 'in a disgraceful manner', with 'sour flax, rope end, and dust sweepings', making them unfit and unsanitary; only 162 of the 2220 examined met the specification. The same magistrate as in the Levy case presided and found the company guilty, fining it £50. *Evening Post*, 26 October 1916, p. 7; *Evening Post*, 1 November 1916, p. 8.

78 *Maoriland Worker*, 10 November 1915, p. 4.

79 *Otago Daily Times*, 25 August 1915, p. 4; also *Nelson Evening Mail*, 28 August 1915, p. 4.

80 *Evening Post*, 18 August 1915, p. 3; *New Zealand Times*, 23 August 1915, p. 4.

81 *Evening Post*, 9 June 1915, p. 6.

82 The full list of rates can be found in *Evening Post*, 24 October 1914, p. 3.

83 If the death was due to 'illness brought on by the fatigue, privation, and exposure incident to active operations in the field before an enemy within twelve months after his having been removed from duty on account of such illness, or if he died in consequence of injuries received in the performance of military duty otherwise than in action within twelve months after having been injured'.

84 The allowance for sons could be paid until they reached 18 and for daughters until marriage or until 21. The age limits could be extended 'in special circumstances'.

85 The regulations also recognised that other

adult female (but not male) relatives might have depended on the dead soldier. Thus mothers of privates or non-commissioned officers could receive £26 a year if they were widows or had an incapacitated husband. If the soldier had no surviving wife, child or mother, a dependent sister or sisters (between them) could qualify, but support would in any event 'cease when the person receiving it marries, or is in any other manner sufficiently provided for'.

86 *Otago Daily Times*, 19 November 1914, p. 6.

87 *New Zealand Times*, 27 May 1915, p. 9. A few days later H. D. Bell, minister of internal affairs and a close ally of Massey, declared, incorrectly in light of how the widows' and old age pensions were assessed, that 'whatever the Government does it does uniformly. There can be no distinguishing men with children as against men with none, and men with parents to support from men with none. When the law is laid down we cannot discriminate between the poor and the better off ... [Pensioners] should not be asked to show the need or to pauperise themselves for the sake of the pension.' He envisaged the privately collected and administered patriotic funds dealing with cases of extra need. *Taranaki Daily News*, 2 June 1915, p. 8.

88 *Evening Post*, 9 June 1915, p. 6. The editorial was approvingly quoted in *Star*, 10 June 1915, p. 4; *Hawera and Normanby Star*, 22 June 1915, p. 4.

89 *New Zealand Herald*, 8 June 1915, p. 6.

90 *Star*, 26 May 1915, p. 4.

91 Baker, *King and Country Call*, p. 57.

92 *Grey River Argus*, 28 May 1915, p. 5.

93 *Evening Post*, 26 May 1915, p. 8.

94 *Timaru Herald*, 10 July 1915, p. 8; *Evening Star*, 9 July 1915, p. 4; *Evening Star*, 10 July 1915, p. 6; *Star*, 3 September 1915, p. 1.

95 See, for example, *Dominion*, 9 July 1915, p. 7.

96 *New Zealand Observer*, 6 November 1915, p. 2. See also *New Zealand Free Lance*, 5 November 1915, p. 8.

97 *Auckland Star*, 24 November 1915, p. 8; *Auckland Star*, 1 December 1915, p. 8.

98 *Dominion*, 30 October 1915, p. 4.

99 *New Zealand Times*, 1 December 1915, p. 7. The board now granted pensions to a father resident in Australia and receiving his old age pension and to war widows who had been living apart from their husbands when the latter enlisted. *Poverty Bay Herald*, 8 December 1915, p. 7; *Dominion*, 14 January 1916, p. 4. In early 1916, Allen explained that the board had not initially interpreted the act 'in the spirit in which it was intended ... but in the last month or two it had been interpreted in a much broader manner'. *Dominion*, 14 January 1916, p. 4. For examples of the board's new largesse, see *Manawatu Standard*, 25 February 1916, p. 3.

100 *Hawera and Normanby Star*, 28 April 1916, p. 8.

101 *Daily News*, 5 May 1916, p. 4.

102 *Marlborough Express*, 9 May 1916, p. 4.

103 *New Zealand Statutes*, 1916, No. 1, 'War Pensions Amendment Act', pp. 3–7.

104 *Evening Post*, 25 May 1916, p. 5.

105 The *New Zealand Observer*, for example, wrote: 'The Commonwealth is more humane. On the arrival of any wounded or sick soldier, it gives him a new uniform. New Zealand allows him to walk around like an animated rag-bag. The Commonwealth gives every returned soldier a free railway pass. New Zealand does not ... The Australian soldier can get all the money due to him at the depot where he joined within 24 hours. Wellington must be warned that a soldier from the wars is back before the Department recognises his pay-book. The Commonwealth pays a pension to a wounded soldier or to his dependents [sic] because the soldier has earned the RIGHT to the pension, and it does not set up a star chamber to humiliate him or his mother or his children.' *New Zealand Observer*, 11 December 1915, p. 16.

106 *Star*, 25 May 1916, p. 5.

107 *Marlborough Express*, 25 May 1916, p. 4.

108 *Timaru Herald*, 27 May 1916, p. 8.

109 For a study of Reform's approach to welfare see Justin Thomas Strang, 'Welfare in Transition: Reform's Income Support Policy, 1912–1928' (MA thesis, Victoria University of Wellington, 1992).

110 *Star*, 21 June 1915, p. 6.

111 *NZPD*, Vol. 173, 8 September 1915, p. 481.

112 *NZPD*, Vol. 173, 7 September 1915, p. 432.

113 *Star*, 29 September 1915, p. 4.

114 *Manawatu Standard*, 1 October 1915, p. 7; *West Coast Times*, 29 September 1915, p. 2.

115 Malcolm McKinnon, *Treasury: The New Zealand Treasury, 1840–2000* (Auckland: Auckland University Press, 2003), p. 85; Everton, 'Government Intervention in the New Zealand Economy', p. 419.

116 *New Zealand Free Lance*, 3 September 1915, p. 9.

117 *Evening Star*, 17 March 1916, p. 6.

118 *Manawatu Standard*, 18 May 1916, p. 4.

119 *Evening Post*, 17 June 1916, p. 4; *Taranaki Herald*, 17 June 1916, p. 2; *Marlborough Express*, 20 June 1916, p. 4.

120 *Southland Times*, 21 June 1916, p. 4. It admitted that dairy and meat farmers were similarly placed, but considered that individually their profits would not be large. Strictly speaking, however, this was irrelevant as the tax was not graduated.

121 *AJHR*, 1916, 'Financial Statement', B-6, p. iv.

122 That would seem, however, to overlook the likelihood that the London government would also be facing big expenses when peace arrived and would need the cash itself.

123 Bassett, *Sir Joseph Ward*, p. 225; ANZ, R15420891,

'Re Budget — Interest and sinking fund on war loan', Ward to Mackenzie, 20 June 1916.

124 *New Zealand Statutes*, 1915, No. 5, 'War Regulations Amendment', section 5(2), p. 10. In August 1916 this duration was further extended to a year after the war. *New Zealand Statutes*, 1916, No. 9, 'War Regulations Amendment', section 7(2), p. 107.

125 *New Zealand Statutes*, 1915, No. 66, 'War Regulations Amendment (No. 2)', pp. 359–60.

126 *New Zealand Gazette*, 15 November 1915, p. 3813; Kathryn Hunter, 'National and Imperial Belonging in Wartime: The Tangled Knot of Australians and New Zealanders as British subjects during the Great War', *Australian Journal of Politics and History*, Vol. 63, No. 1 (March 2017), pp. 31–44.

127 *New Zealand Gazette*, 31 August 1916, pp. 2893–94.

128 *Manual of the War Legislation of New Zealand Compromising Acts of Parliament, Proclamations, Orders in Council, and other Instruments Passed, Issued, and Made in Consequence of the War, and in Force on 30th September, 1916* (Wellington: Government Printer, 1916), pp. 182, 184, 188, 196.

129 Baker, *King and Country Call*, p. 44.

130 *Maoriland Worker*, 1 March 1916, p. 6.

131 *Manawatu Daily Times*, 14 March 1916, p. 4.

132 *NZ Truth*, 26 February 1916, p. 3.

133 Baker, *King and Country Call*, p. 167.

134 Michael Bassett with Michael King, *Tomorrow Comes the Song: A Life of Peter Fraser* (Auckland: Penguin, 2000), pp. 71–72.

135 This resulted in numerous reports on the events and Christchurch diligence saw full transcripts of her lectures and following question-and-answer sessions produced.

136 ANZ, R22434535, 'Publications, instructions, etc. — Publication "Put up the Sword" Miss Pankhurst', Greymouth Report of meeting held by Miss Pankhurst, 30 June 1916.

137 *NZ Truth*, 24 June 1916, p. 3; *Auckland Star*, 16 June 1916, p. 6; H. E. Holland, *Armageddon or Calvary: The Conscientious Objectors of New Zealand and 'The Process of Their Conversion'* (Wellington: The Maoriland Worker Printing and Publishing Co. Ltd, 1919), p. 14.

138 These instructions were printed in *Auckland Star*, 4 April 1916, p. 8.

139 *New Zealand Gazette*, 20 September 1915, pp. 3263–64.

140 *NZPD*, Vol. 175, 19 May 1916, pp. 276–77.

141 ATL, MS-Papers-2531-4, 'New Zealand Freedom League: Minute Books', 15 November 1915.

142 Baker, *King and Country Call*, p. 77.

143 *New Zealand Herald*, 2 November 1915, p. 5.

144 Baker, *King and Country Call*, p. 78.

145 Jared Davidson, *Dead Letters: Censorship and Subversion in New Zealand 1914–1920* (Dunedin: Otago University Press, 2019), p. 35.

146 A rare success for the staff engaged in censoring correspondence to neutral countries occurred late in 1916 when a Dutchman named Jannes Slijm enlisted under a false name, claiming to be a Belgian. 'It was ascertained from letters written to his people and which were intercepted by the Censor that he was disaffected towards the British Government and people, and had enlisted with intent to desert from the Forces as soon as he reached Europe.' ANZ, R3794939, 'Ordinary Outwards Despatches to the Secretary of State — 5 October 1916–28 March 1917', Memo from Acting-Prime Minister James Allen to Governor, 9 January 1917, attached to Governor to Colonial Secretary, 13 January 1917.

147 ANZ, R3885410, 'Censorship of correspondence, National peace conference, June 1915–July 1920', Deputy Chief Postal Censor to Colonel Gibbon, 29 November 1915; Solicitor-General to Chief of General Staff, 17 December 1915; ANZ, R22434529, 'Publications, instructions, etc. — Literature (anti-militarist) — Publication of', Report of N.Z. Military Censor, 22 November 1915; *Maoriland Worker*, 12 January 1916, p. 4.

148 The president of the New Zealand Institute would describe a similar January 1918 proposal as 'ridiculous and undesirable'. *Mataura Ensign*, 26 August 1915, p. 4; *Star*, 14 October 1916, p. 9; *Evening Post*, 25 October 1916, p. 7; *Ashburton Guardian*, 30 January 1918, p. 3.

149 *Otago Witness*, 19 May 1915, p. 5.

150 He further noted an awareness of the possible consequences of such attitudes: 'May I also ask you to call the attention of the deputation to the aftermath of this horrible war. If this unjust spirit is to be bred and cultivated now, what is to be the position when the war is over?' ANZ, R22319706, 'Miscellanous files and papers — Miscellaneous correspondence and papers [Loose papers]', James Allen to J. J. Clark, 7 September 1915.

151 ANZ, R22319681, 'Minister of Defence — Anti-German League, circulars etc'.

152 *NZPD*, Vol. 173, 25 August 1915, p. 132.

153 Andrew Francis, *'To Be Truly British We Must Be Anti-German': New Zealand, Enemy Aliens and the Great War Experience, 1914–1919* (Oxford; New York: Peter Lang, 2012), pp. 164, 167.

154 *New Zealand Statutes*, 1915, No. 67, 'Enemy Alien Teachers Act', pp. 361–62.

155 George William von Zedlitz, *The Search for a Country: The Autobiography of G. W. von Zedlitz* (Hamilton: Paul's Book Arcade, 1963), p. 17.

156 Judith Bassett, 'Colonial Justice: The Treatment of Dalmatians in New Zealand during the First World War', *New Zealand Journal of History*, Vol. 33, No. 2 (October 1999), p. 162.

157 By reports German and Austrian relations with

Dalmatians interned on Matiu Somes Island were unfriendly. ANZ, R22431231, 'Establishments and Recruitment — Enlistment of aliens in NZEF [New Zealand Expeditionary Force]', Memorandum for the Minister of Defence, 9 December 1916.

158 ANZ, R3794939, 'Ordinary Outwards Despatches to the Secretary of State — 5 October 1916–28 March 1917', Report to Minister of Justice, 21 August 1916, attached to Governor to Colonial Secretary, 9 October 1916.

159 *New Zealand Herald*, 20 July 1916, p. 11.

160 *NZPD*, Vol. 175, 10 May 1916, p. 18.

161 For examples see *NZPD*, Vol. 175, 12 May 1916, p. 102; Vol. 175, 18 May 1916, p. 250; Vol. 175, 2 June 1916, pp. 667–68; Vol. 175, 6 June 1916, p. 680.

162 *NZPD*, Vol. 175, 11 May 1916, p. 18.

163 *Oamaru Mail*, 24 May 1916, p. 6.

164 *New Zealand Gazette*, 2 May 1916, p. 1598.

165 ANZ, R10075037, 'Recruiting Board scheme, December 1915–October 1916'. Further details in ANZ, R22431231, 'Establishments and Recruitment — Enlistment of aliens in NZEF [New Zealand Expeditionary Force]'.

166 *Taranaki Daily News*, 14 July 1917, p. 6. The defence minister declared that 'the policy of the Government is to accept for the New Zealand Expeditionary Force men of enemy alien parentage against whose loyalty nothing is known and who were born subsequent to the naturalisation of the father'. ANZ, R22429059, 'Expeditionary Force — Jugo Slavs [Yugoslavs] in Puhoi District — Disloyalty', Allen to Hall, Skelton and Skelton, 5 October 1917.

167 *Wairarapa Age*, 14 January 1916, p. 5.

168 For examples see *Auckland Star*, 22 December 1915, p. 4; *Evening Post*, 7 February 1916, p. 6.

169 *New Zealand Observer*, 26 February 1916, p. 2.

170 *New Zealand Herald*, 26 February 1916, p. 8; Baker, *King and Country Call*, p. 80.

171 ANZ, R22429115, 'Expeditionary Force — Recruiting Wellington District', Robin to Allen, 24 March 1916. The *Evening Post* agreed, noting that it knew of a number of such physical altercations. *Evening Post*, 6 April 1916, p. 6.

172 Baker, *King and Country Call*, p. 81.

173 *Evening Post*, 20 April 1916, p. 6.

174 Baker, *King and Country Call*, p. 83.

175 John Graham, 'The Voluntary System: Recruiting 1914–16' (MA thesis, University of Auckland, 1971), p. 162; Baker, *King and Country Call*, p. 85.

176 *New Zealand Herald*, 28 March 1916, p. 8.

177 *NZPD*, Vol. 175, 30 May 1916, pp. 484–85.

178 ANZ, R22431244, 'Establishments and Recruitment — Enlistment — Return showing number from each district', 'Return showing the number of men that have registered in the different Military Districts'; Glyn Harper, *For King and Other Countries: The New Zealanders who Fought in Other Services in the First World War* (Auckland: Massey University Press, 2019), p. 18.

179 *NZPD*, Vol. 175, 30 May 1916, p. 486. This position was well mirrored within his private correspondence. See, for example, ANZ, R22319674, 'Miscellanous files and papers — Correspondence with Colonels Birdwood and Russell, December 1914–April 1920 and copies of personal letters, 1920 [Loose papers]', Allen to General Russell, 7 November 1916.

180 Paul Baker, 'New Zealanders, the Great War and Conscription' (PhD thesis, University of Auckland, 1986), p. 180.

181 The bill recognised four categories: 'unmarried men', 'men whose marriage took place subsequently to the first day of May, nineteen hundred and fifteen, except such that have a child under sixteen years of age by a previous marriage', 'widowers with no children under sixteen years of age' and 'men whose marriage has been dissolved or who are judicially separated from their wives by decree of judicial separation, separation order, or otherwise, and who have no children under sixteen years of age'. *New Zealand Statutes*, 1916, No. 8, 'Military Service Act', section 4, pp. 85–86.

182 *AJHR*, 1919, H-19, 'Defence Forces of New Zealand', p. 15.

183 *NZPD*, Vol. 175, 11 May 1916, p. 47.

184 *Journals of the Legislative Council of the Dominion of New Zealand*, 9 May 1916–8 August 1916 (Wellington: Government Printer, 1916), p. 32. For further discussion see P. S. O'Connor, 'The Awkward Ones — Dealing with Conscience, 1916–1918', *New Zealand Journal of History*, Vol. 8, No. 2 (October 1974), pp. 118–36.

185 *NZPD*, Vol. 175, 15 June 1916, pp. 884–85.

186 *NZPD*, Vol. 175, 17 May 1916, p. 694.

187 *New Zealand Statutes*, 1916, No. 8, 'Military Service Act', section 18(1)e, p. 90.

188 *NZPD*, Vol. 177, 21 July 1916, pp. 331–32.

189 *Press*, 9 June 1916, p. 9.

190 *NZPD*, Vol. 175, 31 May 1916, p. 572.

191 *NZPD*, Vol. 175, 1 June 1916, pp. 610, 612.

192 *NZPD*, Vol. 175, 30 May 1916, p. 520.

193 See, for example, *NZPD*, Vol. 175, 30 May 1916, p. 529; Vol. 175, 31 May 1916, p. 573; Vol. 175, 1 June 1916, p. 588; Vol. 175, 1 June 1916, p. 610; Vol. 175, 1 June 1916, p. 635.

194 *New Zealand Statutes*, 1916, No. 8, 'Military Service Act', section 50, p. 100.

195 *NZPD*, Vol. 175, 11 May 1916, p. 47.

CHAPTER NINE: A BETTER COURSE TOWARDS VICTORY

1 John Horne, 'Remobilizing for "Total War": France and Britain, 1917–1918', in John Horne (ed.), *State, Society and Mobilization in Europe during the First World War*, ed. John Horne (Cambridge: Cambridge University Press, 1997), pp. 195–211.

2 *Evening Post*, 5 August 1916, p. 9; *New Zealand Herald*, 9 August 1916, p. 9.

3 Some New Zealand officials did not favour the action and, in early 1918, Allen's private correspondence noted that he thought the ongoing investigation of the commission would erode public morale: 'Inquiry has been made into the Gallipoli campaign against my judgement and against the will of the New Zealand Government. However much I may have felt inclined to condemn the policy which was represented by Gallipoli I have felt there could be no good purpose served in making inquiry just now.' Archives New Zealand (ANZ), R24048328, '[Correspondence between] General Sir Alexander Godley [Commander New Zealand Expeditionary Force] and Colonel Hon. [Honourable] Sir James Allen, Minister of Defence, 6 January 1918–28 January 1920', Allen to Godley, 7 January 1918.

4 *Press*, 10 March 1917, p. 8.

5 Ian McGibbon, *New Zealand's Western Front Campaign* (Auckland: Bateman, 2016), p. 86. Andrew Macdonald claims 5848 wounded and 2111 killed. Andrew Macdonald, *On My Way to the Somme: New Zealanders and the Bloody Offensive of 1916* (Auckland: HarperCollins, 2005), p. 245.

6 *North Otago Times*, 2 September 1916, p. 7; *North Otago Times*, 25 September 1916, p. 5.

7 Paul Baker, *King and Country Call: New Zealanders, Conscription and the Great War* (Auckland: Auckland University Press, 1988), p. 95.

8 *New Zealand Observer*, 8 July 1916, p. 13.

9 *New Zealand Parliamentary Debates* (*NZPD*), Vol. 176, 29 June 1916, p. 302.

10 Alexander Turnbull Library (ATL), qMS-0682, Harrold Ennor Diaries, 25 September 1916; 29 September 1916; 2 October 1916; 6 October 1916; 11 October 1916.

11 Fitz Fischer, *Germany's Aims in the First World War* (London: Chatto & Windus, 1967), pp. 295–98.

12 'The Secretary of State to the Ambassadors and Ministers in Belligerent Countries', https://history.state.gov/historicaldocuments/frus1916Supp/d136.

13 *Poverty Bay Herald*, 18 December 1916, p. 3.

14 *Southland Daily News*, 13 December 1916, p. 4.

15 *Sun*, 26 December 1916, p. 6.

16 *Grey River Argus*, 27 December 1916, p. 8.

17 *Poverty Bay Herald*, 29 January 1917, p. 3.

18 *New Zealand Free Lance*, 26 January 1917, p. 26.

19 *Star*, 8 December 1916, p. 6.

20 *Evening Post*, 5 August 1916, p. 9.

21 *New Zealand Herald*, 4 May 1918, p. 6; *New Zealand Herald*, 5 May 1917, p. 5.

22 Gavin McLean, *Spinning Yarns: A Centennial History of Alliance Textiles Limited and its Predecessors 1881–1981* (Dunedin: Alliance Textiles, 1981), p. 34.

23 *Evening Post*, 22 June 1917, p. 9.

24 I. C. McGibbon, *Blue-Water Rationale: The Naval Defence of New Zealand, 1914–1942* (Wellington: Government Printer, 1981), pp. 29–31; Robin Bromby, *German Raiders of the South Seas* (Sydney: Doubleday, 1985), pp. 126–59.

25 Bromby, *German Raiders of the South Seas*, p. 126.

26 Bromby, *German Raiders of the South Seas*, pp. 141–44; McGibbon, *Blue-Water Rationale*, pp. 29–30. Roy Alexander was aboard the *Wairuna* when it was attacked by *Wolf* and was taken prisoner. He later wrote his account of events. See Roy Alexander, *Cruise of the Raider Wolf* (Sydney: Angus & Robertson, 1939).

27 For some time, the loss of the *Port Kembla* was attributed to a bomb believed to be planted on the ship by militant Australian labour. However, official awareness of *Wolf*'s mine-laying actions dawned and an official statement of the existence of mines in New Zealand waters was issued by the naval adviser. In January 1918 two fishing trawlers and a whaler were chartered to be employed as minesweepers and located and removed 47 mines. McGibbon, *Blue-Water Rationale*, pp. 28–30; Bromby, *German Raiders of the South Seas*, p. 143.

28 McGibbon, *Blue-Water Rationale*, pp. 29–31; Bromby, *German Raiders of the South Seas*, p. 144.

29 *Wanganui Herald*, 7 September 1918, p. 9.

30 *Wanganui Herald*, 7 September 1918, p. 9; ANZ, R22434297, 'Chaplains; Prisoners of War; Reservists — Aliens — Enemy — Correspondence with anti-German League'. The exchange was then published in a Nelson newspaper over October–November 1918. See *Colonist*, 25 October 1918, p. 7; *Colonist*, 20 November 1918, p. 6.

31 Bromby, *German Raiders of the South Seas*, pp. 171–88.

32 John Abbatiello, 'Atlantic U-boat Campaign', in *1914–1918-online. International Encyclopedia of the First World War*, ed. Ute Daniel, Peter Gatrell, Oliver Janz, Heather Jones, Jennifer Keene, Alan Kramer and Bill Nasson, issued by Freie Universität Berlin, Berlin 2016-02-01. DOI: 10.15463/ie1418.10818.

33 B. L. Evans, *A History of Agricultural Production and Marketing in New Zealand* (Palmerston North: Keeling & Mundy Ltd, 1969), p. 107.

34 *Evening Post*, 2 April 1917, p. 8; Richard G. H. Kay, 'In Pursuit of Victory: British–New Zealand Relations During the First World War' (PhD thesis,

University of Otago, 2001), p. 158; *Appendix to the Journals of the House of Representatives* (*AJHR*), 1918, H-38, 'Department of Imperial Government Supplies', p. 18.

35 *Evening Post*, 4 July 1917, p. 4; *Evening Post*, 10 July 1917, p. 3.

36 *Evening Post*, 22 June, 1917, p. 19; *Evening Post*, 21 June 1917, p. 4; *Star*, 21 June 1918, p. 3.

37 All mineral phosphatic fertiliser was imported, with the exception of limited quantities mined at Clarendon in Otago.

38 Massey had inquired into the future of Nauru phosphates as early as 1915 and had noted the matter in Parliament. Gerald Chaudron, *New Zealand in The League of Nations* (Jefferson: McFarland & Co., 2012), pp. 10–11; James Watson, *WF Massey: New Zealand* (London: Haus, 2010), p. 77.

39 *Star*, 9 July 1917, p. 8.

40 *Poverty Bay Herald*, 4 July 1918, p. 3.

41 *Oamaru Mail*, 9 February 1917, p. 1.

42 Baker, *King and Country Call*, p. 141; *Evening Post*, 24 July 1917, p. 2; James Watson, 'Patriotism, Profits and Problems: New Zealand Farming During the Great War', in John Crawford and Ian McGibbon (eds), *New Zealand's Great War: New Zealand, the Allies and the First World War* (Auckland: Exisle Publishing, 2007), pp. 534–49; *Star*, 8 December 1916, p. 6.

43 *Mataura Ensign*, 10 January 1917, p. 4.

44 *Otago Witness*, 18 September 1918, p. 11.

45 *Wanganui Herald*, 30 September 1918, p. 7.

46 Alan Everton, 'Government Intervention in the New Zealand Economy 1914–1918: Its Aims and Effectiveness' (MA thesis, Victoria University of Wellington, 1995), p. 354.

47 *New Zealand Official Year-book*, 1919, p. 591.

48 *New Zealand Official Year-book*, 1919, p. 591.

49 ANZ, R22319765, 'Ministerial Files — Coal — General file'. Two hundred and forty-six days were lost on other grievances, and losses due to 'go slow' actions remain unestimated; *Evening Post*, 23 April 1917, pp. 7–8.

50 ANZ, R22319675, 'Miscellanous files and papers — Correspondence between J Allen and WF Massey, 1st September 1916–1st August 1919 [Loose papers]', Allen to Massey, 28 October 1916.

51 *AJHR*, 1918, H-44, 'Board of Trade (Second Annual Report of the)', p. 19.

52 ANZ, R24048328, '[Correspondence between] General Sir Alexander Godley [Commander New Zealand Expeditionary Force] and Colonel Hon. [Honourable] Sir James Allen, Minister of Defence, 6 January 1918–28 January 1920', Allen to Godley, 7 January 1918.

53 H. E. Holland, *The Scandal of the War Profits* (Wellington: Maoriland Worker Printery, 1917).

54 *New Zealand Herald*, 19 April 1917, p. 4.

55 ANZ, R22319764, 'Ministerial Files — Cost of living taxation and fixing prices, etc', Extract from a Transcript of an Interview between the Executive of the Amalgamated Society of Railway Servants and W. H. Herries, 17 May 1917.

56 *Colonist*, 9 August 1918, p. 4.

57 *Ashburton Guardian*, 12 March 1917, p. 4.

58 *NZPD*, Vol. 181, 15 October 1917, p. 179. See also *Evening Post*, 24 July 1917, p. 2.

59 *Mataura Ensign*, 30 April 1917, p. 4.

60 *Hawera and Normanby Star*, 24 July 1917, p. 4.

61 Joan Beaumont, *Broken Nation: Australians in the Great War* (Crows Nest, NSW: Allen & Unwin, 2013), pp. 165–73.

62 James Belich, *Paradise Reforged: A History of the New Zealanders from the 1880s to the Year 2000* (Honolulu: University of Hawai'i Press, 2001), p. 111–12.

63 For further analysis on Massey and trade see James Watson, '"The Greatest Commercial Traveller in the Empire": Massey and Trade', in James Watson and Lachy Paterson (eds), *A Great New Zealand Prime Minister?: Reappraising William Ferguson Massey* (Dunedin: Otago University Press, 2011), pp. 121–28.

64 Kay, 'In Pursuit of Victory', p. 136.

65 *AJHR*, 1917, H-21, 'Meat Export. Correspondence Between the Prime Minister and the Ministry of Shipping re Withdrawal of Ships, etc.', p. 2.

66 Kay, 'In Pursuit of Victory', p. 139.

67 *Waikato Times*, 13 February 1917, p. 5; *New Zealand Observer*, 17 February 1917, p. 7; *NZPD*, Vol. 178, 28 June 1917, p. 1.

68 Watson, *WF Massey*, p. 50.

69 Bentley Brinkerhoff Gilbert, *David Lloyd George: A Political Life: The Architect of Change 1863–1912* (London: B. T. Batsford Ltd, 1987), pp. 11–25.

70 *Auckland Star*, 12 December 1916, p. 5.

71 *Otago Witness*, 6 December 1916, p. 41; *New Zealand Herald*, 8 December 1916, p. 6.

72 *NZ Truth*, 16 December 1916, p. 1; *Maoriland Worker*, 20 December 1916, p. 4.

73 Kay, 'In Pursuit of Victory', p. 143.

74 ANZ, R22319675, 'Miscellanous files and papers — Correspondence between J Allen and WF Massey, 1st September 1916–1st August 1919 [Loose papers]', Massey to Allen, 2 January 1917.

75 *NZPD*, Vol. 178, 3 July 1917, p. 73.

76 Kay, 'In Pursuit of Victory', p. 144.

77 David Lloyd George, *War Memoirs, Vol. 4* (London: Nicholson & Watson, 1933), p. 1733.

78 *New Zealand Statutes*, 1916, No. 13, 'War Legislation Amendment', pp. 123–38.

79 In March 1917, for example, a maximum price for milk sold in Wellington was fixed at 1s 1/2d per

gallon. *AJHR*, 1918, H-44, 'Board of Trade (Second Annual Report of the)', pp. 10–11.

80 *Timaru Herald*, 6 February 1917, p. 7; *AJHR*, 1918, H-44, 'Board of Trade (Second Annual Report of the)', pp. 1, 2.

81 Everton, 'Government Intervention in the New Zealand Economy', p. 282.

82 Everton, 'Government Intervention in the New Zealand Economy', p. 155.

83 *AJHR*, 1919, H-38, 'Department of Imperial Government Supplies', pp. 11–12.

84 *Hawera and Normanby Star*, 18 November 1916, p. 4. See also *Farmers' Union Advocate*, 4 December 1915, p. 5; 23 September 1916, p. 5; 19 May 1917, p. 23.

85 *Evening Post*, 21 October 1916, p. 6; *New Zealand Law Review*, 1917, Vol. 36, 'The Taratahi Dairy Co., and Mangorei Dairy Co. v. Attorney General', pp. 1–2; *Hawera and Normanby Star*, 9 November 1916, p. 4.

86 *Evening Post*, 31 August 1917, p. 6.

87 *AJHR*, 1918, H-44, 'Board of Trade (Second Annual Report of the)', pp. 3–4.

88 ANZ, R22319675, 'Miscellanous files and papers — Correspondence between J Allen and WF Massey, 1st September 1916–1st August 1919 [Loose papers]', Allen to Massey, 2 February 1917.

89 *Ashburton Guardian*, 10 July 1917, p. 7.

90 *AJHR*, 1917, H-44, 'Board of Trade (First Annual Report of the)', p. 11.

91 John E. Martin, 'Blueprint for the Future? "National Efficiency" and the First World War', in Crawford and McGibbon (eds), *New Zealand's Great War*, pp. 516–33.

92 *AJHR*, 1917, H-43, 'National Efficiency Board (Report Of)', p. 1.

93 Andrew Trlin, *Now Respected, Once Despised: Yugoslavs in New Zealand* (Palmerston North: Dunmore Press, 1979), pp. 104–6.

94 Trlin, *Now Respected, Once Despised*, p. 108.

95 ANZ, R3895405, 'Correspondence and Memoranda concerning Government Policy towards Yugoslavs', Auckland Returned Soldiers' Association to Allen, 25 June 1917.

96 ANZ, R3090759, 'Dalmatians on gumfields', W. Ferguson to Massey, 31 May 1917.

97 *AJHR*, 1917, H-43, 'National Efficiency Board (Report Of)', p. 14.

98 *Grey River Argus*, 7 April 1917, p. 2.

99 *Auckland Star*, 24 May 1917, p. 7.

100 *Evening Post*, 19 January 1917, p. 9.

101 *New Zealand Herald*, 6 July 1918, p. 6.

102 *Press*, 24 April 1918, p. 6.

103 *Journal of the Department of Labour*, 25:287 (January 1917), p. 33.

104 *Wairarapa Daily Times*, 15 February 1917, p. 4.

105 ANZ, R22319675, 'Miscellanous files and papers — Correspondence between J Allen and WF Massey, 1st September 1916–1st August 1919 [Loose papers]', Allen to Massey, 23 May 1917.

106 *AJHR*, 1917, H-43A, 'National Efficiency Board (Report Of) On The Liquor Question', pp. 1–2.

107 *New Zealand Gazette*, 5 February 1917, pp. 439–43; *Press*, 8 February 1917, p. 7; *New Zealand Gazette*, 6 June 1917, pp. 2281–82.

108 Kay, 'In Pursuit of Victory', p. 154.

109 *Feilding Star*, 5 February 1917, p. 3.

110 Maurice Ollivier (ed.), *The Colonial and Imperial Conferences from 1887 to 1937, Vol. 2* (Ottawa: Queen's Printer, 1954), p. 182.

111 Kay, 'In Pursuit of Victory', p. 163; ANZ, R15393166, 'Imperial War Conference — Minutes', p. 183; ANZ, R20470310, 'Other Papers laid before the War Cabinet — Minutes of meetings of the sub-committee of the Imperial War Cabinet', 17 April 1917.

112 ANZ, R20470310, 'Other Papers laid before the War Cabinet — Minutes of meetings of the sub-committee of the Imperial War Cabinet', 17 April 1917. Robert Thornton, 'Invaluable Ally or Imminent Aggressor? Australian and Japanese Naval Assistance, 1914–18', *Journal of Australian Studies*, Vol. 12 (1983), p. 5.

113 ANZ, R15393166, 'Imperial War Conference — Minutes', pp. 59–64; Ollivier, *The Colonial and Imperial Conferences, Vol. 2*, pp. 173–74.

114 Kay, 'In Pursuit of Victory', p. 157; ANZ, R17378327, 'Imperial War Conference 1917 — Minutes of meetings 1–14, 20 March–2 May — Imperial War Cabinet', Meeting 8, 5 April 1917.

115 ANZ, R17378327, 'Imperial War Conference 1917 — Minutes of meetings 1–14, 20 March–2 May — Imperial War Cabinet', Meeting 4, 27 March 1917; ANZ, R24503022, 'Date: 7 August 1917 Subject: Circumstances in which the "Rotorua" was sunk', T. E. Donne to The Under Secretary of State, 24 April 1917.

116 Ollivier, *The Colonial and Imperial Conferences, Vol. 2*, p. 175.

117 Ollivier, *The Colonial and Imperial Conferences, Vol. 2*, p. 175; ANZ, R17378327, 'Imperial War Conference 1917 — Minutes of meetings 1–14, 20 March–2 May — Imperial War Cabinet', Meeting 14, 2 May 1917; ANZ, R15393166, 'Imperial War Conference — Minutes', p. 62.

118 Ollivier, *The Colonial and Imperial Conferences, Vol. 2*, pp. 208–9.

119 Ollivier, *The Colonial and Imperial Conferences, Vol. 2*, pp. 198–99.

120 Ollivier, *The Colonial and Imperial Conferences, Vol. 2*, p. 177.

121 Ollivier, *The Colonial and Imperial Conferences, Vol. 2*, p. 191. This point was also raised in the

New Zealand Parliament. See *NZPD*, Vol. 183, 1918, Addendum, p. 1073.

122 Ollivier, *The Colonial and Imperial Conferences, Vol. 2*, pp. 257–58; ANZ, R17378327, 'Imperial War Conference 1917 — Minutes of meetings 1–14, 20 March–2 May — Imperial War Cabinet', meeting 14, 2 May 1917.

123 Kay, 'In Pursuit of Victory', p. 169.

124 John Crawford, '"The Willing Horse is Being Worked to Death": New Zealand's Manpower Problems and Policies during 1917', in Douglas E. Delaney and Nikolas Gardner (eds), *Turning Point 1917: The British Empire at War* (Vancouver: University of British Columbia Press, 2017), p. 122.

125 Kay, 'In Pursuit of Victory', p. 183.

126 Quoted Governor Liverpool to Walter Long, in Crawford, '"The Willing Horse is Being Worked to Death"', p. 123.

127 ANZ, R3796200, 'Inwards and outwards despatches relating to the European War — 15 January–18 February 1917', Liverpool to Long, 15 February 1917.

128 *NZPD*, Vol. 178, 10 July 1917, pp. 257–58.

129 ANZ, R22319700, 'Ministerial Files — Correspondence with General Godley', Godley to Allen, 13 September 1917.

130 Crawford, '"The Willing Horse is Being Worked to Death"', p. 125.

131 Howard Weddell, *Trentham Camp and Upper Hutt's Untold Military History* (Upper Hutt: Howard Weddell, 2018), p. 106.

132 Weddell, *Trentham Camp*, pp. 75, 106, 56.

133 Orlando Figes, *A People's Tragedy: The Russian Revolution 1891–1924* (London: Pimlico, 1996), p. 327.

134 G. J. Meyer, *A World Undone: The Story of the Great War* (New York: Delta, 2006), pp. 516–21.

135 *New Zealand Observer*, 21 April 1917, p. 1.

136 *Sun*, 7 September 1917, p. 6; *New Zealand Herald*, 17 March 1917, p. 6. For further examples of the February Revolution being presented as redefining the war see *Auckland Star*, 17 March 1917, p. 6; *Hastings Standard*, 20 March 1917, p. 2; *Evening Star*, 17 March 1917, p. 5; *Evening Star*, 16 March 1917, p. 8; *Evening Post*, 20 March 1917, p. 6.

137 *Auckland Star*, 17 March 1917, p. 6.

138 *NZPD*, Vol. 179, 7 August 1917, p. 35.

139 *Colonist*, 29 March 1917, p. 3.

140 *New Zealand Herald*, 26 June 1917, p. 4.

141 ANZ, R22319675, 'Miscellanous files and papers — Correspondence between J Allen and WF Massey, 1st September 1916–1st August 1919 [Loose papers]', Allen to Massey, 8 November 1916. For a wider study of the issue see P. S. O'Connor, *Mr Massey and the American Meat Trust: Some Sidelights on the Origins of the Meat Board* (Palmerston North: Massey University, 1973).

142 Kay, 'In Pursuit of Victory', p. 221.

143 *Evening Post*, 21 July 1917, p. 3.

144 *NZPD*, Vol. 178, 3 July 1917, p. 57.

145 *New Zealand Herald*, 5 July 1917, p. 7.

CHAPTER TEN: CONSCRIPTION

1 It is noted that many, arguably the worst, of New Zealand's social upheavals reflected 'not the absolute demands of the war but the equitable sharing of sacrifices'. Steven Loveridge, 'Introduction: A Small Land in a World War', in Steven Loveridge (ed.), *New Zealand Society at War, 1914–1918* (Wellington: Victoria University Press, 2016), p. 31.

2 Richard S. Hill, *The Iron Hand in the Velvet Glove: The Modernisation of Policing in New Zealand, 1886–1917* (Palmerston North: Dunmore Press in association with the New Zealand Police and with the assistance of Historical Branch, Department of Internal Affairs, 1995), pp. 352–53; Paul Baker, *King and Country Call: New Zealanders, Conscription and the Great War* (Auckland: Auckland University Press, 1988), p. 109.

3 Erik Olssen, 'Waging War: The Home Front 1914–1918', in Judith Binney, Judith Bassett and Erik Olssen (eds), *The People and the Land: Te Tangata Me Te Whenua: An Illustrated History of New Zealand, 1820–1920* (Wellington: Allen & Unwin, 1990), p. 317.

4 Baker, *King and Country Call*, p. 109.

5 *NZ Truth*, 18 November 1916, p. 6.

6 *Appendix to the Journals of the House of Representatives* (*AJHR*), 1919, H-19, 'Defence Forces of New Zealand', p. 14.

7 Baker, *King and Country Call*, p. 111.

8 Archives New Zealand (ANZ), R22431244, 'Establishments and Recruitment — Enlistment — Return showing number from each district', Defence Headquarters Christchurch, 22 August 1916.

9 Defects included defective vision, defective intelligence, alcoholism, flat feet and dental problems. Lynette Callon, 'Fighting Fit?: A Study of the Army's Medical Examinations, 1916–1918' (BA Hons thesis, University of Otago, 1980), p. 79.

10 ANZ, R22431244, 'Establishments and Recruitment — Enlistment — Return showing number from each district', Defence Headquarters Christchurch, 22 August 1916.

11 *AJHR*, 1919, H-19, 'Recruits Examined by Military Medical Boards from Commencement of Ballot, November, 1916, To Conclusion of Ballot, November, 1918', p. 15.

12 Baker, *King and Country Call*, pp. 115–16.

13 *New Zealand Statutes*, 1916, No. 8, 'Military Service Act', sections 25–28, pp. 92–3.

14 David Littlewood, 'The Dutifully Reluctant:

New Zealanders' Appeals for Exemption from Conscription, 1916–1918', *New Zealand Journal of History*, Vol. 50, No. 2 (October 2016), pp. 26–43. The 4.76 per cent figure was 'almost certainly an overstatement' as it included individuals who entered appeals on multiple grounds, seemingly out of confusion, but who subsequently made no mention of conscientious objections during their hearings; Littlewood, 'The Dutifully Reluctant', p. 28.

15 Littlewood, 'The Dutifully Reluctant', pp. 30, 36; Alexander Turnbull Library (ATL), qMS-0683, Harrold Ennor Diaries.

16 ANZ, R22429092, 'Expeditionary Force — Recruiting organisation', appendix 6(3); David Littlewood, '"Willing and Eager to Go in Their Turn"? Appeals for Exemption from Military Service in New Zealand and Great Britain, 1916–1918', *War in History*, No. 21 (2014), pp. 338–54; David Littlewood, '"Should He Serve?" The Military Service Boards' Operation in the Wellington Provincial District, 1916–1918' (MA thesis, Massey University, 2010), pp. 60–61; ANZ, R22429092, 'Expeditionary Force — Recruiting organisation', appendix 6(3).

17 *New Zealand Official Year-book*, 1919, p. 257.

18 ANZ, R22319675, 'Miscellanous files and papers — Correspondence between J Allen and WF Massey, 1st September 1916–1st August 1919 [Loose papers]', Allen to Massey, 28 October 1916.

19 ANZ, R22319675, 'Miscellanous files and papers — Correspondence between J Allen and WF Massey, 1st September 1916–1st August 1919 [Loose papers]', Allen to Massey, 28 October 1916. The manifesto was printed in *Maoriland Worker*, 18 October 1916, p. 4.

20 *New Zealand Gazette*, 4 December 1916, p. 3752.

21 *New Zealand Gazette*, 4 December 1916, pp. 3751–53.

22 ANZ, R22319750, 'Ministerial Files — Labour — General file', W. S. MacDonald to Allen, 23 November 1916.

23 ANZ, R22319750, 'Ministerial Files — Labour — General file', Allen to W. H. Herries, 21 November 1916.

24 ANZ, R3794970, 'Confidential Outwards Despatches to the Secretary of State — 3 April–14 December 1916', Alexander Herdman to the Governor-General, Lord Liverpool, 10 June 1916.

25 ANZ, R22319675, 'Miscellanous files and papers — Correspondence between J Allen and WF Massey, 1st September 1916–1st August 1919 [Loose papers]', Allen to Massey, 30 December 1916.

26 *New Zealand Gazette*, 9 February 1917, pp. 535–37.

27 Barry Gustafson, *Labour's Path to Political Independence: The Origins and Establishment of the New Zealand Labour Party 1900–19* (Auckland: Auckland University Press, 1980), p. 114.

28 Melanie Nolan, *War and Class: The Diary of Jack McCullough* (Wellington: Dunmore Press, 2009), pp. 329–30.

29 ANZ, R22319750, 'Ministerial Files — Labour — General file', John Perkins to Allen, 12 December 1916.

30 *Maoriland Worker*, 13 September 1916, p. 3; 6 December 1916, p. 5.

31 *Star*, 18 November 1916, p. 5.

32 H. E. Holland, *Armageddon or Calvary: The Conscientious Objectors of New Zealand and 'The Process of Their Conversion'* (Wellington: The Maoriland Worker Printing and Publishing Co. Ltd, 1919), p. 14.

33 *Maoriland Worker*, 3 January 1917, p. 3.

34 Baker, *King and Country Call*, p. 159.

35 *1916 Sedition Trials: Robert Semple, Fred. R. Cooke, James Thorn, Peter Fraser and Tom Brindle* (Wellington: Maoriland Worker Printing and Publishing Co. Ltd, 1917), p. 5.

36 Michael Bassett with Michael King, *Tomorrow Comes the Song: A Life of Peter Fraser* (Auckland: Penguin, 2000), p. 72.

37 ANZ, R22319675, 'Miscellanous files and papers — Correspondence between J Allen and WF Massey, 1st September 1916–1st August 1919 [Loose papers]', Allen to Massey, 7 December 1916.

38 *1916 Sedition Trials.*

39 Holland, *Armageddon or Calvary*, p. 14.

40 *Ohinemuri Gazette*, 20 December 1916, p. 2; Bassett with King, *Tomorrow Comes the Song*, p. 73; *Maoriland Worker*, 17 January 1917, p. 4.

41 ANZ, R22319675, 'Miscellanous files and papers — Correspondence between J Allen and WF Massey, 1st September 1916–1st August 1919 [Loose papers]', Allen to Massey, 30 December 1916.

42 ANZ, R22319750, 'Ministerial Files — Labour — General file', Arbuckle to Allen, 12 December 1916.

43 ANZ, R22319750, 'Ministerial Files — Labour — General file', Webb to Allen, 13 December 1916.

44 Baker, *King and Country Call*, p. 169. In November 1916, the inspector of factories at Westport doubted that workers in his area, known for its militancy and the production of particularly valuable coal, would strike: 'The Miners here are quiet and do not seem to have any sympathy with the Newcastle Miners. They have no funds and moreover the majority are married with large families and naturally they have no thought of ceasing work. There are a few who are inclined that way but a very small proportion. The Watersiders with a large majority (so the Secretary who is a personal friend informs me) would not cease work no matter if the Federation does instruct them to do so.' ANZ, R22319750, 'Ministerial Files — Labour — General file', T. Fairhall to Chief Inspector of Factories, 9 November 1916.

45 Leicester Chisholm Webb, 'The Rise of the

Reform Party: A History of Party Politics in New Zealand Between 1910 and 1920' (Honours thesis, University of New Zealand, 1928), pp. 166–67; Len Richardson, *Coal, Class & Community: The United Mineworkers of New Zealand, 1880–1960* (Auckland: Auckland University Press, 1995), pp. 170–71; *Go-slow: Policy in the Mines* (Wellington: New Zealand Times Co., Printers, 1917), p. 4; *Evening Post*, 23 April 1917, pp. 7–8.

46 ANZ, R22319675, 'Miscellanous files and papers — Correspondence between J Allen and WF Massey, 1st September 1916–1st August 1919 [Loose papers]', Massey to Allen, 2 January 1917. Some analysis has considered it fortunate that Massey was out of the country in that Allen and MacDonald were able to better manage industrial relations. John Anderson, 'Military Censorship in World War I: Its Use and Abuse in New Zealand' (MA thesis, Victoria College, Wellington, 1952), p. 276; Tristan Egarr, 'The Dominion State at War' (MA thesis, Victoria University of Wellington, 2018), p. 193.

47 James Holt, *Compulsory Arbitration in New Zealand: The First Forty Years* (Auckland: Auckland University Press, 1986), p. 130.

48 Baker, *King and Country Call*, pp. 160–61.

49 Len Richardson, 'Politics and War: Coal Miners and Conscription, 1914–18', in P. R. May (ed.), *Miners and Militants: Politics in Westland, 1865–1918* (Christchurch: University of Canterbury, 1975), p. 140.

50 Richardson, 'Politics and War', p. 141.

51 ANZ, R22319675, 'Miscellanous files and papers — Correspondence between J Allen and WF Massey, 1st September 1916–1st August 1919 [Loose papers]', Allen to Massey, 26 April 1917.

52 Richardson, 'Politics and War', p. 144.

53 Dan Sullivan, who would head the Labour poll by some distance, was anxious to stress that opposing conscription did not mean Labour was 'disloyal'. 'The charge of disloyalty being made against the Labour party is surely not an honest election cry. [Labour] Cr Herbert might declare from the platform that he has given his only son to the war: that his wife has worked for the Red Cross. Substituting the word brother for son, and the present writer might make a similar claim, and show a family record equal to that of his critics.' *Sun*, 21 April 1917, p. 12.

54 *Maoriland Worker*, 9 May 1917, p. 4.

55 Steven Loveridge and James Watson, 'Economic Mobilisation: New Zealand Businesses and the Great War', in Loveridge (ed.), *New Zealand Society at War*, p. 168; *New Zealand Observer*, 28 April 1917, p. 22; Richardson, 'Politics and War', p. 134.

56 *Sun*, 1 May 1917, p. 3.

57 *New Zealand Herald*, 23 April 1917, p. 4.

58 Bruce Brown, *The Rise of New Zealand Labour: A History of the New Zealand Labour Party from 1916 to 1940* (Wellington: Price Milburn, 1962), pp. 28–29.

59 *Maoriland Worker*, 9 May 1917, p. 7.

60 Peter Franks and Jim McAloon, *Labour: The New Zealand Labour Party, 1916–2016* (Wellington: Victoria University Press, 2016), p. 72.

61 *Wanganui Chronicle*, 27 April 1917, p. 4.

62 *Maoriland Worker*, 9 May 1917, p. 7.

63 Langley maintained that to win the election Labour must cease campaigning to repeal the Military Service Act and instead concentrate on demanding 'conscription of wealth' as well as conscription of men: 'Win the war first shall be Labour's motto. It should be remembered that the people are greatly annoyed with another nation, and until the victory is won and they are pacified it would be madness to oppose their wishes . . . Platform: Support full Conscription, meaning that everything essential to victory, life, wealth, in fact everything in the Banks [sic] of New Zealand should be confiscated by the Government. Agitate against exploitation as bitterly as possible. Demand that all previous war profits be handed over to the authorities. Get into the stump and preach it, and when all the turmoil is over Labour would verily receive its reward by acclamation as would be proved by the first elections held.' *Sun*, 5 May 1917, p. 12.

64 Holland, *Armageddon or Calvary*, p. 14.

65 *New Zealand Herald*, 6 June 1917, p. 6.

66 Richardson, 'Politics and War', p. 145.

67 Harry R. Urquhart, *Men and Marbles* (Auckland: H. R. Urquhart, 1917).

68 *Auckland Star*, 30 April 1917, p. 6; *New Zealand Christian Pacifist*, February 1964, p. 5.

69 ANZ, R22434535, 'Publications, instructions, etc. — Publication "Put up the Sword" Miss Pankhurst'.

70 ANZ, R22430468, 'Administration and Miscellaneous — Censorship — Regulations postal', Report on the Postal Censorship, 30 September 1917.

71 Holland, *Armageddon or Calvary*, p. 5.

72 Baker, *King and Country Call*, p. 171.

73 *Evening Post*, 13 April 1917, p. 8; ANZ, R3885385, 'Censorship of correspondence, T Brosnan to Mrs M McCarthy April–December', 8 May 1918; ANZ, R22429752, 'Territorial Force — Exemptions — Religious objectors NZEF [New Zealand Expeditionary Force]', Officer Commanding District [Auckland] to the Director of Personal Services, 23 November 1917.

74 Holland, *Armageddon or Calvary*, pp. 54–55.

75 *New Zealand Statutes*, 1916, No. 8, 'Military Service Act', section 18(1)e, p. 90; Peter Ballis, 'Seventh-day Adventists in New Zealand Politics, 1886–1918', Peter Ballis (ed.), *IN and OUT of the WORLD: Seventh-day Adventists in New Zealand*, (Palmerston North: Dunmore Press, 1985), pp. 69–70.

76 P. S. O'Connor, 'The Awkward Ones — Dealing with Conscience, 1916–1918', *New Zealand Journal of History*, Vol. 8, No. 2 (October 1974), p. 123; Baker, *King and Country Call*, p. 174.

77 Archibald Baxter, *We Will Not Cease* (Auckland: Cape Catley, 2003), pp. 21–22. For an objector's experiences of jail conditions see pp. 34–64.

78 Baker, *King and Country Call*, p. 204; Seán Brosnahan, '"Shaming the Shoneens": The Green Ray and the Maoriland Irish Society in Dunedin, 1916–1922', in Lyndon Fraser (ed.), *A Distant Shore: Irish Migration and New Zealand Settlement* (Dunedin: Otago University Press, 2000), pp. 126–27.

79 *New Zealand Herald*, 8 March 1918, p. 4; Imelda Bargas and Tim Shoebridge, *New Zealand's First World War Heritage* (Auckland: Exisle Publishing, 2015), p. 34; Ann Beaglehole with Alison Carew, *Eastbourne: A History of the Eastern Bays of Wellington Harbour* (Eastbourne: Historical Society of Eastbourne, 2001), p. 101.

80 ANZ, R22430682, 'Personnel — Deserters tracing of', Wilford to Allen, 2 May 1918; Baker, *King and Country Call*, p. 203; *Marlborough Express*, 24 June 1918, p. 2.

81 ANZ, R22319675, 'Miscellanous files and papers — Correspondence between J Allen and WF Massey, 1st September 1916–1st August 1919 [Loose papers]', Allen to Massey, 27 February 1917.

82 *New Zealand Parliamentary Debates* (*NZPD*), Vol. 183, 17 September 1917, pp. 175–76.

83 Baker, *King and Country Call*, p. 208.

84 ANZ, R22429752, 'Territorial Force — Exemptions — Religious objectors NZEF [New Zealand Expeditionary Force]', Memorandum for Major Lilley, 23 November 1917; https://nzhistory.govt.nz/war/the-military-objectors-list. Another study has suggested a significantly higher figure, noting 'at least 670 objectors' were imprisoned in New Zealand. This figure goes beyond those imprisoned for refusing to serve under the terms of the Military Service Act and includes, for example, those convicted for seditious remarks within the category of 'objector'. See Jared Davidson, *Dead Letters: Censorship and Subversion in New Zealand 1914–1920* (Dunedin: Otago University Press, 2019), p. 110. The methodology behind Davidson's revised figure is available at http://blog.tepapa.govt.nz/2016/06/28/dissent-during-the-first-world-war-by-the-numbers/.

85 *AJHR*, 1919, H-20, 'Prisoners (Report on) for the year 1918–19', p. 1.

86 *Evening Post*, 28 April 1917, p. 5; *NZPD*, Vol. 181, 25 October 1917, p. 497.

87 *New Zealand Herald*, 10 June 1918, p. 4; ANZ, R22429779, 'Territorial Force — Registration — Families more than one — Auckland'.

88 Baker, *King and Country Call*, pp. 207–8; *Evening Post*, 8 April 1918, p. 8; *New Zealand Herald*, 9 October 1917, p. 4.

89 Baker, *King and Country Call*, p. 208.

90 ANZ, R22429773, 'Territorial Force — Employment of religious objectors on State farms', Statement, p. 1.

91 O'Connor, 'The Awkward Ones', p. 129.

92 ANZ, R22429764, 'Territorial Force — Exemptions — Religious objectors NZEF [New Zealand Expeditionary Force]', Such to Allen, 24 June 1916; Allen to Such, 28 June 1916.

93 ANZ, R22319706, 'Miscellanous files and papers — Miscellaneous correspondence and papers [Loose papers]', Allen to T. H. Sprott, 6 March 1918.

94 ANZ, R22429764, 'Territorial Force — Exemptions — Religious objectors NZEF [New Zealand Expeditionary Force]', Military Service Act 1916, Religious Objectors, 1 March 1917.

95 A. H. Reed, *An Autobiography* (Wellington: Reed, 1967), pp. 177–78.

96 ANZ, R22429752, 'Territorial Force — Exemptions — Religious objectors NZEF [New Zealand Expeditionary Force]', Chief of the General Staff to Adjutant-General, 9 August 1917.

97 ANZ, R22429764, 'Territorial Force — Exemptions — Religious objectors NZEF [New Zealand Expeditionary Force]', Military Service Act 1916, Religious Objectors, 1 March 1917.

98 ANZ, R22429764, 'Territorial Force — Exemptions — Religious objectors NZEF [New Zealand Expeditionary Force]', Salmond to Tate, 13 March 1917.

99 *New Zealand Gazette*, 24 April 1917, p. 1399.

100 *Timaru Herald*, 22 February 1917, p. 11. For further examples see *New Zealand Tablet*, 15 March 1917, p. 27; 8 March 1917, p. 42; 24 May 1917, p. 26.

101 *New Zealand Tablet*, 7 December 1916, p. 21.

102 *Evening Post*, 27 February 1917, p. 8.

103 *NZ Truth*, 10 March 1917, p. 5.

104 *Wanganui Herald*, 18 July 1917, p. 8.

105 P. S. O'Connor, 'Storm Over the Clergy — New Zealand 1917', *Journal of Religious History*, Vol. 4, No. 2 (December 1966), p. 130.

106 *New Zealand Herald*, 28 February 1917, p. 11.

107 *New Zealand Tablet*, 7 December 1916, p. 21.

108 ANZ, R10075075, 'Roman Catholic priests and Marist Brothers, November 1916–July 1918', O'Shea to Allen, 17 February 1917.

109 O'Connor, 'Storm Over the Clergy', p. 132.

110 *New Zealand Tablet*, 8 March 1917, p. 33; *Evening Post*, 1 March 1917, p. 8.

111 *New Zealand Tablet*, 1 March 1917, p. 34.

112 For details of the men behind the *Green Ray* see H. S. Moores, 'The Rise of the Protestant Political Association: Sectarianism in New Zealand Politics during World War I' (MA thesis, University of

Auckland, 1966), pp. 62–63.

113 *Green Ray*, 1 May 1918, p. 105.

114 Rory Sweetman, 'New Zealand Catholicism, War, Politics and the Irish Issue 1912–1922' (PhD thesis, University of Cambridge, 1990), pp. 145, 157.

115 *New Zealand Tablet*, 26 April 1917, p. 22; 15 November 1917, p. 26; 1 November 1917, p. 13.

116 *New Zealand Tablet*, 5 July 1917, pp. 11, 17.

117 *New Zealand Herald*, 27 February 1917, p. 4.

118 *New Zealand Herald*, 1 March 1917, p. 6; *Auckland Star*, 1 March 1917, p. 4; Moores, 'The Rise of the Protestant Political Association', pp. 155–56.

119 Salmond advised against a prosecution of Elliott in which the Crown would have to prove that the hostility and ill-will caused by his speeches was a danger to public safety in respect of the present war. Sweetman, 'New Zealand Catholicism', p. 136.

120 ANZ, R22429828, 'Territorial Force — Exemption — Reservists under Military Service Act', 27 April 1917.

121 ANZ, R22319675, 'Miscellanous files and papers — Correspondence between J Allen and WF Massey, 1st September 1916–1st August 1919 [Loose papers]', Allen to Massey, 28 April 1917.

122 *New Zealand Herald*, 12 July 1917, p. 6.

123 *New Zealand Herald*, 12 July 1917, p. 6; *AJHR*, 1917, H-19D, 'New Zealand Expeditionary Forces', p. 1.

124 *New Zealand Herald*, 12 July 1917, p. 6; *Dominion*, 12 July 1917, p. 5. *NZPD*, Vol. 180, 13 September 1917, p. 108 covers the texts of some of these letters.

125 *New Zealand Herald*, 12 July 1917, p. 6.

126 Sweetman, 'New Zealand Catholicism', p. 138.

127 Sweetman, 'New Zealand Catholicism', p. 138.

128 *New Zealand Herald*, 10 January 1917, p. 6. *NZ Truth*, 31 March 1917, p. 5.

129 ANZ, R22436341, 'Conscription — Medical examination of members of 2nd Division', A. L. Herdman to Joseph and Nathan, 2 February 1917.

130 *New Zealand Herald*, 4 May 1918, p. 6.

131 At the end of November 1916 it declared under the heading of 'a duty to the soldier' that '[t]he country cannot fairly expect that a man upon whom it lays its hand under the Military Service Act shall sacrifice all his civil interests. It must accept the onus of making some provision to enable him to safeguard those interests.' *Otago Daily Times*, 22 November 1916, p. 4. The editorial was largely reprinted in *West Coast Times*, 25 November 1916, p. 2. See also *Nelson Evening Mail*, 25 November 1916, p. 4.

132 *Evening Star*, 20 February 1917, p. 2.

133 Graham Hucker, 'When the Empire Calls: Patriotic Organisations in New Zealand during the Great War' (MA thesis, Massey University, 1979), p. 47; *New Zealand Herald*, 11 July 1917, p. 8; *Otago Daily Times*, 20 April 1917, p. 7; *Proceedings of the Second Division League Conference Wellington, July 18–20, 1917* (New Plymouth: Taranaki Daily News Print, 1917), pp. 1–2.

134 ANZ, R22319700, 'Ministerial Files — Correspondence with General Godley', Allen to Godley, 23 July 1917.

135 *Evening Star*, 20 February 1917, p. 2.

136 *Proceedings of the Second Division League Conference*, pp. 5, 28.

137 *Maoriland Worker*, 27 June 1917, p. 3.

138 *New Zealand Herald*, 28 February 1917, p. 8.

139 *Evening Star*, 28 February 1917, p. 4.

140 *New Zealand Free Lance*, 18 May 1917, p. 3.

141 *Evening Star*, 28 February 1917, p. 4.

142 *NZPD*, Vol. 178, 20 July 1917, p. 635.

143 *Proceedings of the Second Division League Conference.*

144 ANZ, R22436341, 'Conscription — Medical Examination of Members of 2nd Division', correspondence from A. L. Herdman to Joseph and Nathan, 2 February 1917.

145 ANZ, R22319675, 'Miscellanous [sic] Files and Papers — Correspondence Between J. Allen and W. F. Massey, 1st September 1916–1st August 1919 [loose papers]', Allen to Massey, 7 May 1917; *Proceedings of the Second Division League Conference*, p. 2.

146 *New Zealand Herald*, 20 March 1917, p. 4; ANZ, R22436353, 'Conscription — Ballot — Second Division — Arrangements', memorandum for the Minister of Defence, 21 December 1917.

147 ANZ, R22429828, 'Territorial Force — Exemption — Reservists under Military Service Act', Memorandum for James Allen, 20 May 1918; *New Zealand Herald*, 6 August 1917, p. 4.

148 Lieut-Colonel J. L. Sleeman, 'The Supply of Reinforcements during the War', in H. T. B. Drew (ed.), *The War Effort of New Zealand* (Auckland: Whitcombe & Tombs Limited, 1923), p. 17.

149 ANZ, R22436341, 'Conscription — Medical Examination of Members of 2nd Division', A. L. Herdman to Joseph and Nathan, 2 February 1917; ANZ, R10075043, '2nd Division — General, February–September 1917'.

150 A selection of protest letters is collected with the defence file ANZ, R22433708, 'Establishments and Recruitment — Ages — Recruits for Expeditionary Force'.

151 *Evening Post*, 10 August 1917, p. 7.

152 *Maoriland Worker*, 18 July 1917, p. 1.

153 ANZ, R22433708, 'Establishments and Recruitment — Ages — Recruits for Expeditionary Force', Memorandum, 12 September 1917.

154 *Evening Post*, 4 July 1917, p. 7.

155 Monty Soutar, 'The Maori War Effort at Home and Abroad in 1917', in Maartje Abbenhuis, Neill Atkinson, Kingsley Baird and Gail Romano (eds), *The Myriad Legacies of 1917: A Year of War and*

Revolution (Cham: Palgrave Macmillan, 2018), p. 58.

156 Soutar, 'The Maori War Effort at Home and Abroad in 1917', p. 58.

157 Soutar, 'The Maori War Effort at Home and Abroad in 1917', pp. 59–61, 64–7.

158 *New Zealand Official Year-book*, 1919, p. 257; *New Zealand Official Year-book*, 1925, pp. 77, 105; Athol Anderson, Judith Binney and Aroha Harris, *Tangata Whenua: An Illustrated History* (Wellington: Bridget Williams Books, 2015), p. 301.

159 ANZ, R22429807, 'Territorial Force — Registration — Maoris and half-castes', Memorandum for the Commandant, 31 October 1916.

160 *Auckland Star*, 25 November 1916, p. 10.

161 ATL, MS-Papers-6919-0234, '040 — Papers re Maori in the Second World War'.

162 ANZ, R24048326, '[Correspondence between] General Sir Alexander Godley [Commander New Zealand Expeditionary Force] and Colonel Hon. [Honourable] Sir James Allen, Minister of Defence, 4 January–29 December 1916', Allen to Godley, 19 December 1916.

163 ANZ, R22436335, 'Conscription — Maoris under Military Service Act — Correspondence', Allen to Herdman, 9 March 1917.

164 ANZ, R10075086, 'General file, June 1917–October 1918', petition, 5 August 1918.

165 Interestingly, some Māori in Taranaki had been suspicious of the census in 1901, asking the local enumerator 'whether Government wished to ascertain their numbers, with a view of sending them against the Boers, or otherwise deporting them'. *AJHR*, 1901, H-26B, 'Census of The Maori Population', p. 14. The authors are indebted to Nigel Robson for this detail.

166 ANZ, R10075085, 'General file, March 1917–April 1918', J. D. Gray to James Allen, 23 May 1917.

167 ANZ, R18874766, 'Military Service Act, 1916 — Enrolling Maori Expeditionary Force Reserve'.

168 ANZ, R10075086, 'General file, June 1917–October 1918', Allen to Liverpool, 22 June 1917; *New Zealand Gazette*, 26 June 1917, pp. 2509–10.

CHAPTER ELEVEN: NADIR

1 *Clutha Leader*, 13 July 1917, p. 7.

2 *New Zealand Times*, 7 August 1917, p. 6. See also *Otago Daily Times*, 20 August 1917, p. 5.

3 Ian McGibbon, *New Zealand's Western Front Campaign* (Auckland: Bateman, 2016), p. 115.

4 *Poverty Bay Herald*, 8 June 1917, p. 6; *Manawatu Standard*, 11 June 1917, p. 5; Archives New Zealand (ANZ), R24048327, '[Correspondence between] General Sir Alexander Godley [Commander New Zealand Expeditionary Force] and Colonel Hon. [Honourable] Sir James Allen, Minister of Defence, 6 January–28 December 1917', Godley to Allen, 11 June 1917. A similarly laudatory letter from General Birdwood was widely published. *Taranaki Herald*, 19 September 1917, p. 2.

5 Alexander Turnbull Library (ATL), MS-Papers -0113-01/20, W. H. Field to Field, 18 September 1917.

6 Glyn Harper, 'New Zealand and "the Catastrophic Year 1917", in Maartje Abbenhuis, Neill Atkinson, Kingsley Baird and Gail Romano (eds), *The Myriad Legacies of 1917: A Year of War and Revolution* (Cham: Palgrave Macmillan, 2018), p. 194.

7 P. J. O'Farrell, *Harry Holland: Militant Socialist* (Canberra: Australian National University, 1964), p. 76; Bruce Brown, *The Rise of New Zealand Labour: A History of the New Zealand Labour Party from 1916 to 1940* (Wellington: Price Milburn, 1962), p. 109. The conference report is available at *Maoriland Worker*, 18 July 1917, pp. 3, 5; *Maoriland Worker*, 23 January 1918, p. 4.

8 *New Zealand Tablet*, 23 August 1917, pp. 25–26; 20 September 1917, p. 15.

9 Douglas Newton, 'The Lansdowne "Peace Letter" of 1917 and the Prospect of a Peace by Negotiation with Germany', *Australian Journal of Politics and History*, Vol. 48, No. 1 (2002), pp. 16–39.

10 *Wanganui Herald*, 21 December 1917, p. 9; *Grey River Argus*, 6 December 1917, p. 2.

11 *New Zealand Parliamentary Debates* (*NZPD*), Vol. 178, 10 July 1917, p. 239.

12 *Northern Advocate*, 14 June 1917, p. 3; *Evening Star*, 6 June 1917, p. 6.

13 *NZPD*, Vol. 178, 6 July 1917, p. 213; 12 July 1917, pp. 315–17.

14 *NZPD*, Vol. 178, 6 July 1917, p. 221.

15 *NZPD*, Vol. 178, 3 July 1917, p. 76.

16 *Evening Post*, 9 July 1917, p. 6.

17 *NZPD*, Vol. 178, 13 July 1917, p. 378; 3 July 1917, pp. 67–68.

18 *New Zealand Herald*, 26 June 1917, p. 4.

19 *Evening Post*, 11 July 1917, p. 3; *North Otago Times*, 22 June 1917, p. 8.

20 *New Zealand Herald*, 14 June 1917, p. 6.

21 His biographer claims this might be considered to be one of the greatest speeches of his career. William Downie Stewart, *The Right Honourable Sir Francis H. D. Bell, P.C., G.C.M.G., K.C.: His Life and Times* (Wellington: Butterworth & Co. Ltd, 1937), p. 146.

22 *NZPD*, Vol. 178, 12 July 1917, pp. 332–34.

23 ANZ, R3796204, 'Inwards and outwards despatches relating to the European War — 14 July–3 September 1917', Liverpool to Long, 17 July 1917.

24 ANZ, R21078971, 'New Zealand Expeditionary Force, its provision and maintenance', p. 8.

25 *NZPD*, Vol. 179, 21 August 1917, pp. 456–57.

26 *New Zealand Herald*, 8 August 1917, p. 6; Christopher Pugsley, *On the Fringes of Hell: New Zealanders and Military Discipline in the First World War* (Auckland: Hodder & Stoughton, 1991), p. 254.

27 *New Zealand Herald*, 26 September 1917, p. 6.

28 ANZ, R22319700, 'Ministerial Files — Correspondence with General Godley', Allen to Godley, 11 October 1917.

29 ANZ, R22319700, 'Ministerial Files — Correspondence with General Godley', Allen to Godley, 11 October 1917.

30 *New Zealand Herald*, 15 October 1917, p. 5.

31 McGibbon, *New Zealand's Western Front Campaign*, pp. 86, 142. https://ww100.govt.nz/passchendaele-casualties.

32 Points of comparison include the 1931 Hawke's Bay earthquake, which killed 256, and the 1979 Mount Erebus disaster, in which 257 died.

33 For further details on the reporting of Passchendaele see Jock Phillips, 'Passchendaele: Remembering and Forgetting in New Zealand', in Abbenhuis, Atkinson, Baird and Romano (eds), *The Myriad Legacies of 1917*, pp. 245–67.

34 *Dominion*, 6 October 1917, p. 7; *New Zealand Herald*, 6 October 1917, p. 8; *New Zealand Herald*, 20 October 1917, p. 7.

35 *Wairarapa Daily Times*, 4 October 1917, p. 5; *Te Puke Times*, 5 October 1917, p. 3.

36 *Evening Post*, 9 October 1917, p. 7; *New Zealand Herald*, 8 October 1917, p. 5.

37 *Press*, 9 October 1917, p. 6.

38 *New Zealand Herald*, 20 October 1917, p. 7.

39 *Evening Post*, 16 October 1917, p. 8; *New Zealand Herald*, 27 October 1917, p. 6.

40 *Press*, 15 October 1917, p. 7; *Evening Post*, 17 October 1917, p. 6; *Mataura Ensign*, 19 October 1917, p. 4.

41 ANZ, R22319674, 'Miscellanous files and papers — Correspondence with Colonels Birdwood and Russell, December 1914–April 1920 and copies of personal letters, 1920 [Loose papers]', Russell to Allen, 7 November 1917.

42 ATL, MS-Papers-5507-15, Annis Bracken Hamerton to Frances Hamerton, 21 October 1917, Hirst Family Letters.

43 *NZPD*, Vol. 181, 1 November 1917, p. 745.

44 Paul Baker, *King and Country Call: New Zealanders, Conscription and the Great War* (Auckland: Auckland University Press, 1988), p. 136.

45 ANZ, R24048328, '[Correspondence between] General Sir Alexander Godley [Commander New Zealand Expeditionary Force] and Colonel Hon. [Honourable] Sir James Allen, Minister of Defence, 6 January 1918–28 January 1920', Allen to Godley, 7 January 1918; ANZ, R22319674, 'Miscellanous files and papers — Correspondence with Colonels Birdwood and Russell, December 1914–April 1920 and copies of personal letters, 1920 [Loose papers]', Allen Papers, Allen to Russell, 29 January 1918.

46 ANZ, R21078971, 'New Zealand Expeditionary Force, its provision and maintenance', p. 8.

47 *NZPD*, Vol. 178, 3 July 1917, pp. 69–70.

48 ANZ, R3796204, 'Inwards and outwards despatches relating to the European War — 14 July–3 September 1917', Long to Liverpool, 18 July 1917.

49 *New Zealand Official Year-book*, 1923, p. 219; *Appendix to the Journals of the House of Representatives* (*AJHR*), 1919, H-38, 'Department of Imperial Government Supplies', p. 13.

50 *Mataura Ensign*, 12 November 1917, p. 2.

51 *Evening Post*, 11 October 1917, p. 4; *Evening Post*, 27 October 1917, p. 8; *Evening Post*, 27 February 1918, p. 10; *Evening Post*, 13 June 1918, p. 4; Alan Everton, 'Government Intervention in the New Zealand Economy 1914–1918: Its Aims and Effectiveness' (MA thesis, Victoria University of Wellington, 1995), p. 191.

52 *AJHR*, 1918, H-38, 'Department of Imperial Government Supplies', p. 18.

53 *AJHR*, 1919, H-24, 'Munitions and Supplies Department: Report by Minister in Charge; also, Report on Activities of Coal-control Department', p. 3.

54 *Maoriland Worker*, 31 October 1917, p. 3.

55 *Star*, 9 July 1917, p. 8.

56 *Evening Post*, 30 October 1917, p. 3.

57 *NZPD*, Vol. 177, 2 August 1916, p. 629.

58 *NZPD*, Vol. 181, 15 October 1917, p. 161.

59 *Evening Post*, 18 October 1917, p. 3.

60 *New Zealand Statutes*, 1917, No. 9, 'Finance', pp. 24–58. *Evening Post*, 2 August 1917, p. 8.

61 *New Zealand* Herald, 2 August 1917, p. 6.

62 *Otago Daily Times*, 14 November 1917, p. 4. The editorial was quoted in other newspapers. See, for example, *Wairarapa Daily Times*, 17 November 1917, p. 4; *Hawera and Normanby Star*, 21 November 1917, p. 4; *Wairarapa Age*, 24 November 1917, p. 4; *Colonist*, 26 November 1917, p. 2.

63 *Press*, 2 August 1917, p. 6.

64 *Otago Daily Times*, 2 August 1917, p. 4.

65 *Star*, 2 August 1917, p. 4.

66 *Ashburton Guardian*, 7 August 1917, p. 7; *Press*, 8 August 1917, p. 7.

67 *Star*, 3 August 1917, p. 4.

68 *Sun*, 2 August 1917, p. 6.

69 *Sun*, 2 August 1917, p. 6.

70 *New Zealand Statutes*, 1917, No. 9, 'Finance', pp. 24–58. For further details, see Justin Thomas Strang, 'Welfare in Transition: Reform's Income Support Policy, 1912–1928' (MA thesis, Victoria University of Wellington, 1992), p. 58.

71 *New Zealand Gazette*, 10 September 1917, pp. 3535–36; 22 December 1917, pp. 4609–10.

72 *New Zealand Statutes*, 1917, No. 28, 'Statute Law Amendment', pp. 227–28.

73 The regions were Auckland province, Canterbury province and an area comprising Wellington,

Taranaki, Hawke's Bay and Marlborough provinces along with part of Nelson province. *New Zealand Gazette*, 4 October 1917, pp. 3841–42.

74 *New Zealand Statutes*, 1917, No. 19, 'Sale of Liquor Restriction', p. 94.

75 *NZ Truth*, 3 November 1917, p. 1.

76 *NZPD*, Vol. 180, 4 October 1917, pp. 633–59.

77 While in England 13.4 per cent of New Zealand troops are reckoned to have contracted VD. In response, the social reform campaigner Ettie Rout advocated the issuing of prophylactic kits, arguing that VD should be regarded as a medical, rather than a moral, problem. Although this view was unconventional, her efforts won some quiet supporters among officials such as Russell and Allen, who arranged for Rout to prepare prophylactic kits to be given to New Zealand soldiers. This provision was undisclosed: Parliament, and seemingly Massey, were left in the dark. ANZ, R22319674, 'Miscellanous files and papers — Correspondence with Colonels Birdwood and Russell, December 1914–April 1920 and copies of personal letters, 1920 [Loose papers]', Russell to Allen, 17 May 1918; ANZ, R24048328, '[Correspondence between] General Sir Alexander Godley [Commander New Zealand Expeditionary Force] and Colonel Hon. [Honourable] Sir James Allen, Minister of Defence, 6 January 1918–28 January 1920', Allen to Russell, 28 February 1918; Jane Tolerton, *Ettie: A Life of Ettie Rout* (Auckland: Penguin, 1992).

78 *Evening Post*, 27 September 1917, p. 6.

79 *Evening Post*, 27 September 1917, p. 6. For further commentary see *Southland Times*, 28 September 1917, p. 4; *New Zealand Herald*, 27 September 1917, p. 4; *Sun*, 27 September 1917, p. 4.

80 *New Zealand Observer*, 6 October 1917, p. 12.

81 *Dominion*, 28 September 1917, p. 7.

82 *Ashburton Guardian*, 17 October 1917, p. 5.

83 *New Zealand Herald*, 1 October 1917, p. 4.

84 *Taranaki Daily News*, 25 September 1917, p. 4.

85 P. S. O'Connor, 'Storm Over the Clergy — New Zealand 1917', *Journal of Religious History*, Vol. 4, No. 2 (December 1966), p. 146.

86 *New Zealand Herald*, 21 February 1918, p. 4.

87 *NZ Truth*, 16 February 1918, p. 6.

88 *Press*, 5 February 1918, p. 7.

89 *Press*, 3 May 1918, p. 6.

90 *NZ Truth*, 4 May 1918, p. 5.

91 *NZ Truth*, 4 May 1918, p. 5; *Press*, 29 April 1918, p. 7.

92 ANZ, R10075085, 'General file, March 1917 — April 1918', Tau Henare to Allen, 19 February 1918, and Allen to Tau Henare, 19 February 1918; ANZ, R10075085, 'General file, March 1917–April 1918', Gerard to Allen, 18 February and (date missing) February 1918.

93 *New Zealand Gazette*, 24 July 1917, p. 2963.

94 ANZ, R18874766, 'Military Service Act, 1916 — Enrolling Maori Expeditionary Force Reserve', report from Blenheim police station, 15 February 1918.

95 ANZ, R18874766, 'Military Service Act, 1916 — Enrolling Maori Expeditionary Force Reserve', Pōmare to Allen, 19 February 1918.

96 *New Zealand Observer*, 3 February 1917, p. 16.

97 ANZ, R18874766, 'Military Service Act, 1916 — Enrolling Maori Expeditionary Force Reserve', report from Hāwera police station, 8 February 1918.

98 ANZ, R18874766, 'Military Service Act, 1916 — Enrolling Maori Expeditionary Force Reserve', Report of Constable Doyle, 2 May 1918.

99 ANZ, R18874768, 'Military Service Act, 1916 — Military Service registration and calling up of Maoris in Waikato-Maniapoto district', the Commissioner of Police to the Government Statistician, 7 April 1918.

100 P. S. O'Connor, 'The Recruitment of Maori Soldiers, 1914–18', *Political Science*, Vol. 19, Issue 2 (December 1967), p. 69. In February 1918 another message from Arawa proclaimed conspicuous compliance with registration: 'In view of the reported objections from South Island Waikatoa [sic] and North Auckland to conscription we desire to inform you that Arawas are registering without a murmur being fully determined to fulfill [sic] every requirement of the National Government so that the maximum effort shall be maintained in reinforcing those gallant lads who have and are shedding their sacred blood for the good and freedom of all races.' As with the Second Division League, compliance came with expectations about concessions regarding the dependants of enlisted men and the message noted: 'A large meeting of Arawas takes place tomorrow for purpose of submitting certain proposals affecting dependents [sic] of Maori soldiers when honoured by direct call of their King under the Act.' ANZ, R10075085, 'General file, March 1917–April 1918', Henare Mete Amohau to Allen, 22 February 1918.

101 ANZ, R10075085, 'General file, March 1917–April 1918', Parata to Allen, 13 February 1918.

102 ANZ, R10075085, 'General file, March 1917–April 1918', Note by Gray on Memo Allen to Pōmare, 28 January 1918.

103 ANZ, R10075085, 'General file, March 1917–April 1918', Allen to Parata, 13 February 1918.

104 ANZ, R10075085, 'General file, March 1917–April 1918', Kawiti to Allen, 7 February 1918.

105 O'Connor, 'The Recruitment of Maori Soldiers', p. 70.

106 ANZ, R10075085, 'General file, March 1917–April 1918', Allen to Henare, 7, 8 February 1918.

107 ANZ, R10075085, 'General file, March 1917–April 1918', Tawhai to Allen, 15 February 1918 (translation).

108 ANZ, R10075085, 'General file, March 1917–April 1918', Massey to Allen, 16 February 1918. The precise sequence of telegrams cannot be determined as not all have time stamps and the exchange with Tawhai is in a different part of the file, but the Massey telegram appears first. ANZ, R10075085, 'General file, March 1917–April 1918', Henare to Allen, 16 February 1918.

109 ANZ, R10075085, 'General file, March 1917–April 1918', Allen to Massey, 16 February 1918; ANZ, R10075085, 'General file, March 1917–April 1918', Allen to Henare, 16 February 1918. A more unscrupulous politician than Allen might have seen the use of the term 'intention' as a continuing loophole.

110 ANZ, R10075085, 'General file, March 1917–April 1918', Allen to Tawhai, 16 February 1918.

111 ANZ, R10075085, 'General file, March 1917–April 1918', Memo Allen to Commandant, 16 February 1918. The suggestion that Colonel Porter should be warned not to use the conscription threat appears to have come in a cable from the secretary of the Recruiting Board that was sent to intercept Allen on his journey northwards. ANZ, R10075085, 'General file, March 1917–April 1918', Gray to Allen, 16 February 1918. Three days earlier Gray was enthusiastic about the campaign and believed that the proclamation itself was helping to promote recruiting. ANZ, R10075085, 'General file, March 1917–April 1918', Gray to Allen, 13 February 1918.

112 Michael King, *Te Puea: A Life* (Auckland: Reed, 2003), p. 85.

113 ANZ, R10075085, 'General file, March 1917–April 1918', Tawhai to Allen, 19 February 1918 (translation); ANZ, R10075085, 'General file, March 1917–April 1918', Allen to Tawhai, 22 February 1918.

114 *New Zealand Herald*, 5 July 1917, p. 6.

115 O'Connor, 'The Recruitment of Maori Soldiers', p. 69.

116 *New Zealand Herald*, 5 July 1917, p. 6. The government also received petitions stating that conscription 'runs against the Treaty of Waitangi'. ANZ, R10075085, 'General file, March 1917–April 1918', Whangarei petition, Nau Paraone Kawiti and others to Liverpool, 2 March 1918.

117 *Te Kopara*, 31 August 1917, p. 4.

118 King, *Te Puea*, p. 88.

119 O'Connor, 'The Recruitment of Maori Soldiers', p. 72.

120 ANZ, R18874768, 'Military Service Act, 1916 — Military Service registration and calling up of Maoris in Waikato-Maniapoto district', Huntly Press editorial, 15 March 1918.

121 ANZ, R10075085, 'General file, March 1917–April 1918', Allen to Pōmare, 19 February 1918. Pōmare replied that it was 'impossible for me to make arrangements here as I am very busy with the northern trouble'. ANZ, R10075085, 'General file, March 1917–April 1918', Pōmare to Allen, 20 February 1918.

122 O'Connor, 'The Recruitment of Maori Soldiers', p. 71.

123 *Evening Post*, 12 December 1917, p. 3; *Colonist*, 16 April 1919, p. 1. PPA membership is impossible to verify given the lack of surviving records. However, even permitting significant exaggeration it is evident the Association garnered an exceptionally large following.

124 *New Zealand Herald*, 6 July 1918, p. 9.

125 *Evening Post*, 12 December 1917, p. 3; *Evening Post*, 1 January 1918, p. 2.

126 H. S. Moores, 'The Rise of the Protestant Political Association: Sectarianism in New Zealand Politics during World War I' (MA thesis, University of Auckland, 1966), p. 216; *Wanganui Chronicle*, 18 July 1917, p. 5; *The Betrayal of Labour* (Wellington: Printed and published for the Protestant Political Association, 1918), p. 6.

127 *Evening Post*, 26 September 1917, p. 3; *NZ Truth*, 6 October 1917, p. 1.

128 *AJHR*, 1917, F-8, 'Auckland Post-office Inquiry: Report of Commissioner; Together with Minutes of Evidence', pp. 1–50.

129 'As a state of war has made the establishment of censorship necessary, and as matters connected with and arising out of censorship are, for reasons of state, obviously secret . . . The censor officer can give no information and no reasons for censoring any documents or correspondence within New Zealand, or as to the scope and extent of the censorship established in New Zealand upon the outbreak of the war.' *New Zealand Herald*, 14 August 1917, p. 6. Declassified records indicate that investigation dated back months and include a memorandum concerning the suppression of sectarian literature. ANZ, R3885386, 'Censorship of correspondence, Protestant Political association, December 1916–September 1918'.

130 Catholic groups would continue to contact the Defence Department regarding the distribution of anti-Catholic material through 1918. ANZ, R3885381, 'Inflammatory statements by Auckland Free Press, April–May'.

131 *Auckland Star*, 18 August 1917, p. 6. Salmond's biographer has said of the surveillance, 'Salmond was aware that there was no proper legislative basis for the censorship, but considered that the needs of the situation justified the risk.' Alex Frame, *Salmond: Southern Jurist* (Wellington: Victoria University Press, 1995), pp. 175–77.

132 *AJHR*, 1917, F-8, 'Auckland Post-office Inquiry: Report of Commissioner; Together with Minutes of Evidence', pp. 15, 18, 121.

133 *AJHR*, 1917, F-8, 'Auckland Post-office Inquiry: Report of Commissioner; Together with Minutes of Evidence', p. 2.

134 *AJHR*, 1917, F-8, 'Auckland Post-office Inquiry: Report of Commissioner; Together with Minutes of Evidence', pp. 3–4.

135 *NZPD*, Vol. 180, 13 September 1917, pp. 108–9, 133.

136 *Wanganui Chronicle*, 30 July 1917, p. 6.

137 Further informing the idea of an official provision for the exemption of Catholic theological students was the National Efficiency Board classification of industries, released on 6 June 1917, which recommended educational institutions as essential. *AJHR*, 1917, H-43b, 'Classification of Industries, Professions, And Occupations During The War Period', pp. 1–4.

138 Michael Bassett, *Sir Joseph Ward: A Political Biography* (Auckland: Auckland University Press, 1993), pp. 229–30.

139 ANZ, R10075039, 'MS [Military Service] Act, 1916, amendments, February–September 1917'.

140 Baker, *King and Country Call*, p. 129.

141 *Otago Daily Times*, 13 September 1917, p. 6.

142 *NZPD*, Vol. 181, 25 October 1917, pp. 495–96.

143 *New Zealand Times*, 30 October 1917, p. 4.

144 *New Zealand Tablet*, 8 November 1917, p. 14.

145 *NZPD*, Vol. 181, 30 October 1917, p. 652.

146 *New Zealand Tablet*, 15 November 1917, p. 14.

147 *Dominion*, 16 October 1917, p. 5.

148 *Maoriland Worker*, 24 October 1917, p. 4. The PPA released its own account of the incident in *The Truth About the Elliott Assault Case* (Wellington: Protestant Political Association, 1917).

149 *New Zealand Herald*, 3 November 1917, p. 8; *Press*, 3 November 1917, p. 8.

150 *New Zealand Herald*, 15 February 1918, p. 4; *Wanganui Chronicle*, 15 February 1918, p. 5; *Dominion*, 25 April 1918, p. 8.

151 *NZ Truth*, 10 November 1917, p. 1; *Evening Post*, 15 December 1917, p. 4; *Evening Post*, 1 January 1918, p. 2.

152 *Maoriland Worker*, 1 May 1918, p. 4.

153 *Auckland Star*, 18 May 1918, p. 4.

154 *New Zealand Observer*, 17 November 1917, p. 13.

155 *New Zealand Herald*, 17 September 1917, p. 6.

156 Rory Sweetman, 'New Zealand Catholicism, War, Politics and the Irish Issue 1912–1922' (PhD thesis, University of Cambridge, 1990), p. 169.

157 Rory Sweetman, 'Cleary, Henry William', *Dictionary of New Zealand Biography*, first published in 1996. Te Ara — the Encyclopedia of New Zealand, https://teara.govt.nz/en/biographies/3c22/cleary-henry-william.

158 *New Zealand Herald*, 5 November 1917, p. 4; *NZ Truth*, 7 September 1918, p. 6.

159 ANZ, R21371462, 'W.A.G.L. Resolution', Moore to Herdman, 30 July 1917.

160 *Dominion*, 10 July 1917, p. 3.

161 *Timaru Herald*, 1 August 1917, p. 8.

162 *New Zealand Statutes*, 1917, No. 8, 'Revocation of Naturalization', pp. 22–23; *New Zealand Statutes*, 1917, No. 12, 'Registration of Aliens', pp. 64–66.

163 *New Zealand Gazette*, 10 October 1917, pp. 3845–47; *Wairarapa Age*, 24 October 1917, p. 4.

164 Albert Gudopp and Dorothy Strauch, *St Martin's Lutheran Church, Marton: 1877–1977 Centennial* (Marton: St Martin's Lutheran Church, 1977), p. 17.

165 ANZ, R22429059, 'Expeditionary Force — Jugo Slavs [Yugoslavs] in Puhoi District — Disloyalty', Lance Corporal O. A. Melville to Assistant Postmaster, Auckland, 24 November 1917.

166 ANZ, R22429059, 'Expeditionary Force — Jugo Slavs [Yugoslavs] in Puhoi District — Disloyalty', Captain Tichener to District Headquarters, Auckland, 28 December 1917.

167 ANZ, R22429059, 'Expeditionary Force — Jugo Slavs [Yugoslavs] in Puhoi District — Disloyalty', Telegram Police Commissioner to Police Superintendent, Auckland, 14 December 1917.

168 ANZ, R22429059, 'Expeditionary Force — Jugo Slavs [Yugoslavs] in Puhoi District — Disloyalty', Report by Plain Clothes Constable Lambert, 24 December 1917.

169 *Evening Post*, 17 September 1917, p. 2.

170 *New Zealand Herald*, 23 April 1917, p. 4. It was and is not unusual for individuals who identified as Germans to have Polish names. Poles who lived in the German Empire were obliged to serve in its army, so fighting that force meant possibly confronting them.

171 ANZ, R22429059, 'Expeditionary Force — Jugo Slavs [Yugoslavs] in Puhoi District — Disloyalty', John Schollum jr to Allen, 6 August 1917.

172 *New Zealand Herald*, 30 October 1917, p. 4.

173 For examples see *Auckland Star*, 30 October 1917, p. 2; ANZ, R3895405, 'Correspondence and Memoranda concerning Government Policy towards Yugoslavs', G. L. Scansie to Massey, 31 October 1917.

174 *New Zealand Statutes*, 1917, No. 21, 'War Legislation', section 35e, p. 109.

175 *Dominion*, 28 November 1917, p. 7.

176 P. S. O'Connor, 'The Awkward Ones — Dealing with Conscience, 1916–1918', *New Zealand Journal of History*, Vol. 8, No. 2 (October 1974), p. 122.

177 Imelda Bargas and Tim Shoebridge, *New Zealand's First World War Heritage* (Auckland: Exisle Publishing, 2015), p. 31.

178 Jared Davidson, *Dead Letters: Censorship and Subversion in New Zealand 1914–1920* (Dunedin: Otago University Press, 2019), p. 110.

179 Baker, *King and Country Call*, p. 178.

180 *Maoriland Worker*, 16 January 1918, p. 7.

181 ANZ, R22429752, 'Territorial Force — Exemptions — Religious objectors NZEF [New Zealand Expeditionary Force]', Memorandum for the

Minister of Defence, 10 October 1917.

182 ANZ, R22429765, 'Territorial Force — Conscientious objectors sent abroad', Richardson to Allen, 28 August 1917.

183 The major accounts of the episode are available in Archibald Baxter, *We Will Not Cease* (Auckland: Cape Catley, 2003); H. E. Holland, *Armageddon or Calvary: The Conscientious Objectors of New Zealand and 'The Process of Their Conversion'* (Wellington: The Maoriland Worker Printing and Publishing Co. Ltd, 1919); Baker, *King and Country Call*, pp. 183–89.

184 ANZ, R22429765, 'Territorial Force — Conscientious objectors sent abroad', Godley to Allen, 7 November 1917.

185 Pugsley, *On the Fringes of Hell*, p. 91.

186 Baxter, *We Will Not Cease*, p. 122.

187 *Maoriland Worker*, 18 July 1917, p. 6.

188 ATL, MS-Papers-2597-33/6/05b, 'New Zealand Yearly Meeting of the Society of Friends', Constance Gill to John Holdsworth, 1 August 1918.

189 For examples see ANZ, R22429763, 'Territorial Force — Conscientious objectors sent abroad'; ANZ, R22429765, 'Territorial Force — Conscientious objectors sent abroad'.

190 *New Zealand Free Lance*, 27 July 1917, p. 8.

191 ANZ, R22429752, 'Territorial Force — Exemptions — Religious objectors NZEF [New Zealand Expeditionary Force]', Memorandum Religious and Conscientious Objectors, 10 October 1917.

192 Holland, *Armageddon or Calvary*, p. 39; *Press*, 28 December 1917, p. 4; Baker, *King and Country Call*, p. 191; O'Connor, 'The Awkward Ones', p. 134.

193 https://nzhistory.govt.nz/war/russian-empire-facts; Orlando Figes, *A People's Tragedy: The Russian Revolution 1891–1924* (London: Pimlico, 1996), p. 773.

194 *Dominion*, 6 November 1918, p. 6; *Dominion*, 29 December 1917, p. 7. For a study of the realities of the Red Terror campaign and the programme of cultural revolution enacted in the early period of Bolshevik rule see Figes, *A People's Tragedy*, pp. 499–540, 630–32, 743–48, 775–77; *Auckland Star*, 22 February 1918, p. 5.

195 Herbert Roth, 'The October Revolution and New Zealand Labour', *Political Science*, Vol. 13, No. 2 (September 1961), pp. 45–55; Alexander Trapeznik, 'New Zealand's Perceptions of the Russian Revolution of 1917', *Revolutionary Russia*, Vol. 19, No. 1 (2006), pp. 63–77.

196 Brown, *The Rise of New Zealand Labour*, p. 53.

197 *NZPD*, Vol. 183, 21 November 1918, pp. 443–44.

198 *Auckland Star*, 29 January 1918, p. 3; *NZPD*, Vol. 183, 21 November 1918, pp. 442–44.

199 *Evening Post*, 12 June 1918, p. 7.

200 *Dominion*, 16 December 1918, p. 6.

201 Barry Gustafson, *Labour's Path to Political Independence: The Origins and Establishment of the New Zealand Labour Party 1900–19* (Auckland: Auckland University Press, 1980), p. 147.

202 *Otago Daily Times*, 29 November 1917, p. 4; *The Daily News*, 27 December 1917, p. 4.

203 Figes, *A People's Tragedy*, p. 548.

204 *Auckland Star*, 18 May 1918, p. 4.

205 *Temuka Leader*, 17 August 1918, p. 2; *New Zealand Herald*, 21 July 1917, p. 7; *Sun*, 21 July 1917, p. 11. In April 1918, it was announced that Russian subjects would not be permitted to serve in the New Zealand military. Volunteers and balloted men with Russian parentage were placed on leave without pay until further orders provided attestation. ANZ, R22429092, 'Expeditionary Force — Recruiting organisation', p. 55.

206 *Dominion*, 12 December 1917, p. 5; *Evening Star*, 11 December 1917, p. 8.

207 Robin Bromby, *German Raiders of the South Seas* (Sydney: Doubleday, 1985), pp. 191–94.

208 ANZ, R24048328, '[Correspondence between] General Sir Alexander Godley [Commander New Zealand Expeditionary Force] and Colonel Hon. [Honourable] Sir James Allen, Minister of Defence, 6 January 1918–28 January 1920', Allen to Godley, 28 January 1918; Bromby, *German Raiders of the South Seas*, p. 198.

209 *Evening Post*, 1 January 1918, p. 2.

CHAPTER TWELVE: ENDURANCE

1 G. J. Meyer, *A World Undone: The Story of the Great War* (New York: Delta, 2006), pp. 627–34, 670.

2 Michael Bassett with Michael King, *Tomorrow Comes the Song: A Life of Peter Fraser* (Auckland: Penguin, 2000), p. 79.

3 P. J. O'Farrell, *Harry Holland: Militant Socialist* (Canberra: Australian National University, 1964), p. 79.

4 *New Zealand Times*, 8 February 1918, p. 6.

5 *Dominion*, 14 February 1918, p. 6.

6 *Maoriland Worker*, 20 February 1918, p. 4.

7 *Evening Post*, 25 February 1918, p. 7.

8 *Evening Post*, 14 February 1918, p. 8.

9 *Dominion*, 15 February 1918, p. 7; *New Zealand Free Lance*, 22 February 1918, p. 3.

10 *Maoriland Worker*, 27 February 1918, p. 7.

11 Bassett with King, *Tomorrow Comes the Song*, p. 368.

12 Bassett with King, *Tomorrow Comes the Song*, pp. 79–80, 368.

13 *New Zealand Times*, 1 March 1918, p. 6.

14 Some doubt has been cast on this incident. See Bruce Farland, *Farmer Bill: William Ferguson Massey and the Reform Party* (Wellington: First Edition Publishers, 2008), p. 331.

15 *New Zealand Herald*, 20 March 1918, p. 7.

16 Archives New Zealand (ANZ), R3796209, 'Inwards and outwards despatches relating to the European War — 14 March–16 April 1918', Liverpool to Long, 30 March 1918.

17 ANZ, R3796209, 'Inwards and outwards despatches relating to the European War — 14 March–16 April 1918', The Governor-General of New Zealand to the Secretary of State for the Colonies, 1 April 1918.

18 ANZ, R22319702, 'Ministerial Files — Correspondence with General Godley', Allen to Godley, 30 May 1918; *Baptist*, May 1918, p. 66.

19 ANZ, R22319674, 'Miscellanous files and papers — Correspondence with Colonels Birdwood and Russell, December 1914–April 1920 and copies of personal letters, 1920', Allen to Russell, 17 June 1918.

20 *New Zealand Parliamentary Debates* (*NZPD*), Vol. 182, 11 April 1918, p. 66.

21 *NZ Truth*, 6 April 1918, p. 1.

22 ANZ, R22319674, 'Miscellanous files and papers — Correspondence with Colonels Birdwood and Russell, December 1914–April 1920 and copies of personal letters, 1920', Allen to Russell, 25 April 1918; ANZ, R21078971, 'New Zealand Expeditionary Force, its provision and maintenance', p. 8.

23 Christopher Pugsley, *The Anzac Experience: New Zealand, Australia and Empire in the First World War* (Auckland: Reed, 2004), p. 279.

24 Details were printed in *Maoriland Worker*, 13 March 1918, pp. 4–5; 20 March 1918, p. 4; 27 March 1918, p. 4.

25 O'Farrell, *Harry Holland*, p. 80.

26 *Hawera and Normanby Star*, 21 May 1918, p. 4.

27 *North Otago Times*, 7 May 1918, p. 3.

28 *Hawera and Normanby Star*, 21 May 1918, p. 4.

29 O'Farrell, *Harry Holland*, p. 82.

30 *Greymouth Evening Star*, 13 May 1918, p. 4; *Grey River Argus*, 6 May 1918, p. 3; *Green Ray*, 1 May 1918, p. 108.

31 ANZ, R22319702, 'Ministerial Files — Correspondence with General Godley', Allen to Godley, 30 May 1918.

32 *Grey River Argus*, 31 May 1918, p. 2.

33 O'Farrell, *Harry Holland*, p. 83.

34 H. E. Holland, *Armageddon or Calvary: The Conscientious Objectors of New Zealand and 'The Process of Their Conversion'* (Wellington: The Maoriland Worker Printing and Publishing Co. Ltd, 1919), p. 137.

35 Paul Baker, *King and Country Call: New Zealanders, Conscription and the Great War* (Auckland: Auckland University Press, 1988), p. 195.

36 Holland, *Armageddon or Calvary*, p. 127.

37 *NZ Truth*, 29 June 1918, p. 8.

38 *NZ Truth*, 6 July 1918, p. 6.

39 *New Zealand Times*, 27 June 1918, p. 7; Baker, *King and Country Call*, p. 197.

40 Holland, *Armageddon or Calvary*, p. 49.

41 *NZ Truth*, 4 July 1918, p. 2.

42 ANZ, R22429856, 'Territorial Force — Defaulters undergoing detention and imprisonment'.

43 *New Zealand Observer*, 6 July 1918, p. 3.

44 ANZ, R22429763, 'Territorial Force — Conscientious objectors sent abroad', 14 August 1918.

45 *Wanganui Chronicle*, 2 February 1918, p. 5.

46 Egerton Gill was released from prison in 1919. Alongside his continued involvement in the Society of Friends, Gill was a keen participant in the Auckland council for the League of Nations Union, organised relief for the Spanish Civil War and became involved in activism for penal reform. He died December 1937, aged 60.

47 Harry Urquhart was released from prison in 1919 though he was locked out of teaching due to his refusal to take an oath. Remaining actively involved in Christian pacifism, he became an inspiration for pacifists during the Second World War and is known as the 'father of Christian pacifism in New Zealand'. He died in November 1963, aged 85.

48 *Ashburton Guardian*, 18 May 1918, p. 5. James Chapple was released from jail in early 1919 and continued as a Unitarian minister in Christchurch until 1925, although his fusion of religion and socialism proved a point of some contention. After moving to Auckland, he served as a Unitarian minister from 1939 to 1941, though he elected to stand down out of concern that his public support for the Soviet Union might create controversy for the church. He died on 8 April 1947, survived by his wife, eight daughters and six sons. Chapple's life and character would provide the basis for the 1978 novel *Plumb*, written by his grandson Maurice Gee.

49 *Conscientious Objectors — Field Punishment* (Wellington: Office of Minister of Defence, 1918), p. 2.

50 By Baxter's account, Allen and Myers interviewed him concerning his attitude to military service, his treatment overseas and his health. Holland, *Armageddon or Calvary*, pp. 85–87.

51 Published in London in 1939, *We Will Not Cease* had an inauspicious beginning when almost all the copies were destroyed in the Blitz. However, interest in Baxter's wartime experiences would grow substantially; *We Will Not Cease* has been republished several times since 1968 and is now claimed as a classic of New Zealand anti-war literature. Archibald Baxter, *We Will Not Cease* (Auckland: Cape Catley, 2003), p. 10.

52 ANZ, R22429857, 'Territorial Force — Defaulters undergoing detention and imprisonment'.

53 ANZ, R22429858, 'Territorial Force — Defaulters undergoing detention and imprisonment 1918–

1919', Adjutant General Tate, 22 October 1918. He added that he did not believe 'that men who refuse to obey orders and practise open defiance are treated gently in any penal institution whether civil or military'.

54 ANZ, R22429858, 'Territorial Force — Defaulters undergoing detention and imprisonment 1918–1919', Director of Personnel Services Osborne-Lilly, 10 October 1918.

55 The recommendations, and the episode in general, saw Cabinet begin to discuss a legislative amendment to better distinguish between 'defiant' and 'conscientious' objectors, ultimately made redundant by the end of the war. Baker, *King and Country Call*, pp. 199–200.

56 *Dominion*, 12 April 1918, p. 7.

57 Rory Sweetman, 'New Zealand Catholicism, War, Politics and the Irish Issue 1912–1922' (PhD thesis, University of Cambridge, 1990), pp. 180–81.

58 *North Otago Times*, 22 May 1918, p. 6.

59 *NZ Truth*, 4 May 1918, p. 5.

60 Sweetman, 'New Zealand Catholicism', pp. 191–92.

61 Sweetman, 'New Zealand Catholicism', pp. 186–87.

62 Sweetman, 'New Zealand Catholicism', p. 203.

63 *Evening Post*, 7 June 1918, p. 10.

64 *New Zealand Gazette*, 23 July 1918, pp. 2759–61.

65 ANZ, R22319675, 'Miscellanous files and papers — Correspondence between J Allen and WF Massey, 1st September 1916–1st August 1919 [Loose papers]', Allen to Massey, 6 July 1918; *Waikato Times*, 11 September 1918, p. 6.

66 Seán Brosnahan, '"Shaming the Shoneens": The Green Ray and the Maoriland Irish Society in Dunedin, 1916–1922', in Lyndon Fraser (ed.), *A Distant Shore: Irish Migration and New Zealand Settlement* (Dunedin: Otago University Press, 2000), pp. 126–27; Baker, *King and Country Call*, p. 128.

67 *New Zealand Gazette*, 4 July 1918, p. 2494; *Otago Witness*, 31 July 1918, p. 41.

68 *New Zealand Times*, 30 October 1918, p. 8.

69 *New Zealand Tablet*, 13 February 1919, p. 14.

70 *Otago Witness*, 31 July 1918, p. 1.

71 Sweetman, 'New Zealand Catholicism', p. 206.

72 *Press*, 30 April 1918, p. 6.

73 *Press*, 29 April 1918, p. 7.

74 *New Zealand Herald*, 30 April 1918, p. 6.

75 *Press*, 30 April 1918, p. 7.

76 The full details are available in *Evening Post*, 30 April 1918, p. 6.

77 *Evening Post*, 30 April 1918, p. 6.

78 The following accounts are taken from *Press*, 30 April 1918, p. 6, *NZ Truth*, 4 May 1918, p. 5 and *Evening Post*, 30 April 1918, p. 8. See also P. S. O'Connor, 'Balmy Christchurch: A Melodrama in Three Parts', *Comment: New Zealand Quarterly Review*, 35 (June 1968), pp. 21–28.

79 *New Zealand Herald*, 1 May 1918, p. 6.

80 Baker, *King and Country Call*, p. 149.

81 *Evening Star*, 1 May 1918, p. 4.

82 ANZ, R22319706, 'Miscellanous [sic] Files and Papers — Miscellaneous Correspondence and Papers [loose papers]', Isitt to Allen, 30 April 1918.

83 *Press*, 3 May 1918, p. 6.

84 *New Zealand Herald*, 9 May 1918, p. 4; *Press*, 20 May 1918, p. 6; *North Otago Times*, 22 May 1918, p. 2.

85 *New Zealand Free Lance*, 9 May 1918, p. 8; *New Zealand Herald*, 17 May 1918, p. 6.

86 *New Zealand Herald*, 25 May 1918, p. 6; *New Zealand Herald*, 11 May 1918, p. 8; *New Zealand Herald*, 4 May 1918, p. 7.

87 ANZ, R22319675, 'Miscellanous [sic] Files and Papers — Correspondence Between J. Allen and W. F. Massey, 1st September 1916–1st August 1919 [loose papers]', Allen to Massey, 14 May 1918; *Waikato Times*, 30 May 1918, p. 5.

88 *Lyttelton Times*, 2 May 1918, p. 5.

89 *New Zealand Herald*, 17 May 1918, p. 8.

90 *New Zealand Herald*, 17 May 1918, p. 8; *New Zealand Herald*, 10 June 1918, p. 6.

91 *Appendix to the Journals of the House of Representatives* (*AJHR*), 1919, H-19, 'Defence Forces of New Zealand', pp. 14, 15; Baker, *King and Country Call*, p. 151. Of the second division men balloted, 13,466 were class A, 23,576 were class C, and 17,507 were class B. Of those who embarked, 796 were class A, 32 were class B and 4 were class C.

92 Baker, *King and Country Call*, p. 151.

93 For example, estimates for French war widows stand at 600,000, and estimates for French war orphans range between 760,000 and 1.2 million. Leonard V. Smith, Stéphane Audoin-Rouzeau and Annette Becker, *France and the Great War 1914–1918* (New York: Cambridge University Press, 2003), p. 70. Another study cites an estimated total of six million war orphans resulting from the conflict: see Andrew Donson, 'Children and Youth', in *1914–1918 Online: International Encyclopedia of the First World War*, ed. Ute Daniel, Peter Gatrell, Oliver Janz, Heather Jones, Jennifer Keene, Alan Kramer, and Bill Nasson (Berlin: Freie Universität Berlin, 2014), DOI: 10.15463/ie1418.10265.

94 P. S. O'Connor, 'The Recruitment of Maori Soldiers, 1914–18', *Political Science*, Vol. 19, Issue 2 (December 1967), p. 74.

95 Michael King, *Te Puea: A Life* (Auckland: Reed, 2003), p. 87.

96 Quoted in King, *Te Puea*, p. 78.

97 Quoted in King, *Te Puea*, p. 88.

98 *New Zealand Herald*, 12 June 1918, p. 6.

99 Quoted in King, *Te Puea*, p. 89.

100 Quoted in King, *Te Puea*, p. 90.

101 King, *Te Puea*, p. 90.

102 O'Connor, 'The Recruitment of Maori Soldiers', p. 77.

103 O'Connor, 'The Recruitment of Maori Soldiers', p. 77; ANZ, R10075086, 'General file, June 1917–October 1918', Attitude of Waikato Maoris to Military Service Act.

104 King, *Te Puea*, p. 95.

105 ANZ, R10075086, 'General file, June 1917–October 1918', petition to Allen, 18 March 1918.

106 *Te Kopara*, September 1918, p. 31.

107 Judith Binney, Gillian Chaplin and Craig Wallace, *Mihaia: The Prophet Rua Kenana and His Community at Maungapohatu* (New York: Oxford University Press, 1979), p. 136; ANZ, R18874766, 'Military Service Act, 1916 — Enrolling Maori Expeditionary Force Reserve', report from Te Whāiti police station, 11 March 1918; ANZ, R22319675, 'Miscellanous files and papers — Correspondence between J Allen and WF Massey, 1st September 1916–1st August 1919 [Loose papers]', Allen to Massey, 12 August 1918.

108 *Te Kopara*, 12 September 1918, p. 12. On Tūhoe soliders see http://www.aucklandmuseum.com/war-memorial/online-cenotaph/record/C74537; Athol Anderson, Judith Binney and Aroha Harris, *Tangata Whenua: An Illustrated History* (Wellington: Bridget Williams Books, 2015), p. 302.

109 King, *Te Puea*, pp. 92, 85.

110 James Cowan, *Maori in the Great War* (Christchurch: Willson Scott Publishing, 2011), pp. 32–34.

111 ANZ, R10075086, 'General file, June 1917–October 1918', Attitude of Waikato Maoris to Military Service Act.

112 Alexander Turnbull Library (ATL), MS-Papers-6919-0234; Baker, *King and Country Call*, p. 220.

113 *New Zealand Gazette*, 24 June 1918, pp. 2406–8; *Auckland Star*, 24 June 1918, p. 2; ANZ, R22319675, 'Miscellanous files and papers — Correspondence between J Allen and WF Massey, 1st September 1916–1st August 1919 [Loose papers]', Allen to Massey, 12 June 1918; Andrew Trlin, *Now Respected, Once Despised: Yugoslavs in New Zealand* (Palmerston North: Dunmore Press, 1979), pp. 115–16; *New Zealand Gazette*, 24 June 1918, pp. 2406–8.

114 Judith Bassett, 'Colonial Justice: The Treatment of Dalmatians in New Zealand during the First World War', *New Zealand Journal of History*, Vol. 33, No. 2 (October 1999), pp. 174–75; Trlin, *Now Respected, Once Despised*, p. 116; *New Zealand Herald*, 25 June 1918, p. 4; *NZ Truth*, 10 August 1918, p. 5; *Auckland Star*, 24 June 1918, p. 2.

115 *New Zealand Herald*, 5 September 1918, p. 6; Bassett, 'Colonial Justice', p. 175.

116 Andrew Francis, *'To Be Truly British We Must Be Anti-German': New Zealand, Enemy Aliens and the Great War Experience, 1914–1919* (Oxford; New York: Peter Lang, 2012), p. 148.

117 *AJHR*, 1919, H-33, 'Prisoners of War at Somes Island (Report of Mr. Justice Chapman Respecting the Treatment of)', p. 4.

118 *Star*, 24 March 1915, p. 6.

119 *Ashburton Guardian*, 1 August 1918, p. 7; *Dominion*, 1 August 1918, p. 6.

120 *AJHR*, 1919, H-33, 'Prisoners of War at Somes Island (Report of Mr. Justice Chapman Respecting the Treatment of)', p. 27; David McGill, *Island of Secrets: Matiu/Somes Island in Wellington Harbour* (Wellington: Steele Roberts & Silver Owl Press, 2001), p. 64.

121 Collections of internees' accounts are available in ATL, MS-Papers-2071, 'Somes Island internee's statements' and ANZ, R3796234, 'Copies of letters to and from Dr. Schultz and others'.

122 McGill, *Island of Secrets*, pp. 49, 51, 60, 67.

123 *AJHR*, 1919, H-33, 'Prisoners of War at Somes Island (Report of Mr. Justice Chapman Respecting The Treatment of)', pp. 4–5; Jared Davidson, *Dead Letters: Censorship and Subversion in New Zealand 1914–1920* (Dunedin: Otago University Press, 2019), p. 152.

124 *Star*, 14 May 1873, p. 2; *Star*, 24 March 1874, p. 2; *Press*, 28 April 1890, p. 4; *Sun*, 10 August 1915, p. 11.

125 *Sun*, 16 July 1918, p. 3; *Press*, 17 July 1918, p. 4.

126 *Sun*, 6 August 1918, p. 8.

127 *Press*, 7 August 1918, p. 6.

128 *NZ Truth*, 10 August 1918, p. 5; *Dominion*, 7 August 1918, p. 4.

129 ANZ, R3796208, 'Inwards and outwards despatches relating to the European War — 18 January–13 March 1918', Long to Liverpool, 10 March 1918.

130 *Taranaki Herald*, 19 August 1918, p. 6.

131 This method was seemingly developed in New South Wales by Sir Owen Cox of Birt and Company. *Oamaru Mail*, 15 June 1918, p. 7; *Poverty Bay Herald*, 14 August 1917, p. 4; *Marlborough Express*, 30 January 1918, p. 3; *Northern Advocate*, 21 June 1918, p. 2.

132 *Northern Advocate*, 27 June 1918, p. 1. An inconclusive experiment was made by the Dominion Laboratory to derive it electrolytically from feldspar. *Evening Post*, 19 February 1917, p. 2.

133 *Taranaki Herald*, 19 August 1918, p. 6. Unfortunately, the nutrients in the material were insufficiently soluble to boost feed crops rapidly, unless mixed with artificial manures such as superphosphate. The cost of those manures, the erection of storage facilities and installation of mixing equipment was likely to make the price of the resulting fertiliser too great.

134 *Otago Witness*, 18 September 1918, p. 11; *Sun*, 8 November 1918, p. 5.

135 *Evening Post*, 27 July 1916, p. 3. See also *Evening*

Post, 11 July 1916, p. 8; *Evening Post*, 25 July 1916, p. 7; *Evening Post*, 11 July 1917, p. 4; J. B. Condliffe and H. R. Rodwell, 'The Course of Rural Land Values in Canterbury, New Zealand, 1914–1925', *Economic Record* (May 1927), p. 47. Another concludes that the 'widely accepted picture of rising war-time incomes is clearly incorrect'. See Tod Simpson, 'Origins of Statutory Producer Control Legislation in New Zealand Agriculture, 1914–1925' (MCA thesis, Victoria University of Wellington, 1991), p. 42; *Evening Post*, 11 March 1918, p. 8.

136 Len Richardson, 'Politics and War: Coal Miners and Conscription, 1914–18', in P. R. May (ed.), *Miners and Militants: Politics in Westland, 1865–1918* (Christchurch: University of Canterbury, 1975), pp. 147, 166.

137 *Evening Post*, 14 February 1918, p. 8.

138 Len Richardson, *Coal, Class & Community: The United Mineworkers of New Zealand, 1880–1960* (Auckland: Auckland University Press, 1995), p. 176.

139 ANZ, R22319674, 'Miscellanous files and papers — Correspondence with Colonels Birdwood and Russell, December 1914–April 1920 and copies of personal letters, 1920', Allen to Russell, 30 May 1918.

140 *Evening Post*, 22 July 1918, p. 3; *New Zealand Free Lance*, 15 August 1918, p. 6.

141 ANZ, R3885396, 'Censorship of correspondence, P. Tooker to P. Green, July–September', extract from Brisbane censor's intelligence report for week ended 10 August 1918.

142 Richardson, *Coal, Class & Community*, p. 180.

143 Richardson, 'Politics and War', pp. 154–55.

144 Leicester Chisholm Webb, 'The Rise of the Reform Party: A History of Party Politics in New Zealand between 1910 and 1920' (Honours thesis, University of New Zealand, 1928), p. 179.

145 *New Zealand Free Lance*, 15 August 1918, p. 6.

146 *New Zealand Times*, 4 July 1918, p. 4; *Poverty Bay Herald*, 8 July 1918, p. 4.

147 *New Zealand Statutes*, 1918, No. 2, pp. 5–18.

148 *Railway Review*, 28 June 1918, p. 317; Barry Gustafson, *From the Cradle to the Grave: A Biography of Michael Joseph Savage* (Auckland: Reed, 1986), pp. 100–1.

149 *Evening Post*, 10 April 1918, p. 4.

150 *Evening Post*, 28 May 1918, p. 7.

151 *AJHR*, 1918, H-44, 'Board of Trade (Second Annual Report of the)', p. 3. By Massey's account, the state-owned butcheries were 'not quite a success' and the new method of supplying butchers from the imperial stores was working 'so satisfactorily' that they had become unnecessary. *Evening Post*, 19 February 1918, p. 8; *NZPD*, Vol. 182, 15 April 1918, p. 254.

152 In Gisborne meat prices fell over 8 per cent between the first and third quarters of 1917. *New Zealand Official Year-book*, 1918, p. 750.

153 *Evening Post*, 16 April 1918, p. 2.

154 *AJHR*, 1921, H-44, 'Department of Industries and Commerce', p. 24.

155 *Evening Post*, 1 January 1918, p. 6.

156 *New Zealand Herald*, 9 September 1918, p. 4.

157 *Waikato Times*, 16 September 1918, p. 4.

158 George L. Cook, 'Sir Robert Borden, Lloyd George and British Military Policy, 1917–1918', *The Historical Journal*, Vol. 14, Issue 2 (1971), p. 385.

159 Quoted James Watson, *WF Massey: New Zealand* (London: Haus, 2010), p. 57; Richard G. H. Kay, 'In Pursuit of Victory: British–New Zealand Relations During the First World War' (PhD thesis, University of Otago, 2001), p. 203.

160 E. M. Andrews, *The Anzac Illusion: Anglo-Australian Relations during World War I* (Cambridge: Cambridge University Press, 1993), p. 192.

161 Andrews, *The Anzac Illusion*, p. 192; Joan Beaumont, *Broken Nation: Australians in the Great War* (Crows Nest, NSW: Allen & Unwin, 2013), p. 442.

162 ANZ, R17378330, 'Imperial War Conference 1918 — Minutes of meetings 30–48, 13 August–31 December — Imperial War Cabinet', 13 August 1918.

163 ANZ, R22319739, 'Ministerial Files — Correspondence with Prime Minister, London trip, 1918', Allen to Massey, 30 April 1918.

164 ANZ, R17378330, 'Imperial War Conference 1918 — Minutes of meetings 30–48, 13 August–31 December — Imperial War Cabinet', 14 August 1918; Beaumont, *Broken Nation*, pp. 449–50.

165 ANZ, R17378330, 'Imperial War Conference 1918 — Minutes of meetings 30–48, 13 August–31 December — Imperial War Cabinet', 15 August 1918.

166 Kay, 'In Pursuit of Victory', p. 216.

167 Beaumont, *Broken Nation*, pp. 397–99; Maurice Ollivier (ed.), *The Colonial and Imperial Conferences from 1887 to 1937, Vol. 2* (Ottawa: Queen's Printer, 1954), pp. 336–43; Kay, 'In Pursuit of Victory', p. 209.

168 Shortly before his departure, Massey noted that he was in no hurry to implement the proposal and wanted to consult with Cabinet and Parliament before reaching a final decision. Back in New Zealand, he stalled the appointment process until after the peace settlement. See Rolf Pfeiffer, 'Exercises in Loyalty and Troublemaking', *Australian Journal of Politics and History*, Vol. 38, No. 2 (1992), p. 183.

169 G. T. Allen, 'New Zealand and the Imperial War Cabinet' (MA thesis, University of Canterbury, 1975), p. 132.

170 ANZ, R22319675, 'Miscellanous files and papers —

Correspondence between J Allen and WF Massey, 1st September 1916–1st August 1919 [Loose papers]', Massey to Allen, 30 July 1918; P. S. O'Connor, 'Some Political Preoccupations of Mr Massey, 1918–20', *Political Science*, Vol. 18, No. 2 (1966), p. 19.

171 Ollivier, *The Colonial and Imperial Conferences, Vol. 2*, pp. 310–22, 370–72; Massey argued his call for regulation on the claim that it was a government's duty, when it came to 'businesses which are of a national character', 'to step in and see that on the one side exploitation is avoided, and that on the other side sufficient encouragement is given to the individuals or firms interested to provide a proper service, and one which will be satisfactory to the travelling and trading public'. Ollivier, *The Colonial and Imperial Conferences, Vol. 2*, p. 312.

172 ANZ, R17378330, 'Imperial War Conference 1918 — Minutes of meetings 30–48, 13 August–31 December — Imperial War Cabinet', 14 August 1918.

173 Kay, 'In Pursuit of Victory', p. 221.

174 ANZ, R22281214, 'Formal Government matters — Massey's telegram copy books — August–September 1918', Massey to Allen, 6 July 1918.

175 *Chronicles of the N.Z.E.F.*, No. 48, 19 July 1918, p. 276; For accounts of soldiers' reactions to Massey and Ward see Nicholas Boyack, *Behind the Lines: The Lives of New Zealand Soldiers in the First World War* (Wellington: Allen & Unwin, 1989), p. 203.

176 ANZ, R22281214, 'Formal Government matters — Massey's telegram copy books — August–September 1918', 17 July 1918.

177 *Chronicles of the N.Z.E.F.*, No. 48, 19 July 1918, pp. 276–77; ANZ, R22281214, 'Formal Government matters — Massey's telegram copy books — August–September 1918', 17 July 1918.

178 Glyn Harper, '"Old Bill Was All Right": William Ferguson Massey and the Soldiers', in James Watson and Lachy Paterson (eds), *A Great New Zealand Prime Minister?: Reappraising William Ferguson Massey* (Dunedin: Otago University Press, 2011), pp. 87–95.

179 *New Zealand Herald*, 23 June 1979, section 2, p. 1.

180 Kay, 'In Pursuit of Victory', p. 226; Pfeiffer, 'Exercises in Loyalty and Troublemaking', pp. 184–85.

181 Allen, 'New Zealand and the Imperial War Cabinet', p. 89.

182 ANZ, R15393165, 'Imperial War Conference', 8 July 1918.

183 Nick Lloyd, *Hundred Days: The End of the Great War* (London: Viking, 2013), p. 118; Meyer, *A World Undone*, p. 677.

184 For key steps in this process see Lloyd, *Hundred Days*, pp. 70–72, 178–79, 200–2, 216–19, 237–40.

185 *Wanganui Chronicle*, 11 July 1918, p. 5.

186 ANZ, R22319675, 'Miscellanous files and papers — Correspondence between J Allen and WF Massey, 1st September 1916–1st August 1919 [Loose papers]', Allen to Massey, 12 August 1918 and 19 September 1918; *NZPD*, Vol. 183, pp. 40, 84, 137, 154.

187 For example, *Evening Post*, 17 July 1918, p. 6.

188 *New Zealand Herald*, 16 July 1918, p. 4.

189 ANZ, R21078971, 'New Zealand Expeditionary Force, its provision and maintenance', p. 8; Baker, *King and Country Call*, p. 137.

190 Ian McGibbon, *New Zealand's Western Front Campaign* (Auckland: Bateman, 2016), pp. 216–17; O'Connor, 'Some Political Preoccupations of Mr Massey', p. 18.

191 O'Connor, 'Some Political Preoccupations of Mr Massey', p. 18; ANZ, R24048328, '[Correspondence between] General Sir Alexander Godley [Commander New Zealand Expeditionary Force] and Colonel Hon. [Honourable] Sir James Allen, Minister of Defence, 6 January 1918–28 January 1920', Allen to Godley, 2 July 1918. Allen's concerns were apt given the problems New Zealand authorities faced with a much larger furlough scheme during the Second World War.

192 H. S. Moores, 'The Rise of the Protestant Political Association: Sectarianism in New Zealand Politics during World War 1' (MA thesis, University of Auckland, 1966), pp. 287–310; Bassett with King, *Tomorrow Comes the Song*, pp. 82–86; *NZ Truth*, 28 September 1918, p. 1.

193 *Evening Post*, 2 October, 28 September 1918, p. 3; *Maoriland Worker*, 9 October 1918, p. 4.

194 *Evening Post*, 2 October 1918, p. 3.

195 Bassett and King, *Tomorrow Comes the Song*, p. 83.

196 *NZ Truth*, 28 September 1918, p. 6.

197 *NZ Truth*, 28 September 1918, p. 6; *Evening Post*, 23 September 1918, p. 7.

198 *Dominion*, 4 October 1918, p. 6.

199 Bassett with King, *Tomorrow Comes the Song*, p. 85; *New Zealand Observer*, 12 October 1918, p. 2.

200 *Nation*, October 1918, pp. 2–3.

201 *Evening Post*, 4 October 1918, p. 3.

202 *Otago Daily Times*, 4 October 1918, p. 4.

203 *NZPD*, Vol. 183, 30 October 1918, p. 92; O'Farrell, *Harry Holland*, p. 121.

204 Bassett with King, *Tomorrow Comes the Song*, p. 87.

205 *Star*, 15 October 1918, p. 5.

206 For examples see *Otago Witness*, 30 October 1918, p. 25; *New Zealand Herald*, 2 November 1918, p. 18; *Otago Witness*, 13 November 1918, p. 31.

207 *NZPD*, Vol. 183, 1 November 1918, p. 169; *Evening Post*, 1 November 1918, p. 7.

208 *Dominion*, 9 November 1918, p. 6.

209 *Evening Post*, 7 November 1918, p. 4.

CHAPTER THIRTEEN: PEACE IS DECLARED

1 Geoffrey Rice, *That Terrible Time: Eye-Witness Accounts of the 1918 Influenza Pandemic in New Zealand* (Christchurch: Hawthorne Press, 2018), p. 32.

2 Doris Gordon, *Backblocks Baby-Doctor: An Autobiography* (London: Faber & Faber, 1955), p. 136.

3 Geoffrey Rice, *Black November: The 1918 Influenza Pandemic in New Zealand*, 2nd edn (Christchurch: Canterbury University Press, 2005), pp. 17, 7, 24; Rice, *That Terrible Time.*

4 *New Zealand Parliamentary Debates* (*NZPD*), Vol. 183, 1 November 1918, p. 177; *Evening Post*, 12 November 1918, p. 8.

5 Charlotte Bennett, '"What with the War [and] the Epidemic, Times are Altogether Troublesome": Agency and Endurance in Adolescent Writings', in David Monger, Sarah Murray and Katie Pickles (eds), *Endurance and the First World War: Experiences and Legacies in New Zealand and Australia* (Newcastle upon Tyne: Cambridge Scholars Publishing, 2014), pp. 96–102.

6 Rice, *Black November*, p. 17.

7 *Manawatu Standard*, 8 November 1918, p. 5.

8 Rice, *Black November*, pp. 85, 60.

9 Rice, *Black November*, pp. 17, 159, 261, 222–23.

10 Hermann Joseph Hiery, *The Neglected War: The German South Pacific and the Influence of World War I* (Honolulu: University of Hawai'i Press, 1995), pp. 172–78.

11 For examples see *Colonist*, 8 November 1918, p. 4; *Star*, 7 November 1918, p. 3; Archives New Zealand (ANZ), R3796227, 'Secret Telegraphic Reports on the War Situation — 1 October–29 December 1918', Secretary of State for the Colonies, Walter Long to Governor-General Lord Liverpool, 9 November 1918.

12 *Evening Post*, 7 November 1918, pp. 2–3; *NZPD*, Vol. 183, 6 November 1918, p. 200. For example, the Christchurch City Council announced, 'On receipt of authentic news that Germany has been granted an Armistice by the Allies, six guns will be fired, and a motor fire engine will traverse the streets flying a flag and sounding its siren.' *Star*, 11 November 1918, p. 1.

13 *Press*, 7 November 1918, p. 5; *Timaru Herald*, 7 November 1918, p. 9; *Dominion*, 9 November 1918, p. 6.

14 *Manawatu Standard*, 8 November 1918, p. 4; Paul Baker, *King and Country Call: New Zealanders, Conscription and the Great War* (Auckland: Auckland University Press, 1988), p. 230.

15 *New Zealand Herald*, 9 November 1918, p. 8.

16 *Evening Post*, 8 November 1918, p. 6.

17 *Press*, 9 November 1918, p. 8.

18 *Evening Star*, 8 November 1918, p. 4.

19 Graham Hucker, 'The Armistice: Responses, Understandings and Meanings For a Rural Region', in John Crawford and Ian McGibbon (eds), *New Zealand's Great War: New Zealand, the Allies and the First World War* (Auckland: Exisle Publishing, 2007), p. 576; *Evening Star*, 8 November 1918, p. 4.

20 *Wanganui Chronicle*, 9 November 1918, p. 4.

21 *Evening Post*, 8 November 1918, p. 6.

22 ANZ, R3796227, 'Secret Telegraphic Reports on the War Situation — 1 October–29 December 1918', Secretary of State for the Colonies, Walter Long to Governor-General Lord Liverpool, 11 November 1918.

23 *NZPD*, Vol. 183, 5 December 1918, p. 823.

24 *Stratford Evening Post*, 13 November 1918, p. 5.

25 *New Zealand Herald*, 13 November 1918, p. 6; Rice, *Black November*, p. 79.

26 *New Zealand Herald*, 13 November 1918, p. 6; Rice, *Black November*, p. 79; Alexander Turnbull Library (ATL), qMS 0684, Harrold Ennor Diaries, 12 November 1918.

27 ANZ, R3796227, 'Secret Telegraphic Reports on the War Situation — 1 October–29 December 1918', paraphrase of cypher telegram dated 27 October 1918. Indicating that he expected the war was coming to an end, Australian prime minister Hughes had stayed in London after the 1918 War Cabinet. E. M. Andrews, *The Anzac Illusion: Anglo-Australian Relations during World War I* (Cambridge: Cambridge University Press, 1993), p. 201.

28 *NZ Truth*, 19 October 1918, p. 5.

29 *NZPD*, Vol. 183, 9 December 1918, p. 957.

30 Rice, *Black November*, p. 89.

31 *New Zealand Herald*, 12 December 1918, p. 4.

32 *Poverty Bay Herald*, 25 January 1919, p. 3; James Watson, *WF Massey: New Zealand* (London: Haus, 2010), p. 84.

33 R. C. Snelling, 'Peacemaking, 1919: Australia, New Zealand and the British Empire Delegation at Versailles', *Journal of Imperial and Commonwealth History*, Vol. 4, No. 1 (October 1975), pp. 15–28.

34 *Otago Daily Times*, 11 December 1918, p. 6. He added in Parliament, 'The power of Germany has got to be broken now — and broken effectually — so that she will not again become dangerous for a century, or perhaps centuries to come.' *NZPD*, Vol. 183, 28 November 1918, p. 539.

35 Michael Bassett, *Sir Joseph Ward: A Political Biography* (Auckland: Auckland University Press, 1993), p. 243; *NZPD*, Vol. 183, 28 November 1918, p. 539.

36 Richard G. H. Kay, 'In Pursuit of Victory: British–New Zealand Relations During the First World War' (PhD thesis, University of Otago, 2001), p. 284. Massey's realpolitik appears to have found a measure of commonality with French prime

minister Georges Clemenceau and noted in a letter to Allen: 'I get on very well with Clemenceau and most of the others and I hope that I shall have a better opinion of the American delegates by the time I get back.' ANZ, R22319675, 'Miscellaneous files and papers — Correspondence between J Allen and WF Massey, 1st September 1916–1st August 1919', Massey to Allen, 13 February 1919.

37 Bassett, *Sir Joseph Ward*, p. 242; *New Zealand Herald*, 17 July 1919, p. 7; *NZPD*, Vol. 183, 9 December 1918, p. 1037; Kay, 'In Pursuit of Victory', p. 238.

38 *Otago Daily Times*, 23 January 1919, p. 5.

39 Hiery, *The Neglected War*, pp. 177, 206. Margaret MacMillan, *Peacemakers: The Paris Conference of 1919 and Its Attempt to End War* (London: John Murray, 2001), p. 111.

40 ANZ, R22319675, 'Miscellanous files and papers — Correspondence between J Allen and WF Massey, 1st September 1916–1st August 1919', Allen to Massey, 21 January 1919.

41 *NZPD*, Vol. 183, 9 December 1918, p. 1032.

42 ANZ, R22319675, 'Miscellanous files and papers — Correspondence between J Allen and WF Massey, 1st September 1916–1st August 1919', Massey to Allen, 26 April 1919.

43 MacMillan, *Peacemakers*, p. 56.

44 Erik Olssen, 'Towards a Reassessment of W. F. Massey: One of New Zealand's Greatest Prime Ministers (Arguably)', in James Watson and Lachy Paterson (eds), *A Great New Zealand Prime Minister? Reappraising William Ferguson Massey* (Dunedin: Otago University Press, 2011), p. 27. See also Watson, *WF Massey*, p. vii–viii.

45 *Papers Relating to the Foreign Relations of the United States 1919: The Paris Peace Conference*, Vol. 3 (Washington, DC: Government Printing Office, 1943), p. 749.

46 *Papers Relating to the Foreign Relations of the United States 1919*, Vol. 3, p. 751; Lloyd George, *The Truth About the Peace Treaties, Vol. I* (London: Victor Gollancz, 1938), pp. 522–23.

47 *Papers Relating to the Foreign Relations of the United States 1919*, Vol. 3, pp. 753–54.

48 Joan Beaumont, *Broken Nation: Australians in the Great War* (Crows Nest, NSW: Allen & Unwin, 2013), pp. 537–38.

49 Kay, 'In Pursuit of Victory', p. 257.

50 Kay, 'In Pursuit of Victory', pp. 284, 277.

51 James F. Willis, *Prologue to Nuremberg: The Politics and Diplomacy of Punishing War Criminals of the First World War* (Westport, Conn: Greenwood Press, 1982), p. 75; Watson, *WF Massey*, pp. 101–2; Kay, 'In Pursuit of Victory', p. 280.

52 *Poverty Bay Herald*, 13 May 1919, p. 3. He later noted how 'astonished' he was to find differences of opinion in Paris on how to proceed on war crimes. *NZPD*, Vol. 184, 2 September 1919, pp. 41–42.

53 MacMillan, *Peacemakers*, p. 328.

54 The Treaty of Saint-Germain-en-Laye, signed 10 September 1919, and the Treaty of Trianon, signed 4 June 1920, made peace with, respectively, Austria and Hungary. The Treaty of Sèvres, signed 10 August 1920, made peace with the Ottoman Empire. Under articles 218–220, ownership of the graveyards of Allied soldiers was transferred to the British, French and Italian governments. However, the treaty became void after its terms stirred hostility among the Turks and the Turkish War of Independence broke out.

55 *Otago Daily Times*, 5 July 1919, p. 9; *NZPD*, Vol. 200, 26 June 1923, pp. 298–99.

56 Gerald Chaudron, *New Zealand in the League of Nations* (Jefferson, NC: McFarland, 2012), p. 13; Watson, *WF Massey*, p. 123.

57 *Otago Daily Times*, 5 July 1919, p. 9.

58 *New Zealand Observer*, 5 July 1919, p. 2.

59 *Poverty Bay Herald*, 13 May 1919, p. 3; Kay, 'In Pursuit of Victory', pp. 284–85. Allen was of a similar mind about the League of Nations. In a reply written to a Quaker he noted 'we may be relying on a broken reed if we put our faith in the League of Nations. My own opinion is that had the Empire been better prepared hundreds of thousands of the lives of our best young men might have been saved.' ATL, MS-Papers-2597-33/6/01B, 'Conscientious objection to military service', letter from Allen, 20 October 1919.

60 *NZPD*, Vol. 183, 9 December 1918, pp. 1036–40; Kay, 'In Pursuit of Victory', pp. 238–39.

61 *Grey River Argus*, 12 July 1919, p. 4. It repeated many of these points during the 1919 general election. Bruce Brown, *The Rise of New Zealand Labour: A History of the New Zealand Labour Party from 1916 to 1940* (Wellington: Price Milburn, 1962), pp. 108–27.

62 *NZPD*, Vol. 204, 2 September 1919, p. 71. Holland was also critical of the League of Nations. See *NZPD*, Vol. 183, 5 November 1918, p. 194. Though Labour speeches would later come to include degrees of support for the league, as late as 1932 the Labour Party platform called for 'the industrial unity of all workers of all countries, for the purpose of superseding capitalism by an industrial democracy, and of forming not a League of Nations but a League of Peoples'. Chaudron, *New Zealand in the League of Nations*, p. 48; Kathryn Peters, 'New Zealand's Attitudes to the Reform of the League of Nations: The background of the memorandum to the secretary-general, 16 July 1936', *New Zealand Journal of History*, Vol. 6, No. 1 (April 1972), p. 81.

63 Bassett, *Sir Joseph Ward*, p. 244.

64 ANZ, R18919890, 'Folder of notes on Peace

celebrations as they were held after the First World War; for the Second World War celebrations', G. W. Russell, 2 December 1918.

65 *Evening Post*, 18 February 1919, p. 8.

66 ANZ, R18919890, 'Folder of notes on Peace celebrations as they were held after the First World War; for the Second World War celebrations'. Local bodies spending up to £100 were eligible for a pound for pound subsidy and those committing larger amounts were eligible for a subsidy of 17s 6d for each pound for amounts between £100 and £250, 13s per pound for £250 to £500, 12s 6d for £500 to £750, and 10s above £750. By January 1920 the government had paid £20,676 on £46,337. ANZ, R12333449, 'War [File title incomplete. Please see register]'.

67 For planning alterations see Imelda Bargas, 'Endurance, Ephemerality and New Zealand's 1919 Peace Celebrations', in Monger, Murray and Pickles (eds), *Endurance and the First World War*, pp. 239–46.

68 *Evening Post*, 23 June 1919, p. 8. Details in ATL, Ref: Eph-A-WAR-WI-Peace-1919-1, 'Ephemera relating to peace celebrations after World War I. 1919. Folder 1'; ATL, Ref: Eph-A-WAR-WI-Peace-1919-2, 'Ephemera relating to peace celebrations after World War I. 1919. Folder 2'.

69 *Southland Times*, 14 July 1919, p. 5.

70 *Western Star*, 21 February 1919, p. 3; *Auckland Star*, 8 July 1919, p. 5.

71 *Press*, 21 July 1919, p. 7.

72 Damien Fenton with Caroline Lord, Gavin McLean and Tim Shoebridge, *New Zealand and the First World War: 1914–1919* (Auckland: Penguin, 2013), p. 104; Christopher Pugsley, *The Camera in the Crowd: Filming New Zealand in Peace and War, 1895–1920* (Auckland: Oratia Books, 2017), p. 417.

73 *Otago Witness*, 23 July 1919, p. 17; see also *Otago Daily Times*, 21 July 1919, p. 5. Video footage of Dunedin's celebrations is available at http://www.teara.govt.nz/en/video/32469/armistice-celebrations.

74 *Souvenir Programme of Peace Celebrations, Invercargill, New Zealand, 1919* (Invercargill: Southland Times Office, 1919), p. 3.

75 Imelda Bargas and Tim Shoebridge, *New Zealand's First World War Heritage* (Auckland: Exisle Publishing, 2015), pp. 177, 184–85; Jock Phillips, *To the Memory: New Zealand's War Memorials* (Nelson: Potton & Burton, 2016), p. 124.

76 *Grey River Argus*, 17 May 1919, p. 3.

77 Carina Hickey, 'From Coal Pit to Leather Pit: Life Stories of Robert Semple' (PhD thesis, Massey University, 2010), p. 262.

78 *Maoriland Worker*, 16 July 1919, p. 2.

CHAPTER FOURTEEN: DEMOBILISATION AND LEGACIES

1 Kate Hunter and Kirstie Ross, *Holding on to Home: New Zealand Stories and Objects of the First World War* (Wellington: Te Papa Press, 2014), p. 15.

2 Ian McGibbon, 'Conscription', in McGibbon (ed.), *The Oxford Companion to New Zealand Military History* (Auckland: Oxford University Press, 2000), p. 118.

3 Lieut-Colonel J. L. Sleeman, 'The Supply of Reinforcements during the War', in H. T. B. Drew (ed.), *The War Effort of New Zealand* (Auckland: Whitcombe & Tombs, 1923), p. 11. *New Zealand Official Year-book*, 1919, p. 257.

4 Paul Baker, *King and Country Call: New Zealanders, Conscription and the Great War* (Auckland: Auckland University Press, 1988), p. 138.

5 *Appendix to the Journals of the House of Representatives* (*AJHR*), 1918, H-19C, 'Royal Commission on Defence Department Expenditure, 1918', p. 67.

6 *AJHR*, 1920, H-46, 'Patriotic Funds', p. 1. Figure calculated using the Reserve Bank's Inflation Calculator, http://www.rbnz.govt.nz; H. T. B. Drew, 'War Finance', in Drew (ed.), *The War Effort of New Zealand*, p. 243; John E. Martin, 'War Economy', in McGibbon (ed.), *The Oxford Companion to New Zealand Military History*, p. 582.

7 ANZ, R21078971, 'New Zealand Expeditionary Force, its provision and maintenance', p. 50; McGibbon, 'Casualties', in McGibbon (ed.), *The Oxford Companion to New Zealand Military History*, p. 80.

8 These figures are calculated with data from http://www.nzhistory.net.nz/war/world-at-war and Andrej Mitrović, *Serbia's Great War 1914–1918* (London: Hurst & Co., 2007). Given variations in death statistics, the broad pattern should be regarded as more significant than the exact figures. The apocryphal claim appears to originate in Maurice Shadbolt's assertion that 'per capita it [New Zealand's losses] would be the greatest combatant loss of any nation involved in the war'. *Voices of Gallipoli* (Auckland: Hodder & Stoughton, 1988), p. 122.

9 *NZ Truth*, 17 January 1920, p. 1.

10 Joan Beaumont, *Broken Nation: Australians in the Great War* (Crows Nest, NSW: Allen & Unwin, 2013); Martin F. Auger, 'On the Brink of Civil War: The Canadian Government and the Suppression of the 1918 Quebec Easter Riots', *Canadian Historical Review*, Vol. 89, No. 4 (2008), pp. 503–40; Baker, *King and Country Call*, pp. 101, 168. For further consideration of New Zealand political stability against other English-speaking democracies see also Margaret Levi, 'The Institution of Conscription', *Social Science History*, Vol. 20, No. 1 (1996), pp. 133–67.

11 *AJHR*, 1918, H-29, 'Department of Agriculture Industries and Commerce', p. 1.

12 Avner Offer, *The First World War, An Agrarian Interpretation* (New York: Oxford University Press, 1989), p. 29; Alexander Watson, *Ring of Steel: Germany and Austria–Hungary at War, 1914–1918* (London: Allen Lane, 2014), p. 334; Thierry Bonzon and Belinda Davis, 'Feeding the Cities', in Jay Winter and Jean-Louis Robert (eds), *Capital Cities at War: Paris, London, Berlin, 1914–1919* (Cambridge: Cambridge University Press, 1997), p. 321; Andrew Donson, *Youth in the Fatherless Land: War Pedagogy, Nationalism, and Authority in Germany, 1914–1918* (Cambridge: Harvard University Press, 2010), p. 127.

13 Barry Gustafson, *Labour's Path to Political Independence: The Origins and Establishment of the New Zealand Labour Party 1900–19* (Auckland: Auckland University Press, 1980), p. 96.

14 Alan Everton, 'Government Intervention in the New Zealand Economy 1914–1918: Its Aims and Effectiveness' (MA thesis, Victoria University of Wellington, 1995), p. 280.

15 *AJHR*, 1918, H-44, 'Board of Trade (Second Annual Report of the)', p. 15.

16 Michael Wynd, '"So the end has come . . . I shall see you again": Demobilising the New Zealand Expeditionary Force' (MA thesis, Massey University, 2006).

17 *Evening Star*, 19 April 1919, p. 9.

18 *Quick March*, March 1919, p. 53; April 1919, p. 3.

19 *AJHR*, 1917, H-30, 'Discharged Soldiers' Information Department', p. 7.

20 Bronwyn Dalley, '"Come Back With Honour": Prostitution and the New Zealand Soldier, at Home and Abroad', in John Crawford and Ian McGibbon (eds), *New Zealand's Great War: New Zealand, the Allies and the First World War* (Auckland: Exisle Publishing, 2007), pp. 364–77; Joanna Bourke, *An Intimate History of Killing: Face to Face Killing in Twentieth-Century Warfare* (London: Granta Books, 1999), pp. 345–68. Public awareness and discussion of war-related psychological conditions was much higher than is often appreciated. To take but one example, it was reported in May 1917 that '[t]he soldier son of a widowed mother has just returned in such a troubled mental state as the result of his battlefield experiences that the mental authorities have had to take over his care'. *Wairarapa Daily Times*, 16 May 1917, p. 4.

21 Stephen Clarke, 'Return, Repatriation, Remembrance and the Returned Soldiers' Association 1916–22', in Crawford and McGibbon (eds), *New Zealand's Great War*, p. 158; Stephen Clarke, *After the War is Over: The RSA in New Zealand* (Auckland: Penguin, 2016).

22 ANZ, R22434688, 'Publications, instructions, etc. — Publicity — General file', memorandum for the Adjutant-General, 25 November 1919.

23 Imelda Bargas and Tim Shoebridge, *New Zealand's First World War Heritage* (Auckland: Exisle Publishing, 2015), p. 190.

24 *AJHR*, 1930, C-9, 'Discharged Soldier Settlement', p. 6.

25 *Grey River Argus*, 6 October 1916, p. 2.

26 Ashley Gould, 'Maori and the First World War', in McGibbon (ed.), *The Oxford Companion to New Zealand Military History*, pp. 298–99; Ashley Gould, 'From Taiaha to Ko: Repatriation and Land Settlement for Maori Soldiers in New Zealand After the First World War', *War & Society*, Vol. 28, No. 2 (2009), pp. 49–83.

27 *AJHR*, 1921, H-30, 'Repatriation Department', pp. 2, 4; *AJHR*, 1921, C-9, 'Discharged Soldier Settlement', p. 2.

28 *AJHR*, 1920, H-19, 'Defence Forces of New Zealand', p. 5. For study of disabled servicemen see Elizabeth Anne Walker, 'The Living Death: The Repatriation Experience of New Zealand's Disabled Great War Servicemen' (MA thesis, Victoria University of Wellington, 2013); Russell Clarke, '"Not Mad, But Very Ill": The Treatment of New Zealand's Shellshocked Soldiers 1914 to 1939' (MA thesis, University of Auckland, 1991), p. 49; Gwen A. Parsons, 'The Construction of Shell Shock in New Zealand, 1919–1939: A Reassessment', *Social History of Medicine*, Vol. 26, Issue 1 (February 2013), pp. 1–18.

29 *AJHR*, 1930, H-18, 'Thirty-second Annual Report of the Pensions Department', p. 3.

30 *AJHR*, 1930, H-18, 'Thirty-second Annual Report of the Pensions Department', p. 4.

31 *AJHR*, 1930, H-18, 'Thirty-second Annual Report of the Pensions Department', p. 6.

32 Bargas and Shoebridge, *New Zealand's First World War Heritage*, pp. 199–200.

33 Bargas and Shoebridge, *New Zealand's First World War Heritage*, pp. 199–200; A. D. Carbery, *The New Zealand Medical Service in the Great War 1914–1918* (Auckland: Whitcombe & Tombs, 1924), pp. 502–17; Anna Rogers, *With Them Through Hell: New Zealand Medical Services in the First World War* (Auckland: Massey University Press, 2018), pp. 395–408.

34 Carbery, *The New Zealand Medical Service in the Great War*, p. 513.

35 Bargas and Shoebridge, *New Zealand's First World War Heritage*, pp. 200–4; Neil Frances, *Safe Haven: The Untold Story of New Zealand's Largest Ever Military Camp, 1916–1919* (Masterton: Wairarapa Archive in association with Fraser Books, 2012), pp. 153–61.

36 Howard Weddell, *Trentham Camp and Upper Hutt's Untold Military History* (Upper Hutt: Howard Weddell, 2018), p. 70.

37 *AJHR*, 1919, H-19, 'Defence Department', pp. 38–39.

38 *AJHR*, 1930, H-18, 'Thirty-second Annual Report of the Pensions Department', p. 3.

39 *AJHR*, 1922, H-30, 'Repatriation Department', p. 3.

40 Miles Fairburn, 'The Farmers Take Over (1912–30)', in Keith Sinclair (ed.), *The Oxford Illustrated History of New Zealand*, 2nd edn (Auckland: Oxford University Press, 1996), p. 205; Nicholas Boyack and Jane Tolerton, *In Shadow of War: New Zealand Soldiers Talk About World War One and Their Lives* (Auckland: Penguin, 1990), p. 245. For an overview of the tone of scholarship of the soldier-settler scheme see Ashley Gould, 'Proof of Gratitude? Soldier Land Settlement in New Zealand After World War I' (PhD thesis, Massey University, 1992), pp. 4–41.

41 Bargas and Shoebridge, *New Zealand's First World War Heritage*, p. 208.

42 Gould, 'Maori and the First World War', in McGibbon (ed.), *The Oxford Companion to New Zealand Military History*, pp. 298–99; Gould, 'From Taiaha to Ko', pp. 49–83.

43 Michael Roche, '"A Duty of the Country": Soldier Settlement 1915–1941', in Rachael Bell (ed.), *New Zealand Between the Wars* (Auckland: Massey University Press, 2017), p. 61; Gwen A. Parsons, 'Challenging Enduring Home Front Myths: Jingoistic Civilians and Neglected Soldiers', in David Monger, Sarah Murray and Katie Pickles (eds), *Endurance and the First World War: Experiences and Legacies in New Zealand and Australia* (Newcastle upon Tyne: Cambridge Scholars Publishing, 2014), pp. 72–85; Gould, 'Proof of Gratitude?'; Coralie Clarkson, 'The Reality of Return: Exploring the Experiences of World War One Soldiers after Their Return to New Zealand' (MA thesis, Victoria University of Wellington, 2011).

44 It proposed the establishment of a Soldiers' Civil Re-establishment League to restore some of the former Repatriation Department's duties. In 1930 Parliament obliged and the league came under the authority of the minister of pensions. *AJHR*, 1930, H-39, 'Ex-Soldiers Rehabilitation Commission', pp. 1–30; *New Zealand Statutes*, 1930, No. 38, 'Disabled Soldiers' Civil Reestablishment Act', pp. 179–80.

45 *New Zealand Herald*, 14 January 1919, p. 4. A November 1918 Reform caucus meeting had declared its support for a party merger and Liberal ranks also expressed tension over an abandonment of the partnership with Reform. *Press*, 16 November 1918, p. 9; Michael Bassett, *Three Party Politics in New Zealand, 1911–1931* (Auckland: Historical Publications, 1982), p. 24.

46 ANZ, R22319675, 'Miscellanous files and papers — Correspondence between J Allen and WF Massey, 1st September 1916–1st August 1919', Allen to Massey, 26 April 1919; *Evening Star*, 22 August 1919, p. 7.

47 Gustafson, *Labour's Path to Political Independence*, pp. 144–45; Leicester Chisholm Webb, 'The Rise of the Reform Party: A History of Party Politics in New Zealand between 1910 and 1920' (Honours thesis, University of New Zealand, 1928), pp. 183–96.

48 *Evening Post*, 11 November 1919, p. 3.

49 Keith Sinclair, *A History of New Zealand* (Harmondsworth: Penguin, 1976), pp. 243–44.

50 Peter Franks and Jim McAloon, *Labour: The New Zealand Labour Party, 1916–2016* (Wellington: Victoria University Press, 2016), p. 74; Bassett, *Three Party Politics*, p. 25.

51 *Press*, 30 December 1919, p. 6.

52 *Marlborough Express*, 3 September 1919, p. 7.

53 *New Zealand Times*, 17 December 1919, p. 2; *Wanganui Herald*, 22 August 1919, p. 7.

54 P. J. O'Farrell, 'The Russian Revolution and the Labour Movements of Australia and New Zealand, 1917–1922', *International Review of Social History*, Vol. 8, Issue 2 (August 1963), p. 177.

55 The effects of this stimulus resonated for some years; 'Up to 1921, the hope of world revolution acted as both spur and inspiration, assisting their claim to a dominant role in the Labour Party.' O'Farrell, 'The Russian Revolution', p. 195.

56 *Evening Post*, 20 December 1918, p. 3.

57 *Auckland Star*, 19 February 1919, p. 5.

58 Gustafson, *Labour's Path to Political Independence*, p. 147; P. J. O'Farrell, *Harry Holland: Militant Socialist* (Canberra: Australian National University, 1964), p. 97.

59 P. S. O'Connor, 'Some Political Preoccupations of Mr Massey, 1918–20', *Political Science*, Vol. 18, No. 2 (1966), p. 22.

60 *New Zealand Herald*, 10 July 1919, p. 7.

61 *Press*, 20 August 1920, p. 8.

62 Erik Olssen, 'Towards a Reassessment of W. F. Massey: One of New Zealand's Greatest Prime Ministers (Arguably)', in James Watson and Lachy Paterson (eds), *A Great New Zealand Prime Minister?: Reappraising William Ferguson Massey* (Dunedin: Otago University Press, 2011), p. 23; O'Connor, 'Some Political Preoccupations of Mr Massey', p. 30. Allegations of collusion between Reform and the PPA were also raised in Parliament. *New Zealand Parliamentary Debates* (*NZPD*), Vol. 185, 15 October 1919, pp. 391–92.

63 Gustafson, *Labour's Path to Political Independence*, p. 130.

64 *NZ Truth*, 20 December 1919, p. 2.

65 *New Zealand Herald*, 17 November 1919, p. 6.

66 *Poverty Bay Herald*, 5 December 1919, p. 9.

67 David C. Thorns and Charles P. Sedgewick, *Understanding Aotearoa/New Zealand: Historical Statistics* (Palmerston North: Dunmore Press, 1997), p. 166.

68 David Littlewood, 'The Provision of Opportunities: Politics and the State', in Bell (ed.), *New Zealand Between the Wars*, pp. 44.

69 In contrast to South African and Canadian counterparts, who saw League membership as a milestone towards greater independence, New Zealand officials have been observed as seeing League membership as 'an unwelcome burden' with the organisation 'criticized as a dangerous illusion and potential threat to the empire'. Gerald Chaudron, *New Zealand in the League of Nations* (Jefferson, NC: McFarland, 2012), pp. 7, 27.

70 For an outline of traditional assessments, see Olssen, 'Towards a Reassessment of W. F. Massey', pp. 15–30. Massey and Seddon are deemed as coming second 'after Fraser, who led the country through the gravest challenges that it has ever faced'. Tom Brooking, *Richard Seddon: King of God's Own* (Auckland: Penguin Books, 2014), p. 423.

71 Baker, *King and Country Call*, p. 190.

72 Michael Bassett, *Sir Joseph Ward: A Political Biography* (Auckland: Auckland University Press, 1993), p. 247.

73 *New Zealand Herald*, 18 December 1919, p. 6.

74 *NZ Truth*, 27 December 1919, pp. 4–5.

75 Bassett, *Sir Joseph Ward*, p. 275.

76 *Evening Post*, 8 July 1930, p. 10.

77 *Maoriland Worker*, 24 December 1919, p. 4.

78 Gustafson, *Labour's Path to Political Independence*, p. 150.

79 Nicholas Hoare, 'Harry Holland's "Samoan Complex"', *The Journal of Pacific History*, Vol. 49, No. 2 (2014), pp. 151–69; O'Farrell, *Harry Holland*.

80 A marble figure on his grave was stated as symbolising 'the struggles of humanity, of the onward and upward march of mankind from slavery and serfdom and the tyrannies and cruelties of the past to the Peace and universally shared Prosperity of the Future'.

81 Tim Beaglehole, 'Fraser, Peter', *Dictionary of New Zealand Biography* (*DNZB*), Te Ara — Encyclopedia of New Zealand, https://teara.govt.nz/en/biographies/4f22/fraser-peter.

82 *New Zealand Official Year-book*, 1921–22, p. 259; *New Zealand Official Year-book*, 1927, p. 606; Malcolm McKinnon, 'Post-war Economies (New Zealand)', in *1914–1918-online: International Encyclopedia of the First World War*, eds Ute Daniel, Peter Gatrell, Oliver Janz, Heather Jones, Jennifer Keene, Alan Kramer and Bill Nasson, issued by Freie Universität Berlin, Berlin 2015-02-17. DOI: 10.15463/ie1418.10556.

83 The clause limiting six o'clock closing to expire six months after the war was repealed by section 2 of the Licensing Amendment Act of 10 December 1918.

84 ANZ, R3898752, 'New Zealand's part in the war, March 1917–September 1919', pp. 22–23; *NZPD*, Vol. 183, 4 December 1918, p. 730.

85 ANZ, R3796215, 'Inwards and outwards despatches relating to the European War — 30 October–4 December 1918', Secretary of State for the Colonies, Walter Long to Governor-General Lord Liverpool, 21 November 1918.

86 *Dominion*, 15 November 1918, p. 4.

87 Frances, *Safe Haven*, p. 147.

88 Michael King, *Te Puea: A Life* (Auckland: Reed, 2003), pp. 96–97.

89 Baker, *King and Country Call*, p. 223; Judith Bassett, 'Colonial Justice: The Treatment of Dalmatians in New Zealand during the First World War', *New Zealand Journal of History*, Vol. 33, No. 2 (October 1999), pp. 176–79.

90 Graeme Dunstall, *A Policeman's Paradise?: Policing a Stable Society 1918–1945* (Wellington: Dunmore Press, 1999), pp. 253, 265, 257.

91 *NZPD*, Vol. 187, 24 August 1920, pp. 354, 359.

92 From this position he ordered the censorship of films including *The Te Kooti Trail* and *All Quiet on the Western Front* and banned James Joyce's novel *Ulysses* as indecent.

93 ANZ, R22319675, 'Miscellanous files and papers — Correspondence between J Allen and WF Massey, 1st September 1916–1st August 1919', Allen to Massey, 7 July 1919; Jared Davidson, *Dead Letters: Censorship and Subversion in New Zealand 1914–1920* (Dunedin: Otago University Press, 2019), p. 34.

94 *NZPD*, Vol. 186, 14 July 1920, p. 411; Vol. 187, 10 August 1920, p. 39; Vol. 187, 27 August 1920, p. 493; Vol. 189, 25 October 1920, p. 18; Davidson, *Dead Letters*, p. 49.

95 ANZ, R3885342, 'Intelligence — Imperial bureau establishment in New Zealand March', Liverpool to Allen, 25 March 1919; Allen to Liverpool, 5 June 1919.

96 ANZ, R22434688, 'Publications, instructions, etc. — Publicity — General file', Richardson to Potter, 26 June 1920; ANZ, R22434795, 'Publications, instructions, etc. — Military propaganda in New Zealand — Correspondence re', Extract from Letter from Chief of Imperial General Staff, 14 October 1920. See also Greg Hynes, 'Propaganda, Perspective, and the British World: New Zealand's First World War Propaganda and British Interactions, 1914–1918' (MA thesis, University of Canterbury, 2013), p. 144.

97 Everton, 'Government Intervention in the New Zealand Economy', pp. 17, 408; Martin, 'War Economy', in McGibbon (ed.), *The Oxford Companion to New Zealand Military History*, p. 582; Tod Simpson, 'The Origins of Statutory Producer Control Legislation in New Zealand Agriculture, 1914–1925' (MCA thesis, Victoria University of Wellington, 1991), p. 18.

98 Michael Bassett, *The State in New Zealand, 1840–*

1984: Socialism without Doctrines? (Auckland: Auckland University Press, 1998), p. 130. In 1932 William Sutch completed a PhD thesis in favour of the ambitions of the Board of Trade's endeavours. This was later published as W. B. Sutch, *Price Fixing in New Zealand* (New York: AMS Press, 1968).

99 *New Zealand Statutes*, 1919, No. 15, 'Board of Trade', pp. 46–55; John E. Martin, 'Blueprint for the Future? "National Efficiency" and the First World War', in Crawford and McGibbon (eds), *New Zealand's Great War*, pp. 516–33.

100 *Colonist*, 17 June 1919, p. 3. McKinnon, 'Post-war Economies (New Zealand)'.

101 *Manawatu Times*, 6 December 1920, p. 5.

102 John E. Martin, *Holding the Balance: A History of New Zealand's Department of Labour 1891–1995* (Christchurch: Canterbury University Press, 1996), p. 384; Erik Olssen, 'Negotiating Conditions and Commitment: The Union Movement and the First World War', in Steven Loveridge (ed.), *New Zealand Society at War, 1914–1918* (Wellington: Victoria University Press, 2016), pp. 156–58; *New Zealand Official Year-book*, 1923, pp. 579–81; Everton, 'Government Intervention in the New Zealand Economy', p. 342.

103 *New Zealand Observer*, 5 July 1919, p. 2.

104 For example, see *Wanganui Herald*, 28 May 1919, p. 9. For further details, see Andrew Francis, *'To Be Truly British We Must Be Anti-German': New Zealand, Enemy Aliens and the Great War Experience, 1914–1919* (Oxford; New York: Peter Lang, 2012), p. 261.

105 Millicent Baxter, *The Memoirs of Millicent Baxter* (Whatamongo Bay: Cape Catley, 1981), p. 59.

106 *Sun*, 11 December 1918, p. 4; *Press*, 6 December 1918, p. 6; *Sun*, 6 December 1918, p. 6.

107 *Dominion*, 11 December 1918, p. 4, 17 December 1918, p. 6; *Sun*, 9 December 1918, p. 5; *NZPD*, Vol. 183, 9 December 1918, p. 1025.

108 *Stratford Evening Post*, 14 December 1918, p. 5.

109 *Wanganui Herald*, 12 December 1918, p. 12.

110 *Rangitikei Advocate and Manawatu Argus*, 10 December 1918, p. 4.

111 *Evening Post*, 23 January 1919, p. 8; *Wanganui Chronicle*, 24 December 1918, p. 5; Baker, *King and Country Call*, p. 201.

112 ANZ, R22429771, 'Territorial Force — Defaulters undergoing imprisonment', Christchurch RSA resolution, 5 December 1918; Rotorua RSA resolution, 5 February 1919; ANZ, R22429770, 'Territorial Force — Religious Objectors Advisory Board', Memorandum for the Chairman of the Public Petition Committee, 26 September 1919.

113 Fairburn, 'The Farmers Take Over (1912–30)', p. 191.

114 Mrs Moore's speech noted that she 'could not but remark upon the fact that recognition of the work done by the Women's Anti-German League came from a foreign country, an ally, but not from their own Government'. *Dominion*, 12 July 1919, p. 4.

115 Graham Hucker, '"Bundling out the Hun": The Women's Anti-German League during the First World War', in Loveridge (ed.), *New Zealand Society at War*, pp. 263–65.

116 Brad Patterson, '"We stand for the Protestant religion, the (Protestant) King and the Empire": The Rise of the Protestant Political Association in World War One', in Loveridge (ed.), *New Zealand Society at War*, p. 250.

117 *New Zealand Tablet*, 21 August 1919, p. 26.

118 Rory Sweetman, 'New Zealand Catholicism, War, Politics and the Irish Issue 1912–1922' (PhD thesis, University of Cambridge, 1990), p. 329.

119 On 1 February 1939, aged 61, Kelly died in Hāwera and his grave in Ōkato cemetery is marked by a sizable Celtic cross. His obituary dwelled upon his 'brilliant pen', which was said to explain 'the real situation in Ireland' and refute 'the false despatches circulated by the hostile British and Colonial Press'. 'Only those who read his articles at that time can realise what a friend Ireland has lost in Dr Kelly.' Rory Sweetman, 'Kelly, James Joseph', *DNZB*, Te Ara — Encyclopedia of New Zealand, https://teara.govt.nz/en/biographies/3k6/kelly-james-joseph; *New Zealand Tablet*, 22 March 1939, pp. 8, 41.

120 Jock Phillips, 'The Great War and New Zealand Nationalism: The Evidence of the War Memorials', in Judith Smart and Tony Wood (eds), *An ANZAC Muster: War and Society in Australia and New Zealand 1914–18 and 1939–45* (Clayton: Department of History, Monash University, 1992), pp. 14–29.

121 *Press*, 26 April 1924, p. 9.

122 *Evening Post*, 26 April 1922, p. 8.

123 The history of the practice is outlined in Juliet Nicolson, *The Great Silence, 1918–1920: Living in the Shadow of the Great War* (London: John Murray, 2009), pp. 140–47.

124 *Auckland Star*, 11 November 1920, p. 5.

125 Nicholas J. Saunders, *The Poppy: A History of Conflict, Loss, Remembrance & Redemption* (London: Oneworld, 2014), pp. 111–12.

126 Helen Robinson, 'Lest We Forget?: The Fading of New Zealand War Commemorations, 1946–1966', *New Zealand Journal of History*, Vol. 44, No. 1 (April 2010), pp. 76–91.

127 *Taranaki Herald*, 13 November 1918, p. 2.

128 Baker, *King and Country Call*, p. 231. See also Bell (ed.), *New Zealand Between the Wars*.

129 Erik Olssen, 'Towards a New Society', in W. H. Oliver with B. R. Williams (eds), *The Oxford History of New Zealand* (Wellington: Oxford University Press, 1981), pp. 272–73; James Belich, *Paradise Reforged: A History of the New Zealanders from the 1880s to the Year 2000* (Honolulu: University

of Hawai'i Press, 2001), pp. 121–25, 248–49. All South Island provinces lost males between 1911 and 1916 whereas all North Island provinces saw some growth except Wellington, where the drop was relatively minor. The trend is also evident with regard to the female population and all North Island provinces, except Taranaki, increased their rate of growth between 1911 and 1916, relative to 1906–11, while the rate dropped in all South Island provinces. The greatest movement was in the age 20–30 cohort, largely independent of parents but likely to be unmarried or childless if married. *Census*, 1916, p. 4.

130 Frances McCall Rosenbluth and John A. Ferejohn, *Forged Through Fire: War Peace and the Democratic Bargain* (New York: Liveright Publishing Corporation, 2017), p. 1. For another major example of how wars have shaped social conditions of egalitarian citizenship see Walter Scheidel, *The Great Leveler: Violence and the History of Inequality From the Stone Age to the Twenty-First Century* (New Jersey: Princeton University Press, 2017). For a New Zealand example see David Littlewood, 'We're all equal here, mate: Egalitarianism in Aotearoa New Zealand', in Trudie Cain, Ella Kahu and Richard Shaw (eds), *Tūrangawaewae: Identity & Belonging in Aotearoa New Zealand* (Auckland: Massey University Press, 2017), p. 216.

131 For example, David Thomson and Melanie Nolan have noted the significance of the 1915 War Pensions Act. David Thomson, *A World Without Welfare: New Zealand's Colonial Experiment* (Auckland: Auckland University Press with Bridget Williams Books, 1998), p. 164; Melanie Nolan, *Breadwinning: New Zealand Women and the State* (Christchurch: Canterbury University Press, 2000), pp. 69–102.

132 Justin Thomas Strang, 'Welfare in Transition: Reform's Income Support Policy, 1912–1928' (MA thesis, Victoria University of Wellington, 1992), p. 135.

133 Baker, *King and Country Call*, p. 231.

134 *New Zealand Statutes*, 1918, No. 9, 'Expeditionary Forces Amendment', section 13, p. 75.

135 *NZPD*, Vol. 185, 24 October 1919, pp. 832; Roger Openshaw, 'The Highest Expression of Devotion: New Zealand Primary-Schools and Patriotic Zeal during the Early 1920s', *History of Education*, Vol. 9, No. 4 (1980), p. 342. The Undesirable Immigrants Exclusion Act empowered the attorney-general to deport or bar entry to anyone deemed 'disaffected or disloyal, or of such a character that his presence would be injurious to the peace, order, and good government'. *New Zealand Statutes*, 1919, No. 44, 'Undesirable Immigrants Exclusion', pp. 160–64.

136 Geoffrey Troughton, 'The *Maoriland Worker* and Blasphemy in New Zealand', *Labour History*, No. 91 (November 2006), pp. 113–29; *New Zealand Herald*, 18 March 1922, p. 10. See also Rory Sweetman, *Bishop in the Dock: The Sedition Trial of James Liston* (Auckland: Auckland University Press, 1997).

137 Paul Christoffel, 'Prohibition and the Myth of 1919', *New Zealand Journal of History*, Vol. 42, No. 2 (October 2008), pp. 154–75.

138 For a sense of how many changes associated with the war built on pre-war trends and post-war life extended or renewed many pre-war dynamics see Steven Loveridge, *Calls to Arms: New Zealand Society and Commitment to the First World War* (Wellington: Victoria University Press, 2014).

139 Roberta Nicholis, *The Women's Parliament: The National Council of Women of New Zealand, 1896–1920* (Wellington: Victoria University Press, 1996), p. 111; Betty Holt with Joyce Herd and Dorothea Horsman, *Women in Council: A History of the National Council of Women of New Zealand* (Wellington: The Council, 1980), p. 48.

140 *NZPD*, Vol. 185, 23 October 1919, p. 758.

141 *NZPD*, Vol. 184, 26 September 1919, pp. 964–65.

142 *Wairarapa Age*, 21 November 1919, p. 4.

143 *Otago Witness*, 26 July 1916, p. 59.

144 Thorns and Sedgewick, *Understanding Aotearoa/New Zealand*, p. 62; G. T. Bloomfield, *New Zealand, A Handbook of Historical Statistics* (Boston: G. K. Hall, 1984), p. 138; Shannon R. Brown, 'Female Office Workers in Auckland, 1891–1936' (MA thesis, University of Auckland, 1993), pp. 33, 59. Nolan notes that single women were 'pushed to the bottom of the labour hierarchy and out of the service'. Nolan, *Breadwinning*, p. 27.

145 *New Zealand Herald*, 5 May 1928, supplement, p. 5.

146 James Bennett, 'Maori as Honorary Members of the White Tribe', *The Journal of Imperial and Commonwealth History*, Vol. 29, No. 3 (2001), pp. 43–44.

147 James Cowan, *The Maoris in the Great War: A History of the New Zealand Native Contingent and Pioneer Battalion: Gallipoli 1915, France and Flanders 1916–1918* (Auckland: Maori Regimental Committee, 1926), pp. ix–x.

148 Bennett, 'Maori as Honorary Members of the White Tribe', p. 45.

149 *New Zealand Times*, 19 April 1919, p. 9.

150 *Wanganui Chronicle*, 24 May 1919, p. 5.

151 Quoted Keith Newman, *Ratana: The Prophet* (Auckland: Raupo, 2009), p. 36.

152 Ranginui Walker, *Ka Whawhai tonu Matou: Struggle without End* (Auckland: Penguin, 2004), pp. 183–84; Basil Keane, 'Kotahitanga — unity movements', Te Ara — the Encyclopedia of New Zealand, http://www.TeAra.govt.nz/en/kotahitanga-unity-movements/print.

153 Jock Phillips, 'Race and New Zealand National Identity', in Neil Garnham and Keith Jeffery (eds), *Culture, Place and Identity* (Dublin: University

College Dublin Press, 2005), p. 174; Belich, *Paradise Reforged*, p. 117.

154 Rory Sweetman, '"Who Fears to Speak of Easter Week?" Antipodean Irish Catholic Responses to the 1916 Rising', in Ruan O'Donnell (ed.), *The Impact of the 1916 Rising: Among the Nations* (Dublin: Irish Academic Press, 2008), p. 74.

155 Steven Loveridge, 'Not so Quiet on the New Zealand Front: *All Quiet on the Western Front* and New Zealand Memories of the Great War', *Journal of New Zealand Studies*, No. 18 (2014), pp. 23–40; Scott Worthy, '"Light and Shade": The New Zealand Written Remembrance of the Great War, 1915–1939', *War & Society*, Vol. 22, No. 1 (2004), pp. 19–40; Lawrence Jones, '"The Shadow of That Earlier War": World War I in the Writing of the 1930s', *Journal of New Zealand Literature*, Vol. 18, No. 19 (2000/2001), pp. 67–82.

156 Although it is difficult to study, scholarship also indicates the significance of family history in shaping individuals' sense of the war. Jay Winter, *Remembering War: The Great War Between Memory and History in the Twentieth Century* (New Haven: Yale University Press, 2006), pp. 40–45; Rosa Maria Bracco, *Merchants of Hope: British Middlebrow Writers and the First World War, 1919–1939* (Providence: Berg, 1993), p. 71.

157 E. K. Mulgan and Alan Mulgan, *The New Zealand Citizen: An Elementary Account of the Citizen's Rights and Duties and the Work of Government*, 3rd edn (Auckland: Whitcombe & Tombs, 1922), pp. 20–21.

158 For major studies of this process in the British context see Dan Todman, *The Great War: Myth and Memory* (London: Bloomsbury Academic, 2005) and David Reynolds, *The Long Shadow: The Great War and The Twentieth Century* (London: Simon & Schuster, 2013); Loveridge, 'Not so Quiet on the New Zealand Front'.

159 *The Month*, 2 August 1930, p. 23.

160 *Tomorrow*, 17 February 1937, p. 231.

161 *Evening Post*, 7 November 1939, p. 33; Steven Loveridge, 'Another Great War?: New Zealand Interpretations of the First World War towards and into the Second World War', *First World War Studies*, Vol. 7, No. 3 (2016), pp. 309–10, 312.

162 Michael Bassett with Michael King, *Tomorrow Comes the Song: A Life of Peter Fraser* (Auckland: Penguin, 2000), pp. 186–87.

163 Loveridge, 'Another Great War?', p. 13; David Grant, *Out in the Cold: Pacifists and Conscientious Objectors in New Zealand during World War II* (Auckland: Reed Methuen, 1986), p. 119.

164 Len Richardson, *Coal, Class & Community: The United Mineworkers of New Zealand, 1880–1960* (Auckland: Auckland University Press, 1995), p. 279; Loveridge, 'Another Great War?', p. 13.

165 Ian McGibbon, 'Gallipoli, National Identity and New Beginnings', in Robert G. Patman, Iati Iati and Balazs Kiglics (eds), *New Zealand and the World: Past, Present and Future* (World Scientific Publishing, Singapore, 2018), pp. 39–54. For a study examining this phenomenon across the dominions and in contrast to Britain see Mark D. Sheftall, *Altered Memories of the Great War: Divergent Narratives of Britain, Australia, New Zealand and Canada* (London: I. B. Tauris, 2009).

166 *NZ Truth*, 22 April 1926, p. 1.

167 O. E. Burton, *New Zealand Division* (Auckland: Clark & Matheson, printers, 1936), pp. 120–21. In the Australian context this growth of nationalism has been associated with a tradition of 'radical nationalism', which fused conceptions of a distinctive national character with left-wing political aspirations. The appearance of similar features in the New Zealand intellectual landscape was the potential result of importation, inspiration or parallel development. For consideration of radical nationalism see Carolyn Holbrook, *ANZAC: The Unauthorised Biography* (Sydney: University of New South Wales Press, 2014), p. 5.

168 *NZPD*, Vol. 183, 30 October 1918, p. 114.

169 *NZPD*, Vol. 185, 17 October 1919, p. 519. 'They have ceased to be dependencies of the Empire. They have become partners — partners with all the duties, responsibilities, and privileges that belong to a partnership.' *NZPD*, Vol. 184, 2 September 1919, p. 36.

170 *NZPD*, Vol. 185, 17 October 1919, p. 538.

171 *School Journal*, Part iii, v. xvi (February 1922), p. 16.

172 *Evening Post*, 26 April 1932, p. 8.

173 For example, Maurice Shadbolt noted, 'The war was never New Zealand's. Our territory was not at risk: we could not have been further from it all. Even the causes of the conflict were not clear to us.' Speaking at Gallipoli at Anzac Day 2003 Dame Silvia Cartwright said, 'For New Zealand the suffering and death had added poignancy because New Zealand had nothing to gain from the fight at Gallipoli. It was someone else's war.' Shadbolt, *Voices of Gallipoli*, p. 100; *Dominion Post*, 25 April 2003, p. A4. See also Stevan Eldred-Grigg, *The Great Wrong War: New Zealand Society in WW1* (Auckland: Random House, 2010) and Nicky Hager, *Other People's Wars: New Zealand in Afghanistan, Iraq and the War on Terror* (Nelson: Craig Potton Publishing, 2011), pp. 184–85.

SELECT BIBLIOGRAPHY

Anderson, John. 'Military Censorship in World War I: Its Use and Abuse in New Zealand'. MA thesis, Victoria University College, Wellington, 1952.

Baker, Paul. *King and Country Call: New Zealanders, Conscription and the Great War*. Auckland: Auckland University Press, 1988.

Bargas, Imelda and Tim Shoebridge. *New Zealand's First World War Heritage*. Auckland: Exisle Publishing, 2015.

Bassett, Judith. 'Colonial Justice: The Treatment of Dalmatians in New Zealand during the First World War'. *New Zealand Journal of History*, Vol. 33, No. 2 (October 1999): 155–179.

Bassett, Michael. *Sir Joseph Ward: A Political Biography*. Auckland: Auckland University Press, 1993.

Bassett, Michael with Michael King. *Tomorrow Comes the Song: A Life of Peter Fraser*. Auckland: Penguin, 2000.

Binney, Judith, Gillian Chaplin and Craig Wallace. *Mihaia: The Prophet Rua Kenana and His Community at Maungapohatu*. New York: Oxford University Press, 1979.

Bourke, Chris. *Good-bye Maoriland: The Songs & Sounds of New Zealand's Great War*. Auckland: Auckland University Press, 2017.

Bromby, Robin. *German Raiders of the South Seas*. Sydney: Doubleday, 1985.

Crawford, John and Ian McGibbon (eds). *New Zealand's Great War: New Zealand, the Allies and the First World War*. Auckland: Exisle Publishing, 2007.

Davidson, Jared. *Dead Letters: Censorship and Subversion in New Zealand 1914–1920*. Dunedin: Otago University Press, 2019.

Everton, Alan. 'Government Intervention in the New Zealand Economy 1914–1918: Its Aims and Effectiveness'. MA thesis, Victoria University of Wellington, 1995.

Frances, Neil. *Safe Haven: The Untold Story of New Zealand's Largest Ever Military Camp: Featherston: 1916–1919*. Masterton: Wairarapa Archive/Fraser Books, 2012.

Francis, Andrew. *'To Be Truly British We Must Be Anti-German': New Zealand, Enemy Aliens and the Great War Experience, 1914–1919*. Oxford; New York: Peter Lang, 2012.

Fraser, Malcolm. *Prices: An Inquiry into Prices in New Zealand 1891–1914*. Wellington: Government Printer, 1920.

Graham, John. 'The Voluntary System: Recruiting 1914–16'. MA thesis, University of Auckland, 1971.

Gustafson, Barry. *Labour's Path to Political Independence: The Origins and Establishment of the New Zealand Labour Party 1900–19*. Auckland: Auckland University Press, 1980.

Harper, Glyn. *Johnny Enzed: The New Zealand Soldier in the First World War*. Auckland: Exisle Publishing, 2015.

Holland, H. E. *Armageddon or Calvary: The Conscientious Objectors of New Zealand and 'The Process of Their Conversion'*. Wellington: The Maoriland Worker Printing and Publishing Co. Ltd, 1919.

Hucker, Graham. 'When the Empire Calls: Patriotic Organisations in New Zealand During the Great War'. MA thesis, Massey University, 1979.

Hunter, Kate and Kirstie Ross. *Holding on to Home: New Zealand Stories and Objects of the First World War*. Wellington: Te Papa Press, 2014.

Hynes, Greg. 'Propaganda, Perspective, and the British World: New Zealand's First World War Propaganda and British Interactions, 1914–1918'. MA thesis, University of Canterbury, 2013.

Kay, Richard G. H. 'In Pursuit of Victory: British–New Zealand Relations During the First World War'. PhD thesis, University of Otago, 2001.

King, Michael. *Te Puea: A Life*. Auckland: Reed, 2003.

Littlewood, David. 'The Dutifully Reluctant: New Zealanders' Appeals for Exemption from Conscription, 1916–1918'. *New Zealand Journal of History*, Vol. 50, No. 2 (2016): 26–43.

Loveridge, Steven. *Calls to Arms: New Zealand Society and Commitment to the Great War*. Wellington: Victoria University Press, 2014.

——— 'Another Great War? New Zealand interpretations of the First World War towards and into the Second World War'. *First World War Studies*, Vol. 7, No. 3 (2016): 303–25.

——— (ed.). *New Zealand Society at War, 1914–1918.* Wellington: Victoria University Press, 2016.

Luxford, Sarah, 'Passengers for the War: The Involvement of Women in Employment During the Great War 1914–1918'. MA thesis, Massey University, 2005.

McGibbon, Ian. *The Path to Gallipoli: Defending New Zealand, 1840–1915*. Wellington: GP Books, 1991.

——— (ed.). *The Oxford Companion to New Zealand Military*. Auckland: Oxford University Press, 2000.

Moores, H. S. 'The Rise of the Protestant Political Association: Sectarianism in New Zealand Politics During World War I'. MA thesis, University of Auckland, 1966.

Murray, Sarah, *A Cartoon War: The Cartoons of the* New Zealand Freelance *and* New Zealand Observer *as Historical Sources, August 1914–November 1918.* Wellington: New Zealand Cartoon Archive, 2012.

O'Connor, P. S. 'The Recruitment of Maori Soldiers, 1914–18'. *Political Science*, Vol. 19, Issue 2 (December 1967): 48–83.

O'Farrell, P. J. *Harry Holland: Militant Socialist.* Canberra: Australian National University, 1964.

Olssen, Erik. *The Red Feds: Revolutionary Industrial Unionism and the New Zealand Federation of Labour 1908–1913*. Auckland: Oxford University Press, 1988.

Phillips, Jock. *To The Memory: New Zealand's War Memorials*. Nelson: Potton & Burton, 2016.

Pointer, Margaret. *Niue and the Great War*. Dunedin: Otago University Press, 2018.

Rice, Geoffrey. *Black November: The 1918 Influenza Pandemic in New Zealand*, 2nd edn. Christchurch: Canterbury University Press, 2005.

Richardson, Len. *Coal, Class & Community: The United Mineworkers of New Zealand, 1880–1960*. Auckland: Auckland University Press, 1995.

Reddiex, Glenn. *Just to let You Know I'm Still Alive: Postcards from New Zealanders During the First World War*. Wellington: Grantham House Publishing, 2015.

Soutar, Monty. 'E te Iwi, Whitiki! Whiti! Whiti! E! Call to Arms: The Formation of the Maori Contingent in the First World War'. *Turnbull Library Record*, 46 (2014): 8–23.

Sweetman, Rory. 'New Zealand Catholicism, War, Politics and the Irish Issue 1912–1922'. PhD thesis, University of Cambridge, 1990.

Watson, James, *WF Massey: New Zealand.* London: Haus, 2010.

Watson, James and Lachy Paterson (eds). *A Great New Zealand Prime Minister?: Reappraising William Ferguson Massey.* Dunedin: Otago University Press, 2011.

Weddell, Howard. *Trentham Camp and Upper Hutt's Untold Military History*. Upper Hutt: Howard Weddell, 2018.

Wood, Antony. 'The Origins of the First National Government: A Study in New Zealand Politics, 1914–15'. MA thesis, Canterbury University, 1963.

Worthy, Scott. 'A Debt of Honour: New Zealanders' First Anzac Days'. *New Zealand Journal of History*, Vol. 36, No. 2 (2002): 185–200.

Wright, Natalie J. 'Beyond the Pale of Human Recognition: The Image of the Enemy as Portrayed in the Otago/Southland Press during World War One: Attitudes towards British Propaganda and Censorship'. MA thesis, University of Otago, 1996.

ACKNOWLEDGEMENTS

The authors would like to acknowledge the work and kindness of the many individuals and organisations who help a volume like this to come into being. We warmly thank our respective academic institutions, the Stout Research Centre at Victoria University of Wellington and Massey University, for accommodation while writing the text. Various institutions, and the staff who keep them turning, were also critical in the course of researching this book and we gratefully acknowledge the Alexander Turnbull Library, Archives New Zealand, the Auckland War Memorial Museum Tāmaki Paenga Hira, the National Army Museum, Puke Ariki, the Ministry for Culture and Heritage, Hocken Collections Te Uare Taoka o Hākena, the Engineer Corps Memorial Centre, the National Museum of the Royal New Zealand Navy, and Statistics New Zealand.

Rebecca Johns went beyond the call as a researcher, returning from various eclectic quests with new findings. Roger Swanson, John Crawford, Nigel Robson, Paul Lumsden and Jared Davidson helped in some specialist areas of research. Glyn Harper, Nicola Legat, John Crawford and David Littlewood and Matt Turner read through earlier versions of the text and this book is the better for their expertise and advice. William Main, Sally Page, Matt Pomeroy, Glenn Reddiex, Patricia Smith and Rory Sweetman gave permissions to reproduce images from their private collections and this book is more vivid because of their generosity.

It has been a pleasure to work with Nicola Legat and the team at Massey University Press, notably Anna Bowbyes, Kate Barraclough and Anna Rogers. We are delighted with the support in publishing a complex history and doing so with an attention to design and detail.

This book was commissioned as part of the First World War Centenary History Programme. We gratefully acknowledge the decision and commitment to produce a professional and authoritative history of the home front as part of the programme. A special thanks goes to Glyn Harper, Professor of War Studies at Massey University and our major point of contact with the First World War Centenary History Programme Governance Group. We thank him both for his able work in overseeing this volume and for his presence as a colleague.

Lastly, we gratefully recognise the support of our families, our friends and colleagues, many of whom had to live with our preoccupations with the history, idealism, pettiness, politicking, convictions, compromises and sacrifices of a society at war.

ABOUT THE AUTHORS

Steven Loveridge graduated with a PhD in history from Victoria University of Wellington, works from the Stout Research Centre for New Zealand Studies, and has researched, written and lectured on numerous aspects of the First World War. His work has been published in various scholarly journals and anthology works, and in the international encyclopaedia *1914–1918 Online*. His first book, *Calls to Arms: New Zealand Society and Commitment to the Great War* (Victoria University Press, 2014), examines the social and cultural dynamics behind New Zealand's wartime commitment.

James Watson has recently retired from the post of associate professor in history at the Palmerston North campus of Massey University. His research interests are largely focused on the relationship between New Zealand and the United Kingdom, particularly in the twentieth century, but also include rural history and the history of technology. His most recent book, *WF Massey: New Zealand*, was published in the Haus 'Makers of the Modern World' series in 2010 and considers William Massey's record at the Versailles Conference.

INDEX

Numbers in **bold** indicate illustrations

OTHER BOOKS IN THE CENTENARY HISTORY PROGRAMME PUBLISHED BY MASSEY UNIVERSITY PRESS

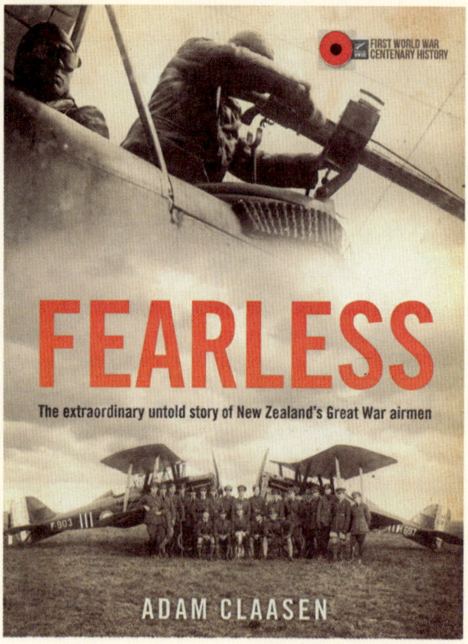

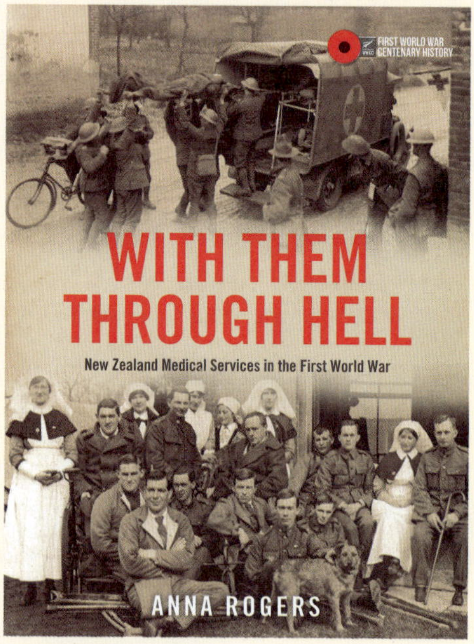

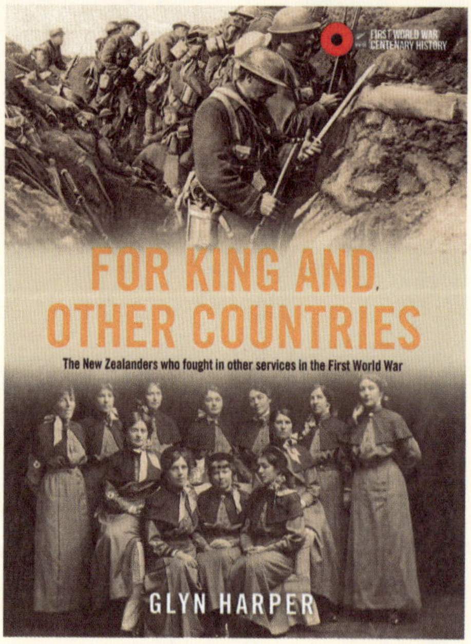

ABOUT THE FIRST WORLD WAR CENTENARY HISTORY PROGRAMME

Massey University, the Ministry for Culture and Heritage (MCH) and the New Zealand Defence Force have joined forces and committed substantial resources to produce a series of authoritative print histories on New Zealand and the First World War. Scholarly yet accessible to broad audiences, the works in this series draw on an extensive range of primary sources held in New Zealand, Britain and elsewhere, and contain high-quality maps and illustrations. Together they form the first complete and detailed account of New Zealand's First World War experience.

These print histories are complemented by digital resources published through the www.firstworldwar.govt.nz website, part of MHC's NZHistory.govt.nz site. The programme's historians have also contributed to other centenary activities, including major international conferences, museum and art exhibitions, television documentaries, heritage trails and commemorative events in New Zealand and overseas.

The Centenary History Programme Governance Group is co-chaired by Gerald Hensley and Massey University Provost Professor Giselle Byrnes. The group includes MCH Chief Historian Neill Atkinson, Defence Force Historian John Crawford, Massey University Professor of War Studies Glyn Harper, and other representatives of the three agencies. More information about the Centenary History series can be found at: http://ww100.govt.nz/first-world-war-centenary-print-histories.

This volume of the Centenary History would not have been possible without generous donations to the Massey University Foundation for this purpose. The Governance Group of the Centenary History Programme acknowledges and thanks the Lotteries Commission and the Auckland War Memorial Museum Tāmaki Paenga Hira.

MASSEY UNIVERSITY TE KUNENGA KI PŪREHUROA UNIVERSITY OF NEW ZEALAND

New Zealand DEFENCE FORCE Te Ope Kātua O Aotearoa NAVY NZ ARMY AIR FORCE

MASSEY UNIVERSITY FOUNDATION

Manatū Taonga Ministry for Culture & Heritage

WW100 FIRST WORLD WAR CENTENARY HISTORY

AM Tāmaki Paenga Hira Auckland War Memorial Museum

MASSEY
UNIVERSITY
PRESS

First published in 2019 by Massey University Press
Private Bag 102904, North Shore Mail Centre
Auckland 0745, New Zealand
www.masseypress.ac.nz

Design by Kate Barraclough
Front cover images: Alexander Turnbull Library, 1/1-008352-G (top) and 1/2-008482-G (below); back cover: Alexander Turnbull Library, 1/2-011079-F (top), *Auckland Weekly News*, 27 July 1916, p. 35 (middle), Alexander Turnbull Library, 1/2-030986-F (below)

A catalogue record for this book is available from the National Library of New Zealand

Printed and bound in China by Everbest Investment Ltd

ISBN: 978-0-9951001-8-3